CADOGAN

David J. J. Evans

Portugal

Cadogan Guides
27–29 Berwick Street, London W1V 3RF, UK
guides@cadogan.demon.co.uk

Distributed in North America by
The Globe Pequot Press
6 Business Park Road, PO Box 833, Old Saybrook,
Connecticut 06475–0833

Copyright © David J. J. Evans 1990, 1992, 1995, 1998
Updated by Alex Robinson
Illustrations © Charles Shearer 1995

Book and cover design by Animage
Cover photographs by: Sylvia Cordaiy Photo Library/Chris North
Maps © Cadogan Guides, drawn by Map Creation Ltd

Series Editor: Rachel Fielding

Editor: Linda McQueen
Proofreading: Lorna Horsfield
Indexing: Ann Hudson
Production: Book Production Services

A catalogue record for this book is available from the British Library

ISBN 1-86011-083-5

Printed and bound in Great Britain by Cambridge University Press.

The author and publishers have made every effort to ensure the accuracy of the information in the book at the time of going to press. However, they cannot accept any responsibility for any loss, injury or inconvenience resulting from the use of information contained in this guide.

'With his highly readable text on Portugal, Evans has added a replete, witty and wonderfully lucid volume to the Cadogan Series. This is an essential tote-along guidebook... Think of a question to ask vis-à-vis your travel planning and Evans, an inveterate roamer with a richly entertaining style, will no doubt have addressed it.'

Travel Publishing News, USA

'An exceptional guide, unique in the English language.'

Jornal de Notícias

'Cadogan Guides: Portugal by David J. J. Evans offers a good blend of cultural and practical information and, like the best companions, challenges assumptions and constantly keeps one amused.'

The Daily Telegraph

'A smooth blend of practical, historical and cultural information, spiced with a dash of wit and irreverence . . . The author is sharp-eyed and does not flinch from telling what he has seen on his journeys around the country.'

The Anglo-Portuguese News

'Keeping the best to last, we come finally to Cadogan Guides' Portugal: the perfect marriage of cultural and practical information, but not confined to the budget end of the scale. Evans' guide is a marvellous collection of treasure and trivia ... description ... and humour. Once again the Cadogan Guide is the pick of the bunch.'

The Daily Telegraph

'It is difficult to praise the Cadogan Guides series too highly. Portugal by David J. J. Evans is typical of the series' blend of good writing, amusing comment and invaluable advice.'

The Independent

iii

For Susan and John

About the Author

David Evans roamed Mediterranean Europe, India, Egypt and Southeast Asia before Portugal seduced him. He studied at Eton and read History at Cambridge. He has lived in New York and London on and off since he was a baby, and has worked as a freelance writer on both sides of the Atlantic. In 1994 he donned a voluminous brown habit and became a novice in the Society of St Francis, an Anglican Franciscan order. He enjoys going for walks amongst trees, making soup, and following his curiosity (which is as omnivorous as a Portuguese goat).

About the Updater

This edition has been updated by **Alex Robinson**. Alex studied Literature and Theology at Bristol and Cambridge and is now a freelance travel writer based in London. He has visited 42 different countries, but has a particular love of all things Latin, especially his wife Gardênia.

A Guide to the Guide

Chapters are divided according to the old ethnic and administrative provinces, each of which has its own distinct character.

Note that the book does not cover Madeira or the Azores.

Please Help Us Keep This Guide Up to Date

We have done our best to ensure that the information in this guide is correct at the time of going to press. But places and facilities are constantly changing, and standards and prices in hotels and restaurants fluctuate.

We would be delighted to receive any comments concerning existing entries or omissions. Significant contributions will be acknowledged in the next edition, and authors of the best letters will receive a copy of the Cadogan Guide of their choice.

Acknowledgements

I could not have undertaken this project, or completed it, without the encouragement and support of my aunt and uncle, Susan and John Mayo. In Lisbon, Michael and Rosita Simpson-Orlebar became my fairy godparents: they welcomed me into their home for several months, and surrounded me with kindness. My mother, Louise Evans, gave me life and lent me a house to write in. I would also like to thank Paula Levey, who offered me the job and saw it through, and Lorna Horsfield, who edited and organized this book. Christopher Cramer tolerated my company for many hours in Portugal, and I am very grateful to Maria Emília Ribeiro for all the transport arrangements.

The Portuguese National Tourist Office have been unstintingly generous with their time and their hospitality. This book would have been impossible without the help of Alberto Marques and Luís Cancela de Abreu. I would also very much like to thank António Serras Pereira, Pilar Pereira, Álvaro de Sousa, Celestino Domingues, Gabriela Ferreira, João Custódio, Isabel Terenas and Alice Martin.

A great many people have shared their enthusiasm and expertise. I am very grateful to: Maria de Lourdes Simões de Carvalho, Eugénio Lisboa, José Maria Montargil, Fernanda dos Santos, Susan Lowndes Marques, Diana Smith, Madalena Cabral, Luís Rebelo, Mark and Ana Hudson, Paula Guimarães, Mafalda Soares da Cunha, Concha Corrêa Botelho, Nono Félix da Costa, Francisco Viegas, Pedro and Lucia Wallenstein, Joanna Clyde, Romeu Pinto da Silva, Joao Barbosa Lisboa, the Conde de Campo Bello, Margaret Aird, Evelyn Hayward, António Madeira, Inês Enes Dias, Gerald Luckhurst, Catherine Mayo, Mark Hewitt, Tanya Garveigh, Rory Macrae, John Delaforce, Angela Delaforce, the Charles Drace-Francis, Jane Fernandes, Maria Deolinda Cerqueira, Manuel Gandra, Fernanda Frazão, Luís Marques da Gama, Salete Salvado, Maria da Graça Teles, Alda Teixeira, Afonso Belarmino, António Capela, Carlos de Matos, Margarida Leite Rio, José Marquês de Fronteira, Alan and Jocelyn Tait, Ruth Briggs, Cristina Gaspar, José Meco, Martins Carneiro, Rosa Costa Gomes, Joao Baptista Martins, César Valença, José Belo dos Santos, and finally Paulo, Isabel, Leonor, Rosa and Armanda.

The following Portuguese regional Tourist Offices have been excellent hosts and have helped me way beyond the call of duty: Viana do Castelo, Monção, Ponte de Lima, Braga, Chaves, Bragança, Lamego, Aveiro, Coimbra, Leiria, Viseu, Covilha, Óbidos, Sintra, Estoril, Setúbal, Santarém, Tomar, Portalegre, Faro, and particularly Oporto. I would also like to thank Enatur in Estremoz and Évora, and the town halls of Évora, Marvão and Castelo Branco.

Updater's Acknowledgements

I would like to thank all the people who helped me in my task, including the many tourist offices and especially my wife Gardênia, plus, at Cadogan Guides, Rachel Fielding and Linda McQueen.

Contents

Contents   ix

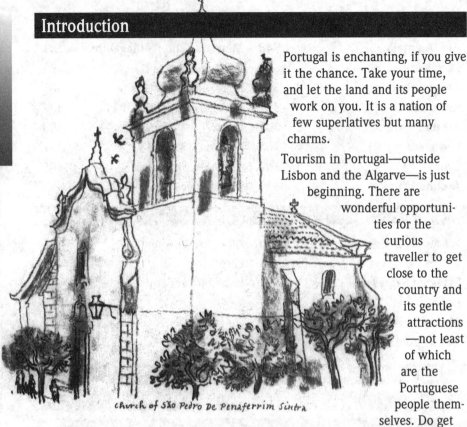

church of São Pedro De Penaferrim Sintra

Portugal is enchanting, if you give it the chance. Take your time, and let the land and its people work on you. It is a nation of few superlatives but many charms.

Tourism in Portugal—outside Lisbon and the Algarve—is just beginning. There are wonderful opportunities for the curious traveller to get close to the country and its gentle attractions—not least of which are the Portuguese people themselves. Do get into the villages: life is easiest to observe in tiny, thrilling walled settlements, such as Monsaraz, Marvão, Monsanto and Óbidos. You may be stared at, but a smile is all it takes to break the ice—after which you might be invited home, to a kitchen with a cauldron over an open fire, for a cup of wine.

Portugal's astonishingly beautiful landscapes range from the simplicity of the Alentejo's vast arid space and strong, pure colours, to the intricacy of the Minho's lush, drowsy smallholdings. The provinces state their identities on every streetcorner and in every field: slim delicate chimneys or no chimneys at all; dogs for herding goats, or wearing nail-studded collars to protect them from wolves; the smell of pine, or eucalyptus, or the sea.

Brazen castles and uplifting cathedrals, a clutch of very good paintings, *azulejos* (tiles) everywhere, and a shower of gilt woodwork attest to Portugal's former wealth. But the Portuguese also have a love for the stuff of rural daily life: stirrups, firedogs and bellows take their place in most museums.

Portugal's prices are catching up with the rest of Europe, but there are still some great bargains at all price levels—particularly in the *Turismo de Habitação* scheme, which offers a highly personal view of rural Portugal by enabling visitors to stay in grand private homes. Most of the country's accommodation is adequate, and the public transport system is decent.

The Best of Portugal

Outstanding natural beauty: around Ponte da Barca, parts of Peneda–Gerês National Park (the Minho); Mirandela to Tua train ride (Trás-os-Montes); Régua to Vila Real train ride (Alto Douro); Tâmega train ride, Amarante–Arco de Baúlhe (Douro Litoral); Sortelha (Beira Alta); south of Monsanto and east of Castelo Branco (Beira Baixa); Serra de Sintra, Serra da Arrábida (Estremadura); north of Constância (Ribatejo); along the River Guadiana (Baixo Alentejo and Algarve); Serra de Monchique (Algarve); the road between Guimarães (the Minho) and Vila Pouca de Aguiar (Trás-os-Montes).

Base for walking in hills: Soajo (the Minho); Sintra (Estremadura).

Base for walking in mountains: Sabugueiro, Manteigas (Beira Alta).

Base for walking beside a river: Ponte da Barca (the Minho); Mértola (Baixo Alentejo).

Wild landscapes: northern Trás-os-Montes, Serra da Estrêla (Beira Alta).

Forest: Buçaco.

Mountains: Serra da Estrêla (Beira Alta).

Spas: Termas de S. Pedro (Beira Alta); Caldas da Rainha (Estremadura).

Undeveloped resorts near good beaches: Vila Nova de Milfontes (Alentejo); Salema, Tavira, Vila do Bispo (Algarve).

Cultured towns and cities with beaches nearby: Viana do Castelo (the Minho); Aveiro (Beira Litoral); Setúbal (Estremadura); Lisbon; Lagos, Faro (Algarve).

Cities and large towns: Viana do Castelo (the Minho); Bragança, Lamego (Trás-os-Montes); Lisbon; Évora (Alto Alentejo).

Small towns: Monção, Ponte de Lima, Ponte da Barca (the Minho); Amarante (Douro Litoral); Tarouca (Beira Alta); Sintra (Estremadura); Serpa (Baixo Alentejo).

Walled villages with infrastructure: Óbidos (Estremadura); Sortelha (Beira Alta); Marvao, Monsaraz (Alto Alentejo).

Walled villages without infrastructure: Marialva (Beira Alta); Monsanto (Beira Baixa).

Other villages: Vilarinho Sêco, Pontido (Trás-os-Montes); Caldas de Monchique, Cacela Velha (Algarve).

Castles and fortresses: Valença (the Minho); Bragança (Trás-os-Montes); Penedono (Beira Alta); Almourol (Ribatejo); Beja (Baixo Alentejo).

Churches, monasteries and convents: Bravães, Braga, Tibães (the Minho); Oporto; Coimbra, Aveiro, Batalha (Beira Litoral); Alcobaça, Mafra (Estremadura); Lisbon; Tomar (Ribatejo); Viana do Alentejo (Alto Alentejo); Mértola (Baixo Alentejo).

Museums: Guimarães (the Minho); Bragança, Lamego (Trás-os-Montes); Oporto; Coimbra (Beira Litoral); Viseu, Caramulo (Beira Alta); Setúbal (Estremadura); Lisbon; Évora (Alto Alentejo).

Azulejos: Barcelos, Viana do Castelo (the Minho); Mangualde (Beira Alta); Évora (Alto Alentejo); Lisbon; Almancil (Algarve).

Market: Barcelos.

Festival: Viana do Castelo; Santarém (Festival de Gastronomia).

Curiosities: staircase at Bom Jesus, Celt-Iberian hill settlement at Citânia de Briteiros, *espigueiros* at Soajo and Lindoso (the Minho); bilingual village of Rio de Onor, rupestral art at Outeiro Machado, Menino Jesus da Cartolinha in the cathedral at Miranda do Douro (Trás-os-Montes); swamped church at Coimbra, lagoon at Aveiro, oxen on the beach at Mira (Beira Litoral); caves at Mira de Aire, the Berlenga islands, westernmost point in Europe at Cabo da Roca, dinosaur footprint at Cabo Espichel (Estremadura); storks at Alcácer do Sal (Alto Alentejo); vultures at Mértola (Baixo Alentejo).

Luxury hotels: Infante de Sagres in Oporto; Palace Hotel in Buçaco (Beira Litoral); Palácio dos Seteais in Sintra, Albatroz in Cascais (Estremadura); York House in Lisbon.

Pousadas: Guimarães (the Minho); Óbidos, Palmela (Estremadura); Évora, Estremoz, Marvão (Alto Alentejo).

Turismo de Habitação: Paço de Calheiros, Casa do Outeiro and Moinho de Estorãos near Ponte de Lima, Paço d'Anha near Viana do Castelo (the Minho); Casa de Rebordinho near Viseu, Casa do Pátio in Sortelha (Beira Alta); Quinta da Capela near Sintra (Estremadura); Quinta de Vale de Lobos (Ribatejo); various, Marvão (Alto Alentejo); Quinta do Caracol and Convento do Sao António in Tavira (Algarve); Horta da Moura (Alentejo).

Moderately priced hotels: Viana Sol in Viana do Castelo (the Minho); São João in Oporto; Astória in Coimbra, Grande Hotel in Luso (Beira Litoral); Infante do Mar in Salema, Albergaria Lageado in Caldas de Monchique (the Algarve).

Cheap accommodation: Hotel Silva and Residencial Rio in Amarante (Douro Litoral); Pensão Silva in Lamego (Trás-os-Montes); Pensão Policarpo in Évora (Alto Alentejo); Residencial Lagôas in Tavira (Algarve).

Travel

By Air

From the UK and Ireland

In peak season, a steady stream of flights spirits the British to Portugal. **To Lisbon**: TAP (the Portuguese national airline) flies from London (Heathrow), and Dublin; British Airways from London (Heathrow and Gatwick) connecting with a British Airways flight from Scotland. **To Oporto**: TAP flies from London (Heathrow); British Airways from London (Heathrow) connecting with a British Airways flight from Scotland. **To Faro**: TAP flies daily except Fridays from London (Heathrow); British Airways from London (Gatwick) connecting with Air UK and British Airways flights from Scotland and Dublin.

TAP's subsidiary, Caravela, handles bookings for *pousadas* and *Turismo de Habitação*, as well as organizing a number of fly-drive alternatives (London ✆ 0171 630 9223 and Dublin ✆ 1 679 8844) from £117 per person. For tailor-made holiday packages (including *pousadas* and some *Turismo de Habitação*) contact: Abreu Travel, 109 Westbourne Grove, London W2 4UL (✆ 0171 229 9905). Speedwing Holidays, 26 Temple Fortune Parade, London NW11 0QS (✆ 0181 905 5252) offer a similar service, but without *Turismo de Habitação* bookings.

TAP Offices in the UK and Ireland

London: Gillingham House, 38–44 Gillingham House, London SW1V 1HL (✆ 0171 828 0262).

Dublin: 54 Dawson Street, Dublin 2 (✆ 1 679 8844).

From the USA and Canada

The frequency of flights to Portugal from the US and Canada is increasing rapidly. TAP offers non-stop services to Lisbon from New York (6½hrs), Boston (6¼hrs), Toronto (7hrs) and Montreal (6½hrs). TWA flies to Lisbon from New York, with connections from San Francisco (5½hrs plus 6½hrs).

Abreu Tours, 317 East 34th Street, New York, NY 10016 (✆ 800 223 1580) handle *pousada* bookings and arrange tailor-made holidays. For cheaper flights try Cosmos/Global Gateway, 92–25 Queens Blvd, Rego Park, NY 11374 (✆ 800 221 0900) who are the leading budget tour operators for Europe in North America.

It can work out cheaper to fly from the USA or Canada to Madrid or London, and head on to Portugal from there, if you have the time.

TAP Offices in the USA

Boston: 1 Exeter Plaza, Boston, Mass MA 02116 (✆ 800 225 7020 toll free).

Newark: 399 Market Street, Newark, New Jersey, NJ 07105 (✆ 800 221 7370 toll free).

Los Angeles: Suite 1, 2221 Rosecrams Avenue, El Segundo, Los Angeles, CA 90245 (✆ 800 365 2359 toll free).

There are no TAP offices in Canada; Canadian passengers should contact the US offices.

By Ferry

There are no direct passenger ferries operating between Britain and mainland Portugal. However, a ferry runs between Plymouth and Santander in northern Spain (*see* 'By Car'). Ferry passengers without cars could take a train from Santander to Valladolid, from where there are connections to Lisbon and Oporto.

By Train

From the UK

A daily rail service operates between London (Victoria) and Lisbon (min. 40hrs), via Paris and Irún/Hendaye. Trains depart from London in the evening, and arrive in Paris early the next morning. In Paris, passengers must change railway stations, to catch the direct train to Lisbon a couple of hours later. This arrives the following morning. Passengers for Oporto change at Pampilhosa.

Details and reservations are available from Rail Europe, Victoria Station, London SW1, ✆ 0990 300 003.

Another option would be to take the Eurostar from London to Paris via the Channel Tunnel, ✆ 0990 186 186 or ✆ 0345 30 30 30. There are between ten and twelve departures daily and the London–Paris journey takes 3hrs, arriving at Gare du Nord.

From Spain

Twice-daily trains from Madrid to Lisbon take between 7 and 9hrs, with connections from Barcelona. Other trains run from Coruña (via Valença and Oporto) and from Salamanca (change at Pampilhosa for Oporto). There are two rail routes to Lisbon from Seville: via Badajoz (change at Entroncamento for Oporto); or via Ayamonte (cross the River Guadiana to Vila Real de Santo António).

special tickets

EU citizens who have been resident for the past 6 months in the European country in which they wish to buy their ticket are eligible for the InterRail pass (currently £259 if you're under 26, otherwise £349, from British Rail or any travel agent), which gives one month's unlimited travel on all European, Moroccan and Turkish railways, as well as up to 30 per cent discounts on trains in Britain, cross-Channel ferries, and ferries between Spain and Morocco.

The equivalent North American EurRail pass can be purchased in the US, for 7, 15, 21, 30, 60 or 90 days: it too saves the hassle of buying numerous tickets, but cost-wise it will only pay for itself if you use it every day, everywhere. The EurRail pass is not valid in Great Britain, Morocco or Eastern Europe, and supplements are payable on many express trains.

Eurotrain offers anyone under the age of 26 inexpensive tickets to a fixed destination. These are valid for two months, and allow travellers to stop off at any stations along the preplanned route. Eurotrain's London office is c/o Campus Travel at 52 Grosvenor Gardens, London SW1W 0AG, ✆ 0171 730 3402. They are not always very clued up, some operators not even realizing that they sell Eurotrain tickets. Assure them that they do. In the US, tickets can be reserved through New York Student Center, 895 Amsterdam Avenue, NYC, NY 10025 (✆ 212 663 5435).

By Bus

Eurolines, ✆ 0171 730 8235, offer services from Victoria coach station on Monday, Wednesday, Friday and Saturday nights to Lisbon (42½hrs), and to the Algarve on Mondays and Fridays only (45½hrs to Faro). Both services require a change of station plus a three-hour stopover in Paris on the following morning. The direct service to Oporto leaves on Saturday morning and takes 33hrs—change at Valladolid in Spain. Tickets are available from any National Express agent, or by credit-card booking over the phone. An under-25 discount is available on the ticket to Oporto.

By Car

More than 2000km of main roads separate Lisbon from Calais. If you prefer a short Channel crossing and a long stint on the *autoroute*, take the ferry from Dover/Folkestone to Calais/Boulogne, and continue to Paris, where you can join the toll *Autoroute de l'Aquitaine* to just beyond Bordeaux. Enter Spain at Hendaye, and drive to Portugal via Burgos and Salamanca. For a longer Channel crossing and less *autoroute*, take a night-time ferry from Portsmouth, and head south via Rennes, Nantes, and La Rochelle before joining the *autoroute*. If you want to take it comfortably, reckon on two overnight stops *en route*.

If you prefer to stay on dry land, Le Shuttle, ✆ 01303 273 300, ✆ 0990 51 52 53, transports cars through the Channel Tunnel on purpose-built carriers between Folkestone and Calais, for between £180 and £200. The UK terminal is off Junction 11a of the M20.

There are a couple of options for cutting down on driving times. A Motorail service operates between Paris and Madrid (daily all year round). Passengers and their cars travel on different trains. The car is loaded onto a train in the evening. Passengers take a train the following morning and arrive in Madrid the next day, when their cars are available for collection. For details, contact Rail Europe, ✆ 0990 300 003, or French National Railroads, Rockefeller Center, 610 Fifth Ave., New York, NY 10020.

Alternatively, Brittany Ferries, Milbay Docks, Plymouth PL1 3EW, ✆ 0990 360 360, operate a twice-weekly 24-hour service from Plymouth to Santander in northern Spain. Costs for passengers are roughly the same as a charter flight to Portugal. There is a special rate for 8-day returns. Santander is approximately 800km from Oporto, 960km from Lisbon, and 1300km from Faro.

Most Spanish/Portuguese **frontier posts** are open 7am–9pm in winter and 7am–11pm in summer. The borders at Tuy/Valença do Minho, Fuentes de Oñoro/Vilar Formoso, Badajoz/Elvas, Alcañices/Quintanilha and Portelo/Calabor are open constantly.

in the UK

Caravela is TAP's tour arm, handling bookings for *pousadas* and *Turismo de Habitaçao*, as well as arranging various fly/drive options—℗ 0171 630 9223; Dublin ℗ 1 679 8844.

Explore Worldwide, 1 Frederick Street, Aldershot, Hampshire GU11 1LQ, ℗ 01252 344161. Hiking specialists who can arrange small group tours in the Gerês and the Douro.

Destination Portugal, 37 Corn Street, Witney, Oxfordshire, ℗ 01993 773269. An excellent agency which can accommodate virtually any needs, from flight only to pilgrimage, wine or *pousada* tours and national park hiking holidays.

in the USA

Abreu Tours, 317 E.34th Street, New York, NY 10016, ℗ 800 223 1580. A Portuguese-run agency with many years of experience.

Cycling Through the Centuries, PO Box 877, San Antonio, FL 33567, ℗ 800 245 4226. This operator organizes cycling holidays in the Alentejo, Minho and the Algarve.

Easy Rider Tours, PO Box 1384, East Arlington, MA 02174, ℗ 617 643 8332. Also offers cycling holidays for all abilities, featuring manor house accommodation and excursions.

Special-interest Holidays

Abreu Travel Agency, 109 Westbourne Grove, London W2 4UL, ℗ 0171 229 9905. Golf holidays, wine tours and pilgrimages.

Alternative Travel Group, 69–71 Banbury Road, Oxford OX2 6PE, ℗ 01865 310399. Art-and-culture tours, manor house, *pousada* and walking holidays.

Cadogan Travel, 9/10 Portland Street, Southampton SO9 1ZP, ℗ 01703 828313. Art-and-culture tours, city breaks, golf, tennis and walking holidays, wine tours and pilgrimages.

Mundi Color, 276 Vauxhall Bridge Road, London SW1V 1BE, ℗ 0171 828 6021. Art-and-culture tours, pilgrimages, wine tours, tailor-made and *pousada* holidays, golf holidays.

North Portugal Travel, 35 Sandford Mill Road, Cheltenham, Glos GL53 7QH, ℗ 01242 262159. Art-and-culture tours, *pousada* holidays, pilgrimages, fishing, golf, tennis and walking holidays, self-catering accommodation.

Portugal Travel Club, 15 Harrow View Road, London W5 1NA, ℗ 0181 810 6010. Golf and tennis holidays, self-catering accommodation.

Portugala Holidays, 1–3 Princes Lane, London N10 3LU, ℗ 0181 444 1857. Self-catering accommodation, pilgrimages, tailor-made and *pousada* holidays, golf and walking holidays.

Roger Taylor Tennis Holidays, 85 High Street, London SW19 5EG, ℗/◉ 0181 947 9727. Tennis holidays at a prestigious centre.

Entry Formalities

Passports and Customs

Holders of British, Irish and EU passports or identity cards can enter Portugal for up to 90 days without a visa. Holders of US and Canadian passports can enter Portugal for up to 60 days without a visa.

These periods may be extended, before they expire, on application to the Foreigners Registration Service, 22 Rua Conselheiro José Silvestre Ribeiro, Lisbon 1600 (℗ 01 714 1027). In practice, visitors are very unlikely to be challenged over how long they have been in the country.

Customs are usually polite and present few problems. It's forbidden to bring fresh meat into Portugal.

Getting Around

By Air

Portugal is such a small country that there should be no need to fly anywhere. If you're in a hurry, TAP's 737s wing their way several times daily from Lisbon to Oporto and Faro, and the airline's subsidiary, LAR, fly smaller aircraft less frequently to Vila Real, Chaves and Bragança. TAP's office in Lisbon is at 3 Praça Marquês de Pombal, ℗ 01 575020.

By Train

Travelling by train is inexpensive, cheaper than travelling by bus, and generally the routes are more picturesque. However, buses are usually faster: Portugal's rail network was cut back severely in 1990, and it's often necessary to travel via junctions or cities to get from A to B. Portugal's trains are nationalized, and are operated by CP (Caminhos de Ferro Portugueses). Their head office is in Lisbon, at Edifício Principal, Santo Apolonia, ℗ 01 8884025/26/27.

Most trains are designated *Regional* or *Inter-Regional (IR)*: the former run shorter routes and stop at most stations along the way. *IR* trains make intermittent stops, while *Rapido IC (Inter-Cidade)* trains stop only at major towns or junctions and *Serviço-Alfa* trains are faster still (the latter two usually require supplements and seat reservation fees to be paid at the time of buying your ticket, pushing the price up by as much as 60 per cent).

Train timetables are generally available if you ask, and are usually posted on station walls. If you plan to travel a lot by train, it's worth asking in the Lisbon or Oporto stations for a copy of CP's official timetable (*Guia Horário Oficial*), which costs 250$00 and gives full details of routes and schedules throughout the country. Alternatively, the Thomas Cook *Continental Timetable* covers the main services. In the UK this can be purchased from any branch of Thomas Cook and costs around £7; in the USA, from Forsyth Travel Library, PO Box 2975, 9154 West 57th Street, Shawnee Mission, Kansas 66210.

Tickets must be purchased at the railway station in advance, rather than on the train— otherwise you are fined. Allow time to queue for buying a ticket.

discount tickets

Various discount schemes are available from major railway stations. CP sell *Bilhetes Turísticos* (railcards for tourists) valid for 7, 14 or 21 days. These are unlikely to cover their costs. Travellers over the age of 65 can buy a *Cartão Dourado* for a nominal sum; this entitles them to 50 per cent off the full fare, but may not be used 6.30–9.30am or 5–8pm. On frequent, designated *Dias Verdes* (Green Days), CP offers a 20 per cent discount on all return fares. Families are eligible for the *Cartão de Família*, which entitles a married couple and at least one of their children under the age of 18 to discount travel on *Dias Verdes*. Young people aged 12–26 are eligible for the *Cartão Jovem*, which allows 50 per cent discounts on journeys over 50km during limited periods. Children under 4 travel free if they do not occupy a seat, and from 4 to 12 pay half-fare.

scenic routes

Four narrow-gauge railway lines are still open in the north, offering an opportunity to get close to country life: at each village, the train is stopped by a lady with a red flag; a sack of maize and a pitcher of wine are heaved aboard, a new pair of shoes is passed out the window, and the train goes on; periodically it hoots to alert villagers walking down the tracks or collecting their dried laundry from the railway sidings. The narrow-gauge routes run from Régua to Vila Real (Corgo line) and Tua to Mirandela (Tua line); both connect with the scenic Oporto–Pocinho railway (Douro line; be sure to get a window seat as the locals pull down the blinds!). The most spectacular train journey in Portugal has recently been re-opened and runs from Amarante to Baulhé (Tâmega line). The route from Aveiro to Viseu (Vouga line) was closed in 1990.

By Bus

Buses are a quick and painless way to get around the country—if you can find out where and when the correct bus departs. Tickets are cheaper than they would be in northern Europe, but they're no bargain. The state-owned Rodoviária Nacional (RN) has been privatized, so there are now many private bus companies, causing some confusion. The main regional companies are mentioned in the text.

For Express travel, check that you're standing in the correct line before queuing to buy your ticket at the bus station. Most Express buses depart from a (fume-laden) central depot. On longer journeys, buses stop for a coffee break every couple of hours. Some of the private buses show films. Night bus drivers have a habit of playing loud music for the duration of the journey.

For local buses, purchase your ticket on board. If you travel in the early morning or mid-afternoon, you'll probably have to scramble for a seat with the children who travel to and from school on local buses (some local bus timetables are devised especially to suit school-children, so if you want to get somewhere out of the way, those are the best times to try).

coach tours

RN Tours serve as a travel agent and organize various regional and national coach tours. Their offices are located as follows:

RN Tours Offices in Portugal

Lisbon: 12th floor, 33 Av. Fontes Pereira de Melo, ✆ 01 353 8846.
Faro: Av. da República (part of the Hotel Eva building), ✆ 089 803305.
Albufeira: 21 Av. 25 de Abril, ✆ 089 55426.
Portimão: 9 Rua Júdice Bicker, ✆ 082 25413.
Oporto: 629 Rua Sá da Bandeira, ✆ 02 380712.
Coimbra: 102 Rua da Sofia, ✆ 039 22944.
Leiria: 3 Rua Cor. Teles Sampaio Rio, ✆ 044 32413.
Évora: 131–133 Rua da República, ✆ 066 24254.

Gray Line, Av. Praia da Vitoria, 12B, Lisbon, ✆ 01 352 2594, also offer tours around the country.

By Car

The charms of Portugal are best appreciated by car, though you pay heftily for the increased convenience of travel: petrol costs around 300$00 per litre for super or unleaded, 310$00 for regular. Street parking is usually no problem, other than in Lisbon and Oporto.

Portugal's road network is improving rapidly but there is still work to be done. Some secondary roads are excellent, others are riddled with potholes (not to mention flocks of sheep and figs laid out to dry). In spring, delightful roadside flowers are sufficient compensation for the slowest of roads. It's difficult to anticipate the time a journey will take, because although traffic is rarely heavy, some roads—particularly in the Minho and parts of the Beiras—are almost entirely made up of hairpin bends.

However bad the roads are, Portuguese drivers are worse. Portugal has one of the highest accident rates in Europe (most accidents occur on the Lisbon–Oporto super-highway, the Lisbon–Algarve highway, or the Lisbon–Cascais Avenida Marginal). Few people think twice before drinking and driving; most show a general disregard for basic rules of the road and each other. The Minho and Trás-os-Montes are notorious in the summer months, when emigrants return to show off their flashy motors.

Foreign-registered cars may enter Portugal for up to 6 months if accompanied by a registration document and a green card proving limited-liability insurance. British and international driving licences are valid; the latter are available through the AA, RAC, or any auto club in the US.

Portugal uses the international road sign system. Drive on the right and overtake on the left; give way to cars approaching from the right. Drivers may overtake stationary trams on the right, when this does not endanger passengers. Seatbelts are obligatory outside built-up areas. Speed limits for cars are: 60kph (37mph) in built-up areas; 90kph (55mph) outside built-up areas; 120kph (75mph) on motorways. There are few toll roads; the Oporto–Lisbon motorway is the only pricey one (2500$00).

For more information, contact the Automóvel Clube de Portugal, 24 Rua Rosa Araújo, Lisbon, ✆ 01 356 3931. The ACP operates a breakdown service: north of Coimbra, call them in Oporto, ✆ 02 316732; south of Coimbra, call them in Lisbon, ✆ 01 942 5095.

Car hire is comparatively cheap by European standards. In Lisbon, all the major firms are represented at the airport. In addition, you'll find Avis at 47 Praça da Vitoria, ✆ 01 356 1176; Hertz at 10 Av. 5 de Outubro, ✆ 01 357 9027/77; and Europcar at Quinta Francelha Baixo Prior Velho. In Oporto, Avis is at 125 Guedes de Azevedo, ✆ 02 315947 (*open Mon–Sat 8.30–7*); Hertz is at 899 Rua de Santa Catarina, ✆ 02 312387. The minimum age for hiring a car is usually 23, and customers must have held a full driving licence for at least one year.

By City Bus and Taxi

Lisbon, and possibly Oporto, are the only towns where you are likely to require a bus; elsewhere, the attractions are within easy walking distance (*see* 'Getting Around' sections in **Lisbon**, p.295, and **Oporto**, pp.149–50). Most city bus journeys cost around 100$00.

Taxis are inexpensive enough to be used by many locals for getting their groceries home. The vehicles are black, with greeny-turquoise roofs. Most are metered: there is a flat rate of about 160$00, plus 10$00 per 117m (with surcharges at night and for heavy luggage)—even in Lisbon, journeys rarely cost more than 500$00. It is difficult to hail a cab from the street: you're much better off going to a taxi rank, or phoning for a radio taxi.

Suggested Itineraries

by car

Portugal is a country to savour, and it would be a pity to rush it. There's quite enough in any one or two provinces to satisfy a single visit to Portugal. All the same, the following routes for drivers may be helpful to those who like their holiday to have a little velocity. These are rough guidelines—all sorts of diversions are listed in the text.

If **high culture** is what you're after, the traditional triangle is Lisbon–Évora–Coimbra. There are numerous sidesteps, which could take in a number of walled villages and other thrills: Monsaraz from Évora, Marvão on your way north from Évora, the forest of Buçaco and the Roman ruins at Conimbriga from Coimbra. You might return south from Coimbra via Batalha and Alcobaça, and perhaps stop over at Óbidos.

It would be a pity to visit Lisbon without taking in the Serra de Sintra or the Serra da Arrábida.

Lisbon is well placed for launching yourself **southwards:** first to Évora, then Beja, via Monsaraz or the church at Viana do Alentejo. From Beja it's a short hop across to Serpa. You could make Mértola the southern extent of your visit, then cut across the width of the country to Vila Nova de Milfontes. You could pass through Santiago do Cacém, and dally in the Serra da Arrábida on your way back to Lisbon.

If you want to keep to **the Algarve**, it's best to tiptoe. From Faro, you could head east to Tavira (and visit Cacela), then inland via São Brás de Alportel (make a diversion to see the church at Almancil) through Silves to Caldas de Monchique. From there it's possible to visit Alvor, Salema and Cape St Vincent.

Castelo Branco is a good place from which to begin an exploration of the **inland Beiras**. From Lisbon, you could drive there via Tomar, or via Marvão and Castelo de Vide. Alternatively, you could get to the inland Beiras from Oporto, via Amarante and Lamego.

Oporto is the obvious place to start a **tour of the north**: drive to Guimarães, then Braga. Head east into the Serra do Barroso, Chaves, Bragança, and back to Oporto via Amarante.

Ponte de Lima or Ponte da Barca are the best bases for getting to know the Minho, because they are at the centre of the province.

A drive **south from Oporto** could take you to Lamego, Viseu, through the Serra do Caramulo to Buçaco, Coimbra, Aveiro, and back to Oporto. For a longer drive, you could go straight to Coimbra or Buçaco, then east into the Serra da Estrêla. North of the Serra, Trancoso and Marialva will repay a visit, before heading back west to Lamego via Tarouca, and Oporto.

by public transport

Travelling north or south on the west coast is fairly straightforward by either train or bus; the problems start when you head inland, and particularly if you want to travel up or down the eastern side of the country. The rail network here is at its least efficient and more often than not you'll have to rely on buses to get from A to B. If you are travelling on one of the various rail passes (*see* p.3), it can sometimes work out quicker to return to the west, make your way up or down the coast, and then cut across to the east again. Note that in the north there are no west–east lines at all above Oporto, from where there is only one line, across to Bragança in the northeastern corner of Portugal.

In theory, Portugal lends itself ideally to exploration by train: some of the routes are amongst the most spectacular in Europe, and travelling at a sedate pace from town to town highlights the diversity of the Portuguese people and landscape. In practice however, this demands patience and a lot of time and, occasionally, a skin thick enough to cope with inquisitive stares from the locals.

Transport information for each town is included in the text. Where connections are given in terms of frequency, 'frequent' means five or more departures daily, 'semi-frequent' three to five departures, and 'infrequent' less than three. This does not include services which run only at certain times of the year and/or on certain days.

Better is the ass that carries me than the horse that throws me.

Portuguese proverb

Practical A–Z

Climate and When to Go

Portugal is a sunny country: even in the north, in December, you can reckon on 3½hrs of sunshine per day. In the south and northeast in July, visitors may fry in 12½hrs of sunshine per day (wearing a hat staves off headaches, and do bring a sunscreen or sunblock for the kids). Winters are chilly in the north—you'll need a decent coat—but delightfully mild in the Algarve. Pack an umbrella and a raincoat if you intend to visit the Minho between October and May—it's the rain that keeps the province green.

Spring and autumn are the best times to visit Portugal; if you can, aim for late April or early May (also coinciding with the wild roadside flowers and hotels' winter rates).

Average maximum daily temperatures (°C)/average number of dry days/ average seawater temperatures (°C)

	January	April	July	October
Viana do Castelo	13°/12/12°	18°/17/14°	24°/26/16°	20°/17/16°
Bragança	8°/14/—	16°/19/—	28°/27/—	18°/20/—
Oporto	13°/14/12°	18°/18/14°	25°/26/16°	21°/18/16°
Coimbra	14°/15/—	21°/22/—	29°/28/—	24°/19/—
Castelo Branco	11°/20/—	19°/22/—	30°/30/—	21°/23/—
Lisbon	14°/16/13°	19°/21/14°	28°/30/16°	22°/22/17°
Évora	12°/17/—	19°/20/—	30°/30/—	22°/22/—
Faro	15°/22/14°	20°/24/16°	29°/31/21°	23°/25/18°

Disabled Travellers

There are few special facilities for disabled travellers, though the Portuguese will always rush to aid anyone who has trouble getting around. There are parking spaces reserved for disabled people in the main cities and adapted WCs and wheelchair facilities at airports and main train stations. The Portuguese National Tourist Office produces some literature for the disabled, including a list of hotels with facilities. In Britain, contact RADAR (Royal Association For Disability and Rehabilitation) at Unit 12, City Forum, 250 City Road, London EC1V 8AF, © 0171 250 3222. They publish *Holidays and Travel Abroad: A Guide For Disabled People* at £5.00. In the USA, a helpful organization is Mobility International, at PO Box 10767, Eugene, Oregon 97400, © 503 343 1286. Also in the USA is SATH (Society for the Advancement of Travel for the Handicapped) at 347 Fifth Avenue, Suite 610, New York 10016, © 212 447 7284.

In Portugal itself, useful associations are: the Portuguese Handicapped Persons Association, Largo do Rato, 1250 Lisbon, © 01 388 9883, and ACAPO (Association of the Blind and Partially Sighted of Portugal), 1st Floor, 86-1 Rua de S. José, 1500 Lisbon, © 01 342 2001.

There are facilities for the disabled at the following Olympic-sized swimming pools: Faro Sports Centre, Loulé Public Swimming Pool (both in the Algarve) and the Piscina Municipal do Areeiro in Lisbon.

Electricity

The current is 220V, 50 cycles, which takes a continental two-pin plug. Some fancy hotels have adaptors—otherwise, bring your own.

Embassies and Consulates

UK: 35–37 Rua da Estrela 4, Lisbon, ℰ 01 395 4082; 3072 Avenida da Boa Vista, Oporto, ℰ 02 618 4789; 7 Largo Francisco A Mauricio, Portimão, ℰ 082 417800.

USA: Avenida das Forças Armadas, Lisbon, ℰ 01 726 5562.

Canadian: 4th floor, Edifício MCB, 144 Avenida da Liberdade, Lisbon, ℰ 01 347 4892.

Irish: 1 Rua da Imprensa à Estrela, 4th floor, Lisbon, ℰ 01 396 1569.

Entertainment and Nightlife

If you want to escape from *bacalhau*, head for the **cinema**: films are cheap (600$00) and are never dubbed. Foreign films are released at the same time as in their native country. All performances have a 10-minute interval, during which 90 per cent of the audience lights up a cigarette. Remember to tip the usherette (20$00). If it's Portuguese cinema you're after, watch out for the films of Manoel de Oliveira, João Botelho, and Paulo Rocha.

Discos and nightclubs are confined to the tourist areas. If they're going to gamble, most Portuguese gamble on the lottery, but there are some **casinos** for hardened addicts. Ask at the local tourist office for details of **concerts**, which tend to be confined to Lisbon and Oporto (*see* **Topics**, pp.49–50).

Festivals

February	Loulé	Carnival
early March	Ovar	Carnival
1st Sun in May	Monsanto	Festa das Cruzes
2 and 3 May	Barcelos	Festas das Cruzes
Easter Thurs	Braga	Ecce Homo procession
1st weekend of June	Amarante	Feast of São Gonçalo
For one week in June (check dates with tourist office)	Silves	Beer festival
12–13, 23–24, 28–29 June	Lisbon	Festas dos Santos Populares
18 June	Monção	Corpus Christi
23 June	Oporto	Festa de São João
24 June	Viseu	Cavalhadas de Vil de Moinhos
1st Sun in July	Tomar	Festa dos Tabuleiros
1st Sun of Aug	Guimarães	Festas Gualterianas
Sun after 15 Aug	Miranda do Douro	Festas de Sta. Bárbara

Fri nearest 20 Aug–Sun	Viana do Castelo	Festas da Senhora da Agonia
End Aug–mid-Sept	Lamego	Festas de N.S. dos Remédios
3rd weekend of Sept	Ponte de Lima	New Fairs
20–25 Sept	Elvas	Festas do Senhor da Piedade, Feira de São Mateus
Last week Oct, 1st week Nov	Santarém	National Gastronomic Festival
26 Dec–6 Jan	Villages around Bragança	Festa dos Rapazes

Food and Drink

Eating Out

The early 18th-century traveller Mrs Marianne Baillie noted that 'the courtly whisper of the highest bred *fidalgo*, loaded with garlic and oil, differed not at all from the breath of the humblest peasant'. Today garlic makes only muted appearances, and Portuguese cooking is not particularly oily, but the gist of her observation holds true: tastes are remarkably democratic, and the best food in Portugal is peasant fare. Fancy restaurants may have extensive wine lists, but for a good meal you'd be better off at an upmarket *tasca* (tavern) or a *restaurante típico* (*see* **Topics**, p.49, for the meaning of '*típico*'). If in doubt, eat where the locals eat and choose the *prato do dia* (dish of the day).

You don't have to be cutting your second set of teeth to ask for a half-portion: helpings tend to be enormous, and many menus list the price of half-portions (usually two-thirds of the full rate).

Dom Duarte (1433–8) advised his subjects to have an interval of 8 hours between their main meals, and his suggestion has been heeded, more or less. Breakfast is usually a cup of coffee with a bread roll and butter, followed by another cup of coffee in the middle of the morning. Lunch begins about 12.30, and lasts until 2 or 2.30. After a mid-afternoon cup of coffee or tea, dinner gets under way around 8.

prices

The restaurant categories in this book correspond to the following prices for an average main course for one person, without wine:

expensive	over 1300$00
moderate	950$00–1300$00
cheap	under 950$00

Portuguese Food

Most Portuguese food is simple and heavy; it's well worth seeking out the more complicated dishes, as these are often the richest and most tasty (particularly the northern meat stews and the coastal fish stews). Regional dishes are the closest you're likely to get to Portuguese home cooking: the best-known are detailed in the text. These regional dishes rely on a narrow range of vegetables, and there are very few vegetable side dishes or salads—although meals often include a vegetable-based soup (usually eaten after the main course). Spices are little used, which is surprising given Portugal's role in the 16th-century spice trade. Vegetarians may strike it lucky in urban areas, but veggie-consciousness has a long way to go. Those who eat fish are well catered for. Vegans will find eating out almost impossible outside the main cities.

Fish and seafood account for 40 per cent of Portugal's protein intake. Fish is usually grilled or boiled; if the latter, you'll be given separate flasks of oil and vinegar, or you could ask for a squeeze of lemon. Portugal is not merely a land of sardines: hake, whiting, *peixe espada* (scabbard fish, not swordfish), *carapaus* (horse mackerel), lampreys, and of course *bacalhau* (*see* below) are popular and widely available. One of the most enjoyable fish dishes is the *caldeirada*, a mixed fish stew, with potatoes and plenty of gravy. Be careful where you choose to order one, as you may end up with a mixture of trimmings.

The pork is excellent, particularly in the Alentejo (or Trás-os-Montes for smoked ham and pork sausages). In 1726 Brockwell wrote that Portuguese pork was the most delicious in Europe: 'their swine are small, short-legged, and generally black, their Bellies oft reaching to the Ground.' The kid is a treat too—it's especially flavourful in the inland Beiras, where the animals graze on wild herbs.

For snacks, the Portuguese favour the *prego* (steak sandwich), *risseak* (deep-fried envelopes of meat or seafood), or *pastéis de bacalhau* (codfish croquettes).

It's an understatement to say that the Portuguese have a sweet tooth: they have a mouthful of sweet teeth. This may be one of the Moors' most persistent legacies, and has been kindled over the centuries by the kitchens of numerous convents—the nuns used to sell confections to supplement their income. Hence some of the more picturesque names: *barriga de freira* (nun's belly); *papos de anjo* (angel's breasts). All are made from egg yolks, sugar and little else. *Pastéis de Nata* (custard tarts), *pão-de-ló* (sponge cake) and *bolos de mel* (honey cakes) are some of the most enjoyable.

bacalhau

It seems perverse that a race whose shores are favoured by so many fish should adopt *bacalhau* as their national dish. This dried, salted codfish looks like ossified grey cardboard, and is cut with a saw before being soaked and cooked in one of (a reputed) 365 different ways. The first official *bacalhau* fleet set sail during the reign of Dom João I (1385–1433), and subsequent fleets made around 150 voyages to Newfoundland during the reign of Dom Manuel (1495–1521); now *bacalhau* is imported from Norway and Iceland.

We unfortunate foreigners are often incapable of appreciating the delights of *bacalhau*: it's only palatable when heavily disguised, as in *bacalhau à Gomes de Sá* (*see* **Oporto**, p.148).

bread

Bread is one of the delights of Portugal: *see* **Trás-os-Montes**, p.101.

Quality wines—including *vinho verde* and Dão—are described in the text, region by region. For port wine, *see* **Oporto**, pp.146–8.

The Portuguese drink a great deal of alcohol, but very rarely get drunk. Wine is extremely cheap—from around 160$00 per litre—and makes a highly enjoyable communion with Portugal. Locally produced wine is regarded as thera-peutic, so you may opt for the *vinho da casa* (house wine)—in the Minho this might arrive in a pottery jug with a couple of porcelain bowls to drink it from. Meals can be chased down with *aguardente*, at its best a brandy-like spirit distilled from wine, or clear *bagaceira*, a throat-burning firewater distilled from the leftovers of pressed grapes.

As for beer (*cerveja*), you'll see *Sagres* all over the place, and very welcome it is too. It's brewed in Lisbon. Keep an eye out for blue-labelled *Super Bock*, and *Sagres Europa*. As for creamy, dark brown *Sagres Preta*, not unlike a British brown ale, proceed with caution. It slips down innocuously enough, but packs quite a punch.

With so many spas, Portugal produces a flood of bottled waters: chalky Carvalhelhos is particularly distinctive. The waters of Monchique and Luso are especially good. It's ridicu-lously difficult to obtain fresh fruit juice.

Geography

Portugal is a small country, as the 10 million Portuguese are fond of remarking. It covers 92,000 sq km. Three rivers serve as boundaries with Spain, but only one river, the Zêzere, originates in Portugal. The hummocky hills of the northwest are balanced by the high, rolling hills of the northeast. South of the latter rises Portugal's only true mountain range, the Serra da Estrêla, which reaches 1993m. The rest of the country is fairly flat, though in places the plains ruck up into hills.

Health and Emergencies

Keep all doctor's and pharmacy receipts. Dial ✆ 115 for an **ambulance**. A fair proportion of doctors speak English, because they have been trained abroad; to be sure you'll be understood, head for the British Hospital at 49 Rua Saraiva de Carvalho, Lisbon, ✆ 01 602020. Pharmacies (*farmácias*) are open Monday to Friday from some time after 9 until 1 and 3–7, if you're lucky, and Saturday mornings.

Don't swim where flags warn you not to. The tapwater is safe to drink throughout the country, except possibly in the Algarve in high season. Delicious bottled water is available.

crime

The vast majority of foreign visitors to Portugal will come and go without a hitch. The farther you are from other foreigners, the less likely you are to get hustled: in the Algarve, Lisbon, and the Estoril coast, watch out for pickpocketing, theft from parked cars, and dodgy property deals.

To call the **police** (and/or ambulance) in an emergency, dial ✆ 115 throughout Portugal.

Insurance

No vaccinations are required for visitors to Portugal from Britain, Ireland, the USA or Canada (though if you are coming from somewhere with a cholera epidemic, you must have an International Certificate of Vaccination).

Portugal has a reciprocal health agreement with Britain: read DHSS leaflet SA30, and fill in forms CM1 and E111. The latter entitles you to free emergency medical treatment while visiting Portugal, on production of the form and your passport. Some charges are made for prescribed medicines and dental treatment. The British National Health Service will not reimburse medical expenses. Travel insurance is advisable for everyone.

Maps and Publications

The tourist offices' most useful handouts are their maps. These vary from illegible photocopies to glossy productions the size of a desktop.

The Automóvel Club de Portugal produces the best road maps: one side represents the whole country, while the reverse depicts the north, centre or south of Portugal in fine detail. Both Michelin and Lascelles produce acceptable maps, should you wish to buy one in advance. Walkers should try their luck at the Instituto Geográfico e Cadastral Geral (Praça da Estrêla, ✆ 01 609925).

newspapers

The Portuguese are not great newspaper readers, and yet Lisbon has ten newspapers (three of which are owned by the state), and Oporto has four morning or evening dailies (one of which is owned by the state). There are ten major national weeklies—of which only a few can scrape together a circulation of more than 100,000.

This situation has its roots in Salazar's dictatorship, when the Press was heavily censored. When the Revolution came, the newspapers were filled with turgid revolutionary propaganda. Thus were the most stalwart of readers turned off their daily or weekly paper.

Before the Revolution of 1974, most newspapers were owned by banks. When the banks were nationalized, the newspapers were tagged on too—which explains the high proportion of state-owned publications. These state-owned newspapers include some of the most prestigious, among them the long-established Lisbon daily *Diário de Notícias*, which is noted for its editorial independence. Independent *Expresso* is the leading privately owned weekly, while the highest circulation goes to *Correio da Manhã*, a tittle-tattle tabloid.

Se7e has the best listings section. Major British newspapers and the *International Herald Tribune* are available in major tourist areas and cities. They arrive in Lisbon the day after publication, and take a while to be distributed from there. *Newsweek* and the European edition of *Time* arrive in Portugal a couple of days after publication. *The Anglo-Portuguese News* is published fortnightly for the British community, and is available on news stands in Lisbon and the Algarve.

television and radio

Go into any cheap eating place of an evening and the patrons are bound to be transfixed in front of a soap opera or a football match. There are 6½ million peak-time viewers in a population of 10 million. The two oldest TV channels are both state-run and state-funded. They are not as independent as the state-owned newspapers, so it is welcome news that private channels have been licensed. Satellite dishes are not uncommon around the main towns.

For 13 years the Roman Catholic church had the only non-state radio station, Radio Renascença. In 1988 this stranglehold was broken, and dozens of new private local stations have been licensed.

libraries

The British Insitute in Lisbon has a well-stocked library in the Rua de São Marçal, ✆ 01 347 6141 (*open Wed 10–7, Thurs 10–5*); between the Bairro Alto and Rato districts. A postal loan service is available. There's also a large stock at the American Cultural Center, 22B Avenida Duque de Loulé, ✆ 01 570102 (*open Mon–Fri 12–6*).

Money

The unit of Portuguese currency is the *escudo*, which is made up of 100 *centavos*. A '$' sign is placed between the *escudos* to the left and the *centavos* to the right. Portuguese currency circulates in notes of 10,000$00, 5000$00, 2000$00, 1000$00 and 500$00. Coins are issued for 200$00, 100$00, 50$00, 25$00, 20$00, 10$00, 5$00, 2$50, 1$00 and $50.

Exchange rates vary from day to day, though unless drastic shifts occur, it's convenient to reckon on 300$00 to the pound, or 250$00 to the dollar—which makes those greeny-blue 1000$00 notes worth around £3.50 or $6.00. There is usually a very hefty commission, which is heavier in banks than at money-changers.

There are banks in every town, and most will change foreign currency or traveller's cheques. In Lisbon, most banks have branches in the Baixa. You may have to look around a bit harder if you wish to cash a Eurocheque (issued by UK banks and guaranteed by a Eurocheque card, these draw money on your UK account in the same way as a normal cheque). Most banks are open Mon–Fri 8.30–2.45. The rate of exchange varies between them, but not significantly. Some fancy hotels and travel agencies will cash traveller's cheques or exchange foreign currency, but the rates sting. The exchange counter at Lisbon airport is open constantly; at Santa Apolônia railway station, Lisbon, it's open every day 8.30–8.30; and in the Praça dos Restauradores it's open Mon–Fri 3.30–7.30 and alternate Saturdays.

Allow a couple of weeks for wiring money from abroad, and work through one of the major banks in Lisbon or Oporto (Banco Espírito Santo, Banco Nacional Ultramarino, Banco Pinto & Sotto Mayor, Banco Português do Atlântico, Banco Totta & Açores).

Credit cards—American Express, Diner's Club, Mastercard and Visa—will be useful for booking airline tickets, car hire, and peace of mind in case of emergency. They are accepted by some, but by no means all, of the upmarket hotels and restaurants. The further you get off the beaten track, the more redundant your plastic will become.

National Holidays

In 1736 Dom Luís de Cunha estimated that there were only 122 working days in the Portuguese year, because of the number of religious festivals. Things have tightened up somewhat, but everything closes on:

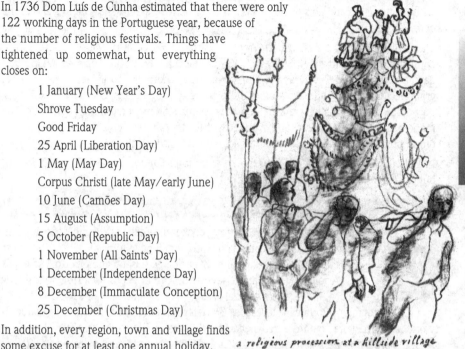

1 January (New Year's Day)

Shrove Tuesday

Good Friday

25 April (Liberation Day)

1 May (May Day)

Corpus Christi (late May/early June)

10 June (Camões Day)

15 August (Assumption)

5 October (Republic Day)

1 November (All Saints' Day)

1 December (Independence Day)

8 December (Immaculate Conception)

25 December (Christmas Day)

In addition, every region, town and village finds some excuse for at least one annual holiday.

a religious procession at a hillside village

Opening Hours

Some **shops** open at 9, but most unlock their doors at 9.30 or even 10. If they close for lunch it will be from 1 to 3: the Portuguese do not take a siesta as such, but prefer long, slow, discursive lunches. On weekdays, shops usually close at 6.30 or 7, though shopping centres stay open till midnight. Most establishments close at 1pm on Saturday.

 The majority of public **museums** are open Tues–Sun 10–12.30 and 2–6: these and the eccentrics are listed in the text. Some do not close for lunch. Admission charges for museums and archaeological sites are usually around 250$00, except for the Fronteira Palace in Lisbon, and the Solar de Mateus near Vila Real.

All small **churches** are kept locked: the keys—giant or otherwise—are with the sacristans or caretakers, who are almost invariably old ladies living nearby, who shuffle over and are delighted to help.

Post Offices

Dom Manuel created Portugal's first postal system before 1520, which makes it one of the longest-running institutions in the country. Portugal's post offices (*correios*) (*open Mon–Fri 8 or 9–12.30 and 2.30–6; main post offices are open at lunchtime and Sat mornings*) are always a hub of activity, partly because they incorporate public telephones (*see* below), and partly because the stamps (*selos*) don't stick, so patrons are kept busy with paintbrushes and pots of glue (*cola*). If you're buying stamps, be sure to stand in the correct queue.

Standard airmail (*por avião*) letters and postcards to EU countries cost 70$00, and to countries outside Europe 90$00 and 130$00 respectively. Reckon on mail taking 5–7 days to Britain, and 7–10 days to North America. There are no air letter-cards (aerogrammes) for postage abroad, though there are letter-cards for postage within Portugal. Post offices also handle telegrams. The poste restante system works well (letters should be marked '*Lista do Correios*', and will be held for the addressee at the designated post office; bring your passport when you collect letters, for which there is a small fee).

In Lisbon, the main post office is in the Restauradores (*open Mon–Sat 8am–10.30pm*), but *poste restante* goes to the Praça do Comércio.

Shopping

Leaving aside the hideous pottery cockerels, there are some good buys in Portugal—but if it's quality you want, you'll have to pay for it. At the upper end of the market are gold and silver filigree (Lisbon and Oporto), Arraiolos rugs (Arraiolos, Évora and elsewhere), leather goods (Oporto), crystal (*see* Alcobaça), large *azulejo* panels (which can be commissioned as a copy of a photograph), Portalegre tapestries (Portalegre and Lisbon), embroidery and lacework from Madeira, embroidered bedspreads (Castelo Branco) and Vista Alegre porcelain. Less pricey alternatives include fun ceramic crockery (Coimbra), pottery figures (Barcelos), black pottery (Chaves, Viseu), basketwork (Lamego and elsewhere), chunky-knit sweaters (Oporto, Lisbon, Nazaré, Sagres), and a supply of olive oil.

If you've brought the car, you could pick up a carved wooden ox-yoke (Barcelos) to serve as a bedhead or, with a couple of pegs attached, as a coat rack. You could stick a lightbulb in an Algarvian chimney to make a night light, or suspend a plant from half a copper *cataplana* (a sealed wok used for steaming food).

Sports and Activities

The Portuguese are crazy about **soccer**, and tend to support one of three clubs: Porto, from Oporto, which won the European Cup in 1987; or Sporting or Benfica from Lisbon (though the latter isn't what it was when Eusébio played for it). Tiny Rosa Mota may have won the 1988 Olympic gold medal for **marathon running**, but few of her compatriots follow in her footsteps.

Water sports make a big splash in summer, but don't expect any infrastructure outside the Algarve and the Estoril coast. (Guincho, on the latter, is renowned for its windsurfing.) Monstrous water parks have sprung up throughout the Algarve. Ask at the Club Naval de Lisboa, Pav. Náutico, Doca de Belém, © 01 363 0061, for a calendar of sailing events.

Portugal is a great place for **golf**, as thousands of Britons have discovered. The Algarve and the Estoril coast are carpeted with golf courses, and there is one course near Espinho, south of Oporto: some of these have been reviewed in the text. Many resort hotels have **tennis courts**, but public courts are hard to come by.

You'll need a licence if you wish to **fish** (trout streams in the north) or **hunt** (wild boar, deer, quail, hare, partridges). Contact the Direcção Geral das Florestas, 26–28 Av. João Crisostomo, Lisbon, ✆ 01 315 6132, and register with the local town hall. For **bull-fighting**, *see* Topics, p.49.

A little, rather tentative **skiing** takes place at Torre in the Serra da Estrêla—but it's certainly not worth going out of your way for.

Telephones

Portugal's fiendish and antiquated telephone system creates problems for even the most straightforward of calls, from Lisbon to Oporto. You'll save yourself a lot of trouble if you phone from a post office (hotels whack on a heavy surcharge for phonecalls): queue in the correct line, and you will be allocated a booth. Make your call, then return to the counter to pay for it. This is a much more efficient system than feeding 25$00 coins into a payphone in a *telefonaria* (a room full of payphones) or trying to use a street phone (most of which are broken). There are so many public phones because private phones are still a luxury in many parts of the country.

There are no cheap rates for dialling abroad. Reckon on 500$00 per minute to the UK, and substantially more for North America. To call the UK from Portugal, first dial ✆ 00 44; for Ireland ✆ 00 353; for the USA and Canada ✆ 097 1. To phone Portugal from the UK, first dial ✆ 00 351 (cheap rate 8pm–8am); from the USA dial ✆ 011 351.

Time

Portugal's clocks go forward one hour on the last Sunday in March and go back an hour on the last Sunday in September. Ordinarily Portugal shares the same time as Britain, and is five hours ahead of Eastern Standard time and eight hours ahead of Pacific time.

Toilets

All the places to stay listed in this book have Western-style toilets rather than squat, as in some Mediterranean countries. In a few of the cheap places, you are requested to put used toilet paper in a bin.

Public facilities are uncommon other than at bus and train stations (bus stations in the marble towns of the Alto Alentejo sport marble urinals) but nobody will mind if you ask to use the toilets of a hotel or restaurant without being a customer.

Tourist Offices

There are tourist offices throughout Portugal, operated by the Ministry of Tourism and signposted as *Turismo*. These are distinct from, and more useful than, the municipal tourist information desks set up in various town halls. Generally, tourist offices try hard to be helpful: more often than not you'll find someone who speaks English. Some know up-to-date hotel prices, but they rarely have timetables for public transport. In theory, opening hours are Mon–Sat 9–6: in fact it varies seasonally and geographically. Few tourist offices will open before 10, some close for lunch 12.30–2, and Saturday afternoon is a long shot.

The Ministry of Tourism has divided the country into regions: tourist offices may have information and pamphlets about other towns in their regions, but not beyond. The exceptions are in Lisbon and Oporto, where the tourist offices offer a gamut of brochures to entice the traveller.

Portuguese national tourist offices offer potential visitors numerous maps, fact sheets, and glossy brochures depicting bikinis in various locations. The offices are in:

UK: 22–25a Sackville Street, London W1X 1DE, ✆ 0171 494 1441.

Eire: c/o Portuguese Embassy, Knocksinna House, Knocksinna, Fox Rock, Dublin 18, ✆ 1 289 3569.

USA: 590 Fifth Avenue, 4th floor, New York, NY 10036, ✆ 212 354 4403.

Canada: 60 Bloor Street West, Suite 1005, Toronto, Ontario M4W 3B8, ✆ 416 921 7376.

Where to Stay

Wide not narrow be my cell
That I may dance therein at will.

Thus spake the hermit in Gil Vicente's 16th-century *Tragicomedia Pastoríl da Serra da Estrêla*. This guide is intended to help you ferret out accommodation that will offer you the very best value for money. There are still a few bargains around, but prices for accommodation in 'undiscovered' Portugal are catching up with the rest of Europe.

Hotels

Most hotels and *pensions* are decent enough, and you are unlikely to have cause for complaint. Should you do so, hotels are obliged to provide an official complaints book (*Livro Oficial de Reclamações*). Hoteliers are not permitted to oblige guests to accept full- or half-board.

Accommodation is divided into a bewildering range of categories, which are allocated according to facilities: hotels (1 star to 5 star); apartment-hotels (2 star to 4 star); *pousadas*; *estalagems* (4 and 5 star); *albergarias* (4 stars); *residencials* and *pensões* (1 to 4 stars). The system is not very helpful, and there are plenty of anomalies. Three-star *residencials* are often more comfortable than one- or two-star hotels. The distinction between *estalagems* and *albergarias* is very slight: both are inns, and usually very pleasant.

Generally, *residencials* are incorporated within larger buildings, and include breakfast in the tariff (unlike some *pensions*).

prices

Establishments are obliged to display prices in their lobbys and guest-rooms. Unless listed or agreed otherwise, single occupancy of a double room is charged at the full rate less the cost of one breakfast. An extra bed installed in a double room will cost 30 per cent of the room rate, though children under the age of eight are charged half that. Single rooms are usually charged at 60–75 per cent of the rate for a double.

Accommodation in this book is listed under six price categories, which are intended as guidelines and nothing more: prices may vary in high and low season or during festivals; and rates vary within some hotels, such as when some rooms have a pretty view and others do not. Inflation is currently running at roughly 5% per annum, and establishments are free to raise their prices from year to year as they wish.

Price ranges for a double room with bath in high season:

luxury	over 18,000$00
expensive	13,000$00–18,000$00
moderate	8500$00–13,000$00
inexpensive	6200$00–8500$00
cheap	4200$00–6200$00
very cheap	4200$00 and below—often with a shared bathroom

Pousadas

Pousadas are government-owned hotels, intended to make use of the best Portugal has to offer. Almost half of them are installed in monasteries, convents, castles or palaces. The rest are in places of outstanding historic or scenic interest. They vary from opulent to modestly comfortable: most of them are reviewed in the text. *Pousadas* can be memorable in their own right, and *pousada* holidays are popular—but their prices have risen steeply. Their restaurants provide good, well-presented food, and are open to non-residents. All *pousadas* are very well signposted.

booking and prices

Pousadas can be booked direct, or through: ENATUR, Empresa Nacional de Turismo EP, 10–A Avenida Santa Joana a Princesa, 1700 Lisbon (© 01 848 1221 or 848 9078, telex 13609 ENATUR P, @ 01 805846).

The *pousadas* have been placed in four categories (B, C, C* and CH), and their prices vary accordingly. These categories are fair and usually offer good value.

High-season prices for bed and continental breakfast are as follows:

Category	B	C	C*	CH
Double room	15,000$00	19,500$00	21,000$00	26,200$00
Single room	13,000$00	17,000$00	18,500$00	23,500$00
Extra bed	4500$00	6300$00	7000$00	8500$00

Solares de Portugal (Turismo de Habitação)

The grand private homes of Portugal have shaken the dust from the tapestries bearing their coats of arms, wafted woodsmoke through their huge kitchens of rough-cut granite, and opened their spare bedrooms to paying guests—under the aegis of the *Turismo de Habitação* scheme. This enables visitors to stay in antique accommodation and receive a highly personal view of rural (or in some cases urban) life.

The name *Turismo de Habitação* is being changed to the more manageable *Solares de Portugal*, although in the text, as in the country, this scheme is still referred to as *Turismo de Habitação*.

The character of the participating houses differs as much as their owners: baronial, baroque or bacchanal. Most are manor houses smacking of faded opulence. Some have ten rooms available, others two. The highest concentration of *Turismo de Habitação* is in the Minho, where the central reservations office in Ponte de Lima handles bookings for some 60 homes. The owners may be there to offer an expansive welcome to the home their ancestors built centuries ago. Most hosts are charming, forthcoming, and not averse to a bit of company. How much you see of the master or mistress of the house depends upon the set-up: some enthuse in English or French at breakfast, in a dining room glinting with crested silver. Most hosts will provide dinner if it is requested in advance.

A few words of warning are in order. Few of the houses are signposted, so it's important to pick up directions from the local tourist office. Most Portuguese antiques are heavy, and these can be oppressive. Sometimes visitors are intimidated by their museum-like surroundings; others feel they are invading their hosts' privacy. Heating is often minimal, so think twice if you're planning a winter visit. *See* below for the booking restrictions.

That said, *Turismo de Habitação* offers an excellent opportunity for a unique experience of accommodation in Portugal—at very reasonable rates.

booking and prices

Manor houses in the Minho are divided into three categories (A, B and C), and their prices vary accordingly.

Category A:	1 pers 13,000$00	2 pers 15,800$00
Category B:	1 pers 10300$00	2 pers 11,800$00
Category C:	1 pers 7500$00	2 pers 8800$00

Elsewhere, participating houses have been allotted one of the five hotel price categories.

Rooms should be booked at least three days in advance, and for a minimum of three nights. Fifty per cent of the total rate should be paid at the time of reservation.

Reservations should be made either with the owners of the houses (who may not speak English) or with an agency representing them. Reservations for the majority of manor houses in Portugal can be made with: TURIHAB (Associação do Turismo de Habitação), Praça da República, 4990 Ponte de Lima (✆ 058 942729, telex 32618 PTPL, ✆ 058 741444).

Other houses are represented by the PRIVETUR association, whose reservations are handled by: CAP (Confederação Dos Agricultores de Portugal), Calçada Ribeiro Sautos, 19–r/c, 1200 Lisbon (℃ 01 674063 or 01 675171/2). ANTER (Associacão Nacional de Turismo Espaço Rural) also represent some houses. Find them at Quinta do Campo, Valado dos Frades, 2450 Nazaré (℃ 062 577135/577126).

Some houses have no agency representing them. Information can be obtained from the Portuguese National Tourist Office in Britain, the United States or Canada.

For **descriptions** of individual houses in the scheme, *see*: Viana do Castelo, Around Monção, Ponte de Lima and Ponte da Barca (the Minho); Sortelha, Guarda, Sabugueiro, Viseu (Beira Alta); Alpedrinha (Beira Baixa); the Aveiro Lagoon (Beira Litoral); Óbidos, Sintra, Cascais, Estoril, Setúbal (Estremadura); Santarém, Constância (Ribatejo); Marvão, Monsaraz (Alto Alentejo); Serpa (Baixo Alentejo); Tavira (Algarve).

Resort Accommodation

Most of Portugal's resort accommodation has been built in the last 15 years and, with the exception of some upmarket 'tourist villages' in the Algarve, offers about as much atmosphere as an unpainted *azulejo*. Expect block bookings from package-tour operators: to get away from them, head for the west coast. The Algarve and Estoril coasts are the most expensive parts of Portugal, but they also have the greatest price variants between high and low seasons, so you can make substantial savings on accommodation by booking out of season.

Cheap Accommodation

Shoestring travellers can find their own kind of Turismo de Habitação: ask at local tourist offices for rooms to rent in people's houses, or look in windows for signs advertising quartos. You may end up with a scrupulously clean little room complete with a religious icon, a lace runner on the chest of drawers and home-made bread for breakfast.

Some of the cheaper *pensions* are a bit unsavoury: you can save money by asking for a room without a private shower room, but pack a pair of flip-flops to wear in the public one. It's advisable to ask to see a room before you commit yourself to renting it. You'll be asked to submit your passport and may have to pay a day in advance. Check whether breakfast is included in the room rate.

youth hostels

Portugal has 14 youth hostels (*Pousadas de Juventude*), 13 of which are open throughout the year. Guests must have a valid Youth Hostel Association membership card. In the USA, these can be obtained from the American Youth Hostels, Inc, PO Box 37613, Washington D.C. 20013–7613 (℃ 202 783 6161). In Portugal, they can be obtained from the Associação Portuguesa de Pousadas de Juventude, 137 Duque d'Avila, 1000 Lisbon (℃ 01 355 9081).

Youth hostels carry the usual grim array of regulations: you must check in 9–12 or 6–9pm; 1 Oct–30 April you must book in advance; you must stay a minimum of three nights;

dormitories must be kept absolutely silent during the night. In short, you'd be better off finding a good *pension*.

camping

Camping is a low-key affair, and can work out remarkably cheap. Ask in bookshops for the *Roteiro Campista*, which offers a detailed listing of all campsites. Unofficial camping is OK if you're discreet, but don't try it in the Algarve.

Women and Children

Sexual harassment is nothing compared with what it is in some Latin countries: in rural areas, single women travellers are a cause of amazement rather than anything else; in large towns and cities, infuriating men on the street hiss or cluck their approval. Steer clear of the areas around bus and train stations at night. For those interested in the feminist movement in Portugal, the Comissão de Condição Feminina (2nd Floor, 32 Avenida da República, Lisbon) has links with feminist groups throughout the country. It also organizes conferences and meetings, encompassing every aspect of women's lives, and is active in social and legal reform.

Portugal is an excellent country in which to travel with small children because the Portuguese are entirely tolerant of them and their ways, though there are few separate amusements for kids. All Portuguese babies are wrapped in several blankets whatever the season.

History and Art

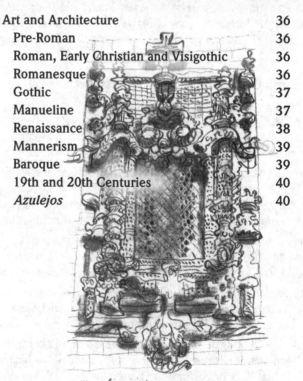

Manueline window, Tomar

Prehistory, the Romans, the Suevi and the Visigoths

When the Celts invaded the Peninsula in the first millennium BC, they mingled with the Iberians—who had been putting down roots since *c.* 8000 BC—and became **Celt-Iberians**. The Phoenicians came in search of metals, and by *c.* 800 BC were trading at Cadiz. Their empire passed to the Carthaginians, and later to the Romans, who occupied Hispania Ulterior (Andalusia) in 202 BC.

The Romans marched inland, where the fierce **Lusitanian** tribespeople of central Portugal waged a successful guerilla war against them. The Lusitanians' leader, Viriatus, was fatally betrayed in 139 BC; so too was the Roman general Sertorius, who briefly championed the Lusitanian cause after 80 BC.

Rome never penetrated deeply north of the Tagus. South of the river, Julius Caesar founded Pax Julia (*c.* 60 BC), to bolster the port of Olissipo (Lisbon) and the towns of Ebora (Évora) and Myrtilis (Mértola). Roman *latifundias* established the pattern of landholding in the Alentejo; Roman roads were used until the Middle Ages, and their bridges are still in use today. They also introduced vines, olives, figs, and almonds.

At the beginning of the 5th century, barbarian hordes entered the peninsula. The Romans enlisted the aid of the **Visigoths**, who disposed of all but the **Suevi**, or Swabians. The Suevi based themselves between the Rivers Minho and Douro, and were converted to Christianity by St Martin: their see of Braga incorporated Lamego, Viseu, Conimbriga and Idanha *c.* 569. The Swabian monarchy was suppressed by the Visigothic ruler, Leovigild, in 585.

The Moorish Occupation and the Christian Reconquest

The Moors were invited into Spain in 711, and nominally conquered the Peninsula within two years. They represented a salad of races—Arabs, Syrians, Persians, Jews, Berbers from Morocco, and Copts from Egypt, who had been Christian—all of whom preferred the sunny climate of the south. Christians rallied together in northern Portugal and Galicia.

In the middle of the 9th century, the Christians crept southwards: Portucale (Oporto) was rebuilt in 868, and the region between the Rivers Minho, Douro, and later the Vouga became known as **Territorium Portugalense**. This territory was administered by successive generations of a ruling family, including Countess Mumadona (around 931).

Ferdinand I, King of Castile, drove the Moors from Lamego (1057), Viseu (1058), and from the city of Coimbra (1064). His successor, Alfonso VI, revived the metropolitan see of Braga—which reinforced the integrity of the province that was to become Portugal.

Alfonso's son-in-law, Henry of Burgundy, ruled the territory between the Rivers Minho and Douro from his capital at Guimarães. Later his widow, **Teresa**, governed Portugal as regent for their son, **Dom Afonso Henriques**.

When Alfonso VII, King of Galicia, invaded Teresa's lands, her barons united behind Dom Afonso Henriques. He defeated his mother at the battle of São Mamede in 1128, and the reign of the **first King of Portugal** had begun.

The House of Burgundy

Although the Pope did not recognize the kingdom of Portugal until 1179, the country had asserted its independence from Spain. It was helped by the fact that none of its rivers were navigable into Spain, and the Spaniards had no need of Portuguese ports.

Moorish chroniclers refer to **Dom Afonso Henriques** (1128/39–85) as 'the cursed of Allah': aided by internal strife amongst the Moors he crusaded southwards, capturing Santarém after the battle of Ourique in 1139, and Lisbon in 1147. But the reconquest was not completed for nearly 150 years. His son Dom Sancho I (1185–1211) continued the subjugation, but in 1191 was driven back north of the Tagus, except for a foothold in Évora. Dom Afonso III (1248–79) captured Faro.

His *Cortes* at Leiria in 1254 was the first at which the commons were represented. **Structures of power** were gradually taking shape. Large parts of the newly conquered lands had been granted to the military and monastic Orders to secure their defence and colonization. The Church fought hard to retain its independence: the bishops were so incensed at the Crown's meddling in the election of bishops, that they declared the deposition of Dom Afonso III. The Portuguese Pope, John XXI, did little to help.

Afonso's son, **Dom Dinis** (1279–1325), became one of the greatest Burgundian kings. He ruled with great foresight—earning Dante's praise in *Paradiso*. Dom Dinis strengthened the nation's defences by building or rebuilding most of her castles, and established the Order of Christ to take the place of the suppressed Knights Templar. Forests were planted, and the king authorized at least 40 fairs. Dom Dinis founded Portugal's first university, the General Studies, in Lisbon in 1290; he also required deeds and official documents to be written in the vernacular. In all this, he was assisted by his peacemaking queen, St Isabel.

The later Burgundian kings became embroiled in a series of **Castilian marriage alliances**: both Dom Pedro I (1357–67), who loved to dance to the sound of the trumpet, and his chivalrous heir, Dom Fernando (1367–83), followed this course. Dom Fernando obeyed his queen, Leonor, and married his heiress, Beatriz, to Juan, King of Castile: if this union produced no fruit, Juan would become King of Portugal.

When Dom Fernando died, Juan ordered the Portuguese townships to proclaim Beatriz queen. He received the backing of the entrenched nobility, who stood to benefit from Castilian-style government—but the spectre of **absorption by Castile** fired the towns and coastal regions in their support for a bastard son of Dom Pedro, **João of Avis**. In Lisbon he was 'accompanied by the common people as if he were dropping precious treasures for them all to grab', and in 1385 João was declared king (1385–1433).

Shortly afterwards he and his lieutenant, **Nun' Álvares Pereira**, defeated Juan at the **battle of Aljubarrota**: this secured the independence of Portugal for nearly 200 years. An Anglo-Portuguese alliance was cemented with the king's marriage to Philippa of Lancaster, sister of England's future Henry IV.

The House of Avis and the Age of Discoveries

Having made peace with Spain, Portugal turned her attention seawards. Fired by the desire for glory, piety and distraction, Dom João I took advantage of a civil war in the Magrib to **capture Ceuta** in 1415. But it was his third son, **Henry the Navigator**, who did most to foster Portugal's maritime exploits. He set up a school of navigation at Sagres, and chanelled his funds into a succession of expeditions. These groped their way down the west coast of Africa; Gil Eanes rounded Cape Bojador in 1434. Madeira and the Azores were rediscovered, but were not colonized until 1445, during the reign of Henry's elder brother, the lawmaker Dom Duarte (1433–8).

Another brother, Dom Pedro, served as regent during the minority of Dom Duarte's heir, Dom Afonso V (1438–81). This riled the young king's half-uncle, the first Duke of Bragança, who fought and killed the regent in 1449.

Like his father and grandfather, Dom Afonso V fought in Morocco, storming to victory at the battle of Alcácer-Seguir in 1458. Also like his forebears, he strengthened the power of the *Cortes*, since expensive expeditions obliged the kings to woo the towns' resources.

His son, Dom João, negotiated peace with Castile. As king (João II, 1481–95) he beheaded the overmighty Duke of Bragança, and received some 60,000 Jews fleeing persecution in Spain.

Overseas explorations were resumed. In 1487 **Bartolomeu Dias** rounded the Cape (of Good Hope) without seeing land, and Pêro de Covilhã was dispatched to India and Ethiopia. The Portuguese crown refused to finance Columbus' plan to find a westward route to the Indies: he took his idea to Ferdinand and Isabella of Spain, sailed in 1492, and discovered America. Now that Spain had a stake in the rest of the world, she and Portugal negotiated its partition. The **Treaty of Tordesillas** of 1493 allocated to Spain all lands west, and to Portugal all lands east of a line running north to south 360 leagues west of the Cape Verde Islands. The Portuguese lands just happened to include Brazil, prompting suspicions that the Portuguese already knew of its existence.

The crown passed to Dom João II's impatient cousin, **Dom Manuel** (1495–1521), whose arms were so long that his hands dangled beside his knees. During his reign, Portugal's position in Morocco and the Congo was consolidated (the former partly because Portugal had begun importing wheat and looked to the wide Moroccan plains). Looking further afield, **Vasco da Gama** set sail in 1497, and returned two years later having discovered a sea route to India and its spices. Pedro Álvares Cabral was dispatched in that direction, but sailed too far west and discovered Brazil, in 1500. Portugal established an administrative capital at Goa, and set about destroying the Indian Ocean's complex web of trading links, to secure the supremacy of her own commerce. A crew sailing under a Spanish flag completed the first circumnavigation of the globe, though their Portuguese captain, Fernando de Magalhãis (Magellan) was killed *en route*.

The profits generated by the spice trade made Dom Manuel the **wealthiest ruler in Europe**—but Portugal's zenith was shortlived. The prospect of quick profit in Africa, India or Brazil lured the nation's entrepreneurs, leaving the home economy and agricultural productivity fatally weakened. Those of the merchant classes who stayed put were hit very badly by the royal monopoly, established in 1506. Nor was the new wealth invested productively. Portugal lost most of her banking and economic expertise in 1496, when the king expelled his Jewish subjects—a prerequisite for his marriage to Princess Isabel of Castile.

Dom João III (1521–57) and Charles V of Spain married each other's sisters (thus providing the basis for Philip II's claim to the Portuguese throne 50 years later). Portugal settled Brazil, and in 1557 was granted Macau to enable her to trade with Canton. But already the prices of spices in Europe were falling, and the mother country was drained of men, ships and money defending the lines of communication that held together her global empire.

In 1536 the New Christians—ostensibly converted Jews—braced themselves against the Inquisition, which established tribunals in Lisbon, Coimbra and Évora. The court grew larger and more slothful, and the countryside became alarmingly depopulated. The Jesuits were invited into Portugal, and were granted their own university at Évora. Other Jesuits did not stay long: St Francis Xavier was preaching in Japan in 1549.

Dom João III's heir became king while still in his mother's womb; his great uncle, Cardinal Henrique served as regent. **Dom Sebastian** (1557–78) was an odd fish, coupling a clear idea of his military calling with a childish impetuosity. The result was disastrous: he led an ill-prepared and clumsy expedition into Morocco, where 15,000 Portuguese were captured at the battle of **Alcácer-Quivir**. Dom Sebastian was killed (*see* **Topics**, p.45), and fewer than 100 escaped; the ransom payments beggared the nation. The elderly cardinal was proclaimed king (1578–80) but died shortly afterwards. In desperation he was replaced by António, Prior of Crato (1580), bastard nephew of Dom João III.

The Spanish Usurpation

Philip II of Spain saw his opportunity. Wealthy Portuguese supported his entry into their country because they wished to avoid the expense of protracted warfare; he may also have had the support of the Jesuits. In addition Portugal's weakening economy needed Spain's American silver. The new king (Philip I of Portugal, 1580–98) abided by his promises to preserve the autonomy of Portugal—though he strengthened those institutions which straddled the two countries, **the Jesuits and the Inquisition**. He closed the Portuguese ports to English and, later, Dutch ships. Undeterred, the Dutch made their own way to the East, where they snatched the spice trade from the Portuguese.

His indolent son, Philip III (II) (1598–1621) had little contact with Portugal, and Philip IV (III) (1621–40) was distracted by the Catalan rebellion.

The Entrenchment of the House of Bragança

The Catalan rebellion gave the Portuguese a chance to rally around the Duke of Bragança, Dom João III's great-nephew. They crowned him King **João IV** (1640–56). Treaties were signed with the Dutch, who had occupied Brazil and had been attacking Portuguese shipping, and with the English, whose **Commonwealth Treaty** of 1654 set out privileges which held for nearly two centuries. At that time, approximately 14 per cent of Portugal's 1.5 million souls were nobility or clergy, thus qualifying for the attendant financial privileges.

Dom Afonso VI (1656–67) was partly paralysed and partly stupid. Fighting against the Spanish dragged on until 1665: they made incursions to Olivença and Elvas in 1658, and to Évora in 1663.

Alarmed by Spain's peace with France, Portugal was desperate to strengthen its alliance with England. Thus **Catherine of Bragança**, Dom Afonso's sister, was married to King Charles II. Her massive dowry included two million cruzados, the right to trade with Portuguese colonies, and the cession of Tangier (Bombay was an afterthought). In return, England agreed to defend Portugal (and its overseas territories) 'as if it were England itself'. The king married Marie-Françoise of Savoy. Shortly afterwards he handed the government and his wife to his brother Dom Pedro.

Dom Pedro II (1667–83) convened a *Cortes* in 1698, the last time the consultative body was ever summoned: the discovery of gold at Mato Grosso in Brazil secured the king's financial independence (and stunted domestic manufacture; only the colonies generated wealth, which was spent on imported goods). In 1703 the **Methuen treaty** implemented a defensive alliance with England and Holland; the subsequent commercial treaty generated favourable terms for Portuguese wine in Britain, and for British cloth in Portugal. The latter terms were the more significant, being the death sentence of the Portuguese textile trade. In the same year, Philip V invaded Portugal, but Spanish and French troops returned to Madrid in 1706.

The wealth created by Brazilian gold was compounded by that of **diamonds**, discovered there in 1728. Although the crown did not always receive its one-fifth share, Dom **João V** (1706–50) reaped an estimated 107 million cruzados over a period of 44 years. However, the money did little to benefit Portugal. The king modelled himself on Louis XIV of France, lavishing much of his fortune on ostentatious building projects—principally at Mafra—and the aggrandizement of his standing in the Catholic world. When he died, there was not enough money left in the royal treasury to pay for his funeral.

His featherbrained son, Dom José (1750–77), was entirely dominated by the tyrannical minister later entitled **Marquês de Pombal**. This 'hairy-hearted' autocrat was made chief minister shortly after the Lisbon earthquake of 1755. He destroyed his enemies, the Jesuits and the entrenched aristocracy, and implemented a policy of **state-aided capitalism** to reduce the foreign deficit and erode Portugal's stultifying network of privileges.

Some 71 manufacturing establishments were set up 1769–78, but economic activity was over-regulated. The state took control of wine production in the Alto Douro, and Pombal reformed the education of the élite.

The benefits of Pombal's rule were temporary, limited, and overshadowed by the cruelty of his subjection. Pombal had no regrets: 'The prisons and the cells were the only means I found to tame this blind and ignorant nation.'

As soon as she acceded to the throne, Dona **Maria I** (1777–92) banished Pombal to his estates. Many of his trading ventures were scuppered, and political prisoners were released. When the queen went screaming mad at Queluz, her son Dom João (later João VI) governed.

The Napoleonic Wars

Napoleon put Portugal back on the European map—if only to decide how best to apportion the country. The French threatened to invade unless Portugal supported their naval blockade of Britain; Portugal refused to commit economic suicide, and a French army under **Junot** marched into Lisbon in 1807. The British had provided a fleet to whisk the royal family to Brazil, out of harm's way; they were to remain there until 1821. The British generals **Wellesley and Beresford** were left to secure the defence of Portugal. Twice the invaders were driven out. They returned, but recalled their final garrison in 1811, having been flummoxed by the Lines of Torres Vedras. The British, for their part, were granted free access to Brazilian ports—enabling them to trade without depending on Portugal as an intermediary. Thus the Portuguese lost a vital source of profit. Their commerce was wrecked and their treasury in debt.

Liberals v. Miguelites and the War of the Two Brothers

Dom João VI (1792–1826) remained in Brazil, and Beresford continued as marshal of the Portuguese army. When he temporarily left the country, an army-backed revolution took place in Oporto. An unofficial *Cortes* was summoned, which devised a sweeping constitution: the *Cortes* was to be a single-chamber parliament elected by universal male suffrage; feudal and clerical rights were to be abolished.

The timid king returned from Brazil in 1821, and agreed to abide by this constitution, though it fettered his power—but his rambunctious queen, Dona Carlota Joaquina, and their younger son, **Dom Miguel**, refused. The latter became the focus of a rural anti-liberal movement.

When Dom João VI died in 1826, his eldest son and heir, **Dom Pedro IV** (1826–8), acceded to the throne. Things were not straightforward: he had already become Emperor of the newly independent Brazil, and was living there. His solution was to abdicate the throne of Portugal in favour of his young daughter, Dona Maria da Glória—on condition that she marry his brother Dom Miguel, and that Dom Miguel accept a **Constitutional Charter**. This was milder than the radical constitution of 1822, but more liberal than the traditional form of government.

The betrothal took place, but Dom Miguel (1828–34) reneged on the agreement. He was declared king with absolute powers, and there followed a purge of liberals. His brother, Dom Pedro, returned from Brazil to **fight for the Portuguese throne**, a bloody task in which he was assisted by excellent generals and British support for the liberal cause. Dom Miguel finally capitulated at Évora-Monte in 1834, and was exiled to Austria.

Liberalism

The state was not only war-weary but bankrupt. The liberals sought wealth by dissolving the country's monasteries and convents in 1834—nearly a quarter of the cultivated land in Portugal changed hands.

Dom Pedro died soon after his victory, leaving the throne to his teenage daughter, Dona **Maria II** (1834–53). Governments came and went rather rapidly: some backed the Constitutional Charter of 1826; others supported the constitution of 1822. Neither was prepared to strike at the roots of the country's financial crisis: the unproductive economy, which relied on foreign investment and loans; and directionless governance. Governments became more stable after 1852, when the Duke of Saldanha introduced modifications to the charter, and a new electoral law had been applied.

During the brief reign of Dom Pedro V (1855–61), Fontes Pereira de Melo set up a **Ministry of Public Works**, to give Portugal the infrastructure necessary for economic growth. Roads and railways were built; agricultural production increased accordingly. However, Portugal's balance of payments took a drastic downturn: the country lacked industrial raw materials, skilled labour (in 1870 there were 150 qualified engineers in Portugal) and investment capital.

Nadir of the Monarchy

When **Dom Carlos** (1889–1908) acceded to the throne, he inherited a country bewildered by the succession of governments in power since 1871. Portugal had sunk into a mire of high unemployment, strikes and public demonstrations. In 1890, Portugal's hopes of gaining control of the territory linking her colonies of Angola and Mozambique were thwarted by an ultimatum from Britain. This rattled the belief that the British Alliance was a guarantee of security, and tipped Portugal into crisis.

The king was the butt of his nation's dishonour, and made matters worse by placing a dictator, João Franco, in charge of the government. Amidst growing discontent, the king and his eldest son Prince Dom Luís Filipe were **shot dead** in Lisbon in 1908. The king was succeeded briefly by his younger son, Dom Manuel II (1908–10).

The monarchy was finally snuffed out in 1910, when the king fled to Britain in the face of a tentative uprising by Republican revolutionaries and their supporters in the navy. This freakish victory led to the **proclamation of the Republic** on 5 October 1910.

The Republic

The Republicans gained the support of the Church, the British, and rural Portugal—but were never democratic. They limited freedom of speech, and muzzled the press. Popular discontent was swelled by Portugal's (limited) involvement in the First World War after 1916, on the side of the Allies. The war exaggerated the weaknesses of Portugal's economy, prompting a series of strikes.

In 1917 a military revolt gained popular support, inaugurating seven years of chaos: there were 45 governments between 1910 and 1926. By 1923 the escudo had fallen to one-twentieth of the value it registered against the pound in 1917. Faced with this intolerable instability, the army overthrew the 'Democratic' regime in 1926.

The New State

Out of the morass emerged Dr António de Oliveira **Salazar**, an economics professor at Coimbra University, who was made Minister of Finance in 1928. With total control of revenue and expenditure, he turned a 330 million escudo deficit into a budgetary surplus—in his first year of office (and his regime continued to balance the budget until it was overthrown in 1974).

In 1932, Salazar became Prime Minister, an office he retained until 1968. His *Estado Novo* (**New State**) stressed nationalism, and Salazar secured the trappings of **dictatorship**: political parties, unions, and strikes were abolished; censorship was enforced; and the hated political police (the PIDE) thrived. Some 100,000 informers supplied the police with details of their friends, families or associates.

Portugal remained neutral during the Second World War, and in the postwar period, communications were extended and modernized. The construction of dams brought hydro-electric power. This enabled Portuguese industry to grow at a rate of 9 per cent per year in the 1950s and 1960s.

The **colonies** ('overseas provinces') formed an integral part of the *Estado Novo*. Local independence movements in Angola (1961), Guinea-Bissau (1963) and Mozambique (1964) ushered in **dirty wars** that were to sap Portugal's meagre resources. By 1968, more than 100,000 Portuguese troops were fighting in Africa.

Democracy

The unpopularity of the wars in Africa, and discontent with the oppressive regime, crystallized into the Movement of the Armed Forces (**MFA**), which toppled the *Estado Novo* in a bloodless coup on 25 April 1974.

The **African territories** were granted their **independence**, and Portugal accommodated three-quarters of a million *retornados* from there. The revolution had a real effect on people's lives: the secret police were dispersed, censorship was lifted, industry, banks and insurance companies were **nationalized**, and nearly 4 million acres of land, especially the large *latifundias* of the Alentejo, was expropriated. Today much of this process is being reversed, as the government pushes through a series of privatization programmes in a rush to meet EU deadlines.

The country came close to civil war in November 1975, when a counter-coup attempted to prevent a communist takeover—but a crisis was averted. In 1976 a new constitution was drawn up, under which the Prime Minister and cabinet were responsible to the popularly elected President and to the Assembly of the Republic, which was elected by proportional representation.

The 1995 elections saw the end of a decade in power by the PSD. Aníbal Cavaco Silva was defeated as prime minister by the socialist mayor of Lisbon, Jorge Sampaio, and Antonio

Gutierres of the PS party gained the largest number of seats in parliament—the first time in 25 years that president and prime minister have come from the same political party. Gutierres has been determined to drag the country into modern Europe. One of his first announcements was a stringency plan, cutting back on social security and attempting to modernize the Portuguese economy. He also promised the business community that Portugal would join the European Monetary System (EMS) in 1999, a promise which is unlikely to be fulfilled. His plans have met with a mixed response from the Portuguese people, the poorest of whom have felt the worst effects of his market-orientated policies; at the same time, through-the-roof property prices in Lisbon indicate an element of confidence in one of the fastest-growing economies in Europe.

Art and Architecture

Pre-Roman

The earliest monuments in Portugal are the megalithic dolmens of the Alto Alentejo (4000–2000 BC). History then leaves a yawning gap until the Iron Age (800–200 BC) when the Celt-Iberians rooted themselves in hill camps: the *Citânias* of Briteiros and Sabroso are chock-full of the foundations of round houses, which had conical roofs (south of the Douro, houses were rectangular, with V-shaped roofs). The contemporary *berrões*, crudely sculpted bulls and boars found throughout Trás-os-Montes, remain mysterious: they may have been the images of a fertility cult, funerary symbols, or territorial markers, or may have been invoked for the protection of flocks and herds. Rupestral art added spice to Celt-Iberian life—best seen at Outeiro Machado—while the *Colossus of Pedralva* (Museu de Martins Sarmento, Guimarães) is a more monumental creation.

Roman, Early Christian and Visigothic

The Romans set about building up the indigenous cities, particularly during the reign of Augustus: they constructed temples (Évora), baths and villas (Conimbriga, Milreu, Miróbriga, and Pisões), amphitheatres, cryptoporticus (Machado de Castro Museum, Coimbra), and a shrine at Braga. Most Roman bridges are still in use, though their roads are not. The best mosaics are at Torres Novas, Conimbriga, Faro and Pisões. There appear to have been few sculptors resident in Portugal: most of the sculpture displayed in museums around the country was carved elsewhere or was the work of itinerant craftsmen.

Lisbon's first bishop was appointed in 357, and Braga's c. 400, but few traces remain of the Early Christians. The Visigoths have left us the Byzantine chapel of São Frutuoso (Braga), and two other buildings subsumed by later ages, the church of São Pedro de Balsemão (near Lamego) and the Sé at Idanha-a-Velha.

Romanesque

Few Moorish buildings survive—the Igreja Matriz at Mértola is an exception—but the Moors bequeathed to Portugal a legacy of whitewashed cuboid houses and shuttered balconies.

The nation of Portugal hatched when the Romanesque was at its prime: monks of Cluny and Cister brought the style from France to the Minho, which is peppered with out-of-the-way Romanesque churches. These granite buildings are decorated with simple capitals, columns, corbels and portal arches: foliage, fabulous animals and human figures ornament churches at Bravães and Longos Vales, while those of Monçao and Melgaço are less lively. Limestone was easily available around Coimbra: the soft stone was easy to carve, which encouraged more elaborate designs, as at the Cistercian Monastery of São João de Tarouca (in Salzedas).

The thick walls and crenellations of Portugal's Romanesque cathedrals (Braga, Oporto, Coimbra, Lisbon, Évora) attest harsh times: their towers served as a refuge in case of invasion. Bragança's *Domus Municipalis* is a rare example of Romanesque civic architecture.

Gothic

The Abbey of Alcobaça (1178) is Portugal's earliest Gothic building, but the style didn't really catch on until the Franciscan and Dominican Orders established themselves during the reign of Dom Afonso III (1248–79). Then the Gothic took hold of Portugal until the second quarter of the 16th century, when it was dislodged by Renaissance sensibilities. The austerity of the mendicant Orders is reflected in sober façades with a rose window above the portal, and three naves divided by slim arches. Gothic capitals sprout realistic flora (grapevines and ivy).

Gothic architecture in Portugal found its supreme expression in the monastery of Batalha. Its progeny includes the Carmo Church in Lisbon, the Sé at Guarda, and the church of São Domingos at Guimarães. Gothic cloisters were added to many cathedrals and churches. There are few traces of Gothic civil architecture: the palaces are ruinous or restored beyond recognition, so it's more worthwhile to look at a humbler level, in parts of Castelo de Vide's *judiaria*.

Most of Portugal's castles are Gothic, with small balconies on the upper storeys of their towers. The castles at Estremoz and Beja are distinguished by their monumental keeps; elsewhere those of Bragança and Óbidos are the most impressive.

The intricate tombs of Dom Pedro I and Inês de Castro at Alcobaça represent Gothic sculpture at its most sublime. The double tomb of Dom João I and Philippa of Lancaster at Batalha created a vogue for monuments on which effigies of the couple rest side by side.

Beyond funerary monuments, fine Gothic sculpture exists in the shrouded *Cristo Morto* in Coimbra's Machado de Castro Museum, and in the Evangelists flanking the portals of the Sé at Évora and the Abbey at Batalha. Portuguese painting was practically non-existent until Nuno Gonçalves (died before 1492) arrived on the scene. His *Panels of St Vincent* (Museu de Arte Antiga, Lisbon) are outstanding as a group portrait and an illuminating historical document.

Manueline

The Manueline style is Portugal's own contribution to the world's architecture: its ebullient forms encapsulate the thrill of the Age of Discoveries, and its treatment of space belongs to generations of horizon-gazers. It developed out of the late Gothic, and reached its peak 1490–1521, during the reign of Dom Manuel, from whom it takes its name. This was Portugal's great age, when wealth from trade with the East generated numerous new artistic ventures, which attracted foreign craftsmen to Portugal.

The Manueline is a disparate style, with substyles derived from the Spanish Plateresque (finely detailed motifs in low relief), the Moorish revival called *mudéjar*, and a concoction of fantastic maritime motifs. Most Manueline work is found south of Tomar, for the court rarely ventured beyond Coimbra.

Boitac's breathtaking Jerónimos Monastery at Belém (Lisbon) is the finest Manueline building, while the window made for the Order of Christ at Tomar is strikingly forceful, and the Torre de Belém (Lisbon) an enchanting blend of Moorish and Manueline styles. The church of Jesus at Setúbal signals the early development of the Manueline style.

Flemish, Spanish, French and mudéjar craftsmen wielded the most influential chisels in Portugal. Manueline architecture required a feast of sculptural embellishment (Unfinished Chapels, Batalha), and thus serves as the finest showcase of Manueline sculpture: elsewhere the sculpture of the age is either late Gothic (the retable of the Sé Velha in Coimbra), early Renaissance, or mudéjar. Mudéjar craftsmen carved and painted wooden ceilings in the chapel of the National Palace at Sintra, in the Igreja Matriz at Caminha, and in the church of São Bento at Bragança. Like contemporary sculpture, the painting of the age followed the Renaissance style.

Renaissance

The Italian Renaissance came to Portugal via Flanders, with whom she had close trading links. Renaissance ornament arrived first: in architecture, full-blown Greco-Roman columns, pilasters and entablature were not embraced wholeheartedly until 1530—when Portugal's wealth was just beginning to wane. The cathedrals of the new dioceses created by Dom João III—Leiria, Portalegre, and Miranda do Douro—take on a Renaissance austerity. Diogo de Torralva's cloister at the convent of Christ in Tomar is the supremely balanced work of the age. The Quinta da Bacalhôa and the Quinta das Torres, both at Azeitão, best represent the civil architecture of the period.

Nicolau Chanterène introduced the Renaissance to Portuguese sculpture: his career in Portugal began with the late Gothic west portal at Belém (Lisbon) and ended with the altarpiece in the Pena Palace at Sintra and the stunningly beautiful tomb now in Évora's municipal museum. His nominal successor, João de Ruão, pales by comparison.

Portuguese Renaissance painting adopts the realism, depth of perspective, and lively colours of Flemish work. Frei Carlos (Museu de Arte Antiga, Lisbon) himself was Flemish. Vasco Fernandes, called Grão Vasco (1475–1541; municipal museums of Viseu and Lamego), Gregório Lopes, Cristóvão de Figueiredo and the Master of Sardoal are the names to watch for.

The finest Portuguese work is in the Setúbal Museum and the Museu de Arte Antiga in Lisbon; the Bruges school is well represented at the municipal museum in Évora.

Mannerism

The Portuguese Renaissance was snuffed out on the death of Dom João III in 1557. Mannerism's cold and frigid classicism set in, and did not thaw until c. 1710. The Spanish takeover in 1580 compounded the decline by dissipating the court and thus removing the focus of artistic patronage.

The newly arrived Jesuits did much to shape the ecclesiastical architecture of the period: true to the spirit of the Counter-Reformation, the pulpit was to be clearly visible from all parts of the church. Lisbon's church of São Vicente de Fora served as a prototype. The Benedictines renovated their monasteries after the early 17th century, preferring large windows in their façades. The palace of the Marquês de Fronteira in Lisbon is the most complete example of 17th-century civil architecture.

At the end of the 16th century, stone sculpture gave way to wooden sculpture: initially, retables simply imitated their stony predecessors, but in the middle of the 17th century they acquired a style of their own—and niches were filled with sculpture (as in the sanctuary at Alcobaça). Josepha de Óbidos (1630–84) cast a rather dim light in the darkness of Portuguese painting. Having been sober, silverwork became richer (Sé, Oporto). The craftsmen of India were set to work on traditionally formed Portuguese furniture, with giddy results. Arraiolos rugs were beginning to appear at the end of the 17th century.

Baroque

The discovery of gold and diamonds in Portugal's colony of Brazil brought a flood of wealth to a monarch who sought glorification through his monumental building works: Dom João V's liberality attracted foreign craftsmen to Portugal, and the arts of Portugal were shaken from their stupor.

Eighteenth-century architecture was dominated by Italian influences. It took two different forms, reflecting the influence of Nasoni's dynamic work in and around Oporto (active 1725–62; simple structures with complex surface ornaments), and of the Italian-trained Ludwig's monumental designs for the palace and monastery at Mafra, as well as his chancel at the Sé in Évora. Baroque architecture in Lisbon was cut short by the earthquake of 1755, which necessitated the economical, unadorned Pombaline style, named after the Marquês de Pombal. At that time the refreshing and much underrated André Soares was working in the north of the country (Casa do Raio, Braga). The rococo's brief flowering gave Portugal the delightful palace of Queluz.

The school of sculpture at Mafra secured an Italian bias to Portuguese Baroque sculpture, not only because Alessandro Giusti (1715–99) taught there, but through the influence of Italian sculptures imported to adorn the basilica itself.

The most exciting sculpture of the age was that architectural form called *talha* (carving) which the Portuguese used with peculiar enthusiasm. It was gilt with Brazilian gold leaf, producing a theatrical effect well suited to Baroque tastes: during its vogue in the 18th century, it spilled from the apse to frame pictures, pulpits and *azulejos* in the nave. In the late 17th century, the retable's concentric arches were ornamented by twisted chestnut columns aflutter with grape vines and phoenix birds (symbolizing the Eucharist and immortality respectively). Dom João V's Italian architects, sculptors and goldsmiths influenced the style, preferring canopies to arches, and adding festoons and volutes—dazzlingly employed in the church of São Francisco in Oporto and the Convent of Jesus at Aveiro. The decorative appeal of gilt- or polychromed-wood imitations of Italian sculpture was soon appreciated.

Many Portuguese painters emigrated to Rome; palettes travelling in the other direction popularized *trompe l'oeil* ceilings. Furniture bent over backwards to accommodate Baroque tastes, but then sobered under the influence of Queen Anne and Chippendale styles. Silverwork veered from Dom João's ostentatious pieces commissioned from Italy for the chapel of São João Baptista, to the supreme French craftsmanship of the Germains' work for Dom José (in the Museu de Arte Antiga and the Ajuda Palace, Lisbon).

19th and 20th Centuries

After a muted period of neoclassicism, Portugal settled into a mishmash of styles known as the 'Eclectic period'. Architectural development was stunted by the dissolution of the religious orders in 1834, and the appropriation of their buildings by the state, which removed the need for any new commissions.

Machado de Castro (1731/2–1822; equestrian bronze in Lisbon's Praça do Comércio) is the only sculptor who approaches the talents of António Soares dos Reis (1847–89), who trained in Paris and Rome, imbuing a classical tradition with more than a dash of Romantic sentiment (Soares dos Reis Museum, Oporto).

Romanticism arrived first in poetry and painting, the latter of which took its lead from foreign artists such as the Swiss Augusto Roquemont. Oporto's Soares dos Reis Museum is the best place to see works by the late 19th-century painters Marques de Oliveira, Silva Porto, and their open-air colleagues José Malhoa, Carlos Reis, and José Júlio de Sousa Pinto. Columbano Bordalo Pinheiro, by contrast, was very much an *atelier* painter.

Twentieth-century Portugal appears to have been in rather too much of a muddle to produce much of artistic merit, other than paintings (Gulbenkian Museum of Modern Art, Lisbon) and literature. Jorge Barradas (1894–1971) was a particularly witty sculptor—a field now dominated by João Cutileiro (Évora's public garden).

Azulejos

Portugal's tiles are one of the most enjoyable and irrepressible facets of her artistic heritage. They are not peculiar to Portugal, but tiles in Portugal are used more extensively and for a greater variety of purpose than anywhere else. *Azulejos* date back to Moorish times; the term itself may be a corruption of two Arabic words, *azraq* (azure) and *zalayja* (a small polished stone).

In the late 15th century, tiles with geometric designs were imported into Portugal from Seville (National Palace at Sintra). To prevent their tin-glazed colours from blending with one another in the furnace, they were separated by rivulets filled with linseed oil, or by ridges in the clay paste.

In the 16th century, the Italians introduced the Majolica technique, by which the clay was covered with white enamel; this could then be painted directly. Andalusian craftsmen brought vitality to Portugal's *azulejos* when she was yoked to Spain 1580–1640, and it was during this period that the Portuguese developed their enthusiasm for *azulejos*.

Early 17th-century tiles were either solid blocks of dark blue or green arranged in simple geometric patterns, or more commonly *azulejos de tapete* (carpet tiles) (church of Marvila, Santarém). The latter imitate Moorish rugs, in yellow and blue. Tiled altar frontals were made to look like textiles, and in the second half of the century the first story-telling *azulejos* emerged. Both Portuguese and Dutch tiles of the period were exclusively blue and white, under the influence of Ming-dynasty porcelain imported into Europe.

The early 18th century saw the introduction of the Dutch-style independent *azulejo*, each of which contained one motif. These cost a fraction of the price of traditional tiles, and during their 40-year vogue a succession of flowers, ships, donkeys, castles and birds sprang up around the country. The same period saw the introduction of large tile panels depicting religious scenes, which mark the apogee of the *azulejo*. These were most perfectly integrated into their architectural settings by the grand master of tile design, António de Oliveira Bernardes (1684–1732) (Lóios Church in Évora, church of N.S. do Terço in Barcelos, Misericórdia in Viana do Castelo). He founded a school in Lisbon, where some of his disciples designed 'cutout' *azulejos*: the most amusing are human figures on staircase landings.

Baroque tiles teem with thick acanthus foliage, scrolls of stone, cherubs and urns sprouting frilled Dutch tulips. The 1730s saw the arrival of *azulejo* scenes depicting the pleasures of an

17th century tile design

idle life, after artists such as Watteau and Boucher. Tones of olive green and burgundy supplemented the blue and yellow, particularly in border garlands and swathes of vegetation.

The reconstruction of Lisbon after the earthquake of 1755 demanded a ready supply of *azulejos*: hasty production required a simplification of the style, which became delicate, decorative, classical and balanced. In the mid-19th century, the custom of decking the exterior of buildings with *azulejos* was introduced from Brazil. Tiles lent themselves to witty Art Nouveau designs, but fared less well with the rigid geometry of Art Deco in the 1930s. Competition from mosaics and marble signalled a lull in *azulejo* design, which was revived in the 1950s, and is still going strong.

Lisbon's Museu de Azulejos provides an overview of the art.

Topics

the Pillory, Elvas

The charm of the Portuguese is one of the most compelling reasons for travelling here. People tend to be gentle and friendly, while retaining great dignity. A genial pessimism pervades much of life, though it's often backed by quiet pride. The Portuguese are unerringly tolerant of foreigners, as George Borrow discovered in 1835: 'I said repeatedly that the Pope...was the head minister of Satan here on earth... I have been frequently surprised that I experienced no insult and ill-treatment from the people.'

Sometimes tolerance is occasioned by passivity. In 1726 Brockwell wrote: 'Be their Business ever so urgent, or the Rains ever so violent, they never hasten their Pace . . . and seem to number each step they take.' But as the receipts from Portuguese emigrants show, the Portuguese can be firm of purpose when they set their minds to it, and highly adaptable. The latter is not always apparent: there's a deep-rooted resistance to change. If you are travelling on a bus and open a window, someone will close it; but if you get on the bus before anyone else, and open a window, it will remain open throughout the journey—as the other passengers see it, the window has always been open, so it had better stay open. On the other hand, 'progress' is sometimes employed for its own sake, as the revamp of various historical buildings attests.

Portuguese women age early, a fact which did not escape Brockwell's attention in 1726: 'No sooner are they in their Perfection than they suddenly decay . . . Thirty once turn'd, they become as justly despicable, as before they were admirable.' Young, urban Marias keep their arms firmly around the necks of lucky Antónios, Manuels or Josés—then, seemingly all at once, they are clad in black and gossiping around a crate of lettuces.

Respectability is very important. The men appear never to remove their subfusc suits, whether they are playing dominoes in *tascas*, or dawdling in town squares. They turn on their heels only to bestow the occasional, single handshake. Few students wear shorts. Respectability also takes the form of courtesy: envelopes are commonly addressed to *excelentíssimo* (most excellent) so-and-so. It was Dom João V who first entitled his secretary of state 'Excellency'. The nobles were disgusted, but found it expedient to use that address for any chance acquaintance, and the custom caught on. Calling cards are distributed liberally—the custom of turning down one corner may hark back to the days when they were proffered by the landed gentry in lieu of immediate payment: turning down the corner made them non-negotiable.

The more fanciful side of the Portuguese temperament may have been shaped at an early age: children are told the bizarre but tragic tale of *Carochinha* (Cockroach), an ugly insect who received numerous proposals of marriage after she discovered a crock of gold. The only sincere candidate was a mouse, who fell into boiling water and died. New Yorkers are not the only people with a fixation for cockroaches.

Sebastianismo

After the disastrous battle of Alcácer-Quivir in 1578, the body of Dom Sebastian could not be found. A whirlwind of rumours proclaimed the return of the king, and speculation gained momentum after Portugal was annexed to Spain in 1580. Dom Sebastian was cast as a hero who would throw off the Spanish yoke and restore the glory of the Portuguese: he became the focus of a messianic cult which received a strong impetus from the New Christians—ostensibly converted Jews—who feared increased persecution under Spanish rule. The upshot of this has lasted far beyond the four pretenders (youth, hermit, pastry cook and Italian) who popped up before 1600: in essence, *Sebastianismo* is akin to *saudade*, and continues to revive in times of national despair. This occurred most forcefully when Prince Dom Miguel returned from Brazil in 1828, and possibly when Salazar—then Minister of Finance—turned around the budgetary deficit in 1928–9.

Saudade

Saudade is a state of mind which lies at the heart of the Portuguese. There's no literal translation: 'longing' or 'yearning' come closest. It is a passive desire for something out of reach, either in the future or in the past. It pricks with an almost religious constancy.

Fado

The musical equivalent of *saudade* is that melancholic, gut-wrenching song called *fado* (fate). The hard, untrained voice of the *fadista* is accompanied by a guitar: together they revel in tragedy, or assume a torpid resignation towards it.

Fado seems to have been born into the lowlife of Lisbon's Alfama district during the 1830s, and is still most at home there. It remains exclusively urban. Coimbra *fado* is quite different: more refined and sentimental, with a listless romantic yearning. The Coimbra guitar style is more chordal than its melodic Lisbon counterpart and has a slower tempo.

The words of the *fado* are not too important: *fadistas* often improvise. However, some *fados* tell the story of Maria Severa, a great *fadista*, whose mother was known as *A Barbuda* (the Bearded Lady). Maria let rip in Lisbon's Mouraria, next to the Alfama, where she conducted a stormy romance with a bull-fighting nobleman, the Conde de Vimioso. What the *fados* fail to mention is that Maria died at the age of 26 not from a broken heart, but from a surfeit of roast pigeon and red wine. The diva of today is Amália Rodrigues. Even she was banished from the airwaves during the initial confusion of the 1974 revolution, when it was illegal to broadcast *fado* on the radio—on the grounds that it encouraged listlessness and fatalism, and was therefore harmful to social progress.

The Church

Black is a popular colour for clothes in Portugal, and not because it's fashionable. Mourning is pervasive: the closer one's relationship to the dead, the longer one wears black. Seven to ten years is par for a parent, two to three for an in-law. Many widows decide to stay in mourning for the rest of their lives. (On the other hand, children's deaths are not formally mourned: they receive a Requiem Mass and no more.) Everyone needs a little colour in their lives, though, and the clues are hanging from the nation's washing lines: people prefer bright underwear.

The Catholic Church inspires greater devotion from Portuguese women than Portuguese men, though on Sundays some village churches attract 90 per cent of the residents. In the village, religion is closely bound up with protection of the household, its animals, and its agriculture ('When there is food in the house, the Saints are left in peace', runs a proverb). The focus is on regional shrines and village pilgrimages—in which the priest serves as a kind of public functionary. Anticlericalism is fairly widespread, which may be evidence of the hiatus in peoples' minds between the local church and the national Church.

In his essay on Portuguese Catholicism, the poet Fernando Pessoa wrote 'Our true God-made-Manifest is…a Catholic Cupid called the Child Jesus. So we pay no attention to the Virgin Mary, but only to Mother Mary.' Hence the two popular images, the pregnant Our Lady of 'O' (named, in part, from the seven antiphons in the Office of the days before Christmas, all of which begin with 'O') and the suckling Our Lady of the Milk. The Mother of Christ became a popular figure for devotion in the 13th century, which preached a more sentimental and direct relationship with God. By the end of the 15th century, more than 1000 of Portugal's churches, chapels and hermitages had been devoted to the Virgin.

Wax ex-votos are an odd but touching feature of many churches. These limbs, heads, chests, breasts, stomachs, pigs, babies and hands are intended to attract divine cures for their respective ailments. They are heaped on altars in a promiscuous jumble, or hung from strings.

Spain

They would have us be Castilian men.
A lizard I would rather be
By the Holy Gospels verily.

So says Jorge, a player from Sardoal, in Gil Vicente's 16th-century *Tragicomédia Pastoril da Serra da Estrêla*. He echoes the sentiments of many of his compatriots. Portugal's only neighbour is more than five times bigger than she is, and the Portuguese maintain a wary dislike of the Spanish—or simply pretend Spain does not exist. There is a saying that from Spain come neither good winds nor good marriages: the east winds are sweltering in summer and piercing in winter, and a series of greedy dynastic marriage alliances made Spain the bogey of Portugal's history.

Yet the Portuguese used to call themselves Spanish—it was an umbrella term for the inhabitants of the Peninsula, and was phased out when Carlos II continued to call himself King of Spain even after Portugal regained her independence in 1640. As late as 1712,

Portuguese delegates negotiating the Treaty of Utrecht insisted that the monarchy in Madrid be referred to as that of Castile, rather than Spain. The EU is forging trade and transport links between the two countries, and each year millions of Spaniards jaunt across the border to stock up on bath towels and bottle corks.

Portugal and Britain

The next time you drink a cup of tea or eat a piece of toast, think of Catherine of Bragança. She popularized the former and is said to have introduced the latter to Britain—with good purpose: she held tea parties to keep an eye on her ladies-in-waiting, who were well within the orbit of her philandering husband, King Charles II.

Portugal is Britain's oldest ally: the tie dates from the Treaty of Windsor in 1386, which is represented in the clasped hands of the effigies of Dom João I and his wife Philippa of Lancaster on their tomb in the Abbey of Batalha. The 600-year-old alliance was invoked most recently during the Gulf War, when Portuguese ships transported British troops.

The Portuguese are fond of the British, and not just those that drink their port wine. But things have not always been rosy. In 1555, the prophet Nostradamus wrote, 'The great empire will be England . . . the all-powerful for more than 300 years; the Portuguese will not be pleased with it' and the truth of his prediction lies in the shift in the relations between the two countries as Portugal's power declined. Britain became the protector of Portugal because her ports were useful, because of trade with her empire, and, most importantly, to offset the power of Spain. Portugal provided Catherine of Bragança with a mammoth dowry (finally settled in the reign of James II), and granted Britain terms of trade which proved so favourable to the British that Pombal severely curtailed them in the following century. When the French invaded in the early 18th century, the King of Portugal fled to Brazil in a British ship, and it was Wellington who expelled the aggressors.

Emigrants

If you come to a village in the north of Portugal and spy a shriekingly incongruous house, built with urban materials and colourfully painted, it's likely to be a *casa de emigrante*. The Portuguese have been emigrating in a big way since the 18th century, when rural proverty drove thousands of men to Brazil. Emigration to France and West Germany, which had begun in the 1950s, surged ahead during the following decade, when young men journeyed abroad to escape conscription for the wars in Africa, and to earn comparatively high salaries: by 1973 an estimated 800,000 Portuguese had left the country. Although many returned after the Revolution of 1974, remittances from hardworking emigrants remain one of the main props of the Portuguese economy.

Most emigrants come from the Minho and Trás-os-Montes, whence they return in August, driving their flashy cars too fast and stuffing their breast pockets with crisp banknotes. Many houses remain half-built until the owner can afford to complete the project, which is intended to symbolize his escape from subsistence farming and ignorance. If he runs into financial difficulties, the pretentious house reverts: the garage becomes a cowshed, the manicured garden becomes a threshing floor. Some labourers return to their previous professions—there are quite a few polyglot shepherds about the place.

The Colonial Legacy

The Portuguese are fond of reminding visitors that their language ranks seventh in the world, in terms of numbers of people speaking it. This hangover from Portuguese colonial rule is still a cause for pride. But in a curious reversal of roles, the Portuguese spoken in Portugal is now being undermined by Brazilian Portuguese: Brazilian soap operas bring slang to their mother tongue.

Portugal fought long and expensive wars in Africa, and pulled out of the continent following the Revolution of 1974. The revolution also brought democracy to Portugal, and thus seems to have served as a kind of exorcism as regards people's attitude towards the empire. Indeed, Cavaco Silva, the Prime Minister, is attempting to rekindle Portuguese influence in southern Africa, particularly in Angola.

Pillories

It's not a fountain or an ornamental garden that stands at the centre of most towns and some villages in Portugal. Right next to the town hall, time after time, there you have it, the pillory: an elegant stone column to which criminals were shackled and whipped. Alternatively, the villain was incarcerated in a cage atop the pillory.

Pillories can be very attractive. They were built from the 13th century to the 18th century, and their detail varies according to current artistic tastes: they can be twisted, or patterned with stone dots, or ornamented with armillary spheres. But still, the deterrent aspect of pillories doesn't seem to justify their prominence: they symbolize something bigger—municipal liberties.

The early kings and great lords of Portugal granted charters to boroughs, indicating their freedoms and guarantees, their taxes, punishments and fines. Judicial power was vested in the *alcaide* (castellan) and was administered at the pillory. Thus pillories came to be associated with decentralized government and local control.

Chimneys

You don't have to be Santa Claus to get a kick out of Portugal's chimneys. They were introduced into the country from south to north: the Algarve's pretty latticed flues hark back to Moorish times; but north of Coimbra, before the 20th century, only town houses and grand manors had chimneys. The discrepancy is rooted in climate and cooking habits: the northerners need to preserve heat in winter, and their stews generate less smoke than the southerners' grills.

In the Minho, some peasant houses still have a *trapeira*—a couple of wooden posts covered with tiles—or simply a hole in the ceiling with a removable cork bung. Smoke seeps through the thatched roofs of Trás-os-Montes, or a few tiles might be left loose. A large hearth is the nucleus of wealthier homes, but the vent itself is often very narrow. Further south, around Santarém, brick chimneys are kept apart from the framework of the house to reduce the risk of fire, while the chimneys of the Alentejo are broad oblongs. (Many of the Alentejo's church belltowers sport gleeful weathervanes—trumpeting angels and cherubs, and one skipping rat.)

Horses and Bulls

The Greek armies were thrown into disarray by 50 Iberian horsemen brought to their country by Dionysius, the despot of Syracuse. Horses have long been important to the Portuguese: King Dom Duarte (1433–8) wrote the first serious treatise on classical equitation since the Greeks held forth on the subject, and thus incorporated the art of riding in the classical revival. This art lingers in Portugal: Lusitano horses are used to refresh the bloodlines of the Lipizzaners at the Spanish Riding School in Vienna. The Portuguese School of Equestrian Art is based in Lisbon, where riders in 18th-century dress (tricorn hats, patent-leather thigh boots, embroidered silk coats) regularly prance about on Alter Real stallions, a strain of the Lusitanian horse.

The breed has maintained its purity due to the tradition of mounted bullfighting, which tests the skill of the rider and horse without killing the bull. The horse's delicate steps incite the bull to charge—the Iberian bull charges repeatedly, and turns in its own length to do so.

Untypical 'Typical'

Típico doesn't quite mean 'typical' in the sense of 'representative': it's more akin to 'quintessential', and ferreting out anything *típico* is a national pastime. Thus Coimbra University is described as a typical university, or Fernando Pessoa a typical poet. Restaurants advertise themselves as *típico* to suggest that they embody something peculiarly Portuguese. The cult of the *típico* was fostered by Salazar's nationalism, and the legacy remains.

Music

Portuguese music is little known and rarely heard. Troubadours appeared in the late 13th century, but it was not until the mid-15th century that polyphony first cleared its throat. It ran out of breath in the mid-17th century, and is now enjoying a muted revival under the aegis of ethno-musicologists—keep an ear open for compositions by **Manuel Cardoso** and **Estêvão Lopes Morago**.

Mannerism brought a certain melancholy to the Portuguese keyboard, which was championed by **António Carreira** (1590–1650). Religious compositions dominated Portuguese music until the late 17th century: during the Spanish domination (1580–1640) there was no court to commission new works, and Dom João IV, who became king in 1640, preferred ecclesiastical music. He required his ambassadors to send him every musical score they could find, which his court musicians were obliged to play. The king then marked the catalogue 'very good', 'good', or 'to Hell'. His music library was the largest in Europe, but both the good and the bad went to Hell in the earthquake of 1755.

Characteristically, Dom João V (1506–50) employed Scarlatti as his daughter's music teacher. Scarlatti was well impressed with **José António Carlos de Seixas** (1704–42), the greatest Portuguese composer of the age. Operas, cantatas and chamber music became more widely known. The late 18th century spawned **João de Sousa Carvalho** (1720–98), who could air his compositions in the new São Carlos Opera House in Lisbon. **João Domingos Bomtempo** (1775–1842) composed a very fine Requiem Mass, but is better known for his sonatas.

The opera house was closed in 1910: music went into decline because it had been closely associated with the court. **Luís de Freitas Brancone** (1890–1955), a contemporary of Bártok, kindled the fire.

The São Carlos Opera House has been reopened. Its orchestra continues to improve, whereas the Gulbenkian orchestra (basically a chamber orchestra, with reinforcements for larger works) tends to rest on its laurels. A new orchestra has been formed in Oporto, but does little to promote Portuguese musical talent—95 per cent of the players are foreign.

Literature

The lyrical streak within the Portuguese has made them better poets than prose writers. It has found expression since the days of Dom Sancho I (1185–1211), whose accomplishments as a poet were later surpassed by Dom Dinis (1279–1325). **Fernão Lopes** (*c.* 1380–*c.* 1459) has been described as the father of Portuguese prose; he was commissioned to write the history of all the Portuguese kings, but only the last three survive—broad, balanced and colourful. **Azurara** succeeded him; through living in the household of Henry the Navigator, the aristocrat was well placed to write the *Chronicle of the Discovery of Guinea*.

The prolific playwright **Gil Vicente** (*c.* 1470–*c.* 1536) was a sort of Brueghel of the stage, who ranged from rollicking farce to solid character portrayal. Portugal's maritime exploits washed up **Luís de Camões** (1524–80), author of the great Portuguese epic *Os Lusíadas* (*The Lusiads*). He served in Ceuta (where his right eye was removed), Goa and Macau, he was imprisoned, and he lost everything except his manuscript in a shipwreck. *The Lusiads* was published (1572) on his return to Portugal, where he died in genteel poverty. In closely structured but wonderfully fluid verse, Camões details Vasco da Gama's voyage to India, overlooked by a panoply of Olympian gods and goddesses. He interprets the greatness of the Portuguese people.

After Camões

After Camões, the pens of Portugal ran dry until **Bocage** (1765–1805) exploded onto the scene, a debauched early Romantic subsequently exiled by Pombal's government. The

Liberal **Almeida Garrett** (1799–1854) was the first of the true Romantics, whose *Travels in My Homeland* combines description of what crosses his path, with musings on what crosses his mind. His contemporary **Alexandre Herculano** (1810–77) used lucid prose to write the history of Portugal up to the reign of Dom Afonso III. He investigated social history, but ceased his project when accused of treason—for pooh-poohing Portugal's foundation myths. The realist novels of **Eça de Quieroz** (1845–1900) were highly admired by Zola. Eça and his generation, 'the Generation of 1870', aimed to effect a national regeneration; his concern with social reform is articulated in his highly enjoyable works, of which *The Maias* is the best known.

The great poet **Fernando Pessoa** (1888–1935) holds a special place in Portuguese hearts—and in their pockets (he features on the 100$00 note). Camões wrote at the beginning of the end of Portugal's empire, Pessoa at its eclipse, but both were concerned with the destiny of the Portuguese. Pessoa created what he called 'heteronyms', who served as vehicles for the poet to write outside his own personality.

Literature under Salazar was smothered by political censorship; one of the best-known works of protest is the *New Portuguese Letters* by **Maria Teresa Horta**, etc., a feminist rallying cry which is sometimes obscure.

The best of the modern novels in translation is **José Saramago**'s *Balthasar and Blimunda*, a painstakingly researched, magical account of a flying machine and the construction of the Palace and Monastery of Mafra. The short story writer **Miguel Torga** was a hot tip for the 1989 Nobel Prize for literature.

Portugal Today

Recent Portuguese politics have been muddled, and nobody is more aware of that than the man in the *tasca*, who sends the whole business to the devil and leaves someone else to sort it out. His passivity goes back a long way. The 18th and 19th centuries lacked a strong liberal tradition, so the population remained ignorant of the powers and limitations of democracy. In the absence of a middle class clamouring for a true parliamentary system, the landed elite dominated politics in Portugal. Salazar's aim to stunt the awakening of political consciousness compounded the situation.

Forty-eight years of dictatorship and two years of revolutionary chaos left a legacy of over-centralized economic structures, flimsy infrastructure, skeletal education, inadequate social welfare and housing. But things are changing rapidly. Portugal joined the EU in 1986, and the Community is pumping billions of dollars into the country to help modernize the economy. Resources are flooding into communications, transport, education and professional training. The tax and financial systems are being reformed, as are agrarian law and labour practices. In the larger cities, construction is booming.

Portugal has few natural resources. She labours under a chronic trade and public-sector deficit, and the economy is heavily dependent on tourism and money sent back by emigrants working abroad—neither of which are dependable. And yet Portugal has the fastest-growing economy in Europe today. There are three main industries: textiles, clothing and shoes (which face competition from southeast Asia); wood pulp (from eucalyptus trees, which some ecologists denounce as too greedy for water, and harmful to neighbouring species); china and earthenware.

The Minho

Sanctuary of Bom Jesús

The northwestern province of Portugal tilts towards the ocean. The mountains in the east reach about 700m, lowering to a hilly central zone divided by broad valleys, covered—particularly in the north—with dense woods of oak and chestnut, and patches of eucalyptus and pine, at about 200m. The low coastal region is fringed with sand beaches, open to the winds and beaten by the wild waves of the Atlantic. At the height of summer the average seawater temperature remains cool—around 16°C.

Not for nothing is this called the Costa Verde—the Green Coast is the wettest province of Portugal. Its high rainfall, temperate climate and relatively rich, granitic soil support intense agricultural development. The introduction of maize in the early 17th century heralded an agricultural breakthrough. Well-suited to the climatic and geologic condition of the Minho, maize was three to four times more productive than the wheat and rye it replaced. The by-products of maize—stalks, leaves, flowers and even the grain itself—were and are fed to cattle, reducing the need for pasture land. The unfailing maize crop ended periodic famines. The population expanded.

Typically, fields are used to cultivate fodder and legumes which were introduced in the 17th century but are still called *novidades* (novelties)—parsnips, beetroot and lupins. Bean plants grow up the maize stalks, providing one of the farmer's most important staple foods. Another nifty use of space was the introduction of climbing vines (*see* below). In the 19th century, many smallholders ditched their goats and planted small pinewoods on unprofitable hilltops, which now provide financial security in case of some extraordinary expense like hospitalization.

It is said that if a Minhoto puts a cow out to pasture in his own field, her dung falls in his neighbour's field. The Minho is a land of smallholdings which are themselves divided, because primogeniture is rare. The Minhotos are conservative as well as pious, devoted both to their land-holdings and to the Virgin Mary, whose image is ensconced in little Romanesque churches. Tractors haven't made much impression, partly because terraces are steep: fields are ploughed by oxen, sometimes using quadrangular ploughs introduced by the Suevi. The Minhotos work with reciprocity, joining to husk the maize then meeting to plant the potatoes.

The people's poverty leads the more dynamic among them to seek work abroad. When they return to the Minho, having made their fortunes, emigrants trumpet their changed status by building ostentatious houses known as *casas de emigrante* (*see* **Topics**, p.47).

The Minho is green and rustic, close knit and alive. Life happens as slowly as the dry stone walls which divide the fields. To many Portuguese, this is the most beautiful province. Cattle with huge, lyre-

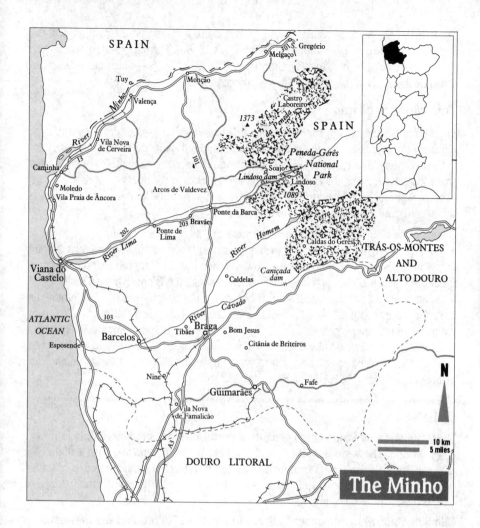

The Minho

shaped horns pull carts with squealing wooden axles—or the untrust-
worthy beasts are led for walks on strings. There are vines everywhere,
creeping up tree trunks, festooned on fences. In *tascas*, people drink
purple wine from white porcelain bowls. On every summer weekend,
some village or other will be celebrating its *festa* or *romaria*.

History

The Minho's system of smallholdings dates back to subjugation of the Celt-Iberians and
Lusitanians by the Romans, who forced them to come down from their hilltop *castros* and
settle the fertile valleys. Agriculture was organized under the auspices of the *villa*. Because
the land was hummocky, each Roman settler was given a parcel of land comprising several
discontinuous plots.

The Minho calls itself the cradle of the nation because it comprised the patrimony of the first King of Portugal, Dom Afonso Henriques (1128–85). Having defeated his mother, Teresa, he established his capital at Guimarães. The see of Braga—which had been established by the Suevi in the 5th century—reinforced the integrity of the region.

Turismo de Habitação

The Minho has the highest concentration of *Turismo de Habitação*, because of the large number of manor houses in the region, especially around Ponte de Lima: most date from the 18th century. The Portuguese Government, and more recently the EU, have made large grants available to offset the cost of adapting these houses to the needs of tourists, in order to encourage tourism in the north of the country, and to preserve houses which the owners can no longer afford to maintain.

Generally the delights of sniffing the woodsmoke in a huge kitchen of rough-cut granite, of wandering through doorways hung with emblazoned tapestries, of peaceful terraces and wild flowers, far outweigh the hitches. However: because these are private homes, rooms should be booked at least three days in advance—though this is not always enforced—and for a minimum stay of three nights; most houses are not signposted—detailed directions from the Tourist Office at Ponte de Lima are a necessity; the small roads are full of potholes, which complicates driving at night. Some of the houses are oppressively heavy and damp—the guide to individual houses around Viana do Castelo, Monção, Ponte de Lima and Ponte da Barca will help you to avoid these. All houses listed for the Minho can be booked through TURIHAB (*see* **Practical A–Z**, p.24).

Vinho Verde

 Vinho verde is one of the delights of Portugal, and it's produced only in the Minho. The wine is light (around 9° of alcohol) and *pétillant*, with a slight acidity balanced by its fruitiness—enough to refresh the most parched of travellers. *Vinho verde* is best drunk very cool, as an apéritif or with shellfish or grilled fish. It's also great for picnics.

Climbing vines were introduced to the Minho in the 17th century, and they have never looked back. The idea was to use space most efficiently by growing other crops beneath the vines, and at the same time protect the grapes from frosts and the damp. So, rather than being pruned back to form low bushes, the vines creep up telegraph poles, oak trees, house walls. Some 60,000 Minhoto farmers sell their grapes to private wine firms, to be marketed under brand names, or to the 21 cooperatives. The more substantial producers have disciplined their runaways to grow along horizontal wires borne a couple of metres off the ground; they harvest the grapes by tractor. The smaller farmers grow vines at the side of their fields, and in September/October harvest them from rickety ladders.

The '*verde*' of *vinho verde* refers to the young age at which the wine is drunk—usually the summer after the grapes were picked—rather than to its colour. It's best to stick to the whites: red *vinho verde* accounts for about 60% of production, and even though it is always drunk fridge cold, it tastes like a mistake. (The reds are fermented in contact with their skins, pips and stalks, whereas the whites are not.) Monção's Alvarinho is the best of the cooperatives' *vinho verde*—though purists argue that it's not a true *vinho verde* owing to its high alcohol content and lower than average effervescence. It costs about 1000$00 in a supermarket. Alvarinho produced by the Palácio da Brejoeira will cost considerably more, if you can find it (wine made from single estates is just beginning to catch on). The best-selling *vinho verde* is the untypically sweet Gatão, which costs less than 500$00.

Minho Specialities

The Minho is as green as its *caldo verde* soup, which is the province's most diffuse culinary export to the rest of the country. The soup takes its colour from shredded galega cabbage, like curly kale, which is stirred up with a warming blend of puréed potatoes, olive oil, and garlic. There will always be a slice of *chouriço* floating in the soup, and there ought to be an accompanying slice of maize bread.

Between October and December the Minhotos slaughter the one or two pigs they have fattened through the year, and eat the spin-offs at least until March. Nothing is wasted, least of all the blood, some of which is used to make *chouriço de sangue* (blood sausages). Like rich black pudding, these are made of cooked pork, blood, bread, oil, wine and other seasonings. Blood comes into its own in *sarrabulhos* (blood stews) made with various organs, rice, onions and blood, and often accompanied by tripe. (The best onions in the Minho come from Barcelos.) The more inventive and frugal pork dishes are not generally available in restaurants or *tascas*.

Lampreys are another great love—made familiar to English schoolchildren by Henry I (1100–35), who died of a surfeit of this eel-like fish. Abundant in the Rivers Minho, Lima and Cávado, lampreys are caught in Lent, on their return to the river to spawn. They make a rich meal, commonly served in a stew with rice, wine and onions, called *arroz de lampreia*. Less oily and more chewy is *polvo com arroz* (octopus rice). Popular wisdom dictates that neither of these dishes should be eaten by a pregnant mother, or her baby will be born with weak bones or no bones at all. No Christmas would be complete without *bacalhau cozido com todos* (salt cod boiled with potatoes, onions, eggs and kale).

Getting Around
by car

The nooks and crannies of the Minho lend themselves to exploration by car or foot: the manor houses in the *Turismo de Habitação* scheme around Ponte de Lima make an excellent base, because of their location at the heart of the province. The main roads are well maintained, and are being improved all the time, mostly through EU funding. The road between Braga and Monção is a slalom of hairpin bends, and it's easy to get stuck behind a tractor or oxcart. Potholes are a problem off the main roads—but more alarming is the crazy driving of emigrants in flashy cars, who come, in the summertime, to visit the folks back home and take them for a spin. The road network is very limited within the Peneda–Gerês park.

by train

The railway network covers major towns, but doesn't venture inland north of Braga. The main line from the south passes through Barcelos and Viana, then continues up the coast and beside the River Minho as far as Valença. Braga and Guimarães are both on branch lines (change at Nine and Lousado respectively). It's best to take a bus between Braga and Guimarães, as the train involves two changes.

by bus

The RN Express bus network in the north of Portugal is very limited. Privatization has opened the way for 60-odd other bus companies, and much confusion. Timetables tend to be kept in people's heads: just keep asking.

Guimarães

First capital of the Portuguese nation, Guimarães busies itself among gently sloping ever-green hills—dominated by the steeper Penha hill—and industrial environs. The superb municipal museum is buffered by a core of well-kept medieval streets, and Afonso Henriques, the first King of Portugal, set eyes on many of the monuments. The town is a centre for linen production, and has been at least since a fair was established at Guimarães in 1258, in which year both linen cloth and household linen were for sale (as well as rabbit fur—by the piece or made-up—black or white feathers, red or green leather, pepper, horseshoes and Moorish slaves). The fair was kept merry by 'buffoons who put up their tents', for which they paid a fee of 3 shillings. Decorative feathers have, alas, disappeared: we must be content with sidewalks paved with brilliant white chipped limestone, and manicured public gardens which feature attractive purple and white cabbages.

History

Afonso Henriques was born in Guimarães, and here he nurtured the embryonic nation. In 1096 Alfonso VI of Castile had bestowed the governance of the hereditary lands of Portucale and Coimbra, which lay between the Rivers Minho and Mondego, on his bastard daughter Teresa and her husband Henry, Duke of Burgundy. They reinforced the 150-year-old earth-and-wood castle built by a local noblewoman, Countess Mumadona, to protect herself and her foundation church of N.S. da Oliveira. Here Teresa bore a son, Afonso Henriques, and she administered the lands on his behalf when Henry died. Though Teresa surrounded herself with French monks from Cluny, the cultural powerhouse of the day, she neglected her son's education. A Coimbra document subscribed by Afonso Henriques, then king, gives some indication of what he may have been getting up to in his youth—the document specifies that vineyards must be carefully protected, especially from small boys, who were to be beaten till the blood came if they were caught trespassing or stealing. Afonso Henriques' upbringing stood him in good stead, though. He became both a sucessful guerilla and a visionary. There was no love lost between mother and son. She leant too much towards Castile, and the emergent nation united behind Afonso Henriques to defeat her at the battle of S. Mamede in 1128. Her tomb and Henry's are at Braga. Seven years later, Afonso Henriques refused to join other north Spanish princes in homage to Alfonso VII of Castile, choosing to swear and pay tribute to the papacy. He took the title Prince of Portugal, but the Pope did not recognize him as such until 1179, by which time he had moved the seat of government from Guimarães to Coimbra.

Guimarães ✆ (053–)   *Getting There*

By **road**, Guimarães is 22km southeast of Braga and 53km northeast of Oporto.

Guimarães is on a branch line: there are frequent direct **trains** from Oporto, but from elsewhere, change at Lousado. Frequent trains run from Lousado to Guimarães (1hr). From Braga, change at Lousado and Nine.

João Ferreira das Neves, ✆ 411756, run frequent **buses** from Oporto (2hrs). Very infrequent REDM buses run from Lisbon (7hrs), Coimbra (4hrs), Oporto (2hrs), and Chaves (3hrs).

Guimarães ✆ (053–)   *Tourist Information*

The sleepy **tourist office** belies its vigorous address: 83 Av. Alameda da Resistência ao Fascismo, ✆ 412450. It displays the town football trophies. From the station, ✆ 412351, walking north past the university will bring you to the tourist office. From the bus station, ✆ 411222, turn right down the Rua Dr A. Pimenta.

English is not spoken in the linen shops. The quality is good, and you pay for it. Best try the Casa dos Enxovais, ✆ 414462, in the Alameda Salazar.

What to See

Dignified on a green hillock, and remarkably toothsome atop a rock outcrop, the **castle** looks like a theatre backdrop: eight square towers of different heights—one bearing a cypress tree—ring the keep. The castle was reconstructed by Count Henry *c.* 1100, and pillaged by 19th-century town councillors, who used the granite for paving stones. Subsequently rescued from such insult, the restored castle lacks atmosphere despite the drama of the living rock. Dom Afonso Henriques was baptized beside the castle in the little Romanesque **church of São Miguel**. Should his ghost choose to revisit the site, he will not come on horseback. A portcullis fell on his leg at the siege of Badajoz, fracturing the bone so badly that he could never ride again.

A lawn links the castle and chapel to the **Ducal Palace**, a building loathed by purists. It was constructed in the early 15th century by Dom Afonso, bastard eldest son of the bastard Dom João I. Having begun life as Count of Barcelos, he died Duke of Bragança; the title was given to him as a sop to placate the head of a strong landed nobility which posed a real threat to the king's authority. Between the changes in his title, he travelled in Europe on diplomatic missions. This, rather than the whim of his wife Beatriz, daughter of (the bastard) Constable Nun' Álvares Pereira, explains why he and his French architect, Anton, built a Burgundian palace. Indeed, the first Duke of Bragança is also the first known emigrant to return to the Minho and build a pretentious home in an incongruous style. Perhaps by way of retribution, it was allowed to fall into ruins until grossly restored as a presidential palace in 1933. Restoration should leave visitors feeling that a work of art, or a monument, has withstood the tide of time: the interior of this *château* is spic and span deodorized history. Nevertheless, there are some good pieces in it, including medieval Persian carpets, numerous 18th-century Flemish tapestries, and two still lifes attributed to Josefa de Óbidos. The ceiling of the banqueting room resembles the inverted hull of a boat. The duke was assured a warm pate while sleeping: a panel at the head of his bed allowed heat through from the fireplace on the other side of the wall.

The Largo da Oliveira

Medieval spirits waft around the **Largo da Oliveira**, dodging the children who play hide and seek around a mid-14th-century Gothic canopy or portico sheltering a stone cross, in front of the **church of N.S. da Oliveira**. The shrine commemorates the miracle to which the church owes its name. In the early 14th century, an olive tree grew at São Torquato, several km away. It provided oil for St Torquato's lamp. The tree was uprooted and transported to Guimarães to perform the same function for the altar of the church of N.S. da Oliveira. Not unreasonably, the tree died. It remained dead until 8 September 1342, when Pedro Esteves placed upon it a cross his brother had brought from Normandy. Three days later, the olive tree broke into leaf. (Perhaps inspired by this example, the Chapter of Guimarães wanted to transport the relics of St Torquato himself into town, because the saint yields large profits in the guise of ex-votos. They attempted to do so forcibly in 1501, 1597, 1637 and 1805. The parishioners of São Torquato love their saint, and are a tenacious lot.) Above the church's portal hovers an elaborately carved and similarly sized window, now bricked up. Both date from Dom João I's reconstruction of the church, and precede the keep-like tower of 1515.

The Museu de Alberto Sampaio

Open summer 10–12.30 and 2–7; winter 10–12.30 and 2–5.30; closed Mon.

The conventual buildings of the collegiate church now house the outstanding Museu de Alberto Sampaio, centred on a rhythmic Romanesque cloister. The balance of the 13th-century cloister was altered in the following century when Dom João I ordered the extension of the church following his victory at Aljubarrota, which secured the kingdom for him. Monks and nuns rubbed shoulders within the wealthy institution after its foundation in the 10th century. Later the pope thought this unwise, and it reopened for men only. The museum is named after an ethnographer/sociologist.

Upstairs the museum's treasures are astonishing. The highlight is a fabulous silver-gilt late 14th-century triptych altarpiece offered by Dom João to Santa Maria of Guimarães. Gaspar Estaço, writing in the 16th century, says it was made from Dom João's silver measuring weights; the older tradition is that it was booty from the travelling chapel of Juan I of Castile. The centre panel shows the Nativity, breathed on by cow heads, whizzed over by cherubs swinging censers, all covered by Gothic arches. Also displayed are a robe said to have been worn by Dom João at Aljubarotta, the heaviest processional cross in the country, weighing in at 22kg, a stunning silver-bound Bible, and a Spanish hand-painted leather altarfront. Do notice the head carved on the back of the lectern, with an aquiline nose and surely an evil glint in his eye.

On the ground floor, beside the entrance to the museum, note the four sculpted saints' figures. St Bartholomew holds a card for folding linen, with a chained devil at his feet. In the ground-floor rooms look at the unusual and delightful 18th-century polychromed wood *Flight from Egypt*. Compassionate and dynamic, it lacks only baby Jesus, who was stolen by a visitor to the museum. The open sarcophagus in the inner cloister was taken from a farm, where it was used as a watering trough.

The Museu de Martins Sarmento

Open 9.30–12 and 2–5; closed Mon.

On the road into town from the bus station, the Museu de Martins Sarmento is named after the 19th-century archaeologist who conserved and continued the excavations at Citânia de Briteiros and at Sabroso. It is crowded with fragments from those Celto-Iberian sites, mostly ceramic and numismatic. The larger objects are more striking, displayed in and around the appropriated 14th-century cloister of the monastery of S. Domingos. The most forceful is the *Colossus of Pedralva*, an awesome and curiously unpublicized 3000-year-old 3m giant. Much debate has focused on the so-called *Pedro Formosa*, a round-topped slab of stone with a bite taken from its bottom. It was once thought to be a sacrificial altar; opinion shifted, and it is now believed to be the façade of a funerary monument, possibly the crematory furnace. Two headless Lusitanian warriors clasp their round shields in front of them.

Festivals

On the first Sunday of August, the *Festas Gualterianas* (Festival of St Walter) coincides with the free fair held in his name, which was first held in 1452. The following night is a much more unusual affair: the *Marcha Gualteriana*, which does not take place every year, is a satiric rather than a devotional procession, based on medieval allegories.

Guimarães ℗ (053–)

Where to Stay

luxury

There are two *pousadas* at Guimãraes, totally different in character, one in town and one 3km outside it. The **Pousada de N.S. da Oliveira**, ℗ 514157, ✉ 514204 (*category C★*), was converted from a block of town houses to make just 16 guestrooms, overlooking a superb medieval square and adjacent to the fine town hall. It is delightfully furnished, like a grand but homey country inn, with good service and a varied menu. Bring ear plugs, as the nearby church bells ring enthusiastically.

The **Pousada de Santa Marinha**, ℰ 514453, ✆ 516234 (*category CH*), Enatur's flagship, is housed in a 12th-century monastery on the Penha hillslope. The monastery was founded for the Augustinian Order in 1154 by Dona Mafalda, wife of Dom Afonso Henriques, in honour of a vow to the patron saint of pregnant women. It was splendidly revamped in the 18th century. The guestrooms used to be monks' cells; they remain small and simply furnished. Many overlook urban Guimarães. Cavernous, whitewashed corridors lead to the drawing room, which is filled with antiques borrowed from Lisbon's Ajuda Palace. The staircase is sided with lively tiles depicting an indulgent lay life, dated 1747 and attributed to Policarpo de Oliveira Bernardes. A columned late Renaissance gallery shelters the heavy 17th-century fountain of São Jerónimos, tinkling with mountain water, and focus of an avenue of trees. The granite-vaulted dining room offers staid meals specializing in beef dishes.

expensive

The **★★★Fundador Dom Pedro**, 760 Av. D. Afonso Henriques, ℰ 513781, ✆ 513786, is the only highrise in Guimarães and offers sound stuff with broad views and a commercial feel. There's no restaurant, but room service deliver international food 8am–midnight. **★★★★Hotel do Tournal**, Largo do Tournal, ℰ 517184, ✆ 517149—the entrance is in the Largo A. L. Carvalha—is a distinctive and very elegant townhouse with luxurious rooms.

moderate

★★★★Albergaria Palmeiros, Rua Gil Vicente, ℰ 410324, ✆ 417261, boasts a garage and swimming pool, but some of the rooms are a bit small.

inexpensive–cheap

The best cheap place to stay is the **Casa de Retiros** of the Padres Redentoristas, 163 Rua Francisco Agra, ℰ 511515 (*cheap*)—beyond the bus station, turn right and uphill. No frills, as you'd expect from pilgrim accommodation, and no pressure but for the 11.30pm curfew. Closer to the centre of town, and without the crucifixes, is **★★★Residencial S. Mamede**, 1 Rua de São Gonçalo, ℰ 513092 (*inexpensive*), which is simple, clean and bare. It tends to get booked up, because the alternative **★★Pensão Imperial**, 111 Alameda Dr. Sá Carneiro, ℰ 415163 (*inexpensive*), is squashed and overpriced.

Guimarães ℰ (053–)   ***Eating Out***

If you're mobile, best head to the top of the Penha hill, where the refined **Danjosé** (*moderate*) offers good service, wooded views and some good *bacalhau*. Otherwise, the choice is uninspiring. **Nicolino**, 106–109 Largo do Toural, ℰ 412083 (*moderate*) is a brown café, with slow service. Cavernous **Jordão**, 55 Av. D. Afonso Henriques, ℰ 411498 (*moderate*)—on the way to the Fundador hotel—is affiliated to a refrigerator factory. **O Telheiro**, 39–41 Rua Dom João 1 (*moderate*) is constantly busy, but it's worth waiting for a table. The *arroz de marisco* is a must.

Of all the cities in Portugal, Braga will get to heaven first: it seems that at one time every other building in Braga was a church or a seminary. The cathedral is the seat of the immensely powerful Primate of Portugal, and his palace is at the heart of Braga.

Because the cathedral is the only church that the casual visitor will wish to visit, it's best to wander around the centre of town in the early morning, before the bustle chases away the angels. For the town has grown into the largest city north of Oporto, and industry has brought its quota of bland buildings (previously the only industries were connected with the Church—carving, organ-making, bell-making, candle-making, stitching and embroidering vestments). The Avenida da Liberdade is a very long, very noisy strip, furnished with car showrooms and supermarkets.

Braga's museums house excellent works of art and craft. The one *palácio* open to the public is delightful. Exceptionally interesting sites surround the city, which has adequate accommodation.

rved window / casa Dos Coimbras
Braga

History

Braga is well sited at the meeting of inland hills and fertile valleys ripe with orchards, market gardens, grasslands and vineyards. In 27 BC the Romans chose the spot to administer the newly conquered territory of Gallaecia, comprised of the Minho and Galicia. Five Roman roads converged on Bracara Augusta, which quickly became a centre for trade and industry: glass, ceramics and other Roman artefacts from Egypt, the Aegean and Germany have been found here, and local products were sold in towns 200km away.

Conquered by the Suevi in 409, Braga became the seat of a bishopric as well as the Suevi's capital until 585. They were cattle-men, farmers—who introduced the quadrangular plough into the region—and robbers. Braga was sacked by the Visigoths and formally incorporated into the Visigothic kingdom by Leovigild in 585 (though the 9th-century *Chronicle of Sebastianus* distinguishes the realm of the Goths from that of the Suevi as late as 701).

Braga's ecclesiastical dominance began with a coup, when at a council in 561 St Martin of Dume (an environ of Braga), also called St Martin of Braga, converted the Suevi to Christianity. The Hungarian saint's other major contribution to Portugal as we know it was his condemnation of pagan names for days of the week. He was a forceful man (his favourite author was Seneca) and now the days of the week are given numbers, Monday being *segunda-feira*, Tuesday *terça-feira*, and so on. St Martin was fond of whispering 'Is this consistent with your promise at the font to renounce the devil and all his works?' Visitors tempted to sin in Braga beware.

Braga was occupied by the Moors from *c.* 730 until they were driven out by Fernando I of Castile. The see was not restored until 1070, after which the bishops squabbled with those of Santiago. The pope adjudicated in favour of Braga's superiority. The Council of Trent awarded the see of Braga the right to its own liturgy.

In 1926 the military coup which facilitated Salazar's dictatorship was launched here.

Getting There

By **road**, Braga is 53km northeast of Oporto and 51km southwest of Viana do Castelo. Braga is on a **rail** branch line. Passengers from Barcelos (frequent, 1hr), Viana do Castelo (frequent, 1¾hrs) and north of Viana must change trains at Nine. There are some direct trains from Oporto, or you can change at Nine (frequent, 1½hrs). From Póvoa de Varzim, change at Famalicão and at Nine (frequent, 1½hrs). From Guimarães, change at Lousado and Nine (frequent, 1¾hrs).

Buses are run by a confusing number of private companies including REDM, Renex and Rodonorte. They all operate out of the bus station on Avenida General Norton de Matos. Very infrequent buses arrive from Viana do Castelo (2hrs), Ponte da Barca (¾hr), Arcos de Valdevez (¾hr), Monção (1½hrs), Melgaço (2¼hrs), Coimbra (2½hrs) Chaves (4hrs), Boticas (3½hrs), and Montalegre (2¾hrs). There are intermittent services to Lisbon (6hrs). Very frequent buses run from Oporto (1¼hrs).

Braga ✆ (053–)   ***Tourist Information***

The **tourist office**, 1 Avenida Liberdade, ✆ 262550, is just off the Praça da República. From the railway station, head straight up the Rua Andrade Corvo, through the Porta Nova and past the cathedral. From the bus station, cross the Praça Alexandre Herculano and continue down the Rua dos Chãos, which leads into the Praça da República. The post office is in the Av da Liberdade, 300m from the tourist office.

Festivals

Easter Week ushers in a series of processions, for which the city is decorated with lights, flowers, and streetside altars. For the *Ecce Homo* procession on Easter Thursday night, hundreds of barefoot penitents carry torches and wand-like cressets, iron baskets holding pitched rope or coal, lighted and mounted on poles.

The Church Christianized the summer solstice by turning it into the Feast of St John the Baptist, here celebrated on 23–24 June with processions including that of King David and the shepherds, whose characters are the descendants of a medieval play (*auto*). Folkloric groups give their costumes an airing.

Around the Town

At the centre of town, a **keep** tufted with green is all that remains of the fortress-palace of 1378. Nearby is the sprawling **Archbishop's Palace**, mixing styles from the 14th to the 18th centuries. It is now an important public library, with books and manuscripts creamed from 20 convents. Its open courtyard, the 18th-century Largo do Paço, contains a curious castellated fountain which is said to be a stylization of the heraldic symbols of Dom Rodrigo de Moura Teles, who commissioned it in 1723. The basin is sided with six spouting castles. The cathedral is almost opposite, entered across the courtyard and through the 18th-century cloister.

The Cathedral

The cathedral is a wonderful place to wander about. It dates from 1070, when the bishopric was restored. Ignore the absurd pin-ball trays of electric candles, and enjoy the veritable salad of Romanesque, Gothic, Renaissance and Baroque styles, of which the last mentioned is the most eye-catching, trumpeting itself in a magnificent pair of organs. These face one another as if in battle, gilt with a crècheful of cherubs, who no doubt delighted in the music of Carlos de Seixas: he was a pupil of Scarlatti. (Cherubs meet a less glorious fate by the font, where they appear to be eaten by lions.) During the Baroque period, the visual impact of organs was considered to be as important as their musical potential—here their façades are illuminated by a lantern. Many Portuguese cathedrals contain multiple organs, simply for show: their close arrangement at Braga quashes any argument about intended antiphonal effects.

The east end of the cathedral was rebuilt in 1532, and contains a finely carved Manueline high altar retable. The building's lichenous main Romanesque façade was embellished with a Gothic porch c. 1500. This shelters a very interesting 12th-century portal whose two arches are carved with scenes of the *Chanson de Roland* and *Roman de Renart*, of Burgundian influence. The porch opens onto the attractive Rua D. Paio Mendes. The cathedral's frilly rooftops are the work of João de Castilho.

The several dependent Gothic chapels are well worth visiting, included in the price of the cathedral museum ticket. The **Capela dos Reis** contains the tombs of the cathedral's founders, Dom Henry and Dona Teresa, parents of Dom Afonso Henriques, the first King of Portugal (*see* 'Guimarães', p.58). With them is the embalmed body of Archbishop Lourenço Vicente. He helped defeat the Castilians at Aljubarrota in 1385, whence the scar on his cheek. Note the stonemason's elaborate mark on the ceiling—stonemasons were paid on the basis of piecework, and had to distinguish their own labour from other people's. In the **Capela da Gloria** the 14th-century tomb of Dom Gonçalo Pereira is very fine: it was commissioned during his lifetime. The figures on one side of the tomb are singing. The man with the keys also has access to the roof and to the *coro alto* or raised choir. Note the splendid breasts of the caryatids on the choir stalls.

The Sacred Art Museum

Open June–Sept, 8.30–6.30.

The large and very rich Sacred Art Museum is installed in the chapter house. It contains some outstanding pieces, but the collection is very badly displayed and disgracefully uncared for. The illuminated manuscripts are damp and wasting away. Worried inquiries will not help: the archbishop chooses not to sanction conservation work.

Among the wealth of embroidered cassocks, a plain cross is striking. It was used at the first Mass in Brazil, in 1500, when Pedro Álvares Cabral had discovered the country (*see* 'Belmonte', p.199). The Hispano-Arab cylindrical ivory coffer, coloured reddish brown, dates from the end of the 10th century and is carved with creatures on unlikely trees. The pre-Romanesque 11th-century chalice of S. Geraldo is inscribed with a reference to Count Mendo, grandson of the Mumadona who founded the monastery at Guimarães, and is said to have been used at the christening of Afonso Henriques. The platform shoes belonged to a very short archbishop. He couldn't reach the altar without them.

The Casa dos Biscainhos Museum

Open 10–12 and 2–5; closed Mon and holidays.

The Casa dos Biscainhos Museum gives a fascinating insight into the refined pleasures and diversions of the 18th-century nobility, from music to falconry, though most of the *palácio* was built in the 17th century. One family lived in it for over 200 years until 1963, when the viscount was outraged by his daughter's marriage to a plebeian. He shot her horse, buried it in the garden, and sold the house to erase her from his memory.

At street level the ground floor is ribbed, to allow precious charges to exit their carriages at the foot of the staircase, which is designed as if it were outdoors. The vehicle would then drive through to the stable block incorporated in the main house, in the French style. The 18th-century gardens follow the Italian fashion: there is a winter house, and a fountain within trained hedges, for cooling the summers. The residents enjoyed the sound of water: the house is built around a fountain cloister, rare in civil architecture. *Azulejos* depict a fraction of 18th-century life, with scenes of falcons and hunting and the priming of a gun. A painting depicts Braga in the 16th century, near the Portuguese copy of a roundbacked Chippendale chair. The Romantic Room includes a working music box and a perfumery for aromatic herbs. The Porcelain Room was formerly the Music Room, as the ceiling paintings show. There are collections of fans and jewellery, and temporary exhibitions downstairs.

Other Sights

At right angles to the façade of the Casa dos Biscainhos is the very beautiful **Town Hall**, attributed to the Baroque André Soares da Silva, whose architecture has received less scholarly study than it deserves. Even more sumptuous is his elaborate **Casa do Raio**. The granite casements accompany a blue tiled front. Down some steps nearby, the **Fonte do**

Ídolo is a Roman sanctuary carved into living granite. The small, simple shrine is dedicated to the God Tongo Nabiacus, as identified by an inscription, but it is not clear whether the carved male figure is the god or the donor, one (Ce)licus. Unusually, there is a votive offering to the goddess Nabia in the same place. Doubtless the god and the goddess, who are symbolized by a carved hammer and dove respectively, are displeased by the stagnant pool beside their sanctuary.

The **Museu Nogueira da Silva** (*open Wed and Fri 3–6*) is one man's collection displayed in his home, financed by the monopoly on lottery tickets over most of Portugal during the dictatorship of his friend Salazar, whose sculpted head is amongst the tusks in the hallway (this is one of the few representations of him not destroyed during the Revolution of 1974). The taste is eclectic, like that of the more civilized crooks in a James Bond movie—from Louis XVI furniture, to a 15th-century Italian chest telling the story of Samson, to Adam chairs and imitation Chippendale, to neoclassical silver in the dining room, and cases of porcelain. The fountain from Tibães is at the bottom of the garden, purchased from the children of the late owner's maid. Under the colonnade are three heads awrithe with sea flowers, concocted by Jorge Barradas in 1969. (His figures at the Museu da Cidade, North Lisbon are even more striking.) Nogueira da Silva enjoyed electric curtains in his ballroom, and financed the completion of the Baroque church tower opposite his residence.

The Environs of Braga

Just outside Braga off the road to Ponte de Lima stands the tiny Visigothic **Chapel of São Frutuoso de Montélios**. Built in the second half of the 7th century, it is one of the oldest Christian buildings in Portugal. The chapel is in the shape of a Greek cross, supported by columns topped with acanthus leaves. The exterior is a series of recessed arches, alternately pointed and round-topped. The columns' ornamentation and the triple arches are probably Visigothic, while the roofing and lateral chapels were contributed by the Moors in the 9th century.

The Hungarian St Frutuoso was Bishop of Braga from 650 to 665: the chapel was adjacent to the monastery he founded, which was destroyed to build the 18th-century church of São Francisco. St Frutuoso's relationship with his adopted country was stormy. He wrote to his friend the Bishop of Saragossa describing Portugal as 'An extremity of the west, an ignorant country where naught is heard but the sound of tempests.' The chapel's atmosphere is not as impressive as its antiquity: though dim and pagan, it does not reek. Latter-day restorers are now setting about it, so it will be further sanitized.

Braga ✆ (053–) **Where to Stay**

expensive

Everything in the ★★★★**Hotel Turismo**, Av. João XXI, ✆ 612200, ✉ 612211, is on a large and impersonal scale. Rooms are gadgety—the bathroom vent hums all night—but have nice balconies overlooking the trees on the main street. The service is efficient, but the bright restaurant offers a limited menu.

Dark corridors at ★★★★**Albergaria Senhora-a-Branca**, 58 Largo da Sra-a-Branca, ✆ 269937/8, ✉ 29937, reek of polish, fresh from the owner's factory. Rooms are spacious and with all mod cons. Entered through a shopping centre, ★★★**Residencial do Central Comercio Avenida**, Avenida Central, ✆ 275722, ✉ 275722—not to be confused with crummy Res. Avenida on Av. da Liberdade— offers big, well-furnished brown rooms with kitchenette.

inexpensive–cheap

★★★**Residencial dos Terceiros**, 85 Rua dos Capelistas, ✆ 270466 (*inexpensive*) is pleasant, though bland, and is approached by an infuriatingly slow elevator. ★★**Residencial Inácio Filho**, 2nd Floor, 42 Rua Francisco Sanches, ✆ 263849 (*cheap*) is interesting because it's in a home, and furnished accordingly—but the landlady is fierce. ★★**Pensão Francafort**, Avenida Central, ✆ 262648 (*very cheap*) was established in 1882, and the large, airy rooms retain period furniture and the original cornicing. A bargain.

Braga ✆ *(053–)*

Eating Out

expensive–moderate

Rustic **Inácio**, 4 Campo das Hortas, ✆ 613235 (*expensive*), is reputed to be the best restaurant in Braga, but the manager may, without provocation, be alarmingly rude to potential diners. The *bacalhau* is good. *Closed Mon.* Next door **Bem-me-quer**, 6 Campo das Hortas, ✆ 262095 (*moderate*) is like a restaurant in a New York brownstone, long, thin, and brick, with old photographs on the walls. It serves very good fish and meat dishes.

cheap

For value, charm and excellent food, you'd be better off at **Abade de Priscos**, 7 Praça Mousinho de Albuquerque, ✆ 276650 (first floor). It's small and intimate, softly lit by bracket lamps and candlelight, and run by a family whose small children wander in if they have nightmares. The menu is brief, but the food is well presented, with rich and subtle tastes, from the excellent—disguised—*bacalhau*, to the slow-cooked beef served on the bone, or pig's trotter with coriander and garlic. For a quick meal in the centre of town, **A Toca**, 127 Rua do Souto, ✆ 263279, serves good food at a counter or booths, with *sarrabulho* an irregular speciality. **Café Astoria**, Praça da República, is a large Art-Deco café with good snacks, small meals and a vegetarian option (usually just a sandwich, but it's a start).

Around Braga

Caldelas

The typical turn-of-the-century spa of Caldelas lies 14km northeast of Braga, a rural niche sheltered by the spurs of the Serra do Gerês, with its complement of neo-Gothic houses. The Romans took advantage of its medicinal qualities: Caldelas is particularly good for gastritis, colitis and other intestinal disorders, and certain dermatological complaints (*spa itself is open 1 June–10 Oct*). Give or take a little global warming, the Romans must also have enjoyed the fresh clean air, which somehow stays pleasant even on sultry days.

Caldelas ☎ (053–)   ***Where to Stay***

The ★★★**Grande Hotel da Bela Vista**, ☎ 361502, 🖷 361136, (*expensive*), on the road to Amares, is built on an elegant platform above the baths to which it is connected by a private elevator. There's a lovely rural panorama from the terrace. *Open 1 June–10 Oct.*

Bom Jesus

Frequent buses for Bom Jesus depart from outside the shopping centre in Braga's Avenida Central. By road, Bom Jesus is 2km east of Braga.

In the 18th century it was deemed unseemly for pilgrims to ascend to their climax by dirt paths. The solution was the Baroque staircase, splendid at Bom Jesus. It climbs the thickly wooded hillslope in a series of terraced zigzags of white plaster, embellished with wall fountains representing the five senses and, higher, the three virtues, and with granite biblical figures who grow more and more rococo as one ascends. Some wear turbans and oriental cloaks. The eye is led up the tier of rich Christmas crackers to the twin-towered church at the top. Penitents climb on their knees, but the fainthearted succumb to the hydraulic funicular from near the base of the staircase.

The lower portion was begun by the Archbishop of Braga in 1723. Cruz Amarante added the upper portion some 60 years later, and the church itself was not completed till 1837. Unlike the church of N.S. dos Remédios at Lamego, the church of Bom Jesus is of no special interest, and there is no sign of the late 15th-century sanctuary on which it was built.

The church is surrounded by manicured gardens, tranquil except at weekends. Amongst the trees are snackbars and hotels, which can be reached by road.

The mid-18th-century vogue for elaborately decorated façades was adopted with special vigour in the region of Braga. Should you wish to continue reeling, this is well illustrated by the rococo **church of Santa Maria Madalena** at **Falperra**, 5km south of Bom Jesus. Designed by André Soares da Silva in 1750, the windows and doors are awrithe with stylized granite vegetation, set against brilliant whitewash.

☎ (053–)   ***Where to Stay and Eating Out***

★★★★**Hotel do Elvador**, ☎ 676611, 🖷 676679 (*expensive*) is small and mellow, with a big view. The good restaurant offers a fixed-price 4-course lunch or dinner; calf's liver is on the menu. ★★★★**Hotel do Parque**, ☎ 676607, 🖷 676679 (*expensive*) is under the same management, but decorated in a weird mix of styles, with puce carpets, frilly lampshades, and very luxurious bathrooms. Drinks are served in the covered courtyard, but there is no restaurant.

Citânia de Briteiros

By road, the site is 10km southeast of Bom Jesus. Frequent buses from Braga (marked Ruães) depart from the corner of the Rua do Carvalho and the Rua de São Vicente. There are infrequent buses from Bom Jesus towards Citânia de Briteiros; if you are using public transport you will have to walk the last km or so, passing vines strapped to tree trunks, and people living in dispersed settlements of two-storey houses above their animals.

Citânia de Briteiros is the largest and most thrilling of the fortified Celto-Iberian hill settlements in Portugal. It's located 10km southeast of Bom Jesus, and is thought to have been the last stronghold against the Romans, c. 26–19 BC. For 200 years the Celto-Iberians and their similarly ferocious neighbours the Lusitanians had kept the Romans south of the Serra da Estrêla. In this they were helped by two brilliant commanders, Viriatus and Sertorius. Times were tough and the locals fought dirty: in *The Georgics*, Virgil extols the advantages of good sheep dogs—with guards like these, you need never fear 'the unpacified Iberians creeping up on you from behind.'

Strabo, writing his *Geographia c.* 20 BC, asserts 'Some authors affirm that...the Celt-Iberians and their neighbours to the north offer sacrifices, on nights of the full moon, to a nameless god, in front of their houses, spending the whole night long with their families dancing, singing in chorus and feasting. The Lusitanians ... practise augury, by observing the entrails of prisoners.' Otherwise, they 'live simply, drink water and sleep on the bare earth...two-thirds of the year they live on acorns, which they roast and grind to make bread. They also have beer. They lack wine but when they have it they drink it up, gathering for a family feast. When they assemble to drink they perform round dances to the flute or the horn, leaping in the air and crouching as they fall.'

Strabo's sources got it wrong about the nameless god: misled by the lack of temples, they overlooked the numerous Celt-Iberian gods venerated in rivers and woods, streams and rocky places. The Celt-Iberians may have left Citânia de Briteiros, but the spirits remain today. The granite walls of the 150 dwellings are now few blocks high; there's enough to divine the primitive urban plan, the water system, and to walk the footpaths. Two wonderful huts were reconstructed by Dr Martins Sarmento after he excavated the site in 1875. They come complete with conical thatched roofs and an unspoilt view. Some of the round huts have no entrances; perhaps they were silos entered by ladder. Downhill stands the most controversial structure, a trench flanked by the granite slabs. Now archaeologists consider this the bath house rather than the funerary chamber, marked no. 17 on the good site plan issued at the entrance.

Castro de Sabroso

Another hill settlement, Castro de Sabroso, is visible from Citânia de Briteiros. It's smaller, older, and better fortified. Unless you are especially interested, there is no need to see both sites. From Taipas, take the Santa Cristina de Longos road to Cancela. Turn right and follow the road to the hilltop *castro*.

Tibães

Six km northwest of Braga, the **convento de Tibães** is a Romantic's dream. Once the greatest Benedictine monastery in the land, Tibães seeps with picturesque decay, but somehow retains its dignity. Blue smoke now rises from its courtyards as the ivy that wrapped them is stripped and burnt, leaving roots like shadows on the plaster. The library is roofless, claimed by the ivy, stilled by the surrounding trees. Now the aqueduct is dry, the pool is stagnant, and the fountain of S. Pedro is watered by hosepipe. São João's obliterated face is blank above his jigsaw garden.

Things were different in the 17th century, when Tibães was enormously wealthy and well-managed, buoyed by generous land grants in addition to its original 12th-century endowment. The abbey was virtually self-supporting—producing wheat, corn, rye, barley, oats, chestnuts, cork and wine as well as pigs, cattle and goats. The lands contained two linen mills: by 1668, textile production was booming, and a justice had to be appointed to adjudicate disputes relating to cloth manufacture. Two years later, probably because textile workers were female, a woman was appointed as justice. Carpenters, potters, tilers, blacksmiths—whose iron was one of the few imports—cobblers, millers, masons and tailors worked for the abbey. The local economy was further diversified by innkeepers, cattle dealers, butchers and fishermen. The abbey promoted the enclosure system to solidify its control over land. The abbot was important to the local community, not just because of his military title. He and his council set prices for cereals purchased from tenants, and even controlled the prices at which they were sold in nearby markets.

The Benedictines chose to show off their worldly wealth: in the late 17th century they decided to do away with all their old-fashioned Romanesque and Gothic architecture to make way for the Baroque. Hence nothing remains of the 12th-century foundation. Visitors seeking more than magnificent decay should head for the gilded glory of the church (*open 9–12 and 2–5; closed Mon and holidays*). André Soares' mid-18th-century retable is an excellent example of Portuguese rococo woodwork, influenced by engravings of rococo work in Augsburg, and by Nasoni's work in Oporto. The garlanded columns are set on Oriental-looking pedestals, probably inspired by the fashion for Chinese art and ceramics. The stalls in the *coro alto* are very odd—draped figures emerge from the backs, beside caryatid partitions. They were brought to life 1666–8, and along with the reliquary chapel at Alcobaça they mark the emergence of a new and particularly Portuguese style of woodcarving, which adopts a sculptural rather than an architectural form, to create the impression of continuous movement. Anyone prepared to risk breaking an ankle on rotting floorboards will be rewarded by the good tiles of Joseph and his brethren in the huge chapter house. One cloister is paved with tombs, which relations etch with artificial flowers.

In 1834, when the religious orders were dissolved, Tibães was sold into private hands. The last owner left the property to her maid's children, who sold off the portable parts: the fountain can be seen at the Nogueira da Silva museum in Braga. The government purchased Tibães some years ago, planning possibly to turn it into a *pousada*, but it hasn't happened yet.

Barcelos is famous for its market, the largest and most illuminating in Portugal, and for its fantastical pottery. The town of about 4500 souls spans the River Cávado, surrounded by deposits of clay, granite and kaolin. Pine trees cloak the gentle hills and open valleys of the outlying region, fertile land planted with maize, vineyards, beans and orchards. Having existed for centuries on agriculture and pottery, the town became a focus for the manufacture of industrial textiles in the first half of this century. Kiln chimneys stretch upwards on the outskirts of town, and barefoot children carry trays of pottery. Centred on the large, elegant Campo da República, Barcelos seems to save all its energy for Thursday, market day.

Barcelos is also responsible for the legend of the cock, which has been immortalized in the hideous pottery cockerel adopted as the Portuguese Tourist Office's motif. In the 14th century, a Galician pilgrim was saved from the gallows when he successfully challenged a roasted cock to crow on a judge's table. That cockerel still has a lot to answer for.

Barcelos makes a good day trip from Braga or Viana do Castelo: there's little choice of accommodation in the town, and finding a bed on a Thursday is virtually impossible.

Getting There

By **road**, Barcelos is 20km west of Braga, and 29km southeast of Viana.

Barcelos is directly connected with all the **railway stations** to the north: Viana (17 daily; ½hr or ¾hr); Afife (6 daily; 1¼hrs); Âncora-Praia (8 daily; 1½hrs); Moledo (5 daily; 1½hrs); Caminha (8 daily; 1¾hrs); Cerveira (9 daily; 2hrs); Valença (8 daily; 2¾hrs). From Oporto, there are 11 trains daily (1¼hrs). From Braga, change at Nine (14 daily; 1hr total). From Guimarães, change at Lousado (1hr), from which there are intermittent trains to Barcelos (¾hr).

Buses run frequently from Braga.

Barcelos ☎ (053–)   ### Tourist Information

The **craft centre** doubles as the **tourist office**, Largo do Porta Nova, ☎ 811882 (*open Mon–Fri 9–12.30 and 2.30–6; Sat and Sun 9–4*), occupying the Torre de Menagem, one of the seven towers of what was the city wall. Note that the craft centre does not ship goods. This can be arranged by its equivalent in Oporto, which also sells Barcelos pottery. From the **railway station**, ☎ 811243, walk straight ahead, and diagonally across the Campo da República to the craft centre. There are two **bus stations**: one is near the Campo in Avenida dos Combatantes da Grande Guerra and the RN depot is in the Avenida Dr Sidónio Pais.

Festivals

The Campo da República is illuminated by innumerable lightbulbs for the **Festas das Cruzes** on 2 and 3 May. Featuring a 'Great Fair' and a carpet of flowers, the festival dates back to 1504, when a peasant who insisted on working on the Day of the Holy Cross saw a luminous, aromatic cross in the land he was digging. The church of Senhor da Cruz is decorated with coloured lightbulbs, until it resembles a giant cake.

Around the Town

The **Campo da República** is Barcelos' huge market square, centred on a beautifully proportioned fountain and surrounded by fine, low buildings. To the north, behind its plain front, the **Igreja do Terço**, or **das Beneditinas**, contains remarkable tiles of the life of St Benedict, created by António de Oliveira Bernardes (1684–1732), who presided over the great period of *azulejo* design. He made these panels in 1713, two years after his work on the Lóios chapel at Évora: the use of space and line is outstanding. One panel depicts three monks bending to lift a platform on which a small, winged, half-goat devil dances. The high dado of Baroque allegorical medallions illustrates contemporary dress. Perched between *azulejo* panels, the vigorous, gilt pulpit probably also dates from 1713. It displays the Hapsburg crowned double-headed eagle, which after the Spanish domination of 1580–1640 remained a popular motif in the art of Portugal. St Michael tops the canopy, attended by statues of children bearing emblems of the Benedictine Order. The ceiling of the church is panelled with the same saint's life.

The attractively plain **Hospital da Misericórdia**, formerly a Capuchin convent, dominates the eastern side of the Campo. More splendid is the 18th-century **Igreja do Senhor da Cruz**, built in a corner of the Campo by Joâo Antunes some 30 years after his Igreja da Santa Engrácia in Lisbon and following its centralized plan. The church's beautiful

Barcelos Pottery

Barcelos pottery was made famous by Rosa Ramalho, a local girl who had a way with clay and produced glazed green tabletop figures, especially Christ on the cross, wearing a crown of thorns. By the time she died several years ago, she had spawned a number of popular potters, who create zany imaginary creatures with distorted features, doing unlikely things like trumpeting. The more representational work is usually religious—whole Last Suppers are produced, and many devils—or simply whimsical, such as hedgehogs stuck with olives. Everything is hand painted in bright colours. It cannot be called beautiful, but it's unique. A selection is on sale in the craft centre/tourist office.

Two of the leading lights of Barcelos pottery are Ana Baraça (© 053 841785) and Mistério (© 053 841227). Ana Baraça's hallmark is her figures' literally pinched faces. Deaf, gummy, and round, she works amongst her grandchildren, eyes shining, laughing silently. Now 91, she's been potting since she was 17. The ideas just don't stop, she says. Mistério produces devils and apostles. His grandmother started him as a potter when he was 12. (When it got too cold for her fingers to make pots, she made socks instead.) Mistério works in a shed, assisted by his 12 children, while his wife wields a broom outside, sweeping the chickens around the courtyard. Where do his ideas come from? He dreams them.

Baroque cupola dominates a garden of obelisks; it contains some very rich giltwork, right up to the tassled pelmets.

The other focus of interest is by the River Cavado, which is crossed by a 15th-century bridge, still youthful-looking despite being held together by a giant iron staple. In the ruined **Ducal Palace** of the eighth Duke of Barcelos, first Duke of Bragança, grass cushions the miscellaneous remains of the **Archaeological Museum** (*open 10–12 and 2–6*). These include the 16th-century crucifix known as the Gentleman of the Cock, which depicts a man being hung. The palace was struck by the 1755 earthquake. Nearby are the Gothic **Igreja Matriz**, and the pillory, apparently draped with neck fetters.

The Barcelos Market

Do plan to be in Barcelos for the Thursday market, which fills the huge Campo da República with row after row of handbags, orange trees, sausage skins, witches' brooms, dog collars, sieves, lace, embroidered linen, carved yokes, cassettes by the tableful, bread by the vanful, fruit and vegetables by the crateful—or laid on a strip of hessian, the entire produce of one smallholding. Swarthy women hawk their wares, nimble and urgent, filigree earrings flapping. A woman in black arrives with a reed basket and a couple of live chickens or pigeons or rabbits, weighs them in her hands, haggles, pokes, and leaves with potatoes or bras or an umbrella. She fumbles in her ample breast for the cloth bag that holds her money. At lunchtime venders drink wine from yoghourt pots. Beggars lie on thoroughfares, displaying their disabilities. In winter, chestnuts roast. The market packs up around lunchtime, so get there early, but don't expect to be tempted to buy anything. An old man on an older cart shifts in his seat to direct his shaggy pony, as it slips on the cobblestones.

Barcelos © (053–) **Where to Stay**

★★★**Residencial Dom Nuno**, 76 Av. D. Nuno Álvares Pereira, © 815084, ✉ 816336 (*cheap*) is opposite the side of the hospital and feels vaguely Spanish. It is fraying at the edges, with reproduction furniture behind its black glass doors.

Two low-budget places overlook the market square: ★★**Residencial Arantes**, Av. da Liberdade, © 811326 (*very cheap*) is frilly and fake in its public parts. Bedrooms can be cramped, windows minimal. ★**Pensão Bagoeira**, 495 Av. Dr. Sidónio Pais, © 811236 (*cheap*) is also frilly and very clean. The restaurant is fun—*see* below.

Barcelos © (053–) **Eating Out**

On market days **Bagoeira** (*see* above) teems with white-hatted chefs racing to satisfy proud new owners who boast, hoot, plot, haggle, and generally have a humdinger. What's more, the food is very good (*cheap*).

Restaurant Casa dos Arcos, Rua Duques de Bragança, ✆ 811975 (*moderate*) is a family-run, entirely stone-built restaurant in the historic part of town. Despite feeling a little like a tourist trap, the seafood is very good and the prices reasonable. For a very sweet snack, **Confeitaria Salvação**, 137 Rua D. António Barroso, is proud of its *laranja de doce*, an orange marmaladed whole, and filled with what is rumoured to be pumpkin. The setting is grand—tablecloths and mirrors, recalling the days of the sweet's invention at this confectionery shop in 1830.

The Minho Coast

The Minho's sand beaches are backed by low dunes, but are exposed to the winds and wild waves of the Atlantic. The best thing to do on these beaches is walk—at the height of summer the average seawater temperature is around 16°C.

Viana do Castelo

An elegant fishing port at the wide mouth of the River Lima, Viana do Castelo is backed by the woody Monte Santa Luzia, and overflown by seagulls. The town is more or less arranged on a grid pattern, but wanderers will come upon *palácios* and rococo churches. Discreetly dispersed among these are a number of hotels, which are successfully attracting racy French and German tourists to mix with the locals among the big waves at the wide Atlantic beach.

Affluence and vitality are returning to Viana, whose fairly low-key fishing industry has been overtaken by the heavy industry on the opposite bank of the river estuary. There are many places to stay in town, though the cheap accommodation is unexciting.

History

Viana served as the port for the north of Portugal until the late 17th century, when it was eclipsed by Oporto. Viana had sent its own ships to France and the Levant in the 13th century. Cloth and cod had been shipped from England to Viana (and, to a lesser extent, to Monção) at least since the 16th century, and bartered on the quayside for the red wine of the Minho—red portugal. Trading links were established with Brazil, Scandinavia and Russia, and Viana's merchants were said to rival those of Venice and Florence. Periodically the canny English and Scottish merchants forsook their Baroque townhouses in Viana, loaded their Carolingian wigs and account books, and set off in flat-bottomed boats up the River Lima. The wine they bought did not travel well: it was frowned on in England. Large quantities were supplied to the British naval commissioners as 'beverage for the sailors'.

Political events then played into the merchants' hands. Colbert, Louis XIV's minister, implemented ultra-protectionist policies, forbidding the import of English cloth into France. Charles II retaliated by banning the import of French wine into England. Demand for red portugal drained the supplies, and the merchants in Portugal looked for new vineyards. They hit upon the Upper Douro—and it was easier to ship wine from the Upper Douro via Oporto: Viana was never the same again.

Trains run directly to Viana from Oporto (frequent, 1¾ or 2½hrs), Barcelos (frequent, ¾hr), and intermittently from all stations north of Viana. From Guimarães, change at Lousado (intermittent, 1hr plus 1½hrs). From Braga, change at Nine (frequent, 1½hrs total).

REDM Express **buses**, ✆ 058 828834 or 01 793 6527, run to Viana infrequently from Lisbon (6hrs), Coimbra (3hrs), Oporto (1¼hrs), Póvoa de Varzim (¾hr), Esposende (½hr). The same company also run frequent buses from Oporto (1¾hrs) and from Póvoa de Varzim (1hr). Intermittent buses run down the coast from Monção.

Viana do Castelo ✆ *(058–)*   ***Tourist Information***

The **tourist office**, Rua Hospital Velho, ✆ 822620 or 24971, used to be a hostelry. It gives away ridiculously small, glossy maps of Viana, and sells blue and white china, crochet work, and embroidery. Gold filigree is a typical embellishment. The railway station, ✆ 822296, is near the centre of town—walk straight ahead down the Av. dos Combatentes. The bus station is on the northeastern edge of town, at the end of the Rua da Bandeira.

Festivals

Viana's ***romaria*** is special: on the Friday nearest 20 August, the image of N.S. da Agonia is carried in procession from the church of the same name, along a route stencilled with coloured sawdust and draped with fishing nets, to the docks, where the boats are hung with flags. The image then goes for a short cruise. Most of the costumes for the religious procession are made by a lady who works in a shoeshop. She spends the year sewing wings onto angels, and then hires them out. Drums announce everything. People camp by their coaches, make coffee on spirit lamps at 4am, play table football, wash in the river, and eat *farturas*, nasty fried sugared flour. Houseplants are put on doorsteps, anyone with gold to wear wears it. For the procession, each village provides a float illustrating the local speciality, be it wine-making, mending fishing nets, picking olives, making bread or killing the pig. One float bears the lady in the publicity poster. Recently someone offered to pay for the poster if his wife could adorn it, but the offer was turned down. (The *romaria* is financed by local subscription.) The last float is the *caravela*, symbol of Viana.

After the *romaria* comes the only bullfight of the year. At the fort on Sunday evening, local costumes are displayed. The costumes of the farm women (*lavradeiras*) get very specific—one for going to church, one for going to the fields, one for collecting seaweed. The ladies of Viana itself wear flowery red headscarves and shawls, white blouses, and pleated red, black and yellow skirts. Traditionally, they keep their wealth in gold—medallions and necklaces of coins—and this Sunday evening is when all the heirlooms get displayed.

Around the Town

Best start at the top: a cobbled road snakes up to Santa Luzia, and makes a pleasant walk; alternatively, the funicular ascends on the hour, 9–12. The hideous grey pilgrimage **church of Santa Luzia**, built early this century in neo-Byzantine style, has been likened to a bowl of sprouting tulips, but it offers a broad view of Viana and the rivermouth. Behind the hotel above the church, **Citânia de Santa Luzia** is a Celt-Iberian settlement dating from the 3rd century BC (*see* 'Citânia de Briteiros'); the 40 dwellings are razed to their stone foundations and guarded by a chihuahua.

The Praça da República

The heart of Viana is the Praça da República, previously cobbled but now nastily paved with modern concrete slabs. The satisfying mélange of 16th-century styles centres on a well-proportioned Renaissance fountain, built by João Lopes the Elder to suit the contemporary Italian taste for water falling from graduated basins. Behind it stand the three arches of the restored **Paços do Concelho** (the old town hall), which is at right angles to the extraordinary three-storeyed façade of the **Misericórdia House**. João Lopes' self-satisfied granite caryatids have borne their load since 1520, as they remained in place when the **Misericórdia** was rebuilt two centuries later. The *azulejos* in the nave were begun in 1720 by António de Oliveira Bernardes, whose work at Évora and Barcelos is so exceptional. Though grand, these biblical scenes lack the others' nobility—they were completed by António's son, Policarpo.

Towards the River

Veering riverwards past the old town hall, the Rua Gago Coutinho passes the rococo chapel of the **Casa da Praça**, which is ornamented with granite shells. There's nothing of interest inside. Nearby, the castellated 15th-century **Sé Catedral** is fronted with horrid stone figures who see, hear, and speak no evil. The interior was burnt by a Napoleonic fire. It contains a fine model of a *caravela*, and a nice juxtaposition of angles at the staircase. Downhill, and running parallel with the cathedral, the once-opulent **Rua de S. Pedro** has now faded, cramping the style of the good Manueline window there. These are the streets to wander.

At the mouth of the docks, the **Santiago da Barra Fort** is uninteresting and disappointing—this is the '*castelo*' in Viana do Castelo. Philip II of Spain, at that time King of Portugal, ordered it to be built in 1592. When they heard the news of the revolution in 1640, the locals besieged the Spanish garrison here, which surrendered.

Inland

From the Praça da República, the Rua Cândido dos Reis leads past the gracious rococo façade of the town hall, formerly the **Palace of the Counts of Carreira**, to a hospice suffused with kindness and good-humour, formerly the **convento de Sant'Ana**. There's an interesting collection of antique wheelchairs in the vestibule; and the chapel (*closed to view at weekends*) is delightful, its ceiling panelled with biblical scenes—Christ is in red—and the gilt retable bursting from the surrounding tiles. The convent was less quiet in former times. In the late 17th century, the nuns were meeting with their lovers in the small buildings on the grounds of the nunnery, which had been built to provide the sisters with somewhere to practise their cooking on days when they were permitted to leave the convent. In 1700 Pedro II ordered these cauldrons of vice to be torn down. Even as the love nests were being razed, the Sisters of Sant'Ana were selling contraband tobacco.

From the Praça da Républica, the Rua Manuel Espregueira runs parallel with the river to the **municipal museum** (*open 9.30–12 and 2–5; closed Mon and holidays*). The museum is housed in a *palácio* built by Vilalobos in 1720, and auctioned 10 years later to a family who lived in it until 1922. The *palácio*'s original *azulejos*, by Policarpo de Oliveira Bernardes, depict the continents personified, aboard unlikely chariots and smiled on by cherubs. The museum contains some good furniture, including a rare Indo-Portuguese table inlaid with ivory dots right down to its feet. Also displayed are a 15th-century Nottingham alabaster depicting Judas' kiss, a Spanish painting of a black magic ceremony—hung near the chapel, a picture of the Praça da República in the 19th century, and a fine anonymous Dutch portrait of a lady.

Viana do Castelo ✆ (058–)   **Where to Stay**

Enatur's hilltop ★★★★**Hotel de Santa Luzia**, Monte de Santa Luzia, ✆ 828891, 🖅 828892 (*expensive*) enjoys broad views of the church of the same name, hills, beaches, the town and its heavy industry. The solid building was recently refurbished in Art-Deco style, right down to the fittings. Bring flip-flops for walking to the swimming pool. The airy restaurant is well finished, with engraved glass candle-guards, but the menu is not inspiring. To the fore of the town, the popular ★★★**Hotel Viana Sol**, Largo Vasco da Gama, ✆ 828995, 🖅 823401 (*moderate*) offers pleasant, sparingly furnished, though viewless bedrooms surrounding a plant-filled atrium; excellent facilities include an indoor swimming pool (be careful—the shallow end is 1½m deep), sauna and a slick discotheque. The gaudy restaurant is grim; the food can be luke-warm and stodgy. Swimmers trudge past, gawking at diners. On the wrong side of the railway line and the Oporto road, ★★★★**Albergaria Calatrava**, 157 Rua Manuel Fiúza Júnior, ✆ 828911, 🖅 828637 (*moderate*) is very comfortable, with a woodburning stove and old photographs; bedrooms have TV and minibar.

Don't be tempted by the riverside location of the **Hotel Aliança,** ✆ 829498—it's very badly maintained. Also on the main street is the ★★★**Residencial Vianamar**, 215 Av. dos Combatentes da Grande Guerra, ✆ 828962 (*cheap*), which is fairly priced and basically comfortable. Rooms have showers. Budget travellers should avoid the crummy **Residencial Terra Linda** and **Residencial Bela Terra**, and head for the **Pensão Guerreiro**, ✆ 822099 (*cheap*), which is clean, spacious and comfortable, and has its own restaurant. ★★★**Residencial Laranjeira**, 45 Rua General Luis do Rego, ✆ 822261, 🖅 821902 (*cheap*) offers small but decent rooms with parquet floors, but many steps. On the south bank of the river, **Apartmentos 'Sandy-Mar'**, ✆ 322982, is a complex of decent apartments, set amongst pine woodlands.

Five km southeast of Viana do Castelo, **Paço d'Anha**, Anha, ✆ 322459 (*category A*), is approached through vineyards which the owners' ancestors established in 1503. The farmbuildings facing the Paço have been converted into three wonderfully rustic two-bedroom bungalows. Expect leather chests around a fireplace, a beamed ceiling above an open kitchen, and a supply of homegrown lemons if you're in season. Squeeze these over a drink and sit on the peaceful lawn behind the bungalows. Another dependent building has been converted into two apartments, sharing a covered patio and a small walled lawn. One has a single bedroom, the other has two, all attractively furnished and equipped with mod cons. Each year the Paço d'Anha produces 50,000 bottles of its own *vinho verde*. Part of the main house's colonnade is taken over by girls sticking labels on the delicious stuff.

Out towards the bus station in Viana, **Casa Grande da Bandeira**, Largo das Carmelitas, ✆ 823169 (*category B*), is homey, quiet, and not dauntingly grand. The three clean-smelling top-floor guestrooms are furnished with reproductions and 19th-century pieces. There are two bathrooms. 'When our guests prefer our company,' says the hostess beneath her bouffant, 'they sit on the veranda overlooking the garden'. Otherwise they have their own basic sitting room, with a stand-up piano.

Off the main road from Viana to Ponte de Lima, **Casa do Ameal**, Meadela, ✆ 822403 (*category B*), offers seven cottagey bungalow apartments, each with its own entrance, in two blocks converted from outhouses. Turn-of-the-century prints, shaggy rugs in front of the log fireplace, patterned bedcovers, and well equipped, discreet kitchenettes characterize the viewless apartments, which come in various sizes. Two stone tables sheltered by a vine are available for eating outside, and the guest dining room has a TV and card table. It's a good place if you're travelling with kids. The house itself was purchased in 1669 for 3500 shillings, by forebears of the present residents.

Viana do Castelo ✆ *(058–)*   ***Eating Out***

A safe bet is always **Os 3 Potes**, 9 Beco dos Fornos, ✆ 829928 (*moderate*)—near the Praça da República—carefully established by an efficient English lady. It began as a bar where locals could meet tourists, and vice versa, and expanded into a cosy convivial restaurant. It's on the site of Viana's first public bakery. Sixteenth-century townspeople would bring their homegrown flour here, pay their fee, stick an emblem in their dough and bake their own bread. Gourds hang from the beamed ceiling, lampshades shed a gentle light, and the good food is subtly adapted to non-Portuguese palates. Consequently, the place can get a bit too touristy, especially on Saturday evenings (and Fridays in August) when folk dancers perform. A cheap weekday set lunch is available. Reservations are recommended in summer.

Alambique, 92 Rua Manuel Espregueira, ✆ 823894 (*moderate*), is decorated with agricultural implements, with the kitchen open to view at the back of the restaurant. The menu is small and ambitious—the snails make a nice change, though the quality of the food varies from day to day. An economical option is the affiliated bar counter, for two-thirds of the price. There's a bar counter option at the pretentious and pricey **Tres Arcos**, 44 Av. J.T. da Costa, ✆ 24014 (*expensive*), where the shellfish are alive. Seafood is also the speciality at **Costa Verde**, 411–413 Rua de Monserrate, ✆ 829240 (*expensive*), which serves good quality food in a bright and featureless restaurant on the northern edge of town towards Valença. Unless you enjoy grit in your food, eschew the astro-turfed seating outside the **Neiva Mar**, 1 Largo Infante Dom Henrique, ✆ 820669 (*expensive*), which is located on the corner of a main road. Inside is a small, tiled haven where bright flowers adorn blue-clothed tables. This is an excellent seafood restaurant— try the stuffed crab. **Jardim**, L. João Tomas Costa, 15, has a good breakfast menu including astoundingly tangy fresh orange juice.

Vila Praia de Âncora

The railway follows the coast from Viana do Castelo to Moledo, passing through Vila Praia de Âncora, a small port with a long beach at the mouth of the Âncora river. The flat expanse of sand is fairly empty, except at weekends, and even then you only need to walk to get away from other people. Behind the beach, dry stone walls separate red-soiled fields into strips. If you prefer not to swim in big waves, head for the sheltered river estuary.

A tourist office functions in the summer on Av. Dr. R. Pereira, ✆ 058 911384, and will arrange rooms in private houses. There's a lot of good fresh fish in the local restaurants. The choice of accommodation includes ★★**Hotel Meira**, 56 Rua 5 de Outubro, ✆ 911111, 🖝 058 911489 (*moderate*), and ★★★★**Albergaria Quim Barreiros**, Av. Dr. Ramos Pereira, ✆ 058 951218, 🖝 951220 (*moderate*).

Moledo

Moledo, Portugal's most northerly Atlantic beach, celebrates its position at the mouth of the River Minho with a semi-ruined castle on a spit. Portuguese families come here on day trips, and the beach is easily accessible from the railway station.

Try ★★★**Pensão Ideal**, Rua Eng Sousa Rego, ✆ 058 721505 (*inexpensive*). *Open 1 May–31 Oct.*

Along the River Minho

Caminha

Caminha was once a mighty riverport, but in the 16th century intermittent border fighting inclined its shipping to Viana do Castelo, draining the small town of any significant revenue. Now Caminha is an unhurried minor frontier post, like a smaller version of Viana do Castelo. A busy road separates Pinhal Praia beach from the town.

The main square is centred on a fountain like Viana's, and dominated by a Renaissance clocktower on an 11th-century base. The carving of a woman who supports the sky deco-rates the portal of the **Misericórdia**. The **fire station** houses a small collection of antique hand-pulled fire engines, to your left as you look at the clocktower. The arch under the tower leads to a charming cobbled street and to a square with a fir tree and two double-decker birdboxes. The **tourist office**, ℗ 058 921952, is situated here.

The **Igreja Matriz** is a fortress-church built in the 75 years after 1480. Pass beneath the Evangelists at the side door. The doors seem to have been made a little later than the rest of the church—though attractive, the figures are a clumsy interpretation of the Renaissance work brought to Coimbra by Frenchmen. The bossed wooden ceiling of the central nave is superbly carved, and represents some of the finest carpentry in the country. Its medallion faces may portray the commissioners of the building, or the craftsmen themselves, the principal of whom is believed to have been Francisco Munoz, from Tuy in Spain. On the outside of the church a stone gentleman points his arse at Spain.

℗ *(058–)*

Where to Stay and Eating Out

Small, clean and friendly, ★★★**Pensão Galo de Ouro Residencial**, 15 Rua da Corredoura, ℗ 921160 (*moderate*), off the main square, has a granite staircase and lovely ceiling mouldings. **Pensão Rio Coura**, ℗ 921142 (*cheap*), and **Residencial Arca Nova**, ℗ 721475 (*inexpensive*) are both near the train station. Arca Nova has the edge with lovely rooms. There's an Orbitur **campsite** at Mata do Camarido, ℗ 921295.

Turismo de Habitação

Casa do Esteiró, ℗ 921356 (*category B*) offers two apartments a few kilometres east of Caminha. **Quinta da Graça**, Vilarelho, ℗ 921157 (*category B*) sits patiently as ivy creeps up its 16th–century walls. The views are great.

For places to eat, there is **O Torre**, under the clock tower, from the main square, and **Alareira**, near the railway station. **Caminhense** (*moderate*) offers superb regional dishes, and **Adega do Chico** near the fire station (*moderate*) is recommended for fish and seafood.

Vila Nova de Cerveira

If you're passing through Cerveira, on the road from Caminha to Valença, the fortress-*pousada* is a great place to stop for a coffee. The village was named after its deer (*cervo*). The defence was built to stem river crossings, and probably dates from the 13th century, when Dom Sancho II granted the settlement to his wife as a wedding present.

℗ *(051–)*

Where to Stay

Cerveira's fortress has become the **Pousada de D. Dinis**, ℗ 795601, ✉ 795604 (*category CH*). Drinks are served on the lawn beside ramparts fronting the river, and guests are cocooned with a chapel, a pillory, and the former town hall, each of which is edged with granite mottled by lichen. The four blocks of box-like guest rooms are decked with grandiose wooden furniture. The *pousada*'s giftshop sells lacework and embroidered table runners. Unless you're staying in the *pousada*, there's no reason to spend the night in Cerveira. However, if you get stuck, the ★★★**Residencial Rainha Santa Isabel**, Av. Heróis, ☎ 795169 (*inexpensive*) is nondescript but clean. Some rooms overlook the railway track and Spain.

Three kilometres southwest of Cerveira, on the road to Caminha, the ★★★★**Estalagem da Boega**, ☎ 795231, ⊕ 7900509 (*moderate*) can be very highly recommended for its excellent service and views down towards the river.

Valença do Minho

Impregnable 17th-century fortress walls enclose the frontier town of Valença, built on a hill overlooking the River Minho. Now the old part of town relents of its hardness, catering to the invasion of Spanish tourists who come to buy bathmats and sackfuls of bottlecorks. They leave in the evening, and the cobbled streets are calm. Geraniums grow on wrought-iron balconies and granite casements. Moss seeps up the splendidly preserved polygonal fosses, embankment, barbican and bastions. A traffic light operates where once visitors were dependent on the trust of the gatekeeper. Valença has outgrown its battlements, and an uninteresting new town clamours below them.

Idrisi, the Muslim geographer who completed his work in Sicily in 1154, wrote of the River Minho as 'a large, wide and deep river: the tide goes far up it, and vessels that go up it stop often because of the great number of villages and castles on its banks.' Valença was one of these stopovers, though at that time the settlement was called Contrasta, explained by a glance across the river to Tuy in Spain. The towns face each other like clenched fists. Dom Afonso V hoped to safeguard the loyalty of Valença by exempting two-thirds of the active male population from participating in raids on Spain. The Spaniards in the War of Restoration and the French in the Napoleonic war failed to take the town.

The **Roman milestone** in front of the church of S. Estêvão was originally near the River Minho jetty, marking the military road from Braga to Astorga.

The Environs of Valença do Minho

A little way east of town, the road to Monçao passes the lichenous granite of the Romanesque **Ganfei Monastery**, rebuilt for the Benedictines in the 18th century.

There are spectacular panoramic views from the **Monte do Faro**, 5km east of Valença. The ascent is fascinating because it gives an almost aerial view of several villages on the way. At the top, the view stretches down the valley of the River Minho to the ocean, and, on a clear day, as far as Pontevedra in Galicia. Some 22km south of Valença, the high village of **Paredes de Coura** makes a pleasant diversion.

Roughly halfway between Valença and Monção, the road passes the well-proportioned Romanesque **church of São Fins de Friestas**, which is all that remains of an early 11th-century Benedictine monastery. The real thrill is the cornice, carved with a collection of bizarre human and animal heads, whereas the portal is decorated with geometric shapes. The first foundation here dates from the 6th century. Subsequently the monks received wild boar in lieu of rent, but this could not sustain them forever. By 1545 there were just three monks, and they were dissolute.

Where to Stay

The **Pousada de São Teotónio**, © 824020, 📠 824397 (*category C*), is a discreet new building within the fortress walls, the only accommodation in town to offer beautiful views of hilly fields towards the river and Tuy beyond it. The service is good and the bedrooms are comfortable. The small restaurant serves very acceptable food on cold plates, with a picture window to distract diners as they eat lamprey or wild rabbit.

★★★**Hotel Lara Residencial**, Lugar de S. Sebastião, © 824348, 📠 824358 (*moderate*), offers neutral bedrooms overlooking the fortifications, but plenty of public space. ★★**Residencial Ponte Seca**, Av. Tito Fontes, © 22580 (*cheap*) is adequate. It's a 10–15-minute walk from the railway station: turn right at the end of the avenue, right at the roundabout, and past the little bridge. Next to the railway station, the ★★**Pensão Rio Minho**, Largo da Estação, © 223331 (*cheap*) is run-down but reasonably clean.

Eating Out

There are three fairly enjoyable restaurants within the fortress walls, as well as the *pousada*'s restaurant. **O Limoeiro**, © 23220 (*cheap*) has a whitewashed arched brick ceiling, lanterns on the walls, pew-like benches, and various meat cutlets on offer. Nearby and more popular is **Parque**, © 23131 (*cheap*). The ingratiating *maître d'* vaunts a broad menu, and keeps the radio on. *Closed Fri.* **Monumental** (*cheap*) is inside the Portas da Coroada and is plain and decent.

Monção

Monção is a charming, mellow little border town nudging the River Minho and centred on two squares ringed with Brazilian chestnuts (not true chestnuts: their fruit is inedible). At dusk an old man plays the accordion in the corner of his shop. An antique barber's chair, complete with a wrought-iron footrest and leather neckrest, awaits customers who can be shaved by a cut-throat razor for 50$00, to the tunes of a harmonica played in an upstairs window. Monção is noted for its lampreys, rich little eels also found on the west coast of Ireland.

A local lady named Deu-la-Deu showed her pluck in 1368 when she and her fellow townspeople were starving under siege by the Castilians. She grovelled about and found enough flour to make two buns. These she threw at the enemy, who left, disheartened by her show of plenty. The heroine and her buns stand gargantuan on Monção's blazon.

Getting There

By **road**, Monção is 19km east of Valença and 39km north of Ponte da Barca.

RN Express **buses** run once daily from Lisbon (8¼hrs), Coimbra (4¾hrs), Oporto (3¼hrs), Braga (1½hrs), Ponte da Barca (¾hr) and Arcos de Valdevez (¾hr). This bus continues through to Melgaço and S. Gregório. Auto-Viação do Minho, ℰ 652917, run infrequent buses from Oporto (3hrs). The bus passes through Viana (1¼hrs), Ancora, Caminha (1hr), Cerveira and Valença (½hr). The **bus station**, ℰ 53620, is in front of the **old train station**. From there, the centre of town is straight ahead and to the right.

ℰ *(051–)*   ***Tourist Information***

The **tourist office** is in the Largo de Loreto, ℰ 652757.

Festivals

On 18 June, Monção celebrates Corpus Christi with a procession which dates back to the 16th century. It includes a blessed ox (*boi bento*), its horns varnished and decorated with flowers and ribbons, a symbol of plenty. A cart of herbs (*carro das ervas*), covered with greenery and filled with nervous or exhibitionist 'little angels', is followed by St George on horseback, wearing a long red cape and toting a sword. A lumbering dragon (*coca*) brings up the rear. After the procession, St George battles the dragon, symbol of evil. The dragon has never yet won.

Around Town

Behind its classical portal in the main square, the **Misericórdia** has a ceiling panelled with cherubs, and a floor paved with sepulchres. An alley to your left as you face the *Misericórdia* leads under an emblazoned arch to the Romanesque **Igreja Matriz**, which contains a cenotaph to Deu-la-Deu, erected by her great-great-grandson, and a Manueline chapel. Most of Dom Dinis' **fortress** of 1306 was destroyed when the now redundant railway line was built. The remains can be seen towards the riverbank, bushy with vegetation. The **spa** is not geared up for tourists. Baths with feet await benchfuls of quiet patients seeking help for rheumatism and bronchitis.

Monção ℰ *(051–)*   ***Where to Stay and Eating Out***

★★★★**Albergaria Atlântico**, 15 Rua General Pimenta de Castro, ℰ 652355/6, ✆ 652376 (*moderate*) is between the two town squares and offers brass bedheads, very wide baths and friendly service. ★★**Residencial Esteves**, Rua General Pimenta de Castro, ℰ 652386 (*cheap*) is 20m in front of the old railway station, comfortable and domestically furnished, with carved wooden furniture. There are even cheaper rooms available above the **Pastelaria Raiano** and from various other unofficial operators around the town—look for their signs in windows.

Plate glass, soft music and air-conditioning are part of the new look at **Mané**, ℰ 652355, ✆ 652376 (*moderate*), next to the Albergaria and recently revamped to suit its international clientele. Friendly, bow-tied waiters serve generous helpings of good food. The *feijoada* is filling and rich. **Restaurant Quinta da Oliveira** (*cheap*), a 10-minute walk from the centre of town, offers a more intimate setting, with wholesome food served by scrubbed ladies in blue headscarves. **El Pollo Rico** (*cheap*), just downhill from the railway station, has very good grilled chicken.

Around Monção

Five km south of Monção at Pinheiros, on the road to Arcos de Valdevez, the simple, balanced façade of the **Brejoeira Palace** (1806–34) was inspired by Lisbon's Ajuda palace. It's closed to the public but easily seen from the road.

In Longos Vales, 8km southeast of Monção on the road to Merufe, a mass of foul and fantastical faces glower from capitals at the back of the 12th-century Romanesque **church of S. João**. To see the round arches of the apse, and more weird creatures, ask for the key at the entrance of the driveway. Continuing a couple of km towards Merufe, take the turning marked Sta Tecla to see long views of the Minho from the defunct **church of S. Caetano**, beside a Celt-Iberian site brightened by jonquils and converted by a cross.

The otherwise unremarkable **Ponte de Mouro**, between Barbeita and Ceivães, 8km east of Monçao, was the bridge on which John of Gaunt, Duke of Lancaster met João I on 1 November 1386. The latter had secured the independence of Portugal at the battle of Aljubarrota in the previous year. Together they planned the invasion of Castile. 'As further proof of friendship and a safeguard for these matters agreed upon,' writes the court historian Fernão Lopes, 'they then decreed and promised that the Duke would give his daughter, the Princess Philippa, to the King of Portugal to be his wife.' The wedding took place in Oporto in 1387 (*see* **Oporto**, p.143). The couple were happily married: in the words of the same chronicler, 'God granted [Philippa of Lancaster] a husband to her taste.'

Ⓒ *(051–)*   **Where to Stay**

Turismo de Habitação

A driveway fenced with slabs of granite stretches through a pine forest towards the sprawling 18th-century **Casa de Rodas**, Ⓒ 652105 (*category B*)—off the road to Arcos de Valdevez; contact the tourist office in Monção for directions. Its reception rooms boast handpainted walls, and light but lordly furnishings. There are four cosy bedrooms fitted with new bathrooms, an old kitchen smelling of woodsmoke, and a comfortable apartment for four. Cabinets display pewter in the cavernous dining room. The owner, Maria Luisa Távora, speaks good English. The construction of a motorway near by reduces Rodas' sublime peace but does not destroy it entirely.

Melgaço

East of Monção, a poorly surfaced but pleasant road runs along the Minho river to Melgaço, past granite villages and opposite their equally humble Galician equivalents. This tiny town in vine land wakes from its sleep on market day, Friday. A wall circles the plain castle **keep** and its rocky outcrop, a frontier watchtower built by Afonso Henriques in 1170. Two viragos fought a memorable battle here in 1383. Inspired by a turncoat hussy—'*A Renegada*'—Castilians infested the castle, where they withstood siege by João

I and the Duke of Lancaster. After seven weeks the renegade spotted Inês Negra amongst her besiegers, and suggested the two of them fight it out, hand to hand, winner take the castle. The renegade fled 'with signs of many punches on her snout', and the castle was Portugal's.

Taking the first left turn from the castle gateway, note the sharp-toothed wolf carved above the side door of the 13th-century Romanesque **Igreja Matriz**—the locals say it represents the Devil.

There's a border crossing into Galicia 9km east of Melgaço, at São Gregorio.

Melgaço ℰ *(051–)*   ***Where to Stay***

 If you want reasonably comfortable accommodation, it's best to stay at the Peso spa 4km west of Melgaço: ★**Hotel das Águas de Melgaço**, Estrada Nacional no.202, ℰ 42262; ★**Hotel Rocha**, Estrada Nacional no.202, ℰ 42356, which has decent food; **Pensão Boavista**, Estrada Nacional no.202, ℰ 42464 (*open 1 June–30 Sept*). (*All inexpensive.*)

In Melgaço itself there's ★★**Pensão Pemba**, Largo da Calçda, ℰ 42555 (*cheap*) or the nicer ★**Residencial Miguel Peireira**, near the cinema, ℰ 42212 (*cheap*).

Along the River Lima

Inland from Viana do Castelo, the terrain is flat between densely forested hills. Hay is stacked like pipecleaners. The route along the north bank of the River Lima is preferable, because it keeps closer to the river's course.

The Romans believed that the Lima was Lethe, the River of Forgetfulness: its beauty would make anyone who crossed its banks forget his native country and his friends. Livy reports that having traversed most of Iberia, the soldiers of Proconsul Decimus Junius Brutus, who took office in 138 BC, refused to cross the 'Flumen Oblivionis'. Brutus grabbed the standard and crossed over with it by himself, persuading them to follow him.

Ponte de Lima

A long, low Roman bridge crosses the river 23km east of Viana, at the point where it builds white sandbanks. Here stands the gracious middling-sized town of Ponte de Lima. The bridge was built as part of the Roman road from Braga to Astorga. Milestones can still be seen along the route, which was a favourite with pilgrims bound for Santiago de Compostela. Dona Teresa granted Ponte de Lima its charter in 1125—in order to strengthen her northern defences—but there are no distinguished monuments. Like Óbidos, the quaint and higgledy-piggledy town recognizes its charms and is taking cosmetic measures to safeguard them—by burying electricity cables.

Ponte de Lima ℰ *(058–)*   ***Tourist Information***

The **tourist office**, ℰ 942335, is off the Praça da República. The **bus station**, at the upstream end of the avenue of trees, includes a waiting room fitted with bus

---

seats—presumably to give the illusion that travellers are already aboard. Buses arrive frequently from Viana do Castelo and infrequently from Braga.

Festivals

On the third weekend of September, the jolly **Feiras Novas** include fireworks, a funfair, a market for agricultural implements, and a religious procession (for which the children of the town are dressed as cherubs and carry anchors and fake palms; a bewigged gentleman bears the cross).

Around the Town

Off the principal road, at right angles to the river, the wide **Igreja Matriz** has been simply beautiful since the 15th century. Note the tracery on some of the ceilings. The **crenellated tower** at the waterfront is all that remains of the town's fortifications. At street level it sells local craftwork; the upper chamber was used as the town prison until 1966. Prisoners used to lower buckets for pedestrians to donate cigarettes and money; the strings have worn incisions in the stone window sill.

The narrow **Roman bridge** caterpillars across the Lima, alternating fat arches with skinny arches, which are wedged on their upstream flanks, to disperse the water. The far side of the bridge was extended in the 14th century. Downstream stands a magnificent **avenue of plane trees**, excellent for lovers, cogitators, and photographing small children. It leads to the **convent of S. António**, which houses a small **museum**.

Since 1125 Ponte de Lima's fortnightly **Monday market** has been held on the sandbank. Cattle are sold on the opposite bank, where the bells of the church of Santo António de Torre Velho used to ring to celebrate good business.

Walks

Ponte de Lima is an important town on the pilgrimage trail to Santiago de Compostela in Spain. The tourist office has information about the route as well as numerous others in the area. If you like a short walk with a target in mind, try the panoramic Hermitage of Santo Ov'dio (across the bridge and a half-hour walk off the road to Valença), or there's the Monte de Santa Maria Madalena (3km to the southeast, approached by a tortuous tarmac road).

Ponte de Lima ✆ (058–)   *Where to Stay*

★★★★**Albergaria Império do Minho**, Avenida Dom Luis Filipe, ✆ 741510, ☎ 942567 (*moderate*), is the centrepiece of a new shopping complex and boasts a swimming pool and quite plush, modern rooms. ★★**Pensão São João**, Largo de São João, ✆ 941288 (*cheap*)

is amiable and charming, though basic. A couple of rooms overlook the river and the low bank beyond. Delicious smells and warm air waft up the stairs from the restaurant below. **Casa do Hospedes O Limiano**, S. Gonçalo, ✆ 742365 (*cheap*) is on the other side of the river and offers good value, breakfast included.

Turismo de Habitação

The central booking office for *Solares de Portugal* (*Turismo de Habitação*) is situated above the tourist office, ✆ 742829/ 742827/ 741672.

There are some 30 houses offering accommodation under this scheme in Ponte de Lima alone. The following is a selection.

The quietly palatial **Paço de Calheiros**, Calheiros, ✆ 947164 (*category A*)—7km north of Ponte de Lima—is the flagship of the *Turismo de Habitação* scheme. Candelabra hang from chestnut ceilings, illuminating the family portraits and antiques, and many of the nine double guestrooms and nearby sitting rooms have fabulous views of the Lima valley. Outside, great magnolia trees shadow the raked gravel driveway, along which stretches the stable block, now converted into five apartments. There's a pool in the grounds and horses for riding. The charming young count is fluent and hospitable. The Calheiros landholding was granted by Dom Dinis and confirmed by Dom Afonso IV in 1336. The present house was built at the end of the 17th century, since when it has not left the family. The count is elected mayor of the village that bears his name. His great-grandfather used to leave a barrel of wine at the manor gates, for the villagers to help themselves.

It's not easy to relax in the dark and heavy **Casa de Crasto**, Ribeira, ✆ 941156 (*category B*)—on the southeastern edge of Ponte de Lima—which feels manorial and is built of dark wood from ceiling to floor. Parts of the 17th-century house were destroyed in 1896, by an owner looking for treasure. The five guestrooms have shower rooms; the comfortable furnishings may include an antique cot and a plant-filled alcove. A stepped garden incorporates tiny-stoned outbuildings and a well.

Also in Ponte de Lima, surrounded by camellia trees, **Casa das Pereiras**, Largo das Pereiras, ✆ 942939 (*category B*) offers three splendid bedrooms and serves the best dinners in town every Friday night.

Casa do Arrabalde, Além da Ponte, Arcozelo, ✆ 742442 (*category B*) is 100m from Ponte de Lima's Roman bridge and offers spartan accommodation overlooking a few fruit trees, in a village. The shared rooms are carpetless, pictureless and almost unfurnished, but for a chess set and some ancient timbers. Not all bathrooms are *en suite*.

Casa do Outeiro, Arcozelo, ✆ 941206 (*category B*), is 1km east of Ponte de Lima and offers a living slice of manorial life: the noble library smells of dried tea, religious paintings agonize on the walls, the family vine (rather than tree) is stuck with photographs, and silver is displayed around the heavy dining room. Huge quantities of quince jelly (*marmalada*) are brewed in the kitchen. The house was restored in

1723, and has been owned by the same family since the early 18th century. In 1809 the invading French Marshal Soult established headquarters here.

The nearby **Quinta do Salgueirinho**, ✆ 941206 (*category C*), is owned by the same family. Pleasant and peaceful, the first-floor terrace overlooks a small orchard. It's furnished in a rustic style, though the carpetless ground floor is chilly, and the kitchen bare—nobody lives here permanently. Still, guests in the four double and one single rooms comment on the housekeeper's hospitality. They share two bathrooms. Adjacent is the **Casa da Vinha**, a small and twee self-contained unit, with a bathroom like a summer-house. *Both open June–Sept.*

Guests' accommodation is across the courtyard from the **Casa de Antepaço**, Arcozelo, ✆ 941702 (*category B*). Freshly decorated with Laura Ashley-style fabrics, the four newly timbered bedrooms are on the ground floor, and some have views up a fertile slope. The first-floor sitting room completes the family farmhouse style. Chicken pots are displayed in the open-plan kitchen.

Beautiful it may be, and swimming pool it may have, but the apartment in **Casa das Torres**, Facha, ✆ 941369 (*category B*)—10km south of Ponte de Lima—feels like a doghouse. The plain ground-floor rooms overlook the parking area and are kept in mothballs.

Moinho de Estorãos, Estorãos, ✆ 941546 (*category B*)—7km northwest of Ponte de Lima—was a watermill, but don't expect a Mississippi-style paddle: the waterwheel decays beside a clear wide stream, by a willow tree and a little Roman bridge. The peace is interrupted only by the strangled quacks of waterside frogs. The miller's house is available for guests. Its simple furnishings are reminiscent of a mountain lodge. The double bedroom is very pleasant, and there are two fold-up single beds. The mill was built in the early 19th century; its 17th-century predecessor was on the opposite bank, and paid an annual rent of one chicken.

The delight of **Casa do Covas**, Nelas, Moreira do Lima, ✆ 941711 (*category C*)—6km northwest of Ponte de Lima—is its peaceful back garden, half of which is given over to wild flower beds, with vines trailing overhead, and silvery trees welling up to a ridge. The apartment which sleeps four is pleasant, with a full kitchen and a games room opening onto the terrace. There are two double apartments, one squashed and unornamented, the other generally unwelcoming.

Casa do Tamanqueiro, Estorãos, ✆ 941432 or ✆ 01 921 3733 (*category C*)—7km northwest of Ponte de Lima—is a stone-walled, family-sized bungalow for the sole use of guests. The heart of the house is the kitchen, hung with onions, chillies and garlic, with a gun on the chimneypiece, a table that seats six, and four gas rings; the only oven is the ancient bread oven. Step over the weedy cement terrace at the back, and follow the pergola to the stream 100m away, overlooking the pine-covered slopes of a hill.

Two minutes away, **Casa da Quinta do Rei**, ✆ 058 941432 (*category C*) is uninspiring and rather gloomy. It overlooks pine hills, the remains of an orchard, and a dilapidated stable. The house is divided into two apartments, the nicer having a double room and a single room, the other two double rooms.

Ponte de Lima ℭ *(058–)*   ***Eating Out***

Ponte de Lima is noted for its *sarrabulho*, rich minced meats and pig's blood. **Restaurante Brazão**, 1 Rua Formosa, ℭ 941890 (*expensive*) has a good reputation and an upmarket feel. The kitchen is open and a roof slopes over it—white-clad women cook good food with great energy. **Beco das Selas**, Beco das Selas, ℭ 943576 (*moderate*) displays curiously carved benches and coat pegs. A saddle hangs on the wall, unaccounted. The atmosphere is warm and the food is pretty good. *Closed Sat.* Granite-walled, dimly lit, and cooled by ceiling fans, **Tulha**, Rua Formosa, ℭ 942879 (*moderate*)—in line with the Roman bridge, but back from the river—serves fish, *sarrabulho*, or grilled skewers of pork and beef in full or half-portions. There's a good selection of local wines. *Closed Mon.* Friendly and cheery thanks to the beaming manager, **Gaio**, Rua Agostinho J. Taveira, ℭ 941251 (*cheap*)—a block over from the tourist office, towards the new bridge—is less polished: best choose the dish of the day. Portions are huge and delicious. *Closed Fri.* **M. Padeiro**, Rua do Bonfim, ℭ 941649 (*cheap*) is beside the crenellated tower and is male and boozy. Onions loop along the ceiling at **Catrina** on the river front, ℭ 941465 (*cheap*). Small and incredibly basic, it's run by a host of cheery women serving large portions of decent food. *Closed Tues.*

Bravães

East of Ponte de Lima the landscape changes as the dense, vinous hills close in on the river. The road to Ponte de Barca is like Salome: exceptionally beautiful and always twisting—to the music of the River Lima.

Twelve km east of Ponte de Lima this road passes through the village of Bravães, whose superb little 11th-century Romanesque **Igreja Matriz** boasts one of the most elaborately carved Romanesque portals in Portugal: clinging quadrupeds, doves, birds of prey and tall figures standing on one another's heads come together in five arches. The pediment, supported by two stylized bull heads—thought to symbolize the death of Christ—depicts Christ flanked by St Peter and St Paul. The dark interior makes it difficult to see the murals of St Sebastian, behind the font, and of the Virgin and Child.

Ponte da Barca

The little town of Ponte da Barca has grown along the river, and is saturated by the lush countryside that surrounds it. The old part of town is delightfully drowsy. Here the river-banks are low, with plenty of space to camp, and the water is great for swimming. An elegant mid-15th-century bridge employs the same thick arch/thin arch principle as at Ponte de Lima.

The bridge was the scene of the *baptizado à meia noite* (midnight baptism), which was practised until the early decades of this century. If her previous child was stillborn, a pregnant woman would go to the bridge at midnight, raise a bucketful of water, and oblige the first male passer-by to dip his fingers into the water and make the sign of the cross on her bared belly. The local priest, it seems, looked the other way, though at a village in the Gerês mountains the priest himself performed the baptism.

Twelve or fourteen trees constitute the **Jardim dos Poetas**, a garden ripe for merry-making beside the river.

© (058–)   *Where to Stay*

*Pensão Freitas, Rua Conselheiro Rocha Peixoto, © 42113, and the marginally more comfortable **Residencial S. Fernando**, Rua das Maceiras, © 42580, 🖃 43766, are both *cheap*. The best place to stay is **Pensão Maria Gomes**, 13 Rua Conselheiro Rocha Peixoto, © 42288 (*cheap*), which has views over the river and bridge. You can breakfast on the balcony to the soothing sound of babbling water.

Turismo de Habitação

Paço Vedro, Ponte da Barca, © 42117 (*category A*) offers a formal, late 18th-century manorial scene: the chandeliered hall with its stiff family portraits, spears and swords leads through to room after shuttered room of heavy antiques, including a harp sumptuously draped with silk. Of its five guest rooms, the doubles are much grander than the singles, but all involve crossing the corridor to get to the bathrooms. There's a tacky bar for guests, opening on to the front garden.

Made grand by its size, **Casa da Agrela**, near Ponte da Barca, © 42313 (*category B*) provides rather normal guestrooms, with views down ramshackle slopes to hills opposite. The price for the view is a steep, nightmare driveway—if you can find it. Above the house is a swimming pool filled with spring water.

© (058–)   *Eating Out*

The basement **Restaurant D. António**, 81 Rua Conselheiro Rocha Peixoto, © 42620 (*moderate*) is keen to please, and says so in English. Coloured cocktails are displayed at the bar. Reasonable trout and steaks are available. Beside the river the aptly named **Bar do Rio** (*moderate*) offers the same specialities, but is submerged when the river floods.

Arcos de Valdevez

Sited in a deep valley overlooked by granite pinnacles, the lovely little town of Arcos de Valdevez has moulded itself into an S-bend in the River Vez. The two parts of town are connected by an elegant, wide-arched bridge with oval portals. Just downstream of the bridge, a leafy island has been made into a public park. Main roads separate the river from the pretty and labyrinthine centre of town, which focuses on a pillory square. Set back from this, the odd Baroque **Igreja de N. S. da Lapa** was built by André Soares in 1767. It's an oval on the outside and an octagon indoors, with a low stone dome and a two-storey entrance porch topped by a weaving cornice.

There are several *pensions* in Arcos, including: ★★★**Pensão Sol do Vale**, Rua Dr Germano de Amorim, which has a garage (*inexpensive*); the modest but clean ★★★**Pensão Ribeira**, Largo dos Milagres, © 65174 (*cheap*), on the riverside beside the bridge; and ★★★**Pensão Tavares**, Rua Padre Manuel José da Cunha Brito, © 66253 (*cheap*). Try to check out **Casa Delfim**. The food is OK, but the main attraction is the proprietor, whose accordions line the walls. The old man considers himself something of a celebrity in the accordion-playing world and is prone to giving spontaneous concerts.

The Peneda-Gerês National Park

The Peneda-Gerês National Park is 70,000 hectares of natural reserve, named after the two mountain ranges it encompasses. Shaped like a horseshoe, it straddles the two provinces of the Minho and Trás-os-Montes, cushioning Spain on its northern edge. It's an excellent place for hiking, and driving can be rewarding, if your car will stand the roads. The park was established in 1971, as Portugal's contribution to International Conservation Year. It includes over a hundred villages, so sometimes it's not apparent that one is in a park at all.

Landscape

Both mountain ranges are dark grey granite, with small schistose strips, rising from tight gorges. A massive granite table mountain separates the Peneda valley from the Gerês valley, and a fissure in the granite produces thermal effects at the spa Caldas do Gerês.

The rock is rounded rather than jagged, which makes it seem more friendly. The barren, biblical scree and weird fields of wind-sculpted boulders are not the crumbs of some giant explosion: they were prised from the bedrock by the freezing and thawing of water held within the rock.

A little glaciation has made dramatic scenery at the headwaters of the Rivers Vez, Homem and Couce-Coucelinho. The River Lima bisects the reserve from north to south, and the River Cávado forms its border in the south. Minor rivers cut deep, narrow valleys through the mountains, fed in winter by hundreds of streams—because granite is impervious—from which the goatherds drink. When it's very wet, there are little waterfalls. Recently six major dams have been built, to provide hydroelectric power. Portuguese visitors, here as elsewhere, view the reservoirs with wonder and affection.

Flora and Fauna

There are spirits in the woods of Gerês: it's not surprising the Celts and Lusitanians worshipped them. The park's flora grows as it does because the land receives up to 2800mm of rainfall annually, the highest in continental Portugal, and varies in altitude from 100m to four peaks over 1400m. The goatherds reckon that the climate is less predictable since Mt St Helena erupted. Mt St Helena or no, the climatic and altitudinal conditions allow a confusion of plant species, whose origins range from the Mediterranean and subtropical regions to Euro-Siberian and Alpine zones. The cork oak (at Ermida), arbutus, Portugal laurel, Gerês fern, royal fern and bilberry can be found on the slopes of the warmer, more sheltered valleys. Woods of English oak (at Matança, Cabril and Beredo), with holly (at Ramiscal) can be found in places where the Atlantic makes itself felt, and at altitudes up to 800–1000m. Higher still come Pyrenean oak and the flora of the Euro-Siberian zone, including the birch (near Mezio) and Scots pine (at Biduiça). Centennial yew trees prefer the high, humid sheltered valleys. Above here there is only scrubland.

Five plants are specific to the Gerês area, including the Gerês fern and the Gerês iris. But for the casual observer in spring, it is the carpets of irises and delicate yellow St John's wort which are most enchanting: the latter lend their colour to the Serra Amarela (the Yellow Mountains).

Over these soar occasional golden and booted eagles, as well as buzzards and goshawks. Eagle owls, tawny owls and Scops owls elude most visitors. The wildlife of Gerês is thrilling but diminished: wild ponies and roebuck. Wolves are now thin on the ground— a more likely sight is a wolf/dog crossbreed, or a wolfskin on a villager's floor. There are lots of black caterpillars with silver linings, and butterflies after them. Sheep and goats need no introduction. Black vipers arrive unannounced—there aren't many, but it's worth keeping an eye open. If you do see a snake, it is more likely to be a grass snake. Brown bears disappeared from here around 1650, Gerês mountain goats around 1890, and subsequently civet cats.

Settlement

Some 15,000 people live in the Peneda–Gerês park, walking the hills their prehistoric predecessors walked 5000 years ago. Prehistoric man has left uninspiring dolmens at Castro Laboreiro, Mezio, Paradela, Cambeses, Pitões and Tourém, plus several now used as shepherds' shelters. Part of the Roman military road that linked Bracara Augusta (Braga) to Asturica Augusta (Astorga) in Spain passes along the River Homem, now on the southeast side of the Barragem de Vilarinho. Milestones are dotted about the place, at Bico da Jeira, Volta do Covo, Albergaria and Portela do Homem.

After the Romans came the Christian Church. The grassy ruined monastery of Santa Maria das Júnias is a 12th-century Romanesque foundation just next to the Campesinho Brook. It doubtless spawned the deserted village of Juriz, at Aldeia Velha de Pitões das Júnias, now surrounded by an oak forest.

In spring about a dozen village communities migrate from the valleys to the mountains. When the maize has been sown, the mountain people leave their granite huts: they move uphill in May, with their beef-cattle and newly born calves. (Bulls live in the mountains year-round.) Their summer quarters are some 300m higher in altitude: here they stay until October, cultivating rye and potatoes. In the valleys they grow meadow grass as cattle-feed for winter.

The park has very little to offer the visitor in the way of infrastructure—this is part of the appeal, though it can be exasperating. Walking maps are hard to come by, and outside Caldas do Gerês, there is very little accommodation available.

Entry to the park is free. Gates are at Lamas do Mouro (Melgaço), Mezio (Arcos de Valdevez), Leonte (Gerês), and Covelães (in Trás-os-Montes, west of Montalegre). All these are served by good asphalted roads. Off the asphalt, some of the roads are terrible: the earthy gravel gets eroded into yawning potholes. Think twice about using your own car. As elsewhere in the Minho, the roads are full of S-bends.

Walking in Gerês can be sublime, set to the music of goatbells (and the occasional chainsaw). The air smells as air should. There are **park offices** in Braga, ✆ 053 600 3480, Caldas do Gerês, ✆ 053 391181, Montalegre, ✆ 076 52281, and Arcos de Valdevez, ✆ 058 65338. They provide some information in English as well as a park map, which is feeble and difficult to follow. If you're serious about walking, plan ahead: the bookshop Porto Editora near the Infante Sagres Hotel in Oporto stocks 1949 and 1962 military maps of Peneda and Gerês, as does the youth hostel in Campo de Gerês. However, once a military map, always a military map—the management is unlikely to sell them to foreigners. Even so, these maps were made before the dams were built.

There are no marked or signposted paths. It's best to walk on cart or goat tracks, furrowed with cleft hoofprints. If you're worried about getting lost, these tracks usually lead to a settlement of sorts, or at least to an asphalt road, from which you should be able to take bearings. Generally the villagers are extremely friendly and helpful. Many of the men have worked abroad, and speak French, or English with American accents. How much climbing you do depends upon where you go—for the most part there's nothing too strenuous.

TG Trote-Gerês organize **pony trekking** and **camping holidays** in the park. They can be contacted through: CRT Verde Minho, Rua Justino Cruz, Edifício Atlântico 84/90 6°, 4700 Braga, ✆ 053 76924. Montes d'Aventura, based in Porto, ✆ 02 208 8175 and at the Youth Hostel in Campo de Gerês at weekends, organizes adventure trips in the park, including **canoeing**, **horseriding**, and **trekking**.

Caldas do Gerês

Caldas do Gerês has something of the parasol about it: a fashionable spa since the 18th century, it is duly primed with turn-of-the-century hotels. It's also a good place to stock up on herb teas—herbs grow wild in some of the surrounding woods. The **tourist office**, ✆ 053 391133, at the upper end of town, provides inadequate maps. If you've been eating too much *pão-de-ló*, the spa is helpful for obesity—also goitre and diabetes. The hospital is open 1 May–31 Oct.

★★Hotel do Parque, Av. Manuel Francisco da Costa, © 39112 (*inexpensive*), is a pleasant has-been, with a swimming pool. *Open 15 May–15 Oct.* The only competition comes from the **★★Hotel das Termas**, Av. Manuel Francisco da Costa, © 39143 (*moderate*). There are many other *pensions* and *residencials* both in Caldas and on the approach to it. Choose your view.

In the mountains above the Caniçada dam, the **Pousada de São Bento**, Cerdeirinhas, Soengas, © 647190 (*category C**)—signposted on the way to Caldas do Gerês—is a timber-beamed lodge, simply furnished, slightly dog-eared, at its best with a roaring fire in the hearth. The sitting room and open dining area share picture windows, mesmerizing when mist is seeping up from below. Bedrooms are in cuckoo-clock style, with tiny shuttered windows. There may be problems with the hot water.

Soajo

The tough, remote village of Soajo strikes a happy balance between a backwater and something more sophisticated. Its view of the Lima valley is slightly marred by *casas de emigrante*, which stand beside granite houses first established in the 12th and 13th centuries. A fantastic group of *espigueiros* huddle on a granite threshing terrace, above the valley, just northwest of the town. These coffers are built of granite slats and set on stilts, for storing winnowed grain out of the reach of rats. Topped with little granite crosses, they seem like strange pagan tabernacles. In town the pillory dates from the 17th century, and bears an image of the sun. If you like walking, the shepherds may be glad of a bit of company—they set out at 6am.

There's a hotel here, or in one of the cafés you could ask for Alexander. He speaks French, he has rooms to let, and he knows a network of people in villages throughout the park, some of whom also have rooms to let.

granite espigueiros (grain stores) Lindoso

Lindoso

The very steep road from Soajo to Lindoso offers great views of the Lima valley, and passes a tall manmade waterfall. '*Lindo*' means 'beautiful'—here it's rugged beauty. The village is set in a dip between hills backed by the 1400m Outeiro Maior peak. Its lichen-encrusted border **castle** was built by Dom Afonso III, the resettler and administrator, some time before 1258, and reinforced by his son Dom Dinis. A line of low walls and battlements was built in the mid-16th century, and strengthened in 1640 for the War of Restoration. Downhill from the castle, chickens peck around a group of coffer-like *espigueiros*, on a threshing terrace overgrown with weeds.

Construction work on new roads around Lindoso can make driving particularly unpleasant. For the moment huge lorries account for much of the traffic, while in places the road almost disappears.

Castro Laboreiro

Castro Laboreiro stands at an altitude of 950m, 20km southeast of Melgaço, at the tip of the Peneda–Gerês park, and its castle dominates the valley of the River Laboreiro, a small tributary of the River Lima. The little town is spoilt by a rash of *casas do emigrante*, which are sometimes hidden by mist. The air is cool even in summer. The tricky road to the ruined castle passes a granite rock shaped like a giant turtle, looking as if the unfortunate creature has been turned to stone by an angry god. Walking requires a proper map: it's simplest to follow the river, which is fine if you don't mind the slant.

Castro Laboreiro gives its name to a muscular breed of dog like a mastiff, used for herding sheep. They are not friendly dogs. The priest breeds them. The sole accommodation, **Pensão Abrigo**, ✆ 051 45126 (*cheap*) is spick and span, following renovation. **Estalagem de Laboreiro**, ✆ 051 45126 (*cheap*) is a good place to eat and may even start to rent out its rooms one of these days.

Trás-os-Montes and the Alto Douro

Trás-os-Montes, behind-the-mountains—the name conjures up the fabulous realm of a campfire witch, not inappropriately. The province is a high plateau (700m) hemmed in by mountains (1300m) to the north and west; it divides into the wild, gritty *terra fria* to the north of Murça or Mirandela, and the more moderate *terra quente* to the south. The southern hillslopes of the *terra quente* are planted with port wine vineyards, which are focused on the infernal gorge of the River Douro.

The mountains of the west wring water from the Atlantic climate, generating Portugal's highest rainfall (3000mm annually) and leaving a mere 600mm for the eastern plains. There, the climate is Continental, with the country's greatest annual variation in average temperature: Torre de Moncorvo averages 24.6°C in summer and 5.6°C in winter.

Where the soil is fairly rich in the *terra quente* of the south, it supports fruit trees—apple, pear, cherry, and almond. Rye grows on the rolling plains of the *terra fria*, which are mottled with woodland in the hollows: poplar and willow and chestnut. Venerable oak and chestnut trees are found to the north, with some walnut. But it is the names of the scrub that most truly evoke the province—woadwaxen and spurgeflax, gum rockrose and gold and silver broom, wild thyme and rosemary (which, George Borrow reported, should be stuck in one's hat to guard against witches and the mischances of the road).

At weekends the *terra fria* is peppered with gunshot: villagers shoulder their shotguns and head for oak copses to shoot roebuck—the males' horns rarely have more than three spikes; or cultivated land to shoot red-footed, white-breasted partridges; or mixed woods and pastureland to shoot wild boars. Young boars have striped coats, alternating light and dark, which turn to a uniform ashen after the first year of life—when they have had time to reckon with the prospect of being shot. Village dogs wear collars spiked with long nails, which prevent their throats being ripped out by wolves. Wolves howl their way into the myth of Trás-os-Montes, enshrined on the jambs of Romanesque church portals, dreaded by children walking to school. As in the Peneda–Gerês park, most visitors' closest encounter with a wolf will be crossbred with a dog—or the fur on a coat collar or stone wall.

Trás-os-Montes is one of the poorest parts of Europe: although there are pockets of relative wealth, away from the main roads the villagers are peasants who eke out a life only marginally less desperate than that of their medieval forebears. Its area is more than twice that of the Minho, its population two-thirds the size. There is almost no industry in the province—its inhabitants depend upon their land and their animals.

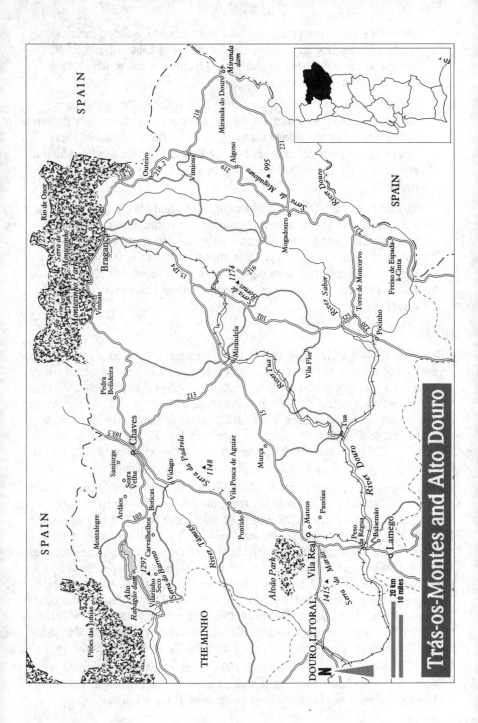

Trás-os-Montes and Alto Douro

Oxen do some of the ploughing, and pull squealing wooden carts, but tractors are making an appearance: the village of Babe, 14km east of Bragança, has 500 residents and 30–40 tractors, many of which have been bought by urban workers.

In the villages the most common complaint is the lack of water in summer—feuds over water are the main cause for murder. Petty disputes can be settled by the village president, who is elected annually. He makes an announcement every Sunday after the church service which is attended by 90 per cent of the villagers, men on one side, women on the other.

In Trás-os-Montes the real monument is man and his life, struggling for sustenance and shelter against burning sun and biting cold. Here, in these desolate conditions, human dignity is more apparent than in more comfortable surroundings. What is important is for the visitor to summon enough of his own dignity to be rid of voyeurism. Trás-os-Montes is a distant, luminous land, and it offers a rare opportunity for travel in Europe.

History

A document of 1096 shows that Count Henry of Burgundy's jurisdiction extended into Trás-os-Montes, opening the way for it to be incorporated in the new nation of Portugal. Its population was very sparse, so Dom Sancho I (1185–1211) attempted to attract settlers. Unlike other parts of the country, vast tracts were never handed over to nobles or military orders: new village societies were established which administered the land, facilities, herds and flocks collectively. There is a popular saying: '*Para cá do Marão, mandam os que cá estão*'—'On this side of the mountains, those who live here command'. Collectivism still exists: history has done little to change Trás-os-Montes.

Spanish troops invaded the province in 1762. Britain sent the 70-year-old Lord Tyrawley to command her trading ally's fleabitten army, but the Spanish Marquis of Sarria was undeterred. He entered Trás-os-Montes, publishing a manifesto that he came to free Portugal 'from the heavy shackles of Britannic dominion'. The army laid siege to Miranda do Douro, whose feeble garrison abandoned hope when their powder magazine exploded. The keys of Bragança were presented to the invaders as soon as they appeared. Chaves too was occupied—the octogenarian Governor of Trás-os-Montes made no attempt to stop the Spaniards. Finally a large number of peasants, reinforced by a few soldiers commanded by Tyrawley's son, O'Hara, repulsed the troops attempting to cross the Douro near Torre de Moncorvo, and successfully held the mountain pass at Montalegre. Pitt sent 8000 British soldiers to beef up the Portuguese army, and a truce was signed in November.

Trás-os-Montes was again in the limelight in 1809, when Soult headed the second French invasion. He entered from Galicia and occupied Chaves, before marching on Oporto. The town was quickly recovered by Portuguese troops under Pinto da Fonseca.

Wine

Red and rosé wines are produced over much of Trás-os-Montes, but it can't match the quality found elsewhere. Valpaços wines are heavy and dark, while the wine of Boticas and Carrazedo is lighter, more like the wines of the Minho.

Bread

There is more to a loaf of bread than meets the palate: in Trás-os-Montes, bread takes on a mystical quality. They say '*O pão é sagrado*'—'The bread is sacred'. It sustains life, like the Communion wafer. For the household it symbolizes the fellowship of eating together, and for the community it symbolizes fertility and a bond with the land, for 'In this land, those who do not work do not eat'. Dough, flour, grain and even the maize plant in the field are called *pão* (bread). Traditionally, for a household to grow its own maize is symbolic of its independence.

In the villages around Bragança, the winter *festas* of the winter solstice, Christmas, New Year and Epiphany revolve around bread, piled into pyramids around wooden structures called *charolos*. The loaves are crafted into fancy shapes—stars, humans, animals—some of them plain bread, some of them baked with honey, eggs, and dried fruits. Each pyramid is topped with a jumble of delicacies. Having processed to the church, the *charolos* are blessed by the priest, and then auctioned off. Buying the bread is a source of great social prestige, not least because of the prophylactic qualities it is believed to have acquired.

Prophylactic qualities or no, eating bread is one of the gastronomic delights of Trás-os-Montes. The maize bread called *broa* is as popular in this province as it is in the Minho. Its crust is hard on the roof of one's mouth, but the crumbly bread is delicious, and curiously rich. Sometimes villagers bake nuggets of pigfat into their bread, making it a meal in itself.

Local Specialities

Trás-os-Montes celebrates with rich peasant stews and sausages; apart from some river trout, fish features less than in the coastal provinces. Chestnuts are sometimes served instead of potatoes, though very rarely in restaurants. The excellent dark runny honey is flavoured by heather.

Fragrant and tasty *feijoada à Transmontana* will warm anyone's cockles. It's best to enjoy this bean stew with your eyes closed—the recipe calls for the ear, snout, and trotter of a pig, as well as different kinds of sausages, cured ham, a little red pepper and an onion. Macbeth's witches may have had a hand in concocting *cozido à Portuguesa*, a boiled medley of blood sausage, pork sausage, spiced sausage, ribs, vertebrae, pigs' ears and lips, kale, carrots, turnips and potatoes.

Transmontane Houses

Houses serve as home, barn and storehouse; their walls of uncemented granite blocks are covered by a single thatched, slated or tiled roof. The ground floor of a rich peasant house will accommodate, say, four oxen and a couple of pigs, whose heat ascends through wooden boards to the bedrooms above. Sometimes the family toilet is a hole in the floorboards above the pigpen. There will be stores of potatoes, maize, walnuts, apples, *marmalada*—rabbits are kept for special occasions, such as the return of an emigrant son. Barrels of wine and *aguardente* ensure that the blood will get pumping on winter mornings. Generally an external stone staircase rises to the wooden veranda of the rich peasant's house. Within, houses are dark and still: doors, windows, and chimneys let heat escape. The kitchen is the heart of the home, where the fire burns and smooths the granite walls with soot. For cooking, a three-legged cauldron is placed over the fire, or in larger houses the cauldron will be suspended from an iron chain. Benches flank the fire, and above it hangs a pole slung with sausages changing from blue to brown in the woodsmoke.

There are incongruities: the occasional television aerial, brought by a returned emigrant, stuck on a chaotic roof with smoke spilling out around it; a Michael Jackson poster sello-taped to the door of a bedroom cupboard that doubles as a store for the pig gutted in December and suspended by a rope through its anus.

Witches

If you come to Trás-os-Montes and feel inexplicably ill, blame it on a spirit, or on someone casting the evil eye. Then seek the help of a white witch. The witch may be either male (*bruxo*) or female (*bruxa*). Witches accept no fees, so bring a sausage, a jar of olive oil or a sack of potatoes. In return for this small gift, you will be healed. Or your future will be laid bare. Or the reason for the failure of your business will be explained. Or you will be equipped with a love potion, to assuage any doubts about your spouse's infidelity. You may prefer a new-fangled witch. These inhabit towns and accept fees. They attract a different kind of clientele, employing 'folk' elements of the Catholic faith which parish priests will no longer sanction. (Catholicism came early to the north of Portugal, and some pre-Christian beliefs and practices crept into its orthodoxy. These practices were disowned by the Church in Portugal as recently as the 1960s—and their protagonists see no inconsistency between them and a creed that sanctions miracles and apparitions.)

Less flagrant but equally authentic are the sausages, not exclusive to Trás-os-Montes, but most at home here. They're eaten grilled, fried, baked and boiled, for snacks, in sandwiches, or as the centre of a meal. *Chouriço* are the most common, filled with lean and fat pork meat, garlic and red-pepper paste. Usually a 2cm in diameter and 15 in length, they are tied in a loop and slung over a wooden pole across the fireplace to

Berrões

Scattered around Trás-os-Montes are more than 200 crude granite sculptures of boars and bulls, usually about 1½m long. They're called *berrões*; they bristle with mystery and are hoofed with paganism, but the locals treat them with affection. The few that have been found *in situ* were within circular stone walls, which may have been sanctuaries. The older *berrões* probably date from before the birth of Christ, perhaps representing deities or divine manifestations, representations of the animals which accompanied the gods, or simply offerings to the gods. The inscriptions on other *berrões* can be dated to between the 1st and 3rd centuries AD, in which case they may represent the Lunones and the Tarboi, which were generally qualified as 'that which roars or moos under the ground'.

Masks

Many people believe that the spirits of the dead return to the land of the living, to safeguard the continuity of their *ideologia*. The spirits are selective about the time of year in which they choose to wreak their anarchic purpose; thus the safeguards to shoo them away are implemented during strictly delimited periods—particularly at the turn of the year. The idea is to use horrid masks to frighten off the malevolent spirits. The villagers create masks that are tangible nightmares: they hit at something deeply human. Usually they are made of wood, sometimes of leather, tin or cork.

The best place to see these masks is in the Museu de Etnologia at Belém in Lisbon. However, the museum has no permanent display, so the masks may not be on show.

Masks are worn at the *Festa dos Rapazes*, celebrated in the villages around Bragança between the feast of St Estevão on 26 December and the feast of Epiphany on 6 January. Unmarried boys over the age of 16 signify their passage from youth to adulthood by dressing in masks and shaggy multicoloured suits draped with huge cowbells. They rampage through houses making grunting noises, terrorizing little boys and demanding sausages from women and wine from men. After the obligatory Mass, the whole village attends a *loas*, in which the young men declaim the events of the past year in the village.

be smoked. Variants include *linguiça*, *paio*, and *salpicão*, the latter two spiced. The *alheira* sausage was perfected by the New Christians, Jews expelled from Spain in the 15th century, who had ostensibly renounced their faith: the Inquisition sent inspectors to check that the 'converts' were eating pork. Smoked sausages were duly produced that tasted like pork—but were made with turkey.

Getting Around

by car

The main road network of Trás-os-Montes is decent enough; but if you're planning on getting to the villages, and a car is the only feasible way of doing so, be prepared for unpaved roads, potholes, mud and flocks of sheep blocking your way. As in the Minho, the summer months are made more hazardous by the dangerous driving of returned emigrants in fancy cars.

by train

The Corgo railway line to Vila Real and the Tua line to Mirandela make some of the most memorable journeys in Portugal, because the traveller gets so close to the land and people. Trains of two wooden carriages ease their way through the granite landscape, clinging to hillsides, stopping at tiny stations when hailed by lone ladies with a red flag pinned to their batons. Sit next to a bag of kale or umbrellas, pass laundry drying on the railway cutting, and listen to the driver's sharp whistle as he alerts pedestrians ambling along the tracks.

by bus

The bus network is exasperating because services are infrequent, and there is no central office to provide details of all the small companies operating here. Timetables are usually kept in people's heads. Tourist offices in the region are generally helpful and reliable and, in the end, all it takes is patience and determination.

Chaves

Chaves is a pleasant town of 13,000 souls, 10km from the Spanish border. Set in a fertile basin, it spans the River Tâmega, a tributary of the River Douro, and is bitten by cold easterly winds. Its isolated, 'top centre' location explain its name: 'chaves' means 'keys', and this was a strategic key to the north of Portugal. Chaves can fill this rôle for the visitor today, serving as a useful base from which to explore the wild surrounding countryside.

Despite its rumbustious history, Chaves today is remarkably calm, though drinking men tend to stress points by table-thumping. Fewer women wear black than elsewhere—either because the mineral water keeps everyone alive, or because they are not so strict in the observance. Spaniards come across the border to shop, so don't be surprised to see prices quoted in pesetas. Mosquitoes whir beside the river, which in summer may be too dry to swim in. Long-haired, green-eyed cats prowl about. The aeons of Chaves' isolation will be shattered by the motorway still under construction, to be completed indefinitely, which will run the length of the country, connecting Chaves with the Algarve. A 180-room hotel is planned, presumably to make the Algarvinhos feel at home.

The **spa** (*open 1 June–31 Oct*) generates water at a fairly stultifying 73°C, the warmest sodium-bicarbonated waters in Europe. It's beneficial to liver troubles, rheumatism, metabolic disorders, intestinal complaints and hypertension.

Local Delicacies

One local delicacy is octopus, which is boiled for Chistmas lunch. Chaves is justly famous for its delicious salty smoked ham, *presunto*, eaten raw like *prosciutto*. *Presunto* should be at least a year old. It's made by a simple but lengthy process: the leg of pork is kept in a paste of salt, paprika, wine and crushed garlic; it spends several weeks in a trough of salt, before the salt is scrubbed off and the pork is hung in the *fumeiro* (the smoking place: literally 'chimney'), for up to two months ending, traditionally, on the first Friday of May.

Hard honey is produced locally, and cafés advertise *pasteis de Chaves*, twinned with Cornish pasties, filled with veal.

History

In 78 AD, the Roman Emperor Flavius Vespasianus founded a burg where two highways crossed, by a thermal spring. He named it Aquae Flaviae. Hydatius, 5th-century Bishop of Chaves, witnessed the beginning of the turbulent history of a place everyone wanted to control, and compiled colourful annals of his time. The Visigoths, he lamented, showed no respect for virgins, whom they abducted (though often returned intact), or for the clergy, who were driven out indecently clothed, while churches were converted into stables and pigsties.

(Hydatius performed a great service to subsequent historians by introducing a new system of chronology, which dated events from the beginning of the Era of Augustus in 38 BC. This, he believed, marked the start of the Roman pacification of the Peninsula. Formerly, chronologies began afresh with the reign of each emperor. In Rome, Dionysius Exiguus proposed another fixed point—the birth of Christ. AD caught on through the work of Bede and the chroniclers of the Carolingians, but the Era of Augustus continued in use in Portugal until 1422, when Dom João I changed it to AD.)

Chaves was destroyed and rebuilt once by the Suevi and twice by the Moors in 250 years. In the mid-13th century the castle was commanded by Portuguese loyal to Spain; and it fell to the Spanish General O'Reilly in the Peninsular War. It was briefly occupied by a monarchist faction rising against the new-born Republic in 1912.

Chaves Pottery

Chaves is renowned for its 'black' pottery, which is coloured like pewter or pencil lead. Burning brushwood subjects ordinary clay pots to a chemical reaction when they are placed in a pit and covered with soil and what looks like coal dust (thus starving them of oxygen). The plain, rounded pots are disinterred, black and heavy-looking. Many of them are made in the village of Nantes, and can be purchased from various shops such as Postigo on Rua do Sol; a pitcher costs about 2000$00.

By **road**, Chaves is 61km from Vila Real, 130km from Braga, and 100km from Bragança.

The nearest **railway station** is at Vila Real.

Rodonorte **buses**, on Rua do Sol, ✆ 333491, run at least one bus daily, plus another 1 July–30 Sept, from Lisbon (9¼hrs), Coimbra (5½hrs), Santa Comba Dão (4½hrs), Viseu (3½hrs), Lamego (2¼hrs), and Vidago (¼hr). There are more frequent services from Vila Real (1¼hrs), Porto (4¼hrs), Amarante (2¾hrs) and Vila Pouca de Aguiar (¾hr).

getting to Spain

On Thursday and Sunday an Internorte bus runs to Vérin (1½hrs) and Orense (3hrs) in Spain. Or it's possible to hitch the 29km to Vérin, from where there are connections to Orense.

The **tourist office** is at 39 Avenida Tenente Valadim, ✆ 333029.

Around the Town

The town has several **squares**; each feels different. Cacti grow in one of them, an extraordinary municipal vanity, covered, in winter, by a polythene igloo. A more understandable source of pride is the town's **Roman bridge**, built across the Tâmega by the Emperor Trajan in AD 98 and 104 and still very functional. There were once a couple more arches than the present 16, but they were land-bound and subsequently built over. One of the two Roman columns on the bridge commemorates an unspecified work—possibly part of the road from Braga to Astorga—constructed by the inhabitants of Aquae Flaviae in conjunction with the soldiers of the Seventh Legion.

On a low hill overlooking the river, the **keep** was built in the 14th century by Dom Dinis. The foundations stand about 5m high, each block marked with a stonemason's hieroglyphic squiggle—stonemasons were paid by piecework, and had to distinguish their own work from that of their colleagues. The keep looks stunted despite its high-toothed crenellations and projecting machicolations, through which were dropped molten lead, boiling oil, and missiles.

Having successfully sacked the keep, Dom João I gave it to his Constable, Nun' Álvares Pereira, who in turn gave it to his daughter Beatriz when she married the king's bastard son, Dom Afonso, Count of Barcelos and future Duke of Bragança. He liked Chaves, and set up home in the keep.

The original protective walls were swallowed up by their 16th-century successors, built to reinforce Chaves for the War of Restoration. The latter period produced ingenious pillarbox corner turrets. Catapult balls retrieved from the bottom of the river are piled at the base of the keep. Dom Dinis' 19-towered escutcheon looms above the keep's entrance: these dominoes were a display of power—lesser men had fewer towers to show. The small military museum within the tower boasts reproductions of ancient armour, but it's mostly 19th- and 20th-century stuff. Note the 16th-century picture of Chaves, depicting the bridge with 14 arches. The top of the building offers a fine view of patchwork fields and the river.

The Museum and the Praça de Camões

Open Tues–Fri 9.30–12.30 and 2–5, Sat and Sun 2–4.30; closed Mon and holidays.

Next to the keep, the Archaeological and Ethnographic Museum is interesting, but there's no feast for the aesthete. To one side of the front entrance door stands one of the original columns of Chaves' bridge—those currently on the bridge may have been intended for elsewhere; to the other side of the door is a Roman milestone with iron bindings, later employed as a gravestone, and a number of post-Roman altars dedicated to Roman gods, including one to the nymphs. The most significant altar, lettered deep, refers to Chaves as a town in AD 78. A framed picture, enlarged from the back of a coin, depicts the Roman emperor who gave his name to the town. Roman terracotta pipes are displayed next to a 19th-century pipe in a splint, made in a nearby village. The similarity of the two types suggests unmodified production.

Up the stairs is a room of fascinating rupestral art, prehistoric figures carved on stone. To the left of the columned room is a 1½m phallus, a smaller statue representing the female sex, and the menhir of a warrior. Articles in the cases have been carbon-dated to 2700 BC. The room of ethnography houses an oxcart, and a triangular device for shaving strips of wood, to weave into baskets. There's also a shepherd's straw suit, of a type still occasionally worn on the mountains when it rains.

Four granite cylinders intertwine to form the turreted **pillory** in the Praça de Camões, a pleasant space fronted by the museum and Chaves' two most notable churches.

The plain façade of the 17th-century **Misericórdia** has been enlivened by an external covered porch with wooden railings. The interior is chock-a-block with 18th-century *azulejos* of New Testament scenes.

The **Igreja Matriz** is at right angles to the *Misericórdia*. The doorway is all that remains of its romanesque beginnings: the church was reconstructed in the 16th century. It houses a fantastical organ decorated with latticework and a head that the Wizard of Oz would have liked to create for himself.

On the other side of town, the inhabited outbuildings of the 17th-century **Fort of São Francisco** generate much laundry and loud music. Beside the fort is an exquisitely proportioned little **chapel**, honey-coloured in the sunlight. Information about it is hard to come by, except that it was moved from elsewhere.

In the 18th century, Dona Maria Ana of Austria, wife of Dom João V, commissioned the octagonal **Igreja da Madalena**, which stands on the far side of the Roman bridge. The interior is disappointing.

Prehistoric Boulders near Chaves

At Águas, 10km east of Chaves, a road leads north to **Pedra Bolideira**, a boulder the size of a small house which can be rocked with the nudge of a shoulder. The phenomenon was discovered by a shepherd, who discovered his horned sheep moving the great rock. The place became known to the wrong sort of people, who tried to blow up the boulder, for building materials. Their plan failed, and now Bolideira is a national monument.

At the village of Sanjurge, 3km northwest of Chaves, follow signs to **Outeiro Machado** or signs indicating 'Arte Rupestre'. Arriving at the dirt track, turn right, then fork left and fork left again. Leave your car at the 'platform' off to the right and walk a short way across the scrubland to the long humped granite boulder pockmarked with prehistoric signs, geometric shapes, and symbols of axes. Like the Pedra Bolideira, the boulder came under threat, from villagers with pick axes convinced that it hid gold. They did little damage. The carvings in themselves are less remarkable than the magic of the place, peopled by spirits on the edge of revealing themselves: this is one of the weirdest places in Portugal. The land is hummocky and soft, the vegetation tough, and the site was once a lake, as indicated by the profusion of rounded stones.

Fairs

The tourist office brochure reports: 'important agricultural centre, [Chaves] is known by its fairies', especially the *Feira dos Santos* held on 1 November, which sells farm and household equipment.

Chaves ℗(076–)   ### Where to Stay

★★Hotel Trajano, Trav. Cândido dos Reis, ℗ 332415, ✉ 27002 (*moderate*), has pleasant rooms decorated in the Portuguese style, with a good view of the old part of town from the terrace. The staff are obliging and uniformed, but the basement restaurant is not promising. Its menu has lots of fish, and a broad assortment of general dishes.

The best place to stay at a more reasonable price is the **★Pensão de Chaves**, 25 Rua de Abril, ℗ 21118 (*moderate*), near the municipal tennis courts. Once fairly grand, it is now fading though still spacious. Floorboards are bare, ceilings are very high, and baths are massive with taps in the middle. It's good value, but hot water may be scarce.

There are several *pensions*, of which the least grim is the **★Hospedaria Flavia**, 12 Trav. Cândido dos Reis, ℗ 22513 (*cheap*), opposite the Hotel Trajano. It costs more than the Hotel Chaves, it's unfriendly and there's not enough hot water.

Turismo de Habitação

Quinta de Santa Isabel, Santo Estêvão, ℗ 351818 (*expensive*) is a traditional manor house standing in an estate filled with pinewood and vineyards. The Sainted Queen Isabel is said to have spent the night here on the eve of her marriage to Dom Dinis—and a good choice she made too; the bedrooms are splendid, with four-poster beds.

Altogether more grand, **Quinta da Mata**, 3km outside Chaves on the road to Mirandela, © 340030 (*moderate*) is a stone manor house dating from the 17th century, set in the Serra da Bruheira, with unexpected facilities including a pool and tennis courts. All five bedrooms are distinctively furnished and there is a terrace restaurant commanding lovely views. There is also a chapel for the spiritually inclined.

Casa da Quinta do Lombo, Estrada de Valpaços, © 21404 (*inexpensive*) is a typical Trás-os-Montes country house with granite walls. There are a number of rooms for eating: one for breakfast, one for lunch and one for dinner. The four bedrooms are pleasant and comfortable and the house has its own mini ethnographic museum, as well as a pool and a warm welcome.

Chaves © (076–)   ***Eating Out***

expensive

Restaurante Carvalho, Largo das Caldas, © 21727, serves tasty regional specialties. *Closed Thurs*. **Restaurante Quatro Caminhos**, 20–23 Rua dos Espirito Santo, © 24772, commands good views from its terrace which complement the good food. The television lurking in the corner is incongruous with the black-tied waiters and classy setting.

moderate

Small, light and simple, **Dyonisios**, 2 Praça do Municipio, © 23751 (by the castle), features good rice dishes. The *tarte maravilha* is mighty tempting.

Just outside Chaves, at Bairro do Retornado, © 23138, is a nameless restaurant run by Fernando da Silva Gomes, very popular with the locals. It's a corrugated-iron shed on a concrete floor, with one side open in summer. In winter they put a brazier of hot coals under each table—keep hold of your paper napkin. The house wine is particularly good. Helpings are enormous.

cheap

Popular for Sunday lunch, probably by default, **Casa Costa**, Rua do Tabulado, © 23568, has reasonably good food served with a sulk. The ceiling is high, with a woodburning stove and grubby paint. The chairs are uncomfortable.

An alternative would be **Caldas**, Rua do Tabulado, © 23579 (behind the Hotel Chaves). Mercifully free of TV, this is a sober place frequented by lone men. The food is not bad.

West of Chaves

The hills around Chaves have large, flesh-coloured bites taken out of them, which are clay mines. Clusters of pollarded chestnut trees grow interspersed with their uncut neighbours, waiting for their eventual transformation into woven baskets.

It took Marshal Soult and the second Napoleonic invasion two days to march from Chaves to Braga. From the fertile river plain the road climbs gently to Sapiãos, from which it rises a further 300m to Cervos—the peaks here divide the tributaries of the River Tâmega and the River Cávado. Villages huddle together for warmth, growing potatoes and rye, separating the woods of pine and oak.

Vidago

The southwesterly road from Chaves to Vila Real follows the course of the River Tâmega as far as the tranquil spa town of Vidago, which is sheltered and framed by tree slopes (*spa open 1 June–15 Oct*). Portugal's most alkaline mineral water claims therapeutic qualities similar to those at Chaves; it also reckons to help asthma (when injected into the blood-stream—seek medical advice!). No doubt beneficial effects are claimed for the 9-hole golf course, too.

✆ *(076–)*   ***Where to Stay***

The enormous pink Edwardian **Palace Hotel** (Parque), ✆ 97356, 🖅 97359 (*expensive*) is grander than ever after recent renovations, but the prices will match its reclaimed status. In the enormous grounds you will encounter the pump room, along with the band-stand, the swimming pool, tennis courts, the lake and of course the splendid park to wander in. Meanwhile, the new ★★★★**Estalagem**, ✆ 97356 (*moderate*), tacked on to the back of the hotel, is the only accommodation available in the park itself. It's modern and a bit beige, but succeeds at being quite upmarket, with polite staff and comfortable rooms.

More down-to-earth options include the ★**Hotel do Parque**, Av. Conde de Caria, ✆ 97157 (*inexpensive; open 1 July–30 Sept*), ★**Pensão Santos**, 2 Estrada Nacional, ✆ 97526 (*very cheap*), which has a nice ivy-covered porch, a brown interior and offers very good value although the rooms are a bit dark and could do with a good airing, and
★**Pensão Primavera**, Av. Conde de Caria, ✆ 97230 (*cheap; open 1 July–30 Oct*).

Spa Pavilion in Vidago

Seara Velha

In the village of **Seara Velha**, some 12km west of Chaves, the donkeys are piled with turnips. Here is the home of Manuel Joâo Carneiro, woodcarver. He never went to school, but worked with a knife and blocks of wood. Now he carves sacred images for local churches, working on his balcony crowded with cobs of maize and a birdcage. The figures are unmistakable—they look startled, as if surprised to see who has created them. The village's communal bakery is now defunct: cats nest in the ovens. The locals brought their own wood and home-grown dough, which they identified with pieces of straw. When it was cold, people slept here.

Capela da Granginha

This Romanesque chapel near Seara Velha is entered through an exceptionally interesting carved portal, depicting animals, plants and people. The face on the left is a devil's, with his tankard-handle ears, placed here so that the church-bound could leave their evil outside. The accompanying creatures look more like dragons than wolves. There's said to be a statue of a half-naked Venus buried outside the chapel—the priest thought it inappropriate. The chapel contains a T-shaped Roman altar excavated from the floor, and a very unusual baptismal font set in one wall which permitted the total immersion of an infant, rather than a token wetting.

Goldmines

The Romans mined this region for gold, particularly at Jales, Três Minas, and near the village of Ardãos, 6km west of Seara Velha and 18km west of Chaves. The gold partly explains the concentration of eight Roman forts in this area. A significant seam of gold was found at Jales in 1988.

Around AD 75, 2000 workers—probably slaves—daily laboured at Três Minas. Pliny describes the system of *ruina monticum* used here: a large amount of water was collected behind a dam; the sluice was opened, and water rushed out through ditches, over ore-bearing rocks which were thus smashed against one another. The loose rock was crushed in rectangular mortars, some of which have been incorporated in the walls of village buildings.

The Ardãos mine is very difficult to find and it should not be approached without a guide, because of the dangers of subsidence—see if the tourist office in Chaves can put you in touch with someone. Amid hills of rosemary and clusters of poisonous purple mushrooms, the entrance to the mine is just a little hole in a boulder: by it are two low parallel mounds of black scorched earth, along which run hairline fissures. Steam issues from them in springtime, an inexplicable phenomenon, as yet uninvestigated. Nearby is a cave hewn by the Romans for storing their gold, now used by shepherds in thunderstorms. The cave is carefully positioned by a 6m-deep sink-hole, down which the unsuspecting will fall, and the unwelcome would have been pushed. Curiously, there are often rainbows over the goldmines—so there's a true crock of gold at the end of the rainbow.

Boticas

Sapiãos is a village of 200 fairly typical transmontane houses, 19km along the Chaves–Braga route, from which a road leads to Boticas. Nudging high and low hills, some treeless, others leafy, Boticas is an airy little place of 1000 souls, half-rustic, half-townified, of no especial interest but for its restaurant and its odd wine.

Boticas and the neighbouring village of Granja produce what is ironically called **Wine of the Dead** (*Vinho dos Mortos*), so named because the wine is buried and is believed to be life-giving. Local farmers buried their bottled wine to hide it from Marshal Soult and his thirsty troops. The French passed by, unaware of what lay fermenting beneath their feet. After the French withdrawal, the locals tentatively dug up their bottles to celebrate. The wine had improved! Of course, this was a miracle—but disappointingly, it has a scientific explanation: the wine benefits from fermenting at a constant temperature, protected from the light. It's available from some local bars, and sometimes in the Restaurant Santa Cruz. Actually it doesn't taste that special, just light and, shall we say, rather earthy.

Eating Out

In Boticas, the wooden chalet-type **Santa Cruz** (*moderate*) is pleasant: the Mayor of Chaves eats here. The farmed trout is a bit tasteless—the beef is far better. Uncommonly, there are bowlfuls of flowers on the tables.

There is no accommodation in Boticas.

The Serra do Barroso

West of Boticas, as far as the border with the Minho, lies the Serra do Barroso—generally abbreviated to Barroso—a very rewarding area for the wandering motorist keen on exploring rude villages lodged in the folds of the hills. Chaves is the most convenient base from which to explore. The hills reach more than 1000m above sea level, but this is not apparent because all the land is high, and there is nothing to contrast it with.

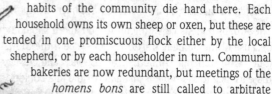

The villages of Barroso were brought together by a common need for defence, and the habits of the community die hard there. Each household owns its own sheep or oxen, but these are tended in one promiscuous flock either by the local shepherd, or by each householder in turn. Communal bakeries are now redundant, but meetings of the *homens bons* are still called to arbitrate disputes over water rights, uncultivated land, broken contracts, and petty crime.

A curious ceremony of fetching the bride applied here at least until the middle of this century: the groom and his relations went to the bride's house, to be asked,

'What seek you here?' 'A wife, honour and wealth', the suitor would reply, to which the traditional riposte was 'She has herded goats, has leapt hedges, and if she has spiked herself on one of them, and you want her as she is, so do I give her to you.' (The maidens of Barroso used to have to wear black stockings if they had been seduced.)

Very occasionally a shepherd will wear a straw suit to keep the rain off, looking like someone from *The Wizard of Oz*, but mostly these odd garments are confined to ethnographic museums. The *capa de honras*, a heavy hooded cloak of brown blanket cloth, is still worn in the villages of the region.

Punishingly cold in winter, with occasional heavy snows, the soil is too poor to support cereal crops. Barroso is soaked with the highest rainfall in Portugal, which at least makes it suitable pastureland. This pastureland buffers the villages, divided by dry stone walls and oak woods. Indeed, so potent is the pasture that the villagers can drink the milk of the small Barroso oxen, unlike that of their cousins from Miranda.

This has not saved the breed from becoming prime movers in the favourite local 'sport' and source of community pride, the **Combate** or **Chega dos Bois**. It's a test of strength between two oxen, each destined only for this purpose. The beasts may weigh up to 1000kg. The oxen are put face to face in a ring. They butt each other, they gore each other, they kick up clouds of dust, and eventually one of them runs away. He is the loser. The oxen used to be communally owned and fed by a village; now they are more likely to be owned by returned emigrants. There are no fixed dates for these spectacles, so there is no way to plan to see one, should you wish to.

Carvalhelhos

Seven km west of Boticas, Carvalhelhos is dominated by its spring-water bottling factory, which spoils the view from the **Castro** a further 1km to the west. The iron-age fort is believed to be about 2800 years old, and has tickled the curiosity of archaeologists because dwellings were built outside the fortified walls, which were restored to a height of 2m around 25 years ago. There's no great atmosphere to the place but should you get stuck and need a room for the night, try ★★★**Estalagem de Carvalhelhos**, ✆ 076 42116, ✎ 076 42174 (*inexpensive*).

Vilarinho Sêco

Some 10km west of Carvalhelhos is the tiny village of Vilarinho Sêco (not to be confused with Vilarinho, beside the Barragem do Alto Rabagão), approached from the peak Alturas do Barroso, 1100m above sea level. This is what travelling in Trás-os-Montes is all about. In a black kitchen, the pockmarks of the granite smoothed by soot, a giant cauldron swings over a heap of blazing logs, with benches either side, on which sit a still cat and a wide-eyed boy, who dunks his hands in the cauldron from time to time, to warm them. The houses and the barns are a jigsaw of granite blocks—the only way to tell the two apart is by the straw peeping under flimsy metal doors. Straw trampled with dung cakes the cobbled street, trod by ruddy women with scythes and layers of wool sweaters. Here the men wear straw suits in the rain, and complain that there is no water in the summer. There is no primary-school teacher, so the kids play with each other, and feed the pigs.

Montalegre

Montalegre is designated the capital of Barroso, a remote castle town of almost 2000 souls lying north of the Braga–Chaves route, 46km from Chaves. Literally the name means 'cheery hill', less appropriate since the construction of whitewashed town houses among their more antique neighbours, in streets leading off the open, modern town square. The café plays sacred music on Sundays. From the town the grey 14th-century castle seems to have three towers, but in fact there are four, the tallest being Dom Afonso's keep. He imitated the style of the towers built by his father Dom Dinis at the end of the 13th century.

There are four *pensions* in Montalegre, the best of which is **Residencial Fidalgo**, on Rua da Corujeira, © (076) 52462 (*cheap*), with pleasant rooms and uplifting views over the valley. If you're here in the summer, trout from the River Cãvado is very tasty—check that the fish hasn't been farmed.

Montalegre is 14km east of Covelães, one of the entry points to the Peneda–Gerês Park (*see* **The Minho**, p.92). The ruins of the monastery at Pitões das Júnias lie a further 10km to the northwest.

Mirandela

For a town which lies at the centre of Trás-os-Montes' road network, Mirandela feels remarkably secluded. Sited beside the River Tua, it stands at the very edge of the *terra quente*: the wide river valley brims with peach and apple orchards, olive groves, and fields of rye.

Mirandela © *(078–)*   ***Getting There***

By **road**, Mirandela is 54km from Chaves, 64km from Bragança, and 70km from Vila Real.

By **train**, © 22517, 5 trains daily take 3½ hours to make the journey from Oporto's São Bento station, via Tua. The journey from Tua to Mirandela can never take long enough—it is a truly spectacular ride.

Buses run twice daily from Chaves and Vila Real (via Murça). Cabanelas operate from behind the fire station on the Rua da República; Rodonorte buses from in front of the railway station. The tourist office is on the main street.

There's not much to see in the airy streets. A long **bridge** crosses the river, built in the 15th century on Roman foundations. The fine **Palace of the Távoras** dominates Mirandela. Its central section rises above the other two, all topped with elaborate granite pediments; the window casements are particularly well balanced. There is nothing interesting within the building, which is now the town hall. The chapel next door fell down several years ago; the most useful pieces of stonework have been removed, but a pile of rubble and an open-air altar remain.

The **Museu de Arte Moderna** (*open Mon–Fri 2.30–6*) displays 20th-century Portuguese paintings and prints, as well as Armindo Teixeira Lopes' images of the town.

★★**Hotel Mira Tua**, 20 Rua da República, ✆ 22403, ✉ 265003 (*inexpensive*), is at the entrance to the old bridge. **Pensão Sá Moreno**, 87 Av. das Amoreiras, ✆ 22434 (*cheap–very cheap*), offers decent rooms at the front and crummy ones at the back. The restaurant downstairs is always busy. **Pensão Praia** (*very cheap*), in a little square just off the main roundabout into Mirandela, offers large, clean and dignified rooms with pretty lace curtains and bright white bedspreads. The proprietor is a kindly soul and the views over the lake make up for what little noise reaches the rooms from the roundabout. Alternatives include: ★★★**Residencial Globo**, Rua Dr Trigo de Negreiros, ✆ 22711 (*cheap*), **Pensão O Lagar**, 120 Rua da República, ✆ 22712 (*cheap*) and ★★★**Residencial Jorge V**, Fontes Frias, ✆ 23126, ✉ 265926 (*inexpensive*).

Bragança

Bragança is a mellow place with quirky ways bred of its isolation. The name conjures something grand and romantic, but Charles II's consort, Catherine of Bragança, has left no trace. Bragança stands at the lordly height of 670m, beside the River Fervença, a small tributary of the River Sabor, and an amphitheatre of low mountains looms in the middle distance. Three roads converge at the cathedral square: from Chaves and Vila Real; from Spain, to the north; and from Bragança's own castle and citadel, which crown a hillock overlooking the rest of town. Ever since Portugal took its present boundaries, Bragança has been synonymous with isolation. This is changing, however: a motorway now connects Bragança with Mirandela to the south, linking up with the Oporto–Vila Real motorway, and another links the town with Zamora (in Spain).

The people of Bragança are more full-bodied than their wine, which they sometimes mix with 7-Up. They favour long-haired Pekinese-type dogs, often called Poochie and rarely on leads. Men grow moustaches, and distraught women give their hair to the Church as a devotional offering, hoping to regain a husband's love.

A mess of remarkably ugly new houses litters the western approach to Bragança. The town's population has recently grown to over 13,000, boosted by emigrants, who fled poverty and have returned with wealth to show.

Bragança is better suited to the ethnographer than the art historian. Famous local son is the Abbot of Baçal (1865–1947), who devoted his life to writing 11 volumes on the ethnography of the region. He publicized the existence of the Marranos, Jews who fled the Spanish Inquisition under Ferdinand and Isabella.

History

Bragança started life as Brigantio, founded by Brigo IV, King of Spain, in 906 BC. Julius Caesar fortified it, building a stronghold at the convergence of Roman military highways. For 400 years the town was destroyed and rebuilt in the battles between Christians and Moors.

It found its final resting place in 1130, when Fernão Mendes, brother-in-law of Afonso Henriques, rebuilt the town on the site of the village of Benquerença, which he obtained from the Monastery of Castro Avelãs. He governed the semi-autonomous province, while the new kingdom attempted to define its frontiers. These had not been fully accepted by Afonso IX of León, who attacked Bragança's newly built castle in 1199. In the late 14th century, the castellan's Castilian sympathies were sufficiently alarming for Dom João I to need to retrieve the town. In 1442 his bastard son, Prince Afonso, eighth Count of Barcelos, was created first Duke of Bragança by the Regent, Dom Pedro.

The eighth duke came to the throne, albeit reluctantly, in 1640. The country united behind the man they made João IV, in order to oust Philip II of Spain. The House of Bragança ruled Portugal until the abolition of the monarchy in 1910. But the dynasts spent scant time in Bragança itself, preferring their seat at Vila Viçosa, in the Alentejo.

Bragança ℂ (073–)   Getting There

The roads from the east and west are still poorly surfaced in parts, and the western approach is tortuous. Bragança is 100km from Chaves and 255km from Oporto, 203km from Guarda and 248km from Viseu.

The **railway station** is now closed.

By **bus**: Rodonorte, ℂ 331870, has an information office by the old railway station on Avenida João da Cruz. Their timetabling is erratic, and it is best to check with them or the tourist office for the latest schedule. They have services from Lisbon (12hrs), via Coimbra (9hrs), Viseu (6¼hrs), Régua (4¼hrs), Vila Real (3½hrs), Vila Pouca de Aguiar (3hrs), and Valpaços (1¾hrs). Buses shake, rattle and roll infrequently from Vidago.

getting to Spain

Rodonorte also runs buses to Sapin, only 34km away, including connect services to Valladolid. A new border crossing has opened at Rio do Onor.

Bragança ℂ (073–)   Tourist Information

The **tourist office**, ℂ 381273, is in a hut on an island in the middle of the Avenida Cidade de Zamora. From the **bus station**, follow the road in to town, past the **train station**, and fork left at the post office to get to the cathedral square.

Around the Town

Bragança's 16th-century **cathedral** is unimpressive. It was a Jesuit college until Pombal expelled the Jesuits in 1759; five years later the diocese was moved here from Miranda. The sacristy is covered with scenes from the life of a skinny St Ignatius, and contains two hulking polychrome sculptures of him and of St Francis Xavier.

The Museu do Abade de Baçal

From the cathedral, head up towards the castle along the Rua do Conselheiro Abilio Beça to the excellent **Museu do Abade de Baçal** (open Tues–Fri 10–5; Sat, Sun 10–6).

Featuring art, archaeology and ethnography, it occupies the 16th-century bishop's palace, an attractive building altered by the bishop of Miranda in 1737. No doubt the bishops would be surprised to see their garden hosting a couple of granite *berrões*. An arcade shelters Roman stone tablets, military, votive and funereal.

Within the palace, two beautiful wooden ceilings canopy an assortment of paintings. The ceiling with carved fruit was removed from the Igreja de S. Bento; its neighbour bears the episcopal arms. A portrait shows the Marquês of Pombal looking winsome. More appealing is Orpheus, who, on another canvas, charms a large rat and various animals.

One room is devoted to episcopal accoutrements. It includes a gold cage to stop wafers blowing away at open-air Masses; an *escrevaninha*, one compartment of which held sand, for 'blotting' wet ink; a deep silver bowl used by the bishop for washing priests' feet. The 16th-century triptych depicting the martyrdom of the Bishop of Antioch, St Ignaçio, hung in the episcopal palace, reminding residents of their brother's sacrifice. Also in this room is a wonderful late 14th-century *Virgin and Child*, gilt and polychromed in the 17th century; and a strange barbed ivory image of Christ with sheep—he wears what they wear.

Another room houses writs issued by Dom Manuel to apportion justice and sanction construction around Bragança. The walls bear framed theses printed onto cloth, following a fashion instigated at the University of Salamanca whereby students would present their doctorates in this form to their home parishes. Such cloths were used within living memory to cover Communion chalices. Poles looking like billiard cues were given to members of the *camara municipal* as symbols of authority. A stunning 900-year-old leather altarfront is displayed among them, decorated with coloured flowers.

The room of ethnography includes a fantastic iron cauldron, and two instruments of 19th-century popular justice: a head brace with a tongue depressor, used to stop a criminal talking; and what may be a woman's chastity belt.

Also notable are Abel Salazar's fluid paintings and Alberto de Sousa's watercolours of the pillories of the district of Bragança. An impressive collection of coins will interest numismatists. The palace's chapel now houses a small collection of magnificent embroidered vestments.

The Route to the Citadel

Bragança is endowed with a pious quota of churches, but sometimes it is difficult to locate their keys.

From the museum, the first church on your right as you walk towards the citadel is the **church of S. Vicente**, with an irregular 17th-century façade—around the other side—beautiful in the evening sunlight. Dom Pedro the Cruel claimed to have clandestinely married Inês de Castro, *c.* 1354, and tradition says the service took place here (*see* 'Alcobaça', p.244). The church is built on a 13th-century base and features a bizarre ceiling: a three-dimensional Christ is caught in the act of ascending, flying like Superman. An *azulejo* panel in the side wall commemmorates General Sepúlveda, who spoke to the people of Bragança from the steps of this church, on 11 June 1809, thus sowing the seeds of the movement which freed Portugal from French domination.

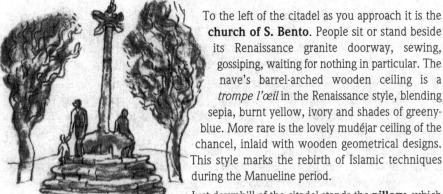

the pillory. Bragança

To the left of the citadel as you approach it is the **church of S. Bento**. People sit or stand beside its Renaissance granite doorway, sewing, gossiping, waiting for nothing in particular. The nave's barrel-arched wooden ceiling is a *trompe l'œil* in the Renaissance style, blending sepia, burnt yellow, ivory and shades of greeny-blue. More rare is the lovely mudéjar ceiling of the chancel, inlaid with wooden geometrical designs. This style marks the rebirth of Islamic techniques during the Manueline period.

Just downhill of the citadel stands the **pillory**, which was moved from outside the Domus Municipalis. For reasons unknown, the base of the shaft has been inserted through one of Bragança's *berrões*, a pig with a hollow in its snout, as if to skewer the unfortunate animal. The citadel wall has also been employed by a later age: a football goal-mouth has been painted on it.

The main gate of the citadel is the Porta de Santo António, and beyond it the ogival Porta da Vila. The citadel is cluttered with live pigs and peasant cottages—there used to be more of these, the place having provided safe accommodation for centuries, but they were razed in the late 1920s, in the interest of 'aesthetics' and 'hygiene'. The wall of the citadel incorporates the Poço do Rei, a well full of rubbish, periodically tidied by the Boy Scouts. The Centro d'Artesanato is here.

The Castle

Fernão Mendes' 12th-century castle was reinforced by João I and Afonso V in the 30 years after 1409. The splendid, formidable schist and granite structure was a clenched fist affirming the king's independence from Castile and León, and his control of the surrounding regions. The battlements overlook rounded, interlacing hills, whose bleating sheep are well within earshot. As well as having a defensive function, the tall, gracious Gothic tower was partly residential, as the wide upper-storey window indicates. The square Princess's Tower stands where the castle wall becomes the wall of the citadel. Now devoid of pale ladies with long blonde hair and conical hats, it must make do with the tale of Dona Leonor, unhappy wife of Dom Jaime, the fourth duke. Suspecting her of infidelity, he locked her in the tower until he murdered her in Vila Viçosa.

It's a great place for children, as there are plenty of nooks and crannies to explore, including the drawbridge, cistern and boringly sanitized dungeon. The doorways in the keep are about 1½m, lit by kitsch electric candles. Having housed a regiment 1855–1928, the keep is now a **military museum** (*open 9–11.45 and 2–4.45; closed Thurs and holidays*). The African weapons were assembled during the 1895 campaigns there. The most bizarre exhibit is the 'Replica of the trousers worn by Gungunhana during his detention in the Açores.' Gungunhana, King of the Vatuas, led many chiefs in their rebellion against the

Portuguese in southern Mozambique in 1895. Mousinho de Albuquerque broke the back of the rebellion when he captured Gungunhana in his own kraal. The African leader was shipped off to the Azores, where he died. (Mousinho de Albuquerque was made tutor of the king's sons. He committed suicide in a Lisbon railway carriage in 1902.)

Within the Citadel

Beside the castle is the **church of Santa Maria**, built between 1701 and 1715, on the site of a Romanesque church. According to tradition, the patron's image was hidden in woods crawling with green lizards, to preserve it from the Moorish invaders. Hence the church is sometimes known as N.S. do Sardão (Our Lady of the Green Lizard). There is nothing reptilian about the belltower incorporated in the inelegant façade, with an elaborate portal. The ceiling of the nave is painted, possibly by the same artist who worked on the church of S. Bento. The key is available from No.133 in the first alley running parallel to the front of the church.

The strange building next to the church is the **Domus Municipalis**, a very rare example of Romanesque civic architecture (because most public meetings took place within churches). It has five unequal sides; the upper storey's round-arched arcade sits on a lower storey of uninterrupted granite. This was the cistern, crucial to a citadel under siege. This importance is reflected in the building's other function: in medieval times it was the meeting place for the *homens bons* of the *vila*, who settled disputes over land rights and waterways. The Abbot of Baçal discovered Dom Sancho I's heraldic seal within the building, which suggests it was built in the first half of the 13th century.

The Back Streets

An interesting route back from the citadel is to turn left immediately past the Porta de Santo António, doubling back along the path as far as the well, then taking the downhill branch back towards the centre of town. The riverbank is planted with small agricultural holdings—urban dwellers like to retain a stake in land. The path becomes a track and finally a road. At the little bridge, head up the **Rua Dos Fornos** (ovens) where all the town's bread was baked. Old people now live in these bakeries, dark dwellings lit by small skylights and the candles that flank religious icons. They exaggerate past bread production to heroic proportions. Spanish Jews lived here when they fled the 16th-century Inquisition.

The road leads into the **Rua das Moreirinhas**. Some say this was named by silk weavers to honour the mulberry tree which silkworms live off; others say the land was given to the Convent of Moreirola in Spain. The houses' sash-windows keep the cold out more efficiently than their shuttered cousins. A wall runs down one side of the street, used for the defence of the town in the 18th century. Near the top of the road, turn right, right and left in quick succession, to the **market**, where people smoke sausages, and sell chickens' feet. Leaving the market, the Rua Dr. Paul Teixeira runs towards the **Jardim António José D'Almeida**, with a caged colonnade for temporary exhibitions or libraries in the summer. The garden used to be the Jesuit college's farm.

expensive

The tranquil **Pousada de São Bartolomeu**, Estrada de Turismo, ✆ 331493, 🖷 23453 (*category B*), relishes its views across a wide ravine to the town and castle, and the surrounding hills and mountains beyond. The all-wood guestrooms have cork ceilings, and are well serviced. The sitting room/bar has a large open fireplace; above this is a boar's head which no longer snorts at the smell of woodsmoke. Guests or visitors can dine on carpeted stone, enjoying good food and views.

moderate

Comfortably furnished and centrally located, **★★★Hotel Bragança**, 15 Rua Dr. Francisco Sá Carneiro, ✆ 331578/9, is a good three-star hotel where guests can sit in wonderful squashy leather chairs and admire fine urban rooftop and castle views.

inexpensive

★★★Residencial Santa Isabel, 67 Rua Alexandre Herculano, ✆ 331427, 🖷 26937, is better value than it used to be, having been stripped of one star and *albergaria* status, and forced to alter its prices accordingly. The rooms remain worn, however, and the varnish could still do with a polish. There's no particular reason to stay at **★★★Residencial Nordeste Shalom**, 39 Av. Abade de Baçal, ✆ 331667, 🖷 331628, which is some way to the west of the town centre. The rooms are OK, if a bit small, with pink frilly bedcovers and thick carpets. They're fond of their colour TV. **★★★Residencial Tulipa**, 8–10 Rua Dr. Francisco Felgueiras, ✆ 331675, provides simple, clean and pictureless rooms, filled with dark-wood furniture, fronted by stand-up balconies, and reached via dark corridors.

cheap

★★★Residencial São Roque, Zona da Estacada, Lote 26–27, ✆ 381481, is a much nicer place than Residencial Santa Isabel (*see* above) and half the price— oddly, they're owned by the same management. Guestrooms are on the seventh and eighth floors, with views over the castle and its surrounds. They are nicely furnished with low beds, attractive lamps, and hygienic bathrooms. Under rather vague management, **★★Residencial Cruzeiro**, Trav. do Hospital, ✆ 331634, offers decent but cold rooms with trimmings, such as wallpaper and suitcase stands. Rooms at the front are noisy, especially on the ground floor.

Turismo de Habitação

Moinho do Caniço, Ponte de Castrelos, Castrelos, ✆ 23577 (*inexpensive*) is a charming old watermill on the bank of the River Baceiro where you can fish for trout. This is truly a rural idyll, very green and quiet. The rooms are cosy and filled with rough wooden furniture.

expensive

There's good cooking to be had at popular and convivial **Lá em Casa** at Rua Marquês de Pombal, ℭ 22111. They serve some unusual fish dishes, but most people go for the beef. One wall is bare stone, the chairs are pine, and hoots come from the family room at the back. **O Geadas**, also called Sol Neve, Rua do Loreto, ℭ 24413, is uncommonly decorated with black wooden trellises between dining booths. It is favoured by business types at lunchtime, who enjoy the grilled trout with *presunto*, or the veal.

moderate

Solar Brangançano, 34 Praça da Sé, ℭ 23875, is housed in attractive first-floor rooms, but the restaurant is pretentious—well-worn napkins are carefully folded, and diners share one candelabrum. They cook with too much salt, and the house wine is nasty, but for all that the restaurant is not so bad. Good rather than very good, **Arca de Noé**, Av. Cidade de Zamora—up from the tourist office, ℭ 381159, specializes in fish dishes, presumably harpooned by one of the bare-breasted cavewomen who parade across the mural at the back of the restaurant.

cheap

O Bolha, Jardim Dr. Antonio José de Almeida, ℭ 23240, offers good *feijoada* but is short of staff in the summer. **Restaurante Poças**, Rua Combatentes da Grande Guerra, ℭ 331428, is attached to the *residencial* of the same name. The two-storey dining room is invariably packed and the simple food is very good and reasonably priced. Worth a look-in, despite the service with a sulk.

Around Bragança

Vinhais

The scenery on the road between Chaves and Bragança is magnificent—great green pastures and clusters of venerable chestnut trees, peppered with settlements whose slate roofs decay lackadaisically. Hillocks stand on hummocks around Vinhais, which lies 32km west of Bragança.

The quiet town of 2000 people is strung out along 1km of the highway, looking southward to a panorama of hills and distant mountains. It was settled in the 13th century, and was once a border post. At the extreme west end of Vinhais stands a long Baroque façade incorporating two churches. The lower part is the **convent of São Francisco**, formerly the seminary of the Diocese of Bragança. The *vila velha* is at the other end of town, entered through a gateway, leading to the ruins of a 13th-century castle. One tower still stands, spectacularly precarious. Chickens, ducks, cats and dogs mooch harmoniously around the pillory, the top of which resembles eagles' heads from some angles.

There's no particular reason to stay in Vinhais. Should you get stuck, **★Pensão Ribeirinha**, Rua Nova, © 71490 (*inexpensive*) has nice, old rooms available, as does the **Casa Leão**, 23 Largo do Arrabalde, © 72450 (*cheap*). The latter provides reasonable food, too.

Castro de Avelãs

Some 7km west of Bragança, off the road from Vinhais, stand the remains of the 12th-century Benedictine **Monastery of Castro de Avelãs**, which was extinguished in 1543—sufficiently long ago for the ghosts to have wandered elsewhere. The original church's triple apse is still intact, though redundant on one side. There is something disturbing about this brick structure composed of blind arcades, as if it was intended to silence something unpleasant. Although this is the sole example of the style in Portugal, it also occurs at Sahagum in León. A pair of remarkably masculine *berrões* sit atop the gate to the monastery, one with a flat head and bared teeth, the other decapitated. Both seem to be saddled.

Parque Natural de Montezinho

Montezinho Park occupies 75,000 hilly hectares in the extreme northeast of Portugal, covering the Montezinho and Corôa *serras*. Altitudes range from 438m in the east, to 1481m in the Montezinho mountains, and down to sea level in the centre. Parts of the west and centre are evergreen. Modest hamlets are scattered amongst the gentle hills; the east, with a lower rainfall, is more sparsely populated. Rivers and streams run from north to south, as does the road network.

The villagers maintain whitewashed circular *pombals* (pigeon coops), which are one of the few distinguishing features of the park. There are some good walks—the River Sabor is particularly beautiful north of França—and a jury of venerable oak and chestnut trees.

Bragança, Vinhais and Gimonde (7km east of Bragança) are the points of entry to the park. Bairro Salvador Nunes Teixeira, Lote 5, Apartado 90, Bragança, © (073) 23734 (*open weekdays 9–12.30 and 2–5.30*), can provide details of self-catering accommodation within the park.

Rio de Onor

Some 22km northeast of Bragança, Rio de Onor is a slate-roofed hamlet within the Montezinho park. It straddles the border with Spain: a chain is slung between two stone blocks marked 'E' and 'P', but nobody takes much notice of it, and the nationalities have been intermarrying for years.

In 1953 the anthropologist António Jorge Dias published a study of Rio de Onor. He found one of western Europe's freak villages, organized on egalitarian collective principles, including the stipulation that no household could graze more than two cows and one calf on the communal meadows. Here were embodied the Germanic pastoral traditions of our ancestors, claimed the anthropologist. Other researchers arrived, documentaries were filmed. And then somebody noticed that the villagers' replies were verbatim quotes from the initial publication.

For all that, there is little apparently different between Rio de Onor and numerous other small villages in Trás-os-Montes.

Outeiro

Roughly 32km southeast of Bragança, the road to Miranda do Douro passes through the village of Outeiro. Its **church of Santo Cristo** was built in 1648, with a coupled portal surmounted by a rose window, itself surrounded by elaborate carvings.

Vimioso

Vimioso, 22km southeast of Outeiro, and just off the Miranda road, is dominated by its hard 17th-century **Igreja Matriz**. The towers support two gargoyles, nicknamed 'Thirst' and 'Hunger': they face, respectively, a water tank and a butcher's shop.

Algoso

It's not really worth travelling the 7km due south of Vimioso to the ruined castle of Algoso—set high between valleys and surrounded by boulders—but there's a nice legend attached to it. The castle is said to have been relocated after a plague of ants made life intolerable. Legend tells of Dom Soeiro, a lecherous 14th-century castellan who lusted after one of the villagers. She was about to be married; Soeiro refused to issue the marriage licence unless the bridegroom brought him two shirts made of nettles. The confounded gallant sought the aid of Aldonsa, a famous witch who lived in a marsh (where doubtless she fumed at not having been consulted about the ants). Aldonsa equipped the bridegroom with two tolerable nettle shirts, and had a word in the ear of King Pedro I, who flew into one of his tantrums, and ordered the execution of Soeiro.

There are fewer bends in the road from Vimioso to Miranda do Douro, and the land flattens out on the approach. Miranda is a very nice place to arrive at.

Miranda do Douro

Miranda is one of the smallest 'cities' in Europe, but happily none of its 2000 inhabitants produce memorabilia announcing the fact. It is located in the eastern corner of Trás-os-Montes, a hop, skip and a jump away from a barren gorge in which the River Douro has been dammed, forming the frontier with Spain; a road across the hydroelectric dam connects Miranda with distant Zamora.

Miranda is a sleepy town that has spilt outside the citadel's five parallel cobbled streets. The Rua da Castanilha is peppered with emblazoned *palácios*, the manifestations of former wealth. A gargoyle on one of these directs its bare buttocks towards Spain. This does not deter the many Spaniards in search of a bargain—the market will sell anything for pesetas, though mostly it offers tough shoes. The shoes may be especially strong because Miranda's walkways are paved in the middle of its streets, so anyone who doesn't pay attention will be run over. To avoid this, head for the cathedral, which contains some superb pieces.

History

In AD 716, Moors conquered the local Visigoths, and called the place Mir-Hândul. When the Moors were expelled in the late 11th century, the Castilians coveted Miranda, a gateway to Portugal. They occupied the town in the second half of the 14th century—until they were expelled by Dom João I—and in 1710, during the War of the Spanish Succession.

In 1762, the city was besieged by Franco-Spanish troops fighting the Seven Years' War. They fired a shell into the powder room of the castle, exploding the 23 tons of gunpowder stored there—which destroyed most of the castle, part of the town walls, and 400 inhabitants. The castle remains an ugly ruin, with a giant bite taken out of it. The blast left the cathedral unharmed; ironically the diocese was transferred to Bragança two years later. The locals comment bitterly, 'The sacristy is in Bragança, but the cathedral is in Miranda.' The people of Bragança say, 'If ever you go to Miranda, see the cathedral and come home.'

More drama came during the Peninsular War: in 1813 Wellington was slung across the gorge in a 'kind of hammock' to inspect about 60,000 Anglo-Portuguese troops who had gathered within Portugal. Not to be outdone, the current Mayor of Miranda remembers whizzing down the gorge as a boy. He reckoned to run from the site on which the *pousada* now stands to the bottom of the gorge, presently flooded to a depth of 60m, in four minutes. (The years have mellowed him.)

Miranda's isolation has left several unique legacies. In some of the surrounding villages, people speak Mirandês, a dialect developed directly from Latin, and the only such patois in Portugal. The ancient dance of the *pauliteiros* is still performed by young men, each dressed in a white flannel skirt covered by the tails of a long linen shirt with embroidered sleeves, a cloth jacket, and a hat decked with flowers. Some ethnographers reckon the dance derives from the Pyrrhic Dance, a war dance simulating the whirring of Hellenic hordes, but there is no place in this theory for the two sticks which each man carries, which suggest a sword dance of sorts. The best time to see the *pauliteiros* is at the *Festas de Santa Bárbara* on the Sunday after 15 August. Miranda has more practical ambassadors, too: its oxen are praised throughout Portugal for their aptitude for work and reproduction.

Getting There

By **road**, Miranda is 83km from Bragança.

The nearest **railway station** is at Pocinho (two trains daily from Oporto, 4¼hrs). The midday arrival at Pocinho connects with a bus to Miranda.

Three **buses** run daily from Bragança (1½hrs)—it can be done as a day trip, if you get up early. Buses stop in the main square.

There is a tiny tourist office with irregular hours, in the new town in front of the the Hotel Turismo.

The dance of the *pauliteiros* (*see* above) is the highlight of the *Festas de Santa Bárbara*, which takes place on the Sunday after 15 August.

What to See

The very good **Terra de Miranda Museum** (*open 10–12.15 and 2–4.45; closed Mon and holidays*) bubbles with intimate insights into people's lives since the turn of the century. The first room includes a small cage to constrain roving babies, a large plate for communal eating, a cork bucket to keep water hot overnight, irons like pincers for making Communion wafers, and a pepper horn. There's also a collection of Spanish ceramic pots. In the next room are displayed a cruciform iron for hanging a pig from the ceiling, a device for making rope from flax, a watermill resembling daggers stuck in a circle, and a wheat-chaff separator embedded with small sharp stones. On the landing upstairs local costumes are displayed on mannequins: one holds inflated pigs' bladders, used for hitting people on the head. In the first floor rooms, an Ancient Hebrew inscription on granite attests to the area's Jewish heritage. A twin-arched building adjoins the museum, fronting the main square: it was formerly the town hall, conveniently next to the town jail.

Miranda's **cathedral** stands in that corner of the citadel nearest the dam.

In 1545, Pope Paul III created a diocese in Miranda. Miranda was unprepared. The bishop needed a cathedral, and construction began seven years later. The austere, windowed façade is the work of Gonçalo de Torralva, the Tomar architect; for the interior, Francisco Velázquez followed the design of Miguel de Arruda. Beneath reinforced rib vaulting, a stunning two-storey altarpiece depicts the elevation of the Virgin: on the lower level 12 wonderfully natural Apostles watch the Virgin rise gracefully on a cloud. The sacristy, to the left, contains an unusual collection of 12 16th-century paintings personifying the months of the year. The cathedral's safe was in the sacristy—the only way in was through a wall vent 4m from the floor. The chest of drawers decorated with mannerist strapwork and fantastic masks may be of Spanish origin—otherwise it is one of the finest pieces of 16th-century Portuguese furniture. The cathedral's organ is beautiful, ornamented with leafy gold and a grim face to banish 17th-century devils.

To the right of the centre nave, in the south transept, a glass case shelters the rosy-cheeked *Menino Jesus da Cartolinha* (the child Jesus in a silk hat). The puppet-like figure is splen-didly dressed. Rings jewel the stumps of his fingers, and he always wears a top hat. The locals make costumes for him: although created in the mid-19th-century, he prefers the fashion of the mid-17th-century, because he commemorates a boy who appeared in Miranda then. This diminutive hero rallied the occupants against the besieging Spanish, and vanished, leaving no doubt that he was the Menino Jesus.

The 16th-century **Bishop's Palace** stood behind the cathedral. It was destroyed by fire in 1706; the ruins include a fine arcade. Note the fountain.

The cathedral's terrace gives an impressive view of the sheer rock gorge and the dam, which was built 1956–60. A small **recreation ground** by the side of the lake offers a swimming pool and facilities for canoeing.

Just beyond the single-arched Roman bridge across the little River Fresno is the 18th-century **Fonte dos Canos**, in a sort of tabernacle, which incorporates five heads apparently in flames. There is a modest **Centro do Artesanato** around the corner from the museum. It sells bagpipes, woven garments, and finely carved *rocas* for hand spinning. Several shops sell high-quality Portuguese handicrafts, including Decorlar at 7A Rua Mouzinho de Albuquerque, which has some nice pieces of china and embroidery amongst a lot of ordinary stuff.

Miranda do Douro ✆ (073–) **Where to Stay**

Poised as if to take a running jump over the gorge, the quiet **Pousada de Santa Catarina**, ✆ 431255, ✉ 41065 (*category C*), offers 12 decent marble-balconied bedrooms with stark views of the barrage and its lake. The light sitting room is attractive, set for chess and draughts/chequers, with plants, magazines, and an odd piece of wood. The dining room is lighter than some of its food, which is not great value. Tiled wild horses run across the walls.

Next to the *pousada* is the **Hotel Turismo**, ✆ 418030, ✉ 431335 (*moderate*). Rooms are clean, modern and comfortable. In the old town, **Pensão Santa Cruz**, 61 Rua Abade de Bacale, ✆ 42474 (*cheap*) has character and is the best option for travellers on a budget.

Miranda do Douro ✆ (073–) **Eating Out**

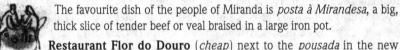

The favourite dish of the people of Miranda is *posta à Mirandesa*, a big, thick slice of tender beef or veal braised in a large iron pot.

Restaurant Flor do Douro (*cheap*) next to the *pousada* in the new town lacks atmosphere but has a good view if the blinds are open, and the food is well presented. **Restaurante Balbina**, ✆ 432394 (*cheap*), in the old town near the cathedral, cooks traditional local dishes.

The Alto Douro

There is no clear boundary between Trás-os-Montes and the Alto Douro: the great river's tributaries penetrate deep into the *terra quente*. Further south, the hills of the Douro valley are terraced with port wine vineyards (*see* 'Visiting the Douro Valley', p.163).

Sendim

The road from Miranda to Mogadouro is pretty in parts, an easy drive because it's flat with long straight stretches. It passes pastureland and fields of cereals, uncultivated land, elms and the occasional ash supporting great storks' nests. At Sendim, the remains of frescoes decay in the 18th-century **Igreja do Senhor do Boamorte**. An *azulejo* panel reminds us that the church was built by Manoel Roanno who travelled on water for four years (illustrated). More curious is the village's **Roman fountain** built like a dog kennel.

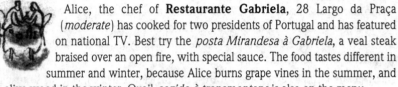

Eating Out

Alice, the chef of **Restaurante Gabriela**, 28 Largo da Praça (*moderate*) has cooked for two presidents of Portugal and has featured on national TV. Best try the *posta Mirandesa à Gabriela*, a veal steak braised over an open fire, with special sauce. The food tastes different in summer and winter, because Alice burns grape vines in the summer, and olive wood in the winter. Quail *cozido à transmontana* is also on the menu.

Mogadouro

There is little to see in the small town of Mogadouro, which lies 46km southwest of Miranda, once made wealthy by its silk industry. Dom Dinis built the **castle** in the 13th century, on Roman foundations. He gave the new building to the Order of the Templars, and on their extinction it passed to the Order of Christ. Donkeys now graze on its ruins and women store their firewood in the sole quadrangular tower, which is inhabited by chickens. The simple **Igreja Matriz**, with its vaulted granite ceiling, dates from the 16th century, though the tower was built in the next century, and the harmonious polychrome altarpiece in the 18th century.

If you'd like a typical Portuguese house, you can buy one in Mogadouro. Made of clay and about 10cm high, with each brick, tile and doorstep lovingly reproduced, they're actually very nice. They are available from the Centro Cultural, Av. da Espanha, priced 2500$00 for a house, 3000$00 for castle ruins.

Buses depart from the kiosk in the central gardens.

Mogadouro ℂ (079–)   **Where to Stay**

There are a few places to stay in Mogadouro including: ★★★**Residencial Estrela do Norte**, 65 Av de Espanha, ℂ 32726 (*cheap*); ★★**Pensão São Sebastião**, Bairro de S Sebastião, ℂ 32176 (*cheap*); or **Pensão Russo**, 10 Rua 15 de Outubro, ℂ 32134 (*cheap*).

Freixo de Espada-à-Cinta

After a monotonous 32km, the flat road south of Mogadouro arrives at the foot of the Reboredo hills, at Freixo's railway station. Some 14km further south, and only 4km west of the River Douro, which forms the border with Spain, lies the town of Freixo de Espada-à-Cinta, surrounded by low hills and thousands of almond trees. The town's odd name, meaning 'ash tree of the girth-sword', is believed to refer to the sword Dom Dinis hung on an ash tree when he took a nap here.

Not a lot happens in Freixo de Espada-à-Cinta, apart from a springtime invasion by Spaniards eager to ogle the almond blossom. At other times, Freixo feels a long way from anywhere else. Several houses have simple Manueline windows and doors.

History

Freixo was a significant settlement before the foundation of the Portuguese kingdom: Dom Afonso Henriques' charter of 1152 refers to its castle. He exempted the inhabitants from paying any tribute, to encourage the growth of an important frontier post. As a further incentive, the town was made a sanctuary for fugitives—provided they were neither fraudulent nor treasonable.

This was the birthplace of Jorge Álvares, the first Portuguese navigator to reach Japan (though the chronicler Antonio Galvão claims this honour for António da Mota, in 1542). Álvares' descriptions of Japan were instrumental in luring thence his friend St Francis Xavier, who was fed up with living in the 'barbarous' Moluccas. The poet Guerra Junqueiro was born here, too. Both are commemorated by statues.

Getting There

By **road**, Freixo is 90km from Miranda and 93km from Guarda.

From Miranda do Douro, change **buses** at the Freixo railway station 14km north of town.

Dom Dinis rebuilt the town's defences. His plan included the almost windowless heptagonal **Torre de Galo** (Cockerel's Tower), which has outlasted other major constructions, including the keep. Dom Dinis did not complete the defences, so in 1342 the people of Freixo obtained permission from his successor, Dom Afonso IV, to use the church tithe to do so. Now it is a bell- and clocktower. From the first storey a spiral staircase leads to the top of the tower, with good views of the countryside.

Freixo's fine 16th-century **Igreja Matriz** stands just below the tower. There are good Manueline portals, but the real delight of the building is the proportions of the interior—a simplified, scaled-down version of the Jerónimos monastery at Belém, with three naves of equal height, separated by cylindrical columns. The retable is painted with 16 panels attributed to Grão-Vasco (*see* 'Viseu', p.179), including *The Annunciation* and *Judas' Kiss*.

Where to Stay and Eating Out

There is a **Hospedaria** (*pension*) in the square where the bus stops (*cheap*). **Restaurante Cinta de Ouro** (*moderate*) is on the southern route out of town, up the hill and on the left. It is rather good with a Spanish flavour to the cooking. There is an atractive patio.

Torre de Moncorvo

Torre de Moncorvo is located halfway up the leafy slope of the Serra do Reboredo, 26km west of Freixo station. Some say the town was named after an 11th-century *senhor*, Mendo Curvo, who lived in a tower; others say Mendo had a *corvo* (a crow). Maybe everyone is correct. Moncorvo's climate shows the greatest annual deviation in the country, averaging a fiery 24.6°C in summer and 5.6° in winter. Some of the largest deposits of iron in Europe, to the east of the town, brought a modest prosperity and spawned blacksmiths. Silk too was a moneyspinner. Now 3000 souls live in Moncorvo, which is noted for its *amêndoas cobertas* (sugared almonds).

The town hall occupies the site of the castle built by Dom Dinis to secure the road from Trancoso to Bragança. About 200m from the central square, the **Igreja Matriz** is the largest church in Trás-os-Montes. It was begun in 1544 and completed some 50 years later, a delay possibly caused by the distance from any stone quarries. The outside is plain and ugly, with a two-storey tower rising above the central section, which gives few clues to the volume and height within. Inside, the gloom and the rectangular plan make the church less uplifting than the cathedral at Miranda do Douro. In 1808 the church plate was hidden on top of the capitals, to escape discovery by French invaders. The church's most remarkable piece is the sumptuous sculpted retable, carved in the 17th century. The upper part shows scenes from the life of Christ, and the lower part depicts two Evangelists, the doubting of St Thomas, the Resurrection, and four church elders. Behind an attractive Renaissance portal, the 16th-century **Misericórdia** houses a fine granite pulpit.

The 7km drive to the top of the **Reboredo mountain** (900m) is excitingly leafy, winding up the forest road, with good views of the surrounding hills and plains.

| *Moncorvo* ✆ *(079–)* | **Where to Stay** |

 There are several places to stay in Moncorvo: ★★★★**Pensão Brasília**, 220 Estrada Nacional, ✆ 22494 (*inexpensive*), which has a children's playground; ★★**Pensão Caçula**, Rua das Amoreiras, ✆ 22218 (*cheap*); ★★**Pensão-Restaurante Campos Monteiro**, 55 Rua Visconde Vila Maior, ✆ 22355 (*cheap*); ★★**Pensão-Restaurante Passarinho**, 23 Rua Infante D. Henrique, ✆ 22319 (*cheap*).

Parque Arqueológico do Vale Côa

In 1989, EDP, the Portuguese state electricity company, had big plans for the Côa river valley: it was to become the site of one of the country's largest hydroelectric power stations. The discovery of thousands of prehistoric engravings and paintings in the area due to be flooded created a six-year feud between the government and a battery of international archaeologists. In 1995, with the giant Côa Dam half-completed, the new socialist government bowed to worldwide pressure, and declared the valley a protected area. A national park was opened in 1996, and new roads, a visitor centre, and a study institute soon followed. It is now possible to visit the archaeological sites with due notice.

| ✆ *(079–)* | **Tourist Information** |

Visiting the Côa Valley is difficult and time-consuming, and you need to be determined. Trips can only be undertaken with a guide, and must be booked through the **Park Office** at 19 Av Gago Coutinho, 5150 Vila Nova de Foz Côa, ✆ 764317. At present they are expensive, too short, and require several months' notice.

However, the visitor centre is open (*open Tues–Sun 9–5.30*) and has a collection of books and literature.

We human beings like to make our mark and the Côa valley site is a great place to be reminded of that. Flints fashioned by our Lower Palaeolithic ancestors some 170,000 years ago have been found at the Quinta da Granja and Quinta do Monte Meão sites, but the valley's most expressive features date from the Upper Palaeolithic and Neolithic periods. Horses are a recurring motif of the former, drawn on the stone at Ribeira de Piscos and Penascosa 40,000 to 10,000 years ago, and etched into the rock at Canada do Inferno, among ox-like aurochs, ibex and fish.

For something more feisty, check out the small caves at Faia, where stylized Neolithic men have been baring their all for the past 5–7000 years. Other sites such as Castelo Velho and Freixo de Numão date from the Copper and Bronze Ages, and Iron Age engravings, depicting armed and mounted warriors, have been discovered at Orgal and Vermelhosa. Seventeenth-century religious motifs are scrawled on the rock at Canada do Inferno, and there is even a graffito of the Douro line steam train crossing the railway bridge over the mouth of the Côa, dated 1944.

℗ (079–)

Where to Stay and Eating Out

There are a few uninspiring *pensões* in Vila Nova de Foz Côa. Try the **Residencial Marina**, Av. Gago Coutinho, 2/4 ℗ 762112 (*cheap*). The **Restaurante Paleocoa**, Cerca do Silvano, Lt 23, ℗ 765166 (*inexpensive*) offers some regional specialities. Otherwise, the Park Office can help you to find accommodation.

Vila Flor

On the road between Torre de Moncorvo and Mirandela is the small town of Vila Flor, named by Dom Dinis as he passed on his way to meet Isabel of Aragon, in the 13th century. He must have had bouquets on his mind: he called it 'Flower Town'.

The only thing worth seeing is the curious country **museum** (*open 9.30–12.30 and 2–5; closed Mon*). The museum was founded in 1946, when three eminent locals donated the contents of their homes. Affectionately inserted among religious images, coins and an 18th-century writing desk are elderly typewriters, walking sticks, snake skins, sewing machines, a suite of zebra-hide furniture, and the sculpture of a boar.

There are a couple of cheap places to eat around the museum. The Vila Flor bus company is called the Soc. de Transportes, and operates from the Av. Marchal Carmona.

Vila Real

Backed by a monolithic hill, and fronted by a steep gorge which plummets in a dramatic jumble of rock shelves to the small River Corgo, Vila Real is the largest town in Trás-os-Montes, with 30,000 souls. Founded in 1272 on an easily defended site, Vila Real became the administrative centre for the territory enclosed by the Rivers Tua, Teixeira and Douro, in the late Middle Ages. Scraps of this medieval heritage remain, swallowed up by emblazoned 18th-century *palácios*. They do little to assuage the town's blandness, though the Solar de Mateus, just outside Vila Real, is worth seeing. The tourist office writes: 'town history has smoothly passed away without any particular events (or excitements).'

Getting There

Vila Real is 107km from Braga, 139km from Bragança and 108km from Oporto.

Three **trains** arrive daily from Oporto; change at Régua (3¾hrs total).

Vila Real is the headquarters of Trás-os-Montes' leading **bus** company, Rodonorte, so it would be sensible to pick up any available timetables from their head office at 19 Rua D. Pedro de Castro, ✆ 059 323234/5 or 322247. Rodonorte has three daily services to Lisbon, Chaves, Mondim de Bastro and Porto. There are two to Braganca and Mirandela.

Auto-Viacao do Tamega, ✆ 322928, on Avenida Carvalho Araujo have services to Porto via Amarante and Coimbra and Lisbon via Viseu and Lamego.

Vila Real ✆ *(059–)*   ### Tourist Information

The **tourist office** is at 94 Av. Carvalho Araújo, ✆ 322819, opposite the cathedral. The **bus station** is behind the Hotel Cabanelas: turn right and walk downhill for the centre of town. Local buses depart from the other end of the Avenida, at No.26. From the **railway station**, ✆ 322193, head up the Rua Miguel Bombarda, and straight across three crossroads, to get to the main strip.

Around the Town

The Avenida Carvalho Araújo is the centre of town. Here stands the **cathedral**, which is all that remains of the Dominican monastery of S. Domingos, constructed for Dom João I in 1427 and burnt to the ground some 400 years later. What's left is unexceptional, Gothic but for the chancel, which was altered in the 18th century.

Diogo Cão was born in one of the three 15th-century houses on the same street. He was the first navigator to reach the mouth of the Congo, where he erected a stone column in 1482, and visited the rich and powerful King Manicongo, who told him 'The kingdom of the Congo shall be like Portugal in Africa.' (Ten years later, news filtered back to Lisbon that the king and queen had been baptized as Christians, and had held a bonfire of ju-jus.) Little more is known of the discoverer—probably because Dom João II ordered all records to be deposited in the Torre de Tombo in Lisbon, to guard the information, especially from the Castilians. The archives were destroyed by the earthquake of 1755.

On the other side of the Avenida, the Rua da Portela bifurcates where Roman-clad archangels flank St Peter on the top of the **Clérigos Church** (also called the Capela Nova). Its Italian Baroque style may be the work of the 18th-century master, Nicolau Nasoni, or of his disciple José de Figueiredo Seixas. The interior has recently been restored.

Parallel with the Rua da Portela runs the **Rua da Misericórdia**, a long, low-built road lined with 16th- and 17th-century houses, resembling a stretched-out London mews.

This road leads to the **Parque Municipal**, which is overlooked by the **Terreiro do Calvário**, an open-spaced terrace with big views of the rounded hills around Vila Real.

The Environs of Vila Real

The Solar de Mateus

For nearly two centuries travellers and historians were ignorant of the Solar de Mateus (3km southeast of Vila Real on the Sabrosa road; *open 9–1 and 2–7; entrance 8500$00; guided tours in summer only*; off season you may persuade a cook to down her meat-cleaver and show you around; Rodonorte run a regular bus service from Vila Real). Now this sumptuous and fantastic palace is known world-wide because its image is on the labels of Sogrape's Mateus Rosé.

Mateus was completed by 1743, at the behest of António José Botelho Mourão. The architect is unknown; on stylistic grounds, it has been attributed to the (Italian) school of Nasoni, who had worked on the cathedral and the Clérigos Church in Oporto, and who was to be the single most important influence on 18th-century architecture in the north of Portugal.

Mateus has a festive air about it: the eye never knows which part of the façade to focus on. Two wings create a deep forecourt enclosed by a carved granite balustrade—the building's effect depends upon the contrast of whitewash and granite. At the centre, a great double staircase diverges and converges beneath the family escutcheon. An obelisk tops every corner.

The chapel stands to the left of the palace, with a similar pediment but too high and too heavy to work very well. The art historian Angela Delaforce attributes the design of the chapel to Nasoni's disciple, José de Figueiredo Seixas. The square reflecting pool in front of the *solar* was added in the 1930s. In it lies the disturbing sculpture of a half-drowned naked lady by the contemporary Évora craftsman João Cutileiro.

The interior retains the atmosphere of the late 18th century, when it was redecorated. Deeply coloured heavy silk hangings still drape the doors to keep the draughts out of a string of rooms with high wooden ceilings. The paintings include remarkably bad royal portraits, rural scenes, and seasonal vegetable heads juxtaposed with women's heads. The small museum includes two exquisite Sèvres vases, wonderful vestments, and one of the 250 copies of an 1817 edition of *The Lusiads*, printed in Paris at the expense of the heir to Mateus, displayed here with three of the original copperplates, by Fragonard and Gerard, which illustrated the work.

Such is the theatricality of the place that it's difficult to stroll around the manicured terraces at the rear of the *solar* without imagining oneself in the 18th century, wearing long shoes with high wooden heels and a buckle or bow, and a wide-brimmed ostrich-feather hat. The darkness of the tunnel of trees trained together is perfect for flirtation, or adjusting one's wig.

The Sanctuary of Panóias

The Sanctuary of Panóias (*staffed 10–12.30 and 2–5 every day except Mon*) is some 8km southeast of Vila Real. Take the Sabrosa road and after 7km follow the signs, through the village of Constatim. On weekdays, Cabanelas operates a single bus to the site from Vila Real; for the return, wait at the stop on the main road.

Three granite boulders are inscribed and carved with troughs. Four inscriptions were tooled at the beginning of the 3rd century, venerating Serapis, Moira, the Mysteries and the Dii Severi (Pluto and Proserpine). Another inscription mentions the sacrifice of animals: their innards were burnt in the larger cavities, and their blood was spilt into the smaller tanks. Other troughs were intended for believers' sacred amputations. Now the receptacles are full of rainwater and sheep impudently graze nearby. Bring your imagination with you.

Vila Real © *(059–)*   *Where to Stay*

***Hotel Mira Corgo**, 76–78 Av 1 de Maio, © 32500, 📧 325006 (*moderate*) is by far the nicest place to stay, with plenty of staff, and comfortable rooms giving dizzy views of the gorge below. There's a 25m pool downstairs, though you have to go outside to get to it.

Hotel Cabanelas, Rua D. Pedro de Castro, © 323153, 📧 323028 (*moderate*), benefits from its recent refit, but remains boringly functional.

Centrally located **Hotel Tocaio**, Av Carvalho Araújo, © 323106 (*inexpensive*) is dark even with the lights on. A stuffed boar lurks in the lobby. Rooms are clean if somewhat comfortless.

*Pensão São Domingos**, 33 Trav. de S. Domingos, © 322039 (*cheap*) is pleasantly atmospheric with uneven floorboards, a rooftop view, and stable-like wooden railings upstairs. The rooms are fine and have a radio to boot.

A few doors down from the tourist office, the **Café Encontro**, 78 Av. Carvalho Araújo (*cheap–very cheap*), has remarkably pleasant rooms, with the cosy atmosphere of a private flat.

Turismo de Habitação

Casa Agrícola da Levada, Timpeira, © 322190 (*expensive*) is part of an estate that still uses traditional farming methods to breed various species of game, including wild(ish) boar. They also produce their own delicious bread, honey, jam and sausages. The four rooms are comfortable, with stone walls.

Casa do Mineiro, Trás do Vale, Campeã, © 979720 (*inexpensive*) only has three rooms, but is built entirely out of granite and occupies an exceptional site at the junction of the Marão and Alvão mountain ranges.

Casa da Cruz, Campeã, © 979422 (*inexpensive*) is another typical house from this region. Inside it has a warm feel with colourful rugs and granite chimneys— one looks to be made from dolmen.

Espadeiro, Av. Almeida Lucena, 🕾 322302, 🖃 72422 (*moderate*) is reputed to be the best restaurant in Vila Real, with regional cooking and a fire place. **Cabanelas**, Rua D. Pedro de Castro, 🕾 323153 (*moderate*) provides a lively snackbar, but the restaurant above it is dead. **Churrasco**, 24 Rua António de Azevedo, 🕾 322213 (*moderate*) offers a very promising barbecue. This windowless haunt is known only to a select bunch. A few kilometres northwest of town, **Quinta da Petisqueira**, an old house in Av. da Noruega, Lordelo, 🕾 341535 (*moderate*) has been converted into a *típico* restaurant.

At **Nevada**, Centro Comercial Mira-Corgo, 🕾 71828 (*cheap*), the restaurant proper is partitioned off from the bar-counter, but everyone shares the air-conditioning. Sometimes the restaurant gets comparatively dressy, rising to stilettos. The food is good, though the choice unimaginative. The bar-counter's fixed-price menu offers the best value in town, including soup, bread, wine and a meat or fish dish.

Pastelaria Gomes, near the cathedral, has a good choice of cakes.

Around Vila Real

Mondim de Basto

Some 45km northwest of Vila Real, the little town of Mondim de Basto makes a good base for hiking in the Alvão hills. The headquarters of the **Parque Natural do Alvão** is in the Rua do Retiro, 🕾 (053) 38209. **Pensão O Sassego**, 🕾 055 381120, and **Pensão Arcádia**, 🕾 (055) 381410, are both cheap. The pine-covered **Monte Farinha**, to the east of town, makes a delightful and not too taxing 2-hour climb: a road leads up to the peak, or there's a path up to the right just past Pedra Vedra, on the Cerva road out of town.

The Castle at Pontido

Some 25km northeast of Vila Real, off the road to Chaves, is a medieval settlement. Five km southwest of the small town of Vila Pouca de Aguiar, take a signposted turning to Pontido/Castelo, to the west of the main road. The track leads through beautiful fields to Pontido. From here it's easiest if you leave your car near the water trough, and walk up the steep right-hand fork to the village called Castel, about 20 minutes away.

Thirteen families live here, essentially in medieval conditions. Smoke seeps through the chaotic stone roofs of houses built of uncemented stone and granite casements, incorporating boulders. The few streets are matted with dung and straw. Behind a gate with slats designed only to contain chickens, there is a yard, kept as common ground, for drying cereals. In summer there is no water because there are no pipes. In winter children are afraid of the starving wolves that follow them on their walk back from school.

The village grew up around a fort, the Castelo da Pena de Aguiar, built on a rocky outcrop strewn with massive boulders. Gaps between the boulders have been filled in, to form the outer wall of defence. The fort was probably sanctioned by 9th-century kings of León eager to push their—Christian—administration further south. The approach is difficult even today: the only access is from slightly below the village, along a path that leads up between smallholdings. The intrepid must squat their way under the low arch of two boulders. Subsequently there is a metre-thick doorway. The most impressive part of the fort is a low-lying shelter with a gently arched roof and a natural rock floor, where the only sound is the squeak of an imperfect horsecart. The view of the valley is wonderful, little changed since the fort was established.

Murça

Murça is a little town strung out along the main road to Mirandela and Bragança, 40km northeast of Vila Real, set in a scoured, rolling landscape crossed by dry stone walls. The main square is the home of the most famous of Portugal's *berrões*, affectionately known as the **Porca de Murça**. The 1½m granite pig inhabits a plinth, impassive, like a hornless rhinoceros.

The small 17th-century **Misericórdia** stands on the main road, its portal flanked by four columns wildly ornamented with vines. The façade is its most notable feature, though the key of the church is kept at house No.6 opposite.

✆ (059–)   ***Where to Stay and Eating Out***

Pensão Maganicha, ✆ 52235 (*cheap*) has good, clean, honest rooms.

There are a couple of places to eat in Murça, and the *pastelaria* on the lower side of the main square sells exquisite pastries.

Régua

Some 25 km south of Vila Real, Régua is the capital of the port wine country, being the nearest river port to Oporto and the westernmost town in the Demarcated Region. Otherwise, the town is of little interest. Its principal worth to the visitor is as the nearest railway station to Lamego.

The **tourist office**, ✆ 054 22846, is opposite the train station on the river bank and can advise about visits to port wine lodges.

Regua ✆ (054–)   ***Getting There***

Trains run fairly frequently from Oporto (2½hrs). They pass through Livração, where they can be joined by passengers from Amarante. From Bragança, change at Tua (from which, ¾hr). Five trains daily run from Vila Real (1hr).

Buses arrive hourly from Lamego; the bus depot in Régua is next to the railway station (for which ✆ 323342).

Residencial Quixote, Av. Sacadura Cabral-Lodim, ☎ 321151 (*cheap*) offers comfortable accommodation a couple of kilometres from the station. The food at **O Malheiro** (on the main street) is good, and the service friendly.

Lamego

The clean and handsome town of Lamego is set in hilly, fertile countryside, 9km south of Régua and the River Douro, surrounded by terraced vineyards and apple, pear, and cherry orchards. The airy settlement of 10,000 souls sits aside the small River Balsemão, a tributary of the Douro, which continues on its course, to the northeast of Lamego, through a steep, leafy valley. Two hills dominate the town, on one of which stands the castle, and on the other, which is wooded and, at 605m, slightly higher, the church of N.S. dos Remédios. The latter can keep an eye on the town, because the church's monumental staircase leads straight on from Lamego's central Avenida. Granite-and-whitewash Baroque *palácios* nudge one another, and in the streets men in flat caps wait for their stubble to grow.

Some of Lamego's accommodation is particularly good value, but the restaurants are not so hot. Do not despair: picnic on the local specialities—cured ham and sparkling wine. Lamego will introduce visitors travelling up from the south to the rich and heavy breads of the north, which are imbued with a mystical significance. This highlights its rôle as a gateway to that wild, remote land beyond the mountains—though it was Lamego's position as a trading post between the east and west of the Peninsula that brought prosperity in the 15th century.

The town had been the seat of a bishopric under the Suevi, and its episcopal status was restored in 1071. Lamego came into its own in the 16th century as a producer of velvet, satin and taffeta, with which it supplied the north of Portugal before the arrival of oriental silks. But the mainstay of the town's economy has always been its wines, described in the 16th century as 'the most excellent and most lasting ones to be found in the realm, as well as the most fragrant.' In the 18th century, Pombal built one of the first decent roads in the north of Portugal from Lamego to Régua, so that the wine could be shipped downriver to Oporto. This is the wine from which port is made, but only a quarter of the crop is so honoured.

Lamego is a 2½hr **drive** from Oporto, via Amarante.

The nearest **railway station** is at Régua, ☎ 23487; in front of it, buses to Lamego depart roughly hourly. Lamego is fairly well connected by the **bus** network, which includes very infrequent daily Rodonorte buses (☎ 63117) from Chaves (2¼hrs), and in the other direction Viseu (1½hrs), Coimbra (3¼hrs) and Lisbon (7hrs). The company Cabanelas run one bus daily except Sundays from Vila Real (¾hr), and in the other direction from Viseu (1½hrs) and Lisbon (5¾hrs).

The bus station is near the cathedral roundabout, from which the Avenida Visconde Guedes Teixeira runs past the **tourist office**, ✆ 62005, which is also the regional headquarters for the Douro Sul. They sell various local handicrafts, including baskets of rye straw bound with bramble bark, and woolly socks. These are made by a charming husband and wife respectively, who work from their balcony overlooking a cabbage patch and carry out each stage of the process, from picking brambles and rearing sheep.

Festivals

Lamego gets its knees up and lets its hair down for the **Festas de N.S. dos Remédios**, a long-drawn-out affair lasting from the end of August to the middle of September, though the early days may feature nothing more spectacular than the mini-golf tournament. There are concerts of rock and classical music, displays of traditional costumes and dancing, a fair, an exhibition of painting, a night-time parade of local floats, and other events, all of which surround 8 September, the day of the religious procession. For this, coupled oxen pull heavy scenes from the life of the Virgin through the streets. Ordinarily, transport by oxen is considered undignified: these beasts participate only by papal dispensation. Kneeling penitents climb the steps to the pilgrimage church, no doubt grateful that they were not born in the 18th century, when sinners scourged themselves with leather thongs ending in balls of solid wax spiked with glass splinters.

Around the Town

The 18th-century pilgrimage **church of N.S. dos Remédios** is an enticing destination. It's best approached as its architects intended, up the granite-and-whitewash double staircase which leads on from the Avenida Dr. Alfredo de Sousa. *Azulejos* and urns enliven the steps, which are fun to climb because it's such a tangible participation in the Baroque. (In the enjoyment of it all, take care not to be run over on the roads between flights of stairs.) Just below the church, the staircase culminates in the splendid **Court of the Kings**, circled by pillars and arches topped with theatrical granite gentlemen in sumptuous attire. The court is centred on an obelisk supported by four unfortunates traced with veins and spouting water from their mouths. The church's elaborate bell towers loom above, atop an unremarkable façade. Except for the portrait room, there's little to look at inside. The hill itself is peaceful and woody, so the road makes a nice walk down.

The road passes the **Raposeira Factory**, now owned by Seagram, where the sparkling wine is made (*guided tours weekdays on the hour, 10–12 and 2–5 inclusive*). The process is heavily mechanized, though the fizz is generated naturally by the second fermentation. An unusual part of the procedure involves the removal of sediment: it is allowed to sink to the cork-end of the inverted bottles; that end is then frozen, and the plastic-and-aluminium cork and ice are removed together.

The Cathedral

Back in town, the cathedral is at the heart of Lamego. Rebuilt in the 16th century and titivated in the 18th century, little remains of its Romanesque beginnings, except the base of the tower. A triple portal opens the façade, built 1508–15; devotees enter through arches ornamented with wild artichokes, pomegranates and other foliage, as well as babies, fantastical monsters, and even a fox munching a bird. Within, the ceiling painted in tapestry colours—sienna and grey-blues—canopies frescoes by Nasoni, who was clearly better at architectural than figurative painting, beautifully carved choir stalls, and a pair of organs dated 1753 (one provides spare parts for the other).

The real highlight is the silver frontal in the Capela do Sacramento—be sure to put the lights on. It was crafted 1758–68 by the master known by his initials MFG, a contemporary of Nasoni from Oporto, to imitate both textile and embroidery. An elegant cloister stands to the left of the church.

The Municipal Museum

Open 10–12.30 and 2–5; closed Mon and holidays.

The Bishop of Lamego did himself well: from 1775 to 1786 the wealthy Dom Manuel Vasconcelos Pereira rebuilt the episcopal palace, a fine building next to the cathedral. It now houses one of Portugal's best regional museums, with very good collections of paintings, tapestries and gilt woodwork.

In early 16th-century Brussels, huge rolls of vertical thread were slung in workshops and knotted with silk and wool, to produce wonderfully rich and lively tapestries, now exhibited in the museum. They include a series depicting the Oedipus story, and a panel vilifying profane music.

The five paintings by Vasco Fernandes (called Grão-Vasco; *see* 'Viseu', p.179) are some of the most excellent ever produced in Portugal. They form part of a retable of 20 panels commissioned for the cathedral by Bishop Dom João de Madureira in 1506. (He was transferred from the Algarve in the—fulfilled—hope that he would mend his un-Christian ways, and his likeness is given to the central figure of the *Circumcision* panel.) The retable was dismantled while the cathedral was revamped in the 18th century; during the process 15 masterpieces were lost. The style of painting is Flemish, and Flanders has crept in to the scenes in a more tangible form: the houses of the middle panel are clearly North European. The *Creation of the Animals* is quite unlike the other panels. It depicts God blessing his creatures, including a unicorn, and may belong to the School of Grão-Vasco, though the contract for the painting states that it is the master's own work.

The museum contains whole, richly gilt 17th-century chapels removed from the Chagas Convent; seeing them in isolation, it's easier to appreciate their artistic merits. Elsewhere, *azulejos* of the same date blossom with the exotica of Brazil. Finally, note the tomb of the Condessa de Barcelos, a big lady who died in the 13th century, and whose lasting memorial is decorated with scenes of pighunting.

Two Neighbourhoods

Lamego's unexceptional **castle** (*open 10–12 and 2–5*) tops the hill to the north of town, reached via the Rua das Olarias behind the tourist office. Surrounded by a huddle of stone houses, the fortification was heroically rescued in the 1970s by none other than the Boy Scouts, who removed 18 truckloads of trash from the place. They have now appropriated it, and are pleased to demonstrate knot-tying to anyone who might have come to look at the view of the town and hills.

It's much more interesting to wander round the **Bairro da Ponte**, a close-knit and archetypal Portuguese neighbourhood, on the southeastern edge of town, across the bridge on the way to Balsemão. A blacksmith works at No.71 uphill from the first junction, with giant bellows and a pit of water. He makes hoes and thingummys and says he used to work from 3 in the morning till 11 at night. There are some swimming places along the river. Here and in the neighbouring villages, look for *Fogos de Artifício* signs; the firework manufacturers add sparkle to the region's *festas* and *romarias*.

The Environs of Lamego

A good road runs northeast of Lamego, through variegated trees along the valley of the River Balsemão, which is white with rapids. After 3km the road peters out at the village of Balsemão. The **chapel of S. Pedro** is slightly set back from the road, up a steep bank. It's a jewel, behind a plain, reconstituted exterior, erected by the Suevi or Visigoths in the 7th century. A large proportion of the fascinating hotchpotch of later medieval additions was instigated by the 14th-century Bishop of Oporto, Dom Afonso Pires, whose effigy is supported by two angels. Amongst the florid capitals and stonemasons' doodles is one of the *Termini Augustales*. In the 4th–5th centuries, these marked the corners of administrative units called *Civitates*, on which the episcopal dioceses were based. Balsemão makes an excellent walk, though most of the return is uphill.

Lamego ☎ (054–)   *Where to Stay*

 On the edge of town, on the road to Régua, ★★★★**Albergaria do Cerrado**, Lugar do Cerrado, ☎ 63154, ✉ 65464 (*moderate*), is bright, fresh, and refined in its public parts, less characterful in the bedrooms. Cigar smoke reels around the bar. Only guests may dine; the food is OK. The private garage is locked at night. ★★**Hotel Parque**, Parque N.S. dos Remédios, ☎ 62105 (*moderate*) is at the top of Lamego's hill, next to the church. Apart from the church bells and a woodpecker, it's a very peaceful place, overlooking trees and the hotel's own miniature garden. The staff are helpful and the building light, with decent bedrooms furnished with reproductions, and a too-large restaurant.

For the three following *pensãos*, be warned that the cathedral bells chime every 15 minutes through the night. ★★**Pensão Solar da Sé**, Largo da Sé, ☎ 26060, ✉ 65928 (*moderate*), is across from the tourist office and good value: rooms, though small, may face the cathedral, the shower rooms are pleasant with very hot water, and the staff are cheerful. Leaving keys at the front desk might be risky, as it's often left unattended with the street door open. **Pensão Silva**, 26 Rua de Trás da Sé, ✆ 62060 (*cheap*) is behind the cathedral and also good value. Once a home, its bedrooms are impressively spacious and clean, with attractive wallpaper and Venetian blinds. The floorboards and screens to hide the sinks give the place an olde-worlde feel. The decoration at ***Residencial Império**, 6 Travessa dos Loureiros, ✆ 62742 (*cheap*), seems to aspire to an Edwardian bordello's, but the large rooms (with bath) are unexpectedly tranquil despite the din of clashing patterns covering every surface. The staff are friendly too. ***Residencial S. Paulo**, 22 Av 5 de Outubro, ✆ 63114, 🖷 62304 (*cheap*), is hygienic and favoured by Portuguese businessmen.

Turismo de Habitação

Casa de Santo António de Britiande, Britiande, ✆ 699346 (*expensive*) is filled with valuable antiques, dating from the 12th to 18th centuries. There is also a dazzling chapel containing panels of *azujelos* with an altar and ceiling in carved gilt. The rooms are airy and thoughtfully furnished.

Casa dos Varais, Cambres, ✆ 23251 (*expensive*) is a burnt-pink, 18th-century manor house magnificently situated on a hillside with views over the River Douro and vineyards. Worth staying for the views alone.

One of the less prestigious members of the *Turismo de Habitação* scheme is **Vila Hostilina/Instituto Kosmos**, ✆ 623947 (*moderate*), up a narrow road 20m beyond the Albergaria. It is part pumping-iron gymnasium, part guestrooms. The latter are none too welcoming, though there are big views from the upper rooms, and the swimming pool is a relief. Tables in the 'rustic' bar stand on the vat for pressing grapes.

Lamego ✆ (054–)   ***Eating Out***

The best of an uninspiring choice is probably **S. Bernardo**, Largo da Preguiça, ✆ 63545 (*moderate*)—towards the edge of town on the road to Régua. The food is good, but beset by television. **A Minha**, 5 Rua Alexandre Herculano, ✆ 63353 (*cheap*), parallel with the garden strip, plunges valiantly into the 'folklore' atmosphere. The menu includes a tasty *bolo de lamego* (ham in pastry). **Combinado**, 89 Rua da Olaria, ✆ 62902 (*cheap*), up the street behind the tourist office, is cosy, and the portions generous. The television may be showing videos of the manager's exploits as a hypnotist. The bar serves various of his weird home-made liqueurs, potent and colourful. Opposite the cathedral, avoid the Restaurante Novo and its cockroaches.

Oporto and the Douro Litoral

Convento de São Gonçalo, Amarante

Cosmopolitan, polluted and higgledy-piggledy, Oporto is Portugal's second city. It spreads itself and 305,000 souls over hillslopes descending to the granitic north bank of the River Douro; dull suburbs stretch to where the muddy river meets the Atlantic 5½km away. Oporto feels rooted in the late 19th century, in commerce and in granite-trimmed buildings. Rarely more than three storeys high, Oporto is a city of wrought-iron balconies and window shoppers, of newspapers in cafés, and of crazy drivers negotiating one-way streets.

The centre of town is the wide and pompous Avenida dos Aliados, at right angles to the river, sloping from the town hall and its clocktower down to the Praça da Liberdade. The straight streets to the east of the Avenida are dressed with boutiques and department stores, some of which have retained their turn-of-the-century fittings, and all of which are more genteel than the earthy Bolhão market at the heart of the shopping district. The area to the west of the Avenida is more stately, as befits such weighty buildings as the law courts, the Hospital of Sto. António, and the university. Small public gardens have sprung up here. From this core radiate the drab residential districts.

The guts of Oporto lie south of the Praça da Liberdade, towards the river. Wide streets provide plenty of elbow room for the merchants' houses that line them. The downward slope briefly halts at the cathedral hillock, which sings to the tune of the speeding traffic to-ing and fro-ing across the Douro on the upper level of the Ponte de Dom Luís. Clustered around the episcopal skirts, both roads and buildings narrow and darken. Among rickety homes always aflap with drying laundry, ragamuffins slide down the steep streets in cardboard boxes. They arrive at the Ribeira, the area around the riverfront, where customs houses face the giant neon signs of the port wine lodges across the river. On summer evenings, restaurants walled with honey-coloured stone spill out on to the streets around the cobbled Praça de Ribeira. Guitarists strum at the fountain, which is a cube balanced on one corner and pimpled with fake pigeons. Kids squirt detergent in, to make it froth, and high to one side cars beam across the bridge.

The Portuguese call the city Porto, prefaced by the definite article 'o', meaning 'the port'. The definite article has been incorporated in the anglicized version of the city's name, to give Oporto.

History

The Romans' route from Lisbon to Braga crossed the River Douro near its mouth, at the Lusitanian settlement of Cale. As the ferry plied its way back and forth, it spawned the village of Portus on the opposite bank. The two were known as Portus-Cale. Briefly occupied by the Suevi and the Moors, Portus-Cale had a jerky start to life. Abandoned in the middle of the 8th century, resurrected by Vimara Peres in the late 9th century, it further had its pride jilted when Count Henry of Burgundy moved the capital of his feudal holding from Portucale to Braga. However, he took the name of the town for the province under his command, which, under his son Afonso Henriques, became the independent country of Portugal.

In 1111, Count Henry's widow, Dona Teresa, equipped the town with a cathedral. By 1208, the bishops of Oporto had begun their struggle for jurisdictional control of their see: when Bishop Martinho refused to accord Dom Afonso II proper honours, the residents were scandalized, and forced the bishop to remain holed up in his palace for five months. The dispute with the Crown focused on the right to collect tolls and disembark merchandise. The Crown tried to safeguard its interests by establishing a royal borough, Gaia, on the riverbank opposite Oporto, but the wrangling continued until 1253. Then, it was agreed that one-third of the ships sailing down the Douro and half those from abroad should unload at Gaia (which was formally christened Vila Nova de Gaia two years later). Suspicion of outside authority could not be waived, and manifested itself in the 14th century, when the burghers of Oporto were privileged to forbid any nobleman to reside within the city walls. Though the privilege was repealed in the 16th century, subsequent *palácios* steered clear of the ancient city limits.

Dom João I and Philippa of Lancaster

The residents certainly knew how to make a new queen, and an English one at that, feel welcome. On Valentine's Day 1387, Oporto hosted Dom João I's marriage to Philippa of Lancaster, a political match to seal the alliance between Portugal and Philippa's father, John of Gaunt, who had a claim to the throne of Castile.

The streets were strewn with herbs as the king and his bride rode forth, on horses blanketed with gold. The procession was announced by pipes and trumpets, and followed by singing noblewomen. After the ceremony in the cathedral, the couple feasted at the palace; the napkin- and cup-bearers were knights. Fernão Lopes (*c.*1380–after 1459) reports that 'When [the entertainments] were over everyone began to dance while the ladies stood around in a group, singing joyfully. Meanwhile the king went to his chamber: and after supper, in the evening, the archbishop [of Braga] and other prelates with many burning torches, blessed his bed... Then the king remained with his wife, and the others all went to their lodgings.' The bedding ceremony took place, incidentally, without papal dispensation for Dom João to break the oath of chastity he swore when he became Master of the Order of Aviz. Less than a week after the wedding, the king was at the head of an army, bound for Castile.

Henry the Navigator

The bedding ceremony was not held in vain. The couple's third son, Henry the Navigator, was born in Oporto. It was on the Douro that he learnt his love of ships, a love that led him to found a School of Navigation at Sagres, and to devote his life to encouraging and financing Portugal's groping exploration down the west coast of Africa. At the age of 19 he commanded 20 war galleys to be built in Oporto as part of the much larger fleet which set out to capture the North African trading post of Ceuta from the Moors in 1415. Azurara, a member of Henry's household, writes proudly that 'Men marvelled to behold' the galleys as they set out adorned with great standards and little flags, with tilts and canopies of rich stuffs, in the white, black, and blue of the Infante, and bearing his device of garlands of holm oak overlaid with silver, surrounding the words 'Power to do well'.

The Inquisition made little headway in Oporto: only one *auto-da-fé* took place, in 1543.

Wellesley

In 1808, while Junot occupied Lisbon and the royal family had fled to Brazil from the first of three French invasions of Portugal, Oporto arrested its French governor, and set up a provisional junta under the presidency of the bishop. By the end of June central Portugal had freed itself of the invaders. Napoleon planned reconquest, and in 1809 Soult captured Oporto. Within two months Sir Arthur Wellesley, later Duke of Wellington, marched north from Coimbra and relieved Oporto in a brilliant surprise attack: the British had no boats, but found a barber who had rowed across the Douro during the night; they used his boat to locate three large barges, in which part of the army could cross the river. Battle ensued, and a flock of white hankies waving from windows in the lower part of town signalled the French retreat.

Dom Pedro

In the 1820s, Oporto became a hotbed of revolt, attempting to force the Braganças to return from Brazil, and to remove Beresford from command of the Portuguese army. In 1820 Oporto's revolt spread throughout the north of Portugal: the city's Military Council hoped to 'call upon a *Cortes* to organize a Constitution, the want of which is the origin of all our evils!' In 1828 Oporto declared its loyalty to the constitutionalist Dom Pedro and his daughter Maria da Gloria; their absolutist brother and uncle respectively, Dom Miguel, had usurped the throne.

In 1831 the idealistic, epileptic Dom Pedro sailed from Brazil to the Azores, and in the following year made his way from there to Oporto with 7500 men. They entered the city in spite of Dom Miguel's garrison of 13,000, who retired only to besiege the newcomers. Cholera broke out and, we are told, 'for most people a slice of dog or cat was a great treat': troops kidnapped their officers' pets. In 1833 Dom Miguel's fleet was captured off Cape St Vincent. As his troops retreated from Oporto, the river ran red—not with blood but with 27,000 pipes of port (each with a capacity of 522 litres) belonging to the Old Wine Company blown up at Vila Nova de Gaia.

Oporto continued to support the liberal cause throughout the 19th century, electing the country's first Republican deputy in 1864.

The British in Oporto

Fee, fie, fo, fum: the British have long been intimately entangled with Oporto's economy and the history of port wine; equally, they have remained foreign.

The first British to come to Oporto in large numbers were crusader-pirates en route for the Holy Land—'plunderers, drunkards and rapists, men not seasoned with the honey of piety', according to Osbern. In 1147 they docked at Oporto, where the bishop dosed them with wine and urged them not to be 'seduced by the desire to press on with your journey, for the praiseworthy thing is not to have been to Jerusalem, but to have lived a good life while on the way.' Thus he requested their assistance capturing Lisbon from the Moors—and promised them as much money as the royal treasury could afford. The brawlers were persuaded, and set sail for Lisbon, toting the bishop and his colleague João Peculiar, Archbishop of Braga, as security for their rewards.

British merchants took root in Oporto in the 13th century, after the Christian conquest of Seville opened the route to the Mediterranean. They traded woollen cloth, cotton, corn and Newfoundland cod for oil, fruit and cash—Viana do Castelo was the base for the export of red portugal, the wine of the Minho. In 1353 the merchants of Lisbon and Oporto made their own commercial treaty with Edward III. But it was the Commonwealth Treaty of 1654 which really sharpened the British commercial edge, codifying the Britons' right to appoint their own judge and to hold Protestant services in their houses, and setting a ceiling of 23 per cent on customs dues.

The viniculture in the Douro Litoral took off in the second half of the 17th century, when Colbert, Louis XIV's minister, forbade the import of English cloth into France; Charles II was suitably miffed, and imposed similar sanctions on the import of French wines into England. With bulging eyes, the British merchants in Portugal saw an opportunity, and bought up any wine they could—which was not enough, so they encouraged the cultivation of vineyards along the River Douro. Consequently the wine shippers—including the founders of Taylor Fladgate and Yeatman, Croft's, and Warre's—gathered their quill pens and their fighting cocks and emigrated south from Viana to the port at the mouth of the Douro. Each year after the vintage the shippers travelled from Oporto to Régua, an uncomfortable three-day journey which required 'sleeping on ye tables for reason of ye insects'. At Régua they tasted the growers' samples, and bought their wines.

Methuen and After

In 1703 the Methuen Treaty lowered the duty on Portuguese wines imported to Britain to a third less than that on French wines, to the despair of claret drinkers. Swift wrote:

> Be sometimes to your country true,
> Have once the public good in view.
> Bravely despise Champagne at Court,
> And choose to dine at home with Port

While Britain was thirsty for Portuguese wine, Thomas Woodmass reported being told in Oporto that 'there is much bad feeling against [the British], inasmuch as the principal trade of the country is in our hands, but that the treaties of commerce are in our favour'.

The British shippers pushed their luck. In 1727 they formed an association to regulate and improve their trade, and to keep down prices paid to the growers. Their high-handed behaviour was repellent to Pombal, who set about squashing them. In 1755, with barely time to straighten his wig after rebuilding an earthquake-torn Lisbon, Pombal decreed that the entire port-wine trade was to be controlled by a state monopoly company, from which all wine for export must be bought, at prices fixed by its officials.

The most permanent effect of the Alto Douro Wine Company was the delimitation of the Douro as the only area from which port wine could be exported. The British shippers uncorked their complaints, but continued to prosper once the laws relaxed. Pombal himself used Company certificates of quality to fob off wine produced on his estates outside Lisbon as port wine.

Exports to England doubled in the last two decades of the 18th century, and the sun shone on British merchants, who played whist and had little contact with the Portuguese. Wellington's officers were made honorary members of the port wine shippers' Factory. With the advent of constitutionalism during the remainder of the 19th century, the British became less insular, though they bathed at their own beach, now polluted, at Foz.

The most controversial of the British was J.J. Forrester, who arrived in Oporto in 1831. He produced exceptionally detailed maps of the Douro and the vine district, and a monograph on *Oidium Tuckeri*, a disease which attacked the vines. For his services to wine the cartographer was made Barão de Forrester by the King of Portugal.

In 1844 Forrester changed tack, publishing *A Word or Two on Port Wine*: in it he accused shippers of encouraging farmers to adulterate the wine with sweeteners. He argued against the newly implemented practice of adding brandy to stop fermentation. Brandy is crucial to port as we know it: without it, port would have become a thin and bitter liquid. But Forrester is regarded as a hero for singlehandedly tackling the port wine establishments of Oporto and London. He died in 1862 when his boat capsized on the Douro; the gold sovereigns in his money belt sunk him. Flags in Oporto flew at half-mast.

Port sales boomed until the early decades of the 20th century, but did not recover after the Second World War. The market for port-and-lemon was as dry as summer in the Douro valley. With the exception of Sandeman's, the shippers considered 'advertising' a dirty word, and ignored its possibilities; port lost out to sherry, which was marketed as an apéritif to rival the American cocktail. Today port wine is Oporto's fourth or fifth industry, and there are only about 900 British registered as resident north of Coimbra; but in Oporto they remain disproportionately influential. They still play cricket, and some live within herbaceous borders—but if you want an enthusiastic account of the city and its river, there are few more willing sources.

Port

The nice thing about drinking port in Portugal is that you can leave behind its crustier connotations, whiskers and all. Good port is like a liquid symphony playing upon the palate: anyone who thinks of it as a dark and sticky drink to send you to sleep after Christmas lunch, is in for a suprise.

Port is distinguished from other wines for two reasons: because the fermentation process is stopped with brandy; and because the climatic and soil conditions in which the vines grow are unique. Fermentation begins as soon as the grapes are pressed: the yeast on the grape skins acts on the natural grape sugar and transforms it into alcohol; the grape skins also provide colouring matter. After about two days, the grape juice or 'must' is run off into vats where pure grape brandy is added in the ratio of 80 per cent 'must' to 20 per cent brandy. This halts the fermentation process, leaving approximately half the natural grape sugar in the wine.

Port wine is born in the world's oldest Demarcated Region, established by Pombal, which runs along the River Douro from Barqueiros to the border with Spain at Barca d'Alva; its uneven edge covers the area north of the river as far as Vila Real and Murça, and south almost to Pinhel. The soil is a powdery, yellow schist, which retains such rainfall as there is, and the slabs of schist retain the heat of the daytime. The climate is extreme—they call it nine months of winter and three months of hell, sinking to −11°C and rising to an infernal 43°C respectively.

The crop is harvested in the hard, merry weeks between 15 September and 15 October: the timing is crucial and depends on the weather, which is assessed by the farmers and the shippers who buy their grapes. Mountain villagers descend for the harvest, arriving at the *quintas en masse* to work from 7.30 in the morning to 7 at night. They earn relatively good money, and when they rest they drink wine. The women cut the grapes and sing, the men transport the basketfuls, bearing over 50kg of fruit on their backs, steadied by a thong around thx forehead.

Until 20 years ago, the men spent their evenings treading grapes in concrete troughs, arms interlinked, purple to their thighs—a custom quite familiar to the Romans. The advantage of this method is that the grape is crushed but not the pip, which releases unwanted tannin, but the problem with doing it by foot is that temperatures in the treading rooms get very high, inducing fermentation and hence volatile acidity. The alternative is the mechanized process called autovinification, by which grapes are crushed and fermented at a controlled temperature; now, 90 per cent of port is produced in this way. Advocates of mechanization say it makes no difference to the taste of the final product.

The finer wines are stored in the *quintas* scattered over the Douro valley, while lesser wines are kept at the equally scattered *adegas* in white concrete balloons called mummers. The cold temperatures of the winter cause the wine to clear and loose the slight cloudiness that follows fermentation. In March of the following year the wine is ready for transportation to the shippers' 'lodges', or warehouses, at Vila Nova de Gaia, opposite Oporto at the mouth of the River Douro. Until 1987 port wasn't port unless it had matured at Gaia. It had to be matured there because that's where it had always matured, prior to being shipped abroad by British merchants, or transported within Portugal. Partly because of congestion in Gaia, port can now mature elsewhere, at the wineries in the Douro Litoral.

The wine that does make the journey is transported by road tankers. Previously, it was sent by railway, and before the damming of the Douro, by flat-bottomed, square-sailed *barcos rabelos*, piled with up to 60 pipes (a pipe is 522 litres). The only *barcos rabelos* still afloat are advertising devices moored at Vila Nova de Gaia.

The port wine lodges in Vila Nova de Gaia provide tours of their premises, with free tastings afterwards (*see* p.158). The **Solar do Vinho** in Oporto and Lisbon, run by the Port Wine Institutes, sell a wide variety of port wines by the glass.

The tourist office at Lamego (© 054 62005) can arrange visits to Sandeman's Quinta da Pacheca, which is off the road between Régua and Lamego. Everything there is highly mechanized, and is really only of interest to specialists.

What to Eat

When Henry the Navigator was preparing his fleet for Ceuta, he requested the Portuenses to donate food to fuel the expedition. Tradition has it that the inhabitants of Oporto were so generous that they kept only tripe for themselves—thus they are called *tripeiros*. It's more likely, though, that the name has its origins in the siege of the city in 1832–3. The Portuenses love tripe, and drape it in extravagant folds from meathooks; most commonly, it's off-white and looks like a honeycombed sheet of rubber. Tripe is cooked in a rich stew, *tripas à moda do Porto*, which includes calves' trotters, sausage, butter beans, chicken, onions, carrots and cumin.

An Oporto *bacalhau* (salt-cod) merchant is credited with inventing the dish named after him, *bacalhau à Gomes de Sá*. For foreigners, this is one of the most delicious forms the fish can take—because it's heavily disguised. The *bacalhau* is soaked first in water, and then in milk for a couple of hours. Next, it's lightly mashed with fried onions, boiled potatoes and eggs, and garlic. When oil has been added, the mixture is baked, briefly.

Oporto © (02–)   *Getting There*

Oporto is a centre for communications in the north of Portugal; it's the obvious place to begin a fly/drive visit to explore that part of the country. The city is 67km from Aveiro, 53km from Braga, 254km from Bragança, 117km from Coimbra, 313km from Lisbon, 123km from Valença, and 70km from Viana do Castelo.

by air

Pedras Rubras **international airport** is about 13km north of town, in the suburb of Maia. Bus no.56 runs from the airport to the square behind the Clérigos church. The journey takes ¾hr, or an hour in heavy traffic.

by rail

There are three **railway stations** in Oporto. Most trains creep across Eiffel's Dona Maria Pia Bridge to arrive at **Estação de Campanha**, © 564141, on the edge of the city. Change trains here for a 5-minute ride to the **Estação São Bento** (© 564141: there is an English speaker on this number), at the heart of Oporto.

Trains from Póvoa do Varzim, Vila do Conde, and Guimarães via Lousado arrive at the smaller **Estação da Trindade**, ✆ 200 5224. From there, walk downhill past the Trindade church and the town hall to the central Avenida dos Aliados.

Quick trains from Lisbon take about 3½hrs, via Coimbra (1½hrs); change at Entroncamento for Portalegre and Elvas, and from Castelo Branco, Covilhã and Guarda. Change at Lisbon for the south of Portugal. Semi-frequent trains to Braga take 1½hrs (many require a change at Nine, 1¾hrs total), and to Guimarães 1¾hrs. There are three trains daily to Vila Real (change at Régua, 3¾hrs total), and two daily to Bragança (change at Tua—and Mirandela in the morning—8½hrs minimum).

by bus

Generally, buses to and from the north are based at Praça Filipa de Lencastre, opposite the Infante Sagres Hotel, just west of the Av. dos Aliados. Most buses to and from the south are based mainly at the Garagem Atlântico on Ruo Alexandre Herculano, behind the Estação São Bento, from where all RN buses depart. There are also international buses to Spain and France. Anyone leaving by bus should check with the tourist office.

RN Express buses run several times daily to Lisbon (3½hrs) via Coimbra (2hrs). Other routes include a frequent run to Leiria (3¼hrs) and infrequent services to Braga (40 mins) and Guarda (3hrs) via Viseu (2hrs). Renex, on Rua Carmelitas, 7 & 32, have express departures for Lisbon and the Algarve.

Oporto ✆ (02–)   **Getting Around**

Most of the points of interest in Oporto are within walking distance if you don't mind the hills, so bring a pair of sneakers. There are plenty of **taxis**, and they're inexpensive—the problem is getting one to stop, and to put the meter on. Drivers in Oporto are in a hurry and take little notice of one another or of pedestrians; the result is hair-raising. It's hard to find parking spaces in the city centre, and the one-way system is baffling. The easiest solution is to go to the taxi rank outside the *Telephonaria* in the Praça da Liberdade, at the bottom of the Avenida dos Aliados. Taxis add a fixed sum for crossing the Dom Luís I Bridge to Vila Nova de Gaia. If you think a taxi driver is ripping you off, call his bluff by asking for a receipt (*recibo*) with the taxi's number on it.

There are numerous places to **hire cars** in Porto. Try AVIS, at Ferro Campanhã railway station, ✆ 518 9122, in town at Rua Guedes de Azevedo, 124, ✆ 311235, or at the airport, ✆ 944 9525. NovaRent, Rua do Paraíso a Foz, 48, ✆ 610 7697, have some of the best-value rentals in the city.

The local **bus** system is difficult to fathom because routes are not marked at bus stops, and because there is no decent map locating bus stops. There are three categories (*módulos*) of fare, for short, medium and long journeys: the driver will indicate which is which. The central point for all local buses is the Praça da

Liberdade. It's economical for those few visitors who are going to use many buses to buy a book of tickets (*caderneta*), or a four- or seven-day *Passe Turístico* (Tourist Pass), from kiosks near the main bus stops and STCP Bus Services (between Rua das Flores and Rua Mousinho da Silveira) respectively.

The **tram** network is not as extensive as it is in Lisbon. The most useful routes are those to Foz—no.1 from the Rua Nova de Alfandega, or no.18 from the Praça Gomes Teixeira.

boat trips

If you'd like a fish's eye view of Oporto, the **Cruzeiro das Quatro Pontes** (Four Bridges Cruise) motors between the city's four bridges (*open May–Oct, weekdays and Sat am, hourly 10–6*). It departs from the dock in front of the Ferreira port lodge in Vila Nova de Gaia.

The alternatives include a three-hour cruise up the Douro, departing twice daily from the Cais da Ribeira (✆ 383235), and longer cruises to Régua (contact Endouro, ✆ 324236).

Oporto ✆ (02–)   **Tourist Information**

There are two **tourist offices** in Oporto; the main one is in the Praça do General Humberto Delgado, near the belltower, ✆ 312740 (*open Mon–Fri 9–7, Sat 9–4, Sun 10–1*). The other tourist office is nearby, in the Praça Dom João I, ✆ 317514. The two are linked by a yellow brick path.

The **GPO**—for Poste Restante—is opposite the tourist office in the Praça do General H. Delgado. If you wish to send a bottle of port home—perhaps white port which is uncommon in Britain and North America—you can buy bottle boxes and packing stuff in the GPO's package section (at the far end of the 1st floor).

Telephones: Oporto's telephone exchange is in the process of being modernized, and all numbers will be changing. Throughout 1998 and 1999, all numbers beginning 31 are due to change to 205, e.g., ✆ 318765 will become ✆ 205 8765. Numbers beginning 32 will change to 332. Further changes may occur after 1999.

There is a **Telephonaria** at 62 Praça da Liberdade (*open daily 8am–11pm*).

As elsewhere in Portugal, **banks** are *open Mon–Fri, 8.30am–3pm.* You can **change money** at the airport and at most banks. In July and August, Câmbios Bank on Rua Sà da Bandeira is *open Mon–Fri 8.30–6, Sat 8.30–1.* There are two 24-hour automatic change machines on Av. dos Aliados, and one by the taxi rank in Praça da Liberdade. There are also money-changing booths throughout the city which charge lower commission rates than banks. Try Portocâmbios on Rua Rodrigues Sampaio 193, next to the Camara Municipal, ✆ 200 0238, also open weekend mornings.

To e-mail those on the Net back home, head for **Intercyber**, at Praça General Humberto Delgado 291, ✆ 200 5922, *intercyber@mail2.intercyber.pt*

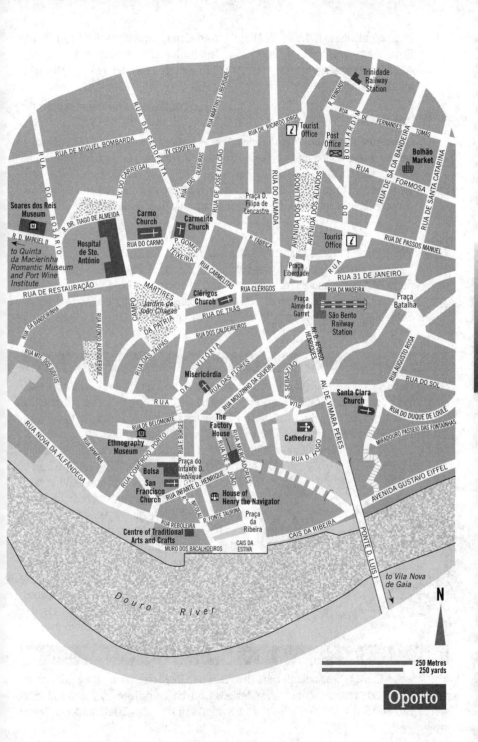

Trinidade Railway Station

Tourist Office

Post Office

Bolhão Market

RUA DE MIGUEL BOMBARDA

RUA DE CEDOFEITA

TV. DO CARREGAL

RUA DAS OLIVEIRAS

RUA DE JOSÉ FALCÃO

RUA MÁRTIRES LIBERDADE

RUA DR. RICARDO JORGE

R. TRINIDADE

RUA

BONJARDIM

DE

FERNANDES TOMAS

RUA DE SÁ DA BANDEIRA

RUA FORMOSA

RUA DE SANTA CATARINA

RUA DO ROSÁRIO

Soares dos Reis Museum

R. D. MANUEL II

to Quinta da Macierinha Romantic Museum and Port Wine Institute

R. DR. TIAGO DE ALMEIDA

Hospital de Sto. António

Carmo Church

Carmelite Church

Praça D. Filipa de Lencastre

RUA DO ALMADA

AVENIDA DOS ALIADOS

AVENIDA DOS ALIADOS

RUA

DO

Tourist Office

RUA DE PASSOS MANUEL

RUA DO CARMO

P. GOMES TEIXEIRA

R. FÁBRICA

Praça Liberdade

RUA CARMELITAS

RUA 31 DE JANEIRO

RUA DE RESTAURAÇÃO

MÁRTIRES

CAMPO

Jardim de João Chagas

DA PÁTRIA

Clérigos Church

RUA CLÉRIGOS

Praça Almeida Garret

RUA DA MADEIRA

Praça Batalha

RUA DA BANDEIRINHA

RUA AFONSO ALBUQUERQUE

RUA DE TRÁS

RUA DOS CALDEIREIROS

São Bento Railway Station

RUA MTE. DOS JÚREOS

RUA DAS TAIPAS

VITÓRIA

RUA AUGUSTO ROSA

RUA DO SOL

Misericórdia

RUA DAS FLORES

RUA MOUZINHO DA SILVEIRA

RUA S. SEBASTIÃO

RUA D. AFONSO HENRIQUES

Santa Clara Church

RUA DO DUQUE DE LOULÉ

RUA NOVA DA ALFÂNDEGA

RUA DE BELOMONTE

Ethnography Museum

RUA ARMÉNIA

RUA F. BORGES

The Factory House

RUA MERCADORES

RUA DE S. JOÃO

Cathedral

RUA D. HUGO

AV. DE VIMARA PERES

MIRADOURO PASSEIO DAS FONTAINHAS

RUA COMÉRCIO PORTO

Bolsa

San Francisco Church

Praça do Infante D. Henrique

RUA INFANTE D. HENRIQUE

R. S. NICOLAU

House of Henry the Navigator

AVENIDA GUSTAVO EIFFEL

RUA REBOLEIRA

R. FONTE TAURINA

Centre of Traditional Arts and Crafts

Praça da Ribeira

CAIS DA RIBEIRA

MURO DOS BACALHOEIROS

CAIS DA ESTIVA

PONTE D. LUIS I

to Vila Nova de Gaia

N

Douro River

250 Metres
250 yards

Oporto

In case of **fire**, dial ✆ 524121. For the **Red Cross**, ring ✆ 666872, and for the Santo António Hospital ✆ 200 7354. The **police** can be contacted on ✆ 200 6821. In **all emergencies**, however, ✆ 115 is more likely to reach someone who speaks English.

For car hire, *see* 'Getting Around', p.149. For **car repairs and maps** contact the Automovel Club de Portugal at 2 Rua Gonçalo Cristovão, ✆ 205 6732.

Decent **walking maps** for the Peneda–Gerês National Park (*see* p.92) do not exist: serious walkers should try to buy a 1949 or 1962 military map from Porto Editora bookshop near the Hotel Infante Sagres, at 1:25000 or 1:50000 scale. The maps are perceived to be crucial to national security, so are sold only to Portuguese. They may predate the hydroelectric schemes, dissipating their usefulness.

Festivals

When the Church Christianized the summer solstice celebration, some of the pagan rites remained: Oporto's annual humdinger is the **Festas de S. João**, on the night of 23 June and the day of the 24th. The streets are filled with bonfires and religious images; people dance till dawn, sustained by roast kid and *vinho verde*. Some hold the traditional lemon balm or hit one another over the head with a leek, or anything they can lay their hands on.

East

Surrounded by Oporto's shopping district, to the east of the Avenida dos Aliados, the vital, screechingly competitive **Bolhão Market** (*weekdays 7–5, Sat 7–1*) is the belly of the city. Swarthy women wrapped with multiple skirts hawk bags at the main entrance to the semi-covered, two-tiered market, watched by an image of Nossa Senhora decorated with wilting flowers. There are stalls piled with baskets of crops, and shawls spread with handfuls of produce. The salt of the earth sell the fruit of the earth, patting flies towards one another with makeshift flyswats of paper and bamboo. They sell all the staples, plus dyed dried flowers, wooden spoons, chicken claws. The cheese sellers, the fishmongers and the butchers are each grouped together; the meat stalls include the severed heads and trotters of pigs and calves. The bakers sell marvellous bread as heavy as bread can be, sawn into fractions with meat cleavers.

West

The Rua dos Clérigos leads uphill from the Praça da Liberdade, confronting pedestrians with the elaborate granite façade of the **Clérigos Church**. Its garlands, festoons and spiral scrolls can be seen most clearly in the early morning sunlight. The architect, Nasoni

(1691–1773), used these motifs in the frescoes he painted at the beginning of his career and later translated them into stone. Constructed between 1732 and 1749, this was the first oval church to be built in Portugal. Its style draws heavily on the Italian Baroque of the previous century: Nasoni introduced the Baroque to the north of Portugal, and his direct influence was felt here at least until his death. His style of architecture suits Oporto, and is very different to the contemporary Pombaline style in Lisbon. The church's audacious granite **tower** is an Oporto landmark, at 75m still one of the highest in the country. It squeezes skywards in segments, and has been likened to an exploding rocket. Cleaning would improve it. A staircase spirals up to the top, which is a good place for getting oriented with Oporto.

There is a fantastic **Neogothic bookshop** at 144 Rua das Carmelitas, which runs uphill from the façade of the Clérigos. Built in the late 19th century, Lello and Irmão looms behind a pinnacled, traceried façade. Books are shelved within Gothic arches, beneath a ceiling of wooden cartwheel shapes. A rounded double staircase reverses back upon itself, leading to an upper storey illuminated by stained-glass windows and hanging lamps like censers.

Uphill, lions with wings spout water into a fountain in the palmy Praça de Gomes Teixeira, fronted on one side by the enormous rectangular university. On the corner roughly opposite this stands the **Carmo Church**, a representative example of the Portuguese Baroque, built by Nasoni's disciple, José de Figueiredo Seixas, in the mid-18th century. The enormous *azulejo* panel was added in 1912. The **Carmelite Church**, next door, was completed in 1628 and subsequently turned into a barracks.

The Soares dos Reis Museum

Follow the Rua do Carmo around the side of the huge Hospital de Sto. António into the Rua de D. Manuel II, where stands the Soares dos Reis Museum (*open Wed–Sun 10–12.30 and 1.30–6; closed Mon and Tues; free on Sun*), the largest and most important museum in Oporto, including comprehensive collections of 19th- and early 20th-century Portuguese painting and sculpture. That said, it's not breathtaking, and can be covered in a single visit.

It occupies the Palace of the Carrancas, a neoclassical edifice which was dogged by its own magnificence. Built in 1795, it housed the Jewish family of Moraes e Castro, whose nickname, Carranca, means 'frown' or 'gargoyle'. They were granted the monopoly of gold and silver thread for the north of Portugal, and thrived on church vestments and military uniforms. The wings of the palace were their workshops. Marshal Soult lived here for 44 days of the Peninsular War, in 1809. Sir Arthur Wellesley chased him out and then, with due aplomb, ate the dinner prepared for the French.

In 1832, during the Civil War between the constitutionalist Dom Pedro IV and his younger brother the absolutist Dom Miguel, Dom Pedro installed himself in the palace, but moved out shortly afterwards having been wounded by a sniper's bullet.

The Carrancas' monopoly lapsed with the liberalization of industry. In 1861, unable to afford to maintain the palace, they sold it to Dom Pedro V. He flattened the small farm at the rear of the palace and built a tennis court surrounded by a stadium for bicycle racing.

The last King of Portugal, Dom Manuel II, willed the palace to the charitable hospital of the *Misericórdia*. Salazar considered the hospital unworthy of such a distinguished setting and shooed it away with a token payment. The museum was installed in 1940, destroying most of the first floor's frescoes in the process.

The Collection

The museum takes its name from the sculptor Soares dos Reis (1847–89), and houses his collected works in marble. These feature *O Desterrado* (the exile), which was completed in a few, feverish months before Soares dos Reis left Rome at the age of 24, when the Portuguese government cut his study allowance. The sentimental appeal of the head of a girl wood carrier, *Flor Agreste*, has ensured its reproduction as tacky paperweights and ornaments. The collection also includes the sepulchral figure of the Conde de Ferreira, who was a slaver, and a mother and child of such humanity that a church rejected them.

Among the paintings are the refreshing works of Henrique Pousão, impressionist in their use of light and colour. Many of his larger canvases were painted in Italy, while the more spontaneous postcard-sized blocks were produced in Portugal. He died in 1884 at the age of 25. There are many works by Silva Porto (1850–93), one of the first naturalists to work outside the atelier, and fiery paintings by Marques de Oliveira. Other artists include Columbano and Sousa Pinto. Among the older paintings are wedding portraits by François Clouet, the 16th-century court painter of Henry II of France, Frei Carlos' *Virgem do Leite*, feeding a remarkably unattractive baby Jesus, and views of Oporto by Jean Pillement (1727–1808).

The dinner service made for the Bishop of Oporto is outstanding amongst the china and ceramics. Much of the glass is Bohemian; the rarest local work is from Vista Alegre, before it became a porcelain factory.

Every museum claims its Indo-Portuguese chest is rare. This museum's chest is distinguished by its legs, which are mermaids with brass nipples. Elsewhere, a crucifix comes complete with articulated joints, for enactments of the Passion.

Towards Foz

Follow the edge of the gardens of the Palácio de Cristal, named after a 19th-century building now replaced by a domed sports pavilion. Bear left down a cobbled lane to the **Quinta da Macieirinha Romantic Museum** at 220 Rua de Entrequintas (*open Tues–Sat 10–12.30 and 2–5, Sun 2–5.30; closed Mon and holidays*). It's decorated and furnished in a style approved by the ghost of Carlos Alberto, abdicated King of Sardinia, who was briefly resident here in 1849. The museum provides a photocopied factual guide in English.

The dressing room is a temple to facial hair, hung with portraits of the ex-king's bewhiskered relations. Carlos Alberto himself had ivory moustache and eyebrow brushes, a lice comb, and brilliantine for errant locks. A screw enabled him to expand his belt when he felt stuffed. He kept some clothes in the corridor outside, with a different drawer for each day of the week, opened in rotation, as his garments were rarely washed. Clearly he was a methodical man: his pocket watch too has seven faces, one for each day of the week. Concerts are still held in the ballroom, which was lit by gas chandeliers.

The lower ground floor of the Quinta is the **Solar do Vinho do Porto**, ✆ (02) 694749 (*open Mon–Fri 11am–11pm, Sat 5–11.30pm; closed Sun and holidays*), a convivial, air-conditioned place to sample many and varied ports. Unlike its snooty sister in Lisbon, the atmosphere here is relaxed and friendly—and the wine is at home. Vintage ports are not available by the glass, because each bottle ought to be consumed on the day it is opened.

Oporto's **Museu de Arte Moderna**, 977 Rua de Serralves, is due to reopen in 1999. Bus no.78 takes about half an hour to get there from the centre of town, or catch it outside the Palácio de Cristal. The museum is housed in a 1930s *palácio*, sympathetically set in beautiful gardens. Check with the tourist office for opening hours and details of temporary and new permanent exhibitions before you set out.

At the extreme west of Oporto is the residential quarter of Foz, bordering the Atlantic. The British had their bathing houses here; the 17th-century **Castelo de Queijo** (Fort of Cheese) takes its name from the rock on which it stands. (Take tram no.1 from Alfândega, downstream of the Ribeira.)

Towards the River

Estação de S. Bento, the main railway station, is a good place from which to begin a visit to the lower and more historic part of Oporto, on the slopes between the Praça da Liberdade and the river. Big panels of inky tiles in the railway station depict scenes from Portugal's history, rendered 1905–15.

Leading down from the Estação de S. Bento, the Rua das Flores is lined with a jumble of 'typical' merchants' houses and their diverse wrought-iron balconies. The imposing and heavy façade of the **Misericórdia** sits rather uncomfortably in this narrow road: the 16th-century church was revamped in the 18th century by Nasoni, who surmounted his creation with the royal crown.

At No.15 next door, the **Misericórdia offices** (*open weekdays 9–12.30, 2–5.30*) contain a *Fons Vitae* painting, one of the finest Renaissance works in Portugal. It was given by Dom Manuel I shortly before his death, c. 1520. Dom Manuel, his third wife Dona Leonor and their eight children are arranged around a basin which collects the blood of the crucified Christ. One of the rear figures may be Dona Leonor, widow of Dom João II, sister of Dom Manuel, and founder of Portugal's charitable hospitals, the *Misericórdias*. The painter is unknown; scholars are even unable to agree on his or her nationality.

The Praça Infante Dom Henrique

Doubling back into the Largo, the Rua Ferreira Borges falls steeply past the Bolsa, and, next to it, the church of S. Francisco.

The **Bolsa** (Stock Exchange) (*guided tours weekdays 9–12 and 2–6; Sat, Sun and holidays 10–12 and 2–5*) stands on the site of the Franciscan monastery which in 1387 was host to Dom João I when he came to Oporto to marry Philippa of Lancaster. The more recent sort of temple, built in the 1830s, incorporates a gross but very expensive pseudo-Moorish ballroom. The audience chamber contains a beautifully inlaid table.

Fantastic and dazzling, the interior of the church of **S. Francisco** (*open 9–5; closed Sun[!] and holidays*) is the country's most overpowering example of giltwork: the walls and ceiling are bathed in a relentless shower of golden foliage—acanthus, grapevine, and laurel—amidst which crouch an assortment of golden cherubs. This is how the wealth of Brazil was spent. It is not the work of Midas, but of Miguel Francisco da Silva (active 1726 until after 1746), who showed little patience for the Gothic church restructured in the early decades of the 15th century: the rose window is one of the few interior indications of an earlier age. Visitors creak their way across the seatless, tombstone floor. There is an early 18th-century tree of Jesse, with roots like seaweed, supporting 12 kings of Judah; a grim rendition of the decapitation of the martyrs of Morocco; and a good mid-16th-century painting of the baptism of Christ. Note the negro monk to the left of the chancel arch.

The Ribeira

Across the road and slightly upstream of the church, the steep Rua da Alfandega runs from the Praça do Infante Dom Henrique towards the river. **Henry the Navigator** is supposed to have been born here in 1394; exhibitions used to be held in the shell of his **house**, but this is now closed to the public whilst archaeological workis being carried out.

Downhill and off to the right, the **Centre of Traditional Arts and Crafts**, 37 Rua da Reboleira, ℂ (02) 320076 (*open Tues–Fri 10–12.30 and 3–7*) provides an exemplary display of northern goodies. Almost everything it stocks is useful or practical, and it can organize shipping. Prices are competitive, and there are reasonably good selections of black pottery, rag rugs, embroidered linen placemats (5000$00 each), lacework (4500$00 plate-sized), signed pottery figures (*see* 'Barcelos', p.73), and reed-like straw handbags and baskets. Walking canes are very good value at 1000$00 each. A shepherd's rainproof straw suit, ideal for *The Wizard of Oz*, costs 6500$00. The 18th-century building was originally used for storing *bacalhau* transported by the ships that docked below. The smell has had time to wear off.

The streets along the river here comprise the **Ribeira**, the most atmospheric district of Oporto.

The Factory House

The Rua de S. João leads uphill from the Praça da Ribeira. Where it crosses with the Rua Infante Dom Henrique, previously known as the Rua Dos Ingleses, stands the inconspicuous headquarters of the British Association (of port wine shippers). The **Factory House** (*Feitoria Inglesa*) takes its name from the factors who belong to it. The building is closed to the public, but it's well worth a visit if you can manage to contact a member. The British Consul John Whitehead designed the building like a Robert Adam town house in London; it was built 1786–90, with sash windows, which are frequently mentioned in contracts as being 'in the English taste'.

The entrance hall was used as a parking place for sedan chairs; the side benches were for bearers. (In the mid-18th century, English ships trading with the American colonies often docked at Oporto and bartered a slave for a pipe of port. The English community liked

Dom Luis I bridge over the River Douro

slaves who spoke their language.) Upstairs the rooms are elegant, light and sober, from the map room with its globes of a world no longer recognizable, to the ballroom, where it's difficult not to click one's heels—a board on the balcony dictates 'Polka' or 'Mélange', which were danced in the candle light of the chandeliers. Outside the ballroom is a portrait of Lieutenant General Sir William Warre. Thereby hangs a tail: born in 1784, he was dismissed from the family firm for fastening the pigtail of one of the Portuguese staff to his desk with sealing wax, as he slept after lunch.

Diners enjoy their port unsullied by the odours of their meal. Keeping the same seating plan, they retire to the pudding room, where smoking is not permitted before 2pm. A glass touched by the lips of Queen Elizabeth is enshrined in a cabinet. A multitude of jelly moulds clutters the top-storey kitchen with crowns and Landseer-type lions: a memo of 1819 states that white port was used for culinary purposes, including wine jelly!

The Cathedral

At the top of the Rua de São João, turn right, up through the narrow, chaotic streets to the imposing hilltop site dominating Oporto's riverside. On it stands the **cathedral** (*open 9–12.30 and 2–6; closed Sun, except for Mass*), which was once a Romanesque fortress church—as were the cathedrals at Braga, Lamego, Coimbra and Lisbon—founded by Dona Teresa, mother of Dom Afonso Henriques. Dom João I and Philippa of Lancaster were married here in 1387 but they would not recognize it now, as much of the 12th-century structure was 'done over' in the 18th century, when the diocese was without a bishop (1717–41). A Baroque doorway has been inserted in the main western façade, surmounted by a beautiful Romanesque rose window.

In the north transept, to your left as you approach the high altar, soft light illumines a magnificent silver retable, created in two stages between 1632 and 1678. Manuel Teixeira and his son-in-law Manuel Guedes made a dozen reliefs depicting figures designed in the flat, elongated Mannerist style, trumpeted by silver cherubs. The second part was the altar front, commissioned of Pedro Francisco 'the Frenchman', who agreed to make it of 'low relief worked with flowers and in the foreign way', which is probably a reference to the swathes of acanthus foliage. In 1809 an ingenious sacristan protected the retable from Soult's troops by hiding it behind a wall of plaster.

Construction of the sober Gothic cloister began in 1385, the year of the battle of Aljubarrota. From it, a good staircase by Nasoni leads to an upper storey. There, the fine grain of the granite and the clean lines of the battlements give the place the feeling of a giant sandcastle. Rich 18th-century *azulejos* of the life of the Virgin and Ovid's *Metamorphoses* decorate the upper tier.

Nasoni designed the porch on the city side of the cathedral, and, most successfully, the prominent **Bishop's Palace** abutting the cathedral. Built in 1772, the palace has now been converted into offices. The terrace of the cathedral overlooks the city and its river. Unsavoury types brood over the view, and boys play football. Behind the cathedral, at 32 Rua Dom Hugo, the **Guerra Junqueiro museum** contains the poet's art collection, furniture and ceramics.

From the cathedral, cross the main road approaching the upper level of the Ponte de Dom Luís I to the Rua Saraiva de Carvalho, off which stands the church of **Santa Clara** which has remarkably ornate giltwork *c.* 1730. If you intend to visit it, do so before seeing the church of S. Francisco, which eclipses even this.

Vila Nova de Gaia

The suburb of Vila Nova de Gaia lies opposite Oporto on the steep south bank of the River Douro, which is spanned on two levels by the Dom Luís I bridge, completed in 1886. Taxis charge a small supplement for crossing the bridge. Otherwise, it's easy to walk across the upper level, if you don't mind heights.

Gaia is dominated by the **port wine lodges,** each of which spells out its name in giant neon letters. Until 1987, port could not be called 'port' unless it matured in Gaia. The area's narrow streets are a logistic nightmare for the road tankers that transport the wine from the Douro valley. The lodges are warehouses rather than cellars simply because Gaia is built on granite. The lodges organize excellent **tours** of their premises, vats, casks, bottles and all—just turn up and wait for an English-speaking group to assemble. The individual companies lay on a small-family-business spiel, though most have been bought out by multinationals. They allow visitors generous samples of the delicious stuff; the cunning crawl from one lodge to the next. It's a good idea to try dry white port, because the lodges serve them properly chilled. Calém have a particularly attractive bar; and are the only lodge that opens on Sundays. Sandeman are said to be especially liberal with the samples. *Most lodges are open weekdays 9 or 10–12 and 2–5.30, later in summer, when some are open on Sat: check at the tourist office.*

Part of the hillslope above the lodges looks wonderfully forested. This has been the private garden of the Conde de Campo Bello for 605 years, complete with maize field, orchard, and the first camellias in Europe, brought from Japan in the mid-16th century. The Condêssa saw a UFO here in 1982.

The upper level of the Dom Luís I bridge leads to the monastery of **Serra do Pilar**, with a round 16th-century church and round cloister, enough to dizzy even the most level-headed monk. Here Wellington planned his crossing of the Douro, in 1809, and the buildings are still occupied by the military. Visitors are not welcomed, but there are great views of the city from the terrace.

Shopping

Except on Sundays, nobody in Oporto need ever be at a loss as to where to buy a bottle of **port**. It's sold all over the place. If you're going to tour one of the wine lodges, it makes sense to buy your bottles there, because you can sample the wares—unless it's a vintage port—and it's fun to see where it comes from.

In the main shopping district to the east of the Avenida dos Aliados, the produce of the local **shoe industry** is much in evidence—ladies' flatties are particularly abundant. **Clothes** are cheaper than in Lisbon, and hand-made **lace** is of very good quality, but not cheap. There is a long tradition of **gold filigree** workmanship in Oporto and the Minho province: in the late 16th-century the goldsmiths of Oporto successfully pleaded the nobility of their profession, which exempted them from guarding the city gates from travellers afflicted with the bubonic plague. Keep an eye open for earrings and brooches.

In the Ribeira, the **Centre for Traditional Arts and Crafts**, at 37 Rua da Reboleira, is the best place to buy useful handicrafts (*see* 'Towards the River', p.156). A stall at the quayside sells excellent **chunky knit sweaters** and cardigans: haggle down to around 3000$00.

In the more administrative part of town to the west of the Avenida dos Aliados, **Livraria Britanica** (184 Rua José Falcão, © 332 3930) is a well-stocked English-language bookshop. But expect to pay about double the UK retail price.

Oporto © (02–)   **Where to Stay**

luxury

With the exception of the Infante Sagres, upper-bracket accommodation is comfortable but lacks atmosphere. The Hotels Dom Henrique and Castor, and the Albergaria Miradouro are surrounded by modern shops and services. It's too far to walk from the centre of town to the Ipanema, and the Meridien is 3km from the centre.

Run by perfectionists, and host to visiting dignitaries, the ★★★★★**Hotel Infante de Sagres**, 62 Praça D. Filipa de Lencastre, © 200 8101, ✆ 314937, strikes an admirable balance between grandiose furnishings, friendly service, and luxury. The carved wood and wrought iron in the public rooms smack of 19th-century opulence, though in fact they date from the early 1950s. Centrally located and fairly quiet, the hotel has 80-odd bedrooms, which are comfortable but colourless, with marble bathrooms. The dining room is formal and businessy, providing quick but unhurried service. Sauces are a speciality. The ★★★★★**Hotel Meridien**, 1466 Avenida da Boavista, ✆ 600 1913, ✉ 6002031, about 3km from the centre of town, is big and glassy, designed to make French business travellers feel at home. ★★★★**Hotel Ipanema**, 156–174 Rua Campo Alegre, ✆ 668061, ✉ 606 3339, has an extraordinarily uninspiring lobby. Beyond that, it's standard stuff, and with no low season, overpriced. The restaurant is big and international.

expensive

★★★★**Hotel Castor**, 17 Rua das Doze Casas, ✆ 570014, ✉ 566076, (will arrange airport pickup), offers very small but nicely furnished, personal rooms which lack the pretensions of the lobby and reflect the oddity of the hotel's name—'*castor*' means 'beaver'—only in their peculiar gadgetry. The dining room is vestigial; the pizzeria/crêperie is a better bet. Comfortable and opulent, but overpriced, ★★★★**Hotel Dom Henrique**, 179 Rua Guedes de Azevedo, ✆ 200 5755, ✉ 201 9451, is somewhat characterless, with lots of gadgetry tastefully incorporated. Some rooms have big views, as does the impersonal restaurant, which features an interesting selection of smoked appetizers. The coffee shop, Tabula, has good food at very reasonable prices, if you don't mind the disco lighting.

moderate

Middle-bracket establishments are generally smaller and offer more character, at the cost of modernity; **Hotel São João** is a good bet.

★★★★**Albergaria Miradouro**, 598 Rua da Alegria, ✆ 570717, ✉ 570717, is cosy and comfortable, 1950s style, with panoramic views of the city. It has managed to keep its prices down and now rates as one of Oporto's best-value establishments. Parking space is limited.

★★★**Hotel São João**, 120 Rua do Bonjardim, elevator to fourth floor, ✆ 200 1662, ✉ 316114, is attractively atmospheric and well positioned, with 14 amply furnished and softly lit guestrooms. The service is very good. Corridors are filled with thrones, plants and tapestries. It's worth paying for the upper category of room, complete with wooden toilet seats.

★★★**Grande Hotel do Porto**, 197 Rua de Santa Catarina, ✆ 200 8176, ✉ 311061, claims to be the oldest hotel in Porto—and that's easy enough to believe. In possession of some grandeur, its central location is a plus: just over five minutes' walk from São Bento station. ★★★★**Residencial Rex**, 117 Praça da República, ✆ 200 4548, ✉ 208 3882, is a fun place to stay, converted from a grandiose house and overlooking a garden square. The ceilings' stucco is amazing, and keeps guests' eyes off the grim carpets. Bedrooms are functional and spacious; one room has a round bed. Parking is available.

inexpensive–cheap

Some of Oporto's inexpensive accommodation is very decent and conveniently located. One or two of the *pensions* feel endearingly semi-residential, but you're likely to freeze in winter, and they fill quickly.

Behind the main tourist office, ★★★**Residencial Pão-de-Açucar**, 262 Rua do Almada, ℰ 200 2425 (*inexpensive*), is well-recommended and very popular. Also very central is the clean but basic ★★★**Pensão Universal**, 38 Av. dos Aliados, ℰ 200 6758, ◉ 200 1055, (*inexpensive*)—guests pay for the location. Noise is not a problem, until you open a window.

Your room at rickety, old-fashioned ★★**Pensão do Norte**, 579 Rua Fernandes Tomás, ℰ 200 3503 (*cheap–very cheap*), might come with some surprisingly personal touches. (It's charming until you find somebody else's nightshirt under the pillow and have to request a room which isn't already occupied.) It is worth paying a little extra for rooms on the lower floors, some of which have bathrooms and look on to the *azulejo*-covered church opposite.

Despite its location to the west of the Avenida dos Aliados, ★★**Pensão Estoril**, 193 Rua de Cedofeita, ℰ 200 2751 (*cheap–very cheap*), feels as if it's set in an unlovely provincial town. The accommodation is bleak, with oddly shaped rooms indicating the building's brutal conversion. ★★**Pensão Astery**, 56 Rua Arnaldo Gama, ℰ 200 8175 (*cheap*), is friendly and homely, run by a small old lady. **Pensão Mondariz**, 139 Rua Cimo da Vila, ℰ 200 5600 (*very cheap*), is situated in the colourful district southeast of São Bento station and run by a booming man who closely resembles Obelix out of the Asterix cartoon strip, down to the twinkle in his eye. Rooms are decent and large, and some have wonderful views over the city. **Pensão Europa**, 396 Rua do Almada, ℰ 200 6971 (*very cheap*), has quite a good restaurant and a lively bar on the ground floor, but the rooms can be a little gloomy. Avoid the windowless ones which face in.

Oporto ℰ *(02–)* **Eating Out**

expensive

Portucale, 598 Rua da Alegria, ℰ 570717, at the top of the Albergaria Miradouro, serves excellent food and has an intimate atmosphere, with stunning views of the city. The walls are hung with tapestries, the tables covered with fine linen and decorated with fresh flowers. The *cabrito á serrana* (kid in red wine) is a speciality. Reservations recommended—ask for a table with a view.

A short walk away from the subsidiary tourist office in the Praça de S. João, **Escondidinho**, 114 Rua de Passos Manuel, ℰ 200 1079, has a good reputation, but can fall rather flat. The décor is informal and old-moneyed, the waiters clubby. The menu includes *entrecôte*, filet of sole, and apple pie. *Closed Sun.*

moderate

The Ribeira is by far the most enjoyable area of Oporto in which to eat, and provides a wide range of restaurants and bars.

Chez Lapin, 42 Cais da Ribeira, ℰ 200 6418, attracts an arty, flighty crowd. A saxophone from the bottom of the Douro exhibits itself on the wall. The many chefs produce good food. Just off the Praça de Gomes Teixeira (the Carmo square),

Papagaio, 30a Travessa do Carmo, ℘ 384855, is a French restaurant run by a gourmand who favours bright colours and is especially skilled with veal. Try the *tarte de cebola*.

Some 50m uphill from the Campanha railway station, **Casa Aleixo**, 216 Rua da Estação, ℘ 570462, appeals to respectable locals in search of a 'typical' *tasca*. The setting is ordinary, the menu is ordinary, but the food is very good, and the half-portions large enough to immobilize most human beings. **Tribunal**, near the Tribunal Law Courts on Rua das Taipas, is fun, attracting a young and stylish crowd who tuck into large portions with gusto. In the Foz district, nestled near the main church is a small and popular Italian restaurant: **Al Forno**, Rua Adro da Foz, ℘ 617 3549 (*moderate–cheap*). The clientele is young and upwardly mobile— some bring their portable phones which seem to be purely for show (thankfully they never ring). The *ementa turistica* is good value at 2500$00.

cheap

Much of Oporto's cheap, counter-top food is to be found in the streets around the university and behind the main tourist office. **Casa Ernesto**, 85 Rua da Picaria, ℘ 200 2600, is located in the latter area, and provides very acceptable food (the half-portions are filling enough and very cheap). Further to the west, **A.F.**, 54 Trav. de Cedofeita, ℘ 325635, is barn-like, with green trimmings and reasonably good food that is not always hot. **Solar Moinho de Vento**, Largo do Moinho de Vento, is an unpretentious place filled with locals.

cafés

There are a couple of large cafés opposite one another in the Praça da Liberdade, both serving omelettes and hamburgers. Mirrored down both sides, the **Café Imperial** terminates in a stained-glass window in which grapes are harvested, a steamer steams, and crates are unloaded at the docks. The clientele is rather male and highbrow. The **Majestic Café**, 2a Rua de Santa Catarina, ℘ 200 3887, is similarly mirrored, but here they reflect cherubs. More elaborate, almost to the point of being camp, is the décor in the **Café Brasileira**, 118 Rua do Bonjardim, uphill from the Estação São Bento. A restaurant is attached, and a counter for hungry business people with no time. At the latter, pay at the till before being served. *Closed Sun.* **Gesto Coop. Cultural**, 13 Trav. do Ferraz, ℘ 320986, is a semi-private café, run by an artists' cooperative, with wonderful views of the city towards the cathedral. Light snacks are served, and local artwork by the coop is for sale. Telephone in advance.

The Douro Litoral

Oporto is such a magnet that the rest of the Douro Litoral seems to have been sapped of its energies. The province stretches along the coast from just south of Esposende to Espinho, and sweeps inland in a broad arc, beyond Amarante.

The best way to see the Douro valley is by **train** from Oporto. The railway joins the broad River Douro near Cinfães, some 50km inland, and follows a spectacular course. It's difficult to call the landscape 'beautiful', though many people do. Rather, it has a kind of brute force. Most Portuguese travellers take the scenery for granted, and pull down the window blinds to keep the sun out—try to preempt them by nabbing a window seat!

Inland, in the Alto Douro, the massive, smooth hills of the river valley are contoured with terraces of vines. The effect of this landscape is changeable: it can be heavy or light, depending on the sunshine—but it's impressive and memorable however you see it. At the moment the vineyards have an open-cast look, because the World Bank gave the port producers an interest-free loan to re-terrace their vineyards to fit two rows per terrace and to allow access by tractor.

Only one train runs daily from Oporto's São Bento station to Pocinho (5¼hrs), the end of the Douro line. This can be done as a day trip, but would require an early start and a late return. Trains run slightly more frequently to Régua (2¼hrs or 2½hrs), which is quite far enough inland to give a good idea of what the Douro is about.

See **Oporto** section, p.150, for details of boat trips up the Douro, though these are limited by the river's dams, which have made it, in effect, a series of giant lakes.

The Atlantic Coast

Oporto is within easy striking distance of the beaches of what are marketed as the Costa Verde (the Green Coast) to the north, and the Costa da Prata (the Silver Coast) to the south. As far as the coasts go, there's little difference between the two: they share chilly water, fairly large waves when it's windy, and patchy development. Both are popular with the residents of the Minho and Trás-os-Montes. To the north of Oporto, the main resorts are at Póvoa de Varzim and Viana do Castelo, and, to the south, Espinho, Aveiro, Figueira da Foz and Nazaré; with the exception of Viana and Aveiro, these offer few diversions other than sea and sun.

Póvoa de Varzim

Póvoa de Varzim is an uninspiring coastal town 30km north of Oporto. Its 2km of wide, sandy beach have incurred heavy development as a resort, butting out most of Póvoa's fishing fleet. The population of 21,000 almost doubles in summer, when the mean temperature is 18°C, most of the increase being residents of the Minho and Trás-os-Montes. They wander the straight streets chewing gum (bring a spare stick and make friends), sometimes venturing into the casino, a rather beautiful pink building on the coast

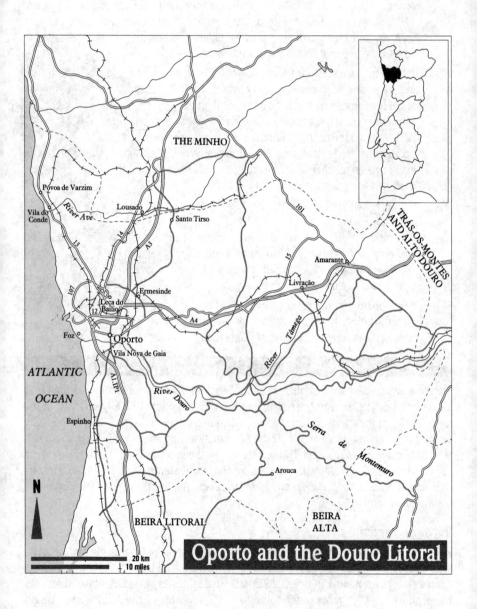

Oporto and the Douro Litoral

road, or to the occasional bullfight. The fishermen keep themselves to themselves in the modest Bairro dos Pescadores. Eça de Quieroz, the brilliant and thoroughly enjoyable 19th-century novelist, was born here.

Getting Around

Oporto's Estação da Trindade is an hour away; **trains** arrive hourly. From the railway station, turn right on to and walk along the Rua Almirante Reis to the Praça do Almada. Bear left there for the seafront.

© (052–) **Tourist Information**

The tourist office is at 166 Avenida Mouzinho de Albuquerque, © 614680, the main road at right angles to the ocean.

The broadly maritime/ethnographical **museum** (*open 10–12.30 and 2.30–6; closed Mon and holidays*) is large and very well researched, but the research is pitched at people with a basic knowledge of the topics it covers, such as fishing for *bacalhau*. The museum includes models of ships and nets, fishermen's clothes and domestic paraphernalia, equipment for collecting seaweed, and a cork life vest.

© (052–) **Where to Stay**

 The glitzy ★★★★**Hotel SopeteVermar**, Rua Imprensa Regional, © 615566, 🖼 615115 (*expensive*), on the coast road, north of town, is comfortable and neutral, trimmed with plants and spotlights. Some of the balconied rooms have sea views. There is a telephone in each bathroom, presumably in case guests run out of toilet paper. Thatched umbrellas are pitched on the grassy poolside. The large, sunny dining room features seafood. Next to the casino, ★★★**Grande Sopete Hotel da Pitch**, 20 Jardim do Passeio Alegre, © 615464, 🖼 615565 (*expensive*), obviously hopes to attract gamblers; it is ridiculously overpriced. Basic furnishings are enlivened with flowers and bowls of fruit; the first-floor sitting room is comfortable and relaxed, and some rooms have sea views from their small windows.

The windows are larger and the rooms more airy at the ★★**Hotel Luso-Brasileira**, 14 Rua dos Cafés, © 615161, 🖼 624713 (*moderate*), though for a view you need an upper-floor room; all have a TV, minibar and desk. Bathrooms are very nice, as is the first-floor bar. **Rua Paulo Barreto** is recommended for cheap accommodation.

© (052–) **Eating Out**

Roughly opposite the fort, **Belo Horizonte**, Rua Tenente Valadim, © 624787 (*moderate*), serves very reasonable food. Boats are painted on the wall. **Estrela do Mar**, 144 Rua Caetano de Oliveira, © 684975 (*cheap*), is undecorated and popular with the locals, who stare inquisitively at foreigners.

Vila do Conde

Vila do Conde is a once-grand boatbuilding harbour at the mouth of the Ave River. The bulk of the charming little town is set back from the wide sandy beach. It's best visited as a day trip from Oporto, 27km away, though there are a couple of places to stay here. Around 870 the settlement was fortified by a count, hence its name. Sold to the Monastery of Guimarães, and later assimilated into crown lands, the town boomed from fishing and trading under Dom João II and Dom Manuel I: in the 16th century, new money built the new town hall and parish church. But the river silted up in the late 18th century, leaving Vila do Conde to a gracious retirement relatively unruffled by the tourists and developers drawn to its larger neighbour, Póvoa de Varzim.

Getting Around

Trains run hourly from Oporto's Estação da Trindade, taking just under an hour. To get to the tourist office, which supplies maps, from the railway station, follow the Avenida Figueiredo de Faria, turn right at the Praça da República, and left into the Rua 25 de Abril.

© (052–)   Tourist Information

The **tourist office** is at 103 Rua 25 de Abril, © 642700, housed in a pretty Hansel and Gretel cottage. Around the corner in the Rua 5 de Outubro, workers at the **Handicraft Centre** (*open Mon, Tues and Sat 10–1 and 3–7, Fri 10–7, and Sun 3–7*) demonstrate the art of *bihrlos*, a type of lace-work using numerous bobbins, pins and a kind of cushion to hold the pricked pattern. The art originated from **Vila do Conde**, and there is a school here where girls between the ages of 5 and 10 are trained in the mind-boggling combination of finger movements required to complete the final work.

Festivals

The **Festival of Corpus Christi** is held in June every four years, most recently in 1997, and features fantastic carpets of flowers. The petals of roses, hydrangeas, carnations and other flowers are collected in sacks from the surrounding quintas. On the night before the festival, they are stencilled on 3km of roads—pink, green, yellow and red—along which the 16kg silver monstrance processes.

What to See

The **convent of Santa Clara** is a prominent bastion in the grand style of the Bishop's Palace in Oporto. The convent was founded in 1318, incompletely rebuilt in 1778, and made defunct 60 years later. Now it's a school, offering access to the finely sculpted tombs in the church (*open 9–12 and 2–6*). The inmates' water was supplied by an aqueduct which once had 999 arches, and looks two-dimensional.

The heart of town is a huddle of interest. Impressive rather than beautiful, the late Gothic **Igreja Matriz** was finished *c.* 1514. João de Castilho crafted the rippling flamboyant

Gothic portal: although it is more sober than his doorway of the Convento de Cristo at Tomar, on the tympanum the sculptor has seen fit to flank St John with a dragon on one side and a naked man on the other. The 17th-century belltower swamps the façade. Flying dragons face one another between each of the arches inside, by beautiful retables. The church now contains the newly opened **Museum of Sacred Art**, © (052) 631424 (*open 10–12 and 2–4*), which houses the Processional Cross from the Chapel of Formariz. A surreal arm bearing a sword projects from the **pillory** nearby, begun in 1538, which is topped by what seems to be a lightning conductor—for divine wrath?

© *(052–)* **Where to Stay**

★★★★**Estalagem do Brasão**, 144 Av. Dr. João Canavarro, © 642016, ✆ 642028 (*inexpensive*), is comfortable, with standard furnishings and lace curtains but narrow beds. Once it was a *palácio*. Now it has a discothèque.

The ★★★**Motel de Sant'Ana**, Monte de Sant'Ana-Azurara, © 641717 (*moderate*) is across the river, and there's also ★★**Pensão Princesa do Ave**, Rua Dr. Antsa do Ave, © 642065 (*inexpensive*).

Turismo de Habitação

Quinta das Alfaias, 515 Rua de António Azevedo dos Santos, Fajozes, © 662146 (*expensive*) is a large box-shaped building standing in its own estate. The garden is a maze of fruit trees, perfect for walks. The large bedrooms are individually furnished, some a bit heavily with too much dark wood. Otherwise, there's a high comfort factor.

© *(052–)* **Eating Out**

Restaurante Ramon, Rua 5 de Outubro, © 631334 (*moderate*) is a warm and happy family *tasca* with its own-label wine. *Closed Tues.* **Le Villageois**, 94 Praça da República, © 052 631119 (*moderate*) serves fairly good food—try the whiting fillets with shrimp sauce. *Closed Mon.*

Espinho

Planned on an unedifying grid, 16km south of Oporto, the resort of Espinho manages to fill its white beach in the summer, but lacks entrepreneurial flair. The beach has receded 200m in the past hundred years, and is divided from most of the town by a railway line.

One of the world's two greatest **violin makers** works in Espinho. António Capela learnt the craft from his father, who made a violin for himself in 1924; then a neighbouring violinist brought an instrument to be repaired, lest he damage his own hands mending it, and the business was under way. António travels to Italy and Germany to select Yugoslavian spruce or the more beautiful maple, the woods with the finest resonance. A large proportion of his creations are outstanding Stradivarius reproductions, which are used by musicians the world over. The strong-armed craftsman has a glint in his eye. He is continually paring, fining and polishing in his workroom, where he plays loud pop on the radio. He's assisted by his son, who made his first violin when he was 13. António is happy to speak French or Italian with musicologists (© 02 720658).

Oporto Golf Club

The golf club is on the coast a couple of km south of town (© 02 722008). It features a difficult 18-hole links course with narrow fairways parallel to one another. Most tourists who play here are Dutch: they feel at home with the flat land. Being so close to the sea has led to difficulties with irrigation, but these appear to be under control. The north wind blows across the course, which is split by a road and includes a fair amount of sand. The rough is not very rough. The new clubhouse includes an uninspired TV room in which to dump children. Green fees are more expensive at the weekend.

© (02–)   *Where to Stay*

★★★★**Hotel Praia Golfe**, Rua 6, © 731 3385, ◉ 731 3397 (*expensive*), near the casino, is pleasant and sporty. Guests receive a 50 per cent reduction on green fees at the Oporto Golf Club 3km away— hence the tartan carpet in the restaurant. Some of the comfortable, neutral bedrooms have big sea views. Equally diverting is the very impressive health centre, which includes a heated indoor swimming pool, squash court, sauna, Turkish bath, gym, and massage room; elsewhere there's a discothèque named Boggie. ★★★**Hotel-Apartamento Solverde**, 77 Rua 21, © 731 3144, ◉ 731 3153 (*expensive*), is part of the casino development at the nub of Espinho, providing space-effective apartments with well-equipped kitchens and curtained-off bedrooms. Bright tiles in the corridors give a beachside feel to the place. The hotel has access to two open-air saltwater swimming pools.

★★**Pensão Espinho**, 326 Rua 19, © 734000 (*cheap*) is 100m up the main street at right angles to the beach, not bad but well worn. Tall windows help if your room smells of cats.

Turismo de Habitação

Vila Maria, 667 Rua 62, © 720350 (*moderate*) is located in the centre of the town, close to the beach. The burnt pink, 19th-century manor house promises well from the street, but the rooms feel rather bare and functional.

© (02–)   *Eating Out*

On the seafront try the *caldeirada* (fish stew) or the *cataplana* (sealed wok) *de tamboril* at **Casa Marreta**, 1355 Rua 2, © 720091 (*moderate*). Pots of fresh herbs ornament the tables. Nearby but back from the seafront is **A Varina**, 1269 Rua 2, © 724630 (*cheap*), featuring fillets of fish and rice-based dishes. The chairs are pine and the green walls weakly hung with fishing nets. For low-budget food served by laconic but multilingual staff, head for **Casa da Feira**, 635 Rua 19, © 720398 (*cheap*). The food is more attractive than the building.

The Church of Leça do Balio

Eight km north of Oporto, and 2km south of the satellite town of Maia stands the fortified Gothic church of Leça do Balio, which was founded as a monastery for men and women in 986, and in 1115, after the first crusade, became the headquarters of the Knights Hospitallers. In 1336 it was rebuilt by the head of the order, since when it has changed little, though it is not grand. The outside is wholly, fiercely crenellated, and the tower resembles a keep—more to emphasize its possession by a military order than for defensive purposes.

The most exciting object in the well-proportioned interior is the baptismal font, carved by Diogo Pires the Younger in 1514: the bowl is supported by toothy, menacing crocodiles with webbed feet and poised tails. Perhaps they drew inspiration from Azurara's chronicle, in which he described 'fish which have beaks three or four palmos [20cms] in length ... and these beaks have teeth on either side, so close to one another that one cannot lay a finger between them... These fish are as great and sometimes greater than sharks.' The basin itself is decorated with pomegranates and maize-like *massaroca* fruits.

Santo Tirso

Roughly 23km inland from Vila do Conde and 25km north of Oporto, the little textile town of Santo Tirso is only of interest for its **Convento de São Bento**, now an agricultural college. A monastery was founded here in 770, by either St Frutuoso or St Martin of Dume, but it was rebuilt in the 13th century; the present building was begun in 1659. Behind a simple triangular façade, the church is rather dull, but do note the gilt woodwork in the altars of the transept, and the impressive pietà. The real reason for coming is to see the two-storeyed Cluniac cloister: built in the 14th century, the arches are supported by twin columns, with vegetable and animal capitals.

Amarante

Amarante is a town as beautiful as its name. Sited 56km east of Oporto, it graciously bridges the River Tâmega, which is edged with willow trees and wooden balconies. These complement the lovely view across the 18th-century bridge to the brooding, disparate convent of São Gonçalo, with the church of São Domingos hovering behind.

The settlement is ancient. It was founded as Turdetanos in 360 BC, but changed its name to honour the Roman Governor Amarantus. Tradition claims that St Gonçalo built the first bridge across the Tâmega in the 13th century, to get to his hermitage on the other side. His bridge fell down in the floods of 1763, but his hermitage became a church and convent. The quaint but strong bridge that now stands was built in 1790. Several years later, in 1809, it was the scene of a heroic resistance by the people of Amarante, who staved off the French Marshal Soult's advance across the bridge for a full 14 days, but had their houses burnt in return.

The town feels somehow benign, despite the lack of pavements. The leafy park beside the river is inhabited by the occasional 10cm charcoal-black slug. A notice warns of polluted water, so swimming is not advisable. This does not deter the town's flock of plump white geese, who motor up and down the river all day and sleep on an island. For the past eight years they've been fed daily by a man with no family and no job. He says he talks to them. Amarante is famous for its egg-yolk-and-sugar **sweets**. The best place to try them is Lailai, near the restaurant Zé de Calçada. Some of Amarante's accommodation offers very good value.

© (055–)   ***Tourist Information***

The **tourist office** (*open daily 9–6*) is in the same building as the museum on the Alameda Teixeira de Pascoaes, © 432259. The small **railway station** is on Rua João Pinto Ribeiro. To reach the tourist office from the train station, turn right outside and walk down to the very bottom of the street, passing the old Turismo. Turn left by the bridge and into the Alameda Teixeira de Pascoaes. Most **buses** stop in the Largo Conselheiro António Cândido; from there, walk along the Rua 31 de Janeiro to get to the Ponte de São Gonçalo.

Festivals

At the **Feast of S. Gonçalo** on the first weekend of June, the town commemorates the patron saint of marriages by baking little phallus-shaped cakes, offered by young men to young women. This is probably a hangover from a Roman fertility cult. (In her cookbook, Edite Vieira does not rise to the challenge: the recipe for *bolos de São Gonçalo* 'would demand elongated tins, but obviously any patty tins will do.')

What to See

The **convento de São Gonçalo** was founded by Dom João III in 1540; it took 40 years to build. To the left of the Renaissance portal stands an arcaded loggia with 17th-century figures. The cupola is tiled with terra cotta, beautiful against the church's mellow granite body. Within, the finely symmetrical organ is supported by three bearded and muscle-bound gentlemen, who have performed their task since 1600. To the left of the altar lies the tomb of St Gonçalo, believed to guarantee a quick marriage to anyone who touches it; underestimating demand, the effigy was made in soft limestone. Consequently the face and foot have been worn away. The cynical will mutter about St Gonçalo reaching the parts other saints cannot reach. The convent has two cloisters, the second of which has been invaded on one side by the town hall.

Upstairs, the **Albano Sardoeira Museum** of modern art is overpowered by Amadeo de Sousa-Cardoso (1887–1918), the greatest Portuguese artist of the 20th century. (His work has found a more fitting home in Lisbon's Gulbenkian Museum of Modern Art.) Born locally, he started his training as an architect, but switched to painting because he loved colours and forms, hoping to express in painting 'what he thought'. In 1906, he moved to Paris and exhibited with Modigliani. He returned to Portugal in 1914, and here he became a close friend of Robert and Sonia Delaunay. In the final year of his life, Amadeo had to limit his painting as the paints damaged his hands; he was killed by Spanish 'flu.

Amadeo's early, figurative work soon ceased to satisfy him; his interest in shapes, colour and light led him to pure abstraction. He later reintegrated figurative elements, painting images as if they were shattered. On his return to Portugal, he became preoccupied by his surroundings and reintroduced representation to his work. His final paintings combine elements from all his periods, and are lumbered with the generic term 'Cubo-photism'.

The Tâmega Railway

The most enjoyable excursion from Amarante is aboard the narrow-gauge Tâmega railway, a single-carriage train which creeps its way northwards past bulging, verdant valley sides and fields of cork trees shorn of their crop, as far as Arco de Baúlhe. This is one of Europe's most enchanting railway journeys and should not be missed if you plan to visit Amarante. There are five trains a day from Porto and four more from Livração.

Amarante ✆ (055–)   ***Where to Stay***

 ★★★**Hotel Navarras**, Rua António Carneiro, ✆ 431036, ✉ 432991 (*moderate*), has neat, clean rooms, and the lobby is large enough for the staff to parade their smart uniforms. Corridor walls are made of fake granite, complete with embedded tinsel. There is a nice rooftop swimming pool. ★★★**Hotel Amaranto**, Edifício Amaranto-Madalena, ✆ 449206 (*inexpensive*) is clean and functional, with sophisticated equipment behind the reception desk and an enormous choice of lighting in guestrooms, which also have balconies. Staff in the hotel's restaurant are very keen to please; they speak English, and serve good food.

★**Albergaria da Margarita**, 53 Rua Cândido dos Reis, ✆ 423110, ✉ 437977 (*inexpensive*) offers excellent value for money. With 32 rooms, it's a pleasant size, decorated in the grand style without being pretentious. Ceilings are high, should you choose to look up rather than out of the window to the lovely view of the river. Breakfast is served on the trellised terrace.

The two cheapest places are on Rua 31st de Janeiro: **Residancial Estoril** ✆ 431291 (*very cheap*) and **Casa Avião**, ✆ 432992 (*very cheap*). Both are adequate though rather basic.

Twenty km from Amarante, off the main road east to Vila Real, the **Pousada de São Gonçalo**, ✆ 461123 (*category B*), is perched 850m up the Serra do Marão. It takes advantage of stunning views of infertile hills, although the peace has been shattered by the first stage of the Oporto–Bragança motorway. The *pousada* is provided with reproduction furniture, in rustic style.

Turismo de Habitação

Casa de Pascoaes, São João de Gatão, ✆ 422595 (*expensive*), is a handsome house facing the Serra do Marão and perched next to the River Tamega and a Roman bridge. Inside, the story continues, with elegant bedrooms often featuring four-poster beds and antique furniture. There is also a museum in which the belongings of the poet Teixeira de Pascoaes are displayed.

Casa do Obra, Fregim, ☎ 425907 (*moderate*) is about 5km out of Amarante and located in a lush estate, awash with vines. The manor house has a curiously triangular outline and perfect symmetry characteristic of French designs from colonial Brazil. Nearby is Amadeo de Sousa-Cardoso's house.

Casa de Aboadela, Aboadela, ☎ 441141 (*inexpensive*) is 9km from Amarante, in the beautiful village of Aboadela, with mountains on one side and impossibly green landscape on the other. The house has few rooms, but its simple style, exhilarating views and low price make it worth a stay.

Amarante ☎ (055–)   ***Eating Out***

Zé da Calçada, Rua 31 de Janeiro, ☎ 422023 (*expensive*), is the upmarket place to eat, furnished like a drawing room, with round rugs for round tables, candlesticks, a fireplace, and plates on the walls. The views are great but the menu is not—the specialities of the house are rarely available, and you may have a choice of only three fish dishes, all of which are fried. **Restaurant Navarras**, Centro Comercial Navarras, ☎ 431036 (*moderate*) is approached through the shopping centre, with views of the street below. It lacks atmosphere, although the food is passable and in half-portions can be surprisingly cheap. **Restaurante Almirante**, Largo Conselheiro António Cândido, ☎ 432566 (*moderate*) has bowls of colourful flowers on the tables and a nice atmosphere. Try the loin of ox with mushrooms. **Restaurante Amaranto**, Murtos Madalena, ☎ 422006 (*cheap*) is a relatively large, wood-panelled place with friendly and giggly service. All three fish dishes are excellent.

Arouca

The village of Arouca is set amongst wooded mountains 55km southeast of Oporto. It's worth a look if you are passing, but don't bother making a special trip to see it. The village was founded by Julius Caesar in the 1st century AD, destroyed by the Moors in 716, and in the early 10th century was chosen as the site for a convent, which is now the **convent of Santa Maria**. The Infanta Dona Mafalda, daughter of Dom Sancho I and ex-wife of the 12-year-old Henry I of Castile, took her vows here in 1220. She later took charge of the convent, bringing it into the Cistercian order. Her body was found uncorrupt in 1616, and is now contained on the right-hand side of the main altar, in an ebony, silver and bronze casket of 1792, about the time when she was beatified. Most of the conventual buildings were reconstructed in the 18th century, with a remarkably austere façade that belies the wealth of the church, in particular its magnificent organ and gilded choir stalls of 1725. The convent's museum contains various paintings, silver, tapestries and furniture.

The Beiras

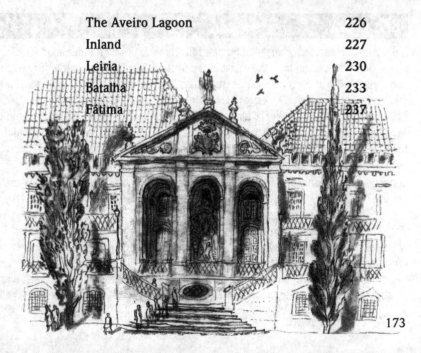

The Beiras occupy almost all the land between the Rivers Douro and Tagus. This vast territory is diverse, and separates into three provinces: Beira Litoral (the Coastal Beira); Beira Alta (the Upper Beira); and Beira Baixa (the Lower Beira).

History

Before the Romans arrived in Portugal, Lusitanian tribespeople inhabited the *Montes Herminios*, which probably corresponds to the eastern slopes of the Serra da Estrêla, in Beira Alta. Hannibal remarked that the people had always lived following their sheep on the mountains with no hope of reward for their perils and fatigues. So many people abandoned their difficult lives in these hills that the eastern Beiras became alarmingly depopulated, and in 1185, in the wake of Leonese aggression, Dom Sancho I launched a resettlement scheme which focused on the restoration of the ancient towns of Covilhã, Guarda and Idanha.

Napoleon's forces entered the Beiras in 1807 under Junot, *en route* for Lisbon. In August 1810 Masséna led 66,000 troops into Portugal through the Beiras, occupying Guarda and Viseu, but their westward march was interrupted by Wellington at Buçaco.

Getting Around

The road network is adequate, and most roads are good. Pampilhosa serves as the Beiras' central railway junction, with connections to the east and on a north–south axis. A railway line runs from Guarda to Castelo Branco via Covilhã—otherwise, the inland Beiras are not well served by the rail network. Similarly, the express bus network is much more comprehensive near the coast, with Coimbra serving as a staging-post for numerous north–south routes.

Beira Alta

Beira Alta is a succession of small granite hills hemmed in by mountains, including the jagged Serra do Caramulo to the east and the massive Serra da Estrêla, the highest mountain range in Portugal, to the southeast. Peaking at just under 2000m, and being a mere 100km from the ocean, the Serra da Estrêla receives an annual rainfall of up to 2500mm. This nurtures a thick blanket of pine trees and supplies the region's rivers, including the Mondego—the only river that is Portuguese from its source to the sea—which run through flat-bottomed valleys from the northeast to the southwest. Rainfall diminishes farther inland, where the thin soil supports few crops.

Settlements are scattered, or grouped in small clusters, and traditionally employ the local granite. To the east the smallholdings support maize and pasture land, whereas to the west the local diet is more dependent on chestnuts, potatoes, and rye bread. In his *Tragicomedia Pastoríl da Serra da Estrêla*, the dramatist Gil Vicente (c. 1470–c. 1536) writes of Lopo, a shepherd who breaks into song and dance 'in the manner of those of the mountains'. But these lapses are not frequent, and the people of Beira Alta seem more sombre and less friendly than those elsewhere. If you want to ingratiate yourself with the locals, you could always try praising the excellent Serra cheese, made from goats' milk.

Very few tourists visit Beira Alta, because even in the large towns there are few monuments of note, and decent accommodation is sparse. But the strange, unpeopled landscapes will appeal to explorers, from the peculiar magnetism of the Serra da Estrêla, to the barren lands pelted with boulders farther to the northeast.

Dão Wines

The southwest of Beira Alta—including Aguiar da Beira, Gouveia, Arganil, Mortágua, Tondela and parts of Viseu—has been demarcated as the Dão wine region, the second most productive in Portugal, named after a minor tributary of the Mondego. Dão reds mature into some of the country's most delicious wines, smooth, full-bodied, and garnet-coloured. Fortunately, 90 per cent of the wine is red, and this is of a far superior quality to the white. Be a bit wary of the young wines, which can taste oddly tannic.

The region is almost entirely granite, though the rock varies in hardness. The scattered plots of some 40,000 farmers are generally terraced, ideally at an altitude of 200–500m, though some vineyards are as high as 800m. The vintage usually begins in late September, at the end of the scorching, dry summer, and before the driving, snowy winter sets in. Most Dãos are matured and blended outside the region: by law, reds must be matured in the cask for a minimum of 18 months, though many remain there for two to four years. Though it is not indicated on the labels, the most balanced wines are produced in oak casks cut from the Forest of Buçaco or the Serra da Estrêla. There is great consistency between the labels—if you like one, you'll like them all—because companies buy from the same suppliers. They are widely available and inexpensive.

Viseu

The capital of Beira Alta commands a plateau on the southern bank of the River Pavia, set at 500m amidst hills forested with Scotch pines, interspersed with gorse, ferns and vineyards. If the wealthy residents of 16th-century Viseu were to wander the town today, they would find much that is familiar. It was they who colonized the upper part of town around the cathedral, and many of their salubrious houses still stand, in wide streets; only the roofs look higgledy-piggledy. This antique part of town focuses on the lovely Praça da Sé, in which the visitor is sandwiched between the very dignified 18th-century façade of the *Misericórdia* and that of the once-Romanesque cathedral. To one side is the plain granite episcopal palace, which houses the Grão-Vasco museum. The modern heart of Viseu stands about 200m distant—as if out of respect—where it operates efficiently around the uncommonly leafy Praça da República.

History

The Romans chose this site for a military camp—the largest yet discovered in Portugal. Close to their roads to Conimbriga, Lamego and other towns, it also offered them relatively easy access to the coastal plain—via the valleys of the Rivers Mondego and Vouga, combined with the benefits of a large, fertile plateau.

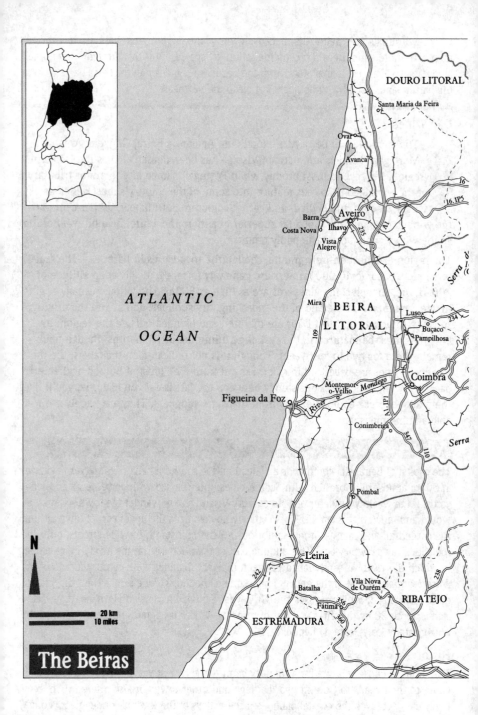

The Beiras

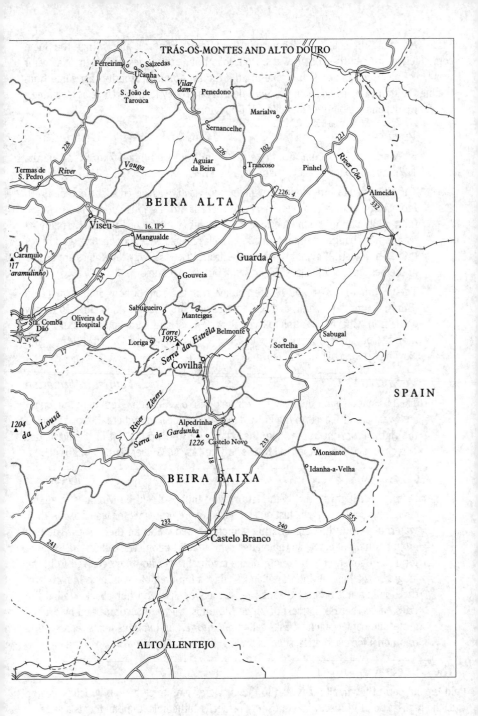

Viseu was made the seat of a bishopric in the mid-6th century, after which the Suevi completely destroyed the Roman walls; Dom João I built new ones. Henry the Navigator was Duke of Viseu, and was thus able to milk the economic prosperity that came from trading the transhumant flocks of the Serra da Estrêla. Today its importance as a commercial centre depends upon the production of Dão wines.

Viseu ✆ (032–) — Getting There

By **road**, Viseu is 85km from Aveiro, 94km from Coimbra, 77km from Guarda, 127km from Oporto, and 110km from Vila Real.

The **railway station**, along with all lines to Viseu, was closed at the end of 1990. From Lisbon, change at Nelas, where there is a direct bus connection to Viseu (min. 4½hrs total). From Oporto, change at either Aveiro or Pampilhosa, followed by another change at either Sernada or Nelas respectively, connecting with buses (min. 3hrs total). If planning your route from Viseu, railway timetables are posted in the bus station so it's possible to work out connections.

The CP **bus** routes, ✆ 27205, are simpler, running from Lisbon (5¼hrs) via Leiria (3hrs), Coimbra (1½hrs), and S. Comba Dão (¾hr). In the other direction, they come from Chaves (3½hrs), via Vila Real (2¼hrs) and Lamego (1¼hrs). In some months, on some days of the week, a CP bus runs from Oporto (2¾hrs) and Covilhã (2½hrs) via Guarda (1¾hrs).

Viseu ✆ (032–) — Tourist Information

The bus station is on the busy Av. António José de Almeida. From here, turn right and walk uphill. To get to the Praça da República, bear left where the road veers to the right. From the Praça, take the Av. 25 de Abril to the left of the Igreja dos Terceiros, and fork left for the **tourist office** (Av. C. Gulbenkian, ✆ 422014).

Festivals

During a drought in the 17th century, the millers of Vil de Moinhos, a village straddling the River Pavia just outside Viseu, were desperate for water to run their watermills—but the neighbouring farmers needed water for their crops. The two groups could not agree, so the matter went to arbitration. The millers prayed to St John the Baptist, and in honour of the favourable verdict they received from the judge, on 24 June, St John the Baptist's day, a hundred of them dress in parody of the nobility and process through the streets of Viseu on horseback. Called the *cavalhadas* (herd of horses) of Vil de Moinhos, they are accompanied by drums, grotesque papier-mâché masks called *gigantones*, and various floats representing traditional local activities, such as sawing pine wood by hand.

The Cathedral

In the old part of town, all roads lead to the dirty-grey granite cathedral, which is located at the highest point in Viseu. Like most of Portugal's cathedrals, the building is a salad of styles: a mannerist façade, dated 1640 and niched with Evangelists, sits uncomfortably between two defensive Romanesque towers which are themselves topped with 18th-century minarets. The cavernous interior is a more elegant affair: 12th-century columns support the church's most interesting feature, the Manueline ceiling tracery representing ropes, which have been knotted loosely like pastry since 1513. Bishop Dom João de Melo tampered with the chancel in the late 17th century; now it is bathed in a yellow light, through which peer dark mermen painted on the ceiling—and the bishop, when he graces his rich throne of Brazilian jacaranda wood. A splendid 18th-century gilt retable glitters in replacement of Grão-Vasco's canvases, removed to the museum next door. A corridor decorated with 18th-century *azulejos* leads to the sacristy—if the door is locked, look through the keyhole at the wooden ceiling painted with exotic birds, whose extravagant plumage would no doubt be plucked by the cherubs, were they more nimble.

A staircase leads from the north transept, on the left of the church, to the *coro alto* and its delightfully carved choir stalls. These are ornamented by embryonic creatures and mask-like faces, as well as a turtle, a whale and, most excitingly, a duck-billed platypus —evidence, to some, that the Portuguese discovered Australia around 250 years before Captain Cook. Lest the little creature's ego swell to continental proportions, it should be pointed out that its form may owe something to the description of a remora offered by the 15th-century chronicler, Azurara: 'another fish, no bigger than a mullet, which has upon the head a sort of crown by which it breathes, doing the office of gills'.

The *coro alto* opens on to the upper storey (*c.* 1730) of the formal, unmeditative cloister, of which the lower storey is interrupted by a late Romanesque/early Gothic portal, discovered in 1918. The upper cloister leads to the chapter house, which is remorselessly decorated with 18th-century *azulejos* depicting Herod's murder of the Innocents. Here is housed the **Cathedral Museum**. One of the curators is determined to lighten the tone, so he makes objects disappear and does other magic tricks between his explanations of precious crosses and a pontifical cloak of white satin bordered with gold. Ask if he'll take you onto the roof, of seemingly uncut, humped granite. In the museum, note especially the two small 13th-century Limoges chests, of turquoise enamelled copper and gilt.

The Museu de Grão-Vasco

Open 9.30–12.30 and 2–5.30; closed Mon and holidays.

The Museu de Grão-Vasco is installed in the bishop's palace, adjacent to the cathedral. During his lifetime, Vasco Fernandes, called Grão-Vasco (*c.* 1475–*c.* 1540), was the most outstanding painter in northern Portugal, rivalled only by Gaspar Vaz. Frei Carlos was working in Lisbon, and together they helped to introduce the Renaissance to Portuguese painting. Viseu is proud of its adopted son; Grão-Vasco is first mentioned in the town in 1501, and he owned a house here from 1512 until the end of his life. His work in Viseu postdates the retable for the cathedral at Lamego, and shows a deeper, fuller style.

On the second floor of the museum, Grão-Vasco's monumental painting of St Peter portrays the apostle as a stern but human Renaissance bishop, with a Portuguese face; his painting of St Sebastian is set against the architecture and landscape of Flanders. Also displayed in the museum are 14 zesty panels following the life of Christ, intended for the cathedral retable: for this work, the master was assisted by his pupils, who were evidently trained in the lively use of reds and yellows. Balthasar has travelled a long way to present his gift to the baby Jesus: at the adoration of the Magi, he is depicted wearing the feathers and pantaloons of an Indian wise man from newly discovered Brazil.

Also displayed upstairs are works by 19th-century naturalists—including Alfredo Morais, Marques de Oliveira, and Malhoa. Elsewhere, there are carved ivories from Central Africa, and swirling Baroque polychrome figures.

Around the Cathedral Square

The **Misericórdia** forms a third side of the cathedral square. Its well-proportioned granite and whitewash structure, with two towers, was designed by António da Costa and dates from 1775.

Head under the arch by the cathedral square, and when the road forks, bear left for the small **Casa-Museu de Almeida Moreira**, who was the director of the Grão-Vasco Museum during the First World War, and bequeathed his house and its contents to the town. Nothing is roped off, nor need it be: the collections of furniture, ceramics and 19th-century paintings are, on the whole, unremarkable.

The Cava de Viriato

On the edge of town across the road from the railway station is an octagonal enclosure dotted with trees: the embankments of the Cava de Viriato were thrown up by a Roman military legion after the campaign of Brutus Callaicus in 138 BC. There's not a great deal to see, except a statue of Viriatus, the Lusitanian guerrilla leader associated with the place on no decent evidence. (Viriatus roused the tribes of the Arevaci, the Belli and the Titti against the Romans, thus reviving the Celt-Iberian wars. Diodorus brings him to life by reporting Viriatus' warning to the citizens of the city of Tucci, who chopped and changed their allegiance between the Lusitanians and the Proconsul Servilianus some time after 141 BC. Viriatus told them of the middle-aged man who went bald because he had two wives: the younger wife plucked out his grey hairs to make him look younger, and the older wife plucked out his dark hairs to make him look as old as her. Thus Viriatus warned the fickle that they would be destroyed by both masters.)

Viseu ✆ (032–)   ***Where to Stay***

 ★★★★**Hotel Grão Vasco**, Rua Gaspar Barreiros, ✆ 423511, ✉ 426444 (*expensive*), offers garden views in a central location near the Praça da República, with an oval swimming pool and staff who try hard to please the mostly Portuguese clientele. The bedrooms and their reproduction furniture are fine, and the bar is conducive to long conversations. In summer, meals are served on the terrace, in winter in the cool, overlaid dining room, which serves local dishes such as roast leg of veal. Across the Parque da Cidade from the tourist office, the more modern ★★★**Hotel Moinho de Vento**, 13 Rua Paulo Emílio, ✆ 424116, ✉ 429662 (*moderate*), abounds with gadgets. The service is pleasant, and breakfast is a buffet.

Characterful **★★Pensão Rossio Parque**, 55 Rua Soar de Cima, ✆ 422085 (*inexpensive*)—next to the Jardim Major Teles—is a fun place to stay, furnished with old knick-knacks and old-fashioned fittings. **★★★Hotel Bela Vista**, 510 Rua Alexandre Herculano, ✆ 422026 (*inexpensive*) is new and perfectly nice, though a little soulless. It has a private car park. Right by the river (which may well be dry), **★★★Residencial Lusitano**, 167 Avenida Emidio Navarro, ✆ 423042 (*cheap*) is good value; rooms are decent, the staff friendly and helpful.

Turismo de Habitação

In Rebordinho, 6km south of Viseu, **Casa de Rebordinho**, ✆ 461258 (*expensive–moderate*) is a peaceful granite and whitewash manor house fronted by its staircase, set in a working farm. Ducks walk across the courtyard, and cows moo. It's furnished with white sofas around the fireplace, Arraiolos rugs on the terracotta floor, hunting prints and lots of flowers. Ground-floor bedrooms are bright and pretty, behind barred windows. Two of the four bedrooms do not have *en suite* bathrooms. The garden contains a Romanesque falcon house, and a 300-year-old rhododendron tree. Apart from breakfast, meals are not normally available.

Quinta de S. Caetano, Viseu, ✆ 423984 (*moderate*) is a distinguished manor house with a splendid chapel dating from 1638. Once the home of the Viscountess of St Caetano, it was the setting of contemporary novelist Augustina Bessa Luis' *Eugénia e Silvina*. The garden hosts a hundred-year-old Atlantic cedar and overlooks the Estrêla mountains. All this added to the simple and elegant feel of the interior of the house, and the good regional food, makes for a comfortable stay.

Viseu ✆ (032–)   **Eating Out**

Trave Negra, 40 Rua dos Loureiros, ✆ 26138 (*expensive*), lit by lanterns and candles, is elegant and quiet. The appetizer platter of cheeses and smoked meats is excellent. There is a fixed-price menu; entrées include veal casserole or roast kid.

Intimate and attractive, granite-walled **O Cortiço**, 47 Rua do Hilário, ✆ 423853 (*moderate*)—just down from the statue of Dom Duarte—offers good food served by grumpy waiters. A couple of doors further up, **Varanda da Sé**, 55 Rua Augusto Hilário, ✆ 421135 (*moderate*) has been decorated with stark, modern colours, a bit like a chain-store pizza house, but it serves good squid and delicious seafood soup (more seafood than soup).

Up the Rua Alexandre Herculano, **Cacimbo** is at No.95, ✆ 422894 (*cheap*) packed with stern-looking locals intent on watching evening TV. A roast suckling pig disappears from the window in portions.

Around Viseu

Termas de São Pedro do Sul

It's refreshing to find a **spa** that has got its act together. Four km southwest of the town of São Pedro do Sul, itself some 22km northwest of Viseu, the healing waters are channelled through an impressive modern complex (✆ 032 71070) on the bank of the River Vouga, and have spawned an array of accommodation, in an airy setting delightfully encroached by pine trees.

The efficiently run spa treats over 10,600 patients throughout the year, for rheumatism, bronchitis, sinusitis, and gout. Treatments normally last two to three weeks, and may include immersion in carbonic baths, lying on a surface slit to allow strips of steam to penetrate through, Turkish baths, a swimming pool for subaquatic douches, and a gym for physiotherapy. Some doctors speak English, and, unlike other spas, the place does not feel like an asylum. There is an initial consultation fee, and a water tax, on top of which patients are charged for individual treatments.

It was the Romans who first appreciated the waters here. They built baths at the time of Emperor Tiberius, but the plug has been pulled from their building complex, which lies in ruins beside its modern equivalent. In the 12th century Dom Afonso Henriques recuperated here from an injury received at Badajoz.

✆ *(032–)*   ***Where to Stay***

There are many places to stay in Termas de S. Pedro do Sul. **★★Hotel Vouga**, Estrada Nacional, ✆ 711263 (*moderate*), is light and airy, perhaps because it is so bare, with balconies overlooking the river.

The Serra do Caramulo

West of Viseu, the Serra do Caramulo shields much of the inland Beiras from the coastal plain; its granite and precambrian schist support a thick cloak of Scotch pine, with rhododendrons and the occasional orchid. The otherwise undramatic range rises to a peak at Caramulinho, at 1074m. It makes a pleasant drive, in spite of the condition of some of the roads. Keep an eye open for women wearing the *capucha*, a hooded black cape which makes them look like goblins, but is intended to stave off the cold and rain.

Caramulo itself is around 43km southwest of Viseu, depending on which route you take. It perches at 800m, an altitude which led the village to be developed in the 1930s as a health resort for sufferers from tuberculosis. There are no special facilities, as one may simply inhale the benefits—this may explain the local bidding, now used infrequently, 'that the blessing of the mountain may accompany you home'.

This remote spot is an unlikely resting place for the excellent **Fundação Abel de Lacerda**, ✆ 032 86270, a miscellaneous collection of painting, sculpture, furniture, silver, archaeology and tapestries. The last category is represented by five early 16th-century Tournai tapestries depicting the first Portuguese in India, complete with weird animals and natives evidently based on garbled reports. There are works by Grão-Vasco and Frei Carlos; Picasso and Dali presented minor pieces to the museum, and Queen Elizabeth II donated a painting by Sutherland.

A road leads uphill from Caramulo, past little granite houses, to the peak of **Caramulinho**. At 1075m, it offers huge 180° views of lesser heights, and is a gentle hour's walk away from town.

About 12km south of Caramulo, a thickly wooded mountainside provides the backdrop for bushy orange trees and a cluster of terracotta roofs, earning the village of **Castelões** the epithet 'the Sintra of the Beiras'. It's a good place for brief walks, as is the **Reserva Botánica de Loendros** at **Cambarinho**, 20km north of Caramulo, just past the village of Campia. In this hilly territory, the horizons are closer, and the land tickled by little streams. The best time to go is in May, when the rhododendrons flower, though their numbers have been depleted by forest fires.

The road veers northeast, and 14km later passes through the larger village of **Vouzela**, of which the only notable feature is the 13th-century **parish church**. Its gutter is supported by carvings of nightmarish human faces, as well as animals and angels, and the bell tower is separate from the church.

℡ *(032–)*   **Where to Stay**

In Caramulo, the **Pousada de São Jerónimo**, ℡ 861291, ℡ 861640 (*category B*), looks like a suburban chalet, with a kidney-shaped swimming pool. The six bedrooms are attractively decorated and homey, with far views from their balconies, and polished granite bathrooms. The dining room takes advantage of the views; diners sit on rustic chairs talking across monastic candlesticks, eating rather plain meals. Also in Caramulo there's the ***Pensão São Cristóvão**, Av. Dr. Jerónimo Lacerda, ℡ 861394 (*cheap*).

Mangualde

Roughly 18km east of Viseu, the little town of Mangualde is surrounded by vineyards and orchards, especially crab-apple trees. Its most distinguished building stands on the extreme south side of town: the splendid **Palácio dos Condes de Anadia** (*open 3–6pm when the owners are in residence, from 9am when they are not; ring the bell and be patient*).

The palace is distinguished by the rigid symmetry of its street façade—but each face of the building is different, including a loggia overlooking the courtyard. It was built in 1740, for the Count of Anadia. His descendants' nanny has clocked up 30 years of service, but her aprons have lost none of their starch as she proudly shows visitors around. She drops her voice in the marvellous kitchen glinting with copper pans, and conspiratorially swaps recipes. There are some lovely handpainted ceilings, Sèvres statues, and various family portraits—the best are in the ballroom, an airy room lined with the most curious *azulejos* in Portugal. They depict a world of reversals: the sun and moon are within the ground, buildings are on clouds; a donkey flogs a man, horses ride men and joust; a man tends his baby while a woman totes a musket. The huge double staircase is sided with ladies and their massive hairdos hunting on horseback, and on panels of the elements, winds puff out their cheeks almost until they pop.

The road to Gouveia, southeast of Mangualde, is a good route into the Serra da Estrêla.

Guarda

The northeastern tip of the Serra da Estrêla is host to the highest town in Portugal: Guarda stands at 1056m, and on clear days it offers views stretching across the plains as far as the Spanish border. Dom Sancho I founded it here in 1199 for just that reason, and chose it to be the successor to the Visigothic episcopal seat of Egitânia. Its name and its ruined castle refer to Guarda's rôle as a frontier-guard; it became known as the city of the four F's: *Fria, Farta, Forte* and *Feia*—cold, well-supplied, strong and ugly. The second of these epithets refers to Guarda's fair, established in 1255. The success of the fair was so important to the welfare of the settlement that all those who came to it were exempt from civil or criminal liability for 30 days; their merchandise included linseed and iron, as well as wine, grain and livestock. Wellington used Guarda as a base for his operations in 1811–12.

The sloping town is charmless and unlovely because it feels bleak and exposed, and when it's cold, people are quite literally wrapped up in themselves. (Dozing beneath local wool blankets is like sleeping with a sheep.) There's little of interest about the place, but several good restaurants and a decent range of accommodation make it a good base from which to explore a wide area, particularly to the north and east.

Guarda © *(071–)*   ***Getting There***

By **road**, Guarda is 140km from Aveiro, 193km from Bragança, 100km from Castelo Branco, 229km from Oporto, and 77km from Viseu.

There are two **train** lines from Lisbon to Guarda (© 211565), but only the more northerly route (6hrs total), via Coimbra-B (3¼hrs) and Pampilhosa (3hrs), is direct. The southerly route runs via Santarém (6½hrs), Castelo Branco (4hrs) and Covilhã, where you have to change (1¼hrs), and takes 7½hrs total. Both run four times daily. From Oporto, Espinho and Aveiro, change at Pampilhosa. From Viseu, take the bus to Nelas (½hr), from where Guarda is 1¾hrs away.

Rede Express **buses** (© 217720) run with similar frequency, taking 6hrs from Lisbon, via Castelo Branco (2hrs) and Covilhã (¾hr). In some months, on some days of the week, RN Express buses run from Oporto (4½hrs) via Viseu (1¾hrs). Joalto, © 211976, also has regular services around the country.

Guarda © *(071–)*   ***Tourist Information***

The extremely helpful regional **tourist office**, © 221817 (*open 9–12.30 and 2–5.30*), is in the Camara Municipal. It has an abundance of information about the region and can help you plan walking and camping expeditions in the Serra da

Estrêla. The railway station is 4km out of town, but there are buses both ways every half-hour. The spanking new bus station is two roads downhill from the Hotel Turismo.

Around the Town

The grim granite **cathedral** took 150 years to build. Construction began in 1390, under the direction of the sons of Mateus Fernandes, architect of Batalha, whose influence is seen in the flying buttresses and the clerestory. Boitac worked on the building 1504–17, shortly before it was completed *c.* 1540. Despite this distinguished parentage and long gestation, the finished product is heavy, both inside and out, though the excellent gargoyles add a touch of wit—some of them have little legs sticking into the air. The interior lacks majesty, despite the twisted columns and high arches. The limestone retable attributed to João de Ruão is peopled by expressionless, insubstantial characters. Quite the opposite is true of the seats of the choir stalls: lift each one to reveal a face with a different expression—grimacing, tipsy, angry, lecherous, smiling. Maybe this is a sardonic comment on the choristers.

Downhill and to the right, the façade of the **Misericórdia** exults in the Baroque of the 18th century, with an elegant granite and whitewash façade. It was built on the site of the old cathedral, which was considered to be too close to the town walls for safety. The façade faces the best-preserved of Guarda's ancient gates, known as the **Torre dos Ferreiros** (the Blacksmiths' Tower). Of the castle itself, little but the keep remains. One block downhill from the *Misericórdia*, the seminary dates from 1601 and now houses the well-displayed **Regional Museum** (*closed Mon*). There's little worth seeing, except an adoration by two of the Magi attributed to the 16th-century master, Frei Carlos. Upstairs, ethnographic curiosities include clay models of traditional games, and a wooden sledge embedded with sharp stones, dragged to separate wheat from chaff.

Guarda ℱ (071–) **Where to Stay**

★★★**Hotel Turismo**, Av. Coronel Orlindo de Carvalho, ℱ 223366, ▨ 223399 (*expensive*)—by the lower end of the Jardim José de Lemos—is a pleasant country inn, large enough to accommodate the contents of a row of tour buses. It's efficient and solid, but parts are fraying. Frilled waitresses offer a very good charcoal grill in the large but not unattractive restaurant. The price of rooms varies with view and equipment. ★★★★**Pensão Residencial Filipe**, Rua Vasco da Gama, ℱ 223659 (*inexpensive*) has decent rooms though some are a bit small.

★★**Casa de Sé**, 17 Rua Augusto Gil, ℱ 212501 (*inexpensive*), is torn at the edges, but it's clean and retains a certain decrepit charm, helped by the cuddly landlady. **Pensão Moreira**, 47 Rua Mouzinho de Albuquerque, ℱ 214131 (*cheap*), is Guarda's newest *pension* and therefore appropriately clean and good-looking. It's OK if you can cope with the doorbell, which you always have to ring to get in and which plays the first three notes of 'Daisy, Daisy' or 'Jesus Christ, Superstar', depending on your imagination. ★★★**Pensão Alianca**, 8a Rua Vasco da Gama,

℗ 212931 (*cheap*) offers budget accommodation and a big smile. There is also a good cheap restaurant.

Turismo de Habitação

Solar de Alarcão, 25 Largo D. Miguel Alarcão, ℗ 214392 (*moderate*) is just uphill from the cathedral and has a promising exterior but is stuffed with bad reproductions. Still, there are nice touches—the emblazoned door drape, the carved dark-wood canopies in the salon. The suite is grand but lacklustre.

Quinta da Ponte, Faia, ℗ 926126 (*moderate*), is well situated in the Serra da Estrêla Park, by a Roman bridge over the River Mondego. The interior stays true to its 18th-century roots, with marzipan-style decorations, combining comfort with a certain grandeur.

Guarda ℗ (071–)	*Eating Out*

Typically Portuguese, **Restaurant Belo Horizonte**, 1 Largo S. Vicente, ℗ 211454 (*cheap*), not to be confused with the *residencial* of the same name, is a family place that shyly serves enormous helpings of delicious food. **Restaurant d'Oliveira**, 1 Rua do Encontro, ℗ 214446 (*moderate*), is also family-run, and worth a visit, if only for its huge rolls. *Both closed Sat.*

Pao Quente bakes good bread opposite the *Misericórdia*. At the top of the cathedral square, **O Ferinho**, 21-23 Rua Francisco do Passos, ℗ 211990, serves good breakfasts and teas. *Closed Sun.*

Northeast of Guarda: the Ribacôa

The road north of Guarda follows the upper edge of the Parque Natural da Serra de Estrêla, through the wide, gently sloping valley of the infant River Mondego. The route is more curvaceous than road maps indicate. North of Celorico da Beira the landscape becomes bare and severe, though stretches of the road are lined with poplars, and with ash and eucalyptus north of Freches.

Trancoso

Some 43km north of Guarda, Trancoso is sited on a hill spur at an altitude of 880m. Much of the town is contained within battlemented curtain walls, which were thrown up by Dom Dinis in the 13th century, so that the town could serve as a base from which to conquer the lands of the Ribacôa, the valley of the River Côa. Trancoso held a special place in Dom Dinis' heart: it was here that he married Isabel of Aragon in 1282. The town was draped with rich wall hangings and branches of ash, but it was the carpet of rose petals that particularly delighted the 12-year-old bride. Dom Dinis presented her with Trancoso as a wedding gift.

The visionary cobbler known as Bandarra (1500–45) composed his *Trovas* in Trancoso. These popular verses were instrumental in creating the messianic cult of Sebastianism, which became widespread during the years of Spanish domination.

Trancoso is a good place to wander around. It's a time warp, a town of wrought-iron balconies and granite casements, where emblazoned *palácios* elbow tiny hovels. Only the web of electricity cables catches at modernity. To the north of the town, the formidable **castle** walls enclose a grassy oval space overlooked by the squat keep, which was also the work of the indefatigable Dom Dinis. In the centre of the walled town, a caged Manueline **pillory** stands in front of the **church of São Pedro**. Appropriately for St Peter, the weathervane is a lion.

Marialva

Seventeen km northeast of Trancoso, the ruined walled village of Marialva occupies a low hillslope overlooking its modern namesake and beyond to the plains of Beira Alta. Crowded with ghosts, the dead village is contained within the walls of a castle built by Dom Sancho I in 1200. It retains its grandeur, though it is covered with weeds and sprinkled with dark rubble and low boulders. Paths of yellowing grass run between former dwellings with empty windows and half-built walls, past olive trees. The 16th-century Igreja Matriz is locked. The Marquis of Távora was governor of Marialva when Pombal condemned him to death in 1759, for alleged conspiracy against the king. The settlement appears to have been tarred with the same brush.

Pinhel

Some 36km east of Trancoso and 34km northeast of Guarda, the attractive and isolated town of Pinhel lies between two tributaries of the River Côa. Dom Afonso Henriques wrested it from the Moors in 1179; subsequently, it has seen little action, apart from stirring itself to greet Catherine of Bragança in 1692. Dom Dinis fortified the settlement in 1312, but much of the town wall was dismantled to build houses.

Two light-stone square castle towers remain, the more northerly with a discrete Manueline window and a Gothic gargoyle. Its twin was used as a prison until recently. The modest 14th-century Gothic **Castle Church of Santa Maria** is contemporary with its Ançâ-stone sculpture from the Coimbra School, attributed to Diogo Pires the Elder: the Holy Mothers are extravagantly draped in white robes. In the chancel, 14 15th-century paintings illustrate the life of the Virgin. The **municipal museum**, Praça de Sacadura Cabral (*open weekdays 10–12 and 2–6*), is fairly humble, but the retable of 1537 is worth a look. It features a quartet of angels playing musical instruments.

Pinhel is the necessary kicking-off point for Almeida if you're dependent on public transport.

© *(071–)*   ***Where to Stay***

 Residencial Falcão, Av. Presidente Carneiro de Gusmão, © 43004 (*very cheap*), and **Residencial Pinhelense**, © 42373 (*cheap*), are the only places to stay—there's not much to chose between them, though the Pinhelense serves quite good meals.

Almeida

Roughly 22km southeast of Pinhel, the beautiful and unspoilt fortified village of Almeida is well worth a visit. The village is surrounded by a bizarre wilderness of plains pelted with boulders. Extraordinarily, the town is contained within star-shaped fortifications, a border fortress whose strength is second only to that of Elvas in the Alentejo.

Dom Sancho I conquered Almeida from the Moors in the 12th century. Such was its strategic importance that the site was refortified three times, by Dom Dinis, Dom Manuel, and Dom João VI. Almeida was captured by the Spanish in 1762, during the Seven Years War, but later in that century it was rebuilt on a Vaubanesque plan—indeed Vauban himself is believed to have completed the works, which have a perimeter of 2.5km. The French took control of the stronghold twice: from the beginning of the Peninsular War until the Convention of Sintra; and in 1810, when Masséna managed to blow up the central magazine.

℗ *(071–)*

Where to Stay and Eating Out

A tinkling horsecart tours the town for guests at the new **Pousada da Senhora das Neves**, ℗ 574283, @ 54320 (*category C*), which has been insensitively dumped on the highest part of the town. There are two *residencials* both by the crossroads outside the fort: **A Muralha**, ℗ 574357, and **Morgado**, ℗ 574412. Both offer decent rooms and are *inexpensive*.

A Tertúlia is run by the same people who manage the Residencial Morgado and serves fine food in a friendly atmosphere (*moderate*). The Pousada has an expensive restaurant. Otherwise there's not too much choice. Ask around.

Castelo Rodrigo

The road north from Almeida passes olive trees and large vineyards, a dry landscape with distant horizons. Castelo Rodrigo lies 19km distant.

This picturesque village mellows and decays beside the Serra da Marofa, a clutch of small-windowed dwellings contained within the broken walls and fat towers of a smashed castle. The castle and its manorial residence were set on fire by indignant locals in the 16th century, disgusted at the traitorous behaviour of Cristóvão Moura, first Marquis of Castelo Rodrigo. He had been instrumental in securing the crown of Portugal for Philip II of Spain.

In the late 14th century, Castelo Rodrigo had sworn allegiance to Beatriz, Queen of Castile, and refused entry to Dom João I. He punished the settlement by decreeing that its coat of arms should always be displayed upside down.

Northwest of Guarda

From Trancoso a leafy road leads northwest through the Serras da Lapa and de Leomil to Lamego and the Alto Douro.

Aguiar da Beira

Some 25km west of Trancoso, it's difficult to tell whether humans or animals live behind medieval doorways in the old part of Aguiar de Beira. Look for telltale straw. The town fountain is surmounted by a roofless granite chamber edged with stone benches, which probably dates from the late 13th century, and may have filled the same rôle as the 12th-century council-chamber at Bragança.

Around the Barragem de Vilar

Twenty-nine km northwest of Trancoso, just southeast of the Barragem de Vilar, the village of **Sernancelhe** boasts a fine pillory topped with a cage, dated 1559. Nearby, the portal of the 13th-century romanesque **Igreja Matriz** is flanked on either side by a niche containing three small sculptures, forming some of the finest Romanesque granite carving in the country. The four Evangelists, St Peter and St Paul wear togas. The portal itself features an arch of angels standing on top of one another. Within, there's not much to look at, except for a tomb depicting a lady on a dragon.

It's possible to swim in the sand-fringed **Barragem de Vilar**, a large man-made lake damming the River Távora, equidistant from Trancoso and Lamego. East of the lake, the village of **Fonte Arcada** worships in a Romanesque **Igreja Matriz**, which was restored in 1502. It contains good Flemish-style paintings of the Passion, and part of the construction appears to use living rock. Thirteen km northeast of the Barragem, the photogenic triangular **castle at Penedono** is worthy of Macbeth: built on a rock outcrop, and mottled with lichen, its crenellated towers are like claws.

Around Tarouca

Nine km northwest of the Barragem de Vilar, a turning south of the main road at Mondim da Beira follows a little trout-filled river to the important monastery church at **São João de Tarouca**. It was the first Cistercian monastery in Portugal, founded in 1124, and has subsequently been filled with delightful oddities. A guide insists on reporting what century these date from; sometimes it's possible to escape from him. Among the vivid paintings from the school of Grão-Vasco is one attributed to the master himself, hung over the third altar to the right of the nave.

Lift the seats of the choir stalls carved from Brazilian wood, to reveal the polished cheeks of the cherubs, against which weary choristers could prop their buttocks. In the chancel, excellent 18th-century *azulejos* narrate the story of the monastery's foundation, complete with a thunderbolt sent to indicate the desired site. The careful use of space and strong blue colouring are combined with a splendid attention to detail, right down to rabbits chomping leaves. Less contented animals appear on the granite tomb of Pedro, Count of Barcelos and illegitimate son of Dom Dinis. Dating from 1354, it depicts a wild boar hunt. Perhaps it was the excitement of the scene that led the gentleman on the front of the organ to wave his arms and open his mouth whenever the organ was played. Considerably less nimble is the whopping 14th-century granite statue of the Virgin, who weighs in at 1000kg. In the sacristy, all 4700 pictorial tiles are different.

One km east of Trancoso, a minor road runs north to the village of **Ucanha**, which is notable for its **fortified bridge**. The bridge itself is odd because it rises to a pointed peak, rather than being flat or humped. The stocky tower that defends it was built by the Abbot of Salzedas in 1465, probably to mark the entrance to the abbey's land, to serve as a customs post for taxes levied on produce, and to trumpet the wealth and importance of the abbey. The river at this point is shallow enough for women to do their laundry.

Small elder trees with dark, heavy leaves grow in the neighbourhood; the berries are harvested and the red dye exported. The minor road continues to **Salzedas**, where the importance of the **Cistercian Monastery** was superseded only by Alcobaça. It was built between 1168 and 1225, under the patronage of Teresa Afonso, widow of Egas Moniz and governess of the five children of Dom Afonso Henriques. The monastic buildings are ruined, but the church remains intact, though mercilessly 'modernized' in the 18th century. Today, the humble houses to the left of the monastery may be more interesting, with an alley right out of the Middle Ages, daub and all.

Returning to the main road to Lamego, a turning to the east just 4km north of Tarouca leads to Ferreirim, where the church of a Franciscan monastery contains panels attributed to Cristóvão de Figueiredo, Garcia Fernandes and Gregório Lopes. The road north to Lamego passes through vineyards and cultivated land, with isolated dwellings among rows of poplars and other trees.

The Serra da Estrêla

Stopping just short of 2000m, the Serra da Estrêla is the highest mountain range in Portugal, and forms a barrier across the centre of the country. They are old-fold mountains: the peaks are rounded and grassy, pelted with granite boulders, where deep, rocky glens split the gently sloping hillsides. There are deep glaciated valleys, with moraines as low as 700m, and glacial lakes. Snow lies on the heights from November to April, and being relatively near the Atlantic, the rainfall is as high as 2500mm. The climate is not so much extreme as variable, shifting quickly from rain to sun, and following only a loose annual pattern. The lower slopes are blanketed with pine and dotted with chestnut trees, though forest fires are common, leaving bald wastelands. Pinaster and birch grow higher up. Heather and broom thrive above the tree line, sometimes level with the clouds. Thousands of crocuses and narcissi flower at the end of April, in shades from deep purple to almost white; the dwarf shrubs flower six weeks later, in the middle of June.

The invigorating, massive views and the pure air make the Serra da Estrêla an excellent territory for walking—the problem, as elsewhere, is the lack of any decent walking map. There's a magnificent walk of 3–3½ hours over easy ground from Penhas Douradas (a winding 20km west of Manteigas) up the gently sloping main ridge, to the summit of Torre, 1993m.

© (075–)   ***Getting Around***

Be careful **driving** in the Serra: roads can be icy or wet, mist descends, and flimsy cars may get blown into the granite posts that line each road. The Gouveia–Manteigas road offers the most spectacular and impressive views in the mountains. From Guarda, the easiest way to approach the highest parts of the Serra is via Valhelhas, 20km southwest of the town. From Valhelhas, a road runs 17km west to Manteigas. Covilhã (Beira Baixa) is a good access point.

Public transport is a problem: **buses** run twice daily from Covilhã (Beira Baixa) to Seia, along the low route via Unhais da Serra, and there is a weekend bus service from Covilhã to Penhas da Saude.

Walking in the Parque Natural da Serra de Estrela, across some of Portugal's most rugged scenery and through some of her most isolated and traditional villages, is a hugely rewarding experience. Trails are easy to follow, and it's possible to spend anything from a day to a week in the park. Manteigas is the best base for **walking expeditions** in the Serra. The village has a very helpful information office, ℂ 982383/3, which sells hiking maps and provides other information about life in the Serra. They also organize guided walks. There are other park offices in Gouveia and Seia, and the regional tourist office in Guarda is also helpful, though they cannot provide maps. Skiers should head for Torre or Sabugueiro, where the Clube Nacional de Montanhismo, ℂ 323364, rents equipment.

Manteigas

The town of Manteigas is the most appealing in the Serra, nestled at the foot of sheer, pale hills, in the glaciated valley of the River Zêzere. The spa town takes pride in its appearance, with the town hall successfully offering incentives for homeowners to paint their

Life in the Serra

All the clustered settlements in the Serra had established themselves by the 16th century, though the isolated hamlets put down their roots more recently. The people of the Serra are sheep farmers, but from April to September they sow rye—a hardy cereal which is well suited to poor soil, and can survive high summer and low winter temperatures—as well as potatoes and a few vegetables. But it is the ewes' milk, wool and lambs that their livelihoods depend on; this is the milk which makes *queijo da Serra*, the superb creamy hard cheese with an 18cm diameter. It takes 4–6 litres of milk to make a single kilo of cheese.

Cheese-making takes place between November and April; many farmers—or more usually their wives—perform each stage of the process, from preparing the milk and rennet to curdling, salting and curing. But industrialization is creeping in, and the farmers are up against strict production requirements from the EU, and competition from other European cheeses. Many of them rent their properties—often just a single, windowless room walled with granite and schist—so there is little incentive to improve them. The thatch must be replaced every year, after the first rains. Around the settlements, or in the hills, it's common to see the *Cão da Serra*, a breed of dog peculiar to the area. They're big, loping things rolling with heavy fur, equipped with collars that bristle with nails, to prevent wolves tearing out their throats.

houses white. Small frogs hop about the place at night. The spa itself helps rheumatism, and is open 1 July–30 September. Two roads lead up into the hills: the forestry road is quicker, but scary. Both pass yew trees growing on the edge of the settlement. Joalta, © 071 211976, have two buses a day on weekdays between Guarda and Manteigas.

Manteigas © (075–)

Where to Stay and Eating Out

luxury

A winding 13km north of Manteigas, **Pousada de S. Lourenço**, © 982450, ● 982453 (*category C★*), perches with a view of the town. It's a harmonious, mellow mountain lodge overlooking smooth, fanning wooded mountains. Double-glazed bedrooms are small and simple beneath wood-planked ceilings, the receptionists dress traditionally, like Gretel, and the comfortable restaurant serves good food at nicely laid tables ornamented by hairy chestnut husks.

moderate

A couple of km from the centre of Manteigas, next to the spa, stands the solid ★★★**Hotel de Manteigas**, © 982400, which is operated by the proprietors of the *pousadas*, Enatur. But for the rush of the Zêzere nearby, it's unexcitingly bare and brown, with odd trellis furniture and blanket curtains. Shower rooms are attached. The bar is comfortably warmed by an open fire, the large restaurant striplit, favouring porks and veals. ★★★**Albegaria Berne**, Quinta de St. António, © 982114, ● 982114, is new, shiny and piney.

cheap

Back in town, ★★**Pensão Estrela**, 5 Rua Dr. Sobral, © 981288, is homey in parts; pumpkins ripen on the windowsills. The bedrooms are basic, and overlook the solar panels that heat the water, to a hill beyond. Gypsy scarves are draped over lamps in the restaurant, which offers stewed rump of veal, or a mixed *cozido serrano*. **Casa de S. Roque**, 67 Rua de Santo António, © 981125, calls itself *Turismo de Habitação*, but it's rather spartan. The best feature is the patio. **Restaurante Berne**, © 981351, is on the better side of ordinary, though the trout may be tasteless.

Gouveia

The road from Manteigas to Gouveia affords dramatic views. About 2km east of the Pousada de S. Lourenço, it passes through a weirdly prehistoric landscape of sandy heather strewn with boulders.

The joy of the little town of Gouveia lies in one of its regular taxis, a 1947 Chrysler De Soto. Invent any excuse to ride in this dream machine. There's an indifferent collection of paintings in the **Sala Abel Manta** (*open 9.30–12.30 and 2–5.30*), only worth a look if you have time to kill. Should you need to stay, ★★**Pensão Estrela do Parque**, 36 Rua da República, © 038 42171 (*cheap*), is charmingly old and dusty. Its restaurant serves quite good food. **Café Cruzeiro**, Avenida 25 de Abril, © 038 42498 (*very cheap*) also offers good budget accommodation.

Around Gouveia

Fifteenth-century houses line narrow cobbled streets in the charming hilltop village of **Linhares**, some 20km north of Gouveia. In the days of the Visigoths the village was a bishopric. The medieval castle offers magnificent views of the plains below.

Linhares ✆ (071–)   ***Where to Stay and Eating Out***

The **Restaurante Bar A Taberna** ✆ 776366 (*cheap*) has comfortable, un-tastefully decorated rooms, a restaurant and very friendly owners.

Seia and Around

The little town of Seia stands 28km southwest of Gouveia. It offers nothing of interest, other than a kicking-off point for a *pousada* and a restaurant.

Seia ✆ (038–)   ***Where to Stay and Eating Out***

 Twelve km southwest of Seia, the **Pousada de Santa Bárbara**, ✆ 52252 (*category C*), occupies the hamlet of Póvoa das Quartas, with bedrooms overlooking the valley. ★★★**Hotel Camelo**, 16 Rua 1 de Maio, ✆ 25555, ✉ 25550 (*moderate–inexpensive*), has a good reputation.

Nineteen km south of Seia, the **Café Montanha**, ✆ 93177 (*moderate*), in the hamlet of **Loriga**, provides hearty, tasty foods, the most delicious of which is the *bróa*, cakey cornbread that melts in your mouth.

Sabugeiro

Eight km east of Seia, Sabugeiro stands, at 1050m, just above the tree line. The old part of the village lies off the main road, remote enough for the 700-odd residents to stare at foreign visitors and instruct their dogs not to growl. Wizened crones lope about the place, shooing chickens with bald necks. Stones keep slates on the roofs of houses and pine branches on top of chicken coops.

Sabugeiro ✆ (038–)   ***Where to Stay and Eating Out***

 The most enjoyable part of the *Turismo de Habitação* at **Casas do Cruzeiro**, ✆ 22825 (*inexpensive*)—next to the church—is the kitchen, where *chouriço* sausages are smoked above the wood fire, and cheese matures in the larder. They smell of popcorn and must respectively. The apartments are low-ceilinged and done-up, a bit bare but OK. One supposedly sleeps six, with a fireplace and TV; there are two other apartments. There are a couple of *residencials* in the new part of the village.

Beside the main road, the rustic *tasca* **Casa Miralva**, ✆ 22629 (*cheap*), serves *miudos de cabrito* (kid giblets) and trout in vinegar, beneath horn lamps. The shop attached sells lovely woolly slippers, mostly in small sizes, sheepskin jackets, and fox pelts. The bar stocks tasty *aguardente zimbrada*, made from juniper berries.

Torre

One of the most forceful parts of the Serra lies southeast of Sabugueiro, just before Torre, around the great rock-cut image of the Virgin, **N.S. da Boa Estrêla**—there's something magnetic, almost cosmic, about the place.

Torre, the highest point in Portugal (1993m), is huddled with corrugated iron huts, from which tentative skiiers emerge. Just below the peak lie dams of drinking water, surrounded by rocks covered with electric-green lichen like some insecticide. The flat light illumines the birth of the River Zêzere, which becomes a tributary of the Tagus.

The road running southeast of Torre towards Covilhã passes through Penhas da Saude, with its campsite, its forbidding disused TB hospital, and its good **youth hostel**, ℂ 075 25375, which is closed in winter.

Sortelha

The tiny, peaceful village of Sortelha, roughly 40km south of Guarda and 33km northeast of Covilhã, is fixed in a landscape of granite boulders; the view from the castle bowls down to a tree-filled valley alive with the sound of running water, and beyond to mountains and plains.

Getting There

The drive south from Guarda or east from Belmonte (Beira Baixa) is beautiful; the only access by public transport is by local **bus**, which runs twice daily from Sabugal.

The old village is contained within the castle walls and built only of granite: houses have been constructed around protruding boulders, and are roofed with lichenous terracotta. A mere dozen people live here permanently. One of them attends a moth-eaten donkey as it wanders home in the luminous evening light, with a bunch of bright grass strapped to its side. The other buildings within the castle walls are second homes, or spartan *Turismo de Habitação*, as most residents live in the more modern village.

The **castle** is excellently positioned for defence; Dom Sancho I chose the site in the 13th century, and took advantage of the rock formation when building its walls. Now ivy wells over the tower. An elegant 16th-century **pillory** stands at the foot of the castle, and there is an **antiquarian shop** opposite its entrance. Although they know their prices, it's a good place to pick up the odd milking stool or spindle.

Sortelha ℂ *(071–)*   ***Where to Stay***

All the accommodation in Sortelha is *Turismo de Habitação*. At the lower end of the village, outside the castle walls, the delightful, cosily furnished wood and granite **Casa do Pátio**, ℂ 68113 (*inexpensive*) is an outbuilding of the Solar de N.S. da Conceição, with which it shares an informal courtyard, where local women stich Arraiolos rugs. A small, well-stocked kitchen leads off the sitting room complete with sofabed, fireplace, woodburning stove and TV. Food and drink are provided; you pay for what you use. Upstairs is a bedroom with two single beds, and a shower room. The chic Viscondessa prattles in French, reserving the right of admission to an independent apartment (*moderate*) on the ground floor of the main house. This includes a double room and a triple room, with a great portico-type chimney in one corner of the dining room. It's cheapest to rent the house during the period 1 June–31 August, because of heating costs.

Three ancient houses are available within the castle walls, of which the dark granite **Casa do Vento Que Soa**, ✆ 68260, is the least uncomfortable. Entered by an unsupported external granite staircase, its many bedrooms are decently but sparsely furnished. Behind its glass front door, the **Casa do Palheiro**, Rua das Escadinhas, ✆ 68182, is tiny, ancient, and slightly claustrophobic. Water leaks about the place. A little staircase climbs beside a granite boulder to the 'bedroom', a rough-cut wooden loft with a mattress on a sprung frame.

Sortelha ✆ *(071–)* **Eating Out**

Within the castle walls, **Alboroque**, ✆ 68129 (*cheap*), is all set for a medieval banquet, without the filth of the original or the kitsch of an imitation. The building is 500 years old, with treetrunk beams and granite walls, and a table made from a huge pair of bellows. At the bar, benches are draped with goatskins, the walls hung with gourds. The menu is brief but the food very good. *Caldeirada de cabrito* is the obvious choice, or there's *bacalhau*, or chicken and French fries.

Restaurante Típico (*cheap*) is traditional and wood-beamed. Be sure to try the *javali* (wild boar) if it is on the menu.

Sabugal

Twelve km east of Sortelha, the early frontier town of Sabugal lies on a low hill overlooking the valley of the River Côa, surrounded by fertile plains.

The imposing early 14th-century **fortress** manages to be both strong and beautiful, but it was not always so: over the ages the high walls and oval ramparts were pillaged, that the locals might wall their kitchen gardens. Now the castle has had its dignity restored, complete with the unusual pentagonal keep. Its predecessor hosted a peace meeting between Dom Sancho II of Portugal and Fernando III of Castile.

Beira Baixa

Beira Baixa, the southeastern or 'lower' Beira, is dominated by mountains in the north including part of the Serra da Estrêla and, running parallel, the craggy grey granite Serra da Gardunha. Snowcapped in winter, the mountains are robed each spring in purple heather blossom, which withers to brown in the heat of summer, only to be relieved by the autumn rains. In the south, the mountains yield to vast plains of Alentejan proportions.

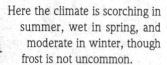

Here the climate is scorching in summer, wet in spring, and moderate in winter, though frost is not uncommon.

In the mountains and hills, pines dominate the trees, oxen and goats the livestock, millet the cereals. But the cultivated area is small: although the rainfall is high, the level ground is poor. Great groves of cork oaks grow on the plains between Idanha-a-Nova and Castelo Branco; other important cash crops include almonds, fruit trees and olive oil, of which Castelo Branco produces some of the best in Portugal. Wool and other textiles buoy the local economy. As in the Alentejo, houses in the south tend to be whitewashed, and the land is held in *latifundias*. The people are affable, tolerant and cordial—no more so than when they are eating superb roast kid, which is particularly aromatic here because the animals graze on wild herbs.

cork harvest

Beira Baixa contains some of the loveliest landscapes in Portugal, combined with places of peculiar magnetism. There are very few monuments of note, so the best thing to do is to drive and discover for yourself.

Built into a wooded hillslope on the southeastern edge of the Serra da Estrêla, Covilhã is a surprisingly large town for such a remote and underpopulated region, with a population of 25,000 souls. The settlement overlooks flatlands to where hills converge in the distance. Its prosperity is dependent on textiles, especially wool, but Covilhã is being promoted as a base for walking in the Serra in summer, and for winter sports. The loiterers wear suits, and watch pine-trees truck through, as there's nothing much else to look at in town.

History

Pêro de Covilhã was born here; of all the Portuguese discoverers, it would have been most interesting to accompany him. Since the 12th century, rumours had been circulating of the 'Lord of Lords and the Greatest Monarch under heaven', who received tribute from 72 kings, who lived in a palace of ebony and crystal, and who was accompanied by giant ants that dug for gold, and fish that squirted purple dye: they called him Prester John. Dom João II was looking for a Christian ally in Africa, so in 1487 he commissioned two men to locate this fabulous kingdom—Pêro de Covilhã, who spoke fluent Arabic, and Afonso de Paiva.

In Alexandria the pair disguised themselves as Arab merchants, and reached Cairo, where Afonso died. Pêro sailed to India, where he spent over a year in the western ports studying the pepper, ginger and gold markets. On his return to Cairo, he passed a written report of his journey to Mestre Joseph, the cobbler of Lamego, one of Dom João II's two Jewish agents there, who in turn delivered it to the king. Doubtless it proved useful to Vasco da Gama a few years later. In Cairo Pêro was told that he would not be welcome in Portugal until he completed his original mission, so in 1490 he headed south. He arrived on the shores of Lake Tana, in what is now Ethiopia, and did indeed find a Coptic kingdom—but the Emperor Naod was not interested in an alliance, and would not allow foreigners to leave the country. Pêro was provided with a wife and an estate. He was still alive when Dom Rodrigo de Lima reached Ethiopia in 1521, though by then he was too weak to return to Portugal. The chronicler Ruy de Pina has the final word: 'Nothing is known of what he finally achieved, for he never came back from his travels.' His route is marked on a granite map in front of the town hall.

In the late 17th century English workers and looms were smuggled to Covilhã to teach the locals to card, spin and weave wool, so that Portugal could supply its own army uniforms. Dom João V was keen to promote the infant industry, but it was tripped up by the Inquisition, because many of the artisans were New Christians, converted Jews. British fears for their virtual monopoly of exports of cloth to Portugal were temporarily allayed, but ultimately the industry took root.

Covilhã ℗ (075–)	**Getting Around**

Covilhã is 55km from Castelo Branco and 38km from Guarda.

Trains, ℗ 331284, run four times daily from Lisbon (4½–6hrs), via Santarém (4½hrs), Entroncamento (4½hrs) and Castelo Branco (1¼hrs). From Oporto, change at Entroncamento after 3hrs. Three trains run daily from Guarda (1¼hrs).

The RN Express **bus** routes are similar, ℗ 33123, making infrequent daily journeys from Lisbon (5¼hrs), via Castelo Branco (1hr), and from Guarda (½hr). In some months, on some days of the week, an RN Express bus runs from Oporto (5¼hrs), via Viseu (2¼hrs).

Covilhã ℗ (075–)	**Tourist Information**

The **tourist office**, ℗ 322170—which seems to have a glossy leaflet for everything—and the booking office for bus tickets are both on the ground floor of the town hall, in the central square.

Covilhã ℗ (075–)	**Where to Stay**
	inexpensive

★★★**Pensão Solneve**, 126 Rua Visconde da Coriscada, ℗ 323001 (in the main square) is very basic and charmless, despite the electric clocks and TVs in the bedrooms. The light restaurant has a separate entrance, popular with men in ties. Dishes can be dry.

Somehow it feels like a soda bar without the ice-cream. Also in the main square, ★★★**Residencial Montalto**, 1 Praça do Municipio, ℂ 327609, is undistinguished, but OK. A nicer place to stay, but on the southern edge of town, is ★**Residencial Santa Eufêmia**, Sitio da Palmatória, ℂ 313308, ✆ 314184, sensibly furnished, with balcony views to the distant hills.

cheap

In a neighbourhoodly street full of life, ★★**Pensão Regional**, 4 Rua das Flores, ℂ 322596 (head downhill from the main square, and continue straight ahead without rounding the bend), offers small rooms with good views, and showers but not toilets. The restaurant gets up a fug. Nearby is a steep-stepped woodsmoky warren, ★★**Pensão São Francisco**, 35 Rua Dr. Almeida Eusébio, ℂ 322263, dilapidated and grotty. ★**Pensão Avenida**, 40 Av. Heitor Pinto, ℂ 322140 (beside the Jardim Público), is all too evidently the home of its toothless proprietress. The grandmotherly trimmings make the damp and the peeling walls forgivable.

Covilhã ℂ *(075–)*   ***Eating Out***

Most of Covilhã's restaurants are affiliated to hotels (*see* above). Otherwise, a fake lobster and crab colonize the back room of **A Traineira**, 19 Rua Pêso da Lá (*moderate*)—between the Rua Visconde da Coriscada and the Rua Marquês da Vila e Bolama—a striplit fish restaurant which fails to peel its prawns for the *arroz de marisco*; better skip the fish and try the *caldeirada de cabrito*. **Restaurante Sporting**, 6 Rua Comendador Mendes Veiga (*moderate*), has a large, vine-covered terrace and a big horse-shoe bar also available for dining. Reliably good food. There are a couple of eating places in the lively Rua das Flores, in the midst of which works an umbrella mender. Tiny, cavernous **Restaurante Tania**, 23 Rua das Flores, ℂ 323499 (*cheap*), is a good place for drinking draught beer while watching one of many compulsive early evening Portuguese soaps.

Belmonte

The village of Belmonte makes a worthwhile detour to the east of the Serra da Estrêla, 21km south of Guarda and 19km northeast of Covilhã, overlooking the flat-bottomed, red-soiled valley of the River Zêzere. Some of its 3000 souls inhabit rude granite houses, which sought protection from the now-ruined castle and the interesting little church of São Tiago.

History

Belmonte has been a stronghold for the *Marranos* for 400 years, housing a cluster of crypto-Jews descended from those forced to convert to Catholicism at the end of the 15th century, but who continued to practise their faith in secret. About 200 of the 4000 village homes belong to direct descendants of *Marranos*: these people incorporate fragments of the Hebraic rituals in their Catholic observance, without knowing their original significance.

The charms of Belmonte were insufficient to detain Pedro Álvares Cabral, who left Belmonte and sailed west until, in 1500, he discovered Brazil. Brazil was all that the sailors could have wished: plump and vibrant naked ladies came to greet them. Pedro Vaz de Caminha, official clerk to the expedition, wrote that this seemingly perfect society lacked only knowledge of the true God. This the Portuguese could put to rights, encouraged by the fact that the natives were not circumcised and were therefore neither Mohammedans nor Jews. A Mass was arranged, which is commemorated by the people of Belmonte on 26 April each year. The Indians knelt beside the Portuguese and, in imitation of their guests, smilingly kissed the crosses that were handed to them.

Belmonte ☎ (075–)	***Tourist Information***

The **tourist office**, ☎ 91488, is in the main town square.

The Town

The pillory square is shaded by *tilia* trees, a genus of lindens, whose leaves are different shades of light green and whose summer blossom can be dried and used to make tea. The tourist office doubles as a workshop for ladies stitching Arraiolos rugs. From there the most interesting route to the castle is the Rua Fonte da Rosa, in which the occupants of tiny windowed houses sit and crochet or bundle kindling wood.

Cabral's ancestors included Fernão Cabral, Giant of Beira, who went into battle with an iron mace weighing more than one *arroba* (15kg); his family had long been the castellans of Belmonte. The filmset **castle** was constructed in the 13th century, on granite, but a sober Manueline window is all that remains of the residence in which Pedro Álvares was born. The toothless granite animals were a later addition to the castle front. On Christmas Eve young men doing military service dance around a flaming tree trunk beside the building, in a ritual similar to the St John's Eve festivities in the Minho and Oporto. Jumping over the fire is seen as an effective means of counteracting the forces of evil which may attack during the following year.

In 1362 the same mellow stone was used to build the fascinating **church of São Tiago** opposite the castle. It has its own tiny belltower on a terrace formerly used as a graveyard, and its shadows cloak a painted 14th-century granite pietà. A side door connects with the pantheon of the Cabral family, though Pedro Álvares is entombed in Santarém. But his spirit lives just a few paces away, down some steps by the church: it takes the form of a pet cockatoo, complete with fluorescent yellow crest, which can say '*Hola*'. '*Cabra*' means 'she goat', so the Cabral family had few options when choosing their emblem: it's one goat on top of another, and can be seen on the wall of the second little church facing the castle.

On the other side of Belmonte, the new **Igreja Matriz** houses a freshly painted granite statue of N.S. da Esperança, which travelled on that first journey to Brazil. The Virgin holds baby Jesus as he feeds grapes to a dove, apparently unperturbed that she was hollowed to lighten the sailors' load.

There are several ordinary little eating places in Belmonte; to stay, readers recommend the **★★Hotel Belsol**, ✆ 912206 (*moderate*), on Quintado Rio, Estrado Nacional—3km away by road, with superb views of the mountains and a pool.

Centum Cellas

Two km north of Belmonte, just off the road to Guarda, stands one of the oddest ruins in Portugal, at Centum Cellas. The three-storeyed granite structure is extraordinary for its large number of windows: it has been classified as a temple or the *praetorium* of a camp, but unconvincingly so. When the surrounding ground is excavated, the tower may prove to have belonged to a villa, possibly dating from the 2nd century, and preserved in isolation because of its use as a watchtower in the Middle Ages.

The Serra da Gardunha

A mere blip compared with the Serra da Estrêla, the Serra da Gardunha runs on a roughly northeast to southwest axis. Between the villages of Casal da Serra and Alpedrinha an infertile wedge of granite is sandwiched between fertile schists: the divide is sudden and apparent. Having peaked at 1223m, the mountains quickly give way to gentle hills.

The cherry trees around **Fundão** blossom at the end of March and bear fruit from the end of April through to June. A mouthful or two wouldn't go amiss, and they could be washed down with a draught of spring water from the roadside fountain southeast of the small town.

Alpedrinha

Twelve km southeast of Fundão, Alpedrinha is a charming, large and relatively affluent village strung out along the main road from Fundão to Castelo Branco, backed by a steep hill slope and looking down over a gentle one. Judging by the amazed looks from ladies carrying their greens, foreign visitors are rare in the higgledy-piggledy tangle of streets off the main road.

Turismo de Habitação

Casa do Barreiro, ✆ 57120 (*moderate*) provides lovely *Turismo de Habitação* at very reasonable rates. Surrounded by delightfully muddled gardens, the solid house was built early this century in that late 19th-century style which topped its residences with little granite obelisks. Two sisters live here, both in their sixties and neither averse to a tipple. One of them speaks French. They prattle around the cool and airy interior, among homey antiques and colourful décor. Guest bedrooms look down the gentle hillslope to the plains beyond, and come with shower rooms—but one room is a dud.

Casa da Comenda, ℗ 57161 (*moderate*), past the Igreja Matriz, is an early 17th-century granite fortress house with elegant, cool rooms and a lovely garden.

For meals, head for the ★★★★**Estalagem S. Jorge**, ℗ 57154 (*moderate*), where the service is courteous, the tables beautifully laid, and the food good. However, guest-rooms are grim, with peeling furnishings, linoleum on the floor, and bathrooms tacked on (*inexpensive*).

Castelo Novo

About 3km south of Alpedrinha, a turning to the right leads to Castelo Novo, a worthwhile detour if you're not in a hurry. The village is set in a basin of dark granite scree which looks so cursed to barrenness as to recall Camões' *Canção IX*, in Roy Campbell's translation: 'There is a mountain, sterile, stark and dry, / Useless, abandoned, hideous, bare and bald, / From whose cursed precincts nature shrinks appalled...' Castelo Novo is a wonderfully sleepy place: sometimes the most lively things there are the potatoes, sprouting.

Castelo Branco

The prosperous capital of Beira Baixa occupies a low hill at the centre of flat lands, 18km from the Spanish border. The town has outlived the '*Castelo*' from which it takes its name: the castle is now ruined, and its place in the hearts of the 27,000 inhabitants has been taken by the surrounding technical colleges. Parts of Castelo Branco are laid out along wide, airy avenues, but it's a rather ordinary place with few traces of its ancient roots. However, the bishop's palace houses a worthwhile museum, and the celebrated palace gardens are filled with a fanciful array of little sculptures. Just outside the town lies a meadow hill with breathtaking views.

Castelo Branco marks the fusion of two Hispano-Roman *vilas*. The Templars built the castle early in the 13th century, and Dom Dinis, on a recce with his Queen Isabel, ordered the extension of the town walls. Being so close to the border, it was the scene of Spanish attacks in 1704 and 1762; in 1807, the French marched in, singing the *Marseillaise*. Junot comandeered the bishop's palace, and his troops pillaged the town before heading towards Lisbon.

Castelo Branco ℗ (072–)   **Getting There**

Castelo Branco is 159km from Coimbra, 100km from Guarda, 80km from Portalegre and 262km from Lisbon.

Around five **trains** travel daily from Lisbon (4hrs) via Santarém (3hrs) and Entroncamento (2¼hrs). From Oporto, change at Entroncamento after 3hrs. In the other direction, they run three times daily from Guarda (3hrs) via Covilhã (1¼hrs). Castelo Branco is the only possible base for visiting Monsanto and Idanha-a-Velha by public transport.

RN Express **buses**, ℗ 23380 or 23301, run infrequently from Lisbon (4¼hrs), Guarda (2hrs), Covilhã (1¼hrs) and Sabugal (2½hrs), with three buses daily from Coimbra (4hrs).

The **tourist office**, ✆ 21002 (*open Tues–Fri 9.30–8.30; Sat–Mon 9–1 and 2–6*), is in a kiosk in the central Alameda da Liberdade. It's a short walk from the **bus station** (turn right), and the **railway station** is ½km to the south (walk up the wide Avenida Nun' Alvares).

What to See

The boringly regular façade of the **Episcopal Palace** does little to enliven the northeastern edge of town. But the appearance is deceptive: it stands on the site of an earlier palace, built in 1596 as the winter residence of the Bishop of Guarda. His 18th-century successors revamped the building in the present manorial style, taking care to include a game park, now vanished.

The town's **Museu de Francisco Tavares Proença Júnior** (*open 9.30–12.30 and 2–5.30*) is installed in the palace, which contains a good archaeological collection, from the Palaeolithic period on, and some rupestral art. The 16th-century Brussels tapestries were used early this century as a pinboard for public notices, and until fairly recently the mounted 'canon ball' spewed random numbers, bingo-style, as a means of apportioning military service. Outstanding among the paintings are *St Anthony* by Francisco Henriques, *c.* 1510—the Franciscan monk holds a red book on which sits a nonplussed baby Jesus—and a *Deposing of Christ in the Tomb* attributed to the early Renaissance master, Garcia Fernandes.

But the most interesting of the museum's collections are the *colchas*, linen bedspreads embroidered with large stitches of silk, like raffia, which have been the local speciality for 300 years. In the 18th century they formed part of the bridal trousseau, and used locally produced silk. This is the sort of thing that fantastical heroines in magic realist novels spend their lives working on, letting their imagination run away with them: the colours are bold yellows and greens, pinks and browns, in a style that might be called Persian Baroque. The motifs are doves, parrots, carnations, pomegranates, all of which are symbolic: a two-headed bird represents two souls in one body; two birds either side of a tree represent lovers; vegetables and trees represent the family. A workshop in the museum keeps the craft alive. Work can be commissioned: it's expensive stuff.

The **Bishop's Garden** is a rare sight, planted with a host of profane little granite statues amidst the boxed hedges and orange trees. This plethora of Baroque whimsy was the brain child of Dom João de Mendonça, who saw the work completed in 1725, and who preferred to meditate in a rowboat on the water tank. The ladies and gentlemen are of little artistic merit, but this does not bother them. They are arranged thematically, including the zodiac, the seasons, the continents, and, most famously, the kings. A few were stolen by French troops in 1807: their memory is not well served by the flowerpots that have replaced them.

Some 200m nearer the centre of town, the **church of São Miguel** served as the cathedral of Castelo Branco 1771–1881, before the bishopric was extinguished. The 13th- or 14th-century building has been reconstructed several times, most notably in the 17th century, which has left bits of Renaissance tracery. Really the only things worth looking at are the locally embroidered copes on show in the sacristy.

The Environs of Castelo Branco

Monte de São Martinho is a stunningly beautiful undiscovered mount of olives just southeast of town. It's an idyllic, enchanted place where the air really is sweet, the butterflies fly fast and meadow flowers nudge miniature irises. Cicadas and cuckoos announce themselves, oblivious to the enormous view towards Spain. It's best to walk the 4–5km; if you're driving, you'll need good suspension. Head for the chapel of N.S. de Mércoles. Continue straight. Take the track to the right past the last town road. The track splits into three; go left. Fork right. Fork right again. Fork left. To go up the hill, head left or right. Please respect it.

Castelo Branco ☎ (072–)　　　　　　　　　　　　　　**Where to Stay**

For very cheap rooms, ask the tourist office to point you towards the area behind the Almeda. ★★★**Residencial Arraiana**, 18 Av 1 de Maio, ☎ 21634, 🖂 331884 (*inexpensive*)—on the very long shopping street leading straight from the centre of town—is bare but decent, with showers, TV and minibar.

Disparate furniture is scattered around ★★★**Residencial Caravela**, 24 Rua do Saibreiro, ☎ 23939 (*cheap*), next to the bus station. Some of the bathrooms have old fittings. Avoid dirty, peeling, noisy ★★**Residencial Martinho**, 41 Alameda da Liberdade, ☎ 21706.

Ten km down the excellent motorway southwest of Castelo Branco, sprawling, split-level ★★★**Motel da Represa**, at Represa, ☎ 98327 (*inexpensive*), has its good moments—the cart wheels, patio and decent-sized swimming pool—but otherwise it's laughably kitsch, especially the bungalows. The honeymoon suite has a ceiling mirror. The 'typical' restaurant is touristy, the international restaurant meaty.

Castelo Branco ☎ (072–)　　　　　　　　　　　　　　　**Eating Out**

A Piscina, ☎ 25105 (*moderate*)—overlooking the municipal swimming pool, the *piscina municipal*—serves some of the best roast kid in Portugal (*cabrito assado na brasa*), complemented by the *batatas do casa*, and the strong and goaty local cheese. It's best to go when the weather is bad—otherwise you'll have to view the unappetizing flesh which surrounds the swimming pool.

Fake ivy covers the arch leading into the **Restaurante Arcadia**, 19 Alameda da Liberdade, ☎ 21933 (*moderate–cheap*). Traditional women smile down at diners from huge wall paintings. Generally the meat dishes are succulent. *Closed Wed.* Alternatively, there's popular, quick and pleasant **Piri–Piri**, Lote 12, Quinta do

Amieiro de Cima, ℂ 21926 (*cheap*), beyond the bus station. If you don't want to leave the town centre, head for Rua Ruivo Godinho, where **Lanterna** at No.5, ℂ 22866, is recommended. The food is better here than at **Floresta** at No.9, ℂ 22330, which serves cold, tough meat to lone males. There's also **Ronda**, further down the hill, ℂ 23128.

East of Castelo Branco

Monsanto

Monsanto is the most dramatic and astonishing of Portugal's hill settlements; come here to know why the birds sing. Here there is no ceiling on life—this is Monte Santo, Sacred Mount. It stands at 758m, some 50km northeast of Castelo Branco by the quickest route. The tiny community is camouflaged by its granite buildings and nourished by magnificent views in every direction, to hills and lakes and unregimented fields.

Getting There

The only way to get to Monsanto by public transport is on the 7.10am bus from Castelo Branco, which, theoretically, returns late morning. However, the bus schedule seems to rely more on whim than timetabling, and it is best to check and double check with the bus station in Castelo Branco. If you're driving to or from Castelo Branco, choose the longer but much more beautiful route via Zebreira.

Festivals

The **Festa das Cruzes** enlivens the first Sunday of May. It commemorates a legendary siege of the stronghold, when the starving inhabitants threw their last calf at the attackers. So demoralizing was this show of plenty that the besiegers withdrew. Now girls and women process to the castle and throw from its walls a 'calf' made of roses and pitchers of flowers. The old women sing and dance with faceless rag dolls called *marafonas*, which are believed to give protection against thunder.

The site was first colonized by the Lusitanians, then by the Romans. Dom Sancho I ejected the Moors from the village in the 12th century. Gualdim Pais reconstructed the castle among still boulders above the village, atop the forbidding rock outcrop of almost volcanic harshness, and Dom Dinis further fortified Monsanto. Now the fortification is ruined; its grass is cropped by goats. In the village, life is intensified: it is difficult not to relish the crack of a carpet being flicked out of a window, or the shudders of a stick brush sweeping the street. There are few inhabitants under the age of 50, for there is little work here. Rabbit hutches are embedded in external staircases, chickens penned in on the dirt beneath overhanging boulders. Monsanto has been voted the most typical (read: quintessential) village in Portugal, so coaches of visitors come and go, assailed by an old woman drumming a square tambourine with her fingers. But Monsanto remains of itself, because there is nowhere for visitors to stay except the rather hard-to-find *pousada*, © 077 32425/34471, ✆ 34481 (*category B*), and just one café.

Idanha-a-Velha

The village of Idanha-a-Velha has been extraordinarily washed by history, and left alone. It occupies a flat, isolated site 48km northeast of Castelo Branco. Most of the inhabitants are ghosts, but some flesh and blood mortals live here too.

History

It was once the Roman city of Igaeditânia, founded by Augustus in 16 BC: in that year Quintus Iallius gave a sun dial to the city. The soil here is fertile alluvium, and was once rich with gold—an altar discovered nearby was inscribed with a dedication to Iuppiter, in thanks for a find of some 40kg of the stuff. Another reason for choosing the site was its proximity to the permanent Roman camp at Medelim, 6km to the north. The settlement became a *municipium* under Vespasian, but the only Roman public monument found so far is the base of a temple probably dedicated to Augustus, on which stands a ruined medieval tower built in the reign of Dom Dinis.

The Visigoths rebuilt Idanha in 534, and tradition has it that this was the birthplace of Wamba, whom they elected as king in 672. He is traditionally credited with having established the ecclesiastical divisions of the Peninsula, but showed little respect for the clergy themselves: he called them up for service in his army, in the wake of a Basque rebellion and an uprising in Gaul. The churchmen took violent revenge, conspiring with the nobles and capturing King Wamba. They shaved his head—as the mark of a slave rather than a grotesque tonsure—and deposed and banished him.

The settlement was destroyed by the Moors in the 8th century, and lay dormant until Dom Sancho I conceded it to the Templars. None of its splendour has been unearthed: it awaits excavation.

Getting There

If you have no transport, it's best to try to hitch a lift from Monsanto, then catch the mid-afternoon bus back to Castelo Branco.

The Cathedral and Around

The Visigoths built a **cathedral** for their bishop in the 6th or 7th centuries, but the pure and simple edifice that now stands is the product of several reconstructions, the most drastic of which was in the 16th century. The horseshoe-shaped colonnade and the flagstones are original. Outside, and at a lower level than the cathedral, is a **baptismal basin**. (The unornamented side door was added much later, in the 16th century.) A little museum displays various ceramics, bones, and a terra-cotta statuette. Wander in the cemetery, composed of eerie Roman and Visigothic ruins which were abandoned, so they say, because of a century-long plague of ants.

Beira Litoral

Beira Litoral occupies the coastal plains from Espinho to Leiria, penetrating about 30km inland to the forested, granitic Serras of Arada, Caramulo and Buçaco. At the province's main city, Coimbra, it broadens to incorporate the Serra da Lousã, stopping short at the Serra da Estrêla. The sand beaches are backed by low, sandy clay dunes which support little more than pine trees. The lower reaches of the Rivers Mondego and Vouga create waterlogged flatlands, the former supporting rice paddies and the latter salt pans. The main appeal of the province lies in specific monuments or features: the economy and land-scape of the estuary of the River Vouga, the Forest of Buçaco, the art and architecture of Coimbra, the excavations at Roman Conimbriga, the Abbey of Batalha.

Coimbra

The noisy, lively university city of Coimbra focuses on a steep limestone hill on the north bank of the River Mondego, 40km inland, halfway between Lisbon and Oporto.

Eight hundred and fifty years ago, Coimbra was the capital of Portugal. Subsequently, it received more than its fair share of the art and architecture of the 15th and 18th centuries, and its 56,000 residents play host to Portugal's most important and popular university. But Coimbra does not relish its past glory. This has been eroded by nibbles and bites, most drastically under the Salazar regime, when featureless modern blocks replaced parts of the old town—which makes it difficult to follow Hans Christian Andersen's advice of 1866: 'Coimbra is a place where one should...live with the students, fly out to the lovely open country around, give oneself up to solitude and let memory unroll pictures from legend and song, from the history of this place.' The city can be divided into upper and lower parts; the walls of the former have almost disappeared, but the steep access roads remain, leading up from the flat land at the foot of the hill.

The dominance of Coimbra's university has made the city into Portugal's think-tank. Its most famous alumnus is the epic poet Camões, who may have been born in Coimbra, *c.* 1524, and who enjoyed his 'bright college years' learning Latin and Greek. There are a handful of outstanding buildings to see, as well as a couple of seductively domestic streets below the university, where music from Bach to Madonna filters through from the fraternities and sororities called *repúblicas*. Coimbra has its own *fado*, a more sophisticated and intellectual version of the Lisbon lament. The guitar which accompanies it appears to be a descendant of the five-stringed lute introduced to Spain in the 9th century by Ziryab, who knew more than a thousand songs (and is also credited with introducing toothpaste to Córdoba). One of the city's less welcome sounds is that of traffic, which tends to run close to the fairly abundant supply of accommodation for visitors.

History

The Romans knew Coimbra as Aeminium, which came into the orbit of their city at Conimbriga, 16km to the south. Conimbriga was abandoned, and in 872 the Moors were driven from the area. By linguistic debasement, Aeminium took the name of the settlement that had previously overshadowed it. The Moors were back in control 987–1064, and again in 1116, when a Moorish army stormed two of the castles erected to defend Coimbra: at Miranda de Beira, the garrison was slaughtered; at Santa Eulália, the governor, Diogo the Chicken, was true to his name, and surrendered. Coimbra itself came next. According to the *Chronicle* of the Goths, Ali, the Almoravid caliph, and his son Yasuf, brought an African army reinforced by Andalucians 'as numerous as the sands of the sea'. The city was sacked, and Countess Teresa sought refuge in the castle. Coimbra's defences lay in ruins until Dom Afonso Henriques built the castle of Leiria as his southern stronghold, in 1135.

He was crowned king in 1139, and transferred the nation's capital from Guimarães to Coimbra, which blossomed. Idrisi, the Muslim geographer who completed his work in Sicily in 1154, describes Coimbra as a flourishing city, whose inhabitants are 'the bravest of the Christians'. Its fertile fields were rich in vineyards and orchards of apples, cherries and plums, for 'the Mondego moves many mills and bathes many vineyards and gardens'.

Coimbra remained the capital during the reigns of Dom Afonso II, Dom Sancho II, and Dom Afonso III, who moved the main royal residence to Lisbon *c.* 1250. Portugal's university also migrated southwards, to Lisbon, after a couple of brief sojourns in Coimbra, but returned finally in 1537. With the university came the Jesuits—who were very influential here until 1772, when Pombal reformed the institution—and the Inquisition, which set up a base in Coimbra. In 1810, Masséna sacked the town, thereby venting some of his frustration at the outcome of the battle of Buçaco.

What to Eat

The Bairrada region, around Anadia and Mealhada just to the north of Coimbra, is renowned for its suckling pig roast in a brick oven (*leitão assado à moda da Bairrada*), served with its skin crispy and golden. The piglets should be between 1 and 1½ months, and suckled on their own mother's milk. Aveiro prides itself on its eel stew (*caldeirada de enguias à moda de Aveiro*), made with potatoes, stale bread, onions, and a little vinegar.

Coimbra © (039–)   *Getting There and Around*

By **road**, Coimbra is 60km from Aveiro, 159km from Guarda, 70km from Leiria, 120km from Oporto, 94km from Viseu and 201km from Lisbon.

Coimbra is better served by public transport on a north–south rather than east–west axis. Frequent **trains** from Lisbon's Santa Apolónia station to Coimbra-B take a minimum of 2hrs, passing Santarém (1¾hrs). The quickest trains from Oporto take 1½hrs (slow trains may have to change at Pampilhosa). Those that pass through Espinho take 1¼hrs, and Aveiro ½hr. Semifrequent trains run from Guarda (3½hrs) via Nelas (1½hrs, connecting with buses from Viseu).

Most **buses** run a couple of times a day from Faro (9¾hrs), Chaves (5½hrs), Lamego (3¼hrs), Viseu (1½hrs), Guarda (3hrs), Monção (5½hrs), Guimarães (3½hrs). The 3¼hr route from Castelo Branco connects with the Braga and Oporto services. Buses are much more frequent from Oporto (1¾hrs), Lisbon (3hrs) and Leiria (1hr). International buses pass through Coimbra on their way from Lisbon to Paris.

Everything within Coimbra is within **walking** distance, but the upper part of town is steep: it may be a good idea to take a taxi to the university, and walk your way down from there. The electrified buses run around the hill rather than up it. A visit to the Santa Clara-a-Nova convent may also warrant a taxi.

Connecting trains run between the two railway stations; Coimbra-B, ℂ 34127, the mainline terminal, and Coimbra-A, ℂ 34998, near the centre of town. Keep your wits about you as trains sometimes leave unannounced.

Coimbra ℂ (039–)   ***Tourist Information***

The main **tourist office** is in the Largo da Portagem, ℂ 33019/33029, at the northern head of the Santa Clara bridge across the

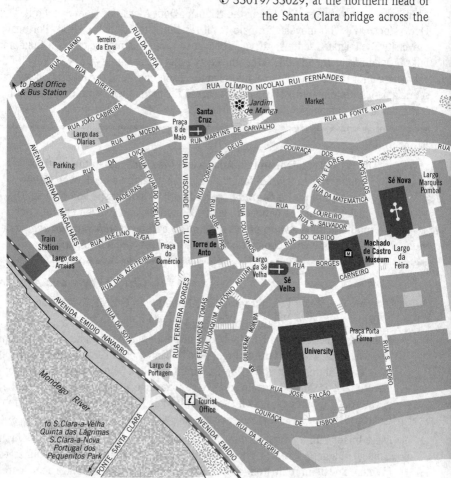

Mondego. There are two other smaller branches in the Largo Dom Dinis and the Praca da Republica near the University.

The **post office** is in the Largo Dom Dinis, with an annexe in the Praça da República.

Supernet, Edifício Golden Shopping Centre, Av. Sa da Bandeira, ✆ 38960, *supernet@mail.telepac.pt*, provides Internet services and coffee.

The Upper Town

The University

Coimbra is dominated by its lofty university, which rides the peak of the city.

In 1288 a trio of Portuguese ecclesiastics requested Pope Nicholas IV to confirm the creation of a university, which they had agreed with Dom Dinis to establish in Lisbon. The Church would finance the venture, as all the students were to become clergymen. Gradually, laymen infiltrated the place, and during the 14th century the university was transferred from Lisbon to Coimbra and back again several times. Standards were mediocre: serious scholars sharpened their quills and headed for Italy or France, particularly Paris. When Paris was split by religious differences in the early decades of the 16th century, Dom João III determined to lick Portugal's university into shape. In 1534 he appointed André de Resende to the faculty, whose searing inaugural speech, at a time 'when nearly the whole of Europe is being reborn', praised the care and patience other nations were devoting to their academic learning, and thundered '... we ought truly to feel ashamed of our gross ignorance and our slothfulness.' The king invited Erasmus to come and teach in Portugal, but the great humanist declined on the grounds of ill health. (In fact, Erasmus disliked the Portuguese as 'a race of Jews', and had criticized the efforts of the Portuguese crown to use its monopoly of the Oriental spice trade to maintain high prices in Europe.)

In 1537 the university was finally re-established at Coimbra, and a decade later the king founded the Royal College of Arts. He recruited a distinguished medley of international professors, only to be embarrassed when some of them were arrested by the Inquisition for precisely that free thinking that had recommended them to the king. In 1555 the College of Arts was handed to the Jesuits.

All was not rosy for the 1500 students. During the minority of Dom Manuel, João III's successor, the *Cortes* urged that the University of Coimbra 'be done away with as noxious to the kingdom, and the revenues be applied to the war [in Magrib], and whomsoever wishes to learn, let him go to Salamanca or to Paris, and there will not be so many graduates in excess, or so many suits.' It was 200 years before Pombal attempted another shake-up at the university: he shooed away corrupt priests who sold doctorates, and added natural sciences to the curriculum. He swept away the castle to build afresh on the top of the hill, and established laboratories and the botanic garden. In future, he determined, entry to the university was to be by examination only.

Coimbra remains Portugal's premier university, held in respect, affection and pride throughout the country.

The Old University

Its core is the Old University, a courtyard with buildings on three sides but open to the south, where a statue of Dom João III stands with his back to views of the River Mondego. The wide river valley winds down from the Lousâ hills, fringed with willow, sedge and poplar, shallow enough to support sandbanks midstream. Since 1634, the Old University has been entered through the **Porta Férrea**, which replaced an earlier, fortified portal. The courtyard incorporates a royal palace donated by Dom João III in 1573, and subsequently much altered.

To the right of the entrance, a theatrical arched gallery, called the **Via Latina**, has engulfed a frontispiece by Cláudio Laprade, who carved figures symbolizing the academic faculties, *c.* 1700—but his work was later remodelled as a monument to Dom José (1750–77). The door marked '*reitoria*' leads to the balcony of the **Sala dos Capelos**, which was formerly the throne room: students defend their doctoral theses under the uncomprehending gaze of various royal portraits, who would no doubt rather be looking at the wonderful view of the city offered by the catwalk, off to one side.

The courtyard is dominated by its unattractive clock tower, in the northwestern corner, which has been calling the students to their lectures since 1733 and has consequently earned the undignified nickname of the '*cabra*' (the 'goat').

To the left of the clock tower is a relic of the former royal palace, a fine Manueline portal, probably by Marcos Pires, one of the stonemasons of Batalha, before 1522. Next to it, a door leads to the **Capela de São Miguel**, which was 'modernized' in both the 17th and 18th centuries, most notably with a blaster of an organ, dated 1733 and gilt with wafting shells and croissant shapes. Pews cushioned with leather anticipate lengthy sermons.

The Library

Press the doorbell under a monstrous national blazon to the left of the quadrangle for entry to the splendid library, the most famous of the university's buildings. The three adjacent rooms, built between 1717 and 1723, were a typically magnificent gift of that vivacious monarch, Dom João V. His portrait stands at one end, past a succession of shelves painted dark green, light green, and fleshy orange, each gilt with restrained ornament. Tapering columns support the galleries, above tables inlaid with ebony, rosewood and jacaranda.

(One of the most inventive characters of the 18th century must have hatched his ideas in these salubrious rooms, which are entirely unconducive to study. In the first half of the 18th century, Bartolomew Gusmão invented a flying machine: it was a sort of fire balloon, which is said to have flown from the castle of St George in Lisbon to the Paço de Povo in the central square. If this is true, it was the first balloon ever to have carried a passenger. He was afraid that the Inquisition would accuse him of black magic, and became an expert on cyphers and how to crack them, before fleeing to Spain, whence he was pursued by his apocalyptic visions. His story is told by José Saramago in his novel, *Balthasar and Blimunda*.)

The Students

If you want to mingle amongst the students, they hang around the Praça da República: walk downstairs from the Praça de Dom Dinis, which is behind the two courtyard blocks that contain the faculties of arts, physics and mathematics, then along the Rua Oliveira Matos.

Students freak out for a week in May called *Queima das Fitas*: fourth years burn their narrow ribbons in chamber pots—each faculty is represented by a different colour—and exchange them for wider ribbons as befits final-year students.

Around the University

The **aqueducto de São Sebastião** terminates just below the Praça de Dom Dinis. The 21 arches of the water course run to the southeast of the university, past an entrance to Pombal's lovely **Botanic Gardens**, which are formally laid out on a circular plan. It's a treat to be surrounded by tall trees and birdsong, but don't come looking for grass.

The so-called **Sé Nova** (New Cathedral) stands to the northwest of the university, in the Largo da Feira. It was begun in 1598 and took nearly the whole of the 17th century to complete, serving as a Jesuit college until the abolition of the order, and shortly afterwards as the seat of the bishopric. The austere façade opens onto a chilly, sober interior which uses space as delicately as does a bomb shelter. Flesh-coloured cherubs zip over the twin baroque organs.

The Rua da Matemática and the Rua de S. Salvador are the two most interesting streets leading down fairly steeply from the Sé Nova and the university. Here small children sing to themselves, to the geraniums, and to the laundry, challenged only by caged songbirds. Impudent ferns sprout from the drainpipes. Many of the university *repúblicas* are here— look especially for the **República Bota-Abaixo**, at the bottom of the Rua de São Salvador. It is decorated with a skull and crossbones, as well as various other large bones, pots and pans, and tin mugs are suspended by bits of string.

The Machado de Castro Museum

Open 10–1 and 2.30–5; closed Mon.

The Rua Borges Carneiro leads downhill from the Largo da Feira, past the **Machado de Castro Museum**, which contains one of the finest collections of sculpture in Portugal, covering particularly the three centuries after *c.* 1330. It's installed in the bishop's palace, most of which dates from the 16th century. An elegant loggia offers views of the river and lower part of the city.

Sculpture

Coimbra became a centre for sculpture because of the qualities of its local stone. *Pedra de Ançã* is a limestone which allows the sculptor a subtlety that is lost in the granite of Oporto and the marble of Lisbon and Évora.

From the early period, note the work of the Master Pêro, who is credited with introducing the Gothic style to Coimbra. His *Nossa Senhora do Ó*, of 1330, and his *Virgin and Child* are more fluid and expressive than the works of his contemporaries, which include a *Sta. Águeda* (Agatha), bearing her breasts on a platter, and a mounted knight brandishing his mace. The latter is a rare Gothic work because it is secular.

The finest works of the Renaissance are by Frenchmen. Nicolau Chanterène, the greatest sculptor working in Portugal in the 16th century, was based in Coimbra 1518–28, after his commission at Belém, and before he had achieved the refinement of his work at Évora. His finest work in the museum is the serene and beautiful *A Virgem Anunciada*.

The prolific João de Ruão (Jean de Rouen, *c.* 1495–1580) was married to the sister of the architect Marcos Pires, creator of the Manueline portal in the Old University. His work is generally overrated, but his *Entombment of Christ* is certainly arresting. Filipe Hodart (active 1522–34) was another Frenchman lured to Portugal by the wealth of the Orient: in 1530 he was commissioned to create the terracotta figures of the Last Supper for the Monastery of Santa Cruz. Their faces express great anguish and concern, their bodies are twisted in disbelief.

Stone sculpture declined in importance in the last quarter of the 16th century, featuring only in sarcophagi, fountains and architectural ornament. Wood took over from stone, a shift represented by a roomful of excellent, theatrical Luso-Flemish wooden sculptures from the 16th century.

Ceramics, Paintings and the Cryptoporticus

Across the loggia and upstairs, one can trace the development of Coimbra's ceramics. It seems that the fanciful animals which poke their heads around the cups and plates on sale in the city today, date back to the 17th century, when artists attempting to fashion animals they had never seen relied on travellers' inaccurate reports.

If you're short of time, it's best to walk straight through the several rooms of paintings to get to the 16th-century Portuguese and Flemish works. These include *A Assunção da Virgem*, from the school of the Master of Sardoal, in the first quarter of the century; the angels' robes are rather more beautiful than their faces. Contemporary with this work, but with a much less formal structure, are two panels from a retable by Quentin Metzys, *Ecce Homo* and *The Flagellation*.

Below the bishop's palace is a two-storey hide-and-seek cryptoporticus; the lower one is closed to the public. These vaulted galleries were built by the Romans as a foundation to give their forum an artificially high position: the cryptoporticus is an alternative to putting up an earthen platform. The forum itself was completely destroyed between the Middle Ages and the 17th century, but taken in conjunction with the cryptoporticus, it must have been one of the tallest buildings in Roman Portugal.

The Sé Velha

The Rua Borges Carneiro continues downhill past what is probably the finest Romanesque cathedral in Portugal, the Sé Velha (Old Cathedral). It was built *c.* 1162, when Coimbra was the nation's capital, and is topped by a square tower, a blue and white fish-scale cupola, and an angel weathervane.

Tradition says that the building was converted from a mosque, which is quite plausible because the first governor of Coimbra, Dom Sisinando, was a Moor who converted to Christianity. His tomb, broken open by the French, lies in the chapter house. An Arabic inscription built into the outer wall of the nave appears to read 'Ahmed-ben-Ishmael built it strongly by order of...'—but the layout of the cathedral is purely Christian.

The austerity of the battlemented western façade is broken by a recessed, round-arched window, which is almost the same size as the portal beneath it. The *Livro Preto* or *Black Book*, covering the period 1162–76, records that a certain Master Robert, a native of the Auverne, came four times from Lisbon to perfect his work on the eight shafts of this portico. Each time, he received four *morabitinos*, plus ten for his expenses, as well as bread, meat and wine for his four apprentices and food for his four asses.

The interior is grand and gigantic; it returned to its simplicity when the *azulejos* of 1508 were wrenched from the walls. Giant shells contain the holy water, so devout sea nymphs will feel at home. Four contented faces look down from the corners beneath the dome. But the retable is the eye-catching feature. Carved by two Flemings, Olivier de Gand and Jean d'Ypres, in 1508, it incorporates a high-relief panel of *The Assumption of the Virgin*, above the four Evangelists. The border of foliage contains figures of mermaids, hunters, a centaur, and a pig playing the bagpipes.

The Lower Town

The Church of Santa Cruz

The church of Santa Cruz is chock-full of goodies. It stands in the Praça 8 de Maio, at one end of Coimbra's main shopping street, the Rua Visconde de Luz. The church was founded by the clerics Dom Telo and Dom João Peculiar in 1131 as a priory of 12 Augustinian monks; São Teotónio, confessor of Afonso Henriques, was the first prior. The dilapidated building was reconstructed and enlarged by Dom Manuel from 1502 onwards.

He endowed Santa Cruz with many privileges: the priors were exempt from the jurisdiction of the bishop, and all the canons were chaplains to the king. In 1539, when the university had moved back to Coimbra from Lisbon, Dom João III made the priors chancellors in perpetuity, a rank they held until the Dissolution of 1834. From the plague of 1423 until it was forbidden in 1641, Santa Cruz was the destination of the eccentric Procession of the Nudes: penitents processed through the streets wearing only their shirts, engrossed in mutual flagellation.

The works of art within the church, mostly by foreign artists, are much more interesting than the body of the building. The façade has suffered from the rise of the street level and an 18th-century triumphal arch, but it was never beautiful. This western front is by Diogo de Castilho, with statues by João de Ruão and Nicolau Chanterène: in 1524 Dom Manuel wrote from Évora ordering 100 gold cruzados to be paid to Diogo and to Master Nicolau for the statues, and two years later another letter granted Diogo the privilege of riding on a mule, 'seeing that he has no horse'.

The Interior

The polygonal **pulpit** is carved in Ançã stone, with a hydra-headed dragon at its base, and attributed to João de Rouão. His tutor wrote to Dom João III in 1522: 'All who see it, say that in Spain there is no piece of stone of better workmanship; for this 20,000 reis have been paid.' In 1520 the bodies of Dom Afonso Henriques, the first King of Portugal, who had died nearly 400 years previously, and his son Dom Sancho I, were disinterred from their graves in front of the old church, and reinstated in thoroughly ornamented anachronistic medieval-style **tombs** sculpted by Chanterène (to the left and right of the high altar), with the effigies in battle dress. The **sacristy**, of 1622, contains furniture of the same date, based on the simple architectural style of the previous century, and some excellent paintings, including a *St Vincent* attributed to García Fernandes (often loaned to exhibitions abroad).

Boitac's Chapter House squeaks with bats, who patently ignore the injunction of the Cloister of Silence, from which stairs lead to the *coro alto*, where a chain of reliefs at the top of the magnificent **choir stalls** (currently closed for restoration) depicts Portuguese vessels doing battle with those of the Turks sailing past rather Germanic cities. These suggest that Master Machim, who started work on the stalls in 1513, had come from northern Europe.

Behind the church of Santa Cruz stands what seems to be a fanciful 20th-century bandstand: the central, circular platform is connected by buttresses to four satellites, and the whole set in a water tank choked by garbage. In fact it was completed in 1535, and its strange name, the **Jardim de Manga** (Garden of the Sleeve) hints at the origin of its design: according to tradition, Dom João III drew the plans for the building on his sleeve.

Across the River

The second left turning across the river leads to the swamped 14th-century Gothic **convent church of Santa Clara-a-Velha**, one of the most bizarre sights in Portugal. The convent was abandoned in the 17th century as a result of the annual flooding of the Mondego, which deposited so much sandy silt that the tops of the church's aisle arches protrude above the water level like Japanese bridges. The sainted Queen Isabel, who refounded the church in 1330, would not like the half-deaf guardian who hawks and spits into 3m of water, where fish swim and green weeds grow. The rose window, to the west, has become a porthole. The sarcophagus with Renaissance decoration was built for Dom Afonso Castelo Branco.

The Rua António Augusto Gonçalves runs several hundred metres from the front of the church to the 18th-century **Quinta das Lágrimas**, where, according to tradition, Inês de Castro was murdered by order of Dom Afonso IV, who considered her unworthy of his son Pedro. When he became king, her demented lover compelled the nobility to pay homage to her exhumed corpse, claiming he had married her (*see* 'Alcobaça', p.244). The *quinta* is in private hands, and closed to the public, but it may be possible to see the **Fonte dos Amores**, the fountain made famous by Camões in *The Lusiads*: 'The nymphs of the Mondego were long to remember, with sobbing, that dark dispatch [of Inês]; and their tears became a spring of pure water, that remembrance might be eternal. The fountain marks the scene of her earlier happiness ...'

Children and their minders can get a kick out of **Portugal dos Pequenitos Park** (*open 9–7.30*), which is entered near the church of Santa Clara-a-Velha: Portugal's monuments are represented in miniature, with pagodas and other exotics from the colonies, including African tribal spears and bottles of locally brewed beer.

The Calçada Santa Isabel rises from the Rossio to the **convent of Santa Clara-a-Nova**, built 1649–77 as a successor to its inundated namesake. Most of it is now used as a barracks and the north wing houses a **military museum** (*open 10–12 and 2–5*). The tank standing outside does little for the building itself. Try to catch the afternoon sun, which shows fabulous 17th-century gilt woodwork to its best advantage. Six panels depict the removal of the body of St Isabel from what threatened to become a watery grave in the church of Santa Clara-a-Velha, and its transference to a silver shrine here, in 1677; her clothes are displayed in the sacristy. The very large cloister was the gift of Dom João V, a man who loved nuns, though he preferred them to come from the convent at Odivelas.

Shopping

Coimbra pottery is delightfully bright and whimsical, painted with unlikely animals and birds which flit through the foliage. Stylistic influences are jumbled: the Hispano-Arab tradition of the 15th century; 16th-century Moghul India and the Orient; and the influence of Delft, transmitted by 17th-century merchants trading with Flanders.

The pottery is on sale throughout Coimbra, especially in the streets leading up to the cathedral from the lower part of town. Chiado, on Rua Ferreira, exhibits some fine ceramics and is a good place to visit before shopping, to get some idea of quality.

expensive

Like an ocean liner with high ceilings, central ★★★**Hotel Astória**, 21 Av. Emídio Navarro, ✆ 22055, ✉ 22057, overlooks the river, bathed in an attractive aura of the late 1930s. The restaurant is a little noisy, but serves good food.

moderate

Its competitors are pedestrian by comparison. Rooms in the grim-looking ★★★**Hotel Bragança**, 10 Largo das Ameias, ✆ 22171, ✉ 36135—next to the railway station—are comfortable but airless. The corridors are horrid, and the staff can be slow and unhelpful.

inexpensive

Furnished with 1950s tack, ★★★**Residencial Avenida**, 37 Av. Emídio Navarro, ✆ 22156—along from the tourist office, overlooking the river—is unappealing but comfortable enough. ★★**Residencial Antunes**, 8 Rua Castro Matoso, ✆ 823048, is very decent and comparatively quiet, but it is uphill from the aqueduct, a fairly long way east of the centre of town.

cheap

★★**Pensão Parque**, 42 Av. Emídio Navarro, ✆ 29202, offers tall, well-finished bedrooms at bargain prices. The same management operates ★★★**Residencial Universal**, 47 Av. Emídio Navarro, ✆ 22444. Neat, spacious rooms and river views from the upper floors are available at **Almedina Coimbra Hotel** ★★★, 203 Av. Fernão de Magalhães, ✆ 29161, in the same road as the bus station and the post office. Bathrooms are sanatorium-style. ★★★**Pensão Moderna**, 49 Rua Adelino Viega, ✆ 25413—off the Praça do Comércio—is dull but has clean rooms complete with televisions. The **Pensão Vitoria**, ✆ 35638, Rua da Sota 9 & 19, is clean, friendly and good value.

very cheap

Close to the railway station, ★**Pensão Flôr de Coimbra**, 5 Rua do Poço, ✆ 23865, is monastically simple, with long hostel-like corridors and sloping wooden ceilings. The restaurant on the first floor serves cheap food. **Hospedaria Simões**, 69 Rua Fernandes Tomás, ✆ 34638 also has simple, monastic rooms. The rooms on the ground floor are noisy, but they cost less.

---

moderate

Fado, coir matting, a tile dado, waiters in bow ties, Coimbra plates on the walls, candles, cushions and a yucca plant accompany the good food at **Trovador**, ✆ 25475, next to the Sé Velha. Try the *chafana à Senhora da Serra* (mutton with red wine). There's a balcony for drinkers who like *fado*. Irresistibly loaded with atmosphere, the walls of **Zé Manel**, 12 Beco do Forno, ☎ 23790, behind the Hotel Astória, are pinned with browning, curling poems, jokes, *fado* songs and compliments. The menu appears to be written by a dyslexic, with flourishes. The upmarket clientele squash in to eat enormous portions of very rich food. The soup is just like granny makes, the *feijoada* superb. A separate staircase leads to an upper chamber, which is brighter and more intimate. **D. Pedro**, 58 Av. Emídio Navarro, ☎ 29108, lacks atmosphere, despite the fountain in the centre of the room, and its menu is none too special.

cheap

Waitresses rush around **Adega Paço do Conde**, 1 Rua Paço do Conde, ☎ 25605, off the Praça do Comércio, an open-sided barbecue mostly under corrugated iron. **Jardim da Manga**, R. Nicolau Rui Fernandes, ☎ 29156, behind the church of Santa Cruz is a self-service cafeteria. *Closed Sat.* **Casa Tica** is tucked away in a street behind the Largo da Portagem. Gourds, wooden wheels, ox yokes, an alarm clock, an army of wine bottles and other random implements hang off the walls. This tiny, whimsical restaurant is populated by bubbly locals, some chatting eagerly in the galleried section around the top. The cheerful proprietor brings raw fish and meat to your table if you have trouble understanding the menu. Delicious food in a fun setting.

An open-air **café** in the Praça da República buzzes with students, below and behind the university. Alternatively, head for the café **Santa Cruz**, a splendid 17th-century construction adjacent to the church, complete with stained glass, ceiling tracery, and dragons tamed to hold lamps. The resident drunk lady at Coimbra-A sings heart-stopping *fado* in the early hours.

Around Coimbra

Conimbriga

Open 15 Mar–14 Sept, 9–1 and 2–8; 15 Sept–14 Mar, 9–1 and 2–6.

Portugal's most elaborate Roman site teems with wonderful mosaics and shrieking schoolchildren. The sprawling site occupies a plateau hemmed in by a V-shaped gorge, surrounded by wild rose bushes and low hills blanketed with umbrella pines and olive trees, girdled by a poorly preserved ceremonial wall. It's accompanied by an excellent museum, and a restaurant.

Although there's plenty to see, only about one-sixth of Conimbriga has been excavated; even the tribunal has not been located.

History

The name of Conimbriga separates into '*conim*', indicating a rocky outcrop or plateau, and '*briga*', the Celtic suffix denoting a defended site. Located midway along the Romans' Lisbon–Braga highway, it was first occupied by the Romans *c.* 200 BC, but fragments have been found dating back as far as 800–500 BC.

In 25 BC there was peace in Lusitania, and the Emperor Augustus determined to expand Conimbriga, to include an aqueduct, a forum with a temple, public baths, private housing and shops. It was Vespasian who made the town a monumental city, AD 69–79. The settlement flowered again in the 3rd century, blooming with those villas and mosaics that remain today. But the boom was shortlived: the Romans lost their grip in western Iberia, and *c.* AD 260–270 Franks and Almans crossed the Rhine and attacked the east of the Iberian peninsula. Although they did not reach as far as Lusitania, there was a general programme of fortifying the province. Conimbriga had to be protected, so a new defensive wall was built using materials wrenched from private houses, the baths, the amphitheatre and even the necropolis. To reduce time and cost, and to cut down on the policing of the walls, the residential part of the city was abandoned. Fear for the safety of the aqueduct led to the construction of a giant reservoir in one wing of the cryptoporticus of the forum.

The Swabians attacked Conimbriga in 465, seizing, amongst others, the wife and child of citizen Cantaber. They captured the city three years later and enslaved its populace—but Conimbriga was not deserted: its bishop attended the Council of Braga in 572. Shortly afterwards the settlement was abandoned in favour of a safer place also on the Lisbon–Braga highway, the Roman settlement of Aeminium. Through linguistic debasement, this became known as Coimbra. The preservation of Conimbriga depended on the departure of its residents.

Getting There

Sixteen km south of Coimbra, Conimbriga makes a good day trip from there. There is a 9am bus every day from the Avic Station on Rua Joao do Ruao, which returns at 3pm. Otherwise, there are direct buses every half-hour to Condeixa-a-Nova, half an hour's walk from the site..

The Site

The Museum

Open 15 Mar–14 Sept, 10–1 and 2–6; 15 Sept–14 Mar, 10–1 and 2–5; closed Mon.

A good place to start, the museum brings the site to life, from needles, hoes, and nails to hairbands, rings, and clips. One whole case is devoted to health and hygiene. Note the maquette of the forum; the real one is not yet open to the public. The labyrinth mosaic, with the Minotaur at its centre, was either a game or a superstitious prophylactic, to bring good health to the family.

Outside the City Walls

There are two main features outside the hastily constructed city walls. To the right (northeast) of the track leading to the excavations is the **House of the Fountains**, constructed during the first half of the 3rd century, on the site of a 1st-century house. The central peristyle of this family home is a pond jigsawed with flowerbeds, which tinkles with a mass of water jets. This design is very unusual, since normally Roman houses had an earthen courtyard in the middle, with only a small pool and flower garden; the Palace of Domitian in Rome is the only known parallel in a Roman town house. Amphoras built into the wall of another of the villa's pools were probably intended as a temporary home for the fish, while the pool they normally lived in was being cleaned. The villa's excellent tiles depict the four seasons, scenes from daily life such as stag hunting, and mythological happenings. They rely less on geometry than other tiles in Conimbriga, probably because they were created a couple of decades earlier.

To the other side of the track, the Roman shops, the two houses with well-preserved geometrical mosaics, and the poorly preserved baths, were disrupted by the hastily erected defensive wall.

Within the City Gates

Through the city gates stand the columns and half-columns of the **Villa of Cantaber**, which was one of the largest city residences in the western Roman world, dating from the 3rd century; the pampered residents had their own baths. On the far side of the villa, to the south, all that remains of the **Christian basilica** are the two semicircles of the baptismal font, and a tiny cruciform chapel whose shape suggests that it dates from the 6th century. When the city was abandoned, the consecrated area was employed as a cemetery.

The track continues past the villa of Cantaber and forks at the **Flavian Forum**. This was made up of two parts: the smooth expanse with the stumps of columns at its edges was the forum square, which was surrounded on three sides by covered porticoes. The upper part was the temple itself, built over a cryptoporticus to raise it to a dominant height.

A paved road ran from the forum to the **Thermae** (baths), past the **Insulae**. These shops, taverns, and storage rooms are now nondescript piles of rubble, but they were not always so dull: one of them produced the mind-boggling phallic vase displayed in the museum. The Augustan baths were at the terminus of the aqueduct; in Trajan's reign they were superseded by a much bigger complex, which is now reduced to large areas of flat stone, a staircase, a buttressed wall, and various sepulchral baths. The baths were supplied with water from one of two tanks fed by Conimbriga's aqueduct, which ran nearly 3500m from Alcabideque. Parts of it are still standing, and the collecting basin at the source is still in use as a fountain, a laundry tub and a watering trough.

The Monastery of São Marcos

Between the villages of São Martinho de Avore and São João do Campo, some 10km west of Coimbra, a minor road leads 4–5km north from the Coimbra–Figueira road to the Monastery of São Marcos, which is well worth a diversion: it contains four fine tombs, one of which is outstanding. Founded in 1452, the conventual buildings were burnt down by peasants in the 19th century in an attempt to injure the landlord who owned them; the buildings that stand in their place are owned by Coimbra University.

The church's Manueline portal opens onto a Baroque nave. Chanterène carved the limestone retable 1522–3, crowded with small and, unfortunately, painted figures enacting scenes of the deposition of Christ. Three tombs contain members of the da Silva family, two of them very elaborate and dated 1522, the third simpler and later, carved by João de Ruão in 1559. These wither by comparison with the beautifully proportioned and elegant tomb of Fernão Teles de Meneses, sculpted by Diogo Pires the Elder in 1481. The young soldier reclines beneath the folds of a draped stone canopy held aloft by hairy men. His sarcophagus is delicately ornamented with artichokes, and some very fine carvings inspired by Africa: a Negro head, seated monkeys and three hippopotami.

Montemór-o-Velho

Set on a hill above the fertile plains of the River Mondego, the **castle** of Montemór-o-Velho looks impressive from the road; it dates from the 11th century, with 14th-century additions, and was built to protect Coimbra. In the early 13th century, Dom Sancho I bequeathed the castle to his daughters Dona Teresa and Dona Mafalda, much to the annoyance of their brother Dom Afonso II, who besieged them there. The pope intervened to calm the unhappy family, resolving that the castle should be administered by the Templars and the lordship of the town by Dona Teresa. There's little to look at within the castle walls, except the delicate twisted Manueline columns in the plain **church of Santa Maria de Alcáçova**, which was restored in 1510, or the skeleton of a 16th-century royal residence.

In the lower part of the village itself, beside a muddy little tributary of the Mondego, the modest 17th-century exterior of the **convento de Nossa Senhora dos Anjos** belies the older and more attractive interior, dating at least from the 14th century. It contains the tomb of Diogo de Azambuja, by the Manueline master Diogo Pires the Younger, *c.* 1518. On the sarcophagus, scenes allude to the trading of gold: Diogo helped to establish an important entrepôt for the metal.

Luso and Buçaco

The **Forest of Buçaco** (Bussaco) covers 105ha (260 acres) of the northern slopes of the Serra do Buçaco, 27km north-northeast of Coimbra. It is a magical, deeply refreshing place—just give it time to work on you. Mossy paths ribbon between the venerable trees, winding through the sharp light past pools and fountains. Walkers can stumble on to crosses and peek into grottoes, which reveal tiny chapels hidden amongst the oaks and cork oaks. For peace of mind, collect a map from the tourist office in Luso, or from the Palace Hotel. Put it in your pocket, and get lost.

The airy spa town of **Luso**—jollier than most—is located some 3km downhill. The water tastes delicious—its high radioactive content is beneficial. If you're serious about a spa treatment, bring your reno-urinary disorders, hypertension, rheumatism, and/or your respiratory complaints.

History

It comes as no surprise that monks lived in this forest. The first were Benedictine hermits, in the 6th century. But it was not until the arrival of the Barefoot Carmelites in 1628 that Buçaco became famous: they walled the forest and planted an arboretum, which was enriched with unlikely species brought back by the Portuguese navigators. Now there are roughly 400 local and 300 exotic varieties, including Mexican cypresses—which look like cedars—and giant ferns, sequoias and ginkgo trees. Such were the qualities of the trees that in 1643 they came under papal protection: Urban VIII threatened to excommunicate anyone who damaged them. As with the trees, so with the monks. Their virtue had been kept intact by that pope's predecessor, Gregory XV, who forbade women to enter the precincts.

Things haven't always been this peaceful: in August 1810, a third French invading force of 66,000 men under Masséna entered the Beiras from Spain, occupying first Guarda and then Viseu. Wellington's guards held the main road to Coimbra, so the French attempted to get there by marching across the Buçaco hills. Wellington took up a position along the line of the ridge, and kept the majority of his 52,000 troops, half of them English, concealed behind it. Against advice, Masséna attacked up the steep slope, but his men were repeatedly thrown back. Eventually they were forced to work their way around the northern edge of the ridge, before turning on Coimbra. Wellington was able to withdraw undisturbed, to take up position at his Lines of Torres Vedras, north of Lisbon.

After the Dissolution of the religious houses, a scene-painter at the San Carlos Opera House designed a neo-Manueline summer palace for the royal family, completed in 1907, adjacent to what remains of the monastery, a small 17th-century church, with a cork-ceilinged cloister. The monarchy was extinguished in 1910, and the king's Swiss cook subsequently started to run the palace as a hotel.

© (031–)   *Where to Stay and Eating Out*

Buçaco

*****The Palace Hotel**, Mata do Buçaco, © 930101, @ 931609, is thrillingly unique, a fantastic, overpowering confection. It induces a camaraderie amongst guests, who respond by swaying down the grandest of staircases—sided with *azulejos* depicting the taking of Ceuta—for the sheer enjoyment of it, rubbing shoulders with the suits of armour, settling in leather chairs beneath billiard-table lamps in the bar, tracing unlikely arches, and peeking at Robin Hood-style murals and lonely lute players. The ceiling of the dining room says it all—its bosses are tipped with starry little lights. Bedrooms are nicely old-fashioned, with fine, highly polished furniture and huge bathtubs. It's tempting to cocoon oneself in the tall velvet curtains. The staff are efficient but stiff, almost too quick in the restaurant, where the food is eclipsed by the superb house wine. Main courses may be quails on toast, or peasant dishes. The choice of desserts is limited. Dinner is served between 7 and 11.30pm; breakfast is available from 8am.

The problem with staying in a tourist attraction is that bus-loads poke their heads through the doors, and sensibly so, from their point of view. The building gives a good indication of what Manueline architecture is not about—the decoration is superfluous, with no tension. The curious should aim for tea or a drink.

Courteous, very respectable, and good value, the large ★★★**Grande Hotel das Termas**, Rua dos Banhos, ✆ 930450, ✉ 930350 (*moderate*), is central and vanilla-coloured and offers smart, spacious bedrooms and a sparkling restaurant. It overlooks the well-maintained Olympic-sized swimming pool, which catches the afternoon sun. *Open 1 May–15 Oct.*

By contrast ★★★**Hotel Eden**, Rua Emidio Navarro, ✆ 939171, ✉ 930193 (*moderate*)—white, at the upper end of town—is characterless, with squashed bathrooms and an uninspiring restaurant. Next door, ramshackle ★★**Pensão Central**, Rua Emidio Navarro, ✆ 939254 (*cheap*), has oddly shaped rooms but is nicely furnished. The terrace restaurant offers *chanfana á Serrana* (mutton with red wine).

Ferns in the corridor and lacy curtains gentrify airy ★★**Pensão Astória**, Rua Emídio Navarro, ✆ 939182 (*inexpensive*)—opposite the Grande Hotel—with a pub attached.

Restaurante O Cesteiro, ✆ 939360 (*moderate*), on the edge of town near the railway station, is very popular with families at the weekend. It lacks atmosphere, but the food is good and fresh. The **Casa de Chá**, ✆ 939411, is a relaxed and civilized teahouse.

Aveiro

Aveiro stands at the eastern edge of a grey, shallow *Ria* (estuary), which extends 45km from Ovar to Mira, with a width of up to 10km, and into which flows the River Vouga. The saltwater estuary was formed by the retreat of the sea and the subsequent formation of coastal sandbanks, which closed up to form a lagoon. Sediment accumulated, and the estuary is now shattered into dunes and meadows of reeds.

In the 16th century, the 14,000 inhabitants were buoyed to prosperity by salt, fishing, and maritime trading. Over the next two centuries, the coastal sandbanks edged southwards until finally they closed up completely, leaving Aveiro high and dry. This combined with the fever-breeding marshes to reduce the population to about 3500 in the second half of the 18th century. Aveiro's fortunes only revived when the sandbar was artificially, permanently breached in 1808, restoring the town's rôle as an important port.

Aveiro is less than half an hour away from good sand beaches, but the town is not a resort. It retains a kind of mellow dignity, with open streets and dragon's-tooth pavements, though its fringe is marred by horrid modern buildings. Three main canals lead in to town from the *Ria*; the only similarity with Venice is that it's often quite smelly, but this can be blamed on the nearby paper factory rather than the canals. Just one building is outstanding, but the *Ria* gives plenty of scope for exploration, and if you dislike swimming in the waves of the Atlantic, the blue lagoon offers a calm alternative. There's a range of good places to stay in Aveiro, and a couple of worthwhile restaurants, although unhurried cafés are sparse.

Salt and Seaweed

Aveiro accommodates two antique industries: salt and seaweed. Brilliant little mounds of salt surround Aveiro in late summer, heaped between the grid of saltpans, before being transported in sober, heavy salt boats. Although it is probably much older, the salt industry dates back at least to AD 959, when Countess Mumadona Dias bequeathed her saltpans at Alvario, as it was known, to the monastery at Guimarães. Now refrigerated tankers bring cod to be salted and transformed into the ubiquitous *bacalhau*.

The estuary supplies a harvest of seaweed, which is used to fertilize Aveiro's crops, though the industry is being eaten away by artificial fertilizers. The green stuff is raked up from the shallow waters into dangerously low-slung, wide-bottomed *moliceiro* boats, which are punted when the wind is slack. The boats' high, curling prows are painted with matters of pride—crude horseriders, saints, women, even the poet Camões, in reds, blues, greens and yellows.

Aveiro ✆ (034–) **Getting There**

Aveiro's **railway station**, ✆ 24485, is served by frequent trains from Lisbon (2½hrs), Coimbra (¾hr) and Oporto (¾hr).

Rodonorte **buses**, ✆ 21755, run infrequently from Lisbon (4¾hrs), via Leiria (2¼hrs) and Figueira da Foz (1¼hrs).

Aveiro ✆ (034–) **Tourist Information**

The **tourist office** is at 8 Rua João Maidença, ✆ 23680, next to the Canal Central, over the bridge at the bottom of the main street.

The **railway station** doubles as the bus terminal, at the top of the main street.

Autoaviação Aveirense run buses along the coast to the nearby **beaches**, every hour during the summer and nearly as frequently in winter.

The Convent of Jesus

Aveiro's **museum** (*open 10–5.30; closed Mon and holidays*)—walk up the Rua Bat. Caçadores from the Praça Humberto Delgado—is installed in the convent of Jesus, which was founded in 1465, and seven years later received the Infanta Joana, daughter of Dom Afonso V, into its starched folds. She was a remarkable woman of celebrated beauty, whose portrait sent Louis XI of France into a swoon, but who was only interested in one crown, the Crown of Thorns.

This she adopted as her personal device, embroidering it on church linen and having it stamped onto her silver. When her brother and father returned from the successful Tangier expedition of 1471, she abdicated her role managing the royal household and asked to enter a convent. At Aveiro she kneaded bread and made prickly hair shirts for the ascetic order, but grew dangerously ill from the diet of bread, herbs and water. She was forbidden to take full vows, to the delight of her father and brother. The latter became Dom João II, and attempted to marry his sister to Richard III of England. She claimed this was impossible, as that king was already dead, and was proved correct. The Infanta Joana was beatified in 1693.

The Church

The convent was revamped in the 18th century: between 1725 and 1729 António Gomes and José Correia transformed its **church** into a fantastic riot of gilt woodwork, with a vaulted chancel like a shower of gold and flesh-coloured cherubs flying up the altar columns. In 1699 Dom Pedro II commissioned the royal architect, João Antunes, to create a tomb to commemorate the beatification of the Princess Infanta Saint Joana. It was 12 years in the making, and its gorgeous Florentine marble inlay fills the lower choir. Two of the supports are phoenixes, symbolizing immortality. The church is lined with scenes from her life—part of which was spent in the low 15th-century cloister that magnifies the sky. In the 18th century, the walls and ceiling of the chestnut *coro alto* were painted with several saints, who rub shoulders with long-feathered birds, parasols, and bows and arrows; perhaps one of the nuns brought a taste for chinoiserie with her from Macau.

The Museum

The museum itself contains unremarkable stone sculpture from the Coimbra school, various Baroque polychromed statues, including a winged St Michael. There are ivory crucifixes and Vista Alegre porcelains, but the most eye-catching works are the primitive paintings. Note particularly the early 16th-century *Senhora da Madressilva*, named after the honeysuckle she holds; St John the Evangelist on a balcony, of the same date; and a portrait of Princess Joana from the third quarter of the 15th century. Cloaked by her red dreadlocks, her arresting face is rather modern.

veiro, Portugal's Venice

Around the Convent

Around the corner in the Rua do Comandante Rocha e Cunha stands the **church of the monastery of São Domingos**, which serves as Aveiro's cathedral. It was founded in 1423, but subsequently remodelled, transformed not only by the façade of 1719, but more brutally by the recent rearrangement of the transepts. The only things worth looking at are the early 18th-century canvases depicting the life of St Domenic, over the choir stalls, and the 15th-century Cruz de São Domingos, a stone cross ornamented with scenes of the Passion, which used to stand outside the monastery but is now housed in the first chapel to the right of the entrance.

Aveiro ℂ (034–)   **Where to Stay**

moderate

The large ★★★**Hotel Imperial**, Rua Dr. Nascimento Leitão, ℂ 22141, ✆ 24148, straight up from the central roundabout, is neutral and efficient, monogrammed wherever possible. Saltpans are visible from the summer terrace. The restaurant caters for tour groups, offering fixed-price meals of dubious value, or *à la carte* steaks, porks, veals, hakes and eels. This is preferable to ★★★**Hotel Afonso V**, 65 Rua D. Manuel das Neves, ℂ 25191, ✆ 381111, farther from the canals, where bedrooms are brown and unexceptional, and the restaurant uninspiring. Patrons may opt to eat less expensively in raspberry booths in the snackbar. A way from the centre of town, ground-floor ★★★★**Residencial Paloma Blanca**, 23 Rua Luis Gomes de Carvalho, ℂ 381992, ✆ 381844, is installed in a lovely old house, though you wouldn't know that from within. It's very nicely done throughout, pretty and sturdy, with minibars.

inexpensive–cheap

More central and noisy, ★★**Hotel Arcada**, 4 Rua de Viana do Castelo, ℂ 23001, ✆ 21886, at the central roundabout, looks grander outside than in. It's old and muddy-coloured, but basically fine, with pleasant staff. Just off the central roundabout, in the Rua José Estêvão, are two tall converted old houses, with mouldings and bare floorboards. Both are clean, but ★★★**Residencial Estrêla**, at No.4, ℂ 23818 (*inexpensive*) is better furnished than ★★**Residencial Beira** at No.18, ℂ 24297 (*cheap*). ★★**Residencial Palmeira**, 7 Rua da Palmeira, ℂ 22521, close to Praça Humberto Delgado, is solid and decent, but rooms don't have bathrooms.

Aveiro ℂ (034–)   **Eating Out**

Head for **Telheiro**, 20 Largo da Praça do Peixe, ℂ 29473 (*moderate*)— by the fish market, not the main market. The food is good but the desserts dull. Aveiro is lucky to have a self-service vegetarian restaurant, **Sonatura**, at 6 Rua Clube dos Galitos, ℂ 24474 (*cheap*), opposite the tourist office. It serves fairly complicated dishes, but can be beset by blandness (the malaise of Portuguese veggies). The fresh fruit juices cannot be faulted. The last meal is served at 7.30pm.

There are some good beaches around Aveiro, and a number of forgettable towns which have come under the sway of the lagoon or the sea itself.

Beaches

The coastline bordering the Aveiro Lagoon is flat and backed by low grassy dunes, which offer meagre shelter from the Atlantic winds. The beaches are not really pretty, but if you're prepared to walk a little way from the access roads, you can sunbathe in splendid isolation. Infrastructure decreases southwards, and there's almost no development between Praia de Mira and Figueira da Foz. To the north, the coastline becomes increasingly developed as it approaches Espinho. The peninsula between São Jacinto and Torreira is only accessible by road at its northern end, so drivers from Aveiro must follow the route via Estarreja. There is a bus link between Aveiro and São Jacinto, but it's much more fun to get there by ferry.

São Jacinto is a humming little port on the *Ria*, with good swimming, and fun dockside cafés. There's a cool, wooded nature reserve just to the north, and the beaches are backed by woods as far as Torreira, a fishing village and resort with a direct ferry link to and from Aveiro. Oxen work on the beach, as at Praia de Mira.

At the mouth of the *Ria*, **Praia de Barra** is backed by ugly modern buildings and, to the rear, the blue lagoon. It tends to be crowded, because it is served by bus from Aveiro.

Costa Nova, a couple of kilometres to the south, attracts an older crowd, and the sand seems whiter than at Barra. The beach houses are painted with red or green or blue vertical stripes.

With its wooden houses built on stilts and its rudimentary development, **Praia de Mira** is one of the most attractive options south of Aveiro, not least because teams of oxen are driven back and forth along the beach, from July to September, hauling in the fishing nets. Small tree trunks serve as rollers for launching the high-prowed fishing boats, and when the catch is landed, it's auctioned on the beach.

decorated moliceiro

© (034-)

Where to Stay

On the peninsula between Torreira and São Jacinto, the glassy **Pousada da Ria**, Bico do Muranzel, Torreira-Murtosa, © 48332 (*category C*), is surrounded on three sides by water. For less exalted living in Torreira itself, try the **★Pensão Albertina**, Av. Arrais Faustino, ✆ 48306 (*cheap*).

Most of the accommodation around Praia de Barra is inland in Gafanha da Nazaré, including **★★★Hotel da Barra**, Av. Fernandes Lavrador, ✆ 369156 (*moderate*) and **★★★Pensão A Marisqueira**, Av. João Corte Real, ✆ 369262 (*inexpensive*).

There are various inexpensive places to stay in Praia de Mira, including **★★★Residencial Arco-Íris**, Av. do Mar, ✆ 471202 (*cheap*), and **★★★Residencial do Mar**, Av. do Mar, ✆ 471144 (*cheap*).

Turismo de Habitação

Mitre-shaped windows indicate that the U-shaped **Quinta do Paço da Ermida** (near Ilhavo, 6km south of Aveiro), ✆ 322496 or ✆ (01) 286 7958 (*moderate*), was a bishop's residence. It's a working farm with attendant dogs and Siamese cats, much polished wood, a canopied terrace with crickets and camellias, marble-topped commodes, and big flower arrangements. The five quiet bedrooms are furnished with heavy, but not oppressive, furniture, and come with elegant bathrooms. Breakfast is served in a dining room like a traditional billiards room. The lady of the house speaks English.

Inland

Ovar

Some 34km north of Aveiro, Ovar marks the northern extent of the waterways. The village makes its living from the timber trade, now that it's landlocked. Decades ago, the dusty, hefty fishwives of the village penetrated as far as Lisbon to hawk their wares, walking barefoot with crates on their heads and training their voices to penetrate every nook and cranny. Their few surviving successors in the capital are still known as Ovarinhas, or Varinhas.

The small, centrally located **Ethnographic Museum** takes particular delight in its collection of pots. The village is renowned for its *pão-de-ló* (a sort of sponge-cake), and its carnival at the beginning of March, which is presided over by clowns with frizzy wigs, and humpty-dumpty suits.

Santa Maria da Feira

Nine km northeast of Ovar, a Gothic castle looms over Santa Maria da Feira, a photogenic, right-angled bastion whose four towers are topped with a confection of cones. Built on the site of a pagan sanctuary, the castle is best seen when swathed in moonlight. It took its present form in the mid-15th century, when four sizzling hearths warmed the vaulted main hall and musicians plucked lutes on the balcony.

There is a *pension* in town, **★Pensão Ferreira**, Rua Dr. Vitorino de Sá, ✆ 056 32859 (*cheap*).

costa Nova

Avanca

At Avanca, 26km north of Aveiro, the **Casa do Marinheiro** is open to view, preserved and furnished in the jolly taste of Dr Egas Moniz, who studied at Coimbra and was awarded a Nobel Prize in 1949 for demonstrating the therapeutic value of removing bits of the brain in cases of mental disorder. He collected Vista Alegre porcelain, and paintings by his contemporaries José Malhoa and Guerra Junqueiro.

Ilhavo

According to legend, Ilhavo, 6km south of Aveiro, was founded by the Greeks, for it was a fishing port until landlocked by the accumulation of silt. Its **museum**, on the northern edge of the village, contains a collection of Vista Alegre porcelain, as well as models of fishing boats, a collection of shells, and models of the *moliceiros* that harvest seaweed.

Vista Alegre

The beauty and delicacy of Vista Alegre porcelain are renowned throughout Portugal. The factory was founded in 1824, to produce both glass and ceramics, and is surrounded by a village of workers' cottages, a couple of km south of Ilhavo. The factory itself is cloaked in secrecy, but it is possible to visit the firm's **museum** (*open weekdays 9–12.30 and 2–5.30*). Though uninformatively labelled, it shows how the porcelain evolved from the early attempts of 1824–32, which yielded only plain and lumpy earthenware. The founder of the factory dreamt of greater things, and went to collect samples of kaolin from Sèvres. Fortune favoured him, and in quarries near Ovar he discovered deposits of kaolin similar to that at Sèvres. He imported French craftsmen to train his workforce, and the way was set for the factory to produce anything from exquisite classic dinner services to fanciful Art Nouveau confections. The manufacture of glass was phased out.

It's worth looking in the adjacent **chapel of N.S da Penha** to see the tomb of its founder, Bishop Dom Manuel de Moura, one of the finest works carved by Cláudio Laprade, *c.* 1697. The bishop's effigy appears to be about to sneeze; in fact, he is gazing towards a low-relief carving of the Virgin Mary as he expires. The figure of Time waits impatiently with a shroud.

Figueira da Foz

'*Foz*' means 'mouth', and Figueira da Foz is a deep-sea fishing port at the mouth of the River Mondego, 40km west of Coimbra and 65km south of Aveiro. Since the beginning of this century, it has been one of northern Portugal's most popular and lively Portuguese family resorts. It also attracts a steady flow of Spaniards—all of whom combine to crowd even this very wide beach. The site has been occupied since Lusitanian times, but you wouldn't know it. The building of a new yacht marina is in progress at the moment.

Figueira da Foz ✆ (033–)   ***Tourist Information***

The **tourist office** is a veritable mine of information and is near the Grande Hotel on the Rua 25 de Abril, ✆ 22610 (*open until midnight during the summer*).

The **Museu Municipal do Dr. Santos Rocha** on the Rua Calouste Gulbenkian is worth a look for the collections of archaeology, ceramics and coins, as well as numerous photographs of 19th-century bathing belles. Overlooking the river, four rooms of the 17th-century **Casa do Paço**, the palace of the bishops of Coimbra, are lined with Dutch tiles, each of which pictures a different horseman, landscape, or religious scene. They form part of a cache shipwrecked here in the 18th century.

The **casino** provides a centre for nightlife, but only gamblers may enter.

Figueira da Foz ✆ (033–)   ***Where to Stay***

The ★★★★★**Clube de Vale de Leão**, Vai, Buarcos, ✆ 33057 (*luxury*), 5km north of town, is the executive's dream with health treatments, conference rooms and the like. It's thoroughly modern, with extensive grounds, and awash with facilities. The basic, heavy ★★★★**Grande Hotel**, Av. 25 de Abril, ✆ 22146 (*expensive*) is a bit grim. ★★★**Hotel Wellington**, 23 Rua Dr. Calado, ✆ 22539, ✇ 27593 (*moderate*), is overpriced, with rather small bedrooms. Good if you don't want to leave your hotel for the duration of the holiday. ★**Hotel Universal**, 50 Rua Miguel Bombarda, ✆ 26228 (*inexpensive*) is spruce, hygienic and well kitted out. The worn carpets of the decent ★★★★**Albergaria Nicola**, 59 Rua Bernardo Lopes, ✆ 22359 (*inexpensive*) make it more appealing. ★★★**Pensão Central**, 36 Rua Bernardo Lopes, ✆ 22308 (*cheap*) is a good bet, and very good value. The high-ceilinged rooms are homey and geraniums line the steps.

Turismo de Habitação

Casa da Azenha Velha, Caceira de Cima, ✆ 25041, ✇ 29704 (*moderate*), is 9km from Figueira da Foz, and stands in its own 12-hectare estate. Geese are raised here. There are riding stables and a riding ring complete with obstacles for the keen equestrian. A fire burns in the large rustic fireplace in the sitting room, setting the tone for the farmhouse comfort.

Figueira da Foz ℭ (033–)	***Eating Out***

Bright, pine **Restaurante O Túnel**, 15 Rua de S. Lourenço, ℭ 26163 (*moderate*), keeps its kitchen in full view. The food is simple but the ingredients are of good quality, served by frenetic waitresses. If you're feeling adventurous, grilled boar is the speciality; otherwise, the beef is good, served with little oven potatoes. English-speaking **Escondidinho**, 60–70 Rua Dr. Francisco A. Diniz, ℭ 22494 (*moderate*), offers Goan food, ranging from spicy hot to spicy tepid. The pork fricassee is good, the prawn curry a bit thin. For dessert, the vaguely caramel *bibinca* is preferable to the chickpea sweet.

Leiria

Set on the flat and fertile coastal plain, 70km southeast of Coimbra and 54km south of Figueira da Foz, at the southern extreme of the Beira Litoral, Leiria is tucked into an elbow of the River Lis. The green and pleasant town of 14,000 souls is built around a castle hillock, and hums with activity, forming a regional centre for small-scale heavy industry, including stonework, cement, steel and dyes. Leiria's main attraction for the visitor is as a base from which to explore Batalha and northern Estremadura, including Alcobaça and the caves at Mira d'Aire.

History

Dom Afonso Henriques built a castle at Leiria in 1135, to serve as his southern stronghold against the Moors, near the site of the Roman town of Collipo. The Moors sacked it two years later, killing 250 of the garrison. Small watchtowers were erected on nearby vantage points, which lit beacons in times of danger and launched horn-blowers into the country-side, shouting '*Mouros ha terra! As armas!*' Knights caught skiving this call to arms were punished with fines and the docking of their horses; lesser mortals had their beards cropped. Nevertheless, the castle had to be rebuilt for the third time in 1144.

In 1254, Leiria hosted the country's first *Cortes* at which the Commons were represented: Dom Afonso III was threatening to solve his monetary difficulties by debasing the coinage, but agreed to accept compensation in lieu of the debasement. A price tax was also intro-duced in the Minho and the Douro, which had previously paid taxes in kind. Dom Dinis and Queen Isabel resided here briefly in the 13th century. Leiria's paper manufacture encouraged local Jews to set up one of the Peninsula's first printing presses, in 1492.

Leiria ℭ (044–)	***Getting There***

By **road**, Leiria is 121km from Aveiro, 70km from Coimbra, 133km from Lisbon, 181km from Oporto, and 162km from Viseu.

Trains, ℭ 882027, run infrequently from Lisbon (2¾hrs), via Caldas da Rainha (frequent, 1hr), and from Figueira da Foz (1hr). Avoid the train from Coimbra, which requires changing at both Alfarelos and Amieira.

Tejo **bus** connections, ✆ 811507, are north–south orientated too, with the most frequent services from Batalha (40mins), Lisbon (2hrs), Aveiro (2¼hrs) and Figueira da Foz (1hr). Buses run very infrequently from Braga (4¼hrs), Bragança (7½hrs) and Chaves (7¼hrs) via Lamego (4¾hrs) and Viseu (3hrs).

Leiria ✆ (044–) — Tourist Information

The **tourist office** is in the Jardim Luís de Camões, ✆ 814748, at one corner of the municipal garden; the **bus station** is on the opposite side of the garden. The railway station, ✆ 882027, is a couple of km northeast of town, with connecting buses.

Around the Town

Perched steep above Leiria, the **castle complex** (*open daily 9–6.30*) is best seen from a distance, and preferably at night. For although the hill is cool and green, the atmosphere is spoilt by electricity cables and lamps, the price to pay for pretty floodlighting. The rigid keep of 1324 is ringed by a defensive wall. This is incorporated in Dom Dinis' palace, flanked by two crenellated towers and centred on a loggia overlooking the town. To the rear of the palace stands the plain roofless Church of N.S. da Penha, built by João I *c.* 1400.

The road downhill opens onto the Largo da Sé, where the tall **cathedral**, completed in the hundred years after 1559, provides the setting for sly glances and anguished prayer in Eça de Quieroz' novel, *The Sin of Father Amaro*. It stands at the edge of the sober and strait-laced old part of town.

Really the only curiosity in Leiria is the modern **Fonte Luminosa**, opposite the tourist office, an Adam and Eve-type sculpture which equips Adam with a semi-erection.

Leiria ✆ (044–) — Where to Stay

moderate

For service and comfort ★★★**Hotel Dom João III**, Av. Dom João III, ✆ 812500, ✉ 812235—on the north side of town, towards Figueira da Foz—is exemplary and good value, though little about it is Portuguese. It attracts a rare type of tailored and sun-glassed clientele, some of whose large-windowed bedrooms overlook the castle. The furnishings are substantial and thoughtful: even the shower nozzle has a massage setting. The cosseted restaurant (*expensive*) offers a large menu with a particularly good choice of soups and simply cooked meats.

★★★**Hotel Eurosol**, Rua D. José Alves da Silva, ✆ 812201, ✉ 811205—on the southern edge of town towards Batalha—is drab, with pokey bathrooms, but otherwise OK. The restaurant (*expensive*) has a good view and nice linen, but the menu is international. The polygonal swimming pool is shared with the ★★★**Hotel Eurosol Jardim**, ✆ 812201, ✉ 811205, next door, which looks like a factory and feels institutional, though the bathrooms are more acceptable than its sister's. The prices are the same for each. Bedrooms are functional leatherette in the ninth-floor ★★★★**Pensão S. Francisco**, 26 Rua de S. Francisco, ✆ 823110, @ 812677 (by the river, on the north side of town), but the views are good, and rooms have TVs.

Rooms in ★★★★**Hotel Liz**, 10 Largo Alexandre Herculano, ✆ 814017, by the river bridge, are very light but sparse. The staff are pleasant.

inexpensive

The public parts of ★★★★**Residencial Ramalhete**, 30 Rua Dr. Correia Mateus, ✆ 812802, @ 815099, are decorated in fun turn-of-the-century style; the bedrooms are fine if you don't mind the stairs to get there.

cheap

★★★**Residencial Leiriense**, 6 Rua Afonso de Albuquerque, ✆ 823054, is airy but plain, except for the mouldings and painted swallows on the ceilings. Nearby ★★**Pensão Alcôa**, 24 Rua Rodrigues Cordeiro, ✆ 32690, is musty and cell-like, but clean. ★★★**Residencial Dom Dinis**, 2 Trav. de Tomar, ✆ 815342, is across the bridge from the tourist office and provides pleasant rooms and a car park—you'll probably need a car to get up the steep road.

Leiria ✆ (044–)   **Eating Out**

Several km from Leiria, **Tromba Rija**, Rua Professores Portelas, Marrazes, ✆ 32022, @ 856160 (*expensive*), offers home-style Portuguese cooking at its best. Square, cosy and wooden, its walls are pinned with the praises of happy gastronomes. There's no written menu. The grill is in full view, but this is a good opportunity to experiment with one of the more complicated dishes like *feijoada tromba rija*, or another of the daily specialities. It's a 500$00 taxi ride away; if you're driving, cross the river heading for Figueira da Foz, take the second right to Marrazes, and the first left after the motorway bridge. *Closed Sun.*

In town, apart from the hotel restaurants, best head for the Rua Dr. Correia Mateus, behind the market, where a string of warm and lively restaurants offer large portions at low and moderate prices. Otherwise there's **Reis**, 17 Rua Venceslau de Morais, ✆ 24834, on the groundfloor of the Centro Comercial (*cheap*), which provides quick and efficient service, large portions, a good choice of wine and a fair *carne de porco Alentejana*. *Closed Sat.* As well as being an open bakery with very good bread and excellent *bolos de mel*, **Pão Quente**, ✆ 31859, opposite, is a bustling pizzeria. **Restaurante Montecarlo**, 32–34 Rua Dr. Correia Mateus (*cheap*), is probably one of the best budget restaurants: the portions are huge so the *meia dose* (half-portion) should satisfy even the greediest.

Batalha

The great Abbey of Batalha stands in flat and verdant pinelands horribly close to the Lisbon–Oporto highway, 11km south of Leiria. The effects of the pollution and vibrations from the N1 are starting to tell, but despite talks of 'moving' the road, there are no actual plans to do anything as yet. The Abbey has spawned a little town which caters enthusiastically to the tourist crowds. The **tourist office** is next to the abbey. There are frequent buses to Leiria and Nazare.

History

When Dom Fernando I died in 1383, his venomous wife Leonor Teles assumed the position of regent, assisted by her lover Count Andeiro. The king had died without a son; his daughter Beatriz was married to the King of Castile, Juan I, who added the arms of Portugal to his standard, and ordered all Portuguese townships to proclaim Beatriz as queen. Those who feared absorption by Castile focused their hopes on one of Dom Fernando's illegitimate half-brothers, Dom João of Aviz, who 'was accompanied by the common people [of Lisbon] as if he were dropping precious treasures for them to grab', according to the chronicler Fernão Lopes.

Having consulted a visionary Castilian hermit, Dom João sought an audience with the queen, who sat doing needlework and wondered why Dom João was armed and 'not wearing gloves as the English do'. She soon found out: Dom João murdered her lover and forced her to flee for her life. He was proclaimed king at the palace window, but did not receive official backing until the *Cortes* met at Coimbra in 1385. Juan I of Castile set his sights on besieging Lisbon, which was held by the Portuguese forces together with the castles around the capital, and much of the Alentejo. As the Castilian forces advanced, they cut off the heads, or hands, or tongues of those Portuguese whom they captured.

On Tuesday, 14 August 1385, Nun' Álvares Pereira commanded the Portuguese army to take up a position at São Jorge on the Lisbon road. For this he used English terminology—the van, the rear, the right and left wings—which had been learnt from the English armies in the Hundred Years War. On their left flank, the 6500 Portuguese troops were supported by about 500 English crossbowmen, sent by Richard II. Together they dug shallow trenches, which were covered with brushwood. In the evening 30,000 Castilian troops came within range, travelling south. Juan I, being ill, rode a donkey, and forbade engagement with the Portuguese army, but his *hidalgos* were impetuous, and broke rank.

The battle of Aljubarotta was over quickly—the Castilian royal standard fell within an hour—but its effects were tremendous: it secured the independence of Portugal from Spanish domination until the dynasty of Aviz was brought to an end 200 years later. João of Aviz became Dom João I, the undisputed ruler of a united kingdom. Many Portuguese nobles were killed, fighting for the Castilian king against the upstart bastard João. The latter's success heralded the reorganization of the nobility, elevating members of the bourgeoisie, artisans and the petty aristocracy. But it also had a more tangible legacy: before the battle João had vowed to build an abbey should he be victorious. Work on the Dominican Battle Abbey started three years later, in 1388, near the site of his victory.

The Abbey of Batalha

The essential parts of the abbey were completed during the reign of João I under the architects Afonso Domingues and Ouguête. These include the church, the royal cloister, and the chapter house. The founder's chapel was concluded in 1434, the year after his death. His eldest son, Dom Duarte (1433–8) commissioned the same architects to build the octagonal 'Unfinished Chapels' as a pantheon for himself and his descendants. This work was continued by Dom Afonso V, who also built a second cloister according to plans by the Alentejan uncle and nephew, Martins Vasques and Fernão de Évora. But it was Dom Manuel who employed Mateus Fernandes and Boitac to alter the Gothic character of parts of the abbey, blending in exotic and extravagant ornament, until the king concentrated all his efforts on his own mausoleum at Belém. Dom João III constructed new dormitories and a cloister (destroyed 1811), a novitiate and an inn—but he stopped building *c.* 1550 as his attention wandered to Tomar.

Manuel Gandra, a geomancer of unorthodox views, offers an alternative explanation for this termination. He believes that the House of Avis connected its emblem, the dove, with the symbol of the Holy Spirit, and intended Batalha as a temple of the Holy Spirit, with themselves at the head of the cult: the pious Dom João III ceased construction because he saw what his ancestors were up to.

The Exterior

The eye wanders over the honey-coloured exterior, over the pinnacles, the flying buttresses and the tracery balustrades, for there is no focus of attention. Nor are there bell-towers, because the Dominicans eschew belltowers. The western portal is very finely carved, with six columns either side of the doorway, on each of which stand modern copies of the 12 Apostles. Above them rises a series of arches niched with biblical kings and queens, the prophets and the angels. On the tympanum, the Creator is surrounded by the four Evangelists. The central octagon of the founder's chapel rises to the right. It all smacks of the English perpendicular style, and indeed Philippa of Lancaster, wife of Dom

Batalha Abbey

João I, may have had a hand in this—she could have imported English architects, during the reign of her cousin Richard II.

The Interior

The exterior belies the sublime interior: the effect is complicated and inexpressible, so thoroughly are the architects manipulating us. It refreshes wonderfully—the secret is in the harmony of the proportions and the purity of the style. The Gothic nave seems impossibly tall. Great plain piers separate the eight bays of the 80m nave from the aisles, which are tinted by modern stained glass. The tomb stone of Mateus Fernandes (c. 1480–1515), who directed the building works during the Manueline period, lies just inside the western entrance.

The Founder's Chapel

To the right is the Capela do Fundador (founder's chapel), designed by Huguet, master of works from 1402 to 1438, and completed in 1434, after the death of João I. It centres on the tomb of João I and Philippa of Lancaster, whose effigies lie hand in hand beneath an exquisite octagonal lantern. He wears the insignia of the Order of the Garter, which was founded by Philippa's father, Edward III. The rear wall is lined with the tombs of their four younger sons. Dom Fernando's is farthest to the left; he was left as a hostage for the return of Ceuta to the Moors, following the capture of the Portuguese army by Sala-ben-Sala in 1437. Dom Fernando was put to work in the vizier's garden and stables at Fez, before being confined to a dungeon, where he died of dysentery after five years of captivity. His body was hung by the feet from the walls of Fez, from which awkward position his Portuguese companions cut out his heart and embalmed it. This was brought to Batalha, and the scant remains of his other parts followed 22 years later, in 1471. Henry the Navigator's tomb is second from the right. The face of his effigy is quite different to that portrayed in the panels of São Vicente (see **Lisbon**, 'Museu de Arte Antiga', p.306).

The Cloisters

The nave opens onto the **Claustro Real**, built by Afonso Domingues, who was master of works from 1388 to 1402. Dom Manuel found it unsatisfying, and ordered Boitac to embellish the arches with marvellous thorny tracery, entwining crosses of the Order of Christ and armillary spheres, employing pearly columns and scaly artichokes (which prevented scurvy and were thus revered by the navigators). An arch opens onto the **Chapter House**, where the forceful unsupported vault provides a suitable setting for the Tomb of the Unknown Soldiers, one from Africa, and one from the Flanders front. The **refectory** is now a military museum and giftshop. At right angles to it stands the sober and elegant Gothic **Claustro de Dom Afonso V**.

The Unfinished Chapels

Dom Duarte, the pious eldest son of Dom João I and Philippa of Lancaster, attached a self-contained octagonal mausoleum to the east end of the abbey, the roofless Capelas Imperfeitas (Unfinished Chapels). Ouguête began work on the seven radial chapels c. 1435, but his design was profoundly altered by the imaginative genius of Mateus

Fernandes, Dom Manuel's master of works, who intended to build an upper octagon, but was able only to begin construction on the forlorn stumps of its buttresses. The true legacy of Mateus Fernandes is the stunning western portal, created in 1509. It is 15m high, and every inch of every arch is exciting: the stone is wrought to a fine filigree of thistles and ivy, chains and rope. At the base are stone snails! Double circles contain Dom Manuel's motto, which seems to read '*Tayas Erey*' or '*Taya Serey*', but which should be '*Tanaz serey*', the old Portuguese for 'I shall be tenacious': the 'y' is a pair of pincers, and the tenacious ivy around each word emphasizes the message. Dom Duarte died in 1438, and was entombed in a chapel opposite the entrance.

The Battleground of Aljubarrota

Four km south of Batalha (and 10km northeast of the village of Aljubarrota), the chapel of S. Jorge marks the battleground of Aljubarrota. The Spaniards were defeated in one hour, which was long enough for Nun' Álvares Pereira, the commander of the Portuguese troops, to get up a sweat; a jug of water stands in the porch of the chapel, to quench his ghost.

Nearby stands an iron statue of a baker's wife, who served her country by hitting Castilians with a baker's shovel. Beckford reports that after the battle the King of Castile scampered off and 'tore his hair and plucked off his beard by handfuls, and raved and ranted like a maniac—the details of this frantic pluckage are to be found in a letter from the Constable Nun' Álvarez Pereira to the Abbot of Alcobaça'.

Batalha ✆ (044–)   *Where to Stay and Eating Out*

The relaxed **Pousada do Mestre Afonso Domingues**, ✆ 96260, ✉ 96247 (*category C*), is a new but unobtrusive building next to the abbey, designed to exclude the noise of the freeway. Its attractive public rooms are paved with dragons' teeth, but the bedrooms feel rather lifeless. The plain dining room offers dishes including roast leg of pork. The **Pensão Gladius**, ✆ 96760 (*cheap*), is very basic but OK. As is **Pensão Vitória**, Largo da Miercórdia, ✆ 96678 (*cheap*).

Turismo de Habitação

The din of traffic doesn't really penetrate hospitable **Quinta do Fidalgo**, ✆ 96114 (*expensive*), just the other side of the main road. A separate block of the unprepossessing house incorporates four guestrooms and a homey sitting room complete with reproduction furniture, a fireplace, cardtable and TV. Bedrooms are comfortably and substantially furnished, with luxurious marble bathrooms, overlooking a sandy garden. There is also a suite with its own entrance.

The exquisitely converted **Casa do Outeiro**, 4 Largo Carvalho, ✆ 96806, ✉ 96808 (*inexpensive*), is preferable, a small house with a swimming pool.

There is a huddle of indifferent touristy restaurants around the abbey.

The Virgin Mary appeared six times at Fátima, 22km southeast of Leiria and 18km east of Batalha. The town has become one of the most important places of pilgrimage in the Catholic world. A giant neo-classical basilica flanked by colonnades overlooks a 15-ha (37-acre) saucer-shaped tarmac esplanade, which penants cross on their knees. It is of no architectural interest; Fátima is not for observers. An official notice puts it like this: 'If you come simply as a visitor, respect the pilgrims at prayer. This place has nothing to satisfy mere curiosity. What matters here is the heart.' Visitors are asked to cover their legs and shoulders. There are pilgrimages on the 12th/13th of each month; crowds reach 100,000 in May and October.

History

On 13 May 1917, three shepherd children saw the Virgin: Lúcia, Francisco and Jacinta, aged 10, 9, and 7. Only Lúcia could converse with her. The children were shown a vision of hell in which 'many souls' were lost through 'sins of the flesh' and because they had 'no one to pray and make sacrifices for them'. The faithful were entreated to 'pray, pray a great deal and make many sacrifices', to 'pray the rosary every day to obtain peace for the world'. If her requests were heard, she promised 'the salvation of many souls, the conversion of Russia, and world peace'. Otherwise, a second war would engulf the world and Russia would 'spread her errors throughout the world, fomenting wars and persecutions against the Church. The good will be martyred, the Holy Father will have much to suffer, various nations will be annihilated ... But in the end, my Immaculate Heart will triumph. The Holy Father will consecrate Russia to me, it will be converted, and a period of peace will be given to the world.'

The Virgin subsequently appeared at the same place on the same day of the month until 13 October, when 70,000 pilgrims and sceptics witnessed the Miracle of the Sun: the sun danced in the sky and then zigzagged towards earth. The Virgin stated that 'the punishment for sin is war' and that 'men must cease to offend God and ask pardon for their sins'.

Pope Paul VI declared the occurrences at Fátima to be 'an affirmation of the Gospel'. Francisco died in 1919 and Jacinta in the following year; their tombs are in the basilica. In 1928 their cousin Lúcia entered the Carmelite convent at Pontevedra in Coimbra. She and Pope Paul VI attended the fiftieth anniversary of the apparitions, along with 1.5 million other pilgrims.

Getting There

Fátima is on the Entroncamento–Coimbra-B **train** route: from Lisbon's Santa Apolónia station, change at Entroncamento (from which Fátima is a mere ¼hr distant); trains from Coimbra-B take 1½hrs. Change there from Oporto, Espinho and Aveiro.

Local **buses** run fairly frequently from Tomar and Leiria. Every day, three RN Express buses make their way from Lisbon (2½hrs) via Santarém (1¼hrs).

Infrequent buses run from Braga (4½hrs), via Oporto (3hrs) and Coimbra (1¼hrs). Just one bus makes the trip from Faro (8hrs), via Santarém (1¼hrs); in the opposite direction, it comes from Coimbra (1½hrs).

Fátima ℰ (049–) **Tourist Information**

The **tourist office** is in the Av. D. José Alves Correia da Silva, ℰ 531139. For the railway station, dial ℰ 46122, and for the bus station, ℰ 531651.

Fátima ℰ (049–) **Where to Stay**

 Among the shops and stalls selling tacky mementos, there are many places to stay in Fátima, but they get heavily booked during the major pilgrimages. Options include ★★★**Hotel Regina**, Rua Cónego Dr Manuel Formigão, ℰ 532303, 🖉 532663 (*inexpensive*) and ★★★**Residencial São Paulo**, Rua de S. Paulo, ℰ 531572 (*cheap*). There's also **Hotel Verbo Divino**, Praça Paulo VI, ℰ 532243 (*inexpensive*).

Ourém Velha

On a high hill surrounded by plains and gentle valleys, 11km northeast of Fátima, 24km southeast of Leiria, 20km northwest of Tomar, and slightly southwest of the market town of Vila Nova de Ourém, the castle-palace of Ourém was rebuilt in the 15th century to satisfy the pretensions of Dom Afonso, son of the first Duke of Bragança, in a style clearly influenced by his travels in Italy. A random arrangement of Gothic windows open on to the courtyard, while balconies are supported by arched brickwork. The ornamental band of ceramic tiles on the north side of the Torre Solar may have been the work of mudéjar craftsmen.

Attached to the 15th-century Igreja Matriz, the **crypt of Dom Afonso** is a simple space which smacks of the synagogue at Tomar, completed in 1460.

Estremadura

water fountain, sintra

Estremadura is a swathe of rolling downland on Portugal's Atlantic coast, incorporating Lisbon in the south. The capital is bracketed by two ranges of hills, each totally different in character; to the southeast, the humped limestone Serra da Arrábida, with its panic of wild flowers; to the northwest, the mossy, craggy Serra de Sintra.

The province was named when it was the southernmost territory occupied by Christians (the Latin *'extrema Durii'* means 'farthest land from the Douro'); after the conquest of the Moors, much of the land in Estremadura was given to the Cistercians and to the canons of St Augustine. North of Sintra, ranks of trees and limestone walls separate orchards and olive groves, vineyards, fields of millet and wheat, and market gardens. Lone settlements straggle between clustered villages, where humble houses are built on two storeys, unlike those of the south. Lisbon exerts a magnetic pull on the economy and attitudes of Estremadura; farm produce is trucked to the capital; people's horizons are a little wider, their senses more canny. Those who live within the orbit of Lisbon are called Saloios, a name derived from the Arabic word *çalliao*, the tribute paid by Moorish bakers in Lisbon.

Perhaps because of the pull of Lisbon, Estremadura has little cultural integrity; there are some remarkable monuments—the palaces at Sintra and Mafra, the abbey at Alcobaça—but the towns, and the people, are rather colourless.

Getting Around

The charming walled settlement of Óbidos is a good base from which to explore the north of the province by car; if you're dependent on public transport, Leiria, at the southern tip of Beira Litoral, would be a better bet.

by car

The road network is good, and incorporates a stretch of motorway from Lisbon to Setúbal. Be particularly careful driving on the Estrada Marginal from Cascais to Lisbon, which is infamous for its high accident rate.

by train

With the exception of suburban lines from Lisbon to Cascais and Sintra, the railway runs north–south from Lisbon to Óbidos, Caldas da Rainha, and Leiria (Beira Litoral)—thus avoiding Estremadura's principal monuments, and offering no route into the Ribatejo. There is no railway bridge across the Tagus, so southbound rail passengers must first take a ferry from Lisbon's Terreiro do Paço to Barreiro.

by bus

Most express buses departing from Lisbon head straight for Santarém (Ribatejo) or Setúbal, so the local bus network is particularly useful for getting around Estremadura. You'll need a car to get the most out of the Serra da Arrábida.

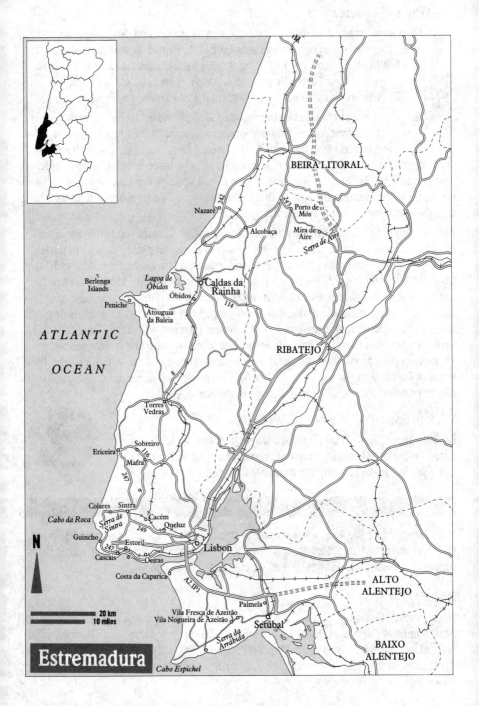

Estremadura

The Wines of Estremadura

The *Oeste* (western) region is Portugal's most productive. Stretching north-west from the Tagus estuary as far as Caldas da Rainha, it makes reds and whites in equal quantity, including the dry yellow *vinho do ano* (wine of the year) of the Torres Vedras Cooperative. The light, cherry-coloured reds are more interesting, particularly the soft red of Óbidos.

There are four small Demarcated Regions near Lisbon, all under threat from rising land and property prices. Indeed, the winery at Carcavelos is virtually extinct. This would have upset King Dom José, who was so proud of Carcavelos wines that in 1752 he sent some to the Chinese court. Wellington and his troops were more partial to the wine of Bucelas, which is produced by fermenting the grapes in open wood vats. This produces a light and slightly acidic wine, that gets very dry with age.

But the wine of Colares takes the biscuit; traditionally, Colares red is the finest and most distinctive in the country. The wine-makers have had plenty of time to perfect their technique—as long ago as 1255, a land grant made by King Dom Afonso III to Pedro Miguel and his wife Maria Estevão required them to plant vines. These peculiar vines are unmistakable: at Colares, dune sands cover the soil's clay base to a depth of 3–10m; the roots of the vine must be planted in clay, so a trench is dug, the roots are planted, and the trunk of the vine is covered with sand. Only the vine branches emerge; these are sheltered from the wind by cane and willow fences. Thus were they protected from the dreadful phylloxera epidemic which ravaged the vines of Portugal in the 1870s and '80s. The aromatic, full-flavoured red takes the colour of black cherries; the white is not in the same league.

What to Eat

Estremadura is renowned for its *açorda de marisco*, which tastes much better than it sounds; prawns, clams and cockles are blended into mashed soaked bread, and topped with eggs.

Alcobaça

The dusty town of Alcobaça was spawned by one of Portugal's most impressive churches, at the confluence of the Rivers Alcoa and Baça, 20km south of Leiria. Fruitful, rolling fields surround the town with dwarfish trees, whose peaches are superb.

History

Dom Afonso Henriques founded the abbey as an offering of thanks for the capture of Santarém from the Moors. Building began in 1178, the year before Pope Alexander III recognized the new Christian nation of Portugal. The king chose the self-sufficient Cistercians, ever in search of lonely places, to colonize and develop the reconquered lands north of Lisbon; the abbey was granted vast estates, including thirteen small towns and three seaports, over which the abbot held civil jurisdiction. He was entitled Lord of the Water and the Wind, because of the estates' many wind- and watermills. He was visitor to all the Benedictine abbeys in the country and was, for over 300 years, until the reign of Cardinal King Henry, the superior of the great military Order of Christ. The abbey yielded nothing to the king, except a pair of boots or shoes when he visited.

Before the Black Death reduced the number to eight, there are said to have been 999 monks. From the mid-13th century, the monks washed their hands of any farm work, to devote themselves to teaching. They founded the country's first public school in 1269, and provided books and money to help Dom Dinis to establish the University of Lisbon, which subsequently moved to Coimbra.

Decadence

Royal interference combined with inept and domineering abbots to foment decadence. But the agricultural activity of the monastery revived in the 18th century: the abbot was almost as dynamic as his cousin Pombal. He drained new land, planted olive groves, and founded an apiary which produced the clearest honey in Portugal. When questioned at the end of the century, the farmers and fruitgrowers of the district reported that it was 'our indulgent landlords and kind friends, the monks' who had taught them to cultivate with such care, to manure with such discernment and to spare their cattle from excessive labour, as Beckford reports.

He visited the abbey in 1794, just five years after Murphy had 'found the greatest temperance and decorum, blended with hospitality and cheerfulness'. Writing 40 years later, Beckford painted a different picture altogether:

> ...In came the Grand Priors hand in hand, all three together. 'To the kitchen,' said they in perfect unison, 'to the kitchen and that immediately.'

The kitchen, next to the refectory, was 'the most distinguished temple of gluttony in all Europe', loaded with every sort and size of river fish, heaps of game and venison, and 'pastry in vast abundance, which a numerous tribe of lay brothers and their attendants were rolling out and puffing up into an hundred different shapes, singing all the while as blithely as larks in a corn-field.'

Junot's soldiers pillaged the abbey in 1810, and the monks were expelled in 1834, when the religious orders were extinguished.

Getting There

Infrequent Rodonorte Express buses run from Lisbon (2 hrs); semi-frequent local buses arrive from Leiria (¾hr), Batalha and Nazaré.

Tourist Information

The **tourist office** is in the Praça 25 de Abril, ✆ 062 42377.

The Abbey of Alcobaça

The celestial simplicity of the Abbey of Alcobaça is awesome and calming. It is the largest church in the country, and its architecture heralds the emergence of the Gothic style in Portugal. But try to see it before Batalha (see 'Beira Litoral', pp.233–5), which is more uplifting. The hybrid façade stretches over 220m. The plain wings, reconstructed in 1725, emanate from the original portal and rose window, but the structure has no fluidity, the eye does not travel. Statues of S. Bento and S. Bernardo were installed either side of the portal, statues of the Virtues flank the rose window, and the Virgin presides over all, between the towers.

The first abbot, Ranulph, was sent by St Bernard himself. He may have brought with him plans for the abbey: the interior is modelled on the Cistercian church at Clairval (1115), in Citeaux, Burgundy. At 106m, it is enormously long, and proportionally narrow, although the truncated pier shafts give breadth to the nave. The Cistercian canon prohibits decorations and statues; the interior has been thoroughly scrubbed in an attempt to restore the original austerity. Terracotta statues of the Kings of Portugal up to Dom José I are shelved in the 18th-century **Sala dos Reis**, to the left of the entrance, which also contains a bronze cauldron captured from the Spanish at Aljubarrota. The *azulejo* dado depicts the history of the monastery.

The Tombs of Pedro and Inês

The unforgettable tombs of Dom Pedro and Inês de Castro stand in the transepts, foot to foot, as requested, so that on Judgement Day they will open their eyes and see one another. The story goes that, after the death of his wife, Prince Dom Pedro fell in love with her Spanish lady-in-waiting, Dona Inês de Castro. Fearful of her brothers' influence, leading nobles poisoned King Dom Afonso V's mind against her. He sanctioned her murder, unaware that the couple had married in secret at Bragança, to legitimize their children. Inês' 'heron-neck' was severed at Coimbra. When Dom Pedro succeeded to the throne two years later, in 1357, two of the three murderers were brought to him at Santarém, tied to an ox-yoke. He is reported to have ripped out their hearts and eaten them, before exhuming Inês' decomposing body and compelling the nobility to do homage to her, prior to her entombment here.

These 14th-century limestone sarcophagi embody the delicacy of Portuguese sculpture at its most magnificent and gracious. Each effigy is attended by six fairylike angels, and the sides of each tomb are entirely covered with reliefs representing biblical scenes, the supplication of various martyrs, and the Passion. A line of musicians play along the top of one side of Inês' tomb, and the dreadful Last Judgement is meted out at her feet, encompassing hell, purgatory and paradise. The figures supporting her tomb have the bodies of dogs and the grim faces of men, including Pedro Coelho, one of her murderers. The wheel of fortune stands still, at the head of Dom Pedro's tomb, bordered with scenes from the life of St Bartholomew. The tombs are inscribed 'Até ao fim do mundo' ('until the end of the world'). Junot's soldiers damaged both monuments as they searched for treasure, pocketing Inês' nose in the process.

The Abbey Buildings

A chapel off the south transept contains the tombs of Kings Dom Afonso II and Dom Afonso III, as well as a mutilated 17th-century terracotta tableau of the death of St Bernard incorporating some 30 figures and their complex hairdos. A pair of frothy, seaflower Manueline portals (*c.* 1520) lead off the Ambulatory behind the high altar, to the Sacristy, which contains pillaged reliquaries, or to the vestibule opposite.

The north aisle connects with the **cloister of Dom Dinis**, whose ground floor was built by Domingo Domingues 1308–11, making it the oldest Cistercian cloister in Portugal, and the model for those of Évora, Lisbon, Oporto and Coimbra. The upper storey was added some 200 years later.

The monks performed their ablutions at the octagonal 14th-century *lavabo*, now primly restored and covered with plants. They ate in silence in the beautiful vaulted **refectory** opposite, while edifying passages from the Bible were read to them. A tributary of the River Alcoa runs through the mammoth 18th-century **kitchen**, adjacent to the refectory, that the monks might feed off fresh fish. Further down the cloister, a staircase leads to the monks' dormitory, now out of bounds. (Until the 17th century, when cells were allowed, monks slept fully dressed in the dormitory, in beds separated by low partitions—high partitions were forbidden by the Chapter's general.) By the staircase is the Parlatory, where the prior gave audiences to the monks, and the square Chapter House, where work was apportioned and friars elected their abbot.

Atlantis Crystal

Alcobaça is also the home of the Atlantis Crystal factory, on the bank of the River Alcoa. Unfortunately it is not open to the public, though the manufacturing process is fascinating. The full-lead crystal is made with 32 per cent red lead (lead oxide)—which gives it weight, brilliance, and a musical ring—mixed with iron-free Belgian sand, and potash. Each stage is worked by hand, from blowing the glass, and remelting the sharp lip of goblets, to cutting with diamond saws and acid polishing. Atlantis export to Britain and North America, and have shops all over Portugal, including one near the factory, in the Avenida Prof. Joaquim Natividade, ✆ 062 540200. Candlesticks cost around 5000$00, decanters from 8500$00 to 15000$00, but since they don't arrange shipping, it's more sensible to shop at your departure point. [Alex is going to ring to check prices—didn't get there]

Alcobaça ✆ (062–)   ***Where to Stay***

★★Hotel Santa Maria, Rua Dr. Francisco Zagalo, ✆ 597395, ✆ 596715 (*inexpensive*), is very decent, with views of the front of the abbey. **★★★Pensão Coraçoes Unidos**, Rua Frei António Brandão, ✆ 42142 (*cheap*)—in the road opposite the entrance to the abbey—offers very basic rooms, with windows opening on to a walkway. The restaurant (*cheap*) is better value, with a fixed-price menu.

Challet Fonte Nova, Estrada da Fonte Nova, ✆ 598300 (*luxury*) is a small, burnt-pink palace in town, near the cloisters, dating from the 1860s and recently restored to its former glory. Everything is furnished in heavy silks (including the affable owner, who speaks French)—the effect is rich indeed. Each of the six bedrooms possesses a different (silky) character—the single room on the first floor has a great draped bed, like a Turkish divan.

Five km north of Alcobaça, on the road to Leiria, the **Casa da Padeira**, ✆ 508272, ✆ 508272 (*moderate*), is undistinguished and impersonal.

Alcobaça ✆ (062–)   *Eating Out*

See Hotel Santa Maria above. The first-floor **Restaurante Trindade**, 22 Praça Dom Afonso Henriques, ✆ 42397 (*moderate*) is beside the abbey and has tables outside in summer, with nicely laid places, though the service can be rather forced. *Closed Sat in winter.*

Around Alcobaça

Nazaré

Some 34km southwest of Leiria and 11km northwest of Alcobaça, the fishing town and popular west-coast resort of Nazaré sits beside a wide, sweeping beach which terminates abruptly at a steep cliff. The first reference to fishing here dates from 1643, but the beach was not formed until the sea withdrew in the following century.

Tourists swell the filthy town, crowding the beach and staking it with tents. Nazaré's 10,000 souls claim Phoenician descent. The women wear elaborate gold earrings, coloured headscarves, dark knitted shawls, pom-pom skirts and eschew stockings, flaunting their bloomers and varicose veins. The men tend racks of splayed sardines and jack-fish drying in the sun on the promenade by the beach, where people walk around eating *tremoceiros* (lupin seeds), reminiscing about the days before the marina, when oxen lived on the sand and dragged boats ashore. The grid-patterned streets are filled with laundry, garbage and birdcages. The **tourist ofice**, ✆ (062) 561194, is near the funicular.

A funicular makes the 110m ascent to the district of Sítio on the promontory overlooking the town, where the 17th-century pilgrimage **church of N.S. da Nazaré** contains some good 18th-century Dutch tiles. The first church built on this site commemorated the miraculous rescue of Dom Fuas Roupinho, castellan of Porto de Mós: in 1182 the stag he was hunting along these cliffs leapt into the sea. His horse was about to follow, when he invoked the Virgin and she halted the beast.

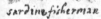

sardine fisherman

There is a wide range of accommodation, including the incongruously modern ★★★**Hotel da Nazaré**, Largo Afonso Zuquete, ✆ 561311, 🖷 561238 (*expensive*), just off the esplanade, which has a rooftop terrace and good views from the upper floors; ★★★**Hotel Praia**, 39 Av. Vieira Guimarães, ✆ 561423, 🖷 561436 (*moderate*), a traditional inn opposite the market with bathroom *azujelos*; ★★**Pensão-Restaurante Riba-Mar**, 9 Rua Gomes Freire, ✆ 551158, 🖷 562224 (*moderate*), on the waterfront, and the good-value **Pensão Central**, 83–85 Rua Monzinho de Albuquerque, ✆ 551510 (*moderate*).

The beach is lined by restaurants with plate-glass windows, which expose diners doing battle with their fishbones. Two of the more popular are **Mar Bravo**, 67-A Praça Sousa Oliveira, ✆ 551180, 🖷 553970, and **Ribamar** next to it (*both moderate*). Do check that the fish isn't frozen. **Casa Lazaro**, Rua Antonio Carvalho Laranjo, near the Residencial Beira-Mar (*moderate*), benefits greatly from being off the main strip. The house wine is as good as the food. **Meu Jardin**, Rua Gil Vicente 67B, ✆ 561784 (*inexpensive*) serves pizza and has some vegetarian options on the menu. **Brisa do Mar**, 10 Av. Vieira Guimarães, ✆ 551197 (*cheap*), opposite the bus station, is mercifully ordinary.

Pinhal Real

North of Nazaré and west of Leiria grows a great pine forest (the Pinhal Real). Dom Dinis planted trees on almost 10,000 ha of land, to produce wood for shipbuilding—Portuguese merchants increased their trade with English ports in the 13th century—and to halt encroaching sand dunes. The same trees were used to construct the first caravels. At the upper end of the forest **São Pedro de Muel** has been developed as a resort, but is said to have severe problems with pollution.

São Martinho do Porto

Twelve km south of Nazaré and 18km southwest of Alcobaça, the little resort of São Martinho do Porto stands beside a semicircular beach which is almost totally sheltered behind natural jetties, making it a good place for children to swim.

Porto de Mós

On a limestone outcrop on the western slope of the Serra dos Candeeiros, 16km northeast of Alcobaça and 25km south of Leiria, the green-coned castle of Porto de Mós dominates the village below it. The fortress was rebuilt by Dom Afonso, son of the first Duke of Bragança, who transformed it into a fortified palace, adding a Renaissance patio and incorporating bits of Roman stonework in the defensive walls. It's not worth going out of your way to come here. The rocky gash to the left of the castle is called the Devil's Nostrils (*Ventas do Diabo*).

Mira d'Aire

The smooth limestone hills of the Serra d'Aire give no indication of their spectacular bellies, a series of caves (*grutas*) bristling with stalactites.

The largest and most accessible of the caves can be entered slightly uphill of the textile town of Mira d'Aire, 14km southeast of Porto de Mós (*open 1 April–30 Sept, 9am–9pm; otherwise 9am–7pm; tours in Portuguese and French; wait for a group to assemble*). They were discovered in 1947 by a boy chasing a sparrow. Rough steps lead down through humid chambers whose roofs drip stone stakes and fragile tentacles, fantastically spotlit in shades of yellow and red. The batless chambers have picturesque names like Hell's Door, Jelly Fish and Church Organ. Around 20m high, they are dizzying rather than claustrophobic.

The visit lasts about an hour, ending beside the underground Black River, with coloured fountains. Then an elevator whisks visitors back through the mountain to the ticket office.

There are more, worthwhile caves near the hamlets of Alvados and Santo António, but one hour underground is enough for most people. The **Grutas da Moeda**, ℃ (044) 190302, at São Mamede, 6km west of Fátima, might be worth a visit if only because one of the underground chambers has been converted into a bar!

Caldas da Rainha

The unexceptional spa town of Caldas da Rainha, 26km southwest of Alcobaça and 5km north of Óbidos, wallows beside clay deposits, which have made it a hive of pottery production.

As she passed through her estates in a carriage, Queen Leonor, wife of Dom João II, noticed a man washing himself. Her eyes widened at this unusual occurrence; she was informed that the sulphuric waters he was bathing in had healing qualities, and, having noted the lack of any large hospital and baths for the poor of Lisbon, founded one here in 1485, at her own expense. A village was designed on the site, privileges were offered to settlers, and the hospital was equipped with linen sheets and feather beds.

Dom João V came three times to take the waters, but William Beckford was unimpressed. On his excursion he noted: 'In my eyes the whole of this famous stewing-place wore a sickly unprepossessing aspect. Almost every third or fourth person you met was a quince-coloured apothecary...and every tenth or twelfth, a rheumatic or palsied invalid, with his limbs all atwist and his mouth all awry, being conveyed to the baths in a chair.'

The pottery industry blossomed in the late 19th century, moulded by Rafael Bordalo Pinheiro, whose favourite creations included smiling wetnurses, open-handed farmers, sacristans, and John Bull. The tradition continues, kneading together wit and gross gaudiness. It's surprising what takes shape—even clay phalluses are sold in the daily market, discreetly bound in brown paper. Kiwi fruits and avocados grow unprotected in the environs, while chrysanthemums require a blanket of plastic tarpaulins.

Infrequent **trains** run from Lisbon (1¾hrs), while local trains arrive from Óbidos in less than 10 minutes. In the other direction, they come from Figueira da Foz (2½hrs), via Leiria (1¼hrs).

Frequent Rodonorte Express **buses** follow a similar route, making the journey from Lisbon in 1½hrs, or from Coimbra in 2½hrs. There are numerous buses from Óbidos (20 minutes).

Caldas de Rainha Ⓒ (062–)   **Tourist Information**

The **tourist office** is in the Praça da República, Ⓒ 831003. From the **railway station**, Ⓒ 831067, follow the Avenida Independéncia Nacional as it veers right, following through to the Praça da República. To get there from the **bus station**, Ⓒ 22067, turn left into the Rua Heróis da Grande Guerra, and take the second left into the Rua Almirante Cândido dos Reis.

Around the Town

Before plunging in, curious visitors to the **spa** (in the Largo Rainha Dona Leonor, Ⓒ 062 832133; a short walk from the Praça da República) should stop at the reception desk, where the weak will be deterred by the all-pervasive stink of sulphur. If you don't want to take your clothes off, the **nasal douche** is worthwhile—but check that nobody is watching: water shoots up one nostril and out the other. Portugal will never smell the same again. Should you choose to go the whole hog, three 35°C **swimming pools** await, in stone-walled rooms (with barrel-vaulted ceilings for people who swim on their backs).

The spa hospital offers a whole gamut of intermediary treatments: note that you may have to pay for a whole day's regimen. Serious visitors should book an appointment with an English-speaking doctor (three consultations cost 3700$00) for advice on a programme of treatment for rheumatism, traumatism, respiratory or female genital complaints, or detoxification.

As you exit the spa, take heart from the **ceramic bacalhau** at the top of a staircase to your right, and go round the back to the early Manueline **church of N.S. do Pópulo**. When this hospital chapel opened in 1496, anyone visiting on certain days of the year was granted a papal indulgence. Beaked, howling gargoyles relieve the heavy exteriors of the church and belltower, while the interior, merry with blue and yellow 17th-century *azulejos*, climaxes in an early 16th-century wooden triptych from the Lisbon school, fitted above the chancel arch. Lilies are painted on the door to the sacristy, which contains a very good pale and doleful *Virgin and Child* by Josefa de Óbidos. The ornate octagonal Gothic font is bunched with grapes.

The **Museu de José Malhoa**, in the Dom Carlos I garden (off the Largo Rainha Dona Leonor), is named after its principal artist, who died in 1933. His chalks and early works are worth a look, but the most rewarding part of the museum is the basement, which is a sort of biblical Madame Tussaud's in pottery. Entered separately, it contains the master-work of Rafael Bordalo Pinheiro, begun in 1887: nine dramatic groups of detailed lifesize ceramic models of characters at the Passion, intended to replace clay figures in the chapels of Buçaco. A colourful and ugly collection of reptilian, caricaturist, and naturalist ceramics is also on show.

Near the park, the **Bordalo Pinheiro Factory** manufactures fun glazed tableware in vegetal forms, 90 per cent of which is exported, including the bright cabbage leaf plates. A small museum displays the factory's wares, and the shop charges around 1250$00 for a large plate. Shipping can be arranged.

The **Ceramic Museum**, at the furthest tip of the park, close to the junction of the Rua Rafael Bordalo Pinheiro and the Av. Visconde de Sacavém, contains some witty pieces including Art-Deco tiles of dragonflies and frogs. Turning up the avenue, a living sculptor's work is displayed in his corrugated-plastic and bolted-iron workshop, the **Atelier Museu António Duarte**. Some pieces are very beautiful; others are wild, and accompanied by striking sketches.

Caldas da Rainha ✆ *(062–)* **Where to Stay**

Writing in 1726, Brockwell warned: 'For persons not admitted into the Hospital, here are the worst Accommodations in the Universe.' The situation has improved somewhat. The large **★★★Hotel Malhao**, 31 Rua António Sérgio, ✆ 842180, ✆ 842621 (*moderate*), is functional but brown, with a swimming pool and maids in frilly uniforms. Local pottery has been smashed and mounted on an interesting collage in the lobby. There's featureless, solid **★★★Residencial Dona Leonor**, 6 Hemiciclo João Paulo II, ✆ 842171, ✆ 842172 (*cheap*). The painter José Malhão was born in **★★Pensão Central**, Largo Dr. José Barbosa, ✆ 831914 (*cheap*). He has left no visible trace.

Caldas da Rainha ✆ *(062–)* **Eating Out**

The restaurant at **Esplanada do Parque**, in the Parque Dom Carlos I, ✆ 832080, is separated from the café by a bookshelf. It's light and leafy, but not the most promising place to experiment with medallions of veal with whisky sauce and dried fruits. **Zé do Barrete**, 16–18 Travessa da Cova da Onça (*moderate*), has to be the best place for grills and spit-roasted meats in no-nonsense surroundings. *Closed Sun.* **Restaurant Portugal**, 30 Rua Almirante Cândido dos Reis, ✆ 34280 (*cheap*), is off the Praça da República, by the tourist office, and offers spruce service at decent prices, though the paintings are fake and muzak plays and the stewed rabbit comes with tinned peas.

Óbidos

Óbidos is an outrageously pretty small town crowning a limestone ridge, 5km south of Caldas da Rainha. Most of its 5000 souls are contained within the 13th- and 14th-century castle walls; the five cobbled streets of white houses, some bordered with mauve or burnt

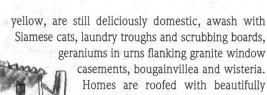

yellow, are still deliciously domestic, awash with Siamese cats, laundry troughs and scrubbing boards, geraniums in urns flanking granite window casements, bougainvillea and wisteria. Homes are roofed with beautifully weathered, lichenous terracotta, whose television aerials are soon to be removed for aesthetic reasons. Tourism has been relatively good for Óbidos; the streets are swept, the dust dampened, and the houses kept in good repair.

In 1148 Dom Afonso Henriques captured the castle from the Moors; he and his troops crept up on it disguised as cherry trees. Dom Dinis gave Óbidos to his queen, Isabel, as a wedding present, and it remained the property of the queens of Portugal until 1834. Josefa de Óbidos (1634–84), whose portraits were sought by fashionable ladies taking the waters at Caldas da Rainha, founded a painting school here. Her better works can be seen in Buçaco, Coimbra, Évora and Cascais.

There are many small places to stay in Óbidos; those in despair of finding anywhere very cheap can console themselves with *ginjinha*, the local morello cherry liqueur, which tastes like celestial cough syrup.

Getting There

Trains arrive infrequently from Lisbon (2hrs) and very infrequently from Figueira da Foz (1¾hrs). There are frequent trains from Leiria (1hr) and Caldas da Rainha (5mins). Local **buses** make the journey from Peniche (¾hr) and Caldas da Rainha (20mins). There are 3 direct buses to Lisbon every day.

Óbidos ☎ (062–)　　　　　　　　　　　　　　　　　　***Tourist Information***

Buses stop beside the Porta da Vila, from which the Rua Direita leads to the astonishingly helpful **tourist office**, ☎ 959231. The **railway station**, ☎ 959186, is at the bottom of Óbidos's hill. Trains still run through although the station is closed. Buy your ticket on the train—the tourist office has timetables.

Around the Town

Óbidos's main entrance gate is the zigzag **Porta da Vila**—scourge of cars' wing mirrors, a gossiping spot, and, since the 18th century, a tiled oratory, all rolled into one. At the opposite end of town, overlooking the flat basin of what was once the lagoon, the castle's high curtain walls with square and cylindrical towers are often used for a filmset. The stronghold was built by Dom Dinis, substantially reconstructed in the third quarter of the 14th century, and altered by Dom Manuel. The 16th-century castellan's residence has been converted into a *pousada*.

Along the main street, the **pillory** bears a little granite shrimping net, symbol of Dona Leonor. The **church of Santa Maria**, in the pillory square, was founded before the Portuguese monarchy, though the present church dates from the Renaissance. Walls of florid late 17th-century *azulejos* support a ceiling painted with 'Indian' masks and reddish cherubs hatched from ideas of Brazil. Here the 10-year-old king Dom Afonso V wed Dona Isabel, two years his junior, in 1444. The tomb of Dom João de Noroha, castellan of Óbidos, stands against the left wall of the church, a prototype Portuguese Renaissance vault (a decorated arch covering a sarcophagus panelled with a plaque, with either a group of biblical figures or a kneeling effigy of the deceased represented on the sarcophagus). Carved 1526–8, perhaps by Chanterène, the intimate relationship of the Ança-stone figures of the pietà, St John and Mary Magdalene, is detailed right down to the tear drops. João da Costa painted the panels over the high altar 1616–18; to the right are panels by Josefa de Óbidos, dated 1661.

To the right of the church, the **museum** (*open 9.30–12.30 and 2–6; closed Mon*) houses excruciating paintings from churches destroyed by the earthquake of 1755; among them are a portrait by Josefa de Óbidos, and double-sided panels still used in the Easter Week procession. There is a Peninsular War room, with guns. Monks spun the 16th-century *Roleta dos Irmãos* (Brothers' roulette) wheel to apportion their daily work, so doubt not: there really is a divine croupier.

The sacristy of the **church of São Pedro** contains a noisemaker, which looks like a portable stocks. It is knocked together to beckon people to church on Good Friday and Easter Saturday, when no churchbells are permitted to ring. Despite its odd pyramidal roof, there is nothing of interest inside the hexagonal **church of Senhor da Pedra** (*open April–Sept, 9.30–12.30 and 2.30–7*) apart from the stone figure on the cross which gives the church its name. It is 500m below Óbidos on the road to Caldas da Rainha. The church was begun and left incomplete during the reign of Dom João V. Chicks hatch in the Nissen huts nearby.

Óbidos ☎ (062–)   **Where to Stay**

                                                            expensive

Installed in the castellan's residence, the excellent **Pousada do Castelo**, ☎ 959105, ℻ 959148 (*category CH*), is both comfortable and ancient. It's very well maintained, with hand axes, a suit of armour, and pewter candlesticks to lend a touch of grandeur. There are just six double bedrooms and three suites. Busy fabrics brighten bedrooms with tiny deep-set windows and wooden ceilings. Approached across the open battlements, the keep contains a cosy medieval maisonette. Stone slabs lead up to the dining room, which is furnished like a provincial *quinta*. Meals do justice to the setting—the kidneys in Madeira sauce are recommended, as is the braised chicken. Try for a table at the Manueline windows, overlooking the courtyard topiary with shrubs like *My Fair Lady* hats. Reservations are necessary for summer lunches.

***Hotel Mansão da Torre, on the Estrada Nacional, ✆ 959247, 🖷 959051, has recently been built around a medieval tower, but it's charmless and spare, despite the showy trimmings. There are two hard tennis courts, and a swimming pool, but no restaurant.

Just outside the town walls, the ******Estalagem do Convento**, Rua Dom João de Ornelas, ✆ 959214, 🖷 959159, used to be a modest nunnery. Its former inmates would relate more to the industrial-sized toilet rolls than to the banknotes tacked onto the ceiling beams at the entrance, or the London Underground signs in the lounge-style pub. Comfortable bedrooms are approached through an irregular courtyard set with tables. The squashed and popular restaurant is a cut above, with a cheerful fireplace and often excellent food. The bass is delicious; if it's not on the menu, try the fried slices of ham.

moderate

The best rooms at the ******Albergaria Rainha Santa Isabel**, Rua Direita, ✆ 959115, 🖷 959115, have balconies overlooking the practically carless cobbled main street, so guests can watch low-key life unravel. Otherwise, the clean rooms are simply but comfortably furnished, with attractive bathrooms. ******Albergaria Josefa d'Óbidos**, Rua Dom João de Ornelas, ✆ 959323, 🖷 959533, is closer to the town's main gate. The bedrooms are as stiff as the bolsters, the reception area sterile, and the restaurant touristy. Its saving grace is the discotheque (*weekends only*), which is a magnet for the surrounding region.

inexpensive–cheap

About 500m downhill from Óbidos, off the road to Caldas da Rainha, ****Residencial Martim de Freitas**, 8 Estrada Nacional, ✆ 959185 (*inexpensive*) is heavily Portuguese, small, plain and clean, with no frills. Outside the town walls, the new **Hospedaria Lauro**, Casal da Canastra, ✆ 950183 (*cheap*) has a pool and private parking. The rooms are comfortable and clean. Ask at the tourist office for details of cheap **accommodation in private houses**.

Turismo de Habitação

Downhill from the castle, the **Casa do Poço**, Trav. da Rua Nova, ✆ 959358 (*moderate*) offers bald rooms entered via a courtyard and lit through terracotta lampshades. Under the same ownership, **Casa do Rológio**, Rua da Graça, ✆ 959282, also feels bare. The stone sundial outside the house gives it its name. **Casal do Pinhão**, Bairro Senhora da Luz, ✆ 959078, is a rural estate 3km from the town. The rooms are light and airy but also feel somehow sparse, despite the proliferation of flowers on the curtains and bedspreads.

Óbidos ✆ *(062–)*   **Eating Out**

Apart from the restaurants in the **Pousada** and the **Estalagem do Convento**, **Alcaide**, Rua Direita, ✆ 959220, 🖷 959159 (*moderate,*) serves very good food in a room draped with ivy and red tablecloths. The proprietors' Azorean specialities include tunafish steak in batter, and a pudding made with biscuits and powdered milk custard. The *ensopado de safio* (eel stew) is very rich, with plenty of gravy to soak into the bread. *Closed Tues and Nov.* On Rua Dom João de Ornelas, there's also **Estalagem do Convento**, ✆ 959214 (*expensive*). The **Vila Infanta** ✆ 959757, on Largo do Santuaro do Senhor da Pedra, serves local specialities, whilst the **Casa do Poço** (*see* above) has a fun bar, dominated by a crane-like winepress built with a treetrunk. There are carvings around the fireplace, and *fado* at around 11 on Saturday nights.

Peniche and Around

Atouguia da Baleia

Fifteen km west of Óbidos, on the bad road from there to Peniche, the village of Atouguia da Baleia was once a port made wealthy by commerce. Its curious name—'*baleia*' means 'whale'—serves as a reminder that whales could be hunted off the coast of Portugal in the 13th century. In 1245, the Abbey of Alcobaça collected the profits from whale oil in the ports which it controlled.

The village is now obscure, but well worth visiting to see the exceptional works of art in its early Gothic **church of São Leonardo**. Behind a plain and pockmarked 13th-century façade, the very good collection of paintings includes a stunning Renaissance representation of São Leonardo backed by a red cloth. Equally exciting is the 14th-century limestone low relief of the Nativity: the Virgin lies tucked in bed beneath a starched sheet, holding a little book in one hand and a flower in the other. The baby Jesus sits on her thighs, warmed by the breath of an ox and an ass, and watched over by angels. Joseph sits at the foot of the bed looking patriarchal. A petrified whalebone lurks in the corner of the church, one of several supposed to have been used to construct the roof.

Exquisite, florid Baroque marble inlay surrounds the retable of the **church of N.S. da Conceição** nearby, fronted by two massive belltowers. The rough pillars beside the church are the remains of a bull stall, probably commissioned by King Dom Pedro I in the 14th century—which would make this the earliest evidence for bullfighting in Portugal.

Peniche

As late as the mid-16th century, the Peniche peninsula was an island in the Atlantic, 22km west of Óbidos, with a perimeter of 8km: siltation formed the narrow isthmus flanked by gently sloping beaches which now joins it to the mainland. The busy, deep-sea fishing port and cannery centre hums around the harbour, to the left of the entrance to the fortifications. During the summer months, 'jolly' Portuguese 'music' is sometimes piped into the main streets. Surprisingly, few people seem deterred by this—however, unless you are in a peculiarly benevolent holiday mood, lengthy exposure is inadvisable.

Peniche ✆ *(062–)* **Getting There**

There is no railway service to Peniche. Semi-frequent Tejo buses, ✆ 782133, run from Lisbon (2hrs), and infrequently from Oporto (5½hrs), via Coimbra (3hrs), Leiria (2hrs) and Nazaré (1¼hrs).

The **tourist office** is on the waterfront between the two bridges, in the Rua Alexandre Herculano, ✆ 789571.

Near the harbour, on the south face of the peninsula, the sprawling **Fortress** (*open 1–7; closed Mon*) was constructed 1557–70, seeing action in 1589 when Norris landed with 12,000 troops in support of the Prior of Crato's claim to the Portuguese crown. It served as a prison under both Pombal and the PIDE, Salazar's hated secret police; it now contains a museum of local archaeology and crafts, incorporating former cells, solitary chambers and the visitors' grille.

The peninsula is fringed with vertical rock cliffs battered by frothy waves and pierced by caverns. It's a breezy 3km walk eastwards to the **Cabo Carvoeiro** and the **chapel of N.S. dos Remédios**, which contains blue and white *azulejos* of the life of the Virgin attributed to the workshop of António de Oliveira Bernardes, *c.* 1711–20. The Berlenga islands are visible on a clear day.

Try **★★Residencial Felita**, 12 Largo do Professor Franco Freire, ✆ 782190 (*cheap*), or **★★★Hotel da Praia Norte**, Av. Monsenhor Bastos, ✆ 781161 (*moderate*), a whitewashed, three-storey concrete block overlooking its swimming pool. There are restaurants along the Avenida do Mar, and fish is cooked outside near the docks.

The Berlenga Islands

Getting There

The **ferry** from Peniche runs from 1 June to 20 September, weather permitting, crossing three times daily during July and August, otherwise once daily. The hour-long trip costs around 1000$00 return.

With a circumference of 4km, Berlenga Grande is the largest and only accessible island of a diminutive archipelago about 12km offshore. It is treeless, craggy and magical, and has been declared a **National Bird Reserve**, accommodating fleets of seagulls, eiders (as in down), rabbits, and a cluster of fishermen. The island is granite, with a preponderance of feldspar. These wonderfully clear waters once harboured pirates. They made life too difficult for those Jeronymite friars who eschewed their brothers at grand Belém and came here in 1513 to assist the survivors of shipwrecks; the monastery was demolished, and a rust-coloured fortress was built on an islet approached by a skinny causeway. In 1666 a garrison of 20 men wounded half of the 1000-strong Spanish assault force unsuccessfully attempting to kidnap and ransom the bride of Dom Afonso VI. She was resting on the island on her way from her father's duchy of Nemours.

A few huts huddle around the small sandy beach near the ferry dock, from which rowboats can be hired to explore the weird rock caves. Paths across the island are marked with stones, to ensure the birds' privacy. The fortress has been converted into an unforgettable **pensão**: check for vacancies with the tourist office at Peniche. There's a campsite above the dock, as well as a little bar-restaurant and a shop for basic supplies.

Torres Vedras and the Coast

Torres Vedras

On the bank of the minor River Sizandro at the southwestern edge of the rippling Serra de Montejunto, 34km south of Óbidos and 33km north of Mafra, the town of Torres Vedras stands at the centre of a wine-producing region; the white is refreshing and light.

Torres Vedras was a royal residence from the mid-13th century to the early 16th century, and gave its name to Wellington's lines of defence for Lisbon early in the Peninsular War. Today it contains little of interest. Tomatoes and green beans are grown for export, and timber is transported from here still dripping with sap. The local *pastéis de feijão* are a treat: made with boiled white beans and almonds, they have the consistency of hard honey, but are not too sweet.

In the Largo de S. Pedro, at the centre of town, winged dragons enliven the Manueline portal of the **church of S. Pedro**, which was rebuilt in the 16th century. Within, 18th-century *azulejos* depict birds in the sky and everyday life with palmtrees, and a tomb contains the remains of João Lopes Perestrelo, who accompanied da Gama on his voyages to India. Behind the church, a Gothic pavilioned fountain, the **Chafariz dos Canos**, dates from 1561. On a gentle hill on the edge of town, Dom Dinis' castle of 1288 was rebuilt for the last time in the 17th century, before being ruined by the earthquake of 1755. Today it is dry and unatmospheric, but for the hairy yellow flowers and geckos in the sun.

The Environs of Torres Vedras

The 15th-century Franciscan **convento de Santo António**, 3km west of Torres Vedras in the hamlet of Varatojo, contains horrid 18th-century *azulejo* panels of a hell where sinners' eyes are pierced with nails. There is a beautiful, rather domestic Gothic cloister, but the rest of the interior has been modernized over the centuries.

Torres Vedras is best known to students of British history for the **Lines of Torres Vedras**. In 1809, Wellington planned to save Portugal from the French by concentrating on the defence of the capital. Reckoning a year in advance, he intended to turn 500 square miles into an impregnable fortress, by constructing chains of mutually reinforcing redoubts, each of which would crown a prominent feature of the landscape. The 152 forts were built secretly: Masséna was unaware of their existence until his advance guard sighted them four days before his arrival, and even the British minister in Lisbon and most of the staff officers in the British army appear to have been kept in the dark. For a whole year, 18 engineers directed 5–7000 local peasants to construct the polygonal redoubts with 4m-thick parapets. Masséna was flummoxed; he dallied, waiting for a false move by Wellington, but retreated on 14 November 1810—a retreat that ended at Toulouse in April 1814.

The British Historical Society of Portugal publishes a pamphlet, *The Lines of Torres Vedras*, which gives details of three day-long walks between various redoubts. Most of these outworks are made up of dull trenches and walls. The simplest to locate is at Torres Vedras itself.

Torres Vedras © (061–) **Where to Stay and Eating Out**

★★Hotel Império Jardim, Praça 25 de Abril, © 314232, ✉ 321901 (*inexpensive*) is central, clean and functional, but give the restaurant a miss.

Try the rabbit stew at **Barrete Preto**, 25 R. Paiva de Andrada, © 22063 (*moderate*), or **Patco**, Trav. J. E. César, © 31496 (*expensive*), where diners sit on lime green chairs and eat off pink table-cloths. **Pensão–Restaurante 1 de Maio**, 3 Rua 1 de Dezembro, © 22875 (*cheap*) is a cheaper and tasty alternative.

Porto Novo

The road to Porto Novo beach, 16km northwest of Torres Vedras, passes a **working windmill** with bucket sails. Maize is jogged through a hole in the top grindstone, to be powdered by its quick rotation. The bow-shaped beach is enclosed by dramatic grey granite cliffs and pummelled by a strong wind.

Porto Novo © (061–) **Where to Stay**

The unexceptional interior of the **★★★Hotel Golf Mar**, © 984157 (*luxury*) is eclipsed by its views over the beach and the ocean—the balconies allow a great feeling of freedom—and by its swimming pools, saltwater outdoors, Olympic-sized indoors. With a 9-hole golf course and two hard tennis courts, the hotel is popular with conferences. The cavernous restaurant offers a limited choice of rather ordinary food. For a cheaper alternative, try **★★Pensão Promar**, Praia de Porto Novo, © 984195 (*inexpensive*), which is across the road from the beach, but cannot boast the same views.

Mafra and the Coast

Mafra

The small, nondescript town of Mafra, 39km northwest of Lisbon, snuggles around its huge 18th-century palace and monastery. Before the construction of the edifice, the settlement was a mere village of a hundred houses gathered around a castle which no longer exists, near a hill which was dynamited on the instructions of Dom João V.

History

In 1711, three years after his marriage to Dona Maria Ana of Austria, the childless King Dom João V pledged to build a monastery should he be favoured with an heir. Dona Maria Bárbara, later Queen of Spain, was born before the end of the year, and the first stone of the palace and monastery was laid in November 1717. It was intended to rival the Escorial and St Peter's in Rome, to express the splendour of the nation and its monarch. The basilica was dedicated at an eight-hour ceremony in 1730 (desperate to relieve himself, the archbishop nearly passed out), but the final works were not completed until 1735. The statistics are boggling. The project cost over 48 million *cruzados*, sufficient to hasten Portugal's economic decline. At the peak of construction, it sapped the energies of 45,000 muddy and flea-ridden civilians, who were marshalled by 7000 soldiers. Their absence from the productive workforce paralysed the country's economy. Some 1270 oxen and 7000 small carts shifted the materials needed to build the 880 halls and rooms, and the 4500 doors and windows. The construction plan was drawn up by a team in Rome co-ordinated by the Marquis of Fontes. Ludwig of Ratisbon (1670–1752), a German trained in Rome, engineered the building and oversaw its construction. The master carpenters, master builders, and master masons were Italian.

Having soaked up the wealth that poured into Portugal from newly discovered deposits of Brazilian gold, Mafra never really caught on as a royal or courtly residence. The blackening south turret, to the right of the façade, was for the king and the north turret, to the left, was for the queen. Dom João V was accompanied by a fleet of lackeys on his night-time forays northwards; on arrival at the queen's chamber, her ladies-in-waiting retired behind an arras, until the king was ready to make his way southwards.

A distinguished School of Sculpture functioned here from 1753 to 1770, under the auspices of Alessandro Giusti, who had come to Portugal from Italy to assemble the chapel of St John the Baptist in Lisbon's church of São Roque. Machado de Castro was one of the school's progeny. In the early 19th century, sweet, bewildered Dom João VI wandered the palace carrying two small boxes in his pocket, one for snuff, and one for grilled chickens' legs. These he gnawed. He retired here to escape the venom of his boundless, bumptious, scheming wife, Carlota Joaquina, who complained, amongst other things, that he was placing too much confidence in his hairdresser. The king fled to Brazil at the insistence of the British, rather than become a puppet of the French invaders. He was accompanied by his wife and most of the furniture from Mafra, which never returned. In 1807, Junot billeted troops in the monastery, which was occupied by Wellington's men shortly afterwards. Parts of the buildings have been in military hands since the mid-19th century.

The Town

Visitors to the **palace** and **monastery** (*open 10–1 and 2–5; closed Tues and holidays*) enter the building where the queen entered, in the middle of the left half of its façade.

The vast, monotonous façade faces west, its flat expanse centering on the basilica topped by high belltowers; the monastery is focused on a square courtyard behind the church, incorporating a refectory, chapter house, kitchen, cells for 280 brothers, and library.

The Basilica and Belltowers

The porch of the basilica houses wonderfully fluid Carrara marble statues of the founders of various religious orders, with curly marble hair, carved by several sculptors in Italy in the style of Bernini. The beautiful proportions of the basilica's interior are complemented by the harmonious paving and panelling of soft yellow, pink, blue, grey, red and black marble. It's a curiously sober memorial to an ostentatious monarch. The arts and crafts of the basilica were imported, right down to the copes, canopies and 3000 walnut panels for the sacristy cupboards and choir stalls. The six organs are almost identical with one another; they were constructed 1792–1807, to replace four earlier organs notable for their ugliness, built by a diminutive Irish monk named Egan.

The belltowers boast the world's largest assemblage of bells, 57 in each tower, 48 of which make up the carillons created in Liège and Antwerp in 1730. The largest carillon bell weighs 10 tonnes, the smallest 30kg. Before these were electrified, the carilloner would shed 2–3kg per concert, for which he wore gloves with separate finger sheaths. Now the carilloner depresses a pedal or a wooden peg—but few people have the skill. **Concerts** are given 4–5pm on Sundays from May to October, as likely as not performed by a TAP pilot called Francisco.

The Palace and Monastery

The palace is kitted out with dull imperial-style furniture dating from the middle of the last century, spanning the reigns of the last four kings of Portugal. Only the whimsical pieces are worthy of attention: the skittle table in the games room, at which monarchs spun tops through the spreadeagled legs of small cherubs; the bathroom's merry bird murals; and the deer horn chandelier, chairs, sofas and wall-mounts in the dining room, made from beasts stalked in the palace's walled hunting ground. The elegant rococo **library** is the longest room in the building, in whose ivory light 30,000 volumes ruminate. The chequered marble floor is conducive to slippered pacing.

Maquettes from the School of Sculpture are displayed in corridors leading to the monastery. The monks' pharmacy is brought to life by a giant syringe displayed on a table—for giving enemas—and the infirmary is *à la* Florence Nightingale, with open cells and shuttered beds, from which insane monks were able to admire the only *azulejos* at Mafra. Sane monks were kept in simple cells, where they could whip themselves and wear millstone necklaces. The delousing booths offered rare luxury: they were made of Brazilian angelin wood rather than Portuguese pine, because it did not splinter.

Mafra ✆ (061–)   ***Where to Stay and Eating Out***

★★Pensão Castelão, Av. 25 de Abril, ✆ 812050, ✉ 51698 (*moderate*) is opposite the palace and not bad value, but nothing special. Its plush restaurant specializes in fish cooked with rice, but the bass is a delicious alternative. **Restaurante Primavera** (*cheap*) is across the road from the palace and serves decent food and rents decent rooms.

Sobreiro

A sculptor has created a **miniature village** for children, at Sobreiro, 3km west of Mafra. Kids shriek about the place, delighting to find artisans at work, several windmills, boats bubbling on a trough of water, and a 'typical' (kitsch) kitchen which sells hot bread. The rustic **bar** marked '*adega*' is hung with cowbells, hoe tops, and bayleaves, flanked by wine barrels, and floored with crazy paving. Salami-style *chouriço* and red wine go down well here. The **restaurant** (*moderate*) itself is dim and quaint. Avoid weekends in summer.

Ericeira

Eleven km west of Mafra, the whitewashed Atlantic fishing village of Ericeira has escaped overdevelopment as a resort.

The cult of Sebastianism leapt to life at Ericeira in 1584, when a hermit proclaimed himself to be the headstrong young monarch killed at Alcácer-Quivir in 1578. The impostor addressed himself as '*infeliz Sebastião*' (unhappy Sebastian), selected a queen, whom he crowned with a diadem pilfered from an image of the Virgin in a nearby church, and collected an 'army' of 1000 peasants armed with pitchforks. He was hung and quartered in 1585. It was from Ericeira that the royal family sailed into exile, on 5 October 1910.

The Praça da República is at the centre of town, surrounded by ugly cuboid houses. From there the Rua Dr. Eduardo Burnay leads down to the stubby sand beach, which is washed by large waves and, off season, lapped by haze. A prettier and less crowded beach lies around a headland to the north, a 25-minute walk away. The **tourist office** is at 33a Rua Dr. Edouardo Burnay, © 061 63122.

Ericeira © *(061–)*   ***Where to Stay***

The long-established ★★★**Hotel de Turismo**, © 864045 (*expensive*), on the coast, appeals to old ladies and congress delegates; anyone more zesty will feel redundant, despite the four swimming pools (two of which are for children). Bedrooms are decent and smell of the sea, with nice wide balconies. The impersonal restaurant offers a no-frills fixed-price dinner.

The best rooms in spruce ★★**Hotel Pedro Pescador**, 22 Rua Dr. Eduardo Burnay, © 864302, ✆ 62321 (*expensive*) are on the top storey, overlooking rooftops, with brightly painted wood furniture. The regimented restaurant is laid for couples. *Open 1 May–9 Oct.*

A holiday atmosphere prevails in ★★★★**Hotel Morais**, 3 Rua Dr. Miguel Bombarda, © 864200 (*moderate*). Rooms overlook the swimming pool and a flowery patio, and there's an attractive restaurant. **Pensão Fortunato**, 7 Rua Dr. Edouardo Burnay, © 62829 (*inexpensive*) is a decent, clean and colourless little place.

Eating Out

Restaurante Poço, opposite Hotel Morais (*moderate*) offers good food outside, amidst trellis vines and sheltered by plastic covering. At **Toca do Caboz**, Rua Fonte do Cabo (*moderate*), savour the *açorda de mariscos* which is particularly good here.

Sintra

On the eastern slope of the Serra de Sintra, 28km northwest of Lisbon, the town of Sintra and its 16,000 souls are swathed by teeming, rich green forests of pine, oak and fern. It makes an easy day trip from Lisbon; once here, walking is the only proper way to relish its woods.

Sintra has been discovered by goats, monks, and the British, who are particularly fond of it. The place has a peculiar magnetism: the Romans knew the Sintra range as Mons Lunae (the Hills of the Moon), and in the 16th century the Jeronymite monastery of N.S. da Penha was built to cover an entrance to the Underworld, so they say. In the summer months of the early years of the 15th century, Dom João I, his English bride and his court took up residence in the National Palace, at the centre of town. Subsequent kings followed his lead, until Dom Ferdinand built the Pena Palace, on a hilltop high above. This ravishing neo-Gothic confection contrasts with a ruined Moorish castle on a nearby peak, floodlit at night, as if suspended in the sky.

Eerie sea mists seep into Sintra's mossy walls and cool the town in summer. Dogs howl across the hollows. Visitors have been inspired to hymn these wonders: in 1529 the Portuguese playwright Gil Vicente hailed Sintra as 'A garden of the earthly paradise / Sent here by Solomon'. Byron lauded it in the opening two stanzas of *Childe Harold*: 'Lo! Cintra's glorious Eden intervenes, / in variegated maze of mount and glen'. Its 'horrid crags' delighted him; later in 1809 he wrote to his mother from Gibraltar claiming the village of Sintra to be 'perhaps the most delightful in Europe ... It unites in itself all the wildness of the Western Highlands with the verdure of the south of France' (neither of which he had visited). Even the Spaniards have a saying: 'To see the world and yet leave Sintra out / Is, verily, to go blindfold about.'

Above all, Sintra appeals to Romantics, and its July **music festival** has adopted a Romantic theme (concerts are performed in the palaces of Sintra—including Seteais—and Queluz). The only reason that visitors might not enjoy the place is that there are too many other people doing just that. In the Praça da República, tour buses are packed together like slices of bread. There's a good range of accommodation, but it usually fills by lunchtime in high season. The town is famous for its *queijadas*, pleasantly sweet cheese cupcakes wrapped in thin pastry. Their secret recipe is protected by two rivals, one of whom is the curate.

Getting There and Around

Frequent trains make the ¾hr trip from Lisbon's Rossio station, via Queluz; local buses run from Mafra and Cascais.

Walking in Sintra is wonderful, if you don't mind hills. There is no walking map. If you're fit, you may reach the Moorish Castle in an hour—but rushing saps the enjoyment. From there, intrepid walkers could get to Pena in 45 minutes. Monserrate is a comfortable 40 minutes from the centre of town.

By **taxi**, expect to pay 2500$00 per taxi for a one-hour return trip to one monument. To cover the Moorish Castle and the Pena Palace will take two hours and 6000$00. A tour around the town and then to the Pena Palace by **horse carriage** will cost 15,000$00.

An occasional bus leaves the Praça da República to visit the Pena Palace, the Capuchos Convent and Cabo da Roca. Check with the tourist office for details.

Sintra ✆ (01–)   **Tourist Information**

The main **tourist office** is near the National Palace at 23 Praça da República, ✆ 923 1157, with a smaller office in the railway station ✆ 924 1623. From the **bus station** and **railway station**, ✆ 923 2605, follow the V-shaped Alameda de Volta do Duche into town.

The National Palace

Open 10–1 and 2–5; closed Wed and holidays.

Sintra has grown up around the grey royal summer palace, an irregular assemblage topped with two conical chimneys. A National Palace has existed on this site since the reign of Dom Dinis. The core of what stands today was inhabited by Dom João I (1357–1433) and his English queen, Philippa of Lancaster; it hosted brilliant court balls and dancing and literary tournaments. Philip the Good, Duke of Burgundy, was received here in 1429, when he came to ask to marry the princess Dona Isabel. The duke brought his painter Jan van Eyck in train. When Dom João III took up residence, his courtiers' Latin, Greek and Hebrew conversations whispered around the palace. In the early 16th century, Dom Manuel made drastic alterations to everything except the proportions of the place. Dom Afonso VI had plenty of time to contemplate these. Childless, he resigned the government of the country in 1667 in favour of his brother Dom Pedro, to ensure the succession, and was subsequently incarcerated here for nine years, without a single lowlife, cockfighting friend to keep him company.

Extra buildings were added after the earthquake of 1755. The National Palace is still used for entertaining foreign dignitaries.

The muddled exterior indicates the palace's gradual evolution. The chimneys are like Kentish oast houses—bottles of champagne, said Hans Christian Andersen—as are the chimneys of various European monasteries. The distinguishing feature here is that there are two of them. The **kitchen** is the first room shown to visitors. Disappointingly bereft of bats, the chimneys would nevertheless accommodate several roasting wild boar.

The **Sala dos Árabes** follows, zigzagged with green, blue and white tin-glaze mudéjar *azulejos*, fabricated in Seville using the *corda sêca* technique and imported by Dom Manuel *c.* 1503, which makes them some of the oldest in the country.

Rooms with Painted Walls and Ceilings

The **chapel**'s rare tile carpet was probably executed by Moorish craftsmen in the 15th century. Painted doves flit every which way over the walls, representing the Holy Spirit and teasing Dom Afonso VI with their freedom; he died of an apopleptic stroke while hearing Mass from the side balcony, in 1683. Perhaps the late 15th-century Sevillian tile floor of his bedroom was worn away by pacing.

Dom Manuel shrewdly reinforced the nobility's novel perception of themselves as a court circle by ordering the coats of arms of 72 families to be painted on the ceiling of the **Sala dos Brasões**. Pombal erased the Távora escutcheon, having executed the marquis by breaking his bones for allegedly attempting to assassinate King Dom José I. The national arms of Portugal at the top is an 18th-century addition, incorporating the dragon crest of the Bragança dynasty, a motif mirrored in the high dado of 18th-century *azulejo* hunting scenes.

Formerly the royal audience chamber, the **Magpie Room** is one of the oldest rooms in the palace; each of the 136 ceiling triangles is painted with a magpie holding a rose in its claws, and clasping a scroll marked '*Por bem*' (gladly or willingly) in its beak: legend claims that Dom João I proffered a rose to a lady of the court when his wife wasn't looking. A magpie stole the rose, drawing attention to the infidelity. The king excused himself by saying '*Por bem*'. There is a more rational explanation: the bird sports the livery colours of the House of Avis—black, blue and white; and the rose could symbolize the House of Lancaster.

The larger and grander **Swan Room** is roofed with octagons of painted swans, each in a different position and each with a gold collar. They may commemorate a wedding present from Philip the Good, or may have been painted when Dona Isabel was to have married her cousin Henry V of England, whose mother's crest was a white swan. The boars' heads on the tables are soup tureens.

The **Archaeological Museum** of fragments in brightly lit cases is situated above the tourist office.

The Environs of Sintra

The Moorish Castle

Open daily, summer 10–6 and winter 10–5.

The road leading westwards out of Sintra passes the **Estalagem dos Cavaleiros**, where Byron stayed in 1809, now boarded up and covered in graffiti, though knights still charge across the signpost. A sharp turning to the left leads to a leafy road, which climbs up to the Pena Palace. Travellers should turn left again to get to the **Moorish Castle**, whose fortifications run along the spine between two pinnacles (454m above sea level), within sight of the Pena Palace—and that was just the point. Finding the ruin too ruined for his Romantic taste, Dom Ferdinand II ordered the castle to be partially rebuilt. It hovers above Sintra, pelted with boulders which seem to be styrofoam, comprising five towers and a keep. The ruined Romanesque church within the enclosure may once have been a mosque. On a clear day, it's worth coming here for the views: southeast to Lisbon and the Serra da Arrábida, southwest to Cabo da Roca, and north to Peniche and the Berlenga islands. A steep path descends into town, emerging between the convento da Trindade and the church of Santa Maria.

The Pena Palace

Guided tours 10–12.30 and 2–5 (open until 6 in summer); closed Mon.

The zigzag road continues uphill to the Pena Palace, a fantastic hilltop confection, begun in 1840, which expresses Dom Ferdinand II's capricious Gothic longings. He and his cousins Albert and Leopold hailed from the obscure state of Saxe Coburg-Gotha. Each married the queen of an empire: Portugal, Britain and Belgium. If he produced a son, the Portuguese consort became king. Ferdinand complied—Dona Maria II had 11 children, the last of which killed her—and became the artist king, a philanthropist tall enough, so they said, to light his cigar from the gas lamps of Lisbon. Ferdinand commissioned Baron von Eschwege—whose statue stands in armour on a peak near the palace—to build it, 30 years before Ludvig of Bavaria let rip.

The exterior is a bonanza of crenellations, minarets, embellished windows and pillarbox turrets. A spreadeagled stone Triton supports a bay window, his legs becoming fishtails, his head sprouting tree roots, unconcerned that the palace's dome imitates that of the Jerónimos Monastery at Belém. It's difficult not to join the delighted children who make ghost noises beneath the portcullis. The best time to bring them here is during a thunderstorm, when the elements are lashing.

At the core of the palace stand the **cloister and chapel** of a 16th-century Jeronymite monastery, otherwise destroyed by the earthquake of 1755. The earthquake provided the patchwork of *azulejos* which wall the cloister. The chapel's superb alabaster retable depicts a variety of dramatic scenes centring on the dead Christ in the arms of angels. It was carved by Chanterène 1529–32, shortly after his work at Óbidos and before he moved to Évora, and resembles a piece of silverwork, tumultuous and delicate. The stained-glass windows are modern.

Visitors are shown through an interminable succession of rooms maintained—right down to the monarch's tooth mug—as they were when the royal family last resided here, in 1910. The frequence of the rose motif is explained by Dom Ferdinand's allegiance to the Rosicrucians, an offshoot of the Masons. Note the furniture designed by Eiffel in a boatlike reception room, the queen's silver hot-water bottle by her bedside, and the grass she stuck in her bed's headboard to dispel bad weather on Palm Sunday, 1910. Dom Ferdinand designed the china in the tea room, and made the engravings. Ceiling holes in the ballroom removed cigar smoke. A room decorated with canvases of naked ladies known to the king has recently been opened to the public—one of them is the queen, but nobody knows which. Be sure to see the kitchens, loaded with copper pans marked F.P.P., for Ferdinand Palácio da Pena, which are rather elaborate considering Dom Ferdinand's favourite foods were quince jam and chocolate.

The artless **grounds** form a splendid natural arboretum, filled with acacias, huge redwoods, and camellia trees. There are two valleys of those strangely prehistoric fern trees native to Australia and New Zealand, some of them 3m tall. The valleys are duplicated because when his queen died, Dom Ferdinand II took a mistress, a feisty German opera singer whom he created Condessa d'Edla. He bequeathed everything to her, rather than to his son, the king. This was intolerable, so the State confiscated her inheritance and fobbed her off with a chalet in the grounds of Pena, where she dabbled in her own garden.

The Convento dos Capuchos

The monastery is currently closed, but is due to open again in 1999. Check with the tourist office for more information.

The first left turning off the road descending from Pena leads 4km west of Sintra through the beautiful upper slopes of the Serra, near its peak at Peninha (490m), coming to a right-hand turning to the Convento dos Capuchos. From 1560, 12 hermits lived in cork-lined cells hollowed from the mountain's rock, sheltered by bursting green vegetation, beneath the grandeur of the sky. With its pure light, the place has retained the force of their spirituality. Look at the shining eyes of the resident curator—which might even have made an impression on Brockwell. Writing in 1726, he shrieked that the hermits were 'living by Theft, Rapine and Murder, of those unhappy Wretches, who are unfortunately Shipwreck'd on that Coast'.

Visitors are dwarfed by the surrounding granite boulders, and then made gigantic by the monks' cells, whose narrow doors are 1½m high and insulated with weirdly insect-like cork bark.

The Quinta de Monserrate

Open daily, summer 10–6 and winter 10–5.

On the road to Colares 2km west of Sintra, a 40-minute walk from the centre of town, the Quinta de Monserrate is a bastard Moorish extravaganza well worth visiting for its **garden**. Flanked by round towers and roofed in rusty orange, it was built for London textile merchant Sir Francis Cook by James Knowles Sr. A thousand men worked on it daily 1858–63; at the end of their labours, Cook furnished it with 'contemporary' Indian furniture, and resided here in April and November. (William Beckford had sublet the Gothic house that previously stood on this site, 1794–1808, adding an English landscape garden—no doubt appetizing to the flock of sheep he had shipped in from Fonthill. In 1809 Byron dropped in, beginning the fashion for visiting the place.)

In the 1850s, the painter William Stockdale created a botanic garden. About a third of the plants came from Australasia, and many were from Mexico. Himalayan rhododendrons were planted here in 1860, just 10 years after they arrived at London's Kew Gardens. Parts of the garden were named after countries—Mexico, Australia, Japan—and parts after mythologies. In 1870 'Thomas of Ercildoune' published a dreadful 300-page poem about Monserrate: 'A blaze of Rhododendrons all around, / Flooding with colour all the enchanted ground'. By 1923 there were a thousand different species growing here. The site was sold to the Portuguese state in 1949 and neglected until an EU grant made possible the employ of three landscape architects and three gardeners.

Sintra ✆ (01–) **Where to Stay**

luxury

The delightfully grand and whimsical ★★★★★**Hotel Palácio de Seteais**, 8 Rua de Barbosa Bocage, ✆ 923 3200, ✉ 923 4277 (1km west of Sintra on the road to Colares), comprises twin blocks joined by a triumphal arch, which were built in 1787 for a Dutch diplomat, and later purchased by the fifth Marquis of Marialva. 'Seteais' means 'seven sighs', which commemorates the Portuguese reaction to the lenient terms imposed on the French by the Convention of Sintra, which was signed here by Wellington in 1808. The furniture combines antiques with good reproductions, set amongst the murals of the main drawing room (watery scenes with trees that branch onto the ceiling), the music room and the card room. Bedrooms number 2, 3 and 4 are also hand-painted. Grandfather clocks chime in the corridors, rivalling the springtime nightingales which sing in trees around the topiary at the rear of the building, which overlooks plains to the sea. The restaurant is elegant but overpriced, serving disappointing food. The management is snooty; casual visitors are frowned at—go for tea or a cocktail.

expensive

★★★★**Hotel Tivoli Sintra**, Praça da República, ✆ 923 3505, ✉ 923 1572 (off the main square), is a very comfortable and efficient modern hotel whose covered balconies offer lovely views of the wooded hillslope opposite. The staff are friendly, helpful, and punctual. The good restaurant lacks atmosphere, and the waiters hover, but try the delicate marinated swordfish appetizer and you'll forgive anything. The nearby ★★**Hotel Central**, 35 Praça da República, ✆ 923 0063 (in the main square), is an honest place with heavy, marbletopped furniture, iron banisters, chipped paint, fake flowers, and no elevator. The wooden restaurant provides simple fare.

moderate

Between Sintra and São Pedro, ★★★**Residencial Sintra**, 12 Trav. dos Avelares, ✆ 923 0738, is a big old place with lumpy beds and gas heating, run by a multilingual German. It could get spooky in winter.

cheap

In a cheaper price range, ★★**Casa de Hospedes Adelaide**, 11 Av. Guilherme Gomes Fernandes, ✆ 923 0873 (downhill from the building with the Gothic tower,

towards the railway station), is preferable. Managed by a very affable ex-comman-
dant of police, it's homey, and some rooms have good views. The **Monte da Lua**,
✆ 924 1029 (*inexpensive*), opposite the train station, is one of the best value and
friendliest hotels in the town, and has good views from the rooms at the back.

Turismo de Habitação

A couple of km west of Sintra, a turning off the road to Colares leads down a long,
very steep, bumpy road to the whitewashed **Quinta de São Thiago**, Estrada de
Monserrate, ✆ 923 2923 (*luxury*), an early 16th-century villa surrounded by trees,
made splendid and cosy by an English family. Much of the furniture is antique,
with vases of flowers, hunting prints, worked leather chairs, silver-framed family
photos, and collections of banister knobs and Madonnas. Candelabra branch on
the breakfast table. There are 10 double guestrooms, whose occupants may use
the swimming pool and tennis court. Meals will be provided on request, for a
minimum of six people.

Further along the road to Colares, the **Quinta da Capela**, Estrada de Monserrate,
✆ 929 0170 (*luxury*), was built by the Duc de Cadaval in the 16th century.
Behind the weathered, time-tested farmhouse exterior lies a surprisingly elegant
and gracious interior, with carefully chosen, simple furniture and cool colours. The
owner is not resident, so the house lacks knick-knacks. Breakfast is the only meal
available in the marble dining room, but a kitchen is provided for guests' use, as
are the basement sauna and fitness room, at extra cost. The peaceful walled garden
overlooks Monserrate to Pena beyond it. A chapel within the grounds is sided with
biblical *azulejos*; other outbuildings have been converted into two self-catering
guest cottages, one accommodating three people and the other four.

On the road to Colares stands the less pricey **Quinta das Seqóias**, Estrada de
Monserrate, ✆ 924 3821 (*expensive*), a converted manor house which nestles in
the hills, with great views over Pena Palace and the coast. The large dining room
was once the kitchen, complete with wooden oven. The tasteful rooms are quietly
understated.

Sintra ✆ *(01–)* **Eating Out**

expensive

Most of the fancy restaurants are in São Pedro, a couple of km south of
Sintra. Rustic **Cantinho de S. Pedro**, 18 Praça Dom Fernando II,
✆ 923 0267, 🖷 923 0317, is one of the best there, with bare brick
walls, hanging plants and good French food. The fillets of sole with
Gruyère sauce are very good. *Closed Mon, Thurs evenings, and Sept.* Steaks are a
speciality at **Solar S. Pedro**, 12 Largo da Feira, ✆ 923 1860, 🖷 924 0678, a
French restaurant where smoochy music oozes through the red light. Waiters are
numerous but not urgent, and the kitchen is open to view. *Closed Wed.*
Restaurante Regional, 1 Travessa do Municipio, next to the Town Hall, ✆ 923
4444, has a cheerful atmosphere, mainly attributable to the bright-eyed waiters.

There is an open kitchen, so you can be entertained by the chef's dramas. The regional food section on the menu is worth a try. **Cintralia**, 1–3 Largo Afonso de Albuquerque, © 924 2299, ✆ 923 2319, crouches awkwardly on a road junction. This large wooden-floored restaurant was most recently a bank and retains a couple of barred doors. The high ceilings have their original mouldings and a fountain lurks under the rather grand stairs. Try the splendid *caldeirada à pescador* which contains virtually all known sea-life and plenty of white wine and aromatic herbs. There is an extensive wine list. *Closed Mon.*

moderate–cheap

Friendly **Tulhas-Bar**, down the street to the right of the tourist office (*moderate*) is a good bet, where the inexpensive fish dishes are especially good; the delicious *bacalhau com natas* is a good introduction to Portugal's favourite fish, because it's disguised with cream and nutmeg. *Closed Wed.* Prices are prominently displayed at the central **Café Paris** (*moderate*), presumably because clients complain they've been overcharged. Be warned. At the **pizzeria** nearby, the pizza base separates from the topping and the cheese isn't stringy (*cheap*).

Cabo da Roca

The westernmost point of Europe focuses the mind on the horizon. Every year more than 70,000 tourists come to this rugged and spectacular place 16km west of Sintra, where no plant grows over 10cm tall. Some of these visitors are North Americans pining for home. Others are Europeans trying to get away from it. Many pay for certificates to say they've been here.

© *(01–)*   ***Getting There***

Direct local buses run from Cascais. From Sintra, take a bus heading for Cascais, from in front of the railway station—a pretty ride past windmills and *quintas*. Get off at Azóia where there is a **tourist office**, © 928 0081, and walk the 4km.

Colares

A very beautiful avenue threads its way through lush and leafy land west of Sintra, arriving 6km later at the village of Colares. Picturesquely sited on a spur of the Serra, it's a quiet place decked with purple camellias, revelling in pines, cypresses and chestnut trees. It was here that the Romans worshipped the sun and moon. The village square is lined with 17th- and 18th-century houses. Be warned that driving through Colares' narrow and steep streets could age even the most fearless a good few years.

Colares © *(01–)*   ***Where to Stay and Eating Out***

Its unreasonable policy of excluding children and singles may explain the lack of visitors to the signposted ★★★**Pensão do Conde**, Quinta do Conde, © 929 1652, ✆ 929 1602 (*moderate*), a new house built around an early 18th-century core. The lovely views are hilly and green; no meals are available. Those with children could try the larger

***Motel das Arribas, Praia Grande, ✆ 929 2145 (*moderate*), which is perfectly respectable and very clean.

Restaurante A Bistro, 2 Largo Dr. Carlos França, ✆ 292 0016 (*expensive*), near the Manueline pillory, occupies what used to be the apothecary's shop, and retains its varnished pine dressers equipped with unlabelled bottles. The German chef prepares good but pricey international food. *Closed Mon.*

Guincho

Rolling Atlantic waves crash against Guincho's two gently sloping sand bays; international windsurfing championships are held here, 9km south of Cabo do Roca and 10km north of Cascais. Free of pollution, inaccessible by public transport, and overlooked by just two buildings, both hotels, Guincho is a welcome relief from the rest of the Estoril coast farther south. The problem is that the undertow is extremely treacherous, strong enough to drown even the most confident swimmers.

Guincho ✆ *(01–)*　　　　　　　　　　　　*Where to Stay and Eating Out*

Lonely *******Hotel de Guincho**, ✆ 487 0491, ✉ 487 0431 (*luxury*) is built on the site of a 17th-century fortress, with a bricked-up well in the glassed courtyard, brick ceilings in the halls, and a wide stone staircase. Crested tureens ornament the baronial dining room, and the living room is welcoming, with an excellent view of the Atlantic. It's comfortable, certainly, but there's something daunting about the bedrooms. Thus daunted, guests may hide under very fine bed linen.

Just across the jagged rock outcrop, the low-key but very expensive restaurant of the *******Estalagem Muchaxo**, ✆ 487 0444 (*expensive*) serves superb seafood—particularly the shrimps, the grilled bass, and the *caldeirada*. Leave room for dessert. With its beach views, the restaurant is decorated like a grotto: chunks of treetrunks, boughs and branches embellish walls of rough stone-chippings. The *estalagem* itself is ornamented in the same style, which is less amusing for protracted periods. Bizarrely, the courtyard is full of seagulls walking in circles.

The Estoril Coast

From Lisbon to Cascais, the south-facing coast has been been glutted by suburban sprawl, and developed as a series of resorts, though now the settlements virtually merge into one another. In summer, the sand beaches are packed with gasping Lisboêtas and basking tourists.

Getting There

Part of the reason for the popularity of the Estoril coast is the excellent public transport link with Lisbon: electric trains depart from the Cais do Sodre approximately every 10 minutes, stopping at stations including Oeiras, Estoril, and usually Monte Estoril, *en route* for Cascais, ½hr away.

Cascais

Cascais is a fishing village turned commuter settlement and sophisticated resort, arranged around three small bays with sand beaches backed by rocks, 1km west of Monte Estoril, shielded from northerly winds by the Serra de Sintra. The mix works very well: in the Rua Frederico Arouca, calloused fishermen squelch past Charles Jourdan shoe shops. The beaches are no less crowded than Estoril's, but they are supposedly less polluted. If you do swim, keep your head above water. There is a shortage of inexpensive accommodation.

Cascais ✆ (01–)   ***Tourist Information***

The **tourist office** is on the Rua Visconde da Luz, ✆ 484 4086. There is a good bookshop with a decent stock of French and English books plus a pile of old *National Geographics* near the train station: **Livraria Glileu**, 24A Avenida Valbom, ✆ 486 6014.

The **church of N.S. da Assunção** stands in a leafy square towards the western edge of town. Its nave is lined with shadowy paintings by Josefa de Óbidos, while busy *azulejos* dated 1748 depict a conference in the clouds. José Malhoa painted the ceiling. The coast road continues westwards past the **Museum of the Counts of Castro Guimarães** (*open 11–5; closed Mon and holidays*), which occupies the late 19th-century home of a family who died heirless in 1927. It retains enough furniture to keep its dignity, but lacks those personal effects which might invade someone's privacy. There is a good portrait by Columbano amongst the silver ewers and samovars, Indo-Portuguese embroidered shawls, and an early 18th-century Indo-Portuguese chest with legs carved like fetishes. A George O'Neil once lived here, which would explain the ceiling decorated with three-leaf clovers. Wide sandy paths wind around the house's garden, which is planted with small-leafed trees and called the **Parque do Marechal Cermona**.

The fishermen's daily catch is auctioned at the **fish market** (between the Praia da Ribeira and the Praia da Rainha beaches, beside a landbound anchor positioned like a great bow about to launch its arrow). From 5 or 6pm, when the fishermen return, the auctioneer starts high and reduces the price of each plastic crate of fish until a bidder grunts loud enough to stop him.

Just west of Cascais, the sea has pounded its way up through a cliff to make a hole known as **Boca do Inferno** (Hell's Mouth).

Cascais ✆ (01–)   ***Where to Stay***

Sited on a rocky promontory which rises above two popular beaches, ★★★★★**Hotel Albatroz**, 100 Rua Frederico Arouca, ✆ 483 2821, ✉ 484 4827 (*luxury; reservations recommended*) is a real treat. It incorporates a 19th-century ducal palace, with fabulous views of the lively Cascais harbour and the coastline stretching east towards Lisbon. The oval swimming pool and sun terrace overlook the ocean, backed by 37 guest rooms and their balconies. The interior decoration is warm and tasteful without being fussy. A covered terrace juts out from the nautical bar, like the prow of a boat. The marble and wood restaurant, sided with picture windows overlooking the coastline, serves very good, and occasionally inventive, food: fish may be served with a turnip sauce, or lamb with walnuts.

Very well positioned overlooking the bay and its fishermen, ★★★**Hotel Baía**, Av. Marginal, ✆ 483 1033, 🖷 483 1095 (*expensive*) provides practical, no-nonsense bedrooms with balconies and a summertime bar on the roof. Corridors are linoleum, elevators unpredictable, and the staff rather serious. The restaurant offers 'monk on the spit'. King Dom Carlos's summer palace has fallen on hard times: rooms at the ★★★**Residencial Solar de Dom Carlos**, 8 Rua Latino Coelho, ✆ 486 8463 (*moderate*) are bright and sparse rather than grand. Slivers of cherubs may flake from the murals onto your bread roll at breakfast. Dirty paint, battered furniture, springless beds and sloppy service await unfortunates at ★★★★**Albergaria Valbom**, 14 Av. Valbom, ✆ 486 5801, 🖷 486 5805 (*moderate*), off the roundabout nearer the water.

Turismo de Habitação

Spruce, elegant, colourful and welcoming, late 19th-century **Casa da Pérgola**, 13 Avenida Valbom, ✆ 484 0040, 🖷 483 4791 (*moderate*), off the seaward round-about, offers a white marble hall and 12 rooms furnished with antique and reproduction Portuguese furniture (heavy, but not oppressively so) and paintings of saints. Garage parking is available. *Open Mar–Nov.*

Cascais ✆ *(01–)*   ***Eating Out***

O Retiro João Padeiro, 12 Rua Visconde da Luz, ✆ 483 0232 (*expensive*)—on the main street at right angles to the waterfront—feels seasoned by time: floors are dragon's-tooth, chairs are leather, and leather panels line the walls. Confident in its specialities of shellfish and fried sole, the restaurant offers veal and pork as the only concessions to meat eaters; the fish tends to be undercooked, though. The efficient waiters can spot a large tipper before he or she sits down.

O Pescador, 10-B Rua das Flores, ✆ 483 2054 (*expensive*) stands out among several restaurants behind the fish market. Prickly brown blowfish and strings of garlic overhang tables where courteous waiters serve paella and good sole, the house specialities. Painted red, green and pink, **Chequers**, 7 Largo Luis de Camões, ✆ 483 0926 (*expensive*) is behind restaurant João Padeiro and serves good, bloody steaks. The groundfloor bar is decorated with film stars and is a nice place for a beer.

If you want to eat with no nonsense, head for **D. Pedro I**, 4 Beco dos Inválidos, ✆ 483 3734 (*cheap*), up a flight of stairs next to the fire station. The house wine is rough, the food solid, especially the ribs. The clientele varies from old men and their crumbs to Portuguese families on holiday.

Coconuts in the Hotel Nau, Lote 14, Rua Dr. Iracy Doyle, ☏ 484 4109, on the western edge of town, is recommended for zappy nightlife.

Estoril

Three km east of Cascais and 26km west of Lisbon, Estoril is marketed as the seaside haunt of fading European aristocrats, who oil themselves on the fine sand beach and enjoy one another to the sound of silver cocktail shakers. Anyone wishing to observe this species will be disappointed; if they are here at all, their villas are patrolled by Alsatians which froth behind flimsy fences, tormented by small boys.

Estoril is a soulless place arrayed around a casino and its gaudy garden, which leads to the crowded beach now almost too polluted to swim at. The garden is dotted with date palms, and enshrines a bust of Fausto Figueiredo, 'patron saint' of Estoril, who founded the casino and brought the railway.

Estoril has assimilated Monte Estoril, slightly to the west, which was the first resort to be developed on this coast line, and has its own railway station. There are no 'sights' in Estoril; most of the good restaurants and boutiques are in Cascais, a couple of km to the west, but, if you have money, Estoril offers some appealing accommodation.

Estoril ☏ (01–) **Tourist Information**

The **tourist office** is at the coastal end of Estoril's public garden, at Arcadas do Parque, ☏ 466 3813. The **railway station**, ☏ 468 6852, is on the beach front.

Estoril ☏ (01–) **Where to Stay**

luxury

The grand and elegant ★★★★★**Hotel Palácio**, Parque do Estoril, ☏ 468 0400, ✉ 468 4867 (backing on to the Estoril Park), was purpose-built in 1930; although it's reputed to be gilt with ex-monarchs, the hotel does not feel exclusive. Public rooms are gracious, human, and light, flanked by tall arched windows opening onto the lawn and thermally heated swimming pool. A cosy piano bar overflows into the marble chequered hall, where bikinis rub shoulders with silk bodices. Two hundred bedrooms and suites are furnished with attractive reproduction furniture, and pampered by 24-hour room service, but only the duplex suites are air-conditioned. A poolside buffet operates in summer, while the dining-room menu includes club sandwiches or stewed quails with dried fruit. Room rates include free golf at the Estoril Golf Club, and there are six tennis courts beside the hotel, half of them floodlit. With an independent entrance, the hotel's excellent **Four Seasons Restaurant-Grill**, ☏ 468 0400 (*expensive; reservations recommended*), is rich, heavy and intimate. Many dishes are prepared at the tableside—the beefsteak *Palácio* leaps to life amid brandy flames, with onions, parsley, and a red wine sauce. Menus, uniforms, linen, china and glasses are changed with the seasons.

The huge, glitzy ★★★★★**Hotel Estoril-Sol**, Parque Palmela, ✆ 483 2831 (on the coast road, between Estoril and Cascais), caters to conferences more than private guests—the bar is friendly if you have the correct delegation name on your lapel—making it hard to relax here, despite the sea views and Olympic-sized swimming pool. The bedrooms are charmless, the bathrooms not up to standard.

★★★★**Hotel Atlântico**, 7–7A Estrada Marginal, ✆ 468 0270, ✉ 468 3619 (on the coast just east of Monte Estoril railway station), overlooks the sea, but is separated from it by a railway line and the hotel's swimming pool. The decent rooms are decorated on a nautical theme; guests read the *Daily Star* newspaper, prefer to eat Mixed Grill Americaine, and drink a lot of tea, slowly.

Attractive new ★★★★**Apart-Hotel Estoril Eden**, Av. Sabóia, ✆ 467 0573, ✉ 467 0848 (next to Monte Estoril railway station), is mostly comprised of studio-suites, with Habitat-style furniture, and beds that pull down from the wall. A chic clientele frequents the disco-bar, the indoor and outdoor swimming pools, and the small supermarket. The sea view is lovely, but noisy should you open a balcony door.

expensive

A comfortable, pleasantly furnished British inn, ★★★★**Lennox Country Club**, 5 Rua Eng. Álvaro Pedro de Sousa, ✆ 468 0424 (parallel with the casino, two blocks towards Cascais), offers small, homey guestrooms named after golf courses, an obliging staff, and a friendly atmosphere fostered by the free coffee and afternoon tea. The restaurant serves roast beef and Yorkshire pudding. Guests receive a discount at Quinta da Marinha golf course. Competent but overpriced ★★★**Hotel Alvorada**, 3 Rua de Lisboa, ✆ 468 0070, ✉ 468 7250 (opposite the casino), is functional but drab, with a roof terrace. The door locks are confusing, so check twice that your room is secure. ★★★**Hotel Lido**, 12 Rua do Alentejo, ✆ 468 4098 (three blocks west of the casino and uphill), is pleasant, ordinary, and equipped with a swimming pool, though the restaurant's menu is small and unimaginative. The winter rates are particularly good.

moderate–cheap

Funky ★★★**Residencial Continental**, 2 Rua Joaquim Santos, ✆ 468 0050 (*cheap*), is at the inland end of the grid of streets to the east of the park and offers high ceilings with mouldings, and sanatorium-style bathrooms. **The Residencial Parsi**, 8 Rua Alfonso Sanchez, ✆ 484 5744 (*cheap*) is scruffy but reasonably clean, and is the cheapest option in town, apart from the **Orbitur campsite** ✆ 487 1014, in Areia, 9km away behind the Praia do Guincho 'beach'.

Estoril ✆ *(01–)*

Eating Out

expensive

Don't shy away from the name: **The English Bar**, Estrada Marginal, ✆ 468 0413, ✉ 468 1254 (next to Monte Estoril railway station), serves very good food, particularly seafood, in sober, wooden surroundings, with pewter ornaments and leather chairs and menus. The waiters know their job well. Sea or stone bass are available; the meat dishes range widely, from *bœuf bourguignon* to shish kebab. The gamut of international cuisine includes **Pak Yun**, 5 Rue de Lisboa, © 467 0691, a good Chinese restaurant, bright and open, specializing in fried spare ribs, roast suckling pig, and satay beef in hot sauce.

moderate–cheap

The pink and white marble interior, with wicker chairs and a mirrored bar, make café **Frolic**, Av. Clotilde, © 468 1219 (*moderate*)—overlooking the Estoril Garden, by the Hotel Palácio—a suitable place to eat a doughnut, a soufflé, or a Godiva golfball. **Casa Gymnopedies Pizza**, 2-E Rua do Viveiro, © 468 5949 (*cheap*)—near Monte Estoril's Experimental Theatre—serves tasty pizzas to take away or eat by candlelight.

Estoril © *(01–)*   **Entertainment and Nightlife**

The cavernous **casino** complex is supposed to be the lifeblood of Estoril, but the lobby is the only part worth checking out, as it's an important venue for exhibiting contemporary Portuguese art.

At 10.15pm diners in the giant restaurant (*expensive*) swallow the last grilled medallion of black grouper, banks of lights dim, ferns are spotlit on the black walls, and a husky voice introduces a troupe of three strolling musicians, who palpitate the ladies and issue red roses. After 45 minutes, ballet and acrobatics take the stage. It is possible to watch the floorshow without buying dinner, at a price.

In the gaming rooms, communication is by taps and gestures; zones of the baccarat tables are labelled in Japanese—but not on behalf of the international clientele. The Portuguese generate 90 per cent of the business. Many of them wear glasses, and smoke cigarettes which burn appreciably faster in the strong air conditioning. The dice game of French bank is popular, as well as roulette amd blackjack. Humourless croupiers dispense their kind of drug. Around 250 slot machines fill a separate room. There is a small cover charge.

Forte Velho, Estrada Marginal, © 468 1337 (*moderate*)—on the edge of Estoril towards Lisbon— is a 17th-century castle, but you wouldn't know that from the dark and smoochy interior, where the music hots up at midnight. *Open 10pm–3.30am.* **Frolic**, © 468 1219 (*moderate*)—in an alley at the seaward end of the Hotel Palácio—is more elegant and better heeled, decorated in shades of grey. *Open 10.30pm–4am.*

Oeiras

In the mid-18th century, people mumbled that the road running 17km west of Lisbon, to Oeiras, was the only decent thoroughfare in the country—because Pombal passed along it to get to his country *quinta*; the omnipotent minister was Count of Oeiras before being dubbed Marquis of Pombal. More recently, the village has been inundated by the Lisbon sprawl.

Pombal's Palace stands just inland of the railway bridge, and now serves as an overflow for the Gulbenkian Foundation; visitors may wander around the garden. The building's design is attributed to the Hungarian architect Carlos Mardel, who clearly built to last: the palace was spared by the 1755 earthquake, which the king considered providential. Without a hint of irony, the plain façade is ornamented with a dozen Carrera marble busts of Roman emperors. Excellent profane and allegorical *azulejos* ornament various minor façades, terraces and staircases.

On a rock jetty facing south, the very well preserved 16th-century **fort of S. Julião da Barra** was designed in the Italian style by Leonardo Torreano, in a broad V-shape with wide esplanades, constructed for almost a century after 1556. Showing no qualms about implementing his policies in his own back yard, Pombal incarcerated 124 Jesuits here in 1759 (45 survived), beginning the fort's long service as a prison. It now provides temporary accommodation to military VIPs.

The circular **Bugio Fort** was built 1586–*c*. 1640 on an islet 2½km off-shore, to protect the mouth of the Tagus.

Estoril Coast ☎ *(01–)*   ***Sports on the Estoril Coast***

With its mild climate, the Estoril coast has long been popular for winter golf. The golf courses are now being supplemented by a variety of other facilities, mainly for tennis and horseriding.

One km inland from Estoril, the long-established **Estoril Golf Club**, Av. da República, ☎ 468 0176, offers 27 holes designed by McKenzie Ross, dividing into a par 69 18-hole course—with good variety, excellent greens, and recently improved tees—and a 9-hole course for beginners. The longer course is fairly short and narrow, but sporty; prospective players must produce evidence of an official handicap. The 9th hole is played over a road. The walk uphill to the 16th is fairly strenuous, and no electric carts are available, so if you prefer to take it easy, you could play the flat 10 holes and then 8 holes of the beginners' course.

Golfball-sized canaries fly around the clubhouse's relaxed reception area, which leads to the trophy-lined sitting room. Meals are available, as are a small swimming pool, changing rooms, caddies, clubs for hire and overnight storage for clubs. Daily rates are available, or visitors can join for five weekdays.

A further 5km inland, the par 66 **Estoril Sol Golf Course**, Linhó, ☎ 924 0331, is prettier. Clubs and trolleys can be hired; squash courts are available.

Surrounded by pine woods, **Cascais Country Club**, Quinta da Bicuda, ☎ 486 9301 (near Bairro da Torre, 4km west of Cascais), is a newly established private tennis club geared up to residents or long-term visitors. Half the six clay courts are floodlit. Members have access to a pretty horseshoe-shaped pool, changing rooms with showers, a restaurant and bar, tennis coaching, and an osteopath. Jazz evenings are arranged sporadically. Family membership includes children under 21, and is available for 1 month or 6 months.

Quinta da Bicuda, Torre, ✆ 484 3233 (3km west of Cascais), is an ivy-clad farmhouse whose outbuildings have been converted into six basic little self-catering apartments, including one in the dove cote. Don't expect great style: the appeal of the place lies in the small swimming pool and quiet garden. The *quinta* incorporates a riding school, which is particularly suitable for children. Meals are served at the poolside bar or in the attractive restaurant (*moderate*).

Attractive and sensibly designed, **Quinta da Marinha**, ✆ 486 9881/9 (5km west of Cascais, 1km inland from the coast road), provides facilities for horseriding, tennis and swimming as well as golf, so non-golfers and children can enjoy themselves too. The layout is compact, though the 200 horse stables and small race track are about 1km away. Three of the six tennis courts are floodlit. Guests stay in wood-and-stone villas tastefully decorated in soft colours. You may find duck on your menu in the restaurant: know that it will be fresh, as the *quinta* runs a thriving duck farm (*luxury*).

Robert Trent Jones designed the *quinta*'s long par 71 course four years ago; the greens are very good but the fairways are not, particularly on the 1st, 3rd, 10th, and 11th holes. It's a beautiful course, though, and the 14th is played over a ravine. A halfway house is available for snacks, separate from the amicable clubhouse, and guards hurry along dawdlers. Players must bring a handicap certificate. There are only six electric carts. Green fees for members rise at weekends; non-members pay 50 per cent extra. Clubs can be rented.

Queluz

Five km northwest of Lisbon, off the road to Sintra, and 12km northeast of Oeiras, the nondescript market town of Queluz is buoyed by Portugal's most elegant royal palace. This charming rococo summer retreat, a sort of intimate Versailles, was built 1758–94; although the garden façade and the garden staircase are the only features of especial architectural interest, the palace gives a lucid insight into the diversions of aristocratic life in the late 18th century.

History

The town takes its name from the Arabic 'Qu'al-Luz' (valley of the almond tree). The palace began life as a small hunting lodge set in rolling parkland, which was granted to the second son of successive monarchs in 1654. In 1747 Prince Dom Pedro, second son of Dom João V, ordered Queluz to be converted into a summer residence (there are still no chimneys). Barracks intended for the Royal Guard were constructed opposite.

Two architects worked on the core of the palace. Mateus Vicente de Oliveira was succeeded by Jean-Baptiste Robillon, a disciple of the French goldsmith Thomas Germain, when Prince Dom Pedro married his niece, the future Queen Dona Maria I. She was incarcerated here when she went insane; she walked in the garden with her white hair streaming in the wind, and saw her father's ghost, 'a calcined mass of cinder'.

In 1794 the royal family's Ajuda Palace in Lisbon was destroyed by fire, and Queluz came to life as their permanent residence. It was then that Queluz became stamped with the spirit of that rambunctious poison dwarf, Carlota Joaquina, the Spanish wife of Dom João VI.

William Beckford was brought here by the young Marquis of Marialva. He came across the regent's wife amid the garden's odiferous thickets, 'seated in the oriental fashion on a rich velvet carpet spread on the grass ... surrounded by thirty or forty young women, every one far superior in loveliness of feature and fascination of smile to their august mistress.' The queen enquired after 'the fat waddling monks of Alcobaça', before insisting that Beckford race the marquis and two Indian girls. The Englishman won, which prompted the queen to 'see whether he can dance a bolero', which Beckford performed 'in a delirium of romantic delight.'

She was fantastically ugly and extremely short, measuring only 137cm (4ft 6in). At Queluz she entwined her dirty hair with pearls and diamonds, and wrapped her body in an old green cloth coat with gold lace frogs, and a split skirt. Outdoors she sported a man's cocked hat. Alternately sniping at her husband and plotting for her favourite son, Dom Miguel, Carlota Joaquina found time to convert one salon into a cocoon-hung house for silk-worms. The royal family fled to Brazil to escape the French invasion. When she returned, as queen, in 1821, Carlota Joaquina was said to be excessively religious. She dressed in a filthy printed cotton gown, equipped with two enormous pockets stuffed with a collection of rotting religious relics.

Queluz is now painted a warm shade of pink. One wing accommodates visiting dignitaries. The palace's paraphernalia followed the royal family to Brazil, and remained there; the thoughtfully restored buildings are furnished with pieces in the Dona Maria I, Dom José and imperial styles.

Getting There

Queluz is a mere ¼hr train ride from Lisbon's Rossio station, or ½hr from Sintra, in the opposite direction. From the **railway station**, walk downhill to the arches. Cross the road and continue (almost) straight, until you see the palace. The entrance is to the left.

Queluz ℂ (01–)   **Tourist Information**

The **tourist office** is on the Palácio Nacional de Queluz, ℂ 436 3415.

The Royal Palace

Open every day except Tues and holidays, 10–1 and 2–5.

The Royal Palace's mirror-lined **Throne Room** opens on to the **Music Room**, where, in the mid-18th century, the queen and her four daughters performed concerts. The queen sang out of tune at the top of her voice. Only she and her brood were equipped with chairs; when overcome with fatigue, courtiers knelt at the back of the room—though the French ambassador preferred to lie on the floor of an antechamber. (The Count de Saint Priest blamed the palace's lack of chairs for the old servants' swollen legs.) The music room is still used for concerts: the acoustics of its curved wooden walls are so good that the window-doors are opened to prevent them being shattered by certain pitches. Beckford considered Queen Dona Maria I's chamber orchestra to be one of the finest in Europe. He heard them play in the **chapel**, in which Dona Maria and her sisters painted the four panels against the walls beneath the cupola. This is a fashionable place to get married; at weekends, couples are scrambled into matrimony every 45 minutes.

The apartments of the Princess of Brazil lead through to the smoking room and dining room—an anachronism, since meals were served wherever the monarch wished, until the 19th century. Hot chocolate, a drink the Spaniards brought from South America, was served in the pot whose handle and spout are at right angles.

Oranges fall from *azulejo* trees in a pretty **corridor**, running to the **Ambassador's Room**, on the ceiling of which Bernardi painted the royal family attending a concert. **Dona Carlota's bedroom** was a square room made to look round, decorated with scenes from *Don Quixote*. Castrati feast on the walls of the **Picnic Room**.

The Grounds

The English lead statues in the **formal garden** used to be painted in flesh colours—perhaps it was their charms which prompted Dona Carlota Joaquina to plunge her legs into the fountains. The palace and formal garden are brilliantly linked to the park by a staircase and cascade of water. At the foot of the staircase, the wall blanketed with puce bougainvillea was frescoed, in 1772, with a scene of blind man's buff. The maze has vanished too, and Dom Miguel's menagerie roars no more. Dom Pedro III grew hot-house pineapples here; his sons kept birds in crystal cages. The Jamor stream runs through the grounds; by means of locks, it could be flooded to fill its canal lined with *azulejo* scenes of river and sea ports, that the royal family might go boating.

Queluz ⓒ (01–)   ***Eating Out***

There is nowhere to stay in Queluz (unless you are a visiting dignitary). The palace's grand kitchen has been converted into a distinguished restaurant, **Cozinha Velha**, ⓒ 435 0232 (*expensive*), which attempts to rekindle the sensuous pleasures of Queluz. Oozing refinement, pineapples ornament a long butcher's table beneath the central chimney and high stone arches, between niches filled with copper. But the expense of eating here exceeds the quality of the cooking. The menu is large; sole is a speciality.

Catering almost exclusively to Lisboêtas, Caparica, on the west coast of the peninsula to the south of Lisbon, offers 8km of sand beaches and coves, which are served by a narrow-gauge railway. Each of the railway's 20 stops has a different character: beaches close to the terminus attract families; no. 9 is gay, and no. 17 is nudist. The little town provides accommodation and restaurants to suit the gamut.

Getting There

Every 15 minutes, ferries run the enjoyable 10-minute route from the Praça do Comércio's Terminal Fluvial to Cacilhas. There, the bus station is next to the ferry dock; take a bus signed 'Caparica'. The more frequent of these take ¾hr (past the Cristo Rei and a corral of disused washing machines). The narrow-gauge railway operates June–September. During those months, buses from Cacilhas stop at the railway's terminus. Out of season, follow the Rua dos Pescadores from Caparica's Praça da Liberdade to the beach.

The direct bus from Lisbon's Praça de Espanha is a quicker but less interesting route to Caparica.

Where to Stay

Caparica ✆ (01–)

★★Hotel Praia do Sol, 12 Rua dos Pescadores, ✆ 290 0012 (*moderate*), offers the best middle-bracket accommodation. It's friendly, efficient and comfortable, with a view of the sea if you crick your neck.

At the north end of Caparica, to your right if you look at the sea, **Pensão Pátio Alentejano**, Rua Prof. Salazar de Sousa, ✆ 290 0044 (*inexpensive–cheap*) is a villa converted into a *pension* run by Belgians. The bedrooms have character but tend to be dark, and some overlook the covered courtyard restaurant. This serves large portions of good food, especially *arroz tamboril*.

Eating Out

Caparica ✆ (01–)

Among the dozens of uniform restaurants on the main street, the Rua dos Pescadores, **O Capote** (*expensive*) shows some individual character. Tankards hang off the ceiling of the bar and the wooden walls of the restaurant are lined with menus from restaurants around the world—this has the potential to confuse at first. The service is efficient and the food good enough, especially the *arroz de mariscos*.

Manie's restaurant, 7E Av. Gen. Humberto Delgado, ✆ 290 3398 (*moderate*) is decked with copper pans and strings of onions. Seafood cooked with rice is the speciality.

On the beachfront, **O Barbas** (*moderate*) is a Copacabana spin-off, with tasty grilled sardines.

The Setúbal Peninsula

The Setúbal Peninsula comprises the delightful, unspoilt southern half of the peninsula formed by the estuaries of the River Tagus in the north and the River Sado in the south. Rising to around 500m in the stunning limestone Serra da Arrábida that skirts its southern shore, it is totally different in character from the sprawling industrial suburbs to the north. Both the eastern towns and Sesimbra are built in the wake of castles, between which shady roads wind through olive groves.

© (065–)   **Getting There**

A drive around the Setúbal Peninsula is an easy day trip from Lisbon, with Setúbal 48km away, and Sesimbra 40km—cross the Ponte 25 de Abril.

Trains run roughly hourly from Barreiro (ferry from Lisbon's Terreiro do Paço, ½hr) to Palmela and Setúbal (¾hr), but it's much easier to take the frequent Belos bus, © 525051, from the Praça de Espanha, which takes an hour to get to Setúbal. Local buses—Covas E. Filhos is the most prolific local company, © 523039—run from Setúbal to Palmela and Sesimbra, from which six buses daily travel to the Cabo Espichel.

Setúbal

The prosperous town and port of Setúbal occupies a curve of the wide mouth of the River Sado, backed by low hills which rise to a single peak in the northeast. The town is home to the sardine canning, cement, and long-established salt industries—in 1640, Setúbal salt paid for Portugal's peace treaty with the Dutch.

Other than the church of Jesus, the Municipal Museum, and the old fishermen's cottages surrounding the Largo António Correia, Setúbal is a charmless place (although the crowd of young, resident foreign-language teachers swear it has hidden appeal). Its main use is as a gateway to the Arrábida peninsula, though the smart pedestrian precinct is a good place to buy shoes. The town has a dark underbelly: drugs are a problem, and Mother Theresa of Calcutta has a home for homeless children. The nuns wear white saris and welcome visitors.

History

When the Roman town of Cetobriga (see 'Tróia', pp.283 and 394) was destroyed by an earthquake at the beginning of the 5th century, Setúbal was constructed on the opposite side of the river mouth, on a site allegedly selected by Túbal, grandson of Noah. The town was in ruins when Dom Afonso Henriques reconquered it from the Moors in the first half of the 12th century, and he ordered it to be repopulated by the inhabitants of Palmela. A century later, the construction of the *Cerca Velha* or old town wall was financed by the country's first conveyancing tax, under Dom Afonso IV. In 1458 a fleet sailed from Setúbal to Morocco with 25,000 men under Dom Afonso V, successfully capturing Alcácer-Seguir. His successor, Dom João II, lived in Setúbal for several years, and it was here that he fatally stabbed the Duke of Viseu in 1484. Philip II of Spain ordered the enlargement of the castle in 1590, to the designs of the Italian Felipe Terzi, with bastions suited to the new developments in cannon.

Bocage

The poet Bocage (1765–1805) was born in the Rua Edmond Bartissol, and lived here until he was 15. He exploded the petrified traditions of the neoclassical period, setting the tone for revolutionary Romantic poets to come: Beckford described him as 'perhaps the most original poet ever created by God', with a fabulous wit and an ungovernable character. Much of his work contained erotic passages, earning him censorship and military exile abroad, under Pombal. He died at the age of 39, warning: '... I stained / Sanctity! Impious folk, if you believe me, / Tear up my verse! Believe eternal life!'

Setúbal © (065–)   ***Tourist Information***

There is a **tourist office** in the Praça de Quebedo, © 534222; but the main one for the region is at 10 Travessa Frei Gaspar, © 524284, between two banks off the Avenida Luisa Todi, where a disconcerting glass floor hovers above the remains of a Roman settlement. It's well worth picking up a copy of their exemplary plan view of the Blue Coast, from Caparica to Sines.

The Church of Jesus

The church of Jesus in the Praça Miguel Bombarda (along the Av. 5 de Outubro from the bus or train stations) is the early work of Diogo Boitac, Languedoc-born architect of the Jerónimos monastery at Belém and originator of the Manueline style. Founded in 1494 by Justa Rodrigues Pereira, Dom Manuel's wetnurse, the church and convent are grounded in the late Gothic style, with Manueline additions—most strikingly, the twisted pillars and spiral ribs which writhe around the interior, formed from faintly polychrome Arrábida marble, which contrive to alter the chancel from a square at its base to an octagon at its top. The nave's dado of 18th-century *azulejos* depicts the life of the Virgin. At a late stage in the construction, Dom Manuel, who was financing the project, required a vaulted nave, causing the architect to alter his plans and add buttresses to sustain the new structure.

The Municipal Museum

Open Tues–Fri 9–12, and 2–5; closed Sun and holidays.

The church's *coro alto* is now incorporated in the municipal museum and hosts the 60cm mummy of Dom João II's illegitimate granddaughter.

The museum's star attractions are 14 canvases, painted in Lisbon probably at the studio of Gregório Lopes, *c.* 1520–30. These are some of the most compassionate and inspiring paintings in the country. They constituted a retable presented to the church of Jesus by Dona Leonor, mother of Dom Manuel—who may be portrayed as St Veronica, offering Christ a piece of cloth as he carries the cross—and hung in three rows: at the top, five scenes of the Passion; below, five scenes of the infancy of Christ; and two saints either side of the altar. There are indications that the paintings are rooted in the theology of the New Christians, those Jews forced by Dom Manuel to convert to Christianity. At Calvary, the Virgin Mary faints in St John's arms, a depiction of human weakness which the Council of Trent labelled heretical. Her figure was painted over, only to be discovered by X-ray in 1939. Wary of the stink, a haloed figure holds his nose while Christ's body is lowered from the cross; thus the painter cocks a snook at ideas of the incorruptibility of the flesh—only the soul is resurrected. On another canvas, the tomb remains closed. Painted at the time of Portugal's Discoveries, one of the Magi is Indian. Note too the coal brazier which warms the crib—similar stoves are still used in the Alentejo.

The museum also has a remarkable collection of ecclesiastical gold and silver, including a 15th-century Gothic processional cross in crystal and gilt.

The Museum of Archaeology and Ethnography (*open 9–12.30 and 2–5.30; closed Sun, Mon and holidays, and on Sat in August*), at the end of the garden strip farthest from the castle, is large and very well displayed. Exhibits include prehistoric rupestral art, excavated pots, fishpots, ex-votos, ploughs, and looms.

Setúbal ℰ (065–)   *Where to Stay*

Setúbal's castle is surmounted by the delightful **Pousada de São Filipe**, ℰ 523844, ℰ 532538 (*category CH*), overlooking the mouth of the River Sado from about 300m above the town. Visitors approach through a wide-stepped tunnel, passing grilles over wells and a chapel whose interior is covered with *azulejo* scenes of the life of São Filipe, created by Policarpo de Oliveira Bernardes in 1736, six years after his work on the church of São Lourenço at Almancil outside Faro. The *pousada's* public rooms are intimate and convivial, while the cool guest-rooms offer very good views and careful attention to detail. Summertime diners are served under dirty awnings on the terrace. Steak and local fish are of high quality but limited selection.

★★★★**Hotel Bonfim**, Avenida Alexandre Herculano, ℰ 534111 (*expensive*) is cosmopolitan and comfortable. Back in town the outmoded, sobering ★★★★**Pensão Esperança**, 220 Av. Luisa Todi, ℰ 525151 (*moderate*), on the garden strip running parallel with the river, near the shopping district, is efficiently run, but antiseptic. The fifth-floor restaurant is insipid despite the views of the town and river. In a quiet street behind the Esperança, ★★★★**Residencial Bocage**, 14 Rua de S. Cristovão, ℰ 21598, ℰ 21809 (*inexpensive*), is small and welcoming, making it pleasant for a short stay. **Pensão Bom Regresso**, Praça de Bocage, ℰ 29812 (*cheap*), on the central pedestrian square, is clean, solid and decent. The best budget accommodation is probably **Pensão Alentejana**, 124 Avenida Luisa Todi, ℰ 21398 (*cheap*), with large, airy rooms, no private bathrooms and no breakfast, but friendly owners and new decoration.

Turismo de Habitação

Take a sharp right on the road up to the castle for the burnt-pink **Quinta do Patrício**, Encosta de S. Filipe, ℰ 37019/98211 (*expensive–moderate*), which is decorated in a fresh, bright style, with good modern pictures, flowery sofas and Arraiolos rugs. The two double guestrooms in the main house share a bathroom; if you're feeling more adventurous, the adjacent windmill has been converted into a guest apartment. The garden of cypress trees overlooks Setúbal and the Sado, with a small swimming pool. Double rooms vary in price.

Setúbal © (065–)   *Eating Out*

Arranged around an open kitchen, **O Caseiro**, 81–85 Av. Luisa Todi, © 29268 (*expensive*)—opposite the Hotel Esperança—offers friendly, helpful service, delicious grilled red mullet, and an electric organ. Gentlemen wear ties. There's a cactus in the pavement outside **Cactus**, 83 Rua Vasco da Gama, © 34687 (*moderate*)—in a road parallel with the garden strip, towards the castle—whose upper walls are hung with black and white photographs of VIP diners. 'There', they point, 'is the chief of the firemen.' The food is very good, the surroundings attractive, the tables well laid. The *churrasco à tio gulherm* is a tasty barbecued steak and sauce. Skip the coffee.

Tróia

Across the mouth of the Sado, Tróia (*see* 'Baixo Alentejo', p.394) has recently been developed as a resort. It helps to have a car to visit the unatmospheric, simple ruins of the Roman town of Cetobriga, on the inland side of the narrow promontory. If you've come for the beach, the sea side of the promontory is less polluted and less crowded.

Ferries run every 45 minutes, taking 20 minutes. The car ferry embarks from the Doca do Comércio (540$00 for car plus driver), the harbour furthest upstream, roughly parallel with the tourist office, and the people ferry embarks near the Doca de Recreio, slightly downstream.

Palmela

Five km north of Setúbal and 39km southeast of Lisbon, Palmela is a clean town of 14,000 souls on the edge of the Serra do Louro, occupying gentle slopes around a castellated hill of 238m.

The first King of Portugal, Dom Afonso Henriques, captured Palmela from the Moors in the mid-12th century, after a surprise attack on the King of Badajoz, 'just as in May, the bull in rut will leap out on the careless passer-by with the blind fury of a jealous lover', as Camões puts it. The knight-monks of Santiago were installed in the castle monastery in 1194, transferring to Mértola in 1239 and returning here in 1423, under the auspices of Dom João I.

Unless you've come to stay or eat in the *pousada*, which now occupies the monastery, Palmela's only exceptional feature is the view from the castle, which the young Southey, writing in 1796, described as the most beautiful he had beheld.

The **castle**, built on Roman foundations, was repaired and enlarged by successive kings until the construction of the bastioned wall in the 17th century. The middle series of walls, surrounding the garrison, the monastery and the church of Sant'Iago, dates from the

15th century. The castle was ruined by the earthquake of 1755, but the views of the massive, dry, reddish hills to the east and west, and the sea to the south, are more than adequate compensation for the visitor, as the wind whistles around the battlements. The view to the southeast is said to stretch to Beja, on a clear day.

One of the more interesting late 15th-century visitors to the castle was Bemoi, formerly Regent of Senegal, where he favoured Portuguese merchants in return for a supply of battle horses; additional military help was to be granted if he converted to Christianity. Thus Bemoi and 25 followers were transported to Portugal. Housed at Palmela, they were given splendid clothes and dined off silver plate. They were received by the king at Setúbal, where they prostrated themselves and made as if to sprinkle dust on their heads. Clearly this endeared Bemoi to Dom João II, who became his godfather at the christening three weeks after his arrival. But there was no happy ending: godson or no, on the return journey Bemoi was executed by the captain of the fleet.

The unquiet ghost of Dom Garcia de Menses, Bishop of Évora and speaker of elegant Latin, tinkles in the cistern. Betrayed by his mistress's brother, his role in the Duke of Viseu's plot to assassinate the king became known to Dom João II, who stabbed the duke to death in 1484 and, unwilling to spill the blood of an ecclesiastic, incarcerated the bishop in the dry cistern, where he was poisoned and found dead with a book in his hand.

The only notable feature in the monastery's 15th-century **church of Santiago** is the funerary urn of Dom Jorge de Lencastre, son of Dom João II and last Master of S. Tiago, built of red Arrábida marble in 1551.

Palmela ✆ *(01–)*   ***Where to Stay***

Within the castle battlements, the **Pousada Castelo de Palmela**, ✆ 235 1395/1226, ✉ 233 0440 (*category CH*), occupies the 15th-century monastery of the Order of Santiago. The whitewashed corridors are floored with stone, arranged around the glassed-in columns of the cloister, filled with armchairs and plants. The rather basic bedrooms are dominated by their views. A light Arrábida marble *lavabo*, dated 1711 and decorated with the scallop shells and pilgrim staff of St James, precedes the elegant, well-trimmed restaurant, which offers excellent shellfish cooked with herbs.

West of Palmela

Vila Fresca de Azeitão

Lording it over the village of Vila Fresca de Azeitão, 8km west of Palmela, the **Quinta de Bacalhôa** (for information, ✆ 01 218 0011) dates from the last quarter of the 15th century, blending Florentine Renaissance loggias with Moorish-looking melon domes. The gardens (*open 1–5 except Sun and holidays*) contain very fine *azulejos*, produced by Moorish techniques but, in part, representing Western design.

In the early 16th century, Bacalhôa was purchased by Afonso de Albuquerque, Viceroy of India; now it is the seat of Mrs Herbert Scoville of Connecticut, who rescued the house and grounds from ruin. Even her valiant efforts are helpless against the pollution and traffic vibrations which are destroying Bacalhôa's *azulejos*. The labyrinthine clipped box hedges are hemmed in by 16th-century tiles depicting the rape of Europa, overlooked by the garden loggia, itself panelled with 17th-century *azulejos* of muscular men with turquoise hair and watery vessels, representing the rivers of Portugal and the world. Beside the water tank which served to irrigate the orchards and shrubs, a pyramid-topped pavilion is walled with geometrical tiles in the Moorish style, incorporating the earliest dated tile panel in Portugal—unhappy Suzanna being mauled by a couple of Moorish-looking elders, of 1565.

The whole process of hand-made **tile production** can be viewed nearby at S. Simão Arte (86 Rue Almirante Reis, ✆ 01 218 3135; at the rear of the Quinta de Bacalhôa). A 60 x 30cm panel costs around 2000$00. Commissions, done from photographs, take about two weeks.

Vila Nogueira de Azeitão

Two km to the west of the Quinta de Bacalhôa, the charming little town of Vila Nogueira de Azeitão takes its name from the Moors' *az-zaytuna* (the place of the green olives). It hosts several grand buildings, including the remains of a Dominican monastery, and the plain **Távora Palace of the Dukes of Aveiro**, dated 1520–3 and said to be Portugal's first purely Renaissance building. In 1758 the duke was extracted from this palace and executed by having his bones broken, accused by the Marquis of Pombal of being accomplice to the ambush and attempted assassination of King José. The Távora escutcheon was subsequently erased from the ceiling of the royal palace at Sintra.

Roughly opposite the *palácio*, visitors can tour the **New Winery of J.M. da Fonseca**, ✆ 01 218 0227 (*open Mon–Thurs 9–12 and 2–5, Fri 9–12 and 2–3*), visiting its cement igloos and mahogany and oak casks, as well as all the sophisticated machinery which takes the romance out of winemaking. It's an interesting excursion for the layman, with a collection of *azulejos* to boot. Fonseca is one of Portugal's largest wine exporters, using Portuguese native varieties of grape as the backbone of all their wines. The Old Winery, in the centre of Vila Nogueira de Azeitão, produces a rich dessert wine, Moscatel de Setúbal, made with grapes bought from farmers on the Setúbal peninsula. Fonseca's best-known brand is smooth, ruby-coloured Periquita, sold in the winery alongside other Fonseca products. (**João Pires**, the Setúbal peninsula's other winery, is based in Pinhal Novo, 12km north of Setúbal, and markets Lancers brand and own-label Mateus Rosé-style wines.)

Azeitão is noted for its creamy derivative of Serra cheese, best scooped from its skin.

✆ *(01–)* **Where to Stay**

The ★★★★**Estalagem da Quinta das Torres**, ✆ 208 0001 (*moderate*)—across the road from Fonseca's New Winery—is a 16th-century baronial mansion with square towers at each corner. Beside it, an odd columned pavilion with a cupola forms an island in the large water tank. Within the *estalagem*, the sympathetic decoration includes candelabra and gun cabinets in the hall, and china ornaments in the 11 high-ceilinged guest bedrooms. The huge suite is particularly good value: frothy bunches of material are attached to the wall above the twin brass beds, whose incumbents are asked to wait three minutes for hot water in the bathroom. In the gallery, two large, imported *azulejo* panels, dated 1570 and 1578, illustrate scenes from the *Aeneid*: the burning of Troy and the death of Dido. Tapestries hang in the dining room, which serves simple, solid dishes, accompanied by Fonseca wines.

The Serra da Arrábida

The enchanted, invigorating Serra da Arrábida is an isolated mass of limestone on the south side of the Setúbal peninsula, running parallel to the coast for about 35km west from Palmela. The rounded, whale-backed mountain rises to no more than 500m, from which it falls in steep scrub-covered cliffs to the sea. Weathering has pitted and flaked the rock, which is strangely beautiful as it lies exposed between pockets of red soil tightly carpeted with Mediterranean vegetation. Over a thousand species of plant have been recorded here, the most common of which are myrtle, aloe, cistus and arbutus. In late March or April the land is awash with wild flowers—Spanish bluebells and coral-pink peonies grow in the shade of dense forests of Lusitanian oak, beside the road leading down to the little village of Portinho da Arrábida. The range is fringed with sandy coves, whose limestone cliffs add a touch of the exotic. The more accessible beaches get quite crowded in season—if you want seclusion, you'll have to brave a steep descent. Try the **Praia dos Coelhos**, to the west of the Praia de Galapos.

The Arabic word *ar-rabat* signifies a fortified hermitage, so there is a precedent for the warren of small cells, a church, and dependent buildings of the Capuchin **Convento Novo** nestled into the slope of the Serra, just below the upper road running through the range, almost at its highest point. Would-be visitors should ask the tourist office in Setúbal for a key to the gates of the monastery—it's worth the effort.

There is something wonderfully simple about the place, as if it has taken the spirit of the hills and blessed it. Sometimes mist accentuates the solitude of the monastery, obscuring the ocean view and wrapping the beautiful hills which surround it. The statue of Frei Martinho near the entrance embodies the philosophy of the Order: his eyes are closed (to the outside world); his lips are closed (in silence); in one hand he holds a candle (of good deeds); in the other he holds a whip (to purge himself); he has two hearts, one locked (to the outside world), the other open (to God).

The monastery was founded by the first Duke of Aveiro for St Peter of Alcantara in 1542. The generous but worldly ducal family endowed the Convento Novo with porcelain crockery, which the monks broke, charmingly, and embedded fragments in some of the walls, with shells. This appears to have been the monks' sole indulgence. When he did things he ought not to have done, a brother banished himself to windowless cell number 11, where he slept with a log pillow on a cork bed until sufficiently purged. Perhaps the voluptuous and hirsute mannequin of Mary Magdalene, lying in a cage, served as example of the temptations others have borne.

The last monk died *c.* 1850; today the Convento belongs to the Duke of Palmela, who makes it available to members of the Unification Church (the Moonies) and their vociferous chihuahuas. The nine pillarbox Stations of the Cross, slightly to the west, are the chapels of the Convento Velho.

℘ (01–)   *Eating Out*

There are several restaurants at the clear-watered **Praia do Portinho da Arrábida**: the **Beira-Mar**, ℘ 218 0544 (*moderate*), overlooking the water, does a good *cataplana*. In high season, best park your car before the descent.

Sesimbra

On the southern side of the Serra da Arrábida, 40km south of Lisbon, the medium-sized town of Sesimbra wells up around a turquoise bay bracketed by limestone hills, overlooked by a hilltop castle. The edge of the town has been developed as a resort, and the beach gets crowded, but the rickety whitewashed back streets resemble a small-scale Greek island resort. Fish are auctioned beside the pretty harbour, at descending prices, and seagulls drop starfish on roads bordered by red-hot pokers.

Sesimbra ℘ (01–)   *Tourist Information*

The **tourist office** is on the seafront at 17 Av. dos Náufragos, ℘ 223 3304.

The five-towered **castle** 240m above sea level is a mere shell, empty but for the town cemetery: it's better seen from a distance. Constructed with the help of Frankish crusaders, it was granted shortly afterwards, in 1236, to the Order of Santiago. Sesimbra's **Santiago Fort** projects on to the beach, outshining the sandcastles around it. Built during the War of Restoration, as a bastion against the Spanish as well as the Algerian pirates, it was designed by a remarkable Fleming called Ciermans (Cosmander in Portuguese). Jesuit, mathematician, engineer and colonel, his combination of skills was so attractive to Philip IV of Spain that he kidnapped Cosmander and compelled him to use his knowledge to assist the Spanish in the siege of Olivença, in 1648. The unhappy genius was shot during the assault, and his fort at Sesimbra suffered the indignity of serving as a bathing hut for three of the four legitimate children of Dom João V. The town's 15th-century *Misericórdia*, several blocks inland from the fort, contains a painting of *Nossa Senhora da Misericórdia* attributed to Gregório Lopes. The two foremost kneeling figures have been variously identified as Dom Manuel and Pope Leo X, or Dom João III and Pope Paul III.

Sesimbra ℘ (01–)   *Where to Stay and Eating Out*

Centrally located **Tony Bar Marisqueira**, 18/19 Largo de Bombaldes ℘ 223 3199 (*expensive*), paved with dragons' teeth and walled with stone, serves good but pricey shellfish.

Slightly to the west of town, the private, relaxed ★★★★**Hotel do Mar**, 10 Rua General Humberto Delgado, ℘ 223 3326, ✆ 223 3888 (*expensive*), is a stepped building with views of the ocean; some balconies overlook the garden and circular swimming pool too. Bedrooms are cosy, bathrooms squashed. An aviary chirps merrily at one end of the reception area. The restaurant is slightly marred by hovering waiters and an unambitious menu. On the promenade in town, the **★★Pensão Espadarte**, Av. 25 de Abril, ✆ 223 3189 (*moderate*), offers both dilapidated old rooms and attractively plain new rooms, all of which are cramped. For cheap accommodation, ask the tourist office about rooms in private houses.

Turismo de Habitação

Quinta dos Medos, Lugar de Fornos, Caixas, ✆ 223 4142 (*moderate*) is an unpretentious house sitting in its own estate.

Cabo Espichel

West of Sesimbra, the hills gradually fall away as they approach the southwestern tip of the Setúbal peninsula, whose steep cliffs are 15km from Sesimbra. There are stone-walled fields of beans and maize, marble quarries, and, on the flat Cabo Espichel promontory, a lighthouse and the **church of N.S. do Cabo**. Built in 1701, it contains embroidered, photographed, and painted ex-votos, as well as the image of the Virgin found by a fisherman guided by its incandescence. Dogs and cats wander into the church at will. Two long arcaded wings of pilgrims' lodgings project forward from the church, derelict but for two inhabitants. It's a quiet place, with an eerie magic about its deserted calm. Heed the warnings about the strong winds when approaching the edge of the cliffs.

Plate-sized **dinosaur footprints and tailmarks** have been found in fossilized mud at the end of Lagosteiros beach, below the church.

Belém

Lisbon

Lisbon is a city of shambolic pomp and straitened circumstance. It blankets a series of hills at the southern edge of the Estremadura plateau, on the north bank of the Tagus. At Lisbon, 10km from the river's mouth, the Tagus broadens into an inland sea, the Mar de Palha (the Sea of Straw). The steep hills make Lisbon a narcissistic city—because there are so many vantage points from which to admire its loveliness. There is no skyline to speak of: the buildings seem to well up from one foundation, behind the docks and waterfronts. They are brilliant white or sorry grey, or, since the 19th century, washed with mellow shades of burnt pink, eau-de-nil and ochre.

The walls of Lisbon are daubed with political graffiti—an art in which the Left are supreme—and pasted with posters advertising concerts. The smell of coffee percolates from cafés whose floors are littered with paper napkins and sugar sachets. In winter, chestnuts are roasted in coal ovens at strategic points and sold in cones of *Yellow Pages*. Beggars wait on the steps of churches, occasionally heaving themselves up to do the rounds of the outdoor cafés. Men and women hawk lottery tickets on a hundred street corners; others shine pedestrians' shoes.

Varinhas—who filled the streets with piercing cries, short skirts, and the fresh fish they sold from wooden trays—are disappearing; a brightly wrapped gaggle of ladies from the Cape Verde islands kindles the tradition opposite the Cais do Sodré. Everywhere, women are knitting: they pass the thread behind their necks and appear, at a glance, to have a limitless supply of wool stored beneath their collars. Kittens play on tiled roofs and dogs sniff at handsome 18th-century street fountains. Inland, to the north, Lisbon's monumental junctions and polluted palm trees give way to faceless housing developments built since the 1930s. Towards the airport, there are shanty towns, where barefoot *retornados* from the colonies fill pitchers at communal water taps.

The web of wires above the streets begins to whistle when a tram approaches. Lisbon's trams are mistakenly likened to those of San Francisco, but the latter are cable cars, which are dragged by leads. Built with British equipment during the 1920s, the trams grind their way to parts of the city that are too steep or narrow for buses to negotiate.

History

Lisbon's excellent natural harbour, fertile hinterland, and easily defensible site led the Phoenicians to settle the hill of São Jorge, which they called Alis ubbo (c. 1200 BC). In 205 BC the Romans occupied what came to be known as Olissipo. They were driven out by the northern Barbarians in 714, shortly followed by the Visigoths and then the Moors. Dom Afonso Henriques, the first King of Portugal, besieged Lisbon for 17 weeks and drove out the Moors in 1147.

The Siege of Lisbon

The king had enlisted the help of Flemish, Rhinelandish and Anglo-Norman knights, who put in at Oporto on their way to the Second Crusade and were lured off course by the promise of booty. Their chronicler, traditionally known as Osbern, records that on the green, upland pastures around Lisbon, 'mares conceived from the wind'. The city was said to contain 60,000 tax-paying families; its great size was attributed to the flowing together of the wickedest men of all nations, as into a cesspool, because there was no proscribed religion. When the siege was under way, the Flemings noticed a posse of Moors creeping out of the city to snatch the half-eaten figs they threw out from their sentry posts. They set snares, and caught three of the infidels. The Anglo-Normans constructed a tower, swathed it with ox hides, and sprinkled it with holy water. Try as they might, the Moors could not set it on fire, and called for a truce. The Crusaders broke the truce by pillaging the city, while the residents departed. The successors' souls were entrusted to the vigorous Gilbert of Hastings, who was chosen as Bishop of Lisbon.

It was Dom Afonso III (1248–79) who first chose Lisbon as his capital. Well sited for the governance of both the north and the south of the country, the city rapidly outstripped Coimbra, Braga, Évora and Silves in size. Its golden age came in the 16th century, when it was a commercial emporium, a hive of merchants, foreigners, and the Inquisition. The maximum population numbered 65,000 in 1527; by 1620 it had swollen to 165,000 and clocked in as the largest city in Iberia, despite the earthquakes of 1531 and 1551, and the yoking of Portugal to Spain under Philip II. King Dom João V organized numerous *festas* in the capital, but the city he had known was to disappear in 1755: two-thirds of the capital was destroyed in the great earthquake.

The Earthquake of 1755

'It began like the rattleing of Coaches, and the things befor me danst up and downe upon the table' wrote Sister Catherine Witham. 'All falling rownd us, and the lime and dust so thick there was no seeing ... We layde under a pair tree, covered over with a Carpett, for Eight days.' In the streets of Lisbon Thomas Jacomb 'saw many coaches, chaises, carts, Horses, Mules, Oxen etc, some entirely some half buried under Ground, many People under the Ruins begging for assistance and none able to get nigh them, many groaning under ground ...' It happened on All Saints' Day, when the churches were bright with candle light; the ensuing fires were almost as destructive as the quake itself (prompting ironic commentary from Voltaire, who places *Candide* in Lisbon when the catastrophe strikes), and the consequent tidal wave swallowed Lisbon's shipping. The Marquês de Alorna's response to the disaster, 'We must bury the dead and feed the living, and close the ports', is often attributed to Pombal—who rose to the occasion. To quash the danger of plague, corpses were set on barges and sunk at sea. Prices were fixed, taxes suspended, emergency hospitals opened. A 4 per cent tax was levied to cover the cost of rebuilding.

In the 19th century, after the flight of the royal family to Brazil, Junot presided over Lisbon—for a mere nine months. Following their defeat by Wellington at the battle of Vimeiro, the French were permitted to withdraw. Wellington's successful military strategy towards the end of the Peninsular War hinged on the defence of Lisbon behind the Lines

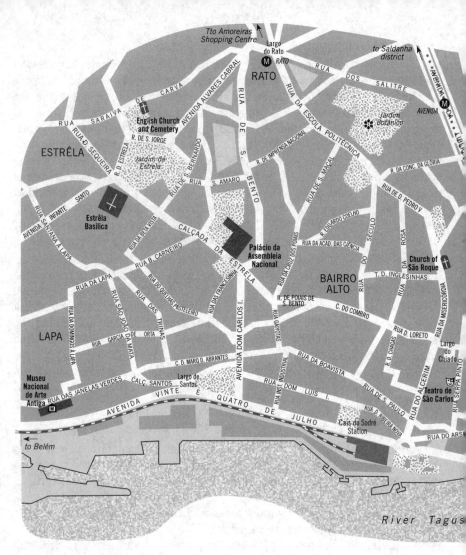

of Torres Vedras. King Dom Carlos and his eldest son were assassinated in the Praça do Comércio in 1908, and the monarchy was overthrown here in 1910. Spies were rife during the Second World War, and the capital was the scene of the bloodless Revolution of 25 April 1974.

Lisbon ☎ (01–)   *Getting There*

Lisbon is an international terminus as well as the centre of Portugal's communications network.

by air

In the 1940s Sacheverell Sitwell recommended visitors to arrive in Lisbon by flying boat. For those of us who are not so lucky, the **airport** is close to town (at Portela;

to Estefânia district

GRAÇA

500 metres
500 yards

N

RUA DO TELHA

R. INST. BACTERIOLOGICO

RUA D. PORTAS D. S. ANTÃO

RUA DA S. JOSE

C. DE SANTANA

RUA DE S.

RUA DA PALMA

RUA D. OLARIAS

RUA DAM. MONTEIRO

CALÇ. DO MONTE

RUA DA GRAÇA

RUA SENHORA DA GLÓRIA

RUA LEITE DE VASCONCELOS

RUA DOSO CÔVO

Tourist Office

RESTAURADORES

National Theatre

RUA DE G. LAZARO

SOCORRO

R. D. JAGRES

CALÇADA DE SANTO ANDRÉ

Largo Martim Moniz

Largo da Graça

C. D. S. VICENTE

RUA DA VERÓNICA

ROSSIO

Praça Dom Pedro IV

Praça da Figueira

RUA DA COSTA DO CASTELO

C. D. GRAÇA

R. DE S. VICENTE

CAMPO D. STA CLARA

to Museu do Azulejo and Church of Madre de Deus

RUA CAMINHOS DE FERRO

onvento do Carmo

evador de nta Justa

RUA GARRET

RUA DE STA JUSTA

RUA AUREA (RUA DO OURO)

RUA N. D. ALMADA

RUA DOS FANQUEIROS

RUA DA MADALENA

R. DE S. MAMEDE

Castle of São Jorge

Museu da Marioneta

Church of Santa Engrácia

Church of São Vicente de Fora

RUA DO PARAÍSO

Museu Nacional de Arte Contemporânea

BAIXA

RUA DA VITORIA

PRATA

RUA DA CONCEIÇÃO

AUGUSTA

RUA S. TIAGO

R. DO LIMOEIRO

Museu-Escola de Artes Decorativas

RUA D. REGUEIRA

RUA DOS REMÉDIOS

ALFAMA

Museu Militar

Santa Apolónia Station

The Sé

R. DE S. PEDRO

RUA JARDIM D. TOBACO

RUA D. ALFÂNDEGA

RUA TERR. DO TRIGO

Post Office

Praça do Comércio

Praça d. Ribeira

AVENIDA INFANTE D. HENRIQUE

A RIBEIRA DA NAUS

Fluvial Station

© 802060 or 804500 for flight information). Reckon on a 20–25-minute taxi ride (around 1300$00 with about 350$00 extra for luggage), or take the airport bus no.91. Other local buses, nos.44 or 45, also serve the airport, as does the metro: take the Green Line to the Praça Marquês de Pombal, the Rossio (for tourist information), and the Cais do Sodre railway station.

by train

Trains from France, Spain, and the north of Portugal arrive at Santa Apolónia Station (© 888 5101 for booking, 888 4181 for information) on the waterfront, a 15-minute walk (or bus nos. 9, 17, 35, 49, 90 or Green Line) east of the Praça do Comércio. Passengers from Sintra and Estremadura north of Lisbon decant at the neo-Manueline Rossio station, whose tracks are several escalator flights above street level. Trains from the Estoril coast arrive at the Cais do Sodré station, on the waterfront just west of the Praça do Comércio. Arrival from the south of Portugal is more spectacular: all trains stop at Barreiro, where they connect with a ferry service which crosses the Tagus to the Fluvial station at the Praça do Comércio.

by bus

The main RN bus station is in the Avenida Casal Ribeiro (near the Praça Duque de Saldanha; served by local bus nos. 1, 21, 27, 31, 32, 36, 38, 44, 45, 49; Ⓜ Saldanha). Most buses from the south terminate at the Praça de Espanha (next to the Gulbenkian; bus no.31, 46; metro Palhava). If you're departing from Lisbon, allow ½hr to buy a ticket, and check you're in the correct line before you queue.

Getting Around

by taxi

If you lose your bearings in Lisbon, fear not: St Anthony is the patron saint of lost things. Maps of Lisbon make the city look deceptively easy to get around: they do not show the hills. Keeping that in mind, the simplest way to move is by taxi. Taxis here are amongst the cheapest in Europe: pay what you see on the meter, plus a 5–10 per cent tip. The initial fare is 250$00, and few rides cost more than 800$00–1200$00. Getting a taxi to stop is another matter—they are free when their 'taxi' sign is illuminated, but it's simpler to find a taxi rank.

by metro

The metro network is none too extensive, but it's simple to use. Stations are signed 'M'. Tickets cost 70$00; a block of them (purchased from metro stations) works out even cheaper. Avoid rush hour, which is considerably worse than in London.

by tram

Anyone visiting Lisbon should take at least one tram (*eléctrico*). Each stop is marked by a tin *paragem* sign hanging from the tramlines. For trams with conductors, enter at the back and exit at the front; otherwise, enter at the front (just watch what everyone else does). Tickets can be purchased on the tram, but it's cheaper to buy a block from the bottom of the Elvador Santa Justa, or from the booth on the north side of the Avenida Fontes Pereira de Melo, near the Praça Marquês de Pombal.

by bus

Buses are often quicker than trams; routes are usually indicated at the stops. Buses accept the same tickets as trams, and the same rules apply.

Lisbon Ⓒ *(01–)*   **Tourist Information**

The **tourist office** is at Praça dos Restauradores (Ⓒ 346 3643). Falkplan produce an invaluable map of Lisbon, which can be purchased from various newsagents. It marks every street (with a useful index), most monuments, and public transport routes. Web Café, 126 Rua do Diario de Notícias ✆ 342 1181, *web1@mail. esotérica.pt*, provides Internet services and good coffee.

Bring flat shoes, as the streets of Lisbon are cobbled and hilly. Comfortable shoes will help you escape from the drug pushers who approach foreigners in the Rossio square and the Praça do Comércio. At night, be wary around the Cais do Sodré—you're unlikely to be in grave danger, but you might come across a brawl.

Festivals

Lisbon gets its knees up in June with the *Festas dos Santos Populares*, a Christianized version of the summer solstice: the Feast of St Anthony (12–13 June) decks the Alfama with bunting, grilled sardines and basil, all of which is washed down with plenty of wine; the Feast of St John (23–24 June) kindles bonfires in the streets and songs in air; and the Feast of St Peter (28–29 June) brings it all to a close.

On the Transience of Saints

St Vincent is the patron saint of Lisbon, but he has gone out of fashion—possibly because he was Spanish. He maintains his place on the emblem of the capital, though. It depicts stylized ravens perching on a barque—in which St Vincent's body was transported to Lisbon, following his arrival (dead) at the cape named after him.

St Vincent's place in the hearts of Lisboêtas has been usurped by St Anthony (called St Anthony of Padua). He was born in Lisbon, opted for life as a missionary but was shipwrecked in Italy, performed a number of miracles, and was canonized the year after his death, in 1232. The Lisboêtas are irrepressibly fond of him, selling little pots of basil, and kindling bonfires during his festival (13–29 June). In the 17th century a regiment entered the name of St Anthony of Lisbon on its membership roll. St Anthony was promoted from private to captain. The regiment's commander sought the saint's promotion to major, stating that 'there is no record of bad behaviour or irregularity committed by him'.

Dragon's-tooth Pavements

In the mid-19th century the Governor of the Castelo de São Jorge set prisoners to work on a queasy wave-patterned mosaic pavement for the Rossio. He may have been inspired by publications on Pompeii. At any rate, the idea caught on, and now Lisbon is delightfully ornamented by complicated and witty pavement designs. Each pale limestone or dark grey basalt cube is about 4cm square—the size of a dragon's tooth—and must be cut by hand. The cubes are pummelled into a bed of sand, from whence they are removed when the sewage pipes need repairing. They get painfully lumpy and uneven if cars drive over them, but they are porous, so they do not interrupt the water cycle. Dragon's-tooth paving prevails in Leiria, Tomar, Caldas da Rainha, parts of Oporto and Santarém and the custom was exported to Brazil, Mozambique and Angola.

The Baixa

The Baixa is the low-lying centre of Lisbon adjacent to the Tagus. A stream probably once flowed through the district into the river; its houses were built on stilts to escape frequent flooding—until the neighbourhood was levelled by the earthquake of 1755. Here was Pombal's chance to build a pristine Lisbon: the new streets should be '40 feet in width, with pavements on either side protected from wheeled traffic by stone pillars, as in London'. He and Eugénio dos Santos, a military engineer, reconstituted the Praça do Comércio as a square open to the river on its south side, and designed a grid pattern of streets stretching 500m inland to the Rossio square and the Praça da Figueira. This has been described as the greatest uniform architectural undertaking of the Age of Enlightenment—but the rationalism of that age has produced a frigid symmetry almost as severe as Pombal himself. All projections and carving were forbidden by law, for reasons of economy and haste. The Baixa was rebuilt for the merchant classes, as the streetnames indicate: Rua da Prata and Rua do Ouro (now the Rua Aurea) were intended for goldsmiths and silversmiths, and the Rua Augusta for cloth-dealers.

The fusty clothes shops remain, along with numerous banks and a huddle of undistinguished restaurants near the Rossio. The central Rua Augusta is reserved for pedestrians, some of whom go paddling and eat ice-creams at the waterfront between the Cais do Sodré station and the Praça do Comércio. The elegant burnt-pink square serves as a parking lot (having previously been apple green and melon yellow, as if it were a traffic light).

The Baixa is the nucleus of the public transport network, so hitch a lift on anything that moves and you'll probably end up here sooner or later. Ⓜ Rossio is the nearest metro station. Buses 39, 40 and 15 may be especially useful, as well as trams 3, 16, 19, 24, 25, 26 and 28.

The Praça do Comércio

The riverfront Praça do Comércio used to be the Terreiro do Paço, which was named after the Ribeira Palace. This stood here from the early 16th century until the earthquake of 1755, enabling the royal family to watch bullfights from their balconies.

A bronze **equestrian statue of Dom José** occupies the centre stage, cast by Machado de Castro (1731–1822). The project took five years to complete, during which time the vacuous king was too ill to have his likeness taken; hence the emphasis is on the helmet rather than the head. The king's horse tramples serpents, and the pedestal is flanked by Triumph leading a horse, and Fame guiding an elephant, in reference to Portugal's conquests in the east. It took more than 1000 people 3½ days to shift the statue into place, with great ceremony. At the front of the pedestal is a bronze medallion depicting Pombal; when the dictator fell from power, the craftsman who had made the medallion was ordered to destroy it. Loath to melt down his work, he bricked it up in a wall of the Arsenal, from which it was retrieved nearly 60 years later.

Manuel Gandra, a geomancer, traces close links between the proportions of the Praça—the monument to Dom José—and the palace and basilica of Mafra, the monument to his father Dom João V. The turrets at the seafront correspond with the turrets at the sides of the palace: accordingly, the equestrian statue occupies the place of the high altar. On 1 February

1908, King Dom Carlos and Crown Prince Luís Filipe were assassinated at the corner of Praça do Comércio and the Rua do Arsenal, near where Lisbon's main post office stands.

West and East of the Praça

The Rua do Arsenal leads westwards to the Cais do Sodré station. Opposite the station, the covered **market** is a riot of eels, *galega* cabbage, chick peas, lettuces, oranges, and almost everything else you're likely to eat in Portugal, pored over by ladies in black with their hands on their cheeks. Most of the arum lilies and carnations are whisked off to gravesides. However early you get there, there is bound to be some action: produce is unloaded during the previous night.

The Rua da Alfândega runs eastwards from the Praça do Comércio, past the **Church of Conceição Velha**, which was built by Dom Manuel on the site of Lisbon's synagogue. King Manuel and Queen Leonor, widow of Dom João II, are among the dignitaries kneeling at the feet of N. S. da Misericórdia, on the tympanum of its richly carved portal. In the parallel street, the Rua dos Bacalhoeiros, the façade of the **Casa dos Bicos** is studded with little pyramids, a curiosity of early 16th-century architecture, built for a bastard of Afonso de Albuquerque. The house subsequently became a *bacalhau* shop. There are similar examples of the design in Italy and Spain.

The Rua Aurea runs parallel to the Rua da Prata; at its junction with the Rua de Santa Justa stands the incongruous iron **elevador de Santa Justa**, whose construction is incorrectly attributed to Eiffel. It was built by Raúl Mesnier in 1902, and is a fun way to get to the Largo do Carmo in the Alfama.

In and Around the Rossio

In the Rossio itself, a statue of the 16th-century playwright Gil Vicente crowns the façade of the **National Theatre** (1842–6). The building stands on the site of the Paço dos Estãos, home of the Inquisition 1534–1820. (In 1726, Brockwell wrote that an *auto da fé* was held every three years: the Inquisitor and Court heard Mass; then 'Prisoners, let their Station or Quality be what it will, almost starved, swarming with Vermine, are separately presented and arraign'd at the Bar'. If they failed to repent they were tortured by 'pressing their Thumbs in a Vice, Drawing the Nails from the Fingers, scalping the Crown, etc'. If convicted a third time, 'The prisoner is arrayed in a pitched Vesture with Flames, Devils, Dragons etc. painted on it, great Weights of Iron Chains are linked to his Hands and Feet'. They were chained to an iron chair 3m from the fire, and roasted.)

The Rua das Portas de Santo Antão runs to the right of the National Theatre, leading to the Geographical Society's **Museu Etnográfico do Ultramar** at 100 Rua Portas de Santo Antão (*open 11–1 and 3–5; closed Tues, Thurs, Sat, Sun and holidays*). It's a jumble of odd things which caught travellers' eyes, displayed around the upper walkways of a tall lecture theatre. The collection includes door locks and musical instruments from Guinea Bissau; *nkonde* statuettes from the Congo, stuck full of iron nails, with mirrors at their bellies; Angolan chieftains' chairs composed of phalluses; tortoiseshell and banjos from Cabo Verde; and heads shrunk by Brazilian Indians. Historically, one of the most significant exhibits is a stone column retrieved from Angola, with an inscription recording that in 1482 'the very high, very excellent and powerful prince King João second of Portugal sent to have this land discovered and these *padrões* placed by Diogo Cão, squire of his household'.

The Alfama

Idrisi, the 12th-century Muslim geographer, referred to the Alfama as *al-hamma* (the bath)—but the only remaining public baths are for the birds. The Alfama's steep and higgledy-piggledy streets are built on stone, which preserved them from the devastations of the earthquake: here, just east of the Baixa, are the antique guts of Lisbon. The Alfama is a warren of narrow alleys and uneven staircases awash with laundry, lit from wrought-iron lamp fittings, hymned by caged budgies and the occasional cockerel, clouded by flies, greened by potplants, protected by half-cannon tiled roofs and, sometimes, by plastic tarpaulins strung out to keep the rain or sun off a doorstep. Behind peeling double doors, children bicycle around street-level vestibules. Be wary of pickpockets and camera thieves.

The Sé (Cathedral)

Gilbert of Hastings required a cathedral. Three years after his appointment as Lisbon's first bishop, Dom Afonso Henriques ordered one to be built for him, possibly on the ruins of a mosque, just east of what is now the Baixa district (tram 28, bus 37). It was designed by Masters Robert and Bernard, the pair who worked on the Sé Velha at Coimbra, in 1150; here they have included two typically Romanesque side towers, and set a rose window in the dignified façade. In 1388 a riotous crowd flung Bishop Martinho Anes from one of these towers, because he was Castilian, and appointed by the Avignonese Pope, Clement VII. The building was damaged and rebuilt after earthquakes in 1337–47 and 1755; now it is heavily restored and rather characterless.

St Anthony passed through the waters of the font: he was baptized in it in 1195. To its left is the chapel of Bartolomeu Joanes, which was built in 1324 and funded by a rich Lisbon merchant. To the left stands Machado de Castro's crib, sculpted in 1766. The organ, a blaster if ever there was one, was added in the 18th century. Chapels lead off the forceful Gothic ambulatory; they contain tombs of João Anes, the first archbishop (d. 1440), and Lopo Fernandes Pacheco, with a dog at his feet. The ambulatory leads through to the gothic cloister, whose arches are split in two.

Dorothy Quillinan, Wordsworth's daughter, visited the cathedral in 1845, and in her journal noted 'two dead infants which we saw carelessly laid on a sort of shelf or projection, behind the High Altar. They were dressed neatly...as if just taken out of the cradle. I insisted upon it that they were wax children. Mr—...assured me they were dead infants—"angels", as they call them and consider them... These are the children of poor people who are allowed to leave them for Christian burial without charge.'

Around the Alfama

Opposite the cathedral, the elegant little **church of Santo António da Sé** shelters the room where St Anthony was born in 1195. His birthplace is now an airless chapel, thick with devotion but little else. The church was built in 1728, to the designs of Mateus Vicente, the architect of Lisbon's Estrêla church. It was paid for from the sale of little altars and images of the saint.

One block inland from the cathedral, the meagre and unatmospheric remains of Lisbon's **Roman Theatre** can be seen from the Rua de São Mamede. An inscription records the dedication of the orchestra in the time of Nero.

The Rua Augusto Rosa leads uphill from the cathedral to the **Museu-Escola de Artes Decorativas** (Museum of Decorative Arts) (*open 10–1 and 2.30–5; closed Sun, Mon and holidays; 30-minute tours twice hourly*; trams 28 or 28B, bus 37) which boasts the most comprehensive display of furniture in the country. The collection—which includes embroidered shawls, 18th- and 19th-century Arraiolos rugs, porcelain, glass, and Portuguese silverwork—was assembled by Ricardo Espírito Santo, and installed in a 17th-century *palácio*, which retains its original *azulejos*.

The Espírito Santo Foundation was set up in 1953 to foster traditional crafts. Bookbinders, gilders, wood carvers, cabinet makers and others can be visited in the 21 workshops next to the museum. Each produces faithful reproductions using original techniques.

The Castle

The route to the castle is complicated: if you keep going uphill, you'll get there eventually. The **castle of São Jorge** (bus 37) was the nucleus of the city, inhabited by the Phoenicians and subsequently by every conquering race. Dom Afonso Henriques initiated the medley of fortifications when he captured the castle in 1147, and rebuilt the Moorish defences. Over-enthusiastic restoration has sucked the atmosphere from the place, turning it over to gardens with tinkling

Castelo São Jorge

fountains, crooning peacocks, black swans and turkeys (find a feather and make an earring). Now the main attraction is the panoramic view of Lisbon and the Tagus.

Three sections of bulwarks can be distinguished: the quadrangular fortress, at the highest point of the hill, with 10 square towers; the citadel, within the first band of walls, built on the site of the Roman acropolis and containing the Paço da Alcáçova, a royal palace until the reign of Dom Manuel; and finally a girdle of walls projecting south, towards the Tagus, built for defence against the Barbarians, and which became the main theatre for the Christian assault.

East of the Castle

The recent revival of satirical puppets may boost the popularity of the **Museu da Marioneta** (Puppet Museum), 19 Largo Rodrigues de Freitas, ✆ 01 887 8396 (*opening has been somewhat erratic of late, so it's best to telephone ahead and make an appointment*), just east of the castle (tram 12). It's intimate, but not a cute museum: puppets have mocked politicians since the 18th century, when puppet operas became fashionable. Puppet plays were banned under Salazar.

Each of the 1¼m puppets takes two months to create; they emerge, say, as Apollo, whose hair is woodshavings, or Dulcineia, whose head is faceless. Occasionally the puppet-featured couple who run the museum perform a puppet opera, with a cast of 12–20. Puppets from Thailand, Burma, Indonesia and Japan are also on show. The paraphernalia of performance includes a tempest machine.

The original **church and monastery of S. Vicente de Fora** (tram 28; due east of the Puppet Museum via the Rua de Santa Marinha) were founded by Dom Afonso Henriques outside (*fora*) the city walls; the buildings that stand today were constructed between 1582 and 1627 by Felipe Terzi, possibly assisted by Juan Herrera, architect of the Escorial.

Its Mannerist style is typical of architecture under the Inquisition: the balanced but frigid white limestone façade (with niches for, from left to right, Saints Vincent, Augustus and Sebastian); the grandiose undivided nave focusing attention on the preacher and celebrant. Dom João V commissioned the canopied baroque altar, which is flanked by eight life-sized wooden sculptures from the Mafra school. In the cloister, late 18th-century *azulejos* depict hunting, rural and court scenes from La Fontaine's *Fables*. These include a rail draped with pocket watches, Dali style. In 1855 the refectory, off the cloister, was selected as the Bragança pantheon: it contains the tombs of most of the kings and queens of Portugal from Dom João IV (died 1656) and Catherine of Bragança through to Dom Carlos (died 1908). The coffins used to have glass tops, so the embalmed bodies could spy on the world.

On Tuesday and Saturday mornings, the **Feira da Ladra** (fleamarket) spreads itself behind the church of S. Vicente. It is unlikely to turn up any interesting nuggets, offering mostly doormats, radios, army surplus, empty soda cans, denim and popcorn. Chunky handknit sweaters are a good bet for around 3000$00, or a machete if the weeds are getting bad back home.

Two blocks downhill from the front of the church, the Rua dos Corvos leads eastwards to the church of Santa Engrácia (*open 10–5; closed Mon*; bus 12), a lofty and uplifting building in the shape of a Greek cross with rounded arms. Panelled with brown, pink and light and dark grey marble, its balanced design influenced a new wave of Italian Baroque architecture. João Antunes drew up the plans in 1682, after the chancel of the previous church crumbled. It became a synonym for unfinished work: the balustraded cupola was not added until 1966. Then, it became the National Pantheon, harbouring the uniform modern cenotaphs of Camões, Henry the Navigator, and Vasco da Gama amongst others. The seatless symmetry yields peculiar echoes, and an elevator goes up to the dome, with views of the port and city.

Beside the river docks, the **Museu Militar** (*open Tues–Sat 10–4; Sun 11–5*; tram 3, 16, 24; bus 13a, 17, 35) traces the evolution of pistols, helmets, the Portuguese flag and the stuff of war in a dull, interminable display.

Xabregas

Xabregas is an eastern suburb whose sole point of interest is the Museu do Azulejo.

The Museu do Azulejo (Tile Museum)

Open Wed–Sun 10–6; Tues 2–6; closed Mon.

Anyone who wants to understand the evolution of Portuguese tile design and technique should visit the Museu do Azulejo (east of the Alfama, one block inland from the Tagus; tram 3, 16, 24, 27; bus 13a, 18, 42): examples are arranged chronologically, from the 16th century to the present day. The museum is installed in the Convent of Madre de Deus.

The collection includes a grotesque rendition of Bacchus, with hairy breasts and a cluster of grapes at his crotch; seven early 19th-century panels illustrating the progress from rags to riches of a hatter called António Joaquim Carneiro; and witty modern tiles of grasshoppers and crabs, with some abstract work. The highlight is a 36m panorama of Lisbon's waterfront, *c.* 1738; many of the buildings no longer exist, including the smoking kilns of factories in the Mocambo district where these very tiles were probably made.

The splendid **church of Madre de Deus** is one of the best places in Lisbon to see rich art *in situ*, and contains some stunning gilt Baroque woodwork. The convent was founded by Dona Leonor, widow of King Dom João II, in 1509; her symbol, the shrimping net, and her husband's, the pelican, ornament the restored side portal.

Little remains of the original foundation, which was enlarged by King Dom João III, and rebuilt after the 1755 earthquake. This restructuring decapitated the tile-painted sheep that accompany Moses as he is addressed by God, in the main body of the church. The headless flock is part of the Dutch *azulejo* dados, which have more spatial depth and use inkier blue than their Portuguese counterparts. Above the tiles, the walls and ceiling are covered with canvases depicting the life of St Francis, attributed to André Gonçalves (1687–1762); note particularly his semicircular *Coronation of the Virgin*. Sixteenth-century paintings from the original church hang in the chancel. The marble stoup (basin for holy water) in the sacristy is said to have belonged to Dona Leonor herself.

The *coro alto* can be entered from the upper cloister. Gilt woodwork frames paintings by André Gonçalves and other 18th-century artists, covering every inch of the ceiling and walls. Graceful *azulejos* are employed as light-reflectors in the window casements.

The Bairro Alto

There are two parts to the Bairro Alto: the *bairro*, or neighbourhood, itself; and the Chiado. The Bairro was laid out on a grid pattern in the 16th century, but the slope of the streets makes them feel slightly wonky. This was, and to some extent still is, Lisbon's Bohemian quarter; the narrowness of the roads and the height of the peeling, balconied houses that overlook them have held on to a lively streetlife, played out around a hive of restaurants, *tascas*, and *fado* houses. The Chiado is slightly closer to the river. It focuses on the Rua Garrett, where the elegant of Lisbon shop in boutiques and turn-of-the-century department stores. In the summer of 1988, a fire began in one such store in the Rua do Carmo. It scarred the face of the Chiado and destroyed a unique part of the city.

The Rua Serpa Pinto runs downhill from the Rua Garrett past Lisbon's fine opera house, the **Teatro de São Carlos** (tram 28), which is supposed to have been modelled on San Carlos in Naples. Construction began in 1792; the draped, columned, mirrored royal box flanked by satyrs recalls grand times. A short way down the Rua Serpa Pinto, the **Museu Nacional de Arte Contemporânea** displays paintings from the second half of the 19th century, and the early decades of the 20th, with an emphasis on the Romantic era. The Gulbenkian Museum of Modern Art (*see* 'Saldanha', p.308) has a far better collection of modern works.

The Calçada do Sacramento leads uphill from Rua Garrett to the Largo do Carmo. Here, the grassy nave and vacant arches of the **Convento do Carmo** (tram 24; Elvador Santa Justa) are Lisbon's most spectacular monument to the great earthquake. The Gothic church perches on the verge of a steep hill, high above the Baixa. It was founded by Dom Nun' Álvares Pereira, the great military leader, in honour of a vow made at the battle of Aljubarrota. The foundations twice gave way, delaying completion until 1423, when the founder himself entered the monastery for the remaining eight years of his life. The church flipped its lid in 1755: the roof collapsed, but the walls, nave arches, and five apses remain intact. Having served as a graveyard, a public refuse pit, and a stable for the neighbouring barracks, the building now houses a muddled **Museu Arqueológico** (*open May–Sept, 10–6; Oct–April, 10–1 and 2–5; closed Sun and holidays*), with miscellaneous Visigothic pieces, pottery, coins and tombs. Note the stone bust of Dom Afonso Henriques at the back of the chancel, which is believed to be the oldest image of the nation's first king.

The Church of São Roque

The Rua da Oliveira leads uphill to the Largo Trindade Coelho, where the austere façade of the church of São Roque gives no hint of the riches within. The church was built in the late 16th century, following Felipe Terzi's plans; in 1642 the great Jesuit Padre António Vieira—missionary, diplomat and economist—delivered his 40-hour sermon here. The third chapel on the right brims with elegant polychrome *azulejos* dated 1585.

But the **chapel of São João Baptista** (to the left of the high altar) steals the show. It encapsulates all Dom João V's magnificence and folly. The king commissioned it in 1742 from Vanvitelli, who built it in Rome, where it was consecrated by Pope Benedict XIV—in return for a gift of 100,000 cruzados. (Traffic between Lisbon and the papal court was not uncommon: the pope had sent a special nuncio to Lisbon bearing consecrated 'nappies' for the Infante Pedro; he was already dead, so they were swathed around the Infante José.) After its consecration the structure was dismantled and shipped to Lisbon, at a total cost of more than £225,000—making it one of the most precious chapels of its size ever built. For all that, its confection of alabaster, amethyst, diaspore, lapis lazuli, porphyry, and several marbles is disappointingly jumbled. The ingredients drown one another. Do look at the magnificent chandelier.

The chapel's fabulous accoutrements are displayed in the **Sacred Art Museum of São Roque**, adjacent to the church. The treasury beggared description (and the people of Portugal): one cope is showered with 15kg of gold, and a mitre is carbuncled with Brazilian rubies. There are some lively Italian Baroque gilt candlesticks.

Next door, the *Misericórdia* almshouse is funded by weekly lotteries—hence the bemusing lifesize sculpture of a lottery ticket seller in the middle of the square, with whom the pigeons have their way.

The Jardim Botánico and Around

Rua de S. Pedro do Alcântara curves uphill into Rua D. Pedro V and the Rato district, where the **Jardim Botánico** blooms beside the Academia das Ciências. It is planted on a hillslope, like almost everything else in Lisbon. Though less exotic than the Estufas, this is one of the few places in the capital where birdsong can be heard in the wild—caged birdsong is like piped music. Visitors can get pleasantly lost on the winding paths, among the cacti and goldfish.

Opposite the Academia, Rua de São Marçal runs steeply downhill, past the **British Institute** (1–3 Rua Luís Fernandes), which occupies what was once the substantial home of Francisco Alves dos Reis, mastermind of the 'Portuguese Bank-note Case'. In 1925, notepaper was obtained from the Bank of Portugal and used to instruct the London firm of Waterlow to print 580,000 500$00 notes—which entered Portugal in the Venezuelan diplomatic bag. The alarm was sounded when duplicate serial numbers surfaced; Messrs Waterlow were sued for the outstanding sum of £610,932.

Estrêla

The Estrêla district is west of the Bairro Alto and north of Lapa.

Where the neighbourhood borders the Bairro Alto, a 10-minute walk downhill from the British Institute, the **Palácio da Assembleia Nacional** (tram 28; bus 6, 13, 39, 49) houses the **Arquivo da Torre de Tombo**, the national archives named after the tower of Lisbon's castle where they were kept until the earthquake. Prior appointments are recommended. The collection includes the Bull of 1179, by which Pope Alexander III conceded the title 'King' to Afonso Henriques, and recognized the independence of Portugal. The Prime Minister's official residence is within the grounds of the National Assembly.

The Estrêla Basilica

From there, the Calçada da Estrêla runs uphill to the **Estrêla Basilica** (tram 25, 26, 28, 29, 30; bus 9), one of the most impressive 18th-century monuments in Lisbon. It was founded by Queen Dona Maria I in thanks for the birth of a son, and the first stone was laid in 1779, under the direction of Mateus Vicente and Reinaldo Manuel, both architects from the Mafra school. The lordly neoclassical façade is well balanced, with twin towers and eight beautiful marble statues; above the church rises a perfectly shaped stone dome. The high, chilly interior dwarfs devotees, who peer through the peculiar light that reflects off multi-coloured marbles.

The mausoleum of the foundress is on the left of the high altar, a sombre memorial to the kindly queen who chose as her confessor the Archbishop of Thessalonica (who started his career as a clown, and then became a soldier). She died in Brazil, from whence her corpse was brought six years later. Only the males of the House of Bragança were embalmed: Dona Maria I had been surrounded by aromatic herbs and enclosed in three coffins. When these were opened, to lay the body in its tomb, one of the two presiding princesses fainted from the stench.

North of the Basilica

Opposite the front of the church, the intimate **Jardim da Estrêla** provides a pond stocked with giant carp, which frighten people drinking beer at the waterside. A curious carved tree trunk stands at the opposite side of the park, which opens onto the Rua de São Jorge. Across the road are the gates of the crowded **English Cemetery**, laid out in 1717 adjacent to the hospital of the English Factory. (Do not be alarmed by the cemetery's postbox; it is for the vicarage.) Previously, Protestants had to be buried by the water's edge, to avoid profaning Catholic soil. Henry Fielding (1717–54) lived long enough to be spared this indignity; the author of *Tom Jones*, who described Lisbon as 'the nastiest city in the world', is buried amongst the cypresses and Judas trees, in the second aisle to the left.

The Amoreiras district, north of Estrêla, is infamous for its **Complexo das Amoreiras** (tram 10, 24, 25, 26, 27, 29, 30; bus 15, 58, 11, 23, 53), a post-modern shopping centre and residential block designed by Tomás Taveira. It appears to be a chrome and glass interpretation of a medieval fortress, totally out of keeping with the rest of the city, but not without a soul. Some people claim it is the most desirable place to live in Lisbon—because then you can't see the building itself. The huge shopping centre is a blend of upmarket boutiques, restaurants and cinemas.

Amoreiras is the destination of the monumental **Aqueduto das Águas Livres**, which gave Lisboêtas their first taste of freely available clean drinking water. Built 1729–48, it was financed by a surcharge on wine, meat and olive oil purchased in the capital. On the last leg of the 19km route, 14 arches bound across Lisbon's Alcântara valley, uninterrupted by the earthquake of 1755. This stretch was open to the public until 1844, the year in which Diogo Alves murdered people by throwing them off it. The internal workings of the aqueduct, the Casa das Águas, may be visited July–October.

Lapa is Lisbon's diplomatic quarter, where ambassadorial residences rub shoulders with humble dwellings, in the west of central Lisbon overlooking the river.

The Museu Nacional de Arte Antiga

Open 10–1 and 2.30–5; closed Mon and holidays.

The Museu Nacional de Arte Antiga (tram 19, bus 27, 40, 49) is the most significant and thrilling Portuguese museum. *Antiga* is misleading: the collection covers Portuguese art from the 11th century to the 19th century. It illustrates the nation's relationship with Flanders, Africa, India, China and Japan, and includes European paintings, and applied arts from magnificent ecclesiastical silverwork to 18th-century furnishings.

The museum's main entrance in the Jardim 9 de Abril forms part of its new wing, which was attached to the 17th-century Palace of the Counts of Alvor and the haunted chapel of the razed Convent of Santo Alberto. The side entrance is in the Rua Janelas Verdes. A small cafeteria issues unexciting salads, which can be eaten in the shady garden.

Portugal in the World

When the first Portuguese landed in Tanegaxima, in 1543, the Japanese called them 'Namban-jin', barbarians from the south. The name stuck, and now applies to all the Japanese plastic arts created during nearly a century of contact with Portugal. Japanese artists were bemused by the exotic Portuguese, and painted them in detail for the home market. The arrival of the missionaries is pictured in two beautifully composed **namban screens**: in each, the Portuguese have bulbous noses—their hosts had never seen such large appendages. Nor had they seen buttons, so every button is detailed. The Portuguese brought Persian horses for the *shōguns*, and dealt in Indian goods, hence the artists imagined (wildly inaccurate) Indian architecture. In one screen, all the priests are Jesuits; the other screen was painted 15 years later, by which time other orders had arrived in Japan.

In India the Portuguese found both skilled craftsmen and abundant raw materials, especially wood and ivory. They took advantage of both from 1498 onwards. One of the most prolific products of this cultural marriage is the many-drawered **Indo-Portuguese chest**, or *contador*, which was based on a European model; but the legs offered Indian craftsmen free rein. **Ivory casks** depict Indian gods beside European hunting scenes. **Embroidered colchas**, used both for wall hangings and as covers for beds, show a broader cultural salad. They are illustrated with European classical mythology and biblical references, as well as hunting scenes. African craftsmen were exploited more selectively—the museum contains a small display of their works in ivory from the little island of Sherbro off Sierra Leone, from Benin, and from Mombasa.

Lisbon was the first market in Europe for the **porcelains** of China, which were shipped by junk to Macau, then westwards. Chinese porcelain was made for three markets: for the imperial family, for domestic use, or for export. Some of the exports are displayed; many of the platters were intended for the Middle East, since Muslims ate communally from large dishes, while the Chinese ate from small, individual bowls. Chinese porcelain had evolved from the blue and white Ming dynasty ware to polychromed designs by the early 18th century, when Portugal began importing it in such quantities as to stunt the home industry. When Pombal forbade the importation of European porcelains into Portugal in 1767, the Portuguese tried to make polychromed faïence copies of Chinese export porcelain tureens and animal-head containers. They created handsome small vases in various sizes. This was the first Portuguese work to come near to matching the grace of Chinese porcelain.

Portuguese Painting

The *Panels of São Vicente de Fora* are of unparalleled significance: they offer a portrait of the generation of the Discoveries. Painted by Nuno Gonçalves 1467–70, the six panels depict 60 uncompromising individuals who were determined to know the world.

The panels were found just over 60 years ago in the defunct church of São Vicente, dismantled and coated with filth—a tiny square has been left uncleaned, at the bottom of the left-hand panel, on the white robe of a Cistercian monk of Alcobaça—so we do not know their intended order. Fishermen are pictured in the panel next to that of the monks; the two right-hand panels show representatives of the army backed by members of the Jewish community. In the centre two panels, St Vincent receives the homage of various dignitaries, backed by an assembly, all painted with a disregard for depth.

Dom Jorge da Costa, Archbishop of Lisbon 1460–1500, is included in the centre right-hand panel. In the centre left-hand panel, the saint is flanked by Henry the Navigator and the widowed Duchess of Bragança, who wears a white headdress. Before the saint kneel Dom Afonso V, in profile, and a lady, possibly Queen Leonor, who had died in 1455. The face in the top left corner of this panel is believed to be the painter's.

Nuno Gonçalves may have learnt his technique from Jan van Eyck, who visited Portugal in 1428 in the suite of Philip the Good, Duke of Burgundy. But there are notable differences from Flemish work: he uses yellow where others use gold; there are no distracting details of the interior. Certainly Gonçalves can stand comparison with the foremost painters of his age.

Of the Luso-Flemish school, note particularly the work of **Frei Carlos**, a Flemish monk who lived in the Alentejo, and was staggered by the quality of light there. Look at his *Annunciation* from an angle, to see what he does with volume in space. The anonymous early 16th-century *Inferno* was a daring work to hang in a convent: Hell is a common kitchen, where the chief devil is a feathered Brazilian Indian.

European Art

European paintings are arranged chronologically rather than thematically, so it is possible to see the evolution of struggles with perspective and space, and of telling a story in cartoon or triptych form. Paintings were required to fit formal categories; when Patinir explored a countryside, he had to justify the subject by tacking on the figure of St Jerome, hung in Room 4. Patinir was doing for external space what Dürer was doing for mental space: his *St Jerome*—hung next to the Patinir—was painted in 1521.

Hieronymous Bosch's *Temptations of St Anthony* takes the biscuit. St Anthony's life spanned the late 3rd and early 4th centuries; much of it was spent in pious meditation in the Egyptian desert. Bosch set him in a kaleidoscope of the Middle Ages, where sinners are punished through excess: the libidinous couple are tied together, the greedy man is being fed gold coins. St Anthony is portrayed four times, but never once looks at the horrifying scenes around him: the saint was strong and pious enough to struggle against exposure to these evils. The artist was admired by contemporaries for his piety and perception at a time when the foundations of society were being shaken by Erasmus, Copernicus, Columbus and, following Bosch's death in 1516, by Luther. Our own uncertain future makes Bosch's apocalyptic vision terrifyingly pertinent.

Small, bright Room 7 offers a change of pace. It includes rare examples of Portugal's coarse early attempts to imitate Chinese porcelain: the Chinese emperor decapitated anyone attempting to reveal its secret. (Europeans guessed at its ingredients in vain, hazarding crushed oyster shells, long-buried dung, snails, or a paste of crushed shellfish and eggs buried for a century.) Genre painting is emerging by Room 8: one panel relishes still life but resolutely titles itself *The Meeting of Jesus and Mary and Martha.*

French Silverware

The world's largest, finest and most varied collection of 18th-century French silverware is gathered here. These works of breathtaking craftsmanship and imagination were made fashionable by the court at Versailles, where monarchs dined in public for eight hours every day. In the 50 years after 1724, the Louvre workshop of Thomas Germain and his son François-Thomas produced an estimated 3000 pieces of gold and silverware for the sovereigns and nobility of Portugal. Much was destroyed by the earthquake of 1755, leaving Dom José I to re-equip the royal tables: kettles spout swans and dragons, mustard pots are oyster shells, and silver toothbrushes stand beside the discreet silver box in which a lady kept her beauty spots. The huge centrepiece illustrates the differences in the work of Germain father and son: Thomas Germain crafted the body in a more classical style than the fantastic lid created by his son. In 1985, the 16 silver-gilt figurines, designed by Cousinet, promenaded at the table of Queen Elizabeth and the Duke of Edinburgh, linked, as their maker intended, by garlands of fresh flowers held between their outstretched arms.

Saldanha

In northern Lisbon, Saldanha is the district north of the Praça Marquês de Pombal and east of the Praça Duque de Saldanha.

The Estufas

In the early 1930s, a gardener noticed that plants grew particularly well in the disused limestone quarry that became the **Estufa Fria**, a botanic garden in the Parque Eduardo VII (from Amoreiras, head down the wide Avenida Duarte Pacheco; tram 24, 27; bus 2, 12, 18, 42, 51; Ⓜ Parque). Originally conceived as a sort of green cathedral, the ferns, fuchsias and what Dr Seuss would call um-pum-pullas are protected by a canopy of matted wooden slats; a giant hothouse proper was added (the *Estufa Quente*), to house a collection of orchids offered to the city. These rub petals with giant poinsettias, assorted cacti and pineapple plants. Birds are caged beside the upper walkways, including parakeets, pheasants and Japanese ducks. The Estufas are well worth a stroll for anyone in need of respite from the city streets.

The Calouste Gulbenkian Museum

Open June–Sept, Wed and Sat 2–7.30; Oct–May, Tues, Thurs, Fri and Sun 10–5; closed Mon and holidays.

The Avenida António Augusto Aguiar runs along the eastern side of the Parque Eduardo VII, leading to the Praça da Espanha and the Parque de Palhava, in which stands the Calouste Gulbenkian Museum (tram 24, 27; bus 16, 26, 30, 56; Ⓜ S. Sebastião, Palhava). The cafeteria in the Gulbenkian Museum of Modern Art is much nicer than that in the Gulbenkian proper: it serves the best salads in Lisbon, but there's always a queue.

Gulbenkian and his Foundation

Calouste Gulbenkian has become the fairy godfather of Portugal's cultural welfare. The Armenian magnate's fortune took on stratospheric proportions just before the First World War, when he negotiated a 5 per cent stake in the newly discovered oil fields of Iraq. He lived in Portugal from 1942 until he died in 1955, at the age of 86; he bequeathed his collection of Oriental and Occidental art to his adopted country, and endowed Portugal with a foundation, the purpose of which was to be 'charitable, artistic, educational, scientific'.

The foundation now has assets of more than one billion US dollars, making it the largest private charitable institution outside the United States; half as much again has been disbursed in grants and scholarships. These include underwriting Portugal's travelling libraries, endowing a museum of modern Portuguese art, building schools, science laboratories, medical clinics and hospitals, funding low-cost housing, orphanages, and centres for the handicapped. Since the early 1960s, many members of the Foundation's own orchestra, choir and ballet have studied abroad.

Gulbenkian had taken British nationality. For a time he intended to bequeath his collection to the British nation; one of the reasons he changed his mind was that Britain declared him a 'technical enemy' during the Second World War (for continuing his rôle as honorary economic counsellor at the Iranian embassy in Paris, after the Vichy regime had been established). Gulbenkian's tact and discretion secured his most spectacular coup: the purchase of works of art from the Hermitage, 1928–30, when the government of the USSR was desperate for foreign currency. He referred to his urge for collecting as 'a disease', but wanted only 'to possess the finest specimens'—if a painting had been damaged or repainted too many times, he was not interested. Gulbenkian believed that a work of art 'must give joy'. He loved paintings 'filled with character and a certain mystery', and with 'a high level of feeling'.

The Museum

The purpose-built Gulbenkian Museum was opened in 1969; leafy views of the Palhavã Park make breathing spaces amid the collection. The museum is intimate and thoughtfully laid out. Everything it contains is worth looking at, and its size makes this possible. Ideally the museum should be visited on two occasions, one for the Oriental and Classical art (covering Egyptian, Greco-Roman, Mesopotamian, Oriental Islamic, Armenian and Far-Eastern art), and one for European art (covering medieval ivories, illuminated manuscripts, Renaissance works, and 18th- and 19th-century sculpture, painting, silver and decorative arts). The gift shop is limited but subsidized, enabling it to sell the cheapest postcards and posters in Lisbon. A series of free printed guides in English thoroughly elucidates each section of the museum.

Egyptian, Greco-Roman and Mesopotamian Art

The small collection of Egyptian art is arranged chronologically, to illustrate its evolution from the Old Kingdom to the Roman era. Note the alabaster bowl (no.1), of magnificent proportions and the simplest of designs, which is sublime but was intended merely for measuring grain—amongst the gods, since it was found in a funerary chamber. Egyptian robes cling to peoples' bodies because their skin was coated with creams to protect it from the severe climate: a flat, ivory spoon (no.9) was used to remove these creams from their pots, and was then floated on water to prevent the ointments from melting.

Around the corner, Gulbenkian's coin collection is unforgettable: he wrote to a dealer that he wanted it 'to reflect Hellenic art when it was at the summit of its beauty and expression'. It leads through to a small arrangement of Mesopotamian art, of which the centrepiece is a low relief of Spring (no.86) sprinkling sacred water on the fields.

Oriental Islamic Art

Gulbenkian paid particular attention to Oriental Islamic art: glass, ceramics, fabrics and illuminated manuscripts of the 12th–18th centuries are given plenty of space, and yet are able to interact with one another. They are linked by the density of their colours, the delicacy of their design, and a tendency towards symmetry. There are some interesting cross-currents, such as the way in which carpet design was influenced by those of book-bindings and silk brocades, or ceramic design by that of architectural tiles. A mosque lamp (no.324) hung in Damascus or Cairo in the 14th century: chains were attached to the six handles. The upper part of the lamp is inscribed with a verse from the Koran describing God as the light of the heavens and the earth.

Oriental Art

One of the most forceful pieces of Oriental Islamic art is displayed in the gallery next door: a superbly proportioned 15th-century jade jug (no.282), from Persia or Samarkand. Jade was believed to split on contact with poison, so a jug such as this came in handy for the wary ruler. Elsewhere in the gallery of Oriental art, cabinets are filled with bright but unlovely Chinese porcelain (the wig stand, no.385, is a curiosity), and with Japanese lacquerware. Every surface required 200 applications of lacquer, each of which took 100 hours to dry. It was ruined if dust settled on the wet lacquer, so many workshops were by the sea, where there is less dust.

Early European Art

The section of European art kicks off with several exquisite medieval ivories, which tell stories to illiterates and were designed for travelling.

The paintings are arranged in chronological order, where possible by schools. Of the early paintings, note van der Weyden's stubbly *St Joseph* (no.897), the fragment of an altarpiece (another section of which is in London's National Gallery), and Diereck Bouts's wordless *Annunciation* (no.895). Domenico Ghirlandaio's *Young Woman* (no.979) is one of the earliest frontal portraits of the Italian Renaissance. Bugiardini, a friend of Michaelangelo, blends the sweet and the sour aspects of the face of a *Young Woman*.

Rembrandt's son Titus posed as *Alexander the Great* (no.966); the subject is sometimes described as Pallas Athena, but would seem too dolorous to be a goddess. His *Portrait of an Old Man* (no.967) shows a dignified greybeard steeped in sadness and bewilderment. You can almost hear the silk russle in Rubens's *Portrait of Hélène Fourment*, his sensual second wife. A couple of years before it was painted, van Dyck had been in Italy, where he painted a *Portrait of a Man*.

Three huge tapestry panels from the series *Children Playing* (nos.1005–7) offer a break from the paintings. The panels were woven in silk, wool and silver and gold thread: more than 200 colours were required to reproduce the tones of Giulio Romano's paintings of cherubs. The little fellows get up to all sorts of tricks, including the torment of frogs.

18th- and 19th-century Art

French paintings and sculpture of the 18th century are displayed near the decorative arts of the same period. One writing table (no.687) came from the apartments of Queen Marie-Antoinette—look at the craftsmanship and the way in which the materials are fused—and a silk hanging (no.1027) was intended to cover her walls at Versailles. Other apartments at Versailles have provided the Gulbenkian with the rolltop desk (no.688) by Riesener, possibly the greatest furniture maker of the 18th century. The museum houses a breath-taking collection of French gold- and silverwork of that age—some of the craftsmen are also represented in Lisbon's Museu de Arte Antiga.

French 18th-century portraiture is best served by La Tour's masterwork, the *Portrait of Duval de l'Épinoy* (no.913). Pastels do not allow the artist to correct his work—hence Duval's head was reworked on an upper sheet of paper. Houdon's smooth marble *Diana* (no.609) was sold to Catherine the Great of Russia. It depicts the naked goddess running.

English portraits and landscapes of the 18th and 19th centuries include works by Gainsborough, Romney and Lawrence. Turner's *Quillebœuf, Mouth of the Seine* (no.976) is charged with swirling, elemental electricity. One room is devoted to luminous works by Guardi (nos.985–1003), and another to 19th-century French sculpture. Gulbenkian was a fan of naturalism—represented by the works of Corot (nos. 929–935) and Daubigny (nos.936–940), amongst others. The collector had a standing contract with René Lalique, the man who put decoration back into French jewellery design, with his delicate and imaginative Art Nouveau creations.

The Gulbenkian Museum of Modern Art

Linked to the Gulbenkian Museum by a sculpture garden, the Gulbenkian Museum of Modern Art is far and away the most important repository of modern and contemporary Portuguese art. *The opening hours are the same as the Gulbenkian's.* Portuguese 20th-century art doesn't really hang together: its main protagonists have either studied in or emigrated to other European capitals.

The first room of the museum is devoted to **Amadeo de Souza Cardoso** (1887–1910; *see* 'Amarante', p.170), who was constantly changing his style, but tied them all together in his final speedy and fragmented works. Amadeo's friend **Eduard Viana** collaborated with him on the review *Orpheu*—as did all the Futurists. **Almada Negreiros**, another Futurist, painted simplified human figures and attempted to foster a Portuguese national identity—which endeared him to Salazar. The dictator wanted a distinct Portuguese style of painting, architecture and sculpture. Expressionist painters such as **Mário Eloy** and **Carlos Botelho** did their best to sidestep this interference, the former painting nature and the latter painting Lisbon. **Vieira da Silva** introduced abstraction to the capital; her style owes much to *azulejos*. In the mid-1940s, the dictatorship prompted artists to paint subjects which would draw attention to the plight of the populace. **Vespeira, Júlio Pomar** and **Rogério Ribeiro** painted workers and peasants to such effect that the secret police withdrew a number of works from the General Exhibition at the Lisbon Society of Fine Arts in 1947.

One -ism gave birth to another: disenchanted Neo-Realists became Surrealists—**Vespeira** and **Fernando de Azevedo** revelled in this apolitical form of revolutionary art. They lived in a regulated society and hoped their work would undermine its rationalism. Both turned to abstraction in the late 1950s.

D'Assumpção and **Vieira da Silva** became renowned for their abstract works; just as the movement was catching on, Pop Art appeared. The 1970s witnessed the exploration of light and time through acrylics and photography. **Paula Rego** is one of the most respected contemporary Portuguese artists: her paintings are sinister and disturbing, harking back to a childhood world of domination.

Sete Ríos

Sete Ríos occupies the northwestern corner of Lisbon.

The Jardim Zoológico

Open April–Sept, 9–8; Oct–Mar, 9–6.

The Avenida Columbano B. Pinheiro runs northwest from the Praça de Espanha to a complicated junction and the Praça General Humberto Delgado, in which stands the Jardim Zoológico (bus 15, 16, 16c, 41, 46, 54, 58, 63; Ⓜ Sete Ríos). The zoo is privately owned; the animals receive corporate sponsorship, providing visitors with many an incongruity. A chocolate drink has adopted the ostriches, but the birds appear unaware of this, and eat their cabbage with resignation. Trees are everywhere except within the cages (perhaps these should be sponsored by hotels). Dogs are included in the menagerie; they alone are afforded a cemetery, the well-signposted *cemitério dos cães*. The zoo is popular with Portuguese families, who lay tablecloths on the tarmac pavements, and picnic.

From the Praça General Humberto Delgado, follow the gently sloping Rua das Furnas to the railway line, cross the railway line, and continue a short way to the Quinta do Marquês de Fronteira.

The Quinta do Marquês de Fronteira

The gates open at 10.45–11am Mon–Sat. Mon–Fri only accompanied visits are available (300$00 for the gardens with an additional 700$00 for the palace). Guided tours are available on Saturdays (max 50 for the gardens, costing 500$00; max 15 for the palace, costing an additional 1000$00) and operate as follows: June–Sept at 10.30, 11, 11.30 and 12; Oct–May at 11 and 12. However, guided tours also operate on the first Sunday of each month, when entrance fees are reduced (400$00 for the garden and the palace); gates open at 3.30pm. Special tours can be arranged (© 01 778 2023) for small groups (1600$00 per person for the gardens and palace). Those wishing to visit on the first Sunday of the month should telephone in advance as numbers are limited. Visitors must bring an identity document. The gardens will not be shown if it is raining.

The Fronteira Palace was built to be lived in, and has been filled with rich pickings over the centuries. It is one of the most enjoyable and stimulating attractions in Lisbon, with mind-boggling *azulejos* and a superb collection of modern Portuguese art.

The first marquis, a general, was active in the War of Restoration. In 1671–2, he built an Italianate hunting lodge 1 hour and 10 minutes' horse-ride north of the Rossio. A new wing was added after the earthquake of 1755, and several loggias were enclosed. The Marquês does not want crowds trekking through his home, which is why access is so restricted and complicated.

The Gardens

The gardens have retained their 17th-century layout, including a formal garden of 365 manicured box trees, quartered to indicate the four seasons. Delightfully bumptious *azulejo* panels personify the months of the year, the signs of the zodiac, and all the planets known at the time, up to Saturn. To one side is an oblong tank, flanked by steps which lead to a walkway above. Reflected in the water are 14 panels of plumed horsemen, influenced by the paintings of Velásquez.

The Palace

Visitors to the **Palace** are shown six rooms, which evolved under the hands of generations of artists. In the Battle Room, tiles of *c.* 1670 depict all the major battles of the War of Restoration (when the Portuguese ended 60 years of Spanish domination). They are clumsy but whimsical: cannons and muskets emit little green plumes of smoke; the forces labelled '*Englezes*' mark a phalanx of English troops who ran out of amunition and used their guns as clubs. The inky Delft panels in the dining room—with finely textured horses' tails—were amongst the first imported into Portugal.

The Delft (dining) room opens onto the Gallery of the Arts terrace, sided with fantastic *azulejo* panels of 1670, depicting personifications of the arts, interspersed with mythological figures. Astronomia is the celestial lady whose breasts are the sun and moon. Apollo is pictured with the flayed skin of Marcius, who dared to defy the God in a music contest. These odd bedfellows overlook Fronteira's Romantic garden, and beyond it to the remains of Monsanto wood. The chapel at the end of the terrace was built in 1584, predating the house; tradition has it that St Francis Xavier said his last Mass here before embarking for India. It is beautifully decorated with shells and the fragments of Ming china broken after King Dom Pedro II and his lackeys supped off it.

The Marquês' collection of modern Portuguese art—which includes work by the Marquesa—is worth a visit in its own right. An old kitchen is devoted to work by Cutileiro, the Évora sculptor of contorted flesh-coloured ladies. Be sure the tap is turned on to bathe the figure sitting in the sink. No other museum dares display Cutileiro's other penchant: sculpted phalluses.

North Lisbon

The Avenida de Berna runs eastwards from the Gulbenkian Museum. It bisects the Avenida da República (which stretches north from the Praça de Duque Saldanha), passing the Moorish-style **Campo Pequeno bullring** (bus 1, 17b, 21, 27, 32, 36, 38, 47, 54; Ⓜ Campo Pequeno). This is built of bricks the colour of dried blood, with cupolas at each axis. It can seat nearly 8500 spectators, some of them on stone benches, which would gather lichen were they given half a chance.

The Avenida da República runs northwards into Campo Grande. At the northwest corner of the Jardim do Campo Grande, the **Museu da Cidade** (City Museum) (*open 10–1 and 2–6; closed Mon*; bus 1, 3, 7, 7a, 17b, 33, 36, 36a, 46a, 47, 50; Ⓜ Campo Grande) puts Lisbon in its historical context, using a variety of media.

The museum is installed in the sober 18th-century Palácio Pimenta, whose most endearing feature is the witty 'cut-out' *azulejos* of hares, swans, fish and other animals hung upside down on the kitchen walls. Upstairs the functions of rooms are illustrated by their *azulejo* dado. Visitors are greeted by two fabulous long-necked, fruit-topped modern ladies sculpted by Jorge Barradas. The collection includes a huge maquette representing the city before the 1755 earthquake, and Dirk Stoop's (1610–86) painting of the Praça do Comércio as it used to be—with merchants weighing their goods around the central fountain, and charlatans bamboozling gullible Lisboêtas. Almada Negreiros's famous portrait of Fernando Pessoa shows the poet with a copy of *Orpheu*, the modernists' journal.

The Museu Nacional do Traje
Open 10–6; closed Mon.
Continuing north, the village of Lumiar has been swallowed by the capital's sprawl. In the Largo Júlio de Castilho, the Museu do Trajo (Museum of Clothing) (bus 1, 7, 7a, 17b, 36) presents temporary exhibitions of aspects of lay dress and fashion, at all social levels, from medieval times to the present. Society has dreamt up some strange and revealing images for us over the ages, which are interesting in themselves, as well as enlivening the study of painting. The museum's photocopied '*Short history of the civil costume in Portugal ...*' includes snippets of information about male and female hairstyles, chips about jewellery, and patches about shoes (all of which were cloaked by foreign influences).

The display is woven into the 18th- and 19th-century Quinta do Monteiro-Mor, which stands in a wonderfully peaceful, mature terraced park (*open 10–5 daily*). In 1793 this was referred to as one of the three most beautiful gardens in Lisbon; a climatic freak gives it a particularly dense and varied vegetation.

The **Museu de Teatro** (Theatre Museum) (*open 10–6; closed Mon*) stands within the grounds. It has a more specialized appeal, featuring costume and backdrop designs, photographs of actors and actresses in performance, and wild, winged, episcopal costumes by Almada Negreiros, in bright appliqué.

The Convento de Odivelas

The Avenida Padre Cruz continues northwards past the Museu do Trajo, feeding the 250–2 road. Just 1km outside Lisbon stands the Convento de Odivelas, founded by Dom Dinis 1295–1305. It was badly damaged by the earthquake of 1755, but the Gothic apse and two side chapels remain. The founder's tomb is here; built during the king's lifetime, it set a fashion for funerary architecture. The flanking sculptures have been decapitated.

Queen Philippa of Lancaster, wife of Dom João I, died here in 1415. Before expiring, she called for three swords with scabbards and guards of gold, pearls and cut stones, to give to her three sons. She showed little fear—small wonder: the chronicler Azurara describes her as 'a woman most acceptable to God'. She was buried at Batalha, during the night, as the heat was excessive.

In the 18th century, the convent was renowned for its poetry recitals. Guests were then invited to drinks, accompanied by glacé pumpkin and lemon peel, meringues, little squares of quince jelly, and *toucinho do céu* (bacon from heaven). Perhaps it was over one such pudding that King Dom João V was introduced to the captivating Dona Magdalena, who bore him a son, Dom Gaspar, the future Archbishop of Braga. But another nun, Madre Paula, caught the king's attention (at the age of 17) and held it for at least 10 years. Their son, Dom José, became Grand Inquisitor. (In his later years, the king resorted to aphrodisiacs, and his last mistress, a French actress called Petronilla, was dismissed for the sake of his health.)

Northeast Lisbon: Expo '98 Site

Getting There

To reach the site, catch a metro or regional train to the impressive new Oriente station, or bus 25A which leaves from the Praça do Comércio.

In 1998 Lisbon hosted Expo '98, a world exhibition to crown the second millennium. Around 60ha of the city's riverfront was renovated for the purpose and it's still possible to visit the principal attraction, Europe's largest **Oceanarium** (*check with tourist office for opening hours and adm*). Four huge tanks are home to 15,000 creatures repatriated from the Antarctic, Atlantic, Pacific and Indian Oceans. Now it's not only navigators who can hobnob with penguins, whale sharks, seals and coral reef fish. The restaurant on the **Vasco da Gama Tower**, also on the site, offers panoramic views of the city. Check for music or sports events at the concert pavilion.

Belém

'*Belém*' means 'Bethlehem': if there is a star over the district, it guides hordes of tourists to the water's edge, 6km west of the city centre. Commuter traffic and rattling trains shatter the calm of Belém's suburban villas. Belém is built on the white stone that was quarried to build the Jerónimos monastery.

Trams 15, 16 and 17 run to Belém, as do buses 14, 27, 28, 29, 43, 49 and 51.

History

Throughout the night of 7 July 1497, Vasco da Gama and his captains kept vigil in the Church of Our Lady of Belém. The following morning, they carried tapers to the riverside, and there made a general Confession. They were absolved of their sins, lest they die on the journey. Almost exactly two years later, da Gama returned to Belém having discovered a sea route to India. A contemporary described da Gama as 'a discrete man, of good understanding and great courage'. Sailing in four *naos*, which were larger and heavier than caravels, he and his crew of not more than 170 men moored at the Cape Verde Islands (off Senegal), the last land they were to see for 62 days. They ate raisins, salt, biscuits, honey and dried beans—but scurvy struck: on the return journey 'all our people again suffered from their gums, which grew over their teeth, so that they could not eat. Their legs also swelled, and other parts of the body, and these swellings spread until the sufferer died.'

At Calicut, the courtiers scorned the copper rings, red berets and hawks' bells which had delighted the Africans. They refused to deliver these tacky gifts to the Zamorin. A Moor at the Zamorin's court spoke a little Castilian, and communicated the potentate's first message to his visitor: 'May the Devil take thee! What brought you hither?' 'We came in search of Christians and spices,' da Gama replied.

The Jerónimos Monastery

Open winter 10–1 and 2.30–5, summer 10–6.30; closed Mon and holidays.

The Jerónimos Monastery (across a little park from the riverside Avenida da India) is the most thrilling and significant building in Portugal. The purest example of Portugal's own Manueline style of architecture has a vital energy and tension, and its treatment of space is breathtaking.

History

In 1460, Henry the Navigator founded a hermitage on this site; friars of the Order of Christ assisted seafarers until 1496, when Dom Manuel gazumped his forebear with plans for a modest Jeronymite monastery. When da Gama returned to Belém in 1499, the king thankfully granted his new foundation the 'pepper penny', a 5 per cent tax on all the spices and precious stones coming from India, and on the gold brought from Guinea. These revenues were deposited with the Medicis' agent in Lisbon. Dom Manuel turned his attention from Batalha Abbey to Belém, employing as his master of works Diogo Boitac, who had flexed his muscles on the church of Jesus at Setúbal. Between 1502 and 1517, Boitac completed the general structure of the buildings, following the tenets of the late European Gothic style. For the decoration, these doctrines were integrated with Manueline ornamentation, which employed ropes, cables, and armillary spheres.

In 1517 João de Castilho replaced Boitac, bringing a new awareness of Renaissance forms. In the doors, the pillars of the nave, and part of the cloister, he and his collaborators harmonized pure classicism with Iberian exuberance—but the new king, Dom João III, became preoccupied with the Convent of Christ at Tomar, and João de Castilho was removed thence. Most of the building was completed in the first quarter of the century. Diogo de Torralva was appointed as master of works in the middle of the century, and worked on the chancel, the choir, and parts of the cloister. Jerónimo de Ruão, son of the sculptor João de Ruão, added some finishing touches to the chancel and the transepts' chapels, 1571–2.

By 1739, the rents received by the monastery had dried to a mere trickle; so severe was the shortage of funds that the monks resorted to selling *pásteis de nata* (custard tarts). It may have been these that appeased the earthquake of 1755, for the buildings were left virtually undamaged. From 1807, part of the building was occupied by the army. When the monasteries were dissolved in 1834, the monastic buildings were occupied by an orphanage for 700 boys. The complex was insensitively 'reconstituted' in the mid-19th century, when the cupola was added.

The Monastery

Facing the river, João de Castilho's elegant, harmonious **south portal** bears more than a trace of Flemish realism—at the top of the portal, even the Virgin's broad hat and ample skirt echo those of a Belgian burgher's wife. Henry the Navigator is represented by a bearded figure between the doors.

Chanterène's **west portal** is stunted by its modern covering. This was his first commission in Portugal; he experimented with ornament, but had not attained the mighty powers that were to come. Dom Manuel and his second wife Dona Maria are portrayed either side of the door, accompanied by their respective patron saints. Above them are niches occupied by the four Evangelists, and buttresses depicting the Apostles.

The navigators provided Manueline architecture with a fund of decorative motifs, and also a concept of space. They had lived with the horizon, and the definition of space in the soaring, ivory-coloured **interior** is more impressive than anywhere else in Portugal.

The nave and aisles are of the same height, united by fanlike vaulting which is supported by polygonal columns decorated with flat classical objects—medallions, skulls, three-headed snakes and harpies, and, on one column, signs of the zodiac. An astonishing unsupported star vault is suspended above the wide transept; after seeing that, the later, classical apse, with its stupendous gilt tabernacle, comes as a mild shock. In the transepts elephants support the tombs of Dom Sebastian and Dom Henrique, the Cardinal-King.

The two-storeyed **cloister** is entered through the giftshop. The cloister's fantastical lower level was decorated by João de Castilho, contemporary with the church. Its wild galaxy of human and animal faces peep through the vegetable ornament bound by ropes and anchors. Strange creatures are here, especially a sort of distorted snail. The upper level, completed in 1544, is more sober. A door leads to the upper choir, with superb choir stalls carved from Brazilian wood *c.* 1560, their sides ornamented by tortured souls in low relief.

The Museu da Marinha

At the west end of the monastery, the Museu da Marinha's naval uniforms and models of ships are best left to school outings. The highlights are a celestial globe *c.* 1700, an early 16th-century map of the coast of Brazil, and the cabin and quarters of the yacht made for Dom Manuel II (1908–10), complete with silver radiators, roulette table and piano. (It was rumoured and later verified that the king had drawn more money from the public treasury than the official accounts showed—his apologists pointed out that the royal allowance had not risen since the late 19th century.)

The Museu de Etnologia

Open 10–12.30 and 2–5; closed Mon.

The Rua dos Jerónimos runs along the eastern side of the monastery. A gentle 10-minute uphill walk leads to the excellent Museu de Etnologia. The presentation is exemplary, and its four simultaneous temporary exhibitions will broaden anyone's horizons.

The Torre de Belém

Open June–Sept, 10–6.30; Oct–May, 10–5.

Returning to the waterfront, the bold and elegant **Torre de Belém** squats at the downstream, or western, side of the district. This is the closest Portugal gets to a national monument, and the finest example of Manueline architecture with Moorish trimmings. Its five-storey tower and projecting bastion were planned by Francisco de Arruda as a lookout post and a base for cannons, to exclude corsairs from the Tagus. When it was built, 1515–21, the tower was surrounded by water; the Tagus nearly lapped the doorstep of the Jerónimos monastery. But the river bank has crept southwards, and now the tower stands beside the shore.

The striking exterior decoration is at its most fanciful in the sentry posts' melon domes, which are based on a design popular in Marrakech. The dome of the northwestern sentry box is supported by a rhinoceros (symbolizing Africa, as elephants symbolized Asia). Moorish balconies and finely carved balustrades ornament the upper storeys, and the crenellations are cross-bearing shields of the Order of Christ. The same cross was echoed in red and white on the sails of the discoverers' ships.

The projecting bastion takes the form of a cloister, below which were the damp storerooms used as dungeons until the time of Dom Miguel. The cloister is topped by a thrilling terrace, which formed the second line of fire. It feels like an enchanted cake (that smells of the sea). Visitors can climb the tower to get good views of Belém and the river.

At the Waterfront

On the opposite side of the dock beside the Torre, the **Museu de Arte Popular** (*open 10–12.30 and 2–5; closed Mon and holidays*) is too large and arid a setting for its display of folksy paraphernalia. It serves as a good introduction to the sausage-dog doorknockers, black pots, baskets, wooden-soled shoes, fire grates, carved horns for pepper, cork jars and cowbells of the regions of Portugal.

In 1960, the 500th anniversary of the death of Prince Henry the Navigator was marked by the construction of the **Monument to the Discoveries**, opposite the monastery and next to the Museu de Arte Popular. The monument resembles the prow of a ship. Henry the Navigator is sculpted at the prow, backed by Camões and others, whose stylized hairdos are respectfully avoided by the seagulls. From the top of the monument, you can hear traffic humming across the **Ponte 25 de Abril**, which clocks in at 1013m, making it the longest suspension bridge in Europe. At its completion in 1966, it was named 'The Salazar Bridge'. Now it commemorates the date of the Revolution, and most of the bridges in Portugal seem to have followed suit.

The Coach Museum

Open daily 10–6; closed Mon.

In 1726 Dom João V purchased a *quinta* in Belém, slightly east of the monastery. Shortly afterwards he annexed it to another, which served as a royal palace and is now the official residence of the President of the Republic. The burnt-pink building is closed to the public, but, just to the south, the royal riding school now houses the **Coach Museum**, in the Rua de Belém. It was built by the Italian architect Jacomo Azzolini for Dom José in Louis XVI style, and hosted various courtly tournaments 1787–1810.

The collection is one of the finest in the world—rivalling those of Versailles and Madrid—though it is incomplete, since Dom João VI took some particularly fine examples with him when he fled to Brazil in 1807. Coaches were not mere vehicles, they were part of the royal razzle-dazzle, propaganda on wheels—and there was plenty of time for such ostentation to make its mark: it took five or six days to get to Oporto. For all that, the museum misses the snort of horses, and the sheer number of coaches dulls the excitement. The most thrilling are those Baroque confections laden with gilt sculpture, at the back of the hall, where mermen ride lions borne by cherubs. The three carriages employed by the Marquês de Fontes on his 1716 embassy to Pope Clement XI glitter with statuary, glorifying Portugal's maritime enterprises and the thrust given to the arts and sciences by Dom João V.

Coaches never recovered from Pombal's austerity measures in the second half of the 18th century: he limited the use of rich fabrics and rich metals in an attempt to avoid imports—and to exalt the king's carriage. It was this period that produced the most curious chaise, a sort of giant gasmask on wheels.

Various spurs and stirrups are displayed in the gallery upstairs. The wooden gentleman with a wraparound moustache is the *estafermo*, literally a 'scarecrow' or 'dullard', but nicknamed 'pain-in-the-arse'. Riders tested their dexterity by attempting to touch him with a lance. If they were too slow, he rotated, whip in hand, and lashed them.

Ajuda

On a hill overlooking the Tagus, the western district of Ajuda is connected to Belém by wide, gently sloping streets. Ajuda is serviced by tram 18 and buses 14, 27, 29, 32, 40 and 42. No.14 runs from the Coach Museum in Belém. The broad Calçada da Ajuda leads inland from the Coach Museum to the **Ajuda Palace**, which dominates a hill high above the Tagus (a 20-minute walk uphill from Belém). Construction began in 1802, on the site of a previous royal palace destroyed by fire: behind the classical façade of white *pedra lioz* stretch interminable rooms stuffed with rich, and for the most part tasteless, 19th-century furnishings acquired by Dona Maria II and her artist husband Dom Ferdinand, who escaped when they could to the Pena Palace at Sintra. It's difficult to see the wood for the trees, but keep an eye open for the Louis XV and XVI commodes, the Gobelins tapestries, assorted stools, writing desks and sideboards, and the silver by Germain. The delightful parquet is different in every room. The Banqueting Room can accommodate 160 guests, and occasionally still does.

Slightly downhill, the Rua do Jardim Botánico leads westwards to the small **church of Memória**, founded by Dom José in 1760, on the site of the attempt to assassinate him two years previously. As the king returned home from an amorous engagement, his carriage was ambushed twice, but not halted. The king received an arquebus shot in the arm, and unknowingly avoided a third trap by ordering his coachman to drive directly to the royal surgeon. The regicide plot proved useful to Pombal. He pinned the blame both on the Jesuits and on the families of the Duke of Aveiro and the Marquis of Tāvora, who were punished with excruciating savagery. Pombal's tomb was transferred to the church's carved marble interior in 1923. Look for the wooden arm pierced by shots, which was Dom José's votive offering.

Across the River

The Cristo Rei Statue

The statue of Christ the King stands, with robed arms outstreched, on a hill opposite Lisbon. It was modelled on Rio de Janeiro's Christ, and inaugurated in 1959, in honour of a promise made by the Portuguese bishops if the country were preserved from the Second World War. An elevator whizzes visitors up the structure, which contains a gift shop and offers heady views of Lisbon. To get to the statue, take one of the frequent ferries from the Praça do Comércio's Terminal Fluvial to Cacilhas—a brief ride—and catch a bus or a taxi from the station next to the ferry dock.

Costa da Caparica and the Setúbal Peninsula

See **Estremadura**, pp.279–83.

Lisbon ✆ (01–)   *Shopping*

Goldsmiths and silversmiths sell the fruits of their craftsmanship in the Baixa, as they have for hundreds of years, so trot along if you fancy a *caravela* for your mantelpiece. Cerâmica Constância, 8C Rua de S. Domingo à Lapa, ✆ 396 3951 (uphill from the side entrance of the Museu de Arte Antiga), design and retail *azulejos*; they can copy photographs, at a price.

For individual *azulejo* items, such as coasters and tablemats, head for Sant'Anna, 95 Rua do Alecrim, ✆ 342 2537; off the Chiado. There are witty *azulejos* for sale in the Rua Academia das Ciências (in the Bairro Alto), as well as Portalegre tapestries (*see* 'Portalegre', p.349). Vista Alegre, the fine porcelain manufacturers, have two outlets in the Bairro Alto: 54 Rua Ivens, © 342 8612; and 18 Largo do Chiado, © 346 1401.

Bookshops cluster in the Chiado; for English-language books, try Livraria Britanica, 168A Rua de São Marçal, © 347 6141, opposite the British Institute, or Livraria Buchholz, 4 Rua Duque de Palmela, near the Praça Marquês de Pombal.

Lisbon © (01–)   **Where to Stay**

luxury

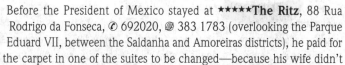

Before the President of Mexico stayed at ★★★★★**The Ritz**, 88 Rua Rodrigo da Fonseca, © 692020, ◉ 383 1783 (overlooking the Parque Eduard VII, between the Saldanha and Amoreiras districts), he paid for the carpet in one of the suites to be changed—because his wife didn't like the colour yellow. The suites are legendary, but some rooms are not at all memorable: what you're paying for is the cachet of the place. That said, The Ritz is especially thoughtful, from its seven types of tea to the sixth floor reserved for non-smokers. The décor is rooted in the late 1950s, when the hotel was built. Its rich, elegant dining room does not have a good reputation; the tartan-carpeted grill serves tastier food. The ★★★★★**Meridien**, 149 Rua Castilho, © 694000, ◉ 354 7164, next door, was opened in 1984. It combines chrome, marble and fountains; being a subsidiary of Air France, the cuisine is French. Across the park at 1 Rua Latino Coelho, © 575757, ◉ 354 7164, stands the ★★★★★**Sheraton** with all the usual Sheraton facilities plus a heated open-air swimming pool. The hotel is the tallest building in Lisbon, with spectacular views from the top-floor bar.

At the edge of the Rato district, on Lisbon's main boulevard, the plush and over-stuffed ★★★★★**Hotel Tivoli**, 185 Av. da Liberdade, © 315 1070, ◉ 357 9461, near the Rato district, surrounds a swimming pool on three sides. Guests can use the solarium and tennis court. The good top-floor restaurant offers views of Lisbon, and grilled steak or chops.

The Avenida da Liberdade runs riverwards, leading to the ★★★★★**Avenida Palace**, 123 Rua 1 de Dezembro, © 346 0151, which overlooks the Rossio square, in the Baixa district. It offers old-fashioned elegance in the centre of town, with marble, marquetry, velvet and tail coats. The hotel was a nest of spies during the Second World War; its secret door on the fourth floor, for discreet exits to railway plat-forms, has been walled over. Bedrooms are sober and can be noisy; the singles are small. Breakfast is the only meal available.

In the Lapa district outside the centre of town, ★★★★**York House** on 32 Rua das Janelas Verdes, © 396 2544, ◉ 397 2793, is installed in a 16th-century convent almost opposite the Museu de Arte Antiga. It is in a class of its own—the four-star *Residencial* grading indicates the lack of gadgets (including elevators) rather than the fresh and pretty bedrooms stocked with homey antiques. Many of the 46 rooms overlook the lush courtyard; those that do not can be noisy. Oozing good taste, Arraiolos rugs warm polished stone corridors lined with low tile dados, and the thick walled dining room is niched with pewter plates and church candlesticks. A set lunch or dinner is available, but the food is not great.

Just up the road, the **York House Annexe** at 47 Rua das Janelas Verdes, ✆ 396 8143, is run by the same management. It's a town house with a spiralling staircase, and turn-of-the-century trappings: beaded lampshades, a tassled piano stool, polished wood, heavy fabrics and large, tiled bathrooms. Upper rooms overlook the Tagus. Breakfast is served in York House itself.

The very comfortable ★★★★**Tivoli Jardim**, 7 Rua Júlio César Machado, ✆ 353 9971, ✇ 355 6566, is on the edge of the Rato district, just off the Avenida da Liberdade, and has access to the swimming pool and tennis court of its five-star sister, next door. Staff are abundant. Single rooms overlook the gardens, and the parking lot overlooks the restaurant, which could spoil an entrecôte sautéed with mushrooms.

expensive

Heading down the Avenida to the Baixa district, ★★★★**Hotel Mundial**, 4 Rua D. Duarte, ✆ 886 3101 (two minutes from the Rossio station), appeals mainly to Iberians. The bedrooms are comfortable but neutral; those at the back are quieter, with views up to the Castelo de São Jorge. The restaurant offers an amazing view of Pombal's Lisbon, with a limited choice of good food, such as the beefsteak *cocotte*. The staff are attentive, as they are throughout the hotel.

On a branch road off the Praça Marquês de Pombal, solid ★★★**Hotel Eduardo VII**, 5 Avenida Fontes Pereira de Melo, ✆ 353 0141, ✇ 353 3879, stands beside the park of the same name. It frequently receives the epithet 'very adequate'. The restaurant's view of the city is panoramic but not boggling, with rich food.

moderate

Most of the accommodation in this bracket is located to the east of the Praça Marquês de Pombal. Light, spacious ★★★★**Residência Roma**, 22-A Travessa da Glória, ✆ 346 0557, ✇ 346 0557 near the tourist office, is the exception. Scruffy in parts, it runs fairly smoothly and owes its popularity to the car park next door.

Sited on the noisy main boulevard itself, ★★★★**Residencial Dom Sancho I**, 202 Av. da Liberdade, ✆ 548648, offers squashed rooms overlooking the ugly well.

Just off the Praça Marquês de Pombal, ★★★**Hotel Dom Carlos**, 121 Av. Duque de Loulé, ✆ 353 9071, ✇ 352 0728, on the edge of the Estefânia district, is efficient, sober, lamplit and wood-panelled. Trees screen the hotel from the main road, muffling it. Further down the road, ★★★**Hotel Embaixador**, 73 Av. Duque de Loulé, ✆ 353 0171, ✇ 355 7596, is OK but nothing special.

Between the Praça Marquês de Pombal and the Jardim Botánico, there's something oddly appealing about the worn carpets and old fittings of the nicely sized ★★★**Hotel Jorge V** at 3 Rua Mouzinho da Silveira, ✆ 356 2525, in the Rato district, where even the bathroom pipes sound like mice chomping.

In the Graça district, ★★★★**Albergaria Senhora do Monte**, 39 Calçada do Monte, ✆ 886 6002 (across the park from the Graça church, inland from the Castelo), offers attractive rooms whose main delights are the broad, dizzy views of Lisbon. Guests without cars will depend on tram no.28, unless they enjoy steep climbs. There is a newly built restaurant.

In Belém, ★★★**Hotel da Torre**, 8 Rua dos Jerónimos, ✆ 363 6262, ✉ 364 5995, on the road at the eastern side of the monastery, is not a friendly place, despite the fine furniture, *azulejo* dado, and pink marble bathrooms.

the pick of the pensions

Three blocks east of the Avenida da Liberdade, ★★★**Pensão Dublin**, 45 Rua de Santa Marta, ✆ 355 5489 (*inexpensive*) is a popular choice with high, chipped ceilings, mouldings, and clean, airy bedrooms.

Further east, in the Estefânia district proper, ★★★**Residência Caravela**, 38 Rua Ferreira Lapa, ✆ 353 9011 (*inexpensive*), off the Avenida Duque de Loulé, is a dark, dull place. On the other side of the Hospital Dona Estefânia, popular, nondescript ★★★**Residencial S. Pedro**, 130 Rua Pascoal de Melo, ✆ 578765 (*moderate*), in the Estefânia district, is clean but tacky. ★★★**Residência Horizonte**, 42 Av. António Augusto de Aguiar, ✆ 539526 (*inexpensive*), in Saldanha district, is hot, clean and functional, arranged around a stair well, northeast of the Praça Marquês de Pombal.

★★★**Residencial Luena**, 9 Rua Pascoal de Melo, ✆ 355 8246 (*inexpensive*), near the bus station in the Estefânia district, is clean and decent, though fairly basic. So too is calm ★★★**Residencial Casa Belmonte**, 5th floor, 95 Av. Duque de Loulé, ✆ 352 1666 (*cheap*), between the bus station and the Praça Marquês de Pombal.

In the Bairro Alto district, a large town house with ceiling mouldings has been converted into ★★**Pensão Londres**, 53 Rua Dom Pedro V, ✆ 346 2203 (*cheap*), near the Port Wine Institute. It's friendly and efficiently run, and most rooms are light and airy. Also in the Bairro Alto, but closer to the Praça do Comércio, the ★★**Residencial Nova Silva**, 11 Rua Victor Cordon, ✆ 0342 4371 (*inexpensive*), near the Academia das Belas Artes, offers a warm welcome, good humour, and superb views of the Tagus from the front. Most rooms have recently been renovated. It is easy to forgive the dilapidations, the small rooms, and the erratic hot water. Long-term rates are negotiable. ★★**Residencial Camões**, 38 Trav. do Poço da Cidade, ✆ 346 4048 (*cheap*) boasts an unbeatable location, right in the heart of the Bairro Alto. The rooms are light and bright and the atmosphere friendly.

The Castelo de São Jorge crowns the Alfama district, and just below the castle walls, ★★★**Pensão Ninho das Águias** (eagle's nest), 74 Costa do Castelo, ✆ 867008 (*cheap*) feels like the top of the world. The plain, simple bedrooms offer vast, exhilarating views of Lisbon. The place is weird. A mad staircase spirals upwards from the lobby, with its stuffed eagle, and there are birdcages on the patio. Without a car, there is a long walk down to the centre of town.

Lisboêtas need no excuse for eating out; they do it frequently and
unhurriedly. The capital caters to all sorts, offering sardines grilled in
the street outside a glorified cupboard, or glittering banquets.

The Baixa

The Rua das Portas de Santo Antão leads north from the Rossio, and contains a
couple of smart restaurants among the indifferent eating places. Beamed
Gambrinus, 25 Rua das Portas de Santo Antão, ✆ 342 1466, ✉ 346 5032
(*expensive*) feels American; the service is excellent, and guests can indulge in
large quantities of shellfish. Just down the road, **Escorial**, 47–49 Rua Portas de
Santo Antão, ✆ 346 3758, ✉ 346 3758 (*expensive*), is rather tacky, with horrid
organ music, a red interior, and Spanish food. Anyone on a tight budget could try
the café at the back of the shopping centre at the bottom of the Avenida (near the
post office), where you get what you pay for.

Alfama

Lautasco, 7 Beco do Azinhal, ✆ 886 0173 (*moderate*), off the Rua de São Pedro,
offers a chance to eat outdoors in a small, shaded residential courtyard, beneath
tall windows, birdcages, wrought-iron balconies, roof weeds, and ubiquitous
laundry. The food is nothing special; braised rabbit is the most adventurous of the
dishes. The music of Mozambique bops through **Cantinho do Aziz**, 5 Rua de S.
Lourenço, ✆ 887 6472 (cheap), in the northeastern corner of the Alfama—until
football comes on TV. The standard of hygiene does not inspire confidence, but the
food is good and spicy. Small children wander about.

The Bairro Alto

The Bairro Alto is Lisbon's kitchen, with the highest concentration of restaurants,
and a mellow atmosphere to aid digestion. Fancy restaurants focus on the Chiado.

The **Tavares**, at 37 Rua da Misericórdia, ✆ 342 1112 (*expensive*), just off the
upper end of the Rua Garrett, is described by a 1913 Baedeker guide as 'tastefully
fitted up in the modern style', and it retains those pre-war heavy gilt mirrors and
stucco. Interior and airless, it started life as a café in 1784. The menu is peppered
with continental dishes. Meats may be served with wine-based sauces, though
bacalhau with potatoes and onions makes an appearance. **Rex**, 1-B Rua Nova da
Trindade, ✆ 346 0114 (*expensive*), is less formal, more clubby, with equestrian
prints on the high wooden dado. Lamb dishes are popular. The **Pap'Açorda**, 57
Rua da Atalaia, ✆ 346 4811 (*expensive*), serves excellent *açordas* in convivial
surroundings. The Bairro Alto's grid of streets is packed with inexpensive restaurants. It's usually necessary to queue for a table at **Bota Alta**, 37 Trav. da
Queimada, ✆ 342 7959 (*cheap*), at the corner of the Rua da Atalaia, a cheerful
and unpretentious bistro with a varied clientele and succulent dishes. **Alfaia**, 24
Trav. Queimada, ✆ 346 1232 (*cheap*), is a gleeful place with *azulejos*, ridiculous

paper vines hanging from the ceiling, and generous helpings of good food. **Bartis**, 95 Rua Diário de Notícias, ✆ 342 4795 (*cheap*), projects a sequence of slides on to its back wall—a shoulder blade, mechanical cogs, that sort of thing. Many of the patrons wear black, but not because they are in mourning. If table space allows, you may be able to drink without ordering a meal.

O Tacão Pequeno, 3A Trav. da Cara (*cheap*), in the alley opposite the funicular, is a theatrical little den, with platefuls of honest food. Off the Rua Garrett, **Cervejaria da Trindade**, 200 Rua Nova de Trindade (*moderate*), is something of a landmark. It was established in 1836, and remains very popular for snacks and entrées. Be careful where you sit, as there is a lot of through traffic. *Azulejo* wall panels depict the elements and the seasons. Near the top of Rua da Atalaia, **De Rua Em Rua**, 51 Rua de São Boaventura, ✆ 346 7164 (*cheap*), is a small, friendly place; the menu is uninspired, but the food good.

Rato

For a humdinger of a meal, try **Comida de Santo**, 39 Calç do Eng. Miguel Pais, ✆ 396 3339 (*expensive*), downhill from the Science Academy, a fun Brazilian restaurant particularly suited to small groups. Brightly painted jungle birds and leaves flit across the wallpanels, washed by mellow music. The exquisite *moquequa* dishes are stewed in coconut milk and palm oil. South African **Como Sequeira**, 30 Rua Gustavo de Matos Sequeira, ✆ 397 7433 (*moderate*), near the British Institute, is a little more earnest, with bright paintings and delicious food— particularly the crêpes. There are no tables for two, so couples may be doubled up.

Estrêla

Cantinho da Paz, 4 Rua da Paz a S. Bento, ✆ 601963 (*moderate*), near the National Assembly, serves a range of subtle Goan curries. It's small and a bit squashed, with a varied clientele. The prawn curry is particularly good, the fish curry nutty and hot, and the chicken curry just plain hot.

Lapa

Sua Excelência, 40–42 Rua do Conde, ✆ 603614 (*moderate*) is two blocks inland from the Museu de Arte Antiga's side entrance and bears the stamp of its manager: intimate, conversational, and protracted. He is a perfectionist who recites the menu—without prices—in the appropriate language. He minces his way through: 'We take a little rabbit. We chop it up ...' The softly lit restaurant is best suited to an evening excursion. The said rabbit is delicious, as is the creamed *bacalhau*. Dessert is a choice of cakes. *Closed Wed in winter and Sat in summer.*

Saldanha

A Gondola, 64 Av. de Berna, ✆ 770426 (*expensive*), opposite the Gulbenkian Museum, offers a rare opportunity to dine outdoors without being gawked at. Patrons eat their good Italian food beneath a mature trellis, or in the smart and sober interior. *Closed Sat evening and Sun.*

Estefânia

Primeiro de Maio, 71 Rua Francisco Sanches, ✆ 822971 (*moderate*), is parallel to the Avenida Almirante Reis, near the Arroios metro station and appeals to respectable Lisboêtas in search of good, hearty food in no-frills surroundings. *Closed Wed.*

Belém

O Caseiro, 35 Rua de Belém, ✆ 363 8803 (*expensive*), between the monastery and the coach museum, is intimate, fun and tasty. Banknotes turn brown on the brick arches which support a beamed ceiling hung with gourds, melons and onions. Loaves of bread dangle from a plough pinned to the wall. *Porco à Alentejana* and simply cooked fresh fish are the house specialities.

Espelho d'Agua, next to the Monument to the Discoveries, ✆ 301 7373 (*expensive*) is favoured by government ministers, who enjoy sitting on the semicircular platform surrounded by glass. The beef is popular.

Along the road, **O Rafael**, 106 Rua de Belém, ✆ 363 7420 (*cheap*) is a modest bistro. **O Alexandre**, 84 Rua Vieira Portuense (*cheap*) is a tiny fish restaurant with great views of the monastery and seating outside. The food is good value and delicious to boot.

Lisboêtas stock up at the **Única Fábrica dos Pastéis de Belém**, an outstanding, long-established *pastelaria* with 'cut-out' *azulejo* figures around the walls.

Cacilhas

A couple of restaurants in Cacilhas, across the Tagus, offer stunning panoramic views of the city, but they have become rather expensive and touristy. Take a ferry from the Praça do Comércio.

A stairway lined with shells leads to **Floresta do Ginjal**, 7 Ginjal, ✆ 276 6013 (*expensive*). The furnishings are outmoded, and the waiters dismissive. Dishes include turbot Trás-os-Montes style, with smoked ham and tomato and onion sauce. Just down the road, **Gonçalves**, 17 Ginjal, ✆ 275 0062 (*expensive*) is a similar set-up, at a slightly greater cost, with well-presented food. *Closed Mon.*

vegetarian restaurants

Lisbon contains a higher concentration of vegetarian restaurants than the rest of the country—which is not saying much. As Portugal is very big on macrobiotics, most vegetarian restaurants are advertised as the former, but all provide vegetarian options on their menus.

Os Tibetanos Restaurante Salão de Chá, Rua do Salitre 117, Metro Avenida, ✆ 314 20 38 (*moderate–inexpensive*), is the best option for vegetarians in Lisbon, serving a variety of sophisticated Asian dishes in delightful surroundings near the botanical gardens. **O Terraço do Finisterra**, 117 Rua do Salitre (*moderate*) is a stripped-pine haven of tranquillity in the Buddhist Centre and features regrettably small portions of weird and very wonderful vegetarian food. The *ementa turistica* is better value. Definitely soul food. *Closed Sun.*

Celeiro, 65 Rua 1 de Dezembro, off Rossio (*cheap*) is a self-service restaurant reminiscent of a school canteen, situated below a healthfood supermarket. It's best to get there early as by 1pm the queue snakes up the stairs, through the shop and out into the street. The wholesome food comes in huge portions. *Open lunchtimes only; closed Sun.* **Centro Macrobiótico Vegetariano**, 25 Rua Mouzinho da Silveira (*cheap*) has the great advantage of having a courtyard in which to eat large portions of healthy, though not always very tasty food. It stops serving food at 8pm. *Closed Sun.*

Espiral, 14a Praça Ilha do Faial, off Largo de Dona Estefânia (*cheap*) is part of Lisbon's 'alternative centre', comprising a health food shop, a bookshop and this large, basement restaurant which displays art for sale on the walls, a noticeboard detailing all sorts of green activities and live music most weekends. The atmosphere is warm and there are Chinese, fish and vegetarian dishes on the menu.

Instituto Kushi, 88 Avenida Barbosa du Bocage (*cheap*) lurks behind a macrobiotic shop and offers standard vegetarian fare in large portions. The staff are noticeably helpful. **Restaurante do Sol**, 25 Calçada do Duque (*cheap*) is up many steps behind Rossio train station. Peeling white walls and long red-clothed tables characterize this simple self-service restaurant which serves excellent fresh juices and good though rather bland food.

Yin–Yang, first floor, 14 Rua dos Correiros (*cheap*) is set in the heart of the Baixa district. This self-service restaurant is a no-frills affair, dishing up huge amounts of delicious vegetarian and macrobiotic food to a varied lunch-time crowd. The fresh juices are also good. Attached is the obligatory healthfood shop and a noticeboard gives information on meditation and yoga classes.

Lisbon ✆ (01–)   ***Cafés and Bars***

Lisbon's once-grand **coffeehouses** are a little seedy, which makes them all the more enjoyable.

At the heart of the Chiado, **Café A Brasileira**, 120 Rua Garrett, ✆ 346 9541, is a Lisbon landmark: its outdoor tables are a great place to watch the fashionable world go by—as the painter Almada Negreiros and the poet Fernando Pessoa were well aware. To mark the centenary of the latter's birth, a lifesized bronze sculpture of him was seated at an outdoor table. In the Rossio Square, **Café Nicola** too has literary ties: a series of wall paintings depict the life of the poet Bocage (*see* 'Setúbal', p.281). Opposite, tourists and Lisboêtas alike queue for outdoor tables at the **Pastelaria Suiça** at 96 Rossio, ✆ 342 8092.

Between Saldanha and Estefânia, ladies sip coffee at **Versailles**, 15A Avenida da República, ✆ 546340, at the south end of the Avenida. Its chandeliers, wall mirrors and fake marble columns make it one of the capital's grandest *pastelarias*.

For somewhere much more earthy, try **Casa de Pasto Alentejana**, 2 Praceta Goa, ✆ 921 9717, off the southern end of the Avenida, between Restauradores and the Rossio. Housed in a splendid old building, with ferns, gilt-mirrored ballroom, chandeliers and *azulejo* tiles depicting scenes from Camões' novels, this semi-private 'club' (anyone can walk in) caters mostly for Alentejans and their friends resident in Lisbon. Upstairs a basic kitchen produces large quantities of Alentejan food (cheap), and all ages stand round the counter drinking beer.

On the edge of the Bairro Alto overlooking the Praça dos Restauradores, the **Solar do Vinho do Porto** (Port Wine Institute), 45 Rua de S. Pedro de Alcântara, ✆ 342 3307, is a pleasant but snooty lamplit bar, flanked by stone walls and tapestries. Like its sister institute in Oporto, it claims to sell 166 non-vintage ports by the glass, though the selection dwindles on closer enquiry. The house once belonged to Ludwig, architect of Mafra, but he has left no traces. A glass of Cockburns 10-Year-Old costs around 250$00. No instruction is available. *Open 10am–12am except Sun and holidays.*

Slightly uphill, **Pavilhão Chinês Bar**, 89 Rua Dom Pedro V, ✆ 342 4729, is a fantastic bar entirely walled with cabinets of fans, sheet music, cigarette holders, china *objets d'art* and a jumble of other curiosities. Admire them from chinoiserie tub chairs. *Open Mon–Fri 2pm–2am; Sat 6pm–2am; Sun 9pm–2am.* **Snob**, Rua do Século, running south from the Praça do Principe Real, is quieter, with green baize, wooden booths, glass cabinets and excellent steaks. Fashionable **Fragil**, 128 Rua da Atalaia, ✆ 346 9578, has a facelift every couple of months to keep the capital's bright young media types queuing at the door late into the night. When they fancy a change, they pile into taxis and chatter loudly until they reach Alcântara, along Belém way, where they strut their stuff at **Alcântara Mar** on the Rua da Cozinha Económica. The seriously trendy can try their luck with the style police parked on the door of **Kapital** (Avenida 24 de Julho, opposite Santos station), which contains three floors of the hippest ravers.

Lisbon's nightlife is increasingly vigorous every year, with the Bairro Alto producing most of the noise. This is the best area of Lisbon to wander through on a Friday or Saturday night. Scores of bars play music from bossa nova and *fado* to trip hop and jazz, and there is usually no entry charge, so you can meander from one to another.

Hot Clube de Portugal, Praça da Alegria, just west of the Avenida da Liberdade (*open Thurs–Sat 10pm–2am*) is one of the capital's foremost **jazz** venues, a sweaty cellar with good live bands on Friday and Saturday evenings, at around 11.30pm. The best places to hear **African music** are **Lontra**, 157 Rua de São Bento, in the Bairro Alto, **Clave de Tó**, 35 Rua do Salvador, in the Alfama, and **Ritz Clube**, 55 Rua da Gloria, west of Avenida da Liberdade, which is Lisbon's largest African club, featuring a resident band and gloriously situated in the premises of an old brothel/music hall. **Clave di Nos**, 100 Rua do Norte, in the Bairro Alto, features music from the Cape Verde Islands, a former Portuguese colony whose rhythms blend those of Africa and Latin America.

Keep an eye out for visiting **Brazilian** singers such as Maria Bethânia, Milton Nascimento and Ney Matogrosso. For up-and-coming **Portuguese bands** (Radio Macau, Xutos e Pontapes, Peste e Sida, GNR, and, for a mixture of rock-and-roll and *fado*, Mler Ife Dada) truck along to an ex-cinema called **Rock Rendez-Vous**, 180 Rua da Beneficência, north of the Gulbenkian museum, near the Rua Francisco T. da Costa. Otherwise, hear it on **Radio Geste** (96.6FM). The Gulbenkian Foundation underwrites most **classical** music concerts, so pick up a programme of events from the museum. They're not well advertised, particularly the 60-odd concerts from October to May.

fado

The Bairro Alto wouldn't be the Bairro Alto without a quiver of *fado* houses. **Machado**, 91 Rua do Norte, ✆ 346 0095 (*expensive;* fado *and folkloric dances 9.30pm–3am*), is a clap-along-with-the-music place where the *fado* is too smooth and pleasant to be genuine. Oil lamps burn on tables served by smiley waitresses in frilled folkloric dresses. In a parallel street, **Arcadas do Faia**, 54 Rua da Barroca, ✆ 342 1923 (*expensive; closed Sun;* fado *and folklore 10.15pm–2am*), is more exclusive and upmarket, with rich décor. The well-varied *fado* is strong and serious, and may be accompanied by dinner. Two streets further west, **O Forcado**, 219 Rua da Rosa, ✆ 368579 (*expensive;* fado *9.30pm–3am*), offers a more genuine atmosphere, although purists accuse it of being touristy. Here the *fado* touches something sad, particularly when Fernanda Pinto sings it. Bullfight posters line the white walls above a tile dado. Dinner is available. Avoid **Luso**, 10 Trav. da Queimada, ✆ 322281, which is kitsch, dirty and dull. For amateur *fado*, try **Mata Bicho**, 18 Rua do Grémio Lusitano, ✆ 346 8868, an *inexpensive* restaurant where the *patron* lets rip.

In the Alfama, photographs of dolorous *fadistas* fill the walls above the tile dado at **Parreirinha de Alfama**, 1 Beco do Espírito Santo, ✆ 868209 (*moderate; after 6.30pm*). Coachlamps cast a gentle light on the renditions. Just west of the Avenida da Liberdade, **Marcia Condessa**, 38 Praça da Alegria, ✆ 346 7093 (*expensive*) provides good late-night *fado* and Portuguese guitar music. In Lapa, **Senhor Vinho**, 18 Rua do Meio á Lapa, ✆ 672681 (*expensive*) is recommended for those in search of the genuine article.

The Ribatejo

Rare in its lack of geographical boundaries, the Ribatejo straddles the River Tagus, which is its main artery ('*ribatejo*' means 'Tagus riverbank'). The river's fecund alluvial plain is rich in pasture and cereals—rice and wheat grow where the soil is compact, millet and vines where the loam is light. Beyond the river's reach stretch yawning grasslands. Until the introduction of railways in the last century, the north-bank river ports were magnets for settlement. These now form the base of the industrial triangle of Torres Novas, Tomar and Abrantes, where textile, cellulose, paper, metallurgical and chemical factories loom. The province is fringed with oak woods.

The Ribatejo is lacklustre; follow the example of the Tagus, and pass through it—but not before you have seen Tomar.

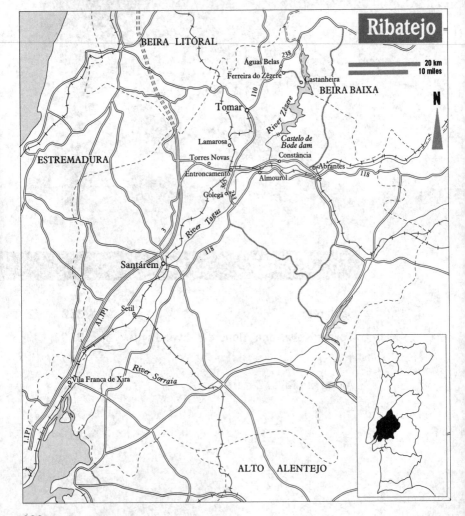

History

In 1147, the chaplain to Hervey de Glanvill, a knight waylaid *en route* for the Second Crusade, wrote of local pride in the fecundity of the Tagus, which was said to be two parts water and one part marvellously flavoursome fish. To the south of the river, the land was potent enough to produce two crops from a single seeding. Later British visitors to the Ribatejo were less reflective: in the second half of the 14th century, Dom Fernando I was so eager to get rid of the riotous English troops sent to assist him in his struggle against Juan of Aragon that he gave them horses and packed them off in the direction of Castile. The knights turned back, entered the Ribatejo and continued to rob, rape and pillage as before. The chronicler Fernão Lopes was shocked by the waste of it all: 'when such-and-such a man felt like eating a cow's tongue, he killed the cow, cut out its tongue, and left the cow to rot.' With time, 'people began to punish this as discreetly as they could, and killed many of [the English] with poisoned bread and in other unobtrusive ways ...'

Camões spent his orphaned childhood in the Ribatejo, nourished not on mother's milk but on that of 'a wild beast', which may have been a cow or a mare, in both of which the Ribatejo abounds. For this is the centre of Portugal's horse- and bull-breeding industry.

Horses used to be necessary for the defence of the realm, and nobody was more aware of this than the king. In 1492 the country's roads were so pitted that anyone wishing to travel in comfort rode a mule, which was smoother than a carriage and more sedate than a horse. So many mares were mated with asses that Dom João II feared the lack of horses threatened the nation's ability to defend itself; he passed a law banishing saddle mules from the kingdom. The clergy let out a shrill objection—and were permitted to keep their mules. But the wily king then passed a decree which forbade every blacksmith to shoe a saddle mule, on pain of death! Horses remain an important part of the Ribatejan economy: the Vale de Santarém hosts the national stud farm, and the country's largest annual horse fair attracts a cross section of traders, riders and breeders to Golegã, 31km northwest of Santarém, in mid-November.

Bulls of the Ribatejo

But it is the Ribatejan bulls which make the greatest impression. They graze the plains; those fortunates which remain uncastrated stoke the powerful tossing muscle which rises between their shoulderblades. They are herded by *campinos*—wild, bow-legged men who wear woolly chaps, and, traditionally, a green stocking cap with a tassel, white blouson shirt, scarlet waistcoat, green cummerbund and black velvet knee-breeches. Before the main bullfights at the July and October fairs, bulls are driven, Pamplona-style, through the streets of Vila Franca de Xira, the Mecca of Portuguese bull fighting. (Should you get trapped, remember that bulls are only flummoxed by immobility.)

The Wine of the Ribatejo

Pombal prohibited the production of wine in the Ribatejo, to boost yields from wheat. The vines have crept back with a vengeance: output from the Ribatejo is second only to the Oeste region of Estremadura, but the quality is less impressive than the quantity. Most wines are red; keep an eye out for those of the Serradayre brand (literally 'Mountain Air'), a smooth, light, fruity wine.

Getting Around

Major roads run through the Ribatejo on a north–south axis, parallel with the River Tagus. The major north–south railway line runs through the province, with a junction at Entroncamento for connections from the east. Northbound express bus services tend to peter out beyond Torres Novas.

Santarém

Built above the west bank of the Tagus 78km northeast of Lisbon, the bustling capital of the Ribatejo was once important for its strategic location; now Santarém's 18,000 souls are preoccupied with the flat pasturelands which surround the town. The moderately attractive settlement lacks exceptional monuments, and sprawls along two parallel shopping streets, the Rua Serpa Pinto and the Rua Capelo Ivens (the latter beloved by timepassers). Santarém is a centre for bullfighting—note the witty bull pavement mosaics.

History

Dom Afonso Henriques was so delighted to capture Santarém from the Moors in 1147, 'by the labour of myself and of my body, and the vigilant subtlety both of myself and of my men', that he founded the Abbey of Alcobaça. The town's first charter indicates his keen interest in the place: it lays down what crops should be cultivated and how much labourers should be paid, recommends that landowners should erect fences to prevent their cattle from straying, and backs the municipal officers in their struggle to avenge damage done to cornfields.

The settlement takes its name from Santa Iria (Irene), whose martyred body was flung in the River Nabão in 653, floated downstream, and made miraculous appearances here during the reign of Dom Dinis. Having erected a stone memorial to the saint, the king died at Santarém in 1325.

The plethora of wild boar attracted a succession of hunting monarchs to Santarém, whose royal palace in turn acted as a magnet for the *Cortes*, which met here occasionally in the 13th and 14th centuries, and fairly frequently in the 15th century. In 1491 Prince Dom Afonso, son of Dom João II, was fatally trampled by his horse while racing along the banks of the Tagus.

Having abandoned hope of breaking through the Lines of Torres Vedras before the onset of winter, Masséna dallied here from November 1810 to March of the following year. When they failed to capture Lisbon, the Miguelites made their last stand at Santarém in 1833–4.

Santarém is well served by links with the north and east of the country, and with Lisbon. Semi-frequent **trains** run from Lisbon (1½hrs) and from Tomar (¾hr). Many services require passengers to change trains at Entroncamento. Semi-frequent trains also run from Guarda (6hrs), via Covilhã (5hrs), Castelo Branco (3¼hrs) and Abrantes (1½hrs); from Oporto (3½hrs), via Aveiro (2½hrs) and Coimbra-B (1¾hrs). Avoid the infrequent service from Elvas (Portalegre) if you can, as it usually requires at least two changes.

Frequent RN Express **buses** take 1¼hrs from Lisbon. Very infrequent express buses run from Faro (7hrs), or from Vila Real de Santo António via Faro from 1 July to 15 Sept. Otherwise, bus connections are fairly local: Fátima (1hr), Tomar (1¼hrs), Abrantes (1½hrs).

Santarém ☎ (043–)   ***Tourist Information***

The **tourist office** is in the centre of town at 63 Rua de Capelo Ivens, ☎ 391512. To get there from the **bus station** (☎ 333201), cross the Av. M. Sá da Bandeira and continue straight ahead. The **railway station**, ☎ 333180, is roughly 1.5km downhill and east of town, to which it is connected by a local bus.

Festivals

Santarém hosts Portugal's premier **agricultural fair** in June, a flower festival in October called **lusoflora** and a massive **national gastronomic festival**, in the last week of October and the first week of November. For this, visitors wander from ex-stable to ex-stable, sampling every region's traditional dishes. Each day a different region takes over the central restaurant and equips it with a folk group.

Around the Town

There are many churches in Santarém, but only a couple worth looking inside.

A grandiose Jesuit **seminary** of 1676 occupies the site of the former royal palace, in the Praça Sá da Bandeira (named after the liberal party leader born here in 1795). The Rua Serpa Pinto leads to the 16th-century **Marvila Church**, whose beautifully proportioned interior lurks behind a snakey Manueline portal. Early 17th-century blue and white carpet *azulejos* line the walls, topped by a row of geometric tiles. The square marble pulpit contains fiery preachers by means of a balustrade.

Past this church and round to the right, the **church of N.S. da Graça** was built 1380–1420, for the canons regular of St Augustine. The portal's tracery is similar to that of Batalha, and harmonizes with the excellent rose window above it, which was carved from a single stone. Within, the three scrubbed and elegant Gothic naves contain tombs of the Menses family, the most impressive being that of Dom Pedro de Menses, whose grandfather founded the church, and who was governor of Ceuta for 22 years until 1437. Effigies of him and his wife hold hands atop the large tomb supported by eight lions, with carved canopies at their heads and leafy pedestals at their feet. If his effigy is anything to go by,

Dom Pedro sported the ultimate rounded haircut. One of the Menses women married Pedro Álvares Cabral (*see* 'Belmonte', p.199), who discovered Brazil and is entombed here.

Back on the Rua Serpa Pinto, the defunct Romanesque-turned-Gothic church of São João de Alporão now contains the jumbled town **museum**. From the outside, the double walls of the chancel are pierced by plain square-headed windows, which are transformed into attractive round-headed openings within. Among the display, the ostentatiously elaborate, scoured tomb of Duarte de Menses steals the show. According to the inscription, he was governor of Alcácer-Seguir and, with 500 troops, successfully defended the town against 10,000 Moors. In 1464 he extricated King Dom Afonso V from a Moorish ambush, but was hacked to death in the process. A cabinet in the museum displays the contents of his sarcophagus: one tooth. Surely he had been fighting hard.

Rising 22m opposite the church, the 15th-century **Tôrre das Cabaças** was built on the orders of Manuel I. He was so disgusted by the resulting edifice that he demanded 8 pots should be placed on high for all to see, symbolizing the empty-headedness of the unfortunates involved in its creation.

Santarém ✆ (043–)   **Where to Stay**

★★Pensão Victoria, 21 Rua 2 Visconde, ✆ 22573, ✉ 28202 (*moderate–inexpensive*), is new and friendly. Some rooms have balconies, some have sitting areas, and others have neither but are a decent size. The hand-woven pictures on the walls are made by the owner. Budget travellers should head for the **youth hostel**, ✆ 333292, on Avenida Dom Afonso Henriques 109, just south of town.

Turismo de Habitação

Quinta de Vale de Lobos, ✆ 429264, (*expensive*) is 6km north of Santarém on the road to Torres Novas—a peaceful olive farm, once the home of Alexandre Herculano (his slippers and bed are there to prove it). Four double rooms, a living room and two chalets are available for guests, as are hunting and walking on the 600-acre estate. The hospitable owners can organize trips to see wild bulls nearby.

Casa de NS da Assumção, 55 Rua 1 de Dezembro, ✆ 25048 (*moderate*) offers the most comfortable accommodation in Santarém itself. Guest rooms, which have a private entrance, are at the back of the house, looking onto a bougainvillaea-filled courtyard. **Casa da Pedra**, 16 Rua das Pedras Negras, Póvoa da Isenta, ✆ 769754 (*moderate*) is in the middle of a game reserve and so offers hunting and riding. It is built of natural stone and has a welcoming and distinctly family atmosphere. The fine food includes home-made bread and sausages.

Santarém ✆ (043–)   **Eating Out**

Portas do Sol, ✆ 29520 (*moderate*), in the garden of that name, offers good local dishes, such as *sável* from the Tagus. *Closed Sun evening and Mon.* At Campo da Feira there's also **O Mal Cozinho**, ✆ 23584, or **Castico**, ✆ 23891 (*both cheap*).

Torres Novas

Torres Novas is an industrial town on the hilly bank of the little River Almonda, 39km north of Santarém and 23km south of Tomar; there are no monuments of note within Torres Novas, but 3km south of town, near Caveira, there are thrilling mosaics at a ruined Roman villa.

The original, 1st-century **Vila Cardílio** was successively remodelled up to the 4th century. Its peristyle is clearly discernible, but little remains above ground. The joy of the otherwise unatmospheric place lies in the figurative and geometric mosaics, which are kept under sand to retain their shades of rust and grey. The sand is swept away by Manuel, who lives in the little white house next to the site, and who left the mosaics to earn his fortune in France, but missed them and returned. The wealth of the mosaics is revealed gradually—a bird becomes a hand, a single face is paired with another. One panel incorporates the words 'May Cardilius and Avita live happily in [their villa] at Torre'.

Back in the Lapas district of Torres Novas, the provenance of smooth, cellar-like **caves** (*key from house 1 in Rua P*) has flummoxed historians. The grotto outside is more sinister: dead frogs rotate in a small black pool edged with primroses. At the highest point in town, wild flowers grow within the **castle walls**, built 1373–6. They overlook a factory yard piled with wood, which is burnt to make steam used in the manufacture of *aguardente*.

Torres Novas ☎ (049–)   *Where to Stay*

Smooth, new, and well-fitted ★★**Hotel dos Cavaleiros**, Praça 5 de Outubro, ☎ 812420, 🖷 812052 (*moderate*) is hung with original art.

Turismo de Habitação

The long white **Quinta Horta do Avô**, ☎ 91116 or (Lisbon) 01 759 2219 (*moderate*) is in Soudos village, a 20-minute drive north-north-east from Torres Novas. It offers farmhouse-style guestrooms, with rugs and the occasional guitar, overlooking a jumbled garden, where flowers spill out of urns, amidst lemon trees, white cobblestones and lilies, with a recently built swimming pool. The one apartment comprises two single beds and a loft for a third.

Almourol

Like something from a child's dream, the fantastic **island castle** of Almourol crowns a rocky little island in the middle of the Tagus, 22km south of Tomar and 15km east of Torres Novas.

Getting There

By road, the castle is invisible from the south bank. Drivers should cross at the railway bridge, go straight ahead, then left, from where the castle is signposted.

Three trains daily leave Tomar for Entroncamento connecting with trains to Almourol, but only one is feasible, leaving Tomar at 8.05am, arriving at

Entroncamento 8.33am, leaving Entroncamento 9.04am, arriving Almourol 9.18am. The trains leave Almourol at 11.35am and 11.57am (then 6.11pm). It's quite a walk from the railway station to the castle.

Built on Roman foundations, the diamond-shaped, battlemented bastion and its 10 towers were constructed by Gualdim Pais, Master of the Order of Templars, in 1171. The setting is ideal for aspiring princesses, who should make a special effort to visit when the river is glassy and the moon is full. This will compensate for the castle's lack of romantic history, which was left high and dry as the Moors were pushed southwards and there was less need to defend this stretch of the Tagus.

A reticent old gentleman nicknamed Bragança rows visitors to and from the bamboo-fringed island, from April to October, depending on the weather; in winter, the river is high because the Spanish open their dams. Expect to pay something over 150$00 for a round trip. Do be careful of the bees on the second storey of the main tower.

Constância

Eighteen km east of Torres Novas and 12km west of Abrantes, the town of Constância occupies an amphitheatre at the confluence of the Rivers Zêzere and Tagus.

Camões was holed up in the **Casa dos Arcos**—now an uninteresting shell—1548–50, following his ill-starred affair with Catarina de Ataide. The restored, hilltop **Igreja Matriz** of 1636 has a nice cockerel weathervane and a bright ceiling painted by José Malhoa, depicting N.S. da Boa Viagem soaring skywards.

Constância ✆ *(049–)*   ***Where to Stay***

Residencial Casa João Chagas, Rua João Chagas, ✆ 99403, ✆ 99458 (*moderate*) provides good, clean rooms and smiley service.

Turismo de Habitação

Built around a terracotta courtyard on the riverbank, immediately opposite a monstrous paper factory, the signposted **O Palácio**, ✆ 99224 (*expensive*) offers a warm welcome, and attractive rooms furnished with light antiques and reproductions. Professor de Azevedo, author of the excellent *Churches of Portugal*, and his wife speak English.

Quinta de Santa Bárbara, off the road to Abrantes, ✆ 99214 (*moderate*) is surrounded by lovely countryside and offers quite grand rooms.

Abrantes

The faintly charming small town of Abrantes stands dominant above the north bank of the Tagus, 26km east of Torres Novas and 72km west of Castelo de Vide. In 1807, Junot and 30,000 troops captured the town (and subsequently requisitioned boots), for which Napoleon entitled him Duc d'Abrantes.

The castle walls enclose the squat **keep** of 1303, which offers distant views of the Ribatejo, and the church of Santa Maria do Castelo, reconstructed in 1433 and now housing the **Museu de Dom Lopo de Almeida** (*open 10–12.30 and 2–5; closed Mon and holidays*). Of the several tombs, the most elaborate is that of Dom João de Almeida (1445–1512), being beautifully carved and well proportioned, though there is no effigy. The chancel houses a collection of 16th-century Sevillian tiles, archaeological fragments, and sculptures including a fascinating late 15th-century Ança-stone *Eternal Father*, seated and deeply sad, holding the crucified Christ.

The **Misericórdia** houses six 16th-century panels depicting the life of Christ from the Annunciation to Calvary, attributed to Gregório Lopes.

Tomar

Sited on the banks of the River Nabão 62km northeast of Santarém, 23km northeast of Torres Novas and 45km southwest of Leiria, Tomar and its 15,000 souls are dominated by the wooded hill on which stands the Templar's convento de Cristo.

Clean, rickety cobbled streets run parallel through the old part of town, where there are spurts of geraniums, and a tinsmith who makes watering cans in a hole-in-the-wall (No.18 Rua Silva Magalhães). A main road bisects the centre of town, passing a wooden water wheel on the near side of the old bridge across the river, and failing to disturb the fish which mass at its far side. There are several good places to stay in Tomar, suited to different budgets, and some enjoyable restaurants.

History

The Order of the Knights Templar was founded during the First Crusade, in 1118, by King Baldwin I, to keep open the pilgrim routes to the Holy Land. Free from all authority except the pope's, they built their first castle in Portugal at Soure, south of Coimbra, in 1128, on land donated by Dona Teresa. The Templars played a key role in assisting Dom Afonso Henriques fight the Moors, and were granted ecclesiastical superiority over Santarém when it was taken in 1147. This the Grand Master, Dom Gualdim Pais, renounced in 1150, in favour of a territory roughly 50km to the north. He built a church and began a castle on the banks of the River Nabão, before abandoning the site in favour of a more secure location nearby, on the levelled knuckle of two hills. The second castle, now ruinous, dates from 1160. Two years later, a church, the *Charola*, was constructed slightly to the west, within the fortified enclosure.

The Templars requested castles and land in return for their services, and so became immensely rich and powerful. (They provided the ransom money for Louis IX of France.) In the early 14th century, Pope Clement V considered them a threat to his authority, and ordered the suppression of the Templars. Jacques de Molay, the last Grand Master of the Templars in Paris, was arrested on charges of blasphemy and sodomy in 1307—but it was rumoured that he managed to send part of his treasure to Portugal. He was a rich man: he is said to have arrived in Paris with 150,000 gold florins and 10 horse-loads of silver.

Dom Dinis dissolved the Portuguese Order of the Templars in 1314. However, he recognized their usefulness to the Crown, and shortly afterwards founded the Order of Christ, which became the Templars' spiritual and worldly successor, as the king intended.

Initially, the headquarters of the new order was at Castro Marim, in the east of the Algarve, but this shifted to Tomar in 1356. Henry the Navigator presided over its most distinguished era; exempted from the Grand Mastership because its vow of poverty was inconsistent with his worldly interests, he was Governor of the Order of Christ 1418–60. Under his aegis, the white sails of the discoverers' caravels bore the order's emblem, the red Cross of Christ.

When Dom João III became Grand Master, he reformed the order into a monastic brother-hood—necessitating the construction of living quarters—and in 1551 swept the Mastership of Portugal's three religious orders into the custody of the Crown. At that time the Order of Christ controlled 21 towns or villages. It declined from the end of the 16th century, and was extinguished together with the other religious orders in 1834.

Getting There

Trains run semi-frequently from Lisbon via Santarém; change at Entroncamento (2¼hrs total). There are frequent local buses to Fatima and Batalha and infrequent express buses from Lisbon (2¾hrs) via Santarém (1¼hrs).

Tomar © *(049–)* ### Tourist Information

The **tourist office** occupies a building constructed in 1930, in the style of a 16th-century mansion, on the Avenida Dr. Cândido Madureira, © 322427. The **railway station**, © 312815, is next to the **bus station**, © 312738; to get to the tourist office, cross the dirt park, continue straight ahead, and turn left at the Avenida Dr. Cândido Madureira.

Festivals

The **Festa dos Tabuleiros** is a harvest festival with a Portuguese twist to it. On the first Sunday in July, 400–500 white-clad 'virgins' (who have been getting younger over the years) carry headdresses as tall as themselves. The headdresses are bread loaves stuck on a cylindrical bamboo frame, decorated with red, yellow and purple paper flowers and leaves, as well as wheat stalks. On the following day a cartload of bread and a cartload of wine are given to 50 poor families.

The Convento de Cristo

Open 9.30–12.30 and 2–5 (till 6 in summer).

The mystical tenets of the Templars are never more apparent than in their architecture: the outer walls of the convento de Cristo are a mirror image of a stellar constellation, with the Charola taking Orion's position.

The Templars' 12th-century **keep** (*closed to the public*) stands beside the entrance to the convento, with crenellations adapted for crossbows, and next to it a triangular cistern whose orientation is said to indicate the location of hidden gold. An inscription records, with exaggeration, that in 1190 'came the King of Morocco, leading 400,000 horsemen and 500,000 foot and besieged this castle for six days', but God was on the side of the Templars. The **Praça de Armas** (terrace) between the keep and the church overlooks the original entrance to the fortifications (topped by granite eggs—either alchemists' eggs or ostrich eggs, which were traded by merchants on the west African coast): a row of plane trees marks the course of a road which led under the terrace and into the stables.

The Charola

The bell-like Charola, begun in 1162, was the Templars' church, which they entered through a portal—now marked by a plaque—where horsemen were blessed. The original church was a 16-sided polygon, based on the design of the Temple of the Dome of the Rock in Jerusalem. João de Castilho's splendid portal of 1515 uses the light carving of his native Spanish Plateresque style. (He worked at Belém too, and his work was pleasing to the king, for when he died in 1553 his daughter received a pension of 20,000 *reis*.) Within the Charola, a circular aisle surrounds a two-storeyed octagon containing the high altar. The early 16th-century panels attributed to Jorge Afonso, which hung in the aisle, have been removed for restoration.

Henry the Navigator built a chapel on the eastern side of the Charola, and dedicated it to St Thomas à Becket. Dom Manuel considered this addition insufficient for the size and wealth of the order, so he broke through the west side of the building and commissioned Diogo de Arruda to construct (1510–14) a *coro alto* above the chapter house. The floor of the latter is peculiarly high, as if something had been hidden beneath it.

The Cloisters and the Chapter House Window

A passage from the nave follows through to the **Claustro do Cemitério** (cemetery cloister) and the Claustro da Lavagem (cloister of ablutions), with tanks once full of water. The opposite side of the nave leads to the upper storey of the supremely balanced and ordered **Claustro Principal**. This magnificent High Renaissance work was commissioned by Dom João III, mostly built 1557–62, and hides much of his father's chapter house. Ironically, the architect of the cloister was Diogo de Torralva, who bricked over one of the elaborate windows his father-in-law had masterminded.

The Claustro Principal overlooks the famous Manueline **chapter house window**, which is much more forceful than would appear from photographs. The window is flanked by two coral-encrusted masts woven with seaweed, writhing with octopus tendrils and bobbing with cork-buoyed ropes, all of which rests on the roots of a tree borne by the sculpture of an old man, believed to represent its anonymous creator. The garter around the right buttress may refer to the Order of the Garter presented to Dom Manuel by the English King Henry VII. The 'ox's eye' above the window allowed the rays of the setting sun to penetrate the rotunda.

Visitors are not normally allowed into the monastic buildings, as they are occupied by the army, but if you do get a chance, look out for the curious blue, yellow and white *azulejos* picturing ladders and flowers which decorate the monks' dormitory.

A short walk downhill from the convento, the road passes the exquisite **church of N.S. da Conceição** (*key from the tourist office*), a Renaissance gem whose austere exterior belies the beautifully proportioned interior flooded with yellow light. It was built *c.* 1530–40, on the initiative of Frei António of Lisbon. Do note the tendinous spiral staircase.

Central Tomar

Back in the Praça da República, the **church of S. João Baptista** is overshadowed by its imposing tower, with a square base and octagonal top. Both church and tower were reconstructed for Dom Manuel in the late 15th century, being completed in 1510. The lively ornament around the north door—boars, dogs, snails and wild asses—is more curious than the western portal's sober motifs of acorns, grapes and armillary spheres.

Within, six excellent panels by Gregório Lopes hang in the side aisles, ill lit (which is ironic for an artist so concerned with the play of light) but rightly kept in the church for which they were painted 1538–9. Pupil and son-in-law of Jorge Afonso, Gregório Lopes is the most sensuous of Portugal's early 16th-century painters, richly detailing clothes, ornaments and particularly the work of goldsmiths. There's more cross-fertilization in the church's ornate limestone pulpit, which is decorated like a piece of contemporary silverware. Its three main faces bear the shield, sphere and cross of Christ respectively. The sacristan, who closets himself away with an electric waffle iron, making communion wafers, has the key to the baptistry, where hangs the fine early 16th-century *Baptism of Christ* triptych, possibly influenced by Quentin Metzys of Antwerp. On the right-hand panel, Christ is tempted by a horned devil.

The Templars sought wisdom in the ancient traditions of Judaism, so it comes as no surprise to find a small Gothic **synagogue** at No.73 Rua Dr. Joaquim Jacinto (in the next street along, to your left as you face the convento), dating from the mid-15th century. Eight inverted pottery jars have been embedded high in the corners of the square chamber, to improve its acoustics. Various stone inscriptions are displayed. The hot baths discovered under the floor of house No.77 in the same road are open to view.

Cross either bridge and take the first right, into the Rua de Santa Iria, to get to the **church of Santa Maria do Olival**. The lower part of its detached belltower is all that remains of the church and castle, initially constructed by Dom Gualdim Pais. His drastically scrubbed tomb is housed inside the church, which was altered by Dom Manuel and Dom João III. The polychrome *N.S. da Anunciação* of 1525 resembles Meryl Streep. Across the road, the private **Museu de Fosforos** (*open erratically*) will kindle the delight of many a pyromaniac.

Tomar is fortunate to have the rambling, untamed **Sete Montes park** near the centre of town. It's a wonderfully peaceful place which formerly belonged to the convento, and can be entered opposite the tourist office.

Festa dos Tabuleiros

moderate

★★★★**Hotel dos Templários**, 1 Largo Cândido dos Reis, ✆ 321730, ✉ 322191 (beside the public garden), offers an excellent view of the *convento* and its wooded hill. The spacious, neutral bedrooms are fine, but the traffic is noisy when the balcony doors are open. Bits of the décor are fraying. The hotel provides a good-sized swimming pool, and a group-oriented restaurant with an uninteresting menu. ★★★★**Residencial Trovador**, Rua Dr. Joaquim Jacinto Ribeiro, ✆ 322567, ✉ 322194 (overlooking the bus station), is pleasant and airy, though outside the centre of town. Bedrooms are equipped with televisions.

cheap–very cheap

With a jolly manager, ★★★**Pensão União**, 94 Rua Serpa Pinto, ✆ 323161 (first and second floors; near the church of São João Baptista), is light and tastefully furnished, though some of the décor needs attention. ★★★**Residencial Luanda**, 15 Av. Marquês de Tomar, ✆ 323200 (across the park from the Hotel dos Templários), offers clean, decent little bedrooms with pretty views but noisy traffic. The **Pensão Tomarense**, near the centre of town at 15 Av. Torres Pinheiro, ✆ 312948, is dirty and bare, beneath warty ceilings. Elsewhere, the type of soap provided here is used for cleaning laundry.

moderate

For excellent home cooking, saunter off to **Chico Elias**, Algarvias, ✆ 311067, a couple of km southwest of town on the uphill road to Torres Novas, a 15–20-minute walk away. Sit at benchlike tables beside a fireplace, beneath rough wood chandeliers, and try the *bacalhau* roasted with pork. *Closed Tues.* In town, **Chez Nous**, 31 Rua Dr. Joaquim Jacinto Ribeiro, ✆ 312294 (near the river, between the bridges), is a successful half-caste. The trimmings are imported—rock opera, prints on the walls—and the menu indigenous, offering very good fried beef with cheese and *presunto* (like parma ham), or *bacalhau gratinado*.

cheap

Across the old bridge, mauve bunches of wisteria cling to rambling **A Bela Vista**, ✆ 312870, but the interior is disappointingly bright, and the menu not well stocked, though popular with children. Concrete-floored **Piri Piri**, 54 Rua dos Moinhos, ✆ 313494 (in one of the central parallel streets), offers some elaborate but bland dishes in large portions. At lunchtime in the market, chicken is barbecued with no nonsense, and eaten at benches, under corrugated iron.

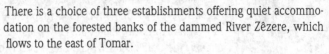

There is a choice of three establishments offering quiet accommodation on the forested banks of the dammed River Zêzere, which flows to the east of Tomar.

Thirteen km southeast of Tomar, the informal and homey **Pousada de São Pedro**, © 049 381159, @ 381176 (*category C*) overlooks the massive Castelo de Bode dam, reflecting the Portuguese fixation with those feats of engineering. Mature trees cloak the dull, interlacing hills around the *pousada*, and do much to hide the power cables. The bathrooms would suit an asylum, but the restaurant serves good, well-presented meals. The 9km road south to Constância follows the bucolic River Zêzere.

Overlooking the aptly named Blue Lake, 28km east-northeast of Tomar, peaceful ★★★★**Estalagem Lago Azul**, 348 Estrada Nacional, © 049 361445 (*expensive*)—in Castanheira—provides an unheated swimming pool, catamaran facilities, a hard tennis court, and a shrubby garden which faces mottled hills across the water, with bald patches caused by forest fires. Bedrooms are furnished like fancy offices, with lively wallpaper. The restaurant serves rather plain food, and dry dessert cakes.

Newer and even more peaceful, the ★★★★**Estalagem Vale da Ursa**, © 074 90981 (*moderate*) is situated on the north bank of the river where it is crossed by the road from Águas Belas to Cernache do Bonjardim. It sits among pinecovered hills on the sandy edge of a reservoir, which holds some of Lisbon's drinking water, 27km northeast of Tomar. Everything feels new, from the polished granite lobby to the spacious, gadgety bedrooms and the marble bathrooms. It's also one of the very few hotels in Portugal designed to be accessible to wheelchairs—all credit to Sr Mariano. Try the restaurant's *achega*, a kind of black bass fished from the lake.

There are some enjoyable walks around the *estalagem*—the village of **Dornes** is a good target (a couple of km west of the bridge), with an earthcoloured **pentagonal tower** built by the Templars. Don't be disappointed by the absence of bears (an '*ursa*' is a female bear); partridges and rabbits are more in line.

If you ask in advance, the RN Express bus from Lisbon to Cernache do Bonjardim may stop near the *estalagem*. If not, the English-speaking management can arrange transport from Cernache.

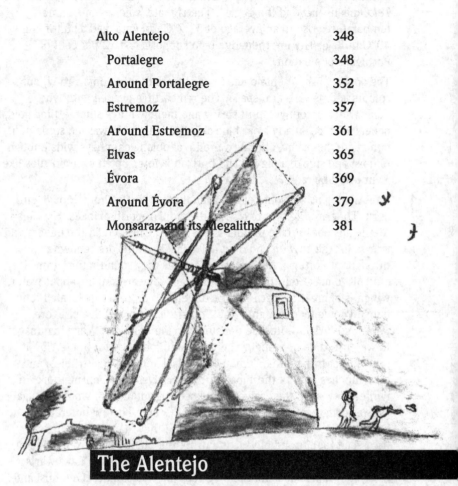

The Alentejo

The Alentejo stretches across just under a third of continental Portugal, to the south of the River Tagus and the province of Ribatejo—'alem Tejo' means 'beyond the Tagus'. The climate is fiery—in summer, temperatures rise to an average of 33.7°C in Évora, and a stultifying 40°C in Beja. The unproductive land supports just 12 per cent of Portugal's population.

The appeal of the Alentejo lies in its austere beauty, in its strong, pure colours and its vast, arid space. The red earth is planted with wheat fields which sprout green in spring and mellow into a summertime gold, beneath the peculiarly clear blue sky. Brilliant, whitewashed settlements punctuate the plains, offering a profile of oblong chimneys wide enough to hoist and smoke a pig in. The horizon is interrupted by grain silos like giant test-tube racks.

The Alentejans are some of the friendliest of the friendly, though stubborn. They are the butt of a recent—familiar—rash of jokes. How many Alentejans does it take to milk a cow? Five. One to hold the udders and four to lift the cow up and down. Their folk choirs are renowned throughout Portugal, but to the unfamiliar they sound rather grim. It's difficult to make out the words—perhaps they are singing about water, which is of great concern (hence the elaborate, centrally located fountains). People fear drought—the *Constituições* of the See of Évora, published in 1534, impose penalties on the practice of carrying images to water in time of drought and threatening them with immersion if they do not bring rain. Women wear black felt hats like trilbies, and pack lunches in cork thermoses for themselves and their menfolk. In winter they wrap themselves in striped rugs of undyed wool. Portugal's gypsies congregate in the Alentejo, and George Borrow noted the banditti who infested the region in 1835: they 'dance and sing, eat fricasseed rabbits and olives, and drink the muddy but strong wine of the Alemtejo'. Peculiar beliefs spice the province: if you have warts, cross your hands and rub them against the ribs of a deceived husband without his knowing.

History

The history of the Alentejo has been shaped by landholding and irrigation. The soil is thin and dry, transport costs are high, and there are few mountains or rivers: hence the Romans introduced huge farms known as *latifúndios* some time between 202 BC and 139 BC. They built 18 dams in the south of Portugal, irrigating fields of wheat planted among olive trees, where pigs grazed when the land lay fallow. Wine production was concentrated on the river valleys and along the main road from Lisbon to Beja via Évora.

The Moors made few changes to the pattern of landholding—though pig breeding declined, given the Koranic injunction. Merchants and representatives of the caliph

The Economy and the Land

Most workers are employed on *latifúndias*; often the more permanent labourers are housed in hilltop homesteads called *montes*. Silviculture offers an alternative to wheat: Baixo Alentejo has been colonized by copses of silvery eucalyptus, planted for pulp and harvested after four years. They are almost as thirsty as the rice that grows at Alcácer do Sal. Plums flourish at Elvas, and the oranges of Vila Viçosa are superb. Alentejan cork-oaks drop acorns, which are hoovered by black pigs. Sheep and goats roam the scrub.

The west-coast port of Sines alone has broken out of the traditional economy: it receives heavy cargoes from the Mediterranean and the Americas, and is a base for heavy industry including petroleum refining, petrochemicals, the extraction of iron from its ore, and naval repairs.

Cork and Olives

The plains of wheat around Évora and Beja yield to fields peppercorned with cork-oak or olive trees, both of which are short, small-leafed and gnarled. Portugal is the world's largest producer of cork. The bark, up to 10cm thick, is cut from the trees every nine years: the trunk and branches are ringed in 2–3m sections with a light axe, and then cut straight down one side. If the weather is too dry, the cork shatters into many pieces; if the weather is too wet and cold, the tree dies of shock. The flayed trunks are a shrieking salmon pink, which blackens with time. Olive trees are shaken until they yield their crop as well as their dignity; mechanized shakers are now edging their way in, requiring a new strain of less tenacious trees.

invested their wealth in land, so in the Alentejo, towns grew into concentrations of absentee landlords.

When the Alentejo was conquered from the Moors, vast tracts of land were doled out to the military orders, though the king retained all important cities and towns. Urban Moslems were compelled to reside outside the town walls, and rural Moslems were milked by heavy taxes—between a third and a half of Moslem town dwellers fled to southern Spain. Dom Sancho I (1185–1211) tried to offset this depopulation by encouraging emigration from Flanders.

From the 14th century, the maritime trade offered rich rewards to speculators, and Alentejan agriculture suffered from lack of investment. The seaports and the cities enthralled villeins, who continued to leave the land. Portugal began importing wheat in the early 16th century. It was not until chemical fertilizers were introduced in 1884 that heathland was brought under new cultivation. Salazar was keen to increase wheat production, but his schemes of 1929 and 1958 met with little success.

The landless rural workers of the Alentejo were the sinews of civilian support for the Revolution of 1974. In July 1975, a law called for the expropriation of properties with more than the equivalent of 500 ha of dry land or 50 ha of irrigated land. (Two years later,

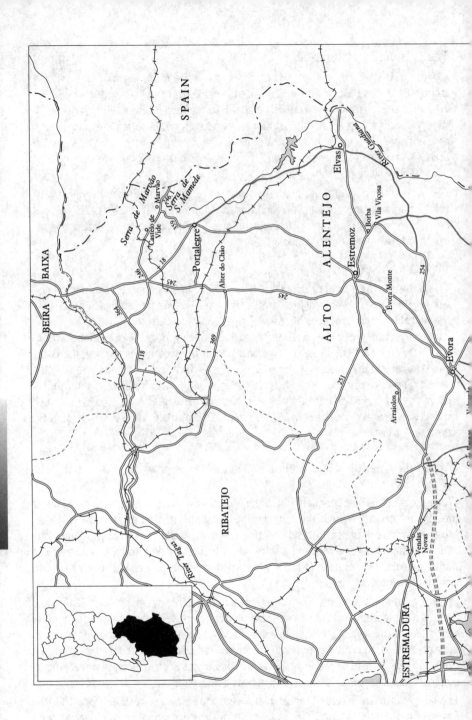

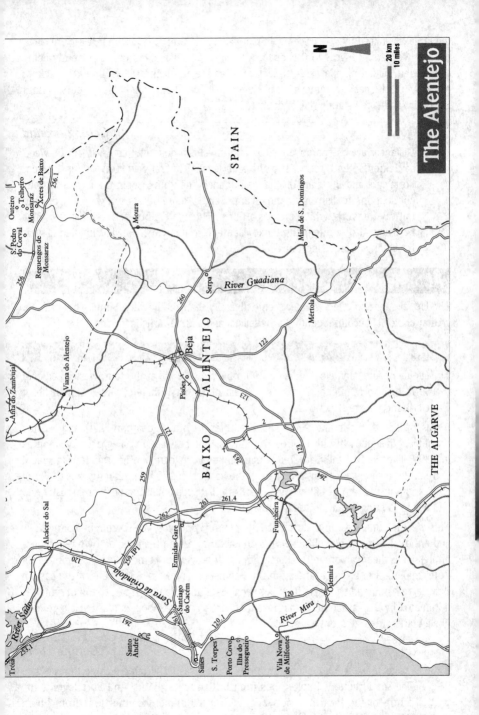

The Alentejo

20 km
10 miles

N

SPAIN

Outeiro
Telheiro
S. Pedro
do Corval
Monsaraz
Xeres de Baixo
256.1
Moura
Reguengos de
Monsaraz
256
Minà de S. Domingos
Serpa
River Guadiana
260
Mértola
Anta do Zambujal
Viana do Alentejo
Beja
122
Pisões
ALENTEJO
123
BAIXO
2
263
123
Alcácer do Sal
259
261.4
264
Funcheira
120
262
261
THE ALGARVE
Ermidas-Gare
259 IP1
Serra de Grândola
120
Santiago
do Cacém
120.1
River Mira
Odemira
261
Tróia
255.1
River Sado
120.1
Santo
André
Sines
S. Torpes
Porto Covo
Ilha do
Pressegueiro
Vila Nova
de Milfontes

the limit was raised by 40 per cent.) In October 1975 *latifúndias* around Beja were occupied by workers. Roughly 900 cooperatives were established—and are currently being dismantled, or falling apart due to lack of initiative and lack of governmental backup. Although most local government is still Communist, the right wing holds the purse strings in Lisbon, and is reinstating the landowners.

Getting Around

Distances are comparatively large, and travel can be monotonous. Roads between settlements tend to be straight and level. The railway network is limited: Portalegre and Elvas are on the main branch line from Lisbon; the former has bus connections to Estremoz and Évora. Baixo Alentejo gets a raw deal from the railway network, which focuses on Beja. The express bus network has few links between Alto Alentejo and Baixo Alentejo, so it's worth considering taking relatively long-distance local buses.

Alto Alentejo

The Upper Alentejo offers greater scenic diversity than the Lower Alentejo, as well as a greater choice of accommodation for travellers, and a firmer artistic footing.

Portalegre

The capital of Alto Alentejo and its 13,000 souls crown a hill at the southwestern edge of the Serra de São Mamede, 109km southeast of Tomar (Ribatejo) and 80km south of Castelo Branco (Beira Baixa).

It was fortified by the Infante Afonso Sanches after his father's death in 1279, and became the subject of a feud with his brother Dom Dinis, who besieged Portalegre for five months in 1299. They settled their quarrel by exchanging Portalegre and Marvão for Sintra and Ourém. Portalegre was briefly occupied by the Spanish in 1704 during the Spanish War of Succession, just when the silk-weaving industry had supplanted the woollen industry and had begun to bring wealth to the town.

This wealth is manifest in a clutch of 18th-century *palácios*, with wrought-iron railings and armorial blazons. The chimneys of cork factories rise on the edge of town—but more impressive is the sycamore in the Rossio Square, whose outer branches have a perimeter of 76m, making it one of the largest on the Peninsula. The Rossio Square is at the base of Portalegre's hill, and shoppers flow between there and the upper part of town, which is dominated by the cathedral. Sometimes there are so many shoppers that Portalegre feels like a market town without a market.

Getting There

Trains make the hour long train ride from Elvas to Portalegre three times a day. The semi-frequent Express bus from Lisbon takes 4¼hrs, and Portalegre is the centre of the local bus network, with semi-frequent connections from Elvas, Estremoz, Castelo de Vide and Marvão.

Wines of the Alentejo

Portugal's most recently Demarcated Region, in the east of the Alentejo, incorporates the towns of Reguengos de Monsaraz, Redondo, Borba and Vidigueira, producing very drinkable, full-bodied, mouth-filling red wines, all of which are matured in cement *depósitos* (except for J.M. da Fonseca's Tinto Velho, from Reguengos, where the lightly crushed grapes ferment in clay pots which are continually sprayed with cold water to keep them cool: the wine is then stored in oak casks to mature and soften for up to two years). The reds approach a powerful 13.5°, while the whites, which are less successful, reach 12.5°.

What to Eat

Alentejan pigs are nourished on the acorns which litter the land, so the gastronomy of the province revolves around their particularly flavourful meat. The favourite local dish is the unusual but rich and tasty *porco à Alentejana* : cubes of pork are marinated, fried and boiled, before being mixed with cockles, and lightly coated with a sauce of tomato concentrate, oil, onions and parsely. *Açorda à Alentejana* is a simpler dish, made of eggs poached in watery bread, with coriander and garlic. The pine-kernel sweets of the western Alentejo are well worth a try. The ewe's-milk cheese of Serpa, served 'fresh' with salt and pepper, is a good idea for a picnic, and if you're planning on doing some of your own cooking, do use the excellent Elvas olive oil.

Portalegre ✆ (045–)   ***Tourist Information***

The main regional **tourist office** is inconveniently located in the upper part of town, at 25 Estrada de Santana, ✆ 331359. Much more convenient is the smaller office, which functions in the Palacio Poroas, just off the Rossio, not far from the **bus station**, ✆ 330723, which is on the Castelo Branco road. The **railway station**, ✆ 96121, is 12km south of town, with connecting buses from the main bus station.

Around the Town

One part of Portalegre's wool industry has achieved world renown: the **Tapestry Factory**, housed in a former Jesuit seminary of 1695, a short walk up from the Rossio Square. The tapestries are extraordinarily detailed, tightly woven woollen reproductions of paintings. A slide is made of a specially commissioned or extant painting, and then projected onto graph paper. On this, each colour is painstakingly numbered, and matched with one of 8000 coloured wools. There are 250,000 knots per square metre, averaging out at a cost of something over 1$00 per knot. Unfortunately, it is no longer possible to visit the factory, but there are sometimes exhibitions in the tourist office.

The Church and Convent of São Bernardo

Across the Parque Miguel Bombarda, the Avenida George Robinson (a late-19th-century English cork entrepreneur) leads to the church and convent of São Bernardo (also called N.S. da Conceição). This is now a training school for the Infantry, who will allow visitors to look at the church if they ask nicely. The convent's whitewash is trimmed with yellow, and its buildings are refreshingly irregular, flaunting an odd half-arch. It was founded in 1518 by Dom Jorge de Melo, Bishop of Guarda, when Portalegre was in his diocese. The church's portico is sided with grand and strongly coloured *azulejos*, dated 1739, picturing the baptism of Christ and other scenes. Dragons decorate the rich Renaissance portal of Estremoz marble.

Within the church is the founder's tomb, which he commissioned *c.* 1540, some eight years before his death. Chanterène's work at the base of the tomb is very delicate; the rest seems too heavy to be the work of the master himself. The bishop was conceited. Not only is his effigy clothed in pontifical robes, but the Virgin Mary attends above, surrounded by angels, waiting to welcome him to Heaven. All this from a man with at least two children, one of them by a nun in the convent! The Virgin is flanked by two pairs of men bearing globes on their heads. The history of the convent is carved into the back of some stalls in the *coro alto*. It stops suddenly in 1779, when the institution was closed by Pombal.

Elsewhere Outside the Town Walls

At the opposite end of the Avenida George Robinson, continue in the same direction through a tangle of streets to the Praça da República, off which stands the **José Régio Museum** (*open 9.30–12.30 and 2–6; closed Mon and holidays*), installed in the home of the poet and teacher who came to Portalegre for one year and stayed for 40, until 1969. An obsessive collector, he amassed 300 naïve images of Christ by unschooled craftsmen, nearly 60 of which are displayed here. Note particularly the 17th–18th-century Christ with angels and doves, and, upstairs, a Christ bleeding rubies. Other collections include firedogs on which to rest skewers, and wooden and bronze pestles and mortars used for culinary, pharmaceutical and magical purposes. There is a 'typical' 17th-century kitchen, and a bedroom designed for meditation.

The desanctified **church of São Francisco**, opposite, was founded in 1275, becoming the first monument to be built outside the castle walls. Some of the simple original Gothic work, including frescoes, remains despite the 16th–18th-century modifications. Note the marble mausoleum of Gaspar Fragoso, who died in 1571 and is depicted in armour with a grim lion at his feet.

An 18th-century *palácio* fronts the Praça da República, just outside the town walls.

The Cathedral Square

Within the walls, to the right are the uninteresting remains of the 13th-century **castle**, and slightly further along to the left the recently restored **convent of Santa Clara**, founded by Queen Dona Leonor Teles in 1376. The Rua 19 de Junho continues to the cathedral square.

Flanked by pinnacled towers which constitute the sole feature of the town's skyline, the **cathedral** was founded by the first Bishop of Portalegre, a Spaniard, in 1556. But it was overhauled in 1795, since when pigeon coos have echoed through its porch. The only remarkable feature is the quantity of paintings in the side chapels—the best are in the fourth chapel on your left approaching the altar, and in the 16th-century high altar retable.

The **municipal museum** (*open 9.30–12.30 and 2–6; Sat 9.30–11.30 and 3–6.30; closed Tues and holidays*) is next to the cathedral, housed in a 16th-century seminary rebuilt in the 18th century. It contains one of the oddest collections in Portugal— hundreds of images of St Anthony, from the Middle Ages to a contemporary lottery ticket. Also displayed are baroque polychrome figures, including *Our Lady of Pain*, with seven silver daggers stuck in her breast, and *Our Lady of the Ascension*, clad in billowing robes. The proceeds from the sale of innumerable sweets, made by the nuns of Santa Clara, paid for the ornate silver and ebony tabernacle. Also downstairs are lots of bloody Christs, chalices, and ivories carved in Bahia. Upstairs there are outstanding collections of fans, silver snuffboxes, and Chinese porcelain cups. Near the last of these are two uncomfortable chairs, identified from paintings as having belonged to the Marquês de Pombal. The museum also displays Portalegre's first car—a buggy—and unlovely collections of ceramics and 20th-century paintings.

Portalegre ✆ (045–)   **Where to Stay**

Three km northeast of town (350$00 in a taxi), on the road to the Serra de São Mamede, ★★★**Estalagem Quinta da Saude**, ✆ 22324, 🖂 27234 (*moderate*) provides rooms in bungalows, with basic glazed-wood furniture. The windows are small, with wooden shutters and without much of a view. The bathrooms are not always clean. However, the restaurant (*expensive*) is probably the best place to eat in or around Portalegre. It's very pleasantly decorated in the style of a grand mountain lodge, with a terracotta floor, plain leather chairs, bracket lamps and an open fire. A board of cured meats is produced as an appetizer. For dessert, try the *touçinho-do-céu*, a deliciously light eggy cake. *Open 12–11.30pm.*

The best place to stay in town is ★★**Residencial Alto Alentejo**, 59–63 Rua 19 de Junho, ✆ 22290 (*inexpensive*), a crisp and charming warren in the road opposite the cathedral, though some bathless rooms have very small windows. Bedrooms are furnished with jolly Alentejan furniture. Some of the baths do not have plugs, and so must be used as showers. This is preferable to ★★★**Hotel Dom João III**, Av. da Liberdade, ✆ 330192 (*moderate*), in the lower part of town, opposite the northeastern corner of the municipal garden, which is composed of large, ugly, empty spaces, and charmless rooms with vestibules. It smells of furniture polish. The enormous restaurant offers a dull menu.

For cheap accommodation, ★★**Pensão Nova**, 28–30 Rua 31 de Janeiro, ✆ 330812 (*cheap*), just up from the Tapestry Factory, is decrepit and basic, painted a gloomy greenish colour. The reception desk also serves nearby **Pensão**

São Pedro (*cheap*), which offers small but decent wallpapered rooms, in an extension of the family home.

Turismo de Habitação

Quinta das Varandas stands in the Serra de São Mamede Nature Park, ℰ 28883 (*moderate*), and is part of the oldest estate in this region. It is well maintained and undauntingly comfortable. The grounds are particularly inviting, with fountains and ponds in the Italian Romantic style.

At 650m above sea level, **Quinta da Fonte Fria**, Serra, ℰ 27575 (*inexpensive*), boasts fine views over the Serra de São Mamede and Marvão, and traces of a traditional Jewish dwelling.

Portalegre ℰ (045–)   *Eating Out*

See **Estalagem Quinta da Saude**, above.

O Abrigo, 74 Rua de Elvas, near the cathedral square, ℰ 331658 (*cheap*) has a very pleasant atmosphere, and the staff are particularly patient with children. The ceiling and lampshades are made of cork, and the windows look onto a pavement at foot-level. The *lulas de caldeirada* (squid stew) tastes better than it sounds. The Nisa cheese is very good too. *Closed Tues*. Opposite the bus station, **O Cortiço**, 17–21 Rua Dom Nuno Alvares Pereira, ℰ 22176 (*cheap*) is much more popular with the locals. The walls are lined with cork, and the food is good and solid. This is a wise choice for a filling meal if you're on a tight budget.

Around Portalegre

Alter do Chão

In the mid-18th century, Dom João V chose to locate his stud farm at Alter do Chão, on a plain 33km southeast of Portalegre and 46km north of Estremoz. Andalucian horses were imported, eventually producing the unique Lusitanian breed.

The operatic **castle** stands in the Praça da República, an irregular pentagon built by Dom Pedro in 1359. On the outside, its walls are a warm brown colour; on the inside, a variety of materials covers the stone. The courtyard is full of orange and cypress trees, ivy and pigeons. Opposite the castle, the *Misericórdia*'s weather vane is a plump, skipping rat. Across the Praça da República, marble columns support the twin cupolas of a fountain dated 1556. It's full of algae, but it makes a nice sound.

Castelo de Vide

Castelo de Vide

When a young couple eloped at the beginning of the 13th century, they galloped off to colonize a rocky mount which Dom Afonso II had given them. They called the place Terra de Vide (Land of the Vine), which changed to Castelo de Vide when the castle was built.

Dom Afonso inherited Castelo de Vide from his father and walled the town in 1280, sparking a conflict with his brother King Dom Dinis, which ended with the Infante exchanging this and other border castles for sites at Sintra and Ourém. The town was involved in another swap in the 14th century, when Dom Fernando gave Castelo de Vide to the Order of Christ in exchange for Castro Marim, thus relieving the townsmen of service as soldiers except in defence of their own fortress.

Castelo de Vide is an appealing little place for a brief visit; its dazzlingly white ancient cottages huddle around the castle, plunge down a hillslope and course up again in six parallel streets off the pillory square. So much dizzy plummeting has earned it the nickname 'Sintra of the Alentejo'. Castelo de Vide's higgledy-piggledy *Judiaria*, the Jewish 'ghetto', has remained intact.

Getting There

From Elvas and Portalegre, only one train daily is feasible: leaving at 8.32am and 9.24am respectively, connecting with the 10.40am from Torre das Vargens. Approximately five local buses run daily from Portalegre. From Marvão, change at Portagem. There are two buses a day from Lisbon.

Castelo de Vide © *(045–)*   **Tourist Information**

The **tourist office** in the pillory square, at 81 Rua de Bartolomeu Álvares da Santa, © 91361, next to the **bus stop,** is very unreliable, so get them to double check their information—particularly bus times. The **railway station,** © 901663, is 4km northeast of town.

Around the Town

The leafy **Praça Dom Pedro V**, at the centre of the lower town, offers a good view of the castle, and is surrounded by handsome houses including the **Torre Palácio**, which is now occupied by a hospital but in 1780 was the birthplace of the statesman Mouzinho da Silva. The church of Santa Maria da Sevesa backs onto the Praça; at the front of the church, the downhill road diminishes as it approaches an irregularly shaped little square in which stands the charmingly worn and uneven **Fonte da Vila**. This 16th-century marble lozenge shelters beneath a columned tabernacle, and once constituted the social centre of the town. The water is delicious, and medicinal for diabetes, and kidney and bone complaints.

An alley rises steeply towards Portugal's oldest synagogue, lined with modest 16th- and 17th-century houses. Each of these has two doorways, one for entry and one for commercial transactions. Some are plain, others are ornamented by stone studs. The excellent view of the town from the top of the alley stretches beyond, to Marvão's rocky hilltop.

From the outside, the **synagogue** looks like any other house. The interior too is plain, but contains a tabernacle with round hollows for sacred oil and a shelf for sacred scriptures. The floor of a room immediately below the place of worship has been hollowed to a depth of about 3m; it was once lined with cork and used for storing cereals. There may have been a tunnel from the synagogue or a house nearby, which emerged outside the castle walls: an escape route at the time of the Inquisition.

The Afonsine Ordinances of 1446 ruled that Portuguese Jews must live in districts set apart for them in cities, into which they were literally locked early each evening. They had their own courts and their own judges, though they were still ultimately responsible to the king; they had to wear a distinctive costume, and Jewish men were forbidden to enter alone the house of an unmarried Christian woman.

In and Around the Judiaria

The Judiaria is a tangled mass of tiny streets at the rear of the synagogue, nestling under lichenous terracotta roofs, with minuscule windows and bulging sides. Masses of plants are potted—with gross irony—in tins which held pig lard, and Friday is laundry and bath day, to be clean for church on Sunday. In the Rua de Santo Antónia, on the very edge of this area, tenants in the unplastered former barracks pay the council a nominal rent of 1$00 per year. The former prison is now a centre for handicrafts called **O Ouriço** (The Hedgehog), where artisans knit, stitch and weave wall-hangings using any material available—even dried pigs' intestines. An old man with wrinkled eyelids makes toy ballerinas and horses. He's chalked numerous dirty pictures onto the walls around him, but keeps his carved masterwork under wraps: a naked man and woman who face one another, joined and unjoined by his pendulum-propelled organ.

The **castle**, completed in 1365, is none too inspiring (*open 9–12.30 and 2–7; only open until 5.30 in winter*), since the keep was mutilated by an explosion in 1705. Its most interesting feature is a 12m-tall brick cylinder, popularly believed to be a funerary chamber. But no skeletons have been found, and it was probably a store-room for munitions, or a lookout post with impressive views of the Serra de São Paulo. In 1630 the household servants of Castelo de Vide contributed funds to build the small **church of Senhora da Alegria** (Our Lady of Joy) within the castle walls, entirely tiled with polychrome *azulejos*.

In the late 17th century the little church of **Senhora da Penha** was built 3km south of town, near some donkey tracks which appeared in the granite when a shepherd invoked the Virgin Mary and she arrived riding the animal.

Castelo de Vide © (045–)   ***Where to Stay and Eating Out***

★★★**Hotel Sol e Serra**, Estrada de São Vicente, © 901301, ✆ 901373 (*expensive–moderate*), overlooking the medium-sized Jardim Grande, is short on character, though there's plenty of space. An electric organ plays ice-rink music during dinner in the dining room, which is sparsely hung with chains like a timid dungeon. The menu is rather ordinary. At the upper side of the municipal garden, ★★★**Residencial Casa do Parque**, 37 Av. da Aramanha, ✆ 901250, 🖅 901228 (*inexpensive*), is a very nice and well-furnished little place: the narrow entranceway has a fireplace, copper kettles, leather chairs and oil paintings. The service is good, if you speak Portuguese, and guestrooms are charming. Some come complete with a beautiful lace tablecloth and a crucifix. Unfortunately the bathrooms tend to be cramped. The restaurant is OK: the *lombo à chef* is your best bet. **Residencial Isabelinha**, Largo do Paço Novo, ✆ 901896 (*inexpensive*), is run by the same people and strikes a more modern note by featuring air-conditioned, rather functional rooms, complete with television.

Round the corner, **Residencial Xinxel**, 5 Largo do Paço Novo, ✆ 901406 (*cheap*)—signposted, set back from the Av. da Aramanha on the upper side of the park—somehow manages a family atmosphere despite the bald rooms with lino floors and bedhead units. Perhaps this is because it's an extension of the proprietor's home, with rooms leading off a communal sitting room. Everything is very clean. ★**Pensão Cantinho Particular**, 9 Rua Miguel Bombarda, ✆ 901151 (*cheap*), in a street just off the main plaza, is the most welcoming place in town—a very friendly, though slightly dilapidated, family-run hotel with attached restaurant.

Marvão

Nineteen km northeast of Portalegre, 12km southeast of Castelo de Vide, and 10km from the Spanish border, Marvão is a medieval walled village of 1000 souls in the Serra de Marvão, built on a steep rock escarpment at an altitude of 860m. It overlooks a barren scene of rough beauty: to the north, south and east stretch endless, almost volcanic, hummocky rock outcrops; to the west lie dark and dusty reds and greens.

The village is enchanted—a muddle of narrow cobbled streets, with very white dwellings built around unexpected shoulders of rock and wide flagstone steps. Granite window casements are mottled with lichen, house numbers are stencilled above the doorways. Plant pots are made from the bark of cork trees, and bags of hearth ash are left on doorsteps, waiting to be collected. Swallows dip in and out of the village, and kites fly above. Marvão appears to have sidestepped several centuries. A variety of houses may be rented under the *Turismo de Habitação* scheme.

History

The Romans knew Marvão as Herminio Minor, since when its location has made it a tough nut to crack. In 715 the Christian Visigoths inhabiting the mount were slaughtered by the Moors, who resettled the place two generations later, under the order of the Lord of Coimbra, Emir Maruan (meaning pleasant or mild), after whom it was named. Dom Sancho II granted it a municipal franchise in 1226, determining that one-third of the men of the borough were to garrison the castle; the rest were to participate in the annual raiding parties into enemy territory.

Marvão–Beirã **railway station** is 13km north of town, near the Spanish border. Very infrequent, indirect trains run from Lisbon, Elvas and Portalegre. Buses are also infrequent. Theoretically, two run daily from Portalegre, making a day trip possible, but the service is erratic, so it is best to check.

© (045–) **Tourist Information**

The **tourist office** is in the Rua Dr. Matos Magalhães, © 93104, (*open 9–12.30 and 2–6*). During the summer another office functions at the Portagem. The **bus stop** is just outside the town walls.

At the northern tip of Marvão, the rugged **castle** seems to grow out of the natural rock. Walls swirl upwards, ever less penetrable. Dom Dinis ordered the construction of the keep *c.* 1300, incorporating a tinkling cistern within the walls, which held half a year's supply of water. Villagers used to play handball on its roof, peace permitting.

The closest building to the castle is the church of Santa Maria, which houses the good little **municipal museum**. Its most interesting section covers popular medicines and prayers. There are also mannequins in traditional dress, Palaeolithic remains, some cannon cleaners about 3m long, and Dom Manuel's charter.

About 300m down Marvão's access road, the **monastery of N.S. da Estrêla** (Our Lady of the Star) takes its name from an image of the Virgin which was found by shepherds guided by a shooting star. The sculpture had been buried by frightened Christian Visigoths as they fled the Moors, and it is popularly believed to protect Marvão from unfriendly armies. The Franciscan monastery was founded in 1448, but revamped by the Bishop of Portalegre in 1772; now it houses the *Misericórdia* hospital. The key to the church is kept opposite the church door, straight through from the entrance to the monastery. The side chapel contains a splendid marble altarpiece, and the 18th-century *azulejos* in the sacristy have been mis-mounted into a strange collage.

Marvão © (045–) **Where to Stay and Eating Out**

The **Pousada de Santa Maria**, 7 Rua 24 de Janeiro, © 93201, ✆ 93440 (*category CH*), is one of the most enjoyable *pousadas* in Portugal, combining civilized living with typically Portuguese furniture and hospitality. There are several reception rooms with log fires, and nicely detailed décor. The nine cosy bedrooms have parquet floors and wonderful views of the bleak rocky hills and plains around Marvão. The dining room is wrapped around the sitting room, taking full advantage of the view. The service is attentive, the plates are hot, and the food is surprisingly cheap for so grand a setting. The menu features lots of local specialities —the Alentejo soup is particularly delicious. **Pensão D. Dinis,** Rua Dr. Matos Magalhães, © 93736, ✆ 93236 (*moderate*), is not really a *pension*: it's simply furnished, with solid wood furniture and spacious bathrooms. The dining room is small and friendly.

It's possible to rent several typically furnished houses within the town walls of Marvão, some of which offer excellent value. All bookings must be made through the tourist office in Marvão, © 93104 (*open 9–12.30 and 2–6*); they will let you know where to collect the house keys. Prices are the same in summer and in winter, when the houses will be cold, despite the gas heaters. Recently many *Turismo de Habitação* houses in the nearby countryside have been closed down. There are plans afoot to open more—contact the tourist office in Marvão for the latest details.

Estremoz

The walled market town of Estremoz climbs up a hillslope, 57km south of Portalegre and 44km northeast of Évora, rising above the undulating plains. Groves of holm oaks and cork oaks, orchards and vineyards thrive in the fertile, well-watered countryside, which includes extensive deposits of pure white marble in its limestone base.

The town blazon is composed of stars (*estrelas*) and a lupin tree (*tremoceiro*), the two elements said to lie behind the name 'Estremoz'. The old fortified hilltop settlement centres on the castle keep. From there, stepped streets lined with low, whitewashed houses run down to the modern heart, the huge, sandy Rossio Marquês de Pombal. Some houses are numbered with stencils, below which women stand and gossip at their two-tiered 'stable' doors, or scrub their marble doorsteps.

History

Three kings—Sancho II, Afonso III and Dinis—built the castle, whose plain keep is known as the Tower of the Three Crowns. Dom Dinis came to Estremoz in 1281 to negotiate for the hand of Princess Isabel of Aragon, subsequently constructing a palace to put her in. Their wedding celebration mortified conservatives when, for the first time in court history, male and female courtiers danced together.

Its strategic location and royal palace boosted the military and political importance of Estremoz, which became one of the key castles in the Alentejo. Dom Pedro I lived here until his death in 1367, and in 1380 Dom Fernando inhabited the tower, shortly before his wife Leonor Teles installed her lover, the Count of Andeiro, in the siesta room. Estremoz later served as a redoubt in the military struggle against Leonor Teles and her Castilian allies, and in the War of Restoration. Vaubanesque fortifications were erected at the end of the 17th century. During the Civil War, the town was staunchly Miguelite, its most grizzly moment coming in July 1833, three days after the liberal victory in Lisbon, when 39 liberal prisoners, including a child of six, were butchered with an axe on the castle's staircase landing.

Getting There

Estremoz station was closed in 1990. This means that each of the two infrequent train routes from Lisbon requires two changes: from Lisbon's Terreiro do Paço, change at Barreiro after ½hr, take a train to Évora (2¼hrs) and change there for the bus to Estremoz (1¼hr). Alternatively, depart Lisbon's Sta. Apolónia (early morning), change at Entroncamento after 1½hrs, and catch a train for Portalegre (2¼hrs), from where a bus runs to Estremoz (1½hrs).

Express buses run infrequently from Lisbon (3hrs), via Setúbal (2¼hrs), and Coimbra. There are more frequent services from Elvas and Arraiolos (each ¾hr), and local Belos buses run frequently from Évora.

Estremoz ☎ (068–)　　　　　　　　　　　　　　　　*Tourist Information*

The **tourist office** is at 26 Largo da República, ☎ 332 2071 (*open weekdays 9.30–1 and 3–6.30*), in a little square off the Rossio Marquês de Pombal; if it's closed, try the tourist hut in the Rossio itself, which is populated by very helpful people. The **bus station**, ☎ 22282 for RN Express, is in the Rossio. The station itself is closed at weekends, so buy your ticket on the bus.

The Castle Keep

Estremoz is dominated by the sober grey castle keep of 1258. It rises 27m above the hilltop, offering huge views—on a clear day you can see Portalegre, Évora and even Palmela—and dizzy glimpses through holes for pouring boiling lead and olive oil. Most of the castle and palace were destroyed by an explosion in the gunpowder room, in 1698. Dom João V restored the latter as a depository for his collection of 40,000 weapons, which were stolen by the French in 1808. The palace is now a *pousada.*

The Sainted Queen Isabel

The **chapel of St Isabel** occupies the little room in the castle where the sainted queen expired in 1336. It is officially closed to viewing but if arranged in advance, possibly the lady from the castle will look kindly and provide the key; ask at the tourist office. Queen Isabel was killed by the journey from Compostela to Estremoz via Coimbra—11 years after the death of her husband, Dom Dinis—having given away most of her income to the poor. She had kept herself and her ladies constantly at work embroidering and weaving, breaking from their routine on Fridays in Lent to wash the feet of 12 poor men, 'the most leprous they could find', according to the chronicler Ruy de Pina.

Dona Isabel was an able peacemaker, mediating between Dom Dinis and his legitimate son Prince Dom Afonso, who became obsessed with the idea that his father would grant the succession to one of his seven bastard half-brothers. It was Dona Luísa de Gusmão, wife of Dom João IV, who founded the chapel in 1659, a time when Dona Isabel's aptitudes as a peacemaker were sorely missed. Now it is lined with 18th-century *azulejos* depicting scenes from the life of the queen, including the conversion of bread into roses: suspicious that his wife was ferreting away her bread for the poor, Dom Dinis asked the queen to drop her skirt. The bread she had been carrying in it was transformed into roses, and Dom Dinis couldn't find a crumb.

Around the Castle Square

In the square at the foot of the keep, the **Igreja Matriz de Santa Maria** was commissioned by Dom Sebastian in the second half of the 16th century. It's usually kept locked, though the building is used for radio broadcasting—try midday on Sunday. The unusual interior is square but for the chancel, with irregularly spaced columns, elegant marble pulpits, and faded frescoes.

The **municipal museum** (*open 10–12 and 2–6; closed Mon and holidays*) occupies an early 17th-century almshouse on the south side of the castle square. Its collection of decorative Estremoz pottery figures illustrates the humour and consistent style of this peasant art, depicting barbers, milkmen, musicians and the like. There's a nice figure of Spring, dressed in a tutu and wearing a tiara of petals and an arc of flowers. In a workshop at the back of the museum, identical twins named Arlindo and Afonso propagate the town's reputation for ornamental pots. The medieval stone discs found in the cemetery at Évora Monte served as signposts, depicting a pair of scissors to advertise a tailor's shop and a pot to advertise a pottery. Upstairs, there are carved horns, rustic furniture, an Alentejan kitchen and some guns. Ask at the museum for the key to its annexe in the former communal granary, hung with modern pictures of variable quality. Next to this is the **Gallery of the Audience Hall**, a Gothic loggia which is all that remains of the 13th-century establishment, except for the keep. The blazon of Estremoz is embedded on the gallery's wall.

It's worth walking round to the quiet, grassy southwestern side of the upper part of town, where the medieval defensive walls run parallel with the 17th-century walls.

The Lower Town

In the lower part of town, the **Town Hall** fronts the south side of the tree-lined Rossio Square, occupying a convent founded by the Archbishop of Évora in 1698; visitors are welcome to look at the excellent *azulejos* of hunting scenes which line its broad staircase. On the east side of the Rossio, facing the castle, the two-roomed **Museu Rural** (*open 10–12 and 3–6; closed Mon and holidays*) is full of curiosities, including bamboo sheaths worn on the fingers of one hand to prevent them being chopped by the scythe held in the other, and large carved horns which stored fieldworkers' cheese and olives. The **church of São Francisco** stands adjacent to the north side of the Rossio. The Gothic structure of three naves and some skew arches dates back to 1213, but the only noteworthy fixtures are a 17th-century tree of Jesse and the tomb of Vasco Esteves Gato, installed in 1401, accompanied by winged angels on bended knee. A water tank edged with marble ripples opposite the entrance to the church, grandly named the **Lago do Gadanha** (the Lake of the Scythe), after the tool held by the statue of Time or Neptune. The **Museum of Agriculture** stands in the Rua Serpa Pinto, which leads off from the *Lago*. Filled with machines, yokes, ploughs and saddles, it is of almost no interest to the non-specialist. Likewise the **C. P. Museum**, near the old station, which exhibits an assortment of trains.

There are **marble quarries** on the edge of town, at the junction with the Elvas road. From here marble is sent to factories nearby to be broken down, and then on to Sintra to be fashioned and polished. The factories are not open to the public, but near the quarries Manuel Véstias (Av. de Santo António, details from the tourist office) has devised a small display.

The Saturday Market in the Rossio Square

The Estremoz market is typical of Alto Alentejo. Vendors arrive in the early light carrying leeks, turnips, maybe a rabbit in a basket, blossom picked from a bush. They lay their goods on hessian mats and sit quietly beside them. Some sell oranges sorted into seven sizes, others crates of hard little cheeses, like white ice-hockey pucks. The men stand together outside the Café Alentejano, pivoting on their heels, dispensing firm, single handshakes, raising a felt hat or a cap. And then, at about midday, everything unsold is packed away, and taken home again.

Estremoz✆ *(068–)*   **Where to Stay**

Installed in the former royal palace, the **Pousada da Rainha Santa Isabel**, ✆ 22618 (*category CH; reservations necessary*), is the most splendid and regal of the country's *pousadas*. Typically, the entrance hall is spacious without being cavernous; charming wooden baroque figures hold snakes for inspection, and in the reception room a statue of the Virgin clasps the baby Jesus to her heart. Don't take the elevator unless you have to—the wide marble staircase and its tile dado are a great treat. Many of the 23 bedrooms have canopied beds, and distant views. The service is snooty though efficient. The restaurant is a hall fragmented by pillars and arches, lit by chandeliers and equipped with baronial chairs. The food is disappointing.

Casa Miguel José, 8 Trav. de Levada, ✆ 22326 (*cheap*)—near the post office—has dark corridors, and solid rooms, with flowers and bits of lace and patterned bedside rugs. At ★★**Residencial Carvalho**, 27 Largo da República, ✆ 22712 (*very cheap–cheap*), windows don't always open, so the ants can't get out, but the water is nice and hot and the furniture decent. ★★**Residencial Mateus**, 39–41 Rua do Almeida, ✆ 222262 (*cheap*) offers honest rooms in the old quarter.

Turismo de Habitação

Monte Dos Pensamentos, ✆ 333166 (*moderate*)—3km out of Estremoz on the Lisbon road, turn right before the service station—is a very pretty country villa with four large rooms each decorated with splendid beds, marble fireplaces, antique screens, Arraiolos carpets and colourful plates. Indeed, plates run riot on all the walls but the effect is cheery—they lift the heaviness of the dining room and complement the airiness of the sitting room.

Estremoz✆ *(068–)*   **Eating Out**

Near the Rossio, the gentle proprietor of **Arlequim**, 15 Rua Dr. Gomes Resende, Jr., ✆ 23726 (*cheap*) is trying hard to keep his attractive, whitewashed restaurant a local haunt, but finding it difficult; the simple food, such as fried plaice with rice, and his French wife's stylish use of local products consistently appeals to visitors. At **Águias d'Ouro**, in the

Rossio, ℂ 333326 (*moderate*) diners sit on uncomfortable cuboid chairs and eat dishes such as *peito de vitela* (calf's heart), served by incongruous black-tied waiters. For a quick snack, **Zé S Pub** (*cheap*), next to the Lago do Gadanha, serves delicious 'toast Alentejana' (ham with a potent mixture of garlic and herbs), popular with a young, cigarette-smoking, hair-flicking, football-watching crowd.

Around Estremoz

Évora Monte

The Estremoz–Évora road passes the western edge of the Serra da Ossa. The one-street village of Évora Monte stands at 474m on a steep hill planted with olive trees and holm oaks, poised with enormous views of the green and gold flatlands; it is said that on a clear day you can see the width of the country. The place is full of idle cats and dogs. Even the bees are drowsy.

The Concession of Évora Monte was signed here on behalf of the warring brothers Dom Pedro and Dom Miguel, in 1834. The latter was permitted to retain his personal belongings, and was granted an annual pension from the government. In return, he agreed to leave Portugal within 15 days, and promised never to return.

Getting There

Buses run infrequently from Évora and Estremoz.

Dom Dinis' **castle** at Évora Monte collapsed during the earthquake of 1531, having provided a home for the contrite fourth Duke of Bragança, who retired here in 1512 after murdering his Spanish wife in a fit of jealousy. Dom João III rebuilt the castle almost immediately, with four massive cylindrical towers. It has recently borne its most disheartening assault—from the restorers. Now it is faced with vanilla-coloured cement.

Évora Monte ℂ (068–)   ***Where to Stay***
Turismo de Habitação

 At **Monte da Fazenda**, ℂ 95172 (*moderate–inexpensive*) a dazzling white and blue exterior masks a mellow interior which is simply and elegantly furnished with pale, wooden furniture and white lace bedspreads. The house offers three apartments each with its own entrance, two rooms and a swimming pool.

Borba

Borba is a small town nestled into the northern slopes of the diminutive Serra de Borba, and serves as a base for marble quarrying at Monte Claros, producing stone of a quality to rival that of Tuscany. Borba makes an important contribution to Portugal's marble exports (in which the country ranks second in the world). The marble has brought modest wealth, though there are no longer opportunities for striking it rich overnight—until the 18th century, emeralds were found in the neighbourhood. In Borba, everything within reason is made of marble—doorsteps, cornerstones, stairs, fireplaces, the municipal crazy paving, even the urinals at the bus station.

The late 16th-century **church of São Bartolomeu** is the only building of note: its treasures are marble, including the altars, tables, porticos, fonts, balustrades, basins and stairs. Rising above all this is a splendid vaulted Renaissance-style ceiling with medallions and crude paintings of religious scenes. The **Fonte das Bicas** is a stylish triangular-shaped fountain carved in the white marble of Montes Claros in 1781, bearing Dona Maria's royal blazon. Among the date palms behind the fountain, two brightly painted railway carriages now house a cramped but curious bar.

Vila Viçosa

Four km southeast of Borba, the tidy, white little town of Vila Viçosa stands on a plain at the base of the eastern slopes of the Serra de Borba. The grid-patterned streets are lined with orange trees, whose fruits unload themselves unceremoniously onto the pavements. Most of the medieval houses which surrounded Dom Dinis' castle of 1270 were torn down in 1663, to make way for defences against the Spanish, who besieged the town two years later.

History

Vila Viçosa is belittled by the massive palace of the Dukes of Bragança. The town had been the property of the first duke; for two generations his heirs neglected their Alentejan estates, preferring to reside in Guimarães, Bragança, Chaves and Barcelos. In the reign of Dom João III, Dom Jaime, the melancholic fourth duke, began the aggrandizement of Vila Viçosa; in 1501 he set in train 101 years of construction on the palace. He also equipped the house with its first malevolent ghosts: suspicious of an affair, he stabbed to death his duchess and her page in front of the whole household. Happier events were celebrated with bullfights in the Terreiro do Paço, close enough for the ladies of the palace to smell blood, with comedies, masques and fireworks, with Italian acrobats on stilts, with dancing to the music of trumpets, kettle drums and wood-wind instruments called shawms. One room of the palace is still called the *Sala da Cabra-cega* (the room of blind man's buff). Perhaps to compensate for the loss of dignity entailed in one such game, trumpets sounded in the ducal palace every time His Grace lifted his cup to take a drink of water, as reported by an Italian cardinal visiting Portugal in 1571.

In 1580 Philip II of Spain trampled on the ducal claim to the throne. Portuguese resentment burst 60 years later, and virtually forced João IV, the eighth duke, to cease composing music, dismount his beloved hunter and take the throne. This marked the beginning of the decline of the palace, which was stripped to furnish the Paço da Ribeira in Lisbon. Subsequent dukes ruled Portugal until 1908, occasionally coming here to hunt in the *tapada*. Dom Carlos left Vila Viçosa one morning in February and was shot dead that afternoon in Lisbon. His successor Dom Manuel II frequented this palace until he was toppled by the Revolution of 1910.

The roads around Vila Viçosa pass meadows and eucalyptus woods, cacti and elegant white egrets. Local buses run from Estremoz or from Évora (1hr).

© *(068–)* **Tourist Information**

The **tourist office** is in the Praça da República, 881101. The **bus station** is in the Rua André Gomes Pereira: to get to the Praça da República, walk along the Rua Dr. António José d'Almeida, almost opposite the bus station, and to get from there to the Terreiro do Paço, continue along the Rua Florbela Espança.

The Ducal Palace

Open 9.30–1 and 2–6, 2–5 in winter; closed Sun, Mon, and holidays; guided tour lasting one hour.

On the northwestern edge of town, the road from Borba passes the large square Terreiro do Paço, which fronts the plain and very, very long marble façade of the Ducal Palace. The entrance is in the middle of the edifice.

Within, most of the furniture is dull and dates from the late 19th century: the notable pieces were removed to Lisbon, where they were destroyed in the earthquake of 1755, or to Brazil, in the train of Dom João VI. The ceiling of the **Sala dos Duques** is covered with paintings of the dukes, similarly dressed, right back to the first duke and his immediate ancestor, Dom João I. Some of them may have been painted by Quillard, a pupil of Watteau, at the invitation of Dom João V in the 18th century. Good 18th-century French tapestries hang in the **Sala das Virtudes**, one from Aubusson and two from Gobelins, depicting the misfortunes of Porus. But the really exceptional tapestry is the portrayal of Alexander the Great in the **Sala de Hercules**, worked with rich tones in Brussels in the 16th or 17th century. In the porcelain room, each nationality is allocated a separate cupboard.

The private apartments are more revealing; they are kept as they were when Dom Carlos and his wife Marie-Amélie left for Lisbon. His uniforms hang in his cupboard, her knick-knacks cover her dressing table. They took sufficient pleasure in their food to equip the kitchen with 2200kg of copper pots and pans.

A simple cloister of 1505 leads through to the **Armoury**, which has a good collection of armour and *epées*. The stables have been converted into a **Coach Museum** (*separate admission*) housing interminable lines of the things.

Around the Terreiro do Paço

The irregular **Convento das Chagas** stands at right angles to the palace, in the Terreiro do Paço. It was founded in 1530 by Dona Joana de Mendonça, the second wife of Dom Jaime—presumably as a bolt-hole in case her husband attempted to dispatch her as he had dispatched her predecessor. Recently restored, it contains the tombs of the duchesses. Since 1677, the tombs of the dukes have been supported by stone lions behind the sober façade of the church of the **Mosteiro dos Agostinhos**, opposite the palace in the Terreiro do Paço. If it's closed, ask at the guard's lodge through a gate to the left.

The fourth side of the Terreiro borders the **Tapada** (Chase), which is surrounded by a wall some 18km long, but no longer reverberates with the snorts of deer and wild boar. The stags' antlers have furnished the ducal dining room. (Dom João, the eighth duke and future king, had a penchant for more exotic animals. For the Infanta's birthday in 1634, he provided a tremendous lion which fought and killed a bull. He sent the pope a rhinoceros for his birthday, but the unhappy creature broke a hole in the side of the ship that was carrying it, sinking the vessel and drowning itself with most of the crew.)

A little way along the main road leading north from the Terreiro stands the **Porta dos Nós** (Gate of Knots), an inelegant example of Manueline whimsy, like the entrance to a dude ranch.

The Castle

In the other direction, the Avenida Duque de Bragança runs uphill from the Terreiro past the Castle. There's not a lot to look at, other than the drawbridge, and the dull vaulted *Sala dos Duques*, for the dukes lived in the castle before the palace was built. The castle walls enclose a tiny, picturesque settlement, with charming wrought-iron streetlamp fittings and the church of **Nossa Senhora da Conceição**. Its 15th-century structure was altered in 1572 and in 1870, when the façade and single tower were revamped. The chapel to the right of the chancel contains *azulejos* by Policarpo de Oliveira Bernardes (1695–1776), whose design is much weaker than his father's work on the Lóios chapel in Évora. The caged pews were occupied by Dominican monks, who may have appreciated the curious offertory box, which is topped with an image of the Virgin and Baby Jesus standing in a cloud, flanked by the sun and the moon. A 16th-century granite **pillory** stands outside the castle walls, looking like a censer on a column.

The Avenida Bento de Jesus runs from the castle to the Praça da República, at the end of which stands the beautifully symmetrical 17th-century **church of São Bartholomeu** which is of no special interest—though the sacristan will be happy to show you the bell tower. He keeps half a bottle of port there.

Vila Viçosa ✆ *(068–)*   **Where to Stay**

There is no hotel accommodation in Vila Viçosa, although private rooms can be arranged through the tourist office and there are a couple of good *Turismo de Habitação* properties.

Turismo de Habitação

Casa dos Arcos, 16 Praça de Martim Afonso de Sousa, ✆ 98518 (*moderate*), dates from the 18th century—its graceful lines ensure the tourist office's classification as a building of public interest. It boasts splendid period decoration and a charming welcome.

Casa de Peixihos, Melo e Faro Passanha, ✆ 98472 (*moderate*) is part of a farm estate, situated about 500m from Vila Viçosa. It has a mercifully cool setting, amidst a grove of orange trees. The six rooms are comfortably furnished with marble scattered throughout.

Framar, 35 Praça da República, Ⓒ 98158 (*cheap*) sells marble pestles and mortars on street level. The restaurant above is deep and wide, with a parquet floor, and is enlivened by a large mural painted on wood. The *ensopado de cabrito a Alentejana* (kid stew) is not bad.

The **Old Bleu Tavern**, 51 Largo Mousinho de Albuquerque, Ⓒ 98882, almost opposite the bus station, is an unexpected psychedelic café: a whole tree stands in the front room, while patrons sit on leather-covered tree stumps. The sound system does justice to the hamburgers, which may be eaten in the back room on plastic chairs amid much plastic ivy.

The unnamed **café** at 70 Rua Gomez Jardim (*cheap*) is a whimsical place with a poster of Linda Lusardi (clothed) in the bar and the hundreds of empty bottles lining the walls, testifying to the place's popularity. The back rooms are slung with fox skins and ivy clambers the low arches. An undiluted slice of local life.

Elvas

Elvas is a busy hilltop frontier town of 15,000 souls, 12km west of the Spanish border and 42km east of Estremoz, close to the southward curve of the River Guadiana.

Within its star-shaped fortifications, Elvas is charming, cobbled, and constantly aware that it is a frontier town: if you look remotely foreign, local salesmen talk to you in Spanish and quote the price of port in *pesetas*. But the modern settlement outside the town walls is dull; the transition is marked by a ring of thick and bushy orange trees. Five hundred years of Moorish occupation has left street names like Alcaiza, Alcamim, Almocovar and Alcáçova, and numerous arches to pass beneath. The monuments are unlikely to detain visitors for long: of the many churches, only one is outstanding (N.S. da Consolação).

Elvas is famous for its candied plums, which are more or less gooey from year to year. Cheap accommodation is scarce, and the town's restaurants are none too inspiring, especially if you don't like fish.

History

Its strategic importance earned Elvas the sobriquet '*chave do reyno*' (key to the kingdom), and rivalry with the defences of Badajoz across the border ensured its heavy fortification. It was recaptured from the Moors in 1230, and subsequently hosted interminable peace and marriage treaties with Spain, right through from the peace treaty between Dom Dinis and his brother Dom Afonso in 1292 to the wedding of the Prince of Brazil, the future King Dom José, to Dona Mariana Vitória in 1729. Philip II of Spain set up court here for a few months in 1581, but during the War of Restoration, in 1644, a garrison of just 2000 men withstood a nine-day siege by Spanish troops who supported his grandson.

Specialists in bastioned military architecture reinforced the stronghold and added a cistern of 2200 cubic metres, capable of withstanding four months' siege. In 1659 Spanish attempts to end the war hinged on their attempt to take Elvas, whose garrison had been decimated by an epidemic to 1000 men. With the help of fog and a relief army from

Estremoz, the Spanish were forced to abandon their encampment and 15,000 muskets. Already the strongest fortress in the country, Elvas spawned complementary works: four forts in the 17th century, including the Forte de Santa Luzia; and the massive Forte de N.S. da Graça, in the later 18th century. Wellington used Elvas as a base prior to the bloody sieges of Badajoz in 1811 and 1812.

Getting There

Trains from Lisbon are infrequent (5¾hrs, change at Entroncamento and/or Torre das Vargens), as are trains from Marvão-Beirã (3¼hrs), via Castelo de Vide (3hrs); change at Torre das Vargens from both, continuing to Elvas, via Portalegre (¾hr). RN Express **buses** run infrequently from Lisbon (4½hrs), Évora (1¾hrs) and Estremoz (¾hr).

Elvas ✆ (068–)   Tourist Information

The **tourist office** is in the Praça da República, ✆ 622236 (*open 9–5.30 including weekends*), beside the **bus station** (✆ 622144 for RN Express). A shuttle bus service runs to and from the **railway station**, ✆ 622816, 3km down the Campo Maior road.

Festivals

The **Festas do Senhor da Piedade** and the **Feira de São Mateús** take place from 20 to 25 September. The fair is mostly agricultural, but there are bullfights and riding competitions, displays of folk dancing, and handicrafts on sale. The first and last days of the fair coincide with religious processions.

The Cathedral and Around

A road leads uphill from the *pousada* and through the **Porta de Olivença**, of 1685, where it becomes the Rua de Olivença. The third turning to the right leads to the unimportant **Museu de António Tomás Pires**, installed in a Jesuit college whose most interesting feature is the portico of 1715 topped by a cupola tiled with zesty geometric *azulejos*. The roomful of *artesanato* is a redeeming feature within, with firedogs, stamps for impressing owners' marks on loaves of bread in the communal bakery, carved horns, and a local speciality—handcut paper doilies.

The Rua de Olivença continues uphill to the Praça da República, at the upper end of which gapes the squat **cathedral** (*closed Tues*), surmounted by a weathervane which is either a devil, or a cherub holding a mace, and enlivened by porcine gargoyles. Elvas was the seat of a bishopric 1570–1882. Francisco de Arruda designed the building *c.* 1517, but it was not completed until the end of the century, and suffered renovation in the 17th and 18th centuries. The Manueline side portals remained unaltered—the south portal, to the left, is the least eroded of the two. Within, the architecture is more sober than the tourist guide, whose fiery breath rises into the conical dome. The altars in the lateral naves were carved of gray and white Estremoz marble in the 18th century, while the retable in the chancel was painted on canvas. The handsome organ is dated 1777 and signed by the Italian Ordoni.

Behind the cathedral stands the fantastic octagonal **church of N.S. da Consolação**, which looks insipid from the outside but is thrilling within. Diogo de Torralva prepared a rough draft for its design in 1543, basing its shape on that of a nearby Templars' hermitage which had been destroyed three years previously. The church feels pagan—at any rate, worshippers would be distracted by the beauty of its ornamentation and proportion. Marble pillars support the cupola, which is decorated with blue and yellow *azulejos* of 1659 right up to the lantern, as are the walls and ceiling. Note the emblem of the Dominican order.

Beside the octagonal church, a recently restored 16th-century **pillory** is covered by spirals of plate-sized 'buttons', like a west African ju-ju. The flippant belvedere behind this is built on the arch of one of the former **Portas do Alcácer**. Passing under the arch, turning left at the Alcáçova church and right at the T-junction, one arrives at the delightful **Rua das Beatas**, in which little dwellings bulge irregularly, and plants flourish. The castle is at the end of this road.

The Castle and the Town Walls

Based on Romano-Moorish foundations, the **castle** (*open 9.30–12.30 and 2.30–7; closed Thurs and at 5 in the winter*) was remodelled both by Dom Dinis and Dom João II, who commissioned the tower. Its exterior is irregular and functional. The inside feels charmingly lived-in, with catapult balls ringing the flowerbed. The structure incorporates the 700-year-old governor's residence, which now displays an atmospheric 'typical' Alentejan kitchen and a bedroom complete with drinking gourds, presumably for nightcaps.

The most interesting route back to the centre of town is via the little roads which run along the town walls, past the **church of the Ordem Terceira de São Francisco** of 1761. The small cemetery contains the graves of Englishmen killed attempting to capture Badajoz in 1811.

The town wall continues past the barracks to the sweeping baroque façade of the **church of São Domingos**, which was founded in 1267 but drastically rearranged in the 18th century. The town walls continue yet further, past the Porta de Oliveira to the Porta de São Vicente, where stands the little marble **Fonte da Misericórdia**, dated 1622: a pavilion shelters Dom Sancho sitting on his steed, which is borne atop various human-faced fish.

the Aqueduct of Amoreira

Outside the Town Walls

Passing through the town gate, the multi-storey **Aqueduct of Amoreira** stands to the right. It was built between 1529 and 1622 and paid for by the country's first royal water tax. The town's blazon, a plumed warrior on horseback carrying a standard, is etched on a panel on the aqueduct. It commemorates Gil

Anes, who trotted over to Badajoz in 1438 and stole its standard. The Spaniards chased him back to Elvas—and round and round the town walls, for his compatriots had closed the gates on him. When the Spaniards caught him, they deep-fried him in a cauldron of oil. As he died, he cried in earnest, 'The man dies but his fame endures.'

The extraordinary **Museum of Ex-Votos** (*open 10–12 and 2.30–6.30*) is attached to the unusually named church of Senhor Jesus da Piedade, a 10- or 15-minute walk to the southwest of town—the custom of naming Jesus with an attribute in the same way as the Virgin may be unique to Portugal. There are five rooms full of ex-voto offerings, old and new—paintings, embroidery, photographs, wax images and, most movingly, crutches.

Elvas ☎ (068–)   ***Where to Stay***

The **Pousada de Santa Luzia**, Av. de Badajoz, ☎ 622194, ✉ 622127 (*category C*)—outside the town walls, at the junction of the continuation of Estrada Nacional 4 and the road to Ajuda—is an unprepossessing building with attractively coordinated bedrooms featuring gay Alentejan furniture and trellised tiles in the bathrooms. The annexe is full of antiques. Convivial public rooms include a popular, mellow bar. The striplit L-shaped dining room can be expanded to accommodate conferences, and suffers accordingly. Fish dishes are a speciality, including the shellfish stew cooked in a *cataplana*.

*****Estalagem Quinta de Santo António, São Brás, 206 Apartado, ☎ 628526 (*luxury*) provides luxurious accommodation set in 800 hectares of land, including an 18th-century garden, a cistern surrounded by Baroque statues, tennis courts, a swimming pool and a plethora of palms and fountains.

***Hotel D. Luís, Av. de Badajoz, ☎ 622756, ✉ 620733 (*expensive*), near the aqueduct, provides well-furnished bedrooms, though the carpets can be worn and lumpy, and the bedspreads grim. There are too many 'fancy' dishes in the over-heated restaurant, with muzak. Desserts are nice though, and Elvas' famous sweet plums may be on offer. Centrally located just off the cathedral square, near the tourist office, ******Estalagem D. Sancho II**, 20 Praça da República, ☎ 622686 (*inexpensive*) offers small but cosy rooms and a friendly atmosphere. The restaurant downstairs offers probably the best value in Elvas. Colourful and calm, it has a wood-beamed ceiling and high-backed chairs. Desserts are local specialities, displayed with bowls of soaking sausages in the middle of the restaurant. Dishes include stuffed pigs' trotters and mussels Spanish style, at very reasonable prices. The *estalagem* also sells the best postcards in town.

Residencial Luzo-Espanhola, Rua Rui de Melo, ☎ 623092 (*inexpensive-cheap*) hopes to attract sojourners from across the border; whether it succeeds or not, it's still one of the cheapest places in town. **Casa de Hóspedes Arco do Bispo, 4 Rua Sineiro, ☎ 623422 (*cheap*)—from Praça da República turn right down the hill and pass the police station—is friendly, clean, and a veritable bargain.

El Cristo, Parque da Piedade, ✆ 628361 (*expensive*) is next to the church of Senhor Jesus da Piedade, a 10-minute walk from town and is more popular for its seafood than its ambience, being large, striplit, and sited in an annexe. The waiters hover, but the food is good. Much of it is sold by the kilo: reckon on 400 grammes per portion. **O Aqueduto**, Av. da Piedade, ✆ 623676 (*moderate*), just down from the Capela de Nossa Senhora da Nazaré, offers reasonably good seafood specialities sold by the kilo and served by waiters in black and white who tarry behind the saloon bar. The floors are crazy-paved with chips of stone, the tablecloths a verdant green, and the lighting not unpleasantly bright. The choice of dishes includes *costeletas de cabrito panadas* (breaded lamb chops). There is a shortage of decent cheap eating places in Elvas, but there are a couple of notable exceptions: **Canal Sete**, ✆ 623593, at 16 Rua dos Sapateiros, opposite the tourist office (*cheap*) is possibly the best budget restaurant in Elvas and unfailingly packed with a varied but lively crowd. The food is very good. There is also a café/restaurant in the **Centro Artistico Elevense**, ✆ 622711, on Praça da República next to the bus station (*cheap*) which serves an excessively good *arroz de marisco*.

Évora

Some 150km east of Lisbon and 77km north of Beja, Évora is one of the joys of Portugal, delightful both to sightseers and to wanderers. Unspoilt and memorable, it occupies the gentle slopes of a wide hill on the Alentejan plain, surrounded by olive groves, wheat fields and vineyards. Its 50,000 souls rank it as one of the country's largest cities; but just 13,500 live within the encircling walls, so it feels like a town. It is this inner town that has been declared part of the World Patrimony by UNESCO. Walking its clean, cobbled streets you come across arches and arcades, whitewashed *palácios* and Renaissance fountains, which together give Évora a wholeness in spite of the range of its monuments.

Houses stretch under the arches of the aqueduct, and it is around here that life is played out. Artisans tap out their trades, making pine coat-hangers or tables; old ladies tend a couple of cratefuls of fruit or vegetables. In winter, children keep themselves warm with fleecy sheepskin jerkins, while old men prefer faded, habit-like capes.

History

Évora's history is as fertile as the title Pliny the Elder gave it—Ebora Cerealis. It was a political centre of Roman Iberia, and its townspeople have been able to claim Roman lineage since *c.* 61 BC, when Julius Caesar sent a group of his countrymen to mingle amongst the natives. Évora may have been the headquarters of Quintus Sertorius, who was sent to govern Hispania and bit the hand of his imperial master when he attempted to make the province independent, around 80 BC. (Sertorius had a pet albino fawn, which he swathed with gold necklaces and earrings, and taught to muzzle his ear as if it were whispering to him. He ordered that good news should be delivered to him secretly, so he could pretend that the doe had brought it to him from the goddess Diana.)

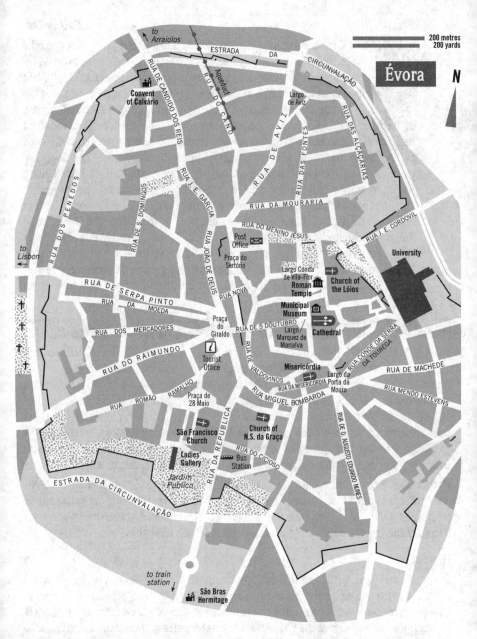

The Visigoths came, and then the Moors, who stayed from 711 to 1165. In the 12th century, Idrisi, the Arab geographer, described Évora as a large, walled town with a great mosque and a castle, surrounded by singularly fertile countryside rich in wheat, fruit and vegetables. The Moors were expelled by Gerald the Fearless, an ingenious outlaw who drove lances into the outer wall of the city to form a staircase, which he mounted by night. Dom Afonso Henriques made Gerald castellan of the town, and he is depicted on the town's blazon, accompanied by two disembodied heads.

In 1166 Dom Afonso Henriques issued Évora with its first charter, in Latin, stating that every man who had a house, a yoke of oxen, 40 sheep, an ass and two beds was obliged to keep a horse and turn it out for military service. When there was a brawl among villagers, wounds were to be taxed, and those who caused them fined according to a fixed penalty.

The Renaissance and After

Évora flourished from the 14th century to the 16th century, enjoying the regal attentions of the locally based House of Avis. The *Cortes* were summoned here, and great artists duly followed. Together they produced a wealth of noble palaces and artworks, and in 1559 Cardinal Henrique founded a university. In 1490, Évora hosted the splendid celebrations for the marriage of Afonso, son of Dom João II, to Infante Isabel of Castile. For this, a wooden hall 44m high and 180m long was built in the garden of the Church of São Francisco, and hung with striped Moroccan cloths. Dancers and musicians were recruited from the Moorish quarters of neighbouring towns, and the whole neighbourhood was scoured for spare beds, each of which was marked, so its owner could identify it, before being carried to Évora. But an outbreak of the plague, just before the jamboree, obliged guests to leave the town for 15 days until the September moon.

Decline set in with the Spanish seizure of the throne in 1580, following the death of Dom Henrique, last ruler of the House of Avis. The limelight left Évora's limewash as future monarchs kept nearer to Lisbon, and its Jesuit university was duly closed by Pombal in 1759. After the 1974 Revolution the town became the centre for agrarian reform, thus circling back to Pliny's denomination.

Getting There

Évora is an easy 3hr drive from Lisbon.

By train from Lisbon, take the ferry to Barreiro for the infrequent rail service direct to Évora (2¾hrs total); the indirect service requires you to change at Casa Branca too (3hrs total). Infrequent trains from Vila Viçosa take 1¾hrs, via Borba (1½hrs), and Estremoz (1¼hrs). Infrequent buses from Reguengos de Monsaraz take 1hr.

Express buses run semi-frequently from Lisbon (2½hrs) via Setúbal (1¾hrs), but infrequently from Beja (1¾hrs), Elvas (1¾hrs), and Moura (1½hrs).

Évora ☎ (066–)   *Tourist Information*

The **tourist office** is in the Praça do Giraldo, ☎ 22671 (*open 9–12.30 and 2–5.30; closed 12.30–2 at weekends*), a short walk uphill from the **bus station** (☎ 22121 for RN Expresses). The **railway station**, ☎ 22125, is less than 1km southeast of town: walk straight ahead and up the Rua da República to get to the Praça do Giraldo. The **post office** is in the Rua de Olivença (*open weekdays 9–6, Sat 9–1*), uphill from the Praça do Sertório. **Lavandaria Ana**, 78 Rua de Aviz, will wash your clothes, and charge by the kilo. The best way to get around Évora is on foot: the points of interest are not far apart, there are no steep hills, and the one-way traffic system is maddening.

The Roman Temple

temple of Diana

Portugal's best-preserved Roman monument stands at the highest point in Évora. The Roman Temple dates from the late 2nd or early 3rd century AD, its granite Corinthian columns topped with Estremoz marble. Although it is popularly known as the temple of Diana, scholars now think that the sanctuary may have been dedicated to the god Jupiter. Perhaps his indignation at the slight resulted in the building's conversion into the municipal slaughterhouse, until 1870. Visitors are requested not to climb on the temple, to conserve it. The neighbouring **sculpture garden** is the best place from which to watch the sun set.

The Church of the Lóios

Admission to the church, which is privately owned, is included in the price of the ticket for the museum at the Palace of the Dukes of Cadaval (250$00).

The church of the Lóios (St John the Evangelist), to one side of the Roman Temple, features the country's most captivating employment of *azulejos*—it would be a great pity to leave Évora without seeing this stunning church. Built on the site of the Moorish castle, the monastic church was founded by Rodrigo Afonso de Melo, Count of Olivença, in 1485, for the Canons Secular of St John the Evangelist, who were nicknamed 'Lóios'. Entered through a Flamboyant Gothic portal, the single nave serves as the pantheon of the de Melo family, whose Gothic and Renaissance tombs include that of Dom Francisco, in the transept, attributed to Chanterène. He tutored the sons of Dom João III.

But one's attention is captured by the very beautiful *azulejos* which subtly complement the internal architecture, with *trompe l'œil* tiles mirroring high windows. The main panels show scenes from the life of St Lorenzo Guistiniani, patriarch of Venice. Created in 1711, they are the master work of António de Oliveira Bernardes, who presided over the greatest period of Portuguese tile production, and they predate his work in Barcelos and Viana do Castelo.

Around the Roman Temple

Downhill in the same road, the two tall towers and courtyard of the **Palace of the Dukes of Cadaval** (*open 9–12 and 2–5*) incorporate a small museum. A finely painted *Virgem do Leite* (milk), from the workshop of Frei Carlos, is stared at by portraits of grim-looking ecclesiastics, whose faces are all the same. There are also two Flemish bronzes and an equestrian portrait of the third duke by Quillard, a pupil of Watteau, *c.* 1730.

In the street behind the Lóios and the palace, the **university** is rather disappointing. Arranged around a two-storeyed classical cloister, it was founded in 1559 by Cardinal Henrique, the future regent, to satisfy the Jesuits' wish for a university they could control, as Coimbra had successfully resisted their influence. But the new foundation never achieved its rival's size or breadth of studies. The corridors are lined with Baroque *azulejos* and all the doors are conveniently numbered, which saves visitors from getting lost.

The Municipal Museum

Open 9–12.30 and 2.30–6; closed Mon and holidays.

Opposite the Roman Temple, the Archbishop's Palace, reconstructed in the late 17th century, now houses Évora's museum, with important collections including sculpture and 15th–16th-century Flemish and Portuguese paintings.

One of the earliest sculptures is the Roman fragment of a vestal, whose legs are clad in a diaphanous marble skirt. Two tombs are outstanding: one can almost feel the softness of the pillows supporting Fernando Cogominho's effigy, or the warmth of the dog at his feet—a faithful friend since 1364. The simple, classical cenotaph of Bishop Dom Afonso de Portugal is one of Nicolas Chanterène's most elegant works, included amongst several pieces by him in the museum. The Frenchman was married in Évora, and here he established a school of sculpture, through which he was able to introduce the sculptural aspects of the Italian Renaissance to Portugal. The museum's modern sculpture includes a disturbing representation of three baby boys fighting, made by Teixeira Lopes in 1910 from a single block of marble. Aggression finds expression rather than representation in João Cutileiro's disembodied women.

Upstairs, note the delicate triptych of the Passion enamelled on copper in Limoges in 1539. Primitive paintings by 16th-century Flemish and Portuguese artists working in Portugal are juxtaposed. Both groups relish colour, but on the whole the Flemish Frei Carlos and Francisco Henriques have a greater depth of feeling and grasp of perspective than Gregório Lopes, Garcia Fernandes or the Master of Sardoal.

The museum's star attractions are the 13 panels of *The Life of the Virgin*, which formed the altarpiece of the cathedral until Ludwig redesigned its apse. The panels were painted by anonymous members of the Bruges School, working under one master, *c.* 1500. They were created in Portugal—there is a typically Portuguese plate in the *Nascimento da Virgem* (the Birth of the Virgin)—with the probable exception of the one larger panel, though Italian Renaissance buildings are used in the background. Saints Ana and Joaquim, the parents of the Virgin, are pictured with a cartoon-like castle, and she is pregnant at her marriage (*casamento*).

The Cathedral

Cathedral museum open 9–12, Sun 9–11, and 2–5; closed Mon and holidays.

Behind the museum, the cathedral seems half-fortress, half-church. Its irregular façade is closest akin to that of the Sé Velha in Coimbra, a good example of the transition from the Romanesque to Gothic styles. According to the chronicler André de Resende, it was begun by the second bishop in 1186, on the site of a mosque, 20 years after the Moors were initially expelled from Évora. Perhaps it served as a mosque again when the Moors retook the town 1192–1211. Construction probably continued through the 13th century.

The bearded gentlemen flanking the portal are the Apostles, standing on ledges of human figures and fantastical animals. These fine medieval Portuguese sculptures were probably commissioned between 1322 and 1340. They all look similar, except St Peter and St Paul, who are the progeny of Telo Garcia of Lisbon.

The interior is very brown; the obtrusive white mortar binding the stonework gives it an oddly Victorian feel. The chandeliers hang on giant rosaries. Because they were considered insufficiently dignified for an archiepiscopal see, Ludwig, the Italian-trained architect of the Convent of Mafra, rebuilt the chancel and high altar in 1718, including a lovely sculpture of the crucified Christ. Ludwig is buried here.

The Cloister and Sacred Art Museum

Tickets down to the cloister and up to the Sacred Art Museum are sold just inside the entrance portal (the museum closes half an hour earlier than the cathedral). The stunning Gothic cloister of *c.* 1323 is pierced by open circles with almost Moorish designs. Sculptures of the Evangelists stand at the corners of the quadrangle, but the most moving sculpture panels the tomb of the 14th-century Bishop Pedro, whose long head is supported by angels. A terrace above the cathedral's west entrance leads to the museum. Filled with a manageable number of reliquaries and embroidered vestments, it features a late 13th-century French Madonna whose seated ivory body parts to reveal scenes from her life. Introspection indeed. Near her is a 16th-century weathervane, looking more like a witch than an angel.

Central Évora

Walking down the steps by the cathedral, and continuing in the same direction, the **Largo da Porta da Moura** is a pleasant place to come upon. It is arranged around a Renaissance orb-fountain whose walls are rippled, presumably by centuries of buttocks. Behind them the Cordovil House sports a hybrid Manueline-mudéjar porch. The beautiful modern building at the upper end of the square comprises the Courts of Justice.

The Rua 5 de Outubro, opposite the cathedral, leads down to the **Praça do Giraldo** and its 15th-century fountain, shaped like a *cataplana*. This is a focus for low-commotion timepassing.

The Rua da República runs downhill from the Praça, from which a road to the left, behind the bus station, opens on to the strange late Renaissance façade of **N.S. da Graça**, which was worked in part by Diogo de Arruda, and is topped by four disgruntled giants in the process of standing up. The nave has fallen down three times.

The Church of São Francisco

Open Mon–Sat 8.30–1 and 2.30–6, Sun 10–11.30 and 2.30–6.

The Rua da República continues downhill past the back of the Gothic church of São Francisco, reconstructed 1460–1501. Gargoyles spew moss down its plastered sides. The church is entered through a gigantic, dizzying porch. As in the cathedral, the mortar is eyecatching. The single nave is daringly high and wide, while the chancel is a jumble of styles including a beautiful 18th-century neoclassical altar. The church hosts Évora's freakiest monument, the **Capela dos Ossos** (Bone Chapel), on ground level. Half-close your eyes and the walls seem built of flint: the macabre truth is more disturbing. For the walls are composed of over 5000 monks' bones. Femurs, tibias, skulls, all are arranged rather neatly, but the effect is horrid. And the decaying skeleton strung on one wall is repellent. A notice at the entrance proclaims *'Nós ossos, que aqui estamos, Pelos vossos esperamos'*—'We bones here are waiting for your bones'. Less threateningly, the chapel's three founding fathers are commemorated with an epitaph of 1629. Note the plaits of hair near the entrance desk, offered as ex-votos.

Southern Évora

The **Museu de Artesanato** (Handicrafts Museum), opposite, includes items for sale. A quick look will suffice for the painted pots and furniture, miniature farm implements, wood- and cork-work, and goat- and cow-bells.

Further downhill along the Rua da República, a public garden contains an uninteresting copy of the **Ladies' Gallery** of the Palace of Don Manuel. On this site Vasco da Gama was given the commission which led to his discovery of the sea route to India. Next to it are some fake Gothic ruins, assembled in 1863 from the remains of the former bishop's palace.

From the 17th-century town walls the odd **São Bras Hermitage** is visible, buttressed by plastered cylinders, and crenellated. Bishop Garcia de Menezo, who founded the hermitage in 1482, was involved in the rebellion of the Duke of Viseu and died ingloriously in a cistern in the castle of Palmela. Now there's nothing particularly significant inside the building.

Northern Évora

On the opposite side of town, not far from the aqueduct, the interesting **convent of Calvário** was founded in 1570 for an offshoot of the Franciscan Order. Knock on the door facing the centre of town, just off the Rua de Cândido dos Reis. The two-storey cloister has a lived-in feel to it, partly because of the caged budgies. These may serve as a memorial to Dona Isabel Juliana de Sousa Coutinho, a girl of 14 forced by the Marquês de Pombal to marry his son. She dug her toes in and for three years she refused to speak when spoken to, after which the unconsummated marriage was annulled. She retired to the convent, whose abbess was Pombal's sister, until the eminent statesman was disgraced, whereupon she married her childhood classmate, Dom Alexandre. (They had been taught by his English tutor, Mr Billingham.) He fathered the first Duke of Palmela.

The church has some good but ill-lit paintings of the life of Mary, attributed to Simão Rodrigues, and some good but flaking frescoes. The gilt woodwork is magnificent, producing a markedly tabernacular effect.

The Environs of Évora

The **Cartuxa** (Charterhouse) is just outside the Porto da Lagoa. The soaring 17th-century façade is wonderful, but the rest of the church is closed to visitors. Although it was founded in 1274, the **monastery of São Bento de Castris**, 3km further on, is unremarkable, except for a single 18th-century *azulejo* panel in the church, forming part of the life of St Bernard. It pictures a pregnant lady with a dog in her womb.

Évora ✆ (066–) **Where to Stay**

luxury

Pousada dos Lóios, Largo Conde de Vila Flor, ✆ 24051, 🖷 27248 (*category CH*)—next to the Roman temple—is a wonderful and memorable place to stay, occupying the old Lóios monastery, which first offered hospitality to travellers in 1491. Now blue habits have given way to the blue blazers of the reception staff. The monastery was founded by Dom Rodrigo de Melo, who became the first Governor of Tangiers.

The building centres on a two-storeyed cloister: the upper level has been glassed in. Guests pass through here to get their snug bedrooms, which are scattered with Arraiolos rugs. Morning churchbells ring loud in some rooms. A swimming pool is available for use.

In warm weather, the ground level of the vaulted cloister is set with dining tables (note the double-horseshoe Manueline doorway). Otherwise, you'll be in the grand hall under iron chandeliers. The food does justice to the setting, and non-residents are welcome. You might try the *migas à Alentejana* (fried pork with bread).

moderate

Situated southeast of the town walls, ★★★★**Albergaria Vitória**, Rua Diana de Lis, ✆ 27174, 🖷 20974, is a comfortable modern set-up, where the uniformed staff work efficiently and seem to enjoy doing so. Rooms have balconies. In the street between the cathedral and the Praça do Giraldo, ★★★★**Residencial Riviera**, 49 Rua 5 de Outubro, ✆ 23304, 🖷 20467 (*moderate–inexpensive*) is alright, but a bit tacky. The breakfast room is homey, though. ★★★**Hotel Dom Fernando**, 2 Avenida Dr Barahona, ✆ 741717, 🖷 741716, is a modern complex which tries to incorporate typical Alentejan styles, notably in the arched ceilings. The rooms are large and comfortable, if somewhat soulless.

★★★**Residencial Diana**, 2 Rua Diogo Cão, ℰ 22008 (off the road running between the cathedral and the Praça do Giraldo) is comfortable and well-established in a solidly built house, with high ceilings, and strong furniture. There's a friendly, chatty atmosphere, especially at breakfast. Be careful not to step on the smelly little dog as you come downstairs. ★★★**Residencial O Eborense**, 1 Largo da Misericórdia, ℰ 22031 (down the steps by the cathedral, take the second right), is installed in a grand 16th-century house, with a whitewashed loggia and sympathetic décor, from cartwheels suspended to hold lights in the breakfast hall, to old photographs hung in corridors that head off at odd angles. Room 112 is especially nice.

In the 16th century, the Count of Lousã built himself a town house, which is now the ★★**Pensão Policarpo**, 16 Rua da Freiria de Baixo, ℰ 22424 (*inexpensive–cheap*)—down the steps by the cathedral, turn left and go past the *Misericórdia* church. The place is atmospheric, with granite columns and open-air corridors. Rooms 102 to 109 are furnished with bright and flowery Alentejan furniture, right up to the pelmets. Room 101 is particularly nice; after 109 the rooms are plainer and not so special. The breakfast room is barnlike and lovely. Parking is available, and some of the staff speak English.

In one of the parallel streets running downhill from the Praça do Giraldo, ★★**Pensão Os Manueis**, 35 Rua do Raimundo, 1st floor, ℰ 22861, is small and decent, with adequate rooms. Another of these streets contains ★★★**Pensão Giraldo**, 15 and 27 Rua dos Mercadores, ℰ 25833, which has high ceilings, plenty of wooden furniture and properly hot water, but is dingy in parts.

Out of Town

A farm's stables and servants' quarters have been converted into an inn, ★★★**Estalagem Monte das Flores**, 4km southwest of Évora, on the road to Alcáçovas, ℰ 25018, ✆ 27564 (*expensive*), that attracts young and beautiful Portuguese, keen on horseriding at 6000$00 per hour. That is the main appeal. When not in the saddle, you may sit on musty-looking armchairs in the dauntingly large sitting room or on ponyskin wallseats in the bar. Bedrooms are furnished with flowery Alentejan furniture. Pork and steak dishes are popular in the dining room.

Turismo de Habitação

There are many houses under this scheme in and around Évora; the tourist office can provide full details, but the pick of the bunch are highlighted below.

Quinta da Nora, Estrada dos Canaviais, 3km from Évora, ℰ 29810 (*inexpensive*) is a charming farmhouse with beautiful grounds, a swimming pool and a working vineyard. The six rooms harbour lovely, heavy furniture and beamed, sloping ceilings. The lounge has its own panel of dazzling *azujelos* and Arraiolos rugs. Ridiculously good value.

Casa de S. Tiago, 2 Largo Alexandre Herculano, ✆ 22686 (*moderate*) is a 16th-century town house dating from the reign of King Manuel I. The rooms display a happy mixture of the simple and the grand, while always feeling comfortable.

Monte da Serralheira, ✆ 741286 (*moderate*) is a Dutch-owned farmhouse about 3km from Évora. There are horses to get dusty on and a lake to cool off in. Three apartments sleep four, and two sleep two. Each has its own entrance and terrace; prices are per day or weekly.

Quinta da Espada, Estrada de Arraiolos, 3km along the Arraiolos road, ✆ 734549 (*moderate*) means 'The Sword Estate'—legend has it that Gerald the Fearless, who liberated Évora from the Moors, hid his sword here. Perhaps it is still lurking in the beautiful grounds, which are distinguished by an aqueduct. Still, the house looks like a typical Alentejan farmhouse, albeit very prettily furnished.

Quinta de S. Luis, Estrada do Igrejinha, ✆ 26983 (*inexpensive*) is 4km outside Évora and presents a more modern façade, set by the L-shaped pool. Horse riding, tennis and hunting parties are on offer, and the interior has a cosy farmhouse feel.

Casa de San Pedro, Quinta de San Pedro, ✆ 27731 (*moderate*) stands in a cool park with family portraits of 19th-century ladies and heirloom-style furnishings. This is not always too relaxing, but the reception is friendly enough.

Évora ✆ (066–)   ***Eating Out***

expensive

St Humberto is the patron saint of hunting, and **Cozinha de S. Humberto**, 39 Rua da Moeda, ✆ 24251, in one of the parallel streets which run downhill from the Praça do Giraldo, is an atmospheric place to celebrate him. The 3–400-year-old building incorporates a trough, now grilled over, which was formerly used for storing wine. Collections of glass, plates and kettles adorn the walls. The *calducho* is good, but the desserts aren't riveting. *Closed Thurs.* Run by two brothers and sometimes a third, **Fialho**, 16 Trav. das Mascarenhas, ✆ 23079, near the theatre, has received a lot of hype, and has a good reputation for regional cooking. Thirty years ago, the prostitution in this side street was so obtrusive that ladies feared they would compromise themselves by coming here. All that's changed now. It's decorated as a tavern, with lots of local pottery and bizarre deer-foot coatpegs. Chairs are leather with bosses, and a huge display of fruit rests under the wood-beamed ceiling. Pork, lamb and game in season are specialities of the large menu. *Closed Mon and Tues; reservations recommended.*

O Aqueduto, 13-A Rua do Cano, ✆ 26373, near the aqueduct, glows with a warm yellow light. It is well run, with plenty of black-tied waiters serving good-quality regional dishes. Shrimps are displayed on a table, bayleaves are stored in tall pots over the earth-coloured floor, and down a couple of steps six huge vessels dwarf the tables they surround. The choice includes *migas com carne de porco* (pork with breadcrumbs). *Closed Wed.* Down the street which runs north from the Praça do Giraldo, past the church of Santo Antão, **Martinho**, 24–25 Largo Luís de Camões, ✆ 23057, attempts a slick décor, with semicircular pink marble 'piano key' steps leading up to the spick and span kitchen, which specializes in rice dishes. The well-presented portions are not enormous. **Luar de Janeiro**, 13 Trav. do Janeiro, ✆ 24895, has giant bottles of wine on the bar, setting the tone for this small restaurant with copper pots, a stag's head and sundry trophies lining rough upper walls. The bow-tied waiters are friendly and the good food comes priced by the kilo.

moderate

Close to the main square, **A Muralha**, 21 Rua 5 de Octubro, ✆ 22284, is inevitably popular with tourists, but has a pleasant lively atmosphere and a short menu of superbly cooked local dishes. It was the recent winner of Évora's gastronomic competition.

cheap

Sobreiro, 8 Rua do Torres, ✆ 29325, near the Calvário Convent off the Rua Cândido dos Reis, comes as a great relief—there is not a bow tie in sight. The interior setting is plain and rustic, with wooden farm equipment on the walls, and bread-bowls made of cork complete with bark. It fills quickly and empties early, but the service is constantly efficient. Most of the locals choose *cozido à Portuguesa*: assorted boiled meats do not make a pretty dish, but it's tasty. *Closed Mon.* **A Semente Barzinho Vegetariano**, 90, Rua Romão Ramalho, ✆ 746190, has some tasty veggie options and offers shiatsu massage.

Puppet Shows

It's worth asking at the tourist office if there is a performance of the Bonecos de Santo Aleixo. These stringed puppets about 30cm tall are manipulated from above, following models created in the mid-19th century by a villager called Nepamoceno. The satirical performances are accompanied by much stamping, singing and shrilling—hilarious whether or not you understand the language.

Around Évora

Arraiolos

Set among low hills 21km north of Évora, beneath the circular walls of a castle, the village of Arraiolos is famous for its **carpetmaking**, comprised of a simple woollen crosstitch in magically beautiful patterns.

Getting There

Arraiolos is a ½hr bus ride from Évora or a ¾hr bus ride from Estremoz. The service runs frequently enough to make an easy day trip.

Arraiolos Carpets

The tradition started at the local monastery in the 17th century, when canvas or linen was embroidered with local wool. By the third quarter of that century, the carpets were being exported to other parts of the country. In 1787 William Beckford noted that at Arraiolos 'I laid a stock of carpets for my journey, of strange grotesque patterns and glaring colours, the produce of a manufactory in this town which employs about 300 persons ... my carpets are of essential service in protecting my feet from the damp brick floors. I have spread them round my bed and they make a flaming exotic appearance.' The patterns were inspired by various sources—Portugal's Moorish heritage, the carpets of Herat and Isfahan brought back by the discoverers, legendary tales of Persian exoticism, and, from the beginning of the 19th century, Aubusson carpets, all of which were sprinkled with a little popular imagination. The carpets have various assets: durability, colours that are slow to blanch, and the possibility of repair in the case of, say, a cigarette burn.

A number of workshops in Arraiolos produce carpets, all of which have their own showrooms. It's cheaper to buy them here than anywhere else: prices currently average out at 30,000$00 per square metre, half of which goes to the hunched sewers. Cushion covers are an alternative, at around 7000$00 each, though the Kalifa shop sells them for less than that. Or you could try asking for do-it-yourself kits in Lisbon.

The Town

The hilltop castle was built by Dom Dinis in 1310, and the great soldier Nun' Álvares Pereira lived here at various times 1415–23. Only the circular walls remain intact; they give the feeling of a giant animal pen. The whitewashed conical buttresses of the **convento dos Lóios** stand 500m to the north of town, surrounded by birdsong. The monastery was given to the Brothers of St John the Evangelist in 1526, and contains tiles dated 1700.

The Convento de Bom Jesus at Valverde

Ten km southwest of Évora on the Alcáçovas road, this monastery is delightfully small and habitable—it even smells of fermenting apples. The tiny cloister leads to a little church built in the shape of a Greek cross, filled with columns of delicate Estremoz marble. Tradition says that Philip II of Spain commissioned the church in 1583, basing the design on the Laurentian Library of the Escorial. Next to the buildings is a platformed water tank edged with oval frames.

Anta do Zambujal

Two km from the convento stands one of the largest dolmens in Europe. It's difficult to find, and is more important for its history than its atmosphere. Coming from Évora, turn right at the Convento and then right at the T-junction. The road becomes a track. Fork left. The track splits into four: take the second from the left. Drive through a stream and fork right. After 100m you will see a corrugated-iron shelter.

In this place 5000 years ago, the dead were buried together in the foetal position. The roofless chamber of their tomb is approached by a corridor of granite blocks propped at unlikely angles, and is walled with obelisks of at least twice human height. Late Neolithic clansmen transported the stone from 1km away, and covered the whole with earth. Personal possessions such as jewellery and chipped stone instruments were buried nearby. Shepherds build fires in the tomb to keep themselves warm at night.

Viana do Alentejo

Some 29km south of Évora, an astonishing fortified **Gothic church** blends with Viana do Alentejo's crenellated castle walls. This produces an extraordinary tiered effect, from the church, to its flying buttresses, to the walls that defended it. These are cornered with massive cylindrical towers, which are miniatured in the church's own pepper-pot pinnacles. The castle is planted with a pretty garden, which can be seen to good effect from the wall-walk; likewise the church's unusually attractive Manueline portal, decorated with granite sea-flowers. Inside the church are octagonal pillars with a fine rhythm, ringed with seaweed and rope. The church is attributed to Diogo de Arruda, and dates from the late 15th century or early 16th century.

Monsaraz and its Megaliths

Getting There

Infrequent **trains** from Lisbon terminate at Évora, where there is one connecting bus daily to Reguengos de Monsaraz, 1hr away. The bus returns after only 2 hours, making a day trip a real rush, but just about feasible.

Express **buses** run infrequently from Lisbon to Reguengos de Monsaraz (3¾hrs), via Setúbal (3hrs) and Évora (¾hr). From Évora, local buses run the same route once daily. There are two daily buses from Reguengos de Monsaraz to Monsaraz itself, making a day trip from Évora just possible, but allowing very little time once you've arrived.

Megaliths

The Alentejo was a centre of megalithic culture between 4000 and 2000 BC, and the area between Reguengos de Monsaraz, 36km southeast of Évora, and Monsaraz, 16km further east, preserves some good examples of menhirs (tombs with large flat stones laid on upright ones) and a cromlech (a circle of upright stones), which can all be visited on a circular tour around the two towns. (The name '*reguengos*' denotes what was once a royal estate, yielding to the crown a quarter to a fifth of the produce of the soil.) The tourist office in Évora produces a glossy booklet detailing the megaliths and their locations.

Some 8km east of Reguengos de Monsaraz, just past S. Pedro do Corval, and about 50m to the left of the road, stands **Lovers' Rock**. It's a natural-standing knobbed fertility stone, just shorter than the trees around it. On Easter Monday, hopeful local single ladies roll up their left sleeves and pelt the rock with fist-sized stones. If a missile stays atop, a baby is due within a year. The base of the rock is littered with disappointments.

Off the road from Telheiro (where there is a whitewashed fountain dated 1422) to Outeiro, a menhir is visible across the fields, about 5½m high. Local farmers found the **Menhir da Bulhoa** lying flat and chopped off a third of it to make an olive-oil press. Decorated with faint zigzag patterns and stars, it is considered too oval and tapering to be a credible phallus, and was probably erected in memory of a chief, or as a geographical marker.

Five km from Monsaraz, on the road to Xeres de Baixo, the **Cromlech do Xerez** stands 300m to the right. Fifty stubby menhirs are arranged in a square, with a great big phallic one in the middle. The splendid central member of the group weighs 7 tonnes. Probably a place for ritual prayer and meeting, it's best seen when the sun is low, casting long shadows from the clusters of natural shrub-studded boulders in the surrounding plough-land. Fertility in an agro-pastoral economy was related not only to people, but also to the land and flocks.

Monsaraz

The walled hilltop village of Monsaraz has held off centuries of development—its medieval streets retain a peculiar magic. You can feel its allure a couple of km away, where the only visible parts of the settlement are its castle and the Igreja Matriz.

The four parallel cobbled streets of Monsaraz offer massive views of the plains of the Alentejo, peppercorned with olive and cork trees. The low, bulging houses are white-washed or built of chaotic grey slate, with mellow terracotta roofs and terracotta jugs used as gargoyles, and whimsical iron dachshund doorknockers. Bitches with distended teats sprawl in the shade, and women wearing black trilby hats sit outdoors and crochet.

Monsaraz was taken from the Moors in 1167 and in the same year was given to the Templars. The joy of the place comes in absorbing the village and its life—there are a couple of churches, but with the exception of a damaged 14th-century marble tomb in the **Igreja Matriz**, they contain little of interest. To the left of that church, the **Paços do Concelho** contains a 15th-century fresco depicting a good and a bad judge: the latter has a devil on his shoulder and is accepting a bribe. Vertical lines scratched into the inner side of the entrance gate were used for measuring material on market days. At the other end of town, the **castle** forms part of a chain of fortresses built by Dom Dinis in the 14th century. Part of it has been converted into a bullring.

Monsaraz © (066–)   ***Where to Stay***

 Sited in a subsidiary settlement below the castle walls, the best feature of ★★★★**Estalagem de Monsaraz**, Largo de S. Bartolomeu, © 55112 (*cheap*) is a wonderfully peaceful and private sinuous garden, backed by natural rock. Below is a swimming pool. Public rooms are decorated in a rustic style, with copper pots and painted plates, and onions suspended from wood beams. The small-windowed bedrooms have heavy furniture and may be dirty. Some of the bathrooms are squashed and ramshackle. The restaurant serves simple food such as liver (*fígado*).

Dom Nuno, 6 Rua Direita, ✆ 55146 (*moderate–inexpensive*) is near the church square, a surprisingly large old house, artistically and comfortably decorated, with stone floors, wooden ceilings and Renaissance doorways. Some of the eight rooms offer fantastic views from their fat beds with handmade bedcovers. A collection of keys hangs on the wall of the galleried sitting room like musical notes. There are very nice modern bathrooms, and a small bar—it's good value.

It is possible to rent two whole houses in Monsaraz. Phone ✆ 55149 or 52179 and ask for Mizette, who speaks English. The larger house has two double rooms: one with a huge foam bed on a cement base, and a typical bamboo ceiling; the other is a loft. The main attraction is the stone-floored sitting/dining room, with a large fireplace, and a cupboard masking a former doorway to the church next door. The well-equipped kitchen has woody fixtures. The other house is delightfully plain and small—it used to be a pigsty and has a garden with a superb view. It has one double room—with a foam bed on a cement platform, above a natural rock outcrop—and one single room. Highly recommended. Prices are quoted per month, week and long weekend. The big house: *moderate–inexpensive*. The little house: *inexpensive–cheap*. Note that prices exclude electricity and gas.

Outside Monsaraz, the **Horta da Moura**, Apartado 64, 7200 Reguengos de Monsaraz, ✆ 55206/55245 (*expensive*) is an impressive converted farmhouse set in extensive grounds and featuring rough white walls, beamed ceilings and terracotta floors. It provides a luxurious base for exploring the River Guadiana—by bicycle, on horse back or even horse-drawn carriage. The many other facilities include tennis. The mellow dining room serves well-cooked regional specialities.

Baixo Alentejo

The Lower Alentejo lacks the dramatic hills of the upper part of the province, but offers an unspoilt coastline. A harsh, slow life unfolds in the remote settlements, with limited accommodation for travellers and few monuments of note. Beja is the principal town of the province, which is at its most beautiful along the banks of the River Guadiana.

Beja

Some 78km south of Évora and 175km north of Faro, Beja occupies the highest point of the plain which separates the catchment areas of the Rivers Sado and Guadiana.

The principal town of the Lower Alentejo is prosperous, purposeful and pedestrian in its new parts, and pleasantly lackadaisical in its old parts. Here shoemenders work in holes-in-the-walls, old people in low houses wait and watch at their street-level windows, and the streets are paved with dragons' teeth and egg-shaped cobbles.

Beja's main appeal today is as a useful stopover point in the corn lands. Fruit is hard to find outside the market—there's a good grocer at 33 Rua dos Infantes, the road opposite the museum entrance.

History

At the beginning of Beja's history, the town was named Pax Julia to commemorate the peace between Julius Caesar and the Lusitanians. It was a commercial centre made up of freemen and foreigners, who practised a variety of Eastern religions: inscriptions have been found dedicated to Cybele, Isis, Serapis and even Mithras. Of the brilliant Muslim court that followed, few traces now remain—only the tiles which wall the Convento. In the mid-15th century, Afonso V made Beja a duchy. Traditionally, it was granted to the second son of the king, until Dom Pedro IV decided that the second-in-line should be Duke of Oporto, and the third-in-line Duke of Beja. During the French occupation, most of Junot's army were stationed in the Alentejo. In June 1808 something snapped, and several French soldiers were killed in a riot in Beja. Junot ordered reprisals; 1200 Bejans were killed in a street battle, and the French commander was moved to report: 'Beja no longer exists, its criminal inhabitants have been put to the sword and their houses pillaged and burned.'

Beja still exists, although its charms are limited to those of the Convento/Museum.

Getting There

Beja offers some transport connections with the south of Portugal. By train from Lisbon's Terreiro do Paço, take a ferry to Barreiro (½hr), connecting with the 1¾hr infrequent train service to Beja.

Trains run infrequently from Vila Real de Santo António (6¼hrs); from here, and all stations in the Algarve, change at Tunes. RN Express buses from Lisbon take 3¼hrs, via Setúbal (2¼hrs). Serpa is a mere ½hr away, Mertola ¾hr and Moura 1¼hrs.

Beja ℭ (084–)   ***Tourist Information***

The **tourist office** is at 25 Rua do Capitão J.F. de Sousa, ℭ 23693 (*open June–Sept, Mon–Fri 9–8, Sat 10–12.30 and 2.30–6; Oct–May, Mon–Fri 10–6, Sat closed 12.30–2.30*), just outside the medieval town walls, not too far from the museum. The **bus station** (ℭ 324044) is in the southeast of town (walk down the street flanking the odd modern Casa da Cultura), while the **railway station**, ℭ 325056, is in the northeast.

The Castle and Around

The castle (*open 10–1 and 2–6*), yet another of Dom Dinis' fortifications, stands on the edge of medieval Beja. Ivy covers its courtyard buildings, which now house a military museum. The philosophical castellan will show visitors the thick-walled keep, and the balcony holes positioned for pouring boiling olive oil on assailants. The building's 40m height allows the luxury of three Gothic windows, and very big views.

In the 18th century, the castle walls supported 40 towers, but they were torn down at the end of the last century. Stepped bungalows follow what remains of the wall of the castle, past a communal patch of grass used by one and all for drying laundry.

To one side of the castle is the church of **Sâo Tïago**, with good pillars of 18th-century *azulejos*. To the other side, the **Igreja de Santo Amaro** houses the new **Museum of Visigothic Archaeology** (*open 9.45–12.30 and 2–5.15; closed Mon and holidays*), with artefacts mostly from the 7th–8th centuries well displayed amongst the whitewashed arches of the church.

Downhill from the castle, on the Lisbon road, stands the **Hermitage of Santo André**. It is not held in great respect locally, despite its foundation in the reign of Dom Sancho I to commemorate the capture of Beja from the Moors in 1162. The whitewash on its cylindrical buttresses has been allowed to lapse, and there has been talk of trying to convert it into the tourist office. (Even this would be preferable to the fate of the shell of the 13th-century Convento de São Francisco, adjacent to the public garden, which is undergoing an extended harvest festival—as a supermarket.)

The porch of the mid-15th-century **Misericórdia**, at one end of the Praça da República, was originally a meat market: as if to prove it, the stonework is nicked like pigskin. Now workmen eat sardines there, and the church itself is used for storing paper.

The Convento de N.S. da Conceição

The convento de N.S. da Conceição houses the municipal **museum** (*open 9.45–12.30 and 2–5.15; closed Mon and holidays*). In the 17th century this was the home of that deserted and reproachful correspondent, Mariana Alcoforado, authoress of the five *Love Letters of a Portuguese Nun*. Her chevalier quit Beja at the end of the Portuguese war with Spain (1661–8). The originals of her letters to him have never been found, but they were published in French in 1669, and subsequently translated into English: 'I do not know why I write to you. You will only take pity on me, and I don't want your pity. I despise myself when I think of all that I have sacrificed for you. I have lost my reputation ...' By the grille where the lovers blew kisses, a flippant curator has displayed Roman ampules created to hold tears, and a nippled jug for a baby.

The Conventual Building

The conventual building, founded in 1459, is a good example of the transition from Gothic to Manueline style; the structure and the ogival arches are Gothic, while the decoration betrays the later influence. The dusty chapel features lots of giltwork and, fourth on the right, an all-marble side chapel dedicated to John the Baptist, though his image was removed in the 19th century. His life is portrayed in good tiles dated 1741, and there's a silver shrine for him and his namesake the Evangelist. A little marble tomb contains the bones of Dona Uganda, the first abbess. The cloister runs the length of the chapel, lined with uneven tiles from various periods, through to the extraordinary, exuberant *Sala do Cap'tulo* (the chapter house), decorated with a dense combination of paintwork and tiles. The painted panels are a bit kitsch, but the ceiling is great. Each pattern of carpet tiles has a single eccentric, because the Moors who made them believed only Allah could be perfect.

The Museum

In the museum's collection, three 16th-century paintings are outstanding: *São Vicente*, from the school of the Master of Sardoal; a Flemish *Our Lady of the Milk*, breast feeding; and a Portuguese *Descent from the Cross*. Note too an 18th-century polychrome sculpture of *N.S. dos Dores*, unusually detailing her toenails, teeth and tears; and a blue and white Ming bowl decorated with horsemen, the name of its first owner and the date of acquisition. There are two curious tombs. One is a stone half-barrel, built for a vintner. The other is Roman, with a little wolf, stating that now the land will be lighter.

Around the Convent

The **church of Santa Maria** (*open at 12 and 6pm*) is next to the museum, with a façade like icing sugar. It's built in the so-called Alentejan Gothic style, with many later additions including an enormous tree of Jesse. Its Moorish foundations are still visible around the gargoyled back of the church.

Behind the museum and towards the bus station, an Alentejan eagle is caged in the public garden. Also on show are some fluffy Chinese chickens.

The Environs of Beja

Ten km southwest of Beja a rough track leads to the ruined Roman villa of **Pisões**, which was inhabited from the 1st to the 4th centuries. There's nothing much to see above ground level: below lie geometric mosaics that blend browns and greens, and occasionally launch into flora and fauna. The villa has a very small peristyle, which gave onto a rectangular basin more than 45m long.

Beja ☎ (084–)   ***Where to Stay***

moderate

★★★★**Residencial Cristina**, 71 Rua de Mértola, ☎ 323035, 🖾 329874—around the corner from the beginning of the road to the Algarve—is functional and very clean behind tinted glass doors. Rooms have thick, patterned curtains, TV and phone, with small bathtubs. Further down the same road, ★★★★**Residencial Santa Barbara**, 56 Rua de Mértola, ☎ 322028, 🖾 32123, provides clean, satisfactory rooms, with stand-up balconies and telephones.

inexpensive

In the central elongated square, near the *Misericórdia*, ★★★**Residencial Coelho**, 15 Praça da República, ☎ 324031, is a very decent, solid sort of place, though the paint's a bit grubby. Rooms come with showers rather than baths.

cheap–very cheap

Fun, faded and characterful ★★**Casa de Hospedes Rocha**, 12 Largo Dom Nuno Alvares Pereira, ☎ 24271 (uphill from the post office) (*cheap*) is furnished with a jumble of old furniture, and high ceilings. The manager manages from his dining table. ★★★**Residencial Bejense**, 57 Rua do Capitâo J. F. de Sousa, ☎ 325001, (near the tourist office) is basic but clean. A gaudy selection of knick-knacks adorns every available space; not all rooms have bathrooms.

| *Beja ✆ (084–)* | *Eating Out* |

Small and whitewashed, **O Portão** (off the Rua dos Infantes, which runs between the Praça da República and the museum) serves carefully prepared and often very good food. MTV by satellite makes conversation a bit difficult. Hope that the *bacalhau à Gomes de Sá* is a dish of the day. In the square next to the museum, **Alentejano**, 6–7 Largo dos Duques de Beja, ✆ 23849, is full of locals in old leather jackets, sitting under the fake wood ceiling and enjoying their meat, rice and potatoes. Portions are large and prices reasonable. **A Floresta**, Largo dos Duques de Beja, ✆ 29578, nearby is popular with locals. The roast lamb is very good, as is the *bolo de rala*, a cake from Beja made with almonds.

Along the street from the tourist office, **Luís da Rocha**, 63 Rua Capitão João Francisco de Sousa, ✆ 23179, is plain and unexciting, adorned only by single carnations. Unusually for Beja, there are several fish dishes on the menu, but the speciality is *cabrito à pastora* (boiled kid).

Along the River Guadiana

Moura

Moura is a small town surrounded by oak and olive groves, some 5km from the Guadiana and 58km northeast of Beja. It is distinguished only by being a bit more Moorish than most, featuring a Moorish quarter, and a coat of arms depicting a Moorish girl dead at the bottom of a tower. This is the unfortunate Salúquiyya, daughter of a Moorish lord, engaged to a neighbouring Moorish mayor. Legend says she opened the gates of the town to her beloved on her wedding day, as any decent girl would, and got more than she'd bargained for. Christians had ambushed her lover and his party, killed them and put on their clothes. Once in the town, the Christians stormed the castle. The remorseful bride flung herself from a tower, to join her beloved in eternal *amour*. Portuguese legends are full of *Mouras encantadas*, enchanted Moorish princesses, who sometimes have a snake's tail in place of their lower limbs.

In fact, Moura was taken from the Moors in 1165 by Gerald the Fearless.

Getting There

Moura is a 1¼hr bus ride from Beja, or can be reached by RN Express bus from Lisbon (3¾hrs), via Setúbal (3¼hrs).

In the 13th century, Moura's dwelling space overflowed the castle walls to form the **Mouraria**, the Moorish quarter, the archetype of other whitewashed Alentejan settlements. No. 11 Travessa da Mouraria has a well with a terracotta lip, and a traditional bamboo ceiling. Note the Pegasus weathervane on the way up to the ruined **castle** of

1290, which was blown up in 1707 by the Duke of Ossuna during the War of Spanish Succession. A round tower still stands, and some walls, which look down on a yard of 15 or 20 large dogs, each with a bell around its neck. They belong to a hunter who lives here, away from other homes, because the dogs howl at the moon. The castle walls used to shelter many people in ramshackle houses, until Salazar bulldozed them away to plant a pretty garden, which never came to fruition.

The **tourist office**, Largo de S. Clara, © 085 22301, is housed in a small, unexciting museum. They have the key to the spacious **Igreja Matriz**, opposite. It's a fine example of the transition from Gothic to Manueline, with a Manueline portal of twisted columns pimpled with balls, and armillary spheres flanking the national blazon. The inferior Sevillian tiles within are dated 1651. The **Convento do Carmo**, on the other side of the castle, was the first Carmelite convent to be founded in Portugal, in the mid-13th century. The chancel was rebuilt in 1725, with a wild-patterned fresco ceiling, and it's said that an inscription on one of the tombs states that the deceased died of laughing.

Moura © (085–)   **Where to Stay**

The once-grand **★★Hotel de Moura**, 1 Praça Gago Coutinho, © 22494 (*inexpensive*) suffers from asylum-like interior fixtures, rendering the pine furniture incongruous but the televisions less so. The recent refit has tried to restore some of its former glory, namely with a boar's head which glowers in the lounge. Alternatively there's the **Residencial Italiana**, 8 Rua da Vitória, © 22348 (*cheap*), by the railway station, with clean rooms in need of an airing. Just up the road is **Pensão Alentejana**, Largo José Maria dos Santos (*very cheap*), which has large, somewhat shabby rooms which manage to retain a certain charm. Some are extremely noisy and the upstairs bedrooms have small skylights in the sloping ceilings rather than windows. For all this, it's friendly and clean.

Moura © (085–)   **Eating Out**

The best place to eat is **O Tunél**, 13 Rua dos Ourives (*cheap*), an attractive little place with a tunnelled ceiling and several brick arches. The food is surprisingly good, though at lunchtime the waiters are overstretched. The *bacalhau à Gomes de Sá* is great. **Clarabóia**, Rua da República, © 22267 (*moderate*) is in a beautiful, sympathetic modern building, spoilt by the bright lighting and lack of intimacy. The simple fare includes roast lamb, and the prawns at the bar make a nice change from *tremoceiros* (lupin seeds).

Serpa

The peaceful little town of Serpa is located where the plains give way to smooth, undulating hills, 28km southeast of Beja. There's something quintessentially Portuguese about the place—its 8000 souls appear to live a life untainted by anything other than the Moors, 750 years ago. Kids stare at visitors, who seem to be invisible to the old people ruminating beside 2000-year-old olive trees. Serpa boasts Portugal's Whitest Street, cobbled and quiet, and also some of the country's finest ewes'-milk cheese.

The western approach to Serpa is very striking—the plain, flat façade of the Solar of the Counts of Ficalho is built into the town walls, supplied by a slender aqueduct and chain pump, beside the conical late 13th-century Gates of Beja. The **Solar** was built in the 17th century by the Bishop of Guarda, a native of Serpa and a member of the Melo family. It remains in private hands.

Getting There

The nearest **train** station is at Beja from where there are connecting buses (½hr), which continue to Moura (½hr).

There are a couple of RN Express **buses** daily from Lisbon (4hrs), via Setúbal (2½hrs) and Beja (½hr).

***

✆ *(084–)*   ***Tourist Information***

The **tourist office** is at the bottom of the steps to the citadel at 2 Largo Dom Jorge de Melo, ✆ 90335 (*open 9–12.30 and 4–7.30*). From the **bus stop** walk along the Rua Soldado and turn right into the Rua dos Cavalos, for the Praça da República and the tourist office.

***

The Castle Hillock

Within the town walls, a wide staircase near the tourist office leads up to the castle hillock, which was first inhabited by the Celts in the 4th century BC. Gnarled olive trees camouflage equally gnarled time-passers on the cobbled terrace fronting the clock tower and the gothic **Igreja Matriz**, whose pale grey capitals are carved with mythological beasts. Beside the church, a huge dislocated chunk of wall perches dramatically above the entrance to the **castle**. It has been there since 1707, when part of Dom Dinis' fortification was blown up by the Spanish Duke of Ossuna during the War of Spanish Succession. The wall blooms with wind-blown flowers, and, high above passers-by, a lemon tree ripens beside the boulder. Behind them, a cockerel weathervane has been peppered with pot-shots.

Elsewhere, the crenellated castle walls are intact, offering beautiful views of the town's terracotta roofs and palm trees, to the wide-open country beyond. When things got too dangerous for the 13th-century residents of Serpa, they abandoned their houses within the castle's outer walls, and rumbled their carts through the zigzagged principal entrance gate of the inner line of defence, which is now visible from the ground floor of the **castle's museum**. Its extensive collection of prehistoric remains includes the tools of daily life employed by *homo erectus*, and a seated lifesize rendition of the Last Supper in plaster of Paris.

In and Around the Walled Town

The great pleasure of Serpa is wandering the irregular streets of the walled town, around the Rua da Figueira (fig tree) and the Rua da Parreira (trellis). At No.4 Rua dos Canos, an old man makes chairs, from start to finish. He gathers and dries reeds from the river, which he plaits for the seat. He collects and strips wood for the frame. Each chair takes him four days, once he has assembled the materials. He charges 2000$00 per chair.

Housed in the old municipal market, the **Ethnographic Museum**, off the Largo do Corro (*open Tues–Sat 9–12 and 2–6*), backs on to the eastern side of the town walls. It displays the tools of cobblers, carpenters, and blacksmiths. There's a press for pork tripe, a huge Sheffield bellows and a swineherd's costume, complete with Mexican-style saddle bag and a pig-whip.

The short Rua de Lampreia runs north from the Largo; at its end, turn right and then left into the Rua da Ladeira, to get to the **convento de Santo António**, founded in 1463 and abandoned at the time of the 1974 Revolution, when it was occupied by students. Now it is annexed to an old people's home; ask there for the key. Its most interesting feature is a series of 18th-century *azulejos* of the life of St Francis, who is shown letting down a rope to help some decidedly naked and breasty people out of Hell, while a winged Christ flies heavenwards with his cross. Cats wander about the church, communing with the angels carved on the retable.

Returning to the Largo do Corro, the Rua A.C. Calisto becomes the Rua do Calvário. Turn right into the Alameda do Correia da Serra for the compact **Botanic Gardens**, fronted by a Roman road lined with olive trees planted by the Romans themselves. The garden is a good place to watch life go by, to the accompaniment of almost continuous radio music. Hollowed oak logs serve as beehives, set in a bed of local shrubs. A moonlight fern also grows here (the seed was smuggled from Switzerland in someone's pocket).

The **Pulo do Lobo waterfall** (translates as Wolf's Leap) can be reached by following the road from Mértola to Beja and turning right after about 3km. This is a better road than the one from Serpa which is really quite rough after the village of São Brás. The waterfall tumbles in singular scenery—the river has cut a profound gorge through the valley which itself is made up of strange and rather creepy rock formations. A powerful and primeval place.

Serpa ✆ (084–)   **Where to Stay**

The **Pousada de São Gens**, Alto de São Gens, ✆ 53724/5 (*category C*), is 2km south of town—turn right where the houses stop. It's on a mount of olives, and the modern building is well designed to exploit the enormous views of endless, chequered yellow and brown plains. Bedrooms are equipped for the heat with air-conditioning and terracotta floors. Bathrooms are pleasant, and there's a swimming pool. The public rooms are habitable, with a fairly elegant dining room featuring a rustic menu. The roast leg of pork is very good, while an *à la carte* choice might be stewed hare in white rice or partridge with nuts. Pastries are homemade.

Occupying a corner slot next to the supermarket, the new **Residencial Beatriz**, 10 Largo do Salvador, ✆ 53423 (*inexpensive*) offers spacious, clean, air-conditioned rooms, complete with bathroom and TV. Comfortable, if rather plain.

The unsigned **Pensão Virgínia**, 75 Rua do Rossio, ✆ 90145 (*cheap*), at the bus stop, has a variety of rooms; some are OK, some are rather mean, with tiny windows. Hot water is hard to come by. It's expensive for what you get. Alternatively, across the square and round the corner to its right, there are very cheap rooms to let above the restaurant **O Casarão**, ✆ 90295.

Turismo de Habitação

Monte da Diabrória, Beringel, ✆ 98177 (*inexpensive*) is a huddle of picturesque farm buildings close to a game reserve. Inside, the rooms are rustic and characterful, with animal skins splayed on the floors, and roaring fires.

Eating Out

The best place to eat inexpensively is the small and cosy **Cuiça-Filho** at 18 Rua das Portas de Beja, ✆ 90566 (*cheap*). One of the more imaginative dishes on the menu is the tasty *arroz de polvo* (octopus rice).

Also near the tourist office there's the **Alentejano**, Praça da República, ✆ 90502 (*cheap*), with brick arches, a blue ceiling, and an almost Italianate feel to its first-floor restaurant. It specializes in long, smoky lunches for business types. **Restaurante O Zé** in Praça da República is simpler but always busy, featuring good *gazpacho* and local cheese (*moderate–cheap*).

The **Cervejaria Lebrinha**, 6–8 Rua do Calvário, ✆ 90311 (near the Botanic Garden) has superb draught beer.

Mértola

The delightfully slow little town of Mértola creeps up the steep bank of the curvaceous River Guadiana, at its confluence with the River Oeiras, 50km south of Serpa and 58km north of Castro Marim. The gritty soil around Mértola hampers agriculture, but the habitat is suitable to partridges, rabbits, hares, foxes, wolves and wild boars. The subsoil is rich in manganese, copper and lead, but they're expensive to extract, and the deposits at São Domingos are almost exhausted. Nowadays the town hall is the only significant employer; most visible wealth comes from contraband, usually televisions bought duty-free in Ceuta in Morocco, and taken to Spain.

Modern Mértola is ugly and nondescript, but tiers of tiny low houses crowd between the river and the castle ruins. The most comfortable place to pass the time is by the wall which runs parallel to the flow. Try leaning against it and you may meet bearded Iléas, an anarchist painter whose aura of untidiness rivals Snoopy's friend Pigpen.

Away from tourists and equipped only with basic accommodation, Mértola is a great base from which to explore the beautiful banks of the Guadiana. Downstream, the river is serene and happy, smooth enough to mirror its own green banks. Turtles peep out at visitors, storks rap undeterred, and snakes serpent themselves away in terror.

History

The Phoenicians sailed up the Guadiana and founded a settlement here, which became an important commercial centre for themselves and the Carthaginians. The Romans made Mirtilis grand, because it occupied a key defensive point on their road from Beja to Castro Marim; it minted coin between 189 and 170 BC. The Moors called it Mirtolah, and built walls around it in the 12th century. These failed to prevent Dom Sancho II conquering the town in 1238. He handed it to the Order of Sant'Iago, to settle and defend.

Getting There

Express buses run from Lisbon (4¼hrs), via Beja (¾hr), or, in the other direction, from Vila Real de Santo António (1½hrs). If you are travelling on a Sunday, the ticket office is only open until 10am so be sure to get up early enough—the inspectors are highly unsympathetic and won't let tourists on the bus without a pre-paid ticket.

℡ (086–)   *Tourist Information*

The **tourist office** is in the Largo Vasco de Gama, in the old part of town, on the road up to the cathedral. The bus station, ℡ 62157, is in the new town, near the main road to Beja.

Around the Town

At the uppermost point of town, the decaying **castle** dates from 1292; it's dramatic only when seen from the southern approach to Mértola, silhouetted above the Moorish town walls. Just downhill, an 11th-century mosque has been converted into the **Igreja Matriz**, without substantially altering the structure. The pineapple-top merlons are typically mudéjar, but the cylindrical towers which buttress the church are native. A bell tower now performs the muezzin's function, and, within the church, an altar stands in front of the *mihrab*, the niche which indicates the direction of Mecca. The square church has five naves, with 13th-century Gothic vaulting.

Further downhill, the **Town Hall** has recently discovered its Roman foundations. These have been adapted into a well-designed museum, with various Roman artefacts and sculptures. Around the corner, the small **municipal museum** contains Moorish pottery, excavated bones, and puppet-like figures—who required only the upper half of their bodies, because their nether regions were hidden by clothes.

The district of Mértola hosts a flock of **black vultures**. The species is in danger of extinction, and the Mértola birds are now dependent upon the munificence of the municipality. Every Monday a jeep deposits animal carcasses for their delectation. They seem to know that a meal is coming, and their wings are audible as they arrive. Would-be spectators should ask nicely at the town hall. It's also worth enquiring there about the plans to run a **tour boat** from Mértola to Vila Real de Santo António at the mouth of the Guadiana and vice versa, which would be a fabulous journey.

A door in the town walls gave access onto the fortified **jetty**, which was probably built by the Moors from Roman materials. Now only stacks remain. Here the tree tops are draped with debris, evidence of river floods. The Guadiana is narrow enough for fishermen to shout across on a Sunday afternoon, as they mend the nets normally buoyed in arcs.

A bridge crosses the Rio Oeiras just south of Mértola. Walking across this, you come to a **convent** planted with kumquats and now inhabited by a Dutch family, who sell bread. Walk through the convent to get to the path by the river.

Mina de São Domingos

Seventeen km east of Mértola lie the old copper mines of São Domingos (*there's a bus from Mertola at around 12.30, returning at around 6pm*). Known to the Romans, they were rediscovered in 1857 and worked by a British firm and some 7000 dependants until about 1960. Then the mines closed and the population was decimated. Now it's something of a ghost town, an ideal setting for a Tarkovsky film. São Domingo was once illustrious enough to be the first town in Portugal to have telephones, trains and electricity. More importantly to the Portugese, it was the first town that allowed foreign players in its football team: two Englishmen played for the town in the 1920s.

Mértola ℂ (086–)   **Where to Stay**

Pensão Beira-Rio, Rua Dr. Afonso Costa, ℂ 62340 (*cheap*) is down by the river, with a good view only slightly spoilt by the small factory opposite, and very nice new shared bathrooms with plenty of hot water if you remember to light the gas boiler. Each of the parquet-floored rooms has a desk, but the beds are a bit lumpy and all the doors stick—you may spend all your time fighting with the locks; to open the front door, pull it towards you as you turn the key. The garden is full of sweet-smelling orange trees. This is preferable to **Pensão San Remo**, Av. Aureliano Mira Fernandes, ℂ 62132 (*cheap*), in the square opposite the bus depot, which is decent but a bit soulless. The reception desk is at the restaurant of the same name, opposite. The back rooms have neither view nor sunshine, though this keeps them cool. The constant and forceful supply of hot water will be a treat for budget travellers coming from other parts of the Baixo Alentejo.

Mértola ℂ (086–)   **Eating Out**

There are no really interesting restaurants in Mértola; most have plain menus, little atmosphere, and reasonable food. The **Restaurante Alengarve**, Av. Aureliano Mira Fernandes, ℂ 62210 (*cheap*), in the square opposite the bus depot, is one of the better ones. The **Restaurante O Churrasco** (*cheap*) is filled with garrulous Portuguese enjoying good food featuring seasonal specialities; in summer the *ensopa de borrego* (spring lamb casserole) is recommended. In winter, try *lampreia* which is an eel-like fish cooked with rice in its own blood (more appetizing than it sounds). Do take time to chat with the charming Tonie, the English-speaking owner.

Alcácer do Sal

After 94km, the route south from Lisbon passes through the attractive town of Alcácer do Sal, which wells up from the Sado river and its flooded rice paddies and salt marshes. Weeds grow on the roofs of houses, and prawns are sold along the promenade.

The Phoenicians established themselves here in the second half of the 7th century BC, discarding those amphorae and striped painted pots which excited subsequent archaeologists. It was the capital of the Moorish province of Al-kassr and, before 1500, it produced some of the purest salt in Europe (assisted by a tiny seaweed present in the Tagus and Sado estuaries, which retained the impurities). From the days of the Moors until the 19th century, this was the chief market town for the Alentejo's cereal crops.

Ornately carved stone or marble fragments embedded in the outside walls of various houses are often the only reminders of Alcácer's past. Today the main reason for stopping here is to see the majestic **storks**, which build basket nests on church roofs, particularly up by the ruined Moorish castle. The castle incorporates the late 12th-century **church of Santa Maria**, whose well-proportioned interior features the Capela do Santissimo, in which babies and angels romp among plants and birds on yellow, blue and green 17th-century *azulejos*.

Below the castle, the classical-style **church of Santo António** was founded by the captain of Dom João II's light horsemen in 1524, and is topped by a dome of semi-transparent jasper. Closer to the river, the former church of Esp'rito Santo now serves as a small **Archaeological Museum**.

Tróia

About 43km northwest of Alcácer, a road runs along a narrow promontory at the mouth of the River Sado to the newly developed resort of Tróia, where highrise hotels look across the river estuary to the port of Setúbal. *Ferries to Setúbal run every 45 minutes and take 20 minutes (540$00 for car plus driver).*

Tróia was first settled by the Phoenicians, and served as the Roman fishing port of Cetobriga from the 1st century AD until it was destroyed by an earthquake in 412. The numerous fish-salting tanks discovered here and at other ports on the Sado estuary are evidence of the preserved fish and *garum* (a blend of fish, oysters, roe and crabs) industries, whose produce was exported in locally manufactured amphorae.

The **Roman ruins** are on the landward side of the promontory, a couple of km from the ferry point to and from Setúbal—but they are unlovely, and not worth a large diversion. At the entrance to the ruins, there is a cemetery which looks like an underground boiler room, and a graveyard. The marble tongues on gravestones mark kneeling spots. The dignitaries' crematorium remains fairly intact, complete with the wall niches where their 4th-century ashes were kept. The path forks: ruins surface along 2km of the left-hand fork, for three-quarters of the site remains unexcavated. If you've come to Tróia for the **beach**, the sea side of the promontory is less polluted and more empty.

The Alentejo Coast

The coast of the Alentejo, stretching south from the mouth of the River Sado to the border with the Algarve just south of Zambujeira, offers the country's best opportunities for low-key beachlife away from the crowds. The grey rock cliffs of the coastline are punctuated by sandy coves and bays, which offer meagre shelter from the wind and waves of the Atlantic, and do little to warm the chilly water, which is noticeably cooler than in the eastern Algarve. The Alentejo coast attracts those Portuguese who are in on the secret (although the word is becoming more widespread), and a mixed bag of world travellers.

There is very little infrastructure—the remoter spots are literally off the beaten track. Elsewhere, accommodation is basic, with one or two exceptions, and getting about is difficult without your own transport.

Getting There

If you're dependent on public transport, there are two access points to the coast: at Santiago do Cacém, from which there are semi-frequent **buses** to the Lagoa de Santo André; and at Odemira, from which there are semi-frequent buses to Vila Nova de Milfontes. Vila Nova de Milfontes can also be reached by the fairly frequent RN Express bus from Lisbon (3¾hrs), via Setúbal (3hrs) and Santiago do Cacém (1¼hrs).

Santiago do Cacém

Some 97km south of Setúbal, the airy town of Santiago do Cacém sweeps across the amphitheatre formed by two hills, in the middle of the hummocky, fertile Serra de Grándola. The squat windmills of the neighbourhood now stand defunct, except for one with kite-like sails.

Legend tells how the town received its name: a blood-curdling leader fled the eastern Mediterranean and armed a squadron of troops. She led them inland from Sines and on St James' Day (*Dia de Santiago*) cut off the head of the town's Muslim ruler, who was called Kassen. Hence Santiago de Kassen. The historians are more sober: the knights of São Tiago (St James) captured the town from the Moors in 1186, only to be driven out by the Caliph Yakub five years later. Things were finally settled in 1217, when the fierce Bishop of Lisbon retook Santiago, with the help of the Templars and the knights of São Tiago.

The landscape of the Serra de Grándola is pretty and friendly rather than dramatic, offering good opportunities for walkers, despite the lack of maps. The old part of town around the castle is decaying, with the exception of several symmetrical *palácios*; the new part is overshadowed by a block of flats built like a battleship. Gypsy horsecarts lollop through, with terriers like mascots, and mirrored harnesses.

Santiago is useful as a base for visiting the sand beach at the Lagoa de Santo André, half an hour away by bus or car.

Santiago's train station was closed in 1990, making connections awkward. Depart from Lisbon's Terreiro do Paço (7.40am or 6.30pm), change at Barreiro and, after 2hrs, at Ermidas-Sado, from where there are connecting **buses** to Santiago (arriving 11.10am and 9.55pm respectively). Services from all stations in the Algarve are similarly infrequent.

Semi-frequent RN Express **buses** from Lisbon take 2¼hrs, via Setúbal (1½hrs), with infrequent buses in the other direction from Vila Nova de Milfontes (1¼hrs). The same company runs two buses daily from main towns in the Algarve, and one from Beja.

℗(069–)   **Tourist Information**

The **tourist office** is in the Praça de Mercado, ℗ 826696. The **bus station** is near the centre of town in the Praça M. Albuquerque.

On a hill to the north of the town, pervaded by a great peace and sense of the past, stand the ruins of Roman **Miróbriga** (*open 9–1 and 2.45–6.45; closed Sun, Mon and holidays*). To get to these, go about 1km up the Lisbon road, where there's a signposted turning, sharp right. Turn left off this after a 10-minute walk. The fenced site occupies several gentle green hillslopes, crossed by paths lined with cypress trees.

Miróbriga probably started life as a Celtic *castro* in the Iron Age, around the 4th century BC. Coins unearthed here indicate that by the 2nd or 1st century BC the settlement was trading with towns in southern Spain. On the highest point stands a temple of Aesculapius, with a temple of Venus; below them a shed protects the market. A path leads down to the baths, complete with gymnasium and massage room. There's enough space to get pleasantly lost, and drift about conjuring up 1st- and 2nd-century Romans—you may even stumble across the housing sector, which remains undiscovered.

Back in town, the excellent **municipal museum** (*open 10–12.30 and 2–5.30; closed Fri, Sat, Mon and holidays*) in the Praça do Municipio, off the straight, modern Av. Dom Nuno Álvares Pereira, displays knick-knacks from the site. The museum is housed in a late 19th-century prison, operational until the Revolution of 1974. The jail doors remain, as does one cell—there was no limit to the number of Salazar's prisoners it would hold. Another cell has been converted into a 'typical country' bedroom, and a third into a noble's room.

On the ground floor, a lively creative spirit flits through the knitted rags, paper decorations, and, in the 'typical kitchen', a *barreleiro*. In this hollowed cork log, boiling water was poured over a muslin cloth containing wood ash and sweet-smelling herbs, to produce suitably alkaline water for washing. Also in the kitchen are a cork baby cage, complete with bell, a collection of birds' nests, and a paddle for punishing urchins.

On a hilltop above the town, the extensively restored **castle walls** are best seen from afar. Around 190m long, they form a parallelogram, with semi-cylindrical walls and a sentinel's path running along the outer line of defence. The walls now encircle a cemetery, with attendant white marble tombs, cypress trees, and a compost heap of decaying flowers.

Santiago do Cacém © (069–) — Where to Stay

The **Pousada de São Tiago**, Estrada National, © 22459 (*category B*), on the Lisbon road, on the edge of town, is a burnt-pink building set back from the road, surrounded by cacti and succulents. It's an attractive and homey little place, quaintly furnished, and in parts looking across the sweep of the town to the castle. However, the bathrooms' linoleum floors and single-bar electric heaters are none too luxurious. The restaurant is kitted out in 'rustic' style, including pottery objects above the windows, but the menu is remarkably unimaginative. All the same, the *migas com carne de porco frita* (boiled bread and fried pork) is good, and may be eaten on the terrace in summer, overlooking the ramshackle garden, and the decent-sized swimming pool.

Pousada Quinta da Ortiga, © 22871 (*category B*) is a simpler affair with rather low ceilings and busy sofa covers. The grounds are nice and quite lush with a good-sized swimming pool.

By contrast, the ★★★★**Albergaria Dom Nuno**, 88–92 Avenida Dom Nuno Álvares Pereira, © 23325, @ 23328 (*moderate*), in the straight, modern street at the bottom of the municipal park, is large, neutral and sanitary, with a kitchen-like restaurant suitable for groups. A better bet is the ★★★**Residencial Gabriel**, 24 Rua Prof. Egas Moniz, © 22245, @ 826102 (*inexpensive*), a short walk from the bus station (in the direction of the old part of town), which is pleasantly furnished, comfortable and adequate. Its annexe, the ★★**Pensão Idéal**, is drab (*cheap*). However, it is preferable to noisy **Pensão Covas**, 8–10 Rua Cidade de Setúbal, © 22675 (*cheap*)—next to the bus station: ask in the café of the same name—where bedroom doors are glassed, toilets are without seats and grandma spends her days shuffling with her zimmer between the bathroom and her bedroom. But it is friendly.

Santiago do Cacém © (069–) — Eating Out

Santiago is short on gastronomic delights. Apart from the *pousada*, try **O Braseiro**, 15 Rua Prof. Egas Moniz, © 22988. The same kitchen serves a 'fancy' restaurant—where diners sit on local wicker chairs under a black ceiling while waiters serve their enjoyable *bife de vacana basa* (*moderate*)—and a very good cheap eating place, with fish swimming in butter (*cheap*). Avoid the house wine.

Lagoa de Santo André

Twelve km northwest of Santiago do Cacém, half an hour by road, a strip of sand separates a lagoon from the sea. The **beach** is large and flat, headed by a collection of fish restaurants arranged around a pleasant, reedy little bay. If you're swimming in the ocean, be particularly careful of the undertow.

There's just one place to stay, though numerous private rooms are offered to let. The ★★★**Residencial Santo André**, ✆ 069 79117 (*inexpensive*) is ugly and box-like, with damp walls and a disappointing view. **A Fragateira** (*moderate*) is a good place to eat, on benches, with bamboo trimmings and fishy murals. Be sure to try the pine-kernel sweets.

Sines

Twenty km southwest of Santiago de Cacém, the Cabo de Sines is a giant pimple on the coastline. Like all pimples, it's better left alone. As you approach, the smell of pinetrees gives way to an industrial stink, emitted by tubular monsters. The town is charmless, the bay planted with oil tankers. This was the birthplace of Vasco da Gama. Presumably his descendants feel similarly impelled to leave Sines.

São Torpes and Morgave

These two beaches are both south of Sines, but still a little too close for comfort. Despite the smooth sand and low waves, there's little to recommend them (except that São Torpes was Nero's chief steward).

Porto Covo

The soil alternates between deep red, light red, and white on the approach to Porto Covo, a laid-back little place with the sea at the end of its straight main street, 6km off the Sines–Odemira road. There used to be no problem camping in the caves around the several small **beach coves**—being careful of the tides—but now that a camp site has opened, the police tell people they're not allowed there or in the woods.

The village has two *pensions*, including the **Abelha**, 40 Rua Vasco da Gama, ✆ 069 95108 (*cheap*), which offers squashed but decent rooms. The **Cácome** is a nice place for a beer, with bullfight posters. Each day, three buses make the journey from Sines.

Ilha do Pessegueiro

Approached from a turning off the Porto Covo–Milfontes route, a tiny settlement huddles together opposite a barren little island about 1km offshore, the main focus of the settlement being the campsite. Sometimes fishermen can be persuaded to ferry visitors to the island, which is topped by a ruined castle built by Dom Pedro II towards the end of the 17th century, to stave off pirates. The mainland offers a very white beach, lots of bottles, campers, dreadlocks, public toilets and showers, and the **Restaurant Ilha** (*cheap*), which plays slow, jazzy music and serves good food, including tuna steak. You can ask here about private rooms. There's no public transport.

Vila Nova de Milfontes

The coast road passes through a barren wilderness between Porto Covo and Vila Nova de Milfontes, an undeveloped town on the estuary of the River Mira. The skyline is low and the street plan pleasantly muddled. This is the most popular resort in the Alentejo, so the limited number of rooms soon gets fully booked. If you choose to swim in the estuary rather than the ocean, watch out for the terrifically strong current.

© (083–) **Tourist Information**

The very helpful **tourist office** is on Rua António Mantes, *©* 96599 (*open 10am–11pm during the summer months*).

© (083–) **Where to Stay**

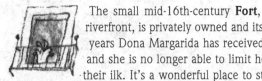

The small mid-16th-century **Fort**, *©* 96108 (*expensive*), on the riverfront, is privately owned and its drawbridge is down. For many years Dona Margarida has received paying guests; times are hard, and she is no longer able to limit her clientele to ambassadors and their ilk. It's a wonderful place to stay, and she remains extremely choosey about who may occupy the seven guestrooms, some of which are kept for friends. The interior is furnished with a suit of armour, animal horns on the stone walls, and a single long dining table with autumn leaves pressed under its glass top, at which all guests dine. The food is said to be excellent. Full board only; picnic lunches by request.

After that, nothing's quite the same. **Casa dos Arcos**, Rua dos Carris, *©* 96264 (*inexpensive*) is built and furnished in emigrant style—everything new and flashy. Similarly uninteresting, but not bad, is ★★★★**Residencial Mil-Réis**, *©* 99223 (*inexpensive*). The unprepossesing exterior and rather lurid reception area of the **Pensão Residencial Eira da Pedra**, *©* 99662 (*inexpensive*) belie comfortable rooms which are rather good value; some come with a sea view and may be rented by the week.

Otherwise there's **Mira Nobre**, *©* 96227 (*cheap*). First, distract the manager from his game of chequers. Then, smile while he whistles to one of his three dogs, Pluto, Nubi and Tucha. Finally, he will mop his brow up two flights of stairs, to a set of five rooms that share a fridge and sink and access to the roof, with laundry facilities. The rooms are a bit bare, with sloping wooden ceilings.

© (083–) **Eating Out**

Portal da Vila, 5-A Rua Sarmento Beires (*expensive*) is a nice little fish restaurant in a walled garden with tiled tables lit by lanterns. Main courses vary with the catch. **A Fateixa**, *©* 96415 (*cheap*) is so relaxed that the chef might forget to cook your food, but the place feels 'authentic' because it's right next to the quay, and the sight of lobster pots induces a belief in the freshness of the food. There is a couple of tables outside.

Odemira

Quizzical looks from the older residents suggest that Odemira has a shock around the corner; the stream of visitors is bound to swell. The town is a useful **junction** for visiting beaches. It nestles in hilly land 20km inland on the River Mira, undisturbed except for the pleas of exotic birds kept on cement floors in the municipal park, and the occasional raised eyebrow at the pipes stuck into a rockface masquerading as a sculpture.

© (083–)   *Where to Stay and Eating Out*

Residencial Rita, Largo do Poço Novo, © 22423 (*cheap*)—turn left out of the bus station; ring bell 2E—can be a bit dark, but is mostly comfortable, in emigrant style, with costly tack in the bathrooms. **Residencial Idálio**, 28 Rua Eng. Arantes Oliveira, © 22156 (*very cheap*) is OK and clean. For a meal, **A Lanchonete**, 3 Trav. 1 Maio (*cheap*) tries hard to please, in French, English and German. Food is well presented.

Rocky coast

The Algarve

The Algarve is a great amphitheatre facing the sea: the landscape changes from the thickly wooded Serra de Monchique (902m) and the rounded, cultivated hills of the Serra do Caldeirão (577m), to a zone of crests running parallel to the coast, cut by the valleys of rivers flowing down from the hills. Here are the orchards of the Algarve—the almonds, the carobs, the olives, and the figs which the Romans lauded and which, in the 17th century, were dried and exported to Flanders and the Levant. The Algarve is also laden with orange trees (though fresh orange juice is almost impossible to buy). The almond trees' pale pink blossom clouds the province from the middle of January to the end of February, above a mantle of bright yellow Bermuda buttercups. (A legendary Moorish king married a legendary Scandanavian beauty and brought her to his capital at Silves. He offered her his all, but she was unhappy: she missed her country's snow. So the king planted thousands of almond trees.) In March and April, the roads of the Algarve are fringed by quince trees' large white blossoms tinged with pink, as well as irises, golden yellow narcissi, jonquils, and tall, freely branched asphodels whose white flowers are veined with red.

The coastal zone separates into two areas: the *sotavento*, east of Faro, with sand dunes, salt lagoons, and a broken spit of sand sheltering the coast; and the *barlavento*, to the west of Portimão, a more humid area of mainly rocky coast, with cliffs up to 80m high, whose sandy bays and coves are separated by weird grottoes and peculiar rock outcrops, exposed to the Atlantic winds. The two are divided by an area of reddish sandy cliffs wooded with pines. The Mediterranean climate brings mild winters and long, warm summers—an equilibrium assisted by the hills, which shelter the province from the northerly winds that blow cold in winter and very hot in summer. The annual rainfall at the coast is just 400–500mm.

Tourism is not the Algarve's only moneyspinner. Fishing is a buoyant source of revenue, as well as brick factories with brick chimneys, and hothouse tomatoes, strawberries, and avocados for export. Inland, dry stone walls pen sheep with pendulous undocked tails, a breed which originated in west Africa, whose coarse wool is used for stuffing mattresses and weaving into heavy blankets. The shepherds wear ex-army swallowtail caps, surplus from the African wars.

Adventurous and independent travellers can take heart: there is not too much development west of Lagos, east of Faro, or inland. Lonely beaches backed by tiny whitewashed settlements do exist, though access is sometimes a problem—but hurry, lest the developers beat you there. Inland, there are some lovely walks in the hills, detailed in the Algarve tourist office's commonsensical *Guide to Walks*.

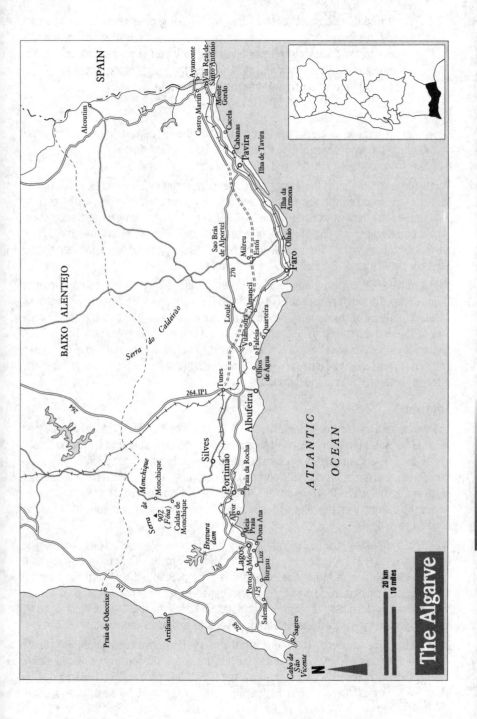

The Algarve

20 km
10 miles

N

403

The rapid development of the Algarve has put great strains on the water supply: it's best not drink tapwater in the summer months, when water levels run low. This sometimes leads to the water supply being cut off for a few hours in the early evening, and usually reconnected just when you're resigned to being salt-encrusted overnight.

History

Drawn by the mineral wealth of the Peninsula, the Phoenicians settled in Spain c. 1364 BC, founding the city of Ossonoba (possibly on the site now occupied by Faro) as an important base for their trade in marble and amber, but little remains of their civilization.

The blood and customs of the Algarve have been much more forcibly influenced by the Moors, who occupied the region from the early 8th century to the mid-13th century, though they too left few material remains. Their legacy is of roof terraces, inner patios, slim chimneys patterned like sugar cellars, through which smoke percolates, and bucket wheels for raising water. The people of the Algarve have darker complexions than their northern counterparts, and tend to be more garrulous and agitated.

The conquest of the Algarve, undertaken by Dom Sancho I, remained incomplete until Dom Afonso III's military successes of 1249. In the 12th and 13th centuries, Christians labelled that part of the country which remained in Moorish hands 'Algarve'. For the Moors themselves, the province of el-Gharb encompassed the western part of the Peninsula as well as the coast of North Africa at Ceuta, Tangiers and Fez. Thus when Tangier surrendered to Dom Afonso V, he styled himself 'King of Portugal and the Algarves, both on this side and beyond the sea'.

Tourism

The Portuguese are fond of saying that 'The Algarve is not Portugal'. This used to be true because the southern province was Moorish; today it is German, Scandanavian, British and French. The 85km stretch of coast between Faro and Lagos is jam-packed with high-rise hotels, apartment blocks, villa complexes, shopping centres and water parks—and more are on the way. Concrete mixer trucks throw up clouds of dust along roads lined with rubble, supplying building sites bustling under the midday sun and the midnight floodlights.

When Faro airport opened in the early 1960s, the Algarve was something of a secret. The Salazar government kept such planning applications as there were under tight control, until the Revolution of 1974 toppled both the government and the controls. Tourism would bring employment to a poor region, so opportunist local councils adopted a more laissez-faire approach. Building did not really take off until the mid-1980s, when Spanish hoteliers upped their prices, and British tour operators looked for new pastures.

In 1964 the Algarve offered 1000 tourist beds; by 1988 this had reached 58,500 and by 1990 the figure was 70,200, accounting for just under half the tourist beds in the entire country. Visitor numbers tell a similar story, with 7.9 million out of a total of 16.5 million visitors to Portugal from abroad holidaying in the Algarve. But, already, things are perceived to have gone too far: growth in visitor numbers to the Algarve has slowed down and restrictions have been imposed to control development in areas where concern is growing for the quality of Portuguese tourism.

The Wines of the Algarve

Vines flourished in the south of Portugal under the Moors, who left the making and selling of wine to Christian Mozarabs. Today, the Algarve is a Demarcated Region, but the wines are undistinguished. All but 3 per cent are reds, with a hefty 13% of alcohol stemming from the grapes' very high sugar content. It's certainly worth trying the Algarvian dry white apéritif wine, matured in wood and similar to an amontillado, as well as the fiery but flavourful *medronho* distilled from arbutus berries in the Monchique hills.

What to Eat

Superb fresh fish is the joy of Algarvian cooking, with an emphasis on sardines (*sardinhas*) and tuna (*atum*), both of which are quite unlike the tinned varieties. Cockles (*amêijoas*) are popular, cooked with smoked pork sausage, cured ham, tomatoes and onions in a *cataplana* (sealed wok). Several different fish can be used to make *xerém*, a kind of maize mash. Inland, you may find hare and partridge served during the hunting season. Algarvian *gaspacho* differs from its Spanish cousin in that the ingredients are diced rather than puréed, leaving the soup pleasantly crunchy. The marzipan sweets of the Algarve, shaped like fruits and filled with sugared egg yolk, may have Moorish origins, since they resemble those sold in North Africa. Figs and almonds are variously combined to make other delicious sweets and desserts. The Moors introduced citrus fruits to the Peninsula: the oranges of the Algarve are succulent, juicy navels.

Getting There

by air

Most visitors to the Algarve fly into Faro's international airport, turn nut-brown, and fly out again.

by car

Car ferries between Ayamonte in Spain and Vila Real de Santo António operate infrequently, now that a new bridge/border crossing has been completed (open constantly). The 'Via da Infante' motorway runs from here to northeast of Albufeira. This will eventually continue to Sagres, and then to Lisbon via the Alentejo coast. The 297km drive from Lisbon to Faro takes about 4hrs.

by train

Semi-frequent trains run to the Algarve from Barreiro (take the ferry from Lisbon's Terreiro do Paço), via Setúbal, Ermidas-Sado (change from Santiago do Cacém and Sines), Tunes (3hrs; change at Tunes for Silves and Lagos, 1¼hrs), Albufeira (4hrs), Faro (4½hrs), Olhão, Tavira (5hrs), Conceicão, Cacela, Castro Marim, and Vila Real de Santo António (5¾hrs).

EVA buses run a twice-daily Alta Qualidade service, complete with stewardess, drinks and video, from Lisbon to Ferreiras (4hrs), Albufeira, Vilamoura (4½hrs), Quarteira, Almancil and Faro (5hrs). Various other companies offer the same service.

Express buses take slightly longer to cover the same route, and continue beyond Faro to Olhão (5½hrs), Tavira (6hrs), Cacela, Monte Gordo and Vila Real de Santo António (6½hrs). These run three times daily, with an additional service to Faro from mid-June to mid-October. Buses run less frequently from Lisbon to Lagos. A single Express bus runs the length of the country from Chaves to Lagos (17hrs), via Vila Real (15½hrs), Viseu (13hrs), Coimbra (11½hrs), Lisbon (6hrs), Setúbal (5hrs), Albufeira (1hr) and Portimão (½hr). EVA buses are the main Algarvian bus company.

Getting Around

Because tourism is relatively new to the Algarve, there is no coast road: the highway runs parallel with the coast, 2 to 10km inland, and feeder roads branch out from there. (The Via Infante, as far as it is open, is the busiest route.) This makes it difficult to get off the beaten track by public transport. Hitch-hiking is demoralizing, because few of the many motorists stop, as most are tourists and already on unfamiliar ground.

In a way, travelling by public transport is simpler here than in other provinces because the bus and train stations are accustomed to baffled foreigners, and make allowances. A railway line stretches from Lagos to Vila Real de Santo António, a 4–4½hr trip serviced by frequent trains: note that some trains do not stop at the smaller stations. (Local buses are detailed in the text.)

West of Lagos

Praia de Odeceixe

On the Algarvian side of the border with the Alentejo, Praia de Odeceixe is a deep, grey stone bay with a flat tongue of sand which breaks the waves of the Atlantic far from the shore line. It's popular with young Germans. Ask for rooms at the café near the parking lot: there is plenty of cheap accommodation in people's homes.

Arrifana

There is something tough about Arrifana, on the west coast, 49km north of Sagres and 6km west of Aljezur. The rounded hills of the coastline, green with glistening cistus, drop in sheer slate-grey cliffs to a smooth bay backed by shingle and dotted with small stacks, against which breaking waves throw up foam. Ask for rooms at the **Restaurante Fortaleza**.

Carrapateira

The best feature of this small town is Bordeira beach a few kilometres to the west. Blissfully quiet, it stretches for miles and is lined with powerful and rugged cliffs rising majestically into the clouds.

Vila do Bispo

Ten km north of Sagres, on a junction of the west and south coast roads, lies a quiet and very sweet little town with a sunny central square and a lovely church, which has a fine Manueline doorway and is ablaze inside with gilding, painting and blue *azulejos*. There is a *pensão* opposite the church: **Pensão Mira–Sagres** (*cheap*), which is perfectly adequate, though it smells rather suspect. Alternatively ask for rooms at No.18 Praça da República, next to the bank (*very cheap*).

The nearest **beaches** are the Praias do Castelejo and Cordoama which lie 5km west of the town. There are no buses and without a car it is a gruelling walk over dusty hills and moors. These beaches are, however, two of the most stunning in the Algarve with stark, slate cliffs covered in a constant film of spray thrown up by the large waves. They stretch for miles, so it is easy to escape what crowds there are. There is a busy restaurant on Cordoama, run by chirpy people and serving good food too.

Cape St Vincent

The invigorating headland on the brink of Europe stands on raw, 60m cliffs, 6km west of Sagres. The landscape is naked: only shrubs and herbs will grow here. There is no settlement to speak of, but the land mass announces itself with one of the most powerful lighthouses in Europe, inhabited by seven families, and a ruined monastery.

The Romans called this the Promontorium Sacrum: at sundown the sun appeared a hundred times larger than elsewhere, and hissed as if it were being quenched. (A freak of atmospherics continues to magnify some of the sunsets, and occasionally the sun appears to yield a green flash as it vanishes.)

Later, St Vincent arrived by water from Valença, dead, in a boat guided by ravens. The promontory became a Christian shrine, and for centuries boats dipped their sails as they passed. The shrine has gone, but the ravens remain (although some of them are believed to have accompanied St Vincent's body on its removal to Lisbon in 1173). A later resident was rather more lively: Henry the Navigator lived and died on the site where the lighthouse stands, commuting to his school of navigation at Sagres. In 1693 these seas bore a naval battle between the French and the combined British and Dutch fleets, and it was here that the British fleet under Jervis and Nelson battled the Spanish in 1797. Sustained by the royal gift they had received when docking in the Tagus—400 bullocks, 400 sheep, chocolate, China tea, and 56 pipes of wine—the British were victorious, and Jervis became Count St Vincent.

There is no public transport between Cape St Vincent and Sagres. The path along the coast there and back is about 26km, making it a long but very pleasant walk.

On a barren rock promontory pelted by northwesterly winds, 36km west of Lagos, the little village of Sagres harbours the spirit of Portugal's groping exploration down the west African coast: a small peninsula some 300m wide juts out from the coast, and on this Henry the Navigator founded his school of navigation.

The wind and the sea are his only true monuments. The insubstantial and modern village is disappointing, laid along three straight parallel streets popular with noisy morning motorbikers. A gang of imitation Madonna pop stars whinge around the Club Recreação Infant Sagres, and world travellers with stories to tell and ham rolls to eat sit outside the Café Conchinha, occasionally playing a guitar. Fishermen with rods like interplanetary receivers lean against the walls at the top of the cliff catching anchovies, eels and snook.

History

In 1437, the Infante Dom Henrique, Henry the Navigator, son of Dom João I and Philippa of Lancaster, was obliged to leave his younger brother Dom Fernando as a hostage for the return of Ceuta to the Moors (*see* 'Batalha', p.235). Crushed by shame, a lesser man than Henry, as his pupil Magellan later remarked, 'would have hidden himself with seven yards of sackcloth and a rosary of oak-apples, to die in the wilds of the Serra de Ossa'.

But Henry found a more useful outlet for his ascetic tastes: he devoted himself—and his revenue as Duke of Viseu, Governor of the Algarve, monopolist of the soap and tunny fishing industries, and Governor of the Order of Christ—to encouraging and financing the exploration of the west coast of Africa. He founded a school of navigation at Sagres, gathering astronomers and astrologers, geographers, cartographers, Jews, seamen, and wandering Arabs, who were able to give first-hand accounts. Jaime Cresques was an early recruit, whose father had produced the Catalan atlas. It was here that the first caravels were built in secret, constructed of Alentejan oak and caulked with pine resin.

The infrastructure of trade developed so quickly that when Cadamosto arrived here in 1454, one of Henry's secretaries showed him 'samples of sugar from Madeira, dragons' blood, and other products', and explained that any merchant could take part in the Infante's trading ventures, on the following conditions: if the merchant provided both ship and cargo, he must pay Henry one-quarter of all he brought back; if the Infante provided the caravel, but the merchant provided the cargo, Henry was owed half of the returns; if nothing was brought back, the Infante would bear the expenses. Such was the volume of trade that at Sagres the apprentice Columbus wrote, 'The Torrid Zone is not uninhabitable, for the Portuguese are sailing to and fro' in it every day.'

The entire library of Henry the Navigator was destroyed when Drake called in at Sagres and set fire to the place, as he sailed home after burning Cadiz in 1587, when Portugal was united with Spain under Philip II of Spain.

Getting There

EVA buses run frequently from Lagos (1hr).

There is a small **tourist** booth in the centre of town which is open only on week-days. **Turinfo** is on Praça da República, ✆ 64520. Being a private company, they have a vested interest in the advice they offer; for rooms it may be better to make your own arrangements.

They usually make the accommodation situation sound desperate, but a quick walk around the square and the town will unearth a plethora of clean and cheap accommodation. They also hire bikes and mopeds, and arrange fishing trips and trips inland.

Around the Town

The Vaubanesque **fortress** which occupies the rocky plateau was completed in 1793—astonishingly, the Ministry of Culture has decreed it's ripe for development: a restaurant and conference centre are in the pipeline. Within its walls stands the simple 14th-century **chapel of NS da Graça** (not open to the public) and a huge, flat, wind compass, discovered in 1928. Named the Rosa-dos-Ventos, it is believed to be contemporary with Henry the Navigator.

Take care not to irritate his thickset, bushy-haired ghost: Azurara, his chronicler and pane-gyrist, reports that 'His aspect...was severe; when anger carried him away—rarely—his countenance became terrifying'. Nor should you try to outfright the ghost of him whose 'heart never knew fear other than the fear of sin'.

Sagres possesses some beautiful **beaches**, all boasting stunningly rugged cliff faces and each with an individual character: Mareta beach is to the right of and below the main square. Waves break against rocks on which people bask like lizards. Baleeira beach is by the harbour and nice enough. Martinhal is a five-minute walk away and popular with windsurfers. As you approach Tonel beach, you pass by some giant burnt-orange rocks of Martian aspect. The beach is sandy and the waves powerful; an ideal combination for surfing and hanging out. This beach has the youngest and coolest crowd. To the right you can clamber over the rocks to reach a small beach colonized by nude Germans. Beliche beach is about a kilometre down the road from Tonel and a beautiful secret with imposing cliffs which have formed many caves and coves. The water here is the warmest, clearest and calmest and there is good shelter from the wind.

To the north of Sagres on the west coast is a handful of virtually deserted beaches which are difficult to get to without your own transport. Take the road to Cape St Vincent and just before it swings left to the Cape, turn right onto an untarmacked road. From here drive on until you reach a dust track on the left, which you can follow to the edge of the cliffs. The views are exhilarating but the climb down to the beach is steep. As with all these beaches, care must be taken when swimming as the current is strong.

Away from other buildings, on a cliff between the fishing harbour and Mareta beach, the **Pousada do Infante**, ✆ 64222, 🖅 64225 (*category C★*), is a large colonnaded villa with good views across the beach cove to the promontory and its fort, and a healthy dose of Algarvian chimneys. Bedrooms are comfortable but not luxurious, with worn furniture, and balconies which look through to one another. In the corridors, dead flies may lie like currants in the striplights' plastic covers, over tatty carpets. Public rooms on the ground floor are more appealing, with striking wall tapestries and views to the small swimming pool. Nevertheless, it's overpriced. Good food is served in the dull dining room; anchovy caught nearby and grilled with butter sauce is a tasty option.

Slightly closer to the village, **★★★Hotel Apartamento O Navegante**, Rua Infante Dom Henrique, ✆ 64354, 🖅 64360, looks like a multilayered motorcoach. New and polite, its small-roomed gadgety apartments are furnished in totally inoffensive modern style. The building is arranged around a shady pear-shaped swimming pool. The best thing about the **★★★Hotel da Baleeira**, ✆ 64212, 🖅 64425, and its coffin-shaped swimming pool, is its site overlooking the harbour, with views stretching east to the cliffs of the Algarve. Inside, things are disappointing: package tours block-book, and bedrooms are floored with linoleum and walled with dirty paintwork.

moderate

If you want fabulous ocean views, head for **★★★★Residência Dom Henrique**, S'tio da Mareta, ✆ 64133, on a cliff above the Mareta beach. It's a middle-class home, with clean, simply furnished guest rooms, and a conservatory from which you can hear the surf. The little restaurant serves grilled squid. The **★★★Residencial Sagres**, Beco da Olaria, Baleeira, ✆ 64612, is located in the centre of Sagres with views over scrubland. Still, it's a clean and friendly place with a balcony to each room.

Otherwise, there are plenty of **very cheap** rooms to let in people's houses—ask at the Café Conchinha.

Sagres' hotels have decent restaurants, and there are a few sandwich bars in the village.

Just off the main square, overlooking the beach, **Mar À Vista**, ✆ 64247 (*expensive–moderate*), serves perfect food in the large, cool restaurant or on the sheltered terrace. The sprightly service is friendly. The bream is excellent.

Another enjoyable option is **Fortaleza de Beliche**, ✆ 64124 (*moderate*), installed in a little fort about a third of the way along the road from Sagres to Cape

St Vincent. Run by Enatur, the *pousada* people, it's decorated in Navigator style, with maps and fake candelabra. The waiters are smartly dressed and courteous, and the food is good.

Bossa Nova, Rua Cte Matoso, © 64566 (*moderate*) is a large and airy restaurant with a continental ambience. On the covered terrace German hippies happily rub shoulders with children dressed in Marks & Spencer's best. The food is a little expensive for what you get—you pay for the atmosphere—but the vegetarian options are cheaper. Avoid the tropical curry, though.

Rosa dos Ventos on the main square, © 64480 (*cheap*), is a bar serving a full range of good snacks and meals. It's owned by two (gracefully) ageing German hippies, complete with matching handlebar moustaches. In the evenings a happy mix of international (mainly German) travellers and locals get drunk together and stagger off to **Topaj** disco around 2am. Great fun.

Between Sagres and Lagos

Getting There

Semi-frequent buses run from Lagos (¾hr to Salema, ¼hr to Burgau and Luz), but you may have to walk from the highway.

Seventeen km east of Sagres and 22km west of Lagos, **Salema** is a rickety fishing village with a sheltered bay, whose rock cliffs fall to a sweep of smooth sand. Development is noticeable, but there is still a happy mix of locals and beach people, who come together to buy fruit and vegetables from the back of a van. The 2km road from the highway passes through a beautiful ravine banked with wild flowers. At the beach, an alley flanked by low and humble houses leads to the left, while to the right a road rises steeply up the cliff.

Eighteen km west of Lagos, **Burgau** is larger and more developed than Salema, with cobbled streets running down to the beach hemmed in by scree. It's popular with the English, though the shore can be quiet. The off-licence sells decorative painted pottery Algarvian housefronts for around 1000$00.

Backed by bare cliffs, **Luz** is popular with English families, who feel sufficiently distant from Faro airport and their loud compatriots. A few cool young dudes sun themselves among the kids.

Just east of Lagos, most of the beach people at **Porto de Mós** are youthful Portuguese. Umbrellas are planted in the sand.

© (082–)   *Where to Stay and Eating Out*

Salema

The characterful and quiet ★★★★**Estalagem Infante do Mar**, Praia da Salema, © 65137 (*moderate*) is encrusted on the cliff top. It's solid and rustic, with sea-view balconies and a small swimming pool. The spick and span restaurant serves good local dishes.

Various houses have **rooms to let**: the one with a green door, opposite the mini-market, offers two double rooms (*very cheap*). Hollyhocks grow in the courtyard, and a boxful of snails leave trails over one another.

There are a couple of places to eat. At the beachside, **Atlântico** has tables outside, and delicious fresh tuna (*cheap*).

Burgau

If you want entertaining accommodation, head for **Casa Grande**, © 65168 (*moderate*). It's a big old house on the edge of town, run by an English lady, and filled with dogs, cats, old cash registers, and excitable Portuguese. Not all the large rooms are tastefully furnished, but that doesn't matter. The restaurant is a wooden barn, with tile-topped tables, dripping candles, and live music every Wednesday and Saturday—just the right kind of place for a drink. The food is basic but good value. *Restaurant open evenings only; closed Sun.*

Luz

Apartments comprise most of the accommodation, though ★★★**Residencial Vila Mar**, 10 Estrada de Burgau, © 789541 (*moderate*), is one possibility. Diners at **A Concha**, 6 Avenida dos Pescadores (*moderate*), sit in rope chairs under a shady trellis. The **O Português**, Rua da Praia, © 788804 (*moderate*) serves grilled fish from an open-plan kitchen. *Closed Thurs.* The deli near the church is a good place to construct a picnic.

Lagos

The Ba'a de Lagos is one of the widest bays of the Portuguese coast, sheltered on the west by the Ponta da Piedade promontory, and on the east by the Ponta dos Trés Irmãos, or do Facho. The harbour town of Lagos commands the bay, on the hilly western bank of the estuary of the River Bensafrim.

Lagos is the principal resort of the western Algarve, particularly popular with Germans, attracting a more varied and sexy crowd than Faro or Albufeira. Yet there's still room for the locals to lead their lives without too much interruption. They shop in the market and let their dogs pick at bones in the wide streets, overflown by seagulls. The vertical rock cliffs of the coast are pocked with weird grottoes, which can be explored by boat.

History

The Lusitanian settlement of Lacobriga was destroyed by an earthquake, making way for its resettlement by the Carthaginians in 350 BC. When Sertorius took Lacobriga from the Romans in 76 BC, it grew into a flourishing town, and never looked back. Many of the early voyages to explore the coast of Guinea departed from this port—spawning the rope- and sail-making industries—after Gil Eanes sailed around Cape Bojador in 1434 and found the imprints of the feet of men and camels. Lançarote returned with a report on elephants, whose 'flesh will suffice to satisfy 500 men, and [the negroes] find it very good'. (The natives discarded the ivory, which was traded by Arabs.) Lançarote also returned with 235

Moorish slaves. The chronicler Azurara, who ordinarily writes dispassionately, seems genuinely moved: 'What heart, even the hardest, would not be moved by a sentiment of pity on seeing such a flock?'

The last Mediterranean crusade departed from Lagos in 1578, under the command of the ascetic, obstinate 25-year-old king, Dom Sebastian, ending in disaster at Alcácer-Quivir. Before he left, the king made the town capital of the Algarve, a title it retained until 1755, when Tavira and finally Faro took over.

Getting There

Frequent **trains** make numerous stops on their way from Vila Real de Santo António (4hrs), including Tavira (3hrs), Faro (2¼hrs), and Albufeira (1¼hrs). From Lisbon, take the ferry to Barreiro, and catch a train to Tunes. Change at Tunes for Lagos (5¼hrs rail travel).

Frequent EVA **buses** arrive from Lisbon (5¼hrs), and infrequently from Vila Real de Santo António (4hrs), via Tavira (3½hrs), Faro (2¼hrs), and Albufeira (1¼hrs), amongst others. Mopeds can be hired from a shop on Rua Direita, between the tourist office and Praça Gil Eanes.

Lagos ℂ (082–)   ***Tourist Information***

The **tourist office** is in the Largo Marquês de Pombal, ℂ 763031, just up from the Praça Gil Eanes, at the centre of town, in which stands the **post office**. The **bus station**, ℂ 762944, is on the harbour front: walk downstream and turn right at the Rua da Porta de Portugal to get to the Praça Gil Eanes. The **railway station**, ℂ 762987, is further away: cross the bridge and turn left, past the bus station.

Around the Town

The sculpture of Dom Sebastian in the Praça Gil Eanes portrays him as a spaceman. Although it looks ridiculous, this is presumably João Cutileiro's way of updating the myth of Sebastianism, the messianic cult fostered by the Spanish domination of 1580–1640, which hoped for a return of the saviour to restore his people to greatness and prosperity, a cult which lingers even today (*see* **Topics**, p.45).

The Rua Direita runs parallel with the river into the Rua da Senhora da Graça. Portugal's only **slave market** was held where this opens into the Praça da República, under the arches of the Custom House. There should be a memorial, but there isn't. Dom Sebastian is supposed to have put fire in the bellies of his troops by speechifying from a window of the **church of Santa Maria**, which overlooks the Praça.

The Rua Henrique Correira Silva leads inland to the tiny **chapel of Sto António**, whose gilt woodwork is among the finest and most ebullient in Portugal. Carved by an unknown sculptor *c.* 1715, the wild animals, monsters, and unlikely vegetation surround scenes from the life of St Anthony—preaching to attentive fish, reinstating the foot which a guilty son had cut off in penance. The painted vault was rebuilt in 1769, after the earthquake. Aesthetes will pay their respects to the grave of Hugo Beattie, an Irish colonel whose motto was '*Non vi sed arte*'.

RUA DAS ESCOLAS PRIMÁ

Fortifications

RUA INFANTE DE CANAL

RUA DO DE SAGRES OLIVEIRA

DA

RUA DO FERRADOR

RUA

Fortifications

RUA DE GIL VICENTE

RUA CÂNDIDO DOS REIS

Cinema

RUA LANÇAROTE DE FREITAS

RUA 25 DE ABRIL

RUA 5 DE OUTUBRO

Church of
Santo António

RUA GENERAL ALBERTO SILVEIRA

Former Slave
Market

RUA DA SRA. DA GRAÇE

Regional
Museum

Avenida dos Descobrim

RUA DO CASTELO DOS GOVERNADORES

Church of
Santa Maria

Praça da
República

Hospital

To Sagres

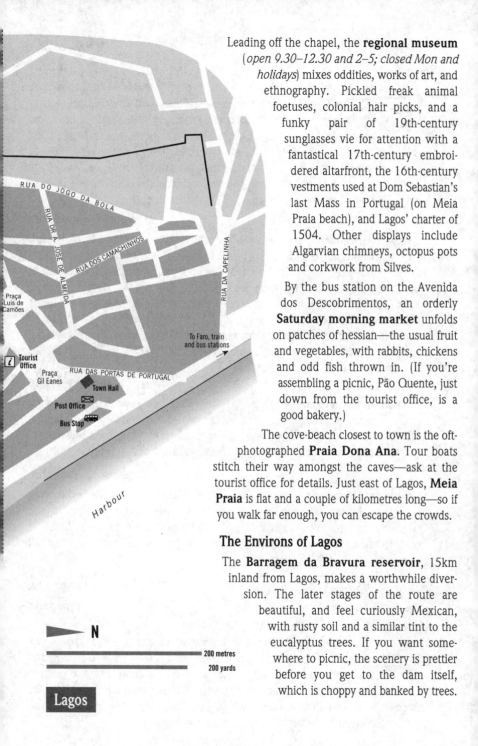

RUA DO JOGO DA BOLA

RUA DR. A. JOSE DE ALMEIDA

RUA DOS CAMACHINHOS

RUA DA CAPELINHA

Praça Luis de Camões

To Faro, train and bus stations →

i Tourist Office

Praça Gil Eanes

RUA DAS PORTAS DE PORTUGAL

Town Hall

Post Office

Bus Stop

Harbour

N

200 metres
200 yards

Lagos

Leading off the chapel, the **regional museum** (*open 9.30–12.30 and 2–5; closed Mon and holidays*) mixes oddities, works of art, and ethnography. Pickled freak animal foetuses, colonial hair picks, and a funky pair of 19th-century sunglasses vie for attention with a fantastical 17th-century embroidered altarfront, the 16th-century vestments used at Dom Sebastian's last Mass in Portugal (on Meia Praia beach), and Lagos' charter of 1504. Other displays include Algarvian chimneys, octopus pots and corkwork from Silves.

By the bus station on the Avenida dos Descobrimentos, an orderly **Saturday morning market** unfolds on patches of hessian—the usual fruit and vegetables, with rabbits, chickens and odd fish thrown in. (If you're assembling a picnic, Pão Quente, just down from the tourist office, is a good bakery.)

The cove-beach closest to town is the oft-photographed **Praia Dona Ana**. Tour boats stitch their way amongst the caves—ask at the tourist office for details. Just east of Lagos, **Meia Praia** is flat and a couple of kilometres long—so if you walk far enough, you can escape the crowds.

The Environs of Lagos

The **Barragem da Bravura reservoir**, 15km inland from Lagos, makes a worthwhile diversion. The later stages of the route are beautiful, and feel curiously Mexican, with rusty soil and a similar tint to the eucalyptus trees. If you want somewhere to picnic, the scenery is prettier before you get to the dam itself, which is choppy and banked by trees.

luxury

The clever, irregular design of the ✱✱✱✱**Hotel de Lagos**, Rua António Crisógono dos Santos, ✆ 769967, ✆ 769920, sprawls over 3 acres of Lagos hilltop, offering spacious, well-furnished bedrooms which overlook the town, the swimming pool or a courtyard filled with lush exotics and birdsong. The cavernous main dining room serves fairly good food, and guests enjoy fringe benefits such as membership of Duna Beach Club and reduced green fees at Palmares golf course. Smooth, helpful service, impressive facilities and relatively well-hidden package tourists distinguish the hotel.

expensive–moderate

Less pricey, but offering good value in the centre of town, ✱✱**Pensão Mar Azul**, 13 Rua 25 Abril, ✆ 769143, is very pleasant and well maintained. All rooms have private bathrooms, but for one room this means crossing the corridor to reach it. Under the same ownership, **Albergaria Marina Rio**, Av. dos Descobrimentos, ✆ 769859 (*expensive*), is well kitted out and efficiently run. Most of their clients are German block-bookings, making it difficult for the independent traveller to get a look-in. It's worth contacting them anyway as rooms are sometimes available. Another option is ✱✱✱**Pensão Lagosmar**, 13 Rua Dr. Faria e Silva, ✆ 63722 (*moderate*).

inexpensive–cheap

✱✱✱**Pensão Dona Ana**, Praia Dona Ana, ✆ 762322 (*inexpensive*), makes a good cheaper option near the beach. The English-owned ✱✱✱**Pensão Rubi-Mar**, 70 Rua da Barroca, ✆ 763165 (*cheap*) is pleasant and good value. You could also try ✱✱✱✱**Pensão Sol e Sol**, 22 Rua Lançarote de Freitas, ✆ 61290 (*inexpensive*).

Turismo de Habitação

Quinta da Alfarrobeira, Estrada de Palmares, Odiáxere, ✆ 798424 (*expensive*), is an excessively pretty country house, set in about 10 hectares of grounds and combining proximity to Lagos and Meia Praia with a quiet and mellow setting. The beamed-ceiling interior contains two double bedrooms and one apartment, all decorated in the cool, Algarvian style.

---

expensive

Dom Sebastião, 20–22 Rua 25 de Abril, ✆ 762795, near the tourist office is usually humming with activity. It's a split-level tavern with a dragons'-tooth floor, a black beamed ceiling, leatherbound menus, and very good food—including clams cooked in a *cataplana*, and oysters. *Closed Sun in winter; reservations recommended.* Between mirrored walls, **Os Arcos**, also on Rua 25 de Abril, ✆ 763120, huddles around a big white pillar. The service can be curt although the food is often excellent.

Inland from the Praça Gil Eanes, **Alpendre**, 17 Rua António Barbosa Viana, ✆ 62705, is more pricey. The wood-beamed restaurant is well presented and serves very good food, though the leather armchairs dispel intimacy, the menu is rather too large to find one's way around, and smoochy muzak plays away. Fillets of sole are flambéed with vermouth. *Closed off season; resevations recommended.*

Up by the fortress walls, at the top of the Rua Infante de Sagres, **Muralha**, 15 Rua da Atalaia, ✆ 63659, puts on *fado* for tourists. The floor is dragon's tooth, the tablecloths tartan and the bracket lamps are fake gaslamps. Scallops of veal with Madeira go down well.

Cataplana (cooking pan)

moderate

Slightly off the tourist trail, **O Escondidinho** ('the hideaway'), Beco do Cemitério, ✆ 760386, was a well-kept secret until the Hotel de Lagos started sending guests there. Portions are huge and the atmosphere jovial, verging on boisterous. Close by, **O Alberto**, 27 Largo Convento Sra. da Glória, ✆ 769387, has an open kitchen, where you can watch waiters burning themselves on the hot plates. On Rua 25 de Abril, teeming with bars and restaurants, is the friendly **O Lamberto**, ✆ 763746, a first-floor establishment boasting a nice terrace, good food and a buoyant atmosphere. **O Pousada de Juventude de Lagos**, 50 Rua Lançarote de Freitas, ✆ 761970, is the best budget option in town.

cheap

If you just want a bit of normal Portugal, small, plain **Ritinha**, 25 Rua do Canal, ✆ 63791, is popular with local families and has no menu in English. There's also basic, unpretentious **Ocean e Lagos** (next to a bookshop, beyond Praça João de Deus at the very top of town), where Joaquim serves good seafood to his loyal clientele. From the outside, **Adega da Marina**, 35 Avenida dos Descobrimentos, ✆ 764284, looks like all the restaurants along this road. However, a peek inside will surprise: this is a huge, barn-like dining room with long refectory-style tables, fishing nets, anchors, and a swordfish along the walls and a beamed, vaulted ceiling. The garrulous clientele is mostly Portuguese and the quality of the food matches the wonderful atmosphere. **O Terraco**, 12 Rua Lançarote de Freitas, near the youth hostel, has a filling, cheap breakfast menu to set you up for the day.

There are many bars; largest, and probably the best of the young and trendies, are **Zanzibar** at 93 Rua 25 de Abril and its various imitators in the same stretch of street.

Alvor

The higgledy-piggledy port at the mouth of the Alvor estuary has escaped tourist development; surely, it has a powerful patron saint. Eighteen km east of Lagos, Alvor (not to be confused with Montes de Alvor) was known to the Romans as Portus Hannibalis, before the Moors named it Albur. In 1495, the 40-year-old Dom João II and 25 *fidalgos* billeted themselves on the castellan of Alvor, Alvaro de Ataide, after the king caught a chill in Monchique. Physicians drugged him into a stupor. The chronicler Garçia de Resende takes up the tale: Dom João begged those around him 'for the love of God to wake him up and not let him die like a beast'. They tried. Dom Diogo de Almeida seized the monarch's beard and shouted, 'Senhor, wake up.' He woke, saying, 'Prior, that hand could with more decorum be placed elsewhere, for there are feet!' Shortly afterwards, the Bishop of Tangier was closing Dom João's eyes and mouth, when the king murmured 'Bishop, it is not yet time.' With that he died. (The Lisbon city council commiserated by forbidding all barbers to shave a beard or cut any hair for six months.)

The narrow streets, of almost unsullied whiteness, lead up a low hill to the yellow-bordered 16th-century **Igreja Matriz**. Its fascinating Manueline portal is carved in reddish stone: the concentric arches depict sea flowers, dragons, lions, and musicians, all wrapped by a giant octopus tentacle. There is nothing of interest inside the church.

The long beach is a little way off, backed by low dunes. It attracts some beautiful young people, but it's overlooked by a clutch of horrid Lego-like hotels.

fishermen prepare their boat

Eating Out

There are a number of restaurants. Down by the river quay, **Os Pescadores** serves good, honest food in a pleasant setting (*cheap*). Plastic chairs are arranged under umbrellas, from which diners watch their fresh fish being grilled gently and lovingly. Fish is priced by the kilo and served with salad and unskinned potatoes.

Portimão and Around

Seventeen km east of Lagos and 28km west of Albufeira, Portimão fumes on the western bank of the River Arade, a couple of kilometres from the coast. The built-up town with a population of 33,000 is a major port and sardine-canning centre—with a crazy one-way system. It has little to recommend it.

Portimão ✆ (082–)   ***Tourist Information***

The **tourist office** is in the Largo do 1 de Dezembro, ✆ 23695, and the **British Consulate** is at 7 Largo Francisco A Mauricio, ✆ 417800.

The Environs of Portimão

Portimão sprawls a couple of kilometres towards its beach, **Praia da Rocha**, at the mouth of the River Arade. The beautifully flat sand beach backed by 70m cliffs in earthy shades must have been idyllic, once. Now it is packed with monster hotels. There are a couple of vantage points equipped with telescopes, presumably to aid sunbathers find a space large enough to lie down on. Twelve km east of Portimão, **Carvoeiro** is an unappealing, over-built town with a small beach.

Portimão ✆ (082–)   ***Where to Stay and Eating Out***

There are numerous hotels for all budgets, including ★★★★**Hotel Oriental**, Av. Tomás Cabreira, Praia da Rocha, ✆ 413000 (*luxury*), an exotic, Xanadu-type affair which gets away with it; ★★★**Hotel Globo**, 26 Rua 5 de Outubro, ✆ 416350 (*moderate*), and **Pensão Residencial Toca**, Rua Eng. Francisco Bivar, ✆ 24035, ✆ 24035 (*cheap*).

The most enjoyable part of Portimão is the row of cheap fish restaurants by the river bridge, which serve sardines. Diners can follow the action on the lively quay.

Inland from Portimão

Serra de Monchique

Beginning 17km inland from Portimão, the breathtaking Monchique hills form a barrier between the Algarve and the Alentejo. The highest points are at Fóia (902m) and Picota (744m), sufficient to shelter the Algarve from northerly winds and trap the rain blown inland from the coast, to give the western end of the range the highest rainfall in the Algarve, most of which falls between the end of November and the beginning of May. Steep streams bubble out of the schist, making it easier to irrigate terraced plots of land.

The hills are thickly wooded with eucalyptus like cheerleaders' pom-poms, and every shade of pine tree. When the commercially grown eucalyptus is cut—usually in February—the small leafy branches are lopped off and left to rot *in situ*, thus making a slippery surface to slide the trunks down. The roads are flanked by yellow-flowered mimosa. Peonies and pale purple rhododendrons bloom before the end of April, while small arbutus trees flourish throughout the range—keep an eye out for their large, dark green, toothed leaves, and globular, warty, red fruits. Better still, try the flavourful *medronheira* brandy distilled from the berries. It's not the brandy but the flat light that makes the hills appear to be superimposed on one another.

Caldas de Monchique

North of Portimão, houses quickly give way to beds of tall reeds and carpets of little yellow flowers. The good tarmac road rises to Caldas de Monchique, 18km from Portimão, 22km northwest of Silves and 76km west-northwest of Faro. The tiny spa town is set in a niche in the Serra de Monchique, 250m above the beachy plains. Simply refreshing, it is lulled to sleep by a tide of trees. There are some delightful walks through the woods.

Having designated Dom Manuel as his successor, Dom João II visited Monchique in 1495. He was pleased to see one of his courtiers victorious in a wrestling match against the locals, one chilly Sunday morning. His doctors advised that it was too cold to swim, but the king bathed twice. He also insisted on following the hounds when they found boars in the woods, a combination which rendered him gravely ill. He and his retainers decanted to Alvor, where the king died.

Caldas de Monchique was popular with the Spanish bourgeoisie in the 19th century. They left a casino, which now houses a **handicraft market**. (If you'd like an attractive alternative to net curtains, have a look at the drapes here, for 7000$00 each.)

The grim buildings just below the settlement are the water-bottling factory and the spa (*open 1 June–15 Nov*), which is particularly good for rheumatism and respiratory disorders. Water emerges from the ground at 32.1°C.

Caldas de Monchique © (082–)   **Where to Stay**

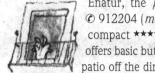

Enatur, the *pousada* people, run lacklustre **Albergaria Velha**, © 912204 (*moderate*), furnished like a child's playroom. The small, compact ★★★★**Albergaria do Lageado**, © 912616 (*inexpensive*) offers basic but pleasant bedrooms: its charm begins with the trellised patio off the dining room, from which a path leads up through a rock garden to a lovely family-sized swimming pool (open to non-residents for 1200$00, with showers). Guests lie on deckchairs surrounded on three sides by tree-covered slopes and birdsong. The restaurant serves simple dishes. *Open 1 May–31 Oct.* Genial **Pensão Central**, © 912203 (*cheap*) overlooks a mass of eucalyptus. It combines faded respectability with the sparseness of a summer house—floorboards are bare, the hot water is erratic, and there is a bowl of pinecones in the hallway. It's worth considering the half-board (*see* below).

Caldas de Monchique © (082–)   **Eating Out**

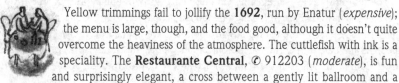

Yellow trimmings fail to jollify the **1692**, run by Enatur (*expensive*); the menu is large, though, and the food good, although it doesn't quite overcome the heaviness of the atmosphere. The cuttlefish with ink is a speciality. The **Restaurante Central**, © 912203 (*moderate*), is fun and surprisingly elegant, a cross between a gently lit ballroom and a wooden schoolroom. Pretty plates decorate the walls, and a Siamese cat enjoys the woodburning stove. The food is very good, though the service can be obtrusive—if you're travelling on a tight budget, this would be a good place for a splurge. Try the *bacalhau à Central*, cooked with cream and mushrooms. The cheap eating place near the Albergaria do Lageado closes early in the evening.

Monchique and Around

The road winds 7km north from Caldas de Monchique, climbing 200m to **Monchique**, a little town of 10,000 souls. The views of the coastal plain are fabulous, as are the camellia trees. Amongst a jumble of unsightly, fairly modern houses, a cobbled street leads up from the main square to the **Igreja Matriz**, which boasts an odd Manueline portal from which five carved knots radiate. Well sited above the town are the flower-clad ruins of the Franciscan monastery of **N.S. do Destêrro**, founded in 1632 by Dom Pero da Silva, later Viceroy of India. Some of the locals make their living as potters and basket makers. The latter pollard their willow trees, to produce flexible shoots. These are tied in bundles and weighted down at the bottom of irrigation tanks until they are used for basket-making in the summer.

Climbing up to the Picota peak makes a wilder and more interesting walk than Fóia, through farms and chestnut coppices.

West of Monchique, the road climbs past stacks of logs, and eucalyptus trees. Recalcitrant cows are led along the road, which suddenly enters a land of heather and scrub. The peak of the range is **Fóia**, 8km from Monchique, forested with broadcasting aerials.

Monchique is the best place to buy the wooden chairs which fold like scissors and which can be spotted in hotels and homes around the country. This simple design was brought to Portugal by the Romans and is considered evidence of Roman presence in Monchique. José Leonardo Salvador, the 'Monchique Chair Man' makes them from alder wood (a relative of the birch) and has derived more complicated designs from the original and even branched out into tables. He is something of a local celebrity, having starred in a BBC documentary, among others. His shop is called Casa Dos Arcos, Estrada Velha, ✆ 082 92692, and displays his work beautifully. Chairs cost from 3500$00 to 7000$00.

Monchique ✆ (082–)   ***Where to Stay and Eating Out***

Rooms at **Residencial Miradouro da Serra**, Rua Combatentes do Ultramar, ✆ 912163 (*cheap*), which is near the main square in Monchique, are clean and tastefully decorated; those at the back have no view. Guests are given a key to the front door, as there is no full-time receptionist in the off season. There are a couple of inexpensive restaurants in Monchique; **Charette** is recommended.

Several km uphill from Monchique, the ★★★★**Estalagem Abrigo da Montanha**, Estrada da Fóia—Corte Pereiro, ✆ 912131, ✉ 913660 (*expensive–moderate*), is a peaceful lodge with a garden full of camellias, mimosas and arbutus. Guestrooms are prettily furnished with iron bedheads, and the view from their shuttered windows stretches down to the sea. The restaurant (*moderate*) serves very good local specialities, though the service is rather slow. Dishes include the delicate *assadura* (pork with lemon juice and garlic). The *morgado de figo* is a delicious and unusual dessert made of alternate layers of figs and almonds. **Restaurante Paraiso De Montanha**, on the road up to Fóia, ✆ 912150 (*moderate*), has a wide terrace commanding breathtaking views and a small menu featuring good chicken piri–piri. Two boisterous dogs frolic at your feet. *Closed Thurs.*

Silves

Situated among gentle hills beside the River Arade, 8km inland from Lagoa and 29km northwest of Albufeira, Silves was the 30,000-strong capital of the Moorish province of al-Gharb from the mid-11th century to the mid-13th century.

By the 16th century, the river had silted up and the population was reduced to just 140. Subsequent earthquakes have destroyed much of the character of the place—the only living monuments to the Moors are the orange and almond groves which surround the town, which is now home to 10,000 people.

History

Idrisi, the 12th-century Arab chronicler and geographer, remarked on the 'fine appearance' of Xelb, a port with 'attractive buildings and well-furnished bazaars', praising the purity of the Yemenite Arabs' language and pronunciation, as well as the region's 'delicate, appetizing and delicious' figs. For all its opulence, Silves had a troubled history. Soon after the Moors had installed themselves, the city was captured by al-Mu'tadid, of Seville, who planted flowers in the skulls of his decapitated enemies and used them to decorate his palace gardens. Returning to Moorish control, Silves was besieged by Dom Sancho I in 1189. The king had flagged down lusty English crusaders on their way to Jerusalem, promising booty. They set to work, in July and August, just when the figs were bursting with ripeness. The parched garrison surrendered on 1 September, and filed out of the stronghold bearing nothing but their clothes—which the Crusaders removed, to the disgust of the king. The allies occupied the city, and spent most of that night torturing the remaining inhabitants into revealing the location of their hidden treasure. Two years later the Caliph of Morocco recaptured Silves, along with the rest of Portugal south of the Tagus, except Évora. The Moors were finally driven out in 1242, during the reign of Dom Afonso III.

Silves ✆ (082–)   ***Getting There***

Silves is on the east–west railway route, ✆ 442310. Semi-frequent buses, ✆ 442338, make the ¼hr journey from Portimão.

Silves ✆ (082–)   ***Tourist Information***

The **tourist office** is in the centre of town, on the Rua 25 de Abril, ✆ 442255 (*open weekdays 9.30am–7pm, weekends 9–12.30 and 2.30–5*). The **railway station** is 2km south of Silves, from which a connecting bus runs every half-hour.

A beer festival is held within the castle walls in the first two weeks of June—an ironic fate for a Muslim establishment.

Around the Town

The earthy red **cathedral** was built of local sandstone in 1189, and reconstructed after the Reconquest, in 1242. It was the seat of the Algarve's bishopric until 1580, when that honour was transferred to Faro. The Gothic parts of the cathedral have been altered, and although the building is a peaceful place, few interesting architectural features remain. Note the curious gargoyles on the exterior of the apse. Dom João II's coffin was buried here in 1495, having been lined with quicklime to speed the decay of the body. Four years later, it was disinterred: the quicklime had destroyed the shroud and almost burnt through the wooden coffin, but the body was incorrupt. Truly, a miracle. The splinters of the coffin were set aside as holy relics, and the king, placed in a new coffin, was translated to Batalha. Several fine tombs have remained here, including one decorated with a coiled serpent.

Uphill from the cathedral, it's exciting to walk along the top of the thick, rust-coloured curtain walls of the **castle**, built by the Moors on Roman foundations, and restored *c.* 1835. The defences encircle a grove of lemon trees and hibiscus, planted above both a cistern that once held a year's supply of water, and a Roman copper mine later used for storing grain.

At the east end of town, on the road to Messines, the **Cruz de Portugal** is an ornate 16th-century white limestone cross, 3m high. One side depicts Christ crucified, the other the descent from the Cross.

Silves ⓒ (082–)   ### Where to Stay and Eating Out

★★★★**Albergaria Solar Da Moura**, Horta Pocinho, ⓒ 443106/7 (*moderate*) is a rather ugly low-rise new hotel which crouches over Silves, affording great views. It is modern and comfortable, and the excellent Marisqueira Rui restaurant (*expensive*) is an added bonus. **Estabelecimentos Dom Sancho**, Largo do Castelo, ⓒ 442437 (*inexpensive*), has a historical setting next to the castle. Otherwise, try **Residencial Sousa**, 17 Rua Samora Barros, next to the post office, ⓒ 442502 (*cheap*) or **Residencial Ponte Romana**, Horta Cruz, ⓒ 443275 (*cheap*), which also has a tasty restaurant.

The recently restored **Quinta Do Rio** (*moderate–inexpensive*), ⓒ 445528, ✉ 445528, is 6km out of Silves, beautifully situated in an orangery in the hills. The Italian management is charming and will arrange excursions and horse riding. Details from the tourist office.

Oysters bubble in their tank at **Rui**, 27 Rua Comendador Vilarinho, ⓒ 442682 (*expensive*), which serves fish and shellfish by the kilo in no-

nonsense surroundings. *Closed Tues off season.* **Mesquita**, Rua Policarpo Dias, ℂ 442747 (*cheap*), is a good *tasca*, with a fence around the walls. *Closed Sat.*

Albufeira to Almancil

Albufeira

Getting There

Frequent trains and buses run from Faro (1hr) and from Lagos (1hr), stopping at each stage along the way.

Albufeira ℂ *(089–)*   ***Tourist Information***

The **tourist office** is in the Rua 5 de Outubro, ℂ 585279, on the way to the beach tunnel. It's a 5-minute walk from the **bus station**, ℂ 589755, to the centre of town: to get to the tourist office, walk along the Avenida da Liberdade, turn right at the tip of the gardened Largo Eng. Duarte Pacheco, then left into the Rua 5 de Outubro. The **train station**, ℂ 571616, is 6km north of town, with connecting buses.

Some 39km northwest of Faro and 50km east of Lagos, the pretty, hilly seaside village of Albufeira has become one of Portugal's most popular package resorts. Part of the settlement was submerged by a tidal wave following the earthquake of 1755; for the summer months, the whole of the Albufeira is submerged by a different kind of tidal wave—one that takes longer to drain away. The whitewashed, pedestrian streets seethe with sun lovers, who are supplied with cheap beer and saucy postcards. Touts in the main square sell time-share apartments. That said, there are no enormous hotels in Albufeira, and a rock-hewn tunnel leads directly to the beach, which is edged by weird cliffs. Brightly painted fishing boats rest on the sand, beside the transparent sea; the catch makes interesting viewing at the fish market.

Albufeira ℂ *(089–)*   ***Where to Stay***

★★★**Hotel Rocamar**, Largo Jacinto D'Ayet, ℂ 586990 (*expensive*), is along the road from the Church of Sant'Ana and provides standard, airy rooms, with private balconies overlooking the beach. The Rua Coronel Águas leads to the Avenida do Ténis; they meet at the ★★★**Residencial Vila Bela**, 15 Rua Coronel Águas, ℂ 512101 (*moderate*), which is attractively layered and beflowered, with bright rooms and balconies overlooking the small swimming pool.

★★★**Residencial Vila Branca**, Rua do Ténis, ℂ 586804 (*inexpensive*)—head inland from the Largo Jacinto D'Ayet—is nothing special: both bedrooms and shower rooms are pokey. There is not much cheap accommodation outside rooms in private houses (ask at the tourist office), though ★★**Pensão Silva**, 18 Trav. 5 de Outubro, ℂ 512669 (*cheap*)—down an alley opposite the tourist office—offers six pleasant rooms in an old building with flaking ceilings. In addition to these and countless other hotels, there are numerous rooms offered by touts meeting buses at the station.

Overlooking the beach, near the fish market, **A Ruina**, Cais Herculano, ℗ 512094 (*expensive; reservations sometimes necessary*), is a fun place to eat delicious seafood. The lower part is more atmospheric: dripping candles, turtle shells, stone-studded walls, treetrunk tabels and the menu on a blackboard justify the high prices. Some diners choose to sit in a cordoned-off area right on the beach. **Atrium**, 20 Rua 5 de Outubro, ℗ 515755 (*expensive*), near the tourist office, attempts elegance, with little success. The menu is international, including a smoked swordfish starter. At the other end of the scale, unsigned *tasca* **Ana**, right next to the fish market, is accustomed to intrepid travellers. It serves one dish only, which should be collected from the kitchen (*cheap*).

Olhos de Água

Nine km east of Albufeira, Olhos de Água is a working fishing beach backed by ochre-coloured cliffs, with a clutch of small restaurants. It's a pleasant place, though sometimes dirty: if there are too many people for your liking, just head round the eastern promontory to a huge stretch of beach. On the beach front, **O Caizote**, ℗ 089 501230 (*cheap*), is a lively but simple restaurant under English management, with good charcoal-grilled chicken, and octopus salad.

Falésia

At Falésia, 8km to the east, the coastline changes from coves to an uninterrupted expanse of sand, backed by smooth cliffs. These are liable to subside should you get too close to their edge, though the irresistible smell of pine woods wafts across the clifftop paths. The **Aldeia das Açoteias** holiday village, 1 or 2km inland, is composed of concrete hutches, and is only recommended for athletes who have access to good training facilities.

To get to Falésia by public transport, take a regular bus from Albufeira to Aldeia das Açoteias, then catch the beach-bound shuttle from there.

Vilamoura

Roughly 22km northwest of Faro, and 4km from Quarteira beach, Vilamoura is the largest touristic development in Portugal. Building is still in progress—as it is everywhere else—but the target is 55,000 beds and agricultural self-sufficiency. (The herd of dairy cattle inhabits a giant silo.) High-rise hotels vie with one another for air space, though there is no heart to the settlement.

Vilamoura has two mature **golf courses**: every hole of Frank Pennink's peaceful Number One course has tight fairways and character—holes 10 and 15 are over gulleys. All the par 3s are difficult, as can be discussed at the bar on the 12th tee. The Number Two course may still have to recover from rebuilding, and may be a bit scraggy. It's best to book two days in advance. There is one pro, but generally no caddies; 10 buggies are available for each course. Players are limited to 4 hours on the course, and a maximum handicap of 28 for men, 36 for ladies.

Vilamoura ✆ (089–)   **Where to Stay**

luxury

The sumptuously neutral ★★★★★**Marinotel**, ✆ 389988, offers state-of-the-art for its own sake: room keys are flat electronic dominoes, poolside cages filter a modicum of sunshine. It is equipped with all the trimmings—including an aviary, putting, and a watergarden—plus fabulous views of the marina or the sea, and a lobby layered with giant ring binders. The fat-cat clientele can rest assured that the presidential suite has bullet-proof doors. Other luxury hotels include ★★★★**Hotel Dom Pedro**, ✆ 315450 and ★★★★**Estalagem da Cegonha**, ✆ 66271.

Quarteira to Quinta do Lago

Quarteira, on the coast just east of Vilamoura, 6km from the east–west highway, is a jungle of apartment-hotels. Neighbouring **Vale de Lobo** is a more ritzy development, where the sprinklers are always at work to keep the lawns green, and where the emphasis is on low-rise whitewashed 'village' complexes elaborated from the local style of architecture, with a liberal sprinkling of lattice-work chimneys. Slightly further to the east sprawls the **Quinta do Lago resort**.

Almancil

Thirteen km northwest of Faro, the interior of the little **church of São Lourenço**, in the sleepy town of Almancil, is covered with astonishingly beautiful **azulejos** depicting the life of the saint, dated 1730 and signed by Policarpo de Oliveira Bernardes. This is unquestionably his finest work, which elsewhere does not live up to the masterful craft of his father, António, in Évora, Barcelos and Viana do Castelo. The tiles have been designed to complement the architectural features of the church, best seen in the *trompe l'oeil* cupola.

Faro

Some 297km from Lisbon, and 53km from the border at Vila Real de Santo António, the capital of the Algarve is built around a charming harbour at the edge of a wide lagoon, 9km from the beach.

Nothing is quite the same since the airport was built: now Faro is the destination of hundreds of charter flights. The less imaginative visitors who fly in to Faro tend to remain here, soaking up the sun and the beer. Tourism has brought affluence to some, but gypsy children beg in the streets, and Faro is fringed by a polythene shanty town. Without a booking, finding somewhere to stay can be very difficult.

History

Faro was captured from the Moors in 1249, after which Dom Afonso III rebuilt the town walls. In the 15th century these encircled a group of Jewish residents who set up a press to print Hebraic texts. The bishopric of the Algarve was transferred from Silves to Faro in 1580; the Earl of Essex may have been the bishop's first English visitor. Returning home in 1596, after sacking and burning Cadiz, he landed at Faro beach with Lord Howard of Effingham, Raleigh, and 3000 troops: Portugal was under the rule of Philip II of Spain, and hence a fair target. The city had been deserted, and Essex installed himself in the bishop's palace—from which he stole 200 black leather volumes tooled in gilt. Two years later he presented the clerical collection to his friend Sir Thomas Bodley, who had recently founded a library at Oxford. (The first Bodleian librarian subsequently complained that 'diverse sentences' had been censored by the Inquisition.) Having removed the books, the English set Faro on fire and departed. Parts of the city were destroyed by earthquakes in 1722 and 1755.

Getting There and Around

Six kilometres out of town, the new terminal at **Faro airport** can, and does, cope with 4.5 million visitors per year. A taxi to the centre of town will cost about 1200$00 (1600$00 at night)—agree on the price first, as meters are habitually broken—or take bus nos.18 or 16. Airport buses depart from opposite the bus station (see below).

From the **railway station**, walk down the Avenida da República, past the **bus station**, to get to the harbour; the **tourist office** is on the far side of the Jardim Manuel Bivar.

If you feel impelled to go to Faro beach, **bus** nos.16 and 14 leave every half-hour from opposite the bus station on Avenida da Republica, 200m southwest of the Jardim Manuel Bivar. Bus 16 also serves the airport.

Faro © (089–)   ### Tourist Information

Expect a queue in the **tourist office**, 8 Rua da Misericórdia, © 80360; (*summer hours 9.30am–7pm daily*). **American Express** is represented by Star Travel Service, 36 Rua Conselheiro Bivar, © 805525. For information on buses, call © 899760, and for trains © 801726. Both these numbers will reach English speakers.

The Old Town: The Cathedral and Archaeological Museum

The old part of town rests secure behind fortified walls, entered near the tourist office through the 18th-century Italianate **Arco da Vila**, a gate with space for storks to nest and a niche for St Thomas Aquinas, who was invoked to save the city from a plague in the 17th century. Follow the pretty, cobbled Rua do Município; it opens on to a square edged with orange trees, in which stands the Renaissance **cathedral** (*open 10–12 daily*). Although it has appropriated the tower of its Gothic predecessor, the building is of little architectural interest, with a wide nave flanked by 18th-century *azulejos*, and a wild, cote-like Baroque reliquary. The fun chinoiserie organ was painted in 1751, to look like an elaborate version of something a monkey would grind.

Behind the cathedral, the Convento de N.S. da Assunção now houses the **Archaeological Museum** (*open Mon–Fri 9–12 and 2–5*), whose illuminating collection was retrieved locally. Part of it is displayed in the stunning two-storey cloister of 1543, with beady gargoyles and a peaked and lichenous terracotta roof. The convent was built by Dona Leonor, third wife of Dom Manuel; her blazon ornaments the portico, complete with shrimping net. The two 1st-century busts of Hadrian and Agrippina, wife of Emperor Claudius, were discovered at Milreu—circle Agrippina to see her elaborate hairstyle—while the excellent 3rd-century mosaic detailing half

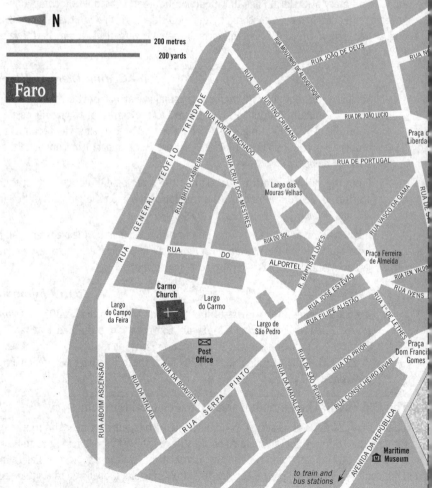

Neptune's face, surrounded by two of the four winds, was found close to the railway station. A cabinet near the mosaic displays Roman ampules intended to hold tears. There are some good woodcuts upstairs.

Outside the Old Town

Two of Faro's other museums are worth a visit if you have time to spare. On the dock past the Hotel Eva, the **Maritime Museum** (*open 2–5.30; closed Sat, Sun and holidays*) contains numerous models of fishing boats from past and present, labelled in English.

Algarvian handicrafts, photographs of typical houses and peasants in traditional dress, and reconstructions of domestic interiors are on display at the **Ethnographic Museum** (*open Mon–Fri 9.30–12 and 2–5*), on the third floor of the District Assembly, beside the Jardim da Alagoa.

There are two curious churches outside the Old Town. From the Jardim Manuel Bivar, the Rua Dom Francisco Gomes leads into the Rua de Santo António. Veer right at the Praça da Liberdade, into the Rua do Pé da Cruz, at the end of which stands the small 17th-century **church of Pé da Cruz**. Knock on the door.

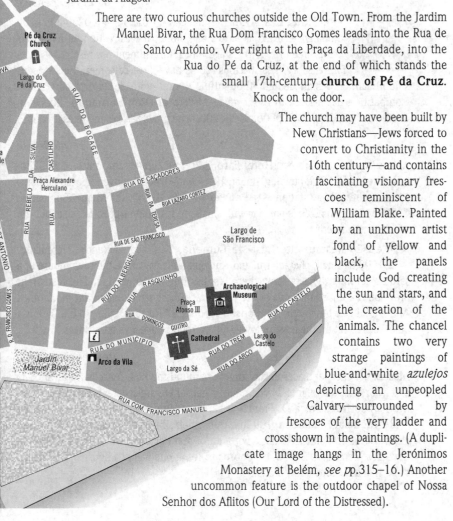

The church may have been built by New Christians—Jews forced to convert to Christianity in the 16th century—and contains fascinating visionary frescoes reminiscent of William Blake. Painted by an unknown artist fond of yellow and black, the panels include God creating the sun and stars, and the creation of the animals. The chancel contains two very strange paintings of blue-and-white *azulejos* depicting an unpeopled Calvary—surrounded by frescoes of the very ladder and cross shown in the paintings. (A duplicate image hangs in the Jerónimos Monastery at Belém, *see p*p.315–16.) Another uncommon feature is the outdoor chapel of Nossa Senhor dos Aflitos (Our Lord of the Distressed).

Tower blocks loom behind the **Carmo Church** in the Largo do Carmo, wrecking the effect of its grand façade of 1713. Lovesick angels support the richly gilt retable; to the right, a door leads to the panelled sacristy, and thence to the freaky **Capela de Ossos** (the Bone Chapel). The walls of this simple, uniform, and ghoulish chamber are entirely lined with some 1250 skulls and other monks' bones, extracted from graves around the church in 1816.

There are some excellent **beaches** within easy striking distance of Faro—on the islands off Olhão, 8km to the east (train or bus to Olhão, then regular ferries)—so avoid the intolerable **Faro beach**, which is jam-packed.

Faro ✆ (089–)   **Where to Stay**

luxury–expensive

★★★★**Hotel Eva**, Av. da República, ✆ 803354, ✆ 802304, is traditionally regarded as Faro's best hotel. It was resting on its laurels until three or four years ago, but refurbishment has restored it to its former glory. The spacious rooms have large balconies, the service is smooth and the management thoughtful. Rooms with sea views cost more. Competition has arrived in the form of ★★★**Hotel Dom Bernando**, Rua Gen. Teófilo da Trinidada, ✆ 806806, ✆ 806800, which feels as expensive as it is.

moderate

Across the main square, ★★★**Hotel Faro**, 2 Praça D. Francisco Gomes, ✆ 803276, feels like a grey office building, only darker. Some balconies overlook the harbour. Close to the railway station, ★★★**Pensão Afonso III**, 64 Rua Miguel Bombarda, ✆ 803542, ✆ 805185, is popular with small groups. Rooms are a fair size, but the whole is nondescript.

★★★**Pensão Restaurante Casa de Lumena**, 27 Praça Alexendre Herculano, ✆ 801990, is small, characterful and Anglophile. It was once the town-house of a sardine-canning dynasty; now there is a bar under a grapevine. The restaurant preys on the unadventurous palate (*moderate–expensive; restaurant moderate*). And if it all gets too much, ★★★**Pensão Iorque**, 37 Rua de Berlim, ✆ 823973, is a quiet(er) retreat on the edge of town, where rooms have TVs and fridges.

inexpensive–cheap

Most of the cheaper places to stay are in or around the Rua Conselheiro Bivar or its extension the Rua Infante D. Henrique, where there are several grocery stores, off the harbourfront Praça D. Francisco Gomes. Almost opposite, there's friendly ★★**Residencial Madalena**, 109 Rua Conselheiro Bivar, ✆ 805806, which offers clean rooms and dark corridors. For a bit of real Portugal, Dona Adelaide, 9 Rua Cruz dos Mestres, ✆ 29693, has **rooms to let** in one half of a house; rooms in the other half are occupied by students.

If all else fails (as it could well do in high season), there is a **youth hostel** of sorts on the Rua do Matadouro, near the police station (but not for any particular reason). Avoid **Pensão Dina**, which rents by the hour.

Faro ℰ (089–)

expensive

Cidade Velha, 19 Rua Domingos Gueiro, ℰ 27145, in the cathedral square, is an elegant and romantic little place. Fresh flowers and a dim Art Deco lamp accompany each pink tablecloth. There are prints on the walls. The proprietor is the gourmand who invented fillet of pork stuffed with dates and walnuts in port wine—which could be preceded by the smoked swordfish with horseradish, and followed by the iced whisky tart. *Open for lunch and dinner Mon–Fri, and dinner on Sat.*

Restaurante O Gargalo, 30 Largo do Péda Cruz, ℰ 27305, is set in a pretty square with a small blue and white church at its mouth and a spouting fountain in its middle. There are tables outside, but the cool, calm interior is a treat. The multi-domed ceiling canopies heavy wooden furniture, and stained-glass windows add an ecclesiastical note. The food is excellent—this may be the place to experiment with *bacalhau.*

moderate–cheap

Doubtless a reflection of the treatment they receive from foreign visitors, Faro's inexpensive restaurants are a touch-and-go affair: waiters can be rude or downright hostile, and prices have a habit of changing while the food is being cooked. Do always check your change.

There are exceptions to every rule, though, and in Faro the most memorable one is **Tasca O Chalaver**, 120 Rua Infante D. Henrique, ℰ 822455 (*cheap*), where you choose your dinner from a large fish- and meat-covered slab, before it is transferred to a huge open grill which smokes away under a black hood. The white walls are satisfyingly soot-marked, and covered by gnarled vines, which snake across the sloping, corrugated-iron ceiling. Hearty regulars talk ten to the dozen while the local drunk mumbles amiably to himself in one corner.

Vasco da Gama, 49a Rua Vasco da Gama, ℰ 21666 (*moderate*) is another 'pick your own' place; this time it's still alive, and staring with beady eyes from the tank at the door. For picnic food, there's a delicious **bakery** and *croissanteria* at 33 Rua de Santo António.

Inland from Faro

Frequent buses run to Estói from Faro (¼hr).

Estói, Milreu and Louié

The Algarve's only *palácio* is decaying 9km north of Faro at **Estói**. Recently purchased by Faro Town Council, the late 18th-century building itself is closed, but the fanciful façade and garden are viewable—mashing together styles from the neoclassical to Art Nouveau. The weathervane is a horse, perhaps indicating an equestrian streak in the Counts of Carvalhos, who lived here.

A short walk to the west, along roads bordered with arum lillies, lie the **Roman ruins at Milreu**, once a patrician's villa. Little is left standing above ground, and the site lacks atmosphere, but there are some witty fish mosaics in the baths next to the residential area. The entrance was remodelled in the 4th century, becoming a small vestibule with two semicircular fountains on either side. The temple consecrated to water deities is another 4th-century building. The agricultural quarters, to the southeast, are divided into small rooms for farm labourers. An excellent English-language guide to the site is pasted by the entrance.

Twenty km northwest of Estói, **Loulé** hosts a **carnival** in February. Don't expect it to be sexy and Brazilian. Mamas photograph their daughters dressed as fairies, and their sons dressed as gangsters—who wave when they remember—on floats pulled by tractors. It's charming.

© *(089–)*   *Where to Stay*

Two km north of São Brás de Alportel, 16km north of Faro, a grassy driveway curves up a gentle hill planted with olive trees to the low-key **Pousada de São Brás**, © 842305 (*category C*). It's a beautiful, quiet, but rather run-down villa, smelling of wood polish. Bedrooms are sparsely furnished, with small bathrooms and views to the town of São Brás and the low hills around it. The restaurant is mellow, but the food is indifferent and the selection limited.

Olhão to Vila Real de Santo António

Olhão

Eight km east of Faro, the fishing town of Olhão is sheltered from the open sea by a series of offshore islands which comprise part of the Rio Formosa estuary. Ferries run from Olhão to the two flat islands of Armona and Culatra, hidden from view, which are fringed with uncrowded white sand beaches.

Olhão's cubic houses with flat roofs and external staircases were inspired by trade with North Africa, and brought a modest fame—they owe nothing to the Moors, as the town was founded in the 16th century. Its moment of glory came in 1808, when two local fishermen sailed to Rio de Janeiro in a caique without navigational charts, to tell the fugitive King Dom João VI that Napoleon's troops had left Portugal. As a reward the king granted Olhão the status of a town, and renamed it Olhão da Restauraçao. (The cognomen was dropped because it brought back unpleasant memories of the subsequent War of Restoration.)

Frequent buses and trains both take ¼hr from Faro. Inexpensive **ferries to the islands** depart from the quay, a short walk from the tourist office. Buy your ticket at the kiosk before boarding. The trip to **Armona** takes 15mins and runs every 60 or 90 minutes June–Sept, three times daily in May and Oct, and twice daily otherwise. Ferries to the **Ilha da Culatra** depart seven times daily June–Sept, and four times daily for the rest of the year.

© (089–)   *Tourist Information*

The **tourist office** *(open Mon–Fri 9–12 and 2.30–5, Sat 9–12; July and Aug, Mon–Fri 9–7pm, Sat and Sun 9–12 and 2.30–5)* is in the Rua do Comércio/Largo da Lagoa, © 713936, on the seaward side of the two churches. From the **bus and train stations**, walk down the wide Avenida da República.

The town is decaying sleepily; all the action happens at the harbour, which is edged with restaurants. The jumble of old streets has overflowed into a dull grid pattern, and many of the residents are rickety. At the centre of town stand two churches roofed with terracotta. An angel with a bell skirt serves as a weathervane for the **Igreja Matriz** of 1698. At the rear of the church, the Capela dos Aflitos (Chapel of the Suffering) is always open, for the wives of fishermen to pray during storms. Should you be wondering, the Pastelaria Elvis and Brian, near the churches, is named after the manageress's sons.

Ferries regularly make the short trip to **Ilha da Armona** (*see* above). Passengers disembark at Armona's single settlement, facing the mainland, where there are a couple of laid-back restaurants, and swimmers enjoying the warm, sheltered water. Follow the main path for 20 minutes, past interminable prefabricated beach huts, to the smooth, fine beach, which has a friendly atmosphere and is long enough to offer escape from other people.

You can also easily visit the **Ilha da Culatra** (*see* above). Along the sand spit, several rundown fishing villages face the mainland, mixing uncomfortably with a rash of beach huts. The ferry's first stop is **Culatra**, a grim settlement—it's better to stay on board to get to **Farol**, ¾hr from Olhão, a village of beach huts flanked by sand beaches.

Olhão © (089–)   *Where to Stay*

Pensão Bicuar, 5 Rua Vasco da Gama, © 714816 (*cheap*), has decent colourful rooms, while both ***Pensão Boémia, Rua Dr. Estevão, near Largo da Liberdade, © 721122, and ****Pensão Bela Vista**, 65–67 Rua Dr. Teófilo Braga, © 702 538, are small, clean, decent and cheap. ****Hotel Ria Sol**, 37 Rua General Humberto Delgado, © 705267 (*moderate–inexpensive*), is slightly more upmarket.

There is no accommodation on Armona, though you could ask the tourist office if there are any beach huts to let. On Culatra, **Hotel Bar Tropical** offers the only accommodation.

Tavira

Thirty km northeast of Faro and 23km southwest of Vila Real de Santo António, the most beautiful town in the Algarve has hardly been affected by tourism: the only tide to sweep through it is that of the Gilão River, whose banks are lined with both grand and humble houses, and crossed by a once-Roman bridge.

Founded by the Turduli *c.* 2000 BC or by the Greeks *c.* 400 BC, Tavira's fortune was for long based on tuna fishing. Shoals of the fish were harpooned off Faro from the end of April to the end of June, swimming eastwards to spawn in the Mediterranean, and off Tavira, when the fish returned westwards, thinner, in July and August. Tuna are now only found on the high seas, but the Tavirans have retained a taste for the firm grey meat.

Tavira's gentle hillslopes and 21 churches make lovely rooflines of peaked and weathered terracotta. The people are exceptionally friendly, and the streets smell of sawdust and baking bread. There are wonderful beaches nearby. Accommodation is decent but not luxurious, with one exception.

Tavira ℂ (081–)   ***Getting There and Tourist Information***

Frequent buses and trains run from Faro (both ¾hr). The new **bus terminus** is on Rua dos Pelames, from which you turn left and walk 2 minutes to reach the **tourist office**, ℂ 22511, at 9 Rua da Galería, while the **railway station** is 1km away, along the Rua da Liberdade. Please note: there is no Bureau de Change in Tavira and banks are not open on Saturdays; the tourist office can do nothing for distressed, poverty-stricken tourists except despair of them.

What to See

Most of Tavira's churches are permanently locked, but wanderers will be delighted by various stone or wood windows and doors around the town. At the highest point in Tavira, the **churches of Santa Maria and Santiago** are a beautiful, Moorish ensemble, topped by the former's cockerel weathervane. The **Misericórdia**, just up from the tourist office, has an attractive Renaissance portal, built 1541–51, with Saints Peter and Paul at its corners. There is a fine pair of 18th-century bench seats in the **Carmo Church** (across the

Roman bridge over the Gilão at Tavira

river from the Praça da República and up through the Largo de São Braz; huge key from house No.22 opposite).

The **Ilha de Tavira** is an offshore sandbank stretching 11km west from Tavira. Get there by taking the bus marked *Quatro Águas (frequent service June–Sept; three or four times daily Mar–May, and Oct)* from the stop next to the cinema. The 10-minute ride connects with a ferry *(8am–11pm)*. During the summer there is a direct ferry which leaves from near the market. The quay is on the eastern tip of the island, surrounded by beach huts. It takes a small walk to get away from the crowds on this white-sanded beach lapped by the warmest, jade-green waters in the Algarve. A handful of restaurants and bars have sprung up on the Ilha, aiming largely at the population of the campsite, which harbours a varied crowd, from families to young travellers growing dreadlocks. **The Sunshine Bar** is run by a jolly Anglo/Irish couple and has a youthful and fun feel.

Tavira ℮ (081–)

Where to Stay

A couple of km east of Tavira, the ***Eurotel**, Quinta das Oliveiras, ℮ 324324 *(expensive)* is booked up by package tour operators. Spruce **Residencial Princesa do Gilão**, 10–12 Rua Borda de Agua de Aguiar, ℮ 325171 *(inexpensive)* overlooks the river, with very good views towards the main part of town. Tiled floors help to keep the bedrooms cool. Bedrooms in the 'plush' **Residencial Mirante**, 83 Rua da Liberdade, ℮ 322255 *(inexpensive)*, uphill from the tourist office, come complete with fake rose, glass droplet bedside lamps, and marbled walls. Tiny shower rooms have no toilets, and single rooms may be dark.

There is a good atmosphere at **Residencial Castelo**, 4 Rua da Liberdade, ℮ 323942 *(inexpensive–cheap)*, opposite the tourist office. Rooms are large and solidly furnished. The best cheap place to stay is **Residencial Lagôas**, 24 Rua Almirante Cândido dos Reis, ℮ 322252 *(very cheap–cheap)*, across the river from the Praça da República—turn right off the Praça Dr. António Padinha. Small and clean, it is run by cheerful Maria, who dispenses hugs and grapes from her farm. There are communal fridges, and laundry facilities on the roof, which has excellent views of the 'typical' roofs of the Algarve, and makes a great place to look at the stars with a bottle of wine or two.

Turismo de Habitação

Quinta do Caracol, ℮ 322475 *(luxury)*—on the landward side of the railway station—is a wonderful 200-year-old converted farmhouse, whitewashed and draped with bougainvillea. The seven homey apartments include a basic kitchenette and a shower room; some overlook the raised circular pool once used for washing laundry, now painted, and intended for wallowing. Other facilities include a hard tennis court and a self-contained bar frequented by the resident owners, 83-year-old grandfather and year-old baby included. The railway track is nearby, but trains are infrequent. There is one 2-person apartment, six 4–5 person apartments.

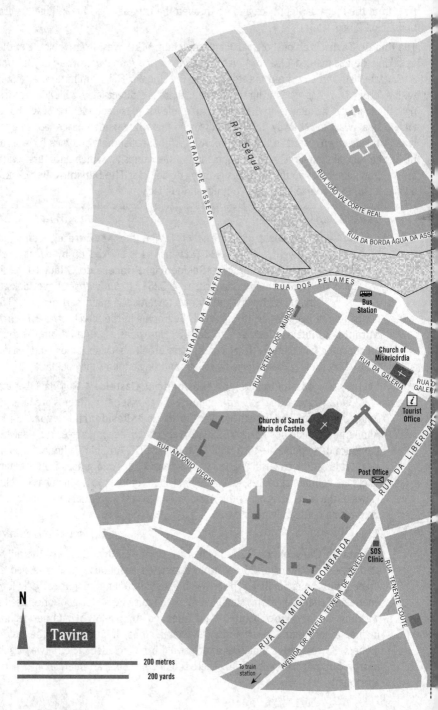

RUA JOÃO VAZ CORTE REAL

RUA DA BORDA ÁGUA DA ASSE

Rio Séqua

ESTRADA DE ASSECA

RUA DOS PELAMES

Bus Station

ESTRADA DE BELAFRIA

RUA DETRAZ DOS MUROS

Church of Misericórdia

RUA DA GALERIA

RUA D GALERI

Tourist Office

Church of Santa Maria do Castelo

RUA ANTÓNIO VIEGAS

Post Office

RUA DA LIBERDAD

SOS Clinic

RUA DR MIGUEL BOMBARDA

AVENIDA DR MATEUS TEIXEIRA DE AZEVEDO

RUA TENENTE COUTE

To train station

N

Tavira

200 metres
200 yards

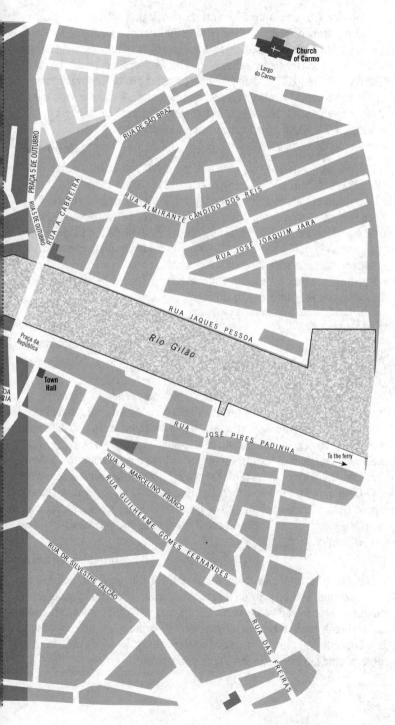

The newly opened **Convento do São Antonio**, 56 Atalaia, ✆ 325632 (*expensive*), behind the army barracks, is a converted 17th-century monastery, lovingly converted and filled with antiques. It's been in the family of the charming Isabel for two centuries, and is patently her passion. The six bedrooms retain the calm aura of monks' cells. If luxury is more your line, opt for the suite. The watchtower, baked in Tavira sunshine, overlooks the salt marshes, and the circular swimming pool is flanked by an ancient bucket-mill well. Guests are free to eat or linger in the central courtyard. Excellent value for the warmest of welcomes.

villa rentals

If you'd like to rent a villa, the two excellent tourist villages called **Pedras d'el Rei**, ✆ 325352, and **Pedras d'el Rainha**, ✆ 370181, located at Sta. Luzia, 3km west of Tavira, and at Cabanas, 5km east of Tavira, are well designed and close to undeveloped beaches (*moderate*). The villas' wooden-trellised windows overlook communal lawns, so the sites feel spacious and private, while the interiors are simply furnished in cool local materials. Both villages incorporate a swimming pool, restaurant, post and telephone facilities, babysitter and a well-stocked supermarket, which sells firewood for chilly winter evenings. The beach is a short walk away. Villas range in size, from two to ten beds.

Tavira ✆ *(081–)*

Eating Out
expensive

The excellent **Quatro Aguas**, ✆ 325329, on the harbour where the ferry departs for the Ilha, is a cool, elegant restaurant with a fish tank harbouring beady-eyed crustaceans which don't end up on your plate, as opposed to the catch of the day which does. An army of rooftops lays seige to the eponymous **Patio Restaurante**, 30 Rua António Cabreira, ✆ 23008, a boisterous-looking place with an incongruously rarefied atmosphere inside. The extensive seafood menu is of the highest quality and the huge portions are served by the amiable and trilingual Edouard. Try the grilled tiger prawns flambéed in cognac. **O Caneção**, 162 Rua José Pires Padinha, ✆ 819211, is the new face of the quayside—big windows, ceiling fans, waiters in black tie, and a long bar, but the atmosphere is rather dry. The meat and fish are good; the vegetables are not. Next door, fishermen mend their nets.

moderate–cheap

A little closer to the centre of town, **Imperial**, 22 Rua José Pires Padinha, ✆ 22234 (*moderate*) gets up a fug on the quayside, with wicker chairs and a dirty fish tank (for pets). *Sarrabulho de marisco* (pork and shellfish) comes in double portions, or there's tuna steak. The surprise dessert is the bridal bolster, of soft meringue. **Bica** (on the ground floor of the Residencial Lagôas—*see* above) is very plain but serves the most delicious fresh tuna steaks (*cheap*).

Cabanas

A short walk from Conceicão, 5km east of Tavira, Cabanas is a relaxed and simple fishing village sheltered from the sea by a sand spit, with a couple of restaurants on the promenade. It's possible to squelch out to the sandbank at low tide, when the locals are digging for shellfish with trowels, and when fossils can be found on the beach at the end of the coast road. The sandbank beach is one of the friendliest in the Algarve, popular with families, but not exclusively so. The mainland sand beach is backed by grassy dunes and a ruined fort.

Cacela Velha

If anywhere in the Algarve deserves the epithet 'unspoilt', it's the hamlet of Cacela, on the coast 8km east of Tavira. Surrounded by ploughed fields, the settlement focuses on a whitewashed church and a little 18th-century fortress perched atop a gentle cliff. Most of the mainland beach has been colonized by silvery bushes, but there are sheltered spots amongst them, or you could try to persuade someone to row you over to the sand spit which shelters Cacela from the sea. This is a great place to watch the sun go down, accompanied by tinkling goat bells, and afterwards you could sit outside at the hamlet's only restaurant, **Casa Velha** (*cheap*).

Vila Nova de Caçela

The sole reason for coming to Vila Nova de Cacela, 10km east of Tavira and 9km west of Vila Real de Santo António, is to eat huge portions of wonderfully fresh grilled fish at low prices at **A Camponesa**, © 081 95351 (*moderate*), off the main road. The surroundings are about as simple as you can get: concrete floor, corrugated-iron roof, formica tables, paper placemats, and no walls. It's a popular restaurant full of people delighted to have found the Real Thing. Forget the starters or desserts, take your time, and listen to the chef whistle like a bird when each portion is cooked. The menu varies with the catch.

Monte Gordo

Four km west of Vila Real de Santo António, the joyless modern resort of Monte Gordo has little to recommend it. Grid-patterned streets of no-frills gardened houses are being elbowed out by tall hotels and large restaurants, which vie for space overlooking the very wide fine white beach popular with the British and Dutch.

Monte Gordo © *(081–)*   ***Tourist Information***

There is a **tourist office**, © 44495 (*open 9.30–7*), on the beach front just before the casino, which is usually filled with tourists demanding bus and train timetables for excursions 'to anywhere'!

Should you wish to escape, **bicycles** may be hired at 23 Rua Pedro Álvares Cabral, near the pharmacy.

Monte Gordo ✆ (081–) — *Where to Stay*

All is not lost: very pleasant low-rise ★★★★**Hotel Casablanca**, Rua 7, ✆ 511444 (*expensive*) is set back from the beach and is equipped with small indoor and outdoor swimming pools, a poolside snackbar and a walled sun area. Bedrooms are cool and attractive. Make strenuous efforts to avoid the ★★★**Hotel Alcazar**, around the corner, which recently lost a star to prove the point. The ★★**Baia de Monte Gordo**, Rua Diogo Cão, ✆ 43672 (*moderate*) is clean and functional. In the west of town, **Residencial Prómar**, Rua Dom Francisco de Almeida, ✆ 512184 (*inexpensive*), is uninviting and requires full board. You might do better at **Pensão Espanhola**, R. Pedro Álvares Cabral, ✆ 42359 (*cheap*), although there's not much in it.

Monte Gordo ✆ (081–) — *Eating Out*

Copacabana, Avenida Infante Dom Henrique, ✆ 41536 (*expensive*) is a jazzy affair, serving reliable food. **Mota**, ✆ 42650 (*cheap*), is a large hamburger grill on the beach, with seats outside. In the centre of town, **Bar Stop**, 29 Rua Gonçalo Velho, ✆ 43672 (*moderate*) is not as cheap as it looks, but it's a good place for fuel food—especially the juicy stews.

Vila Real de Santo António

Tourist Information

Buses and trains run frequently from and to all major stations in the Algarve.

At the eastern tip of the Algarve, the frontier town and tunny-processing port of Vila Real de Santo António vegetates at the mouth of the River Guadiana. Ferries cross to and from Ayamonte in Spain, and a bridge across the river has recently been constructed.

When Dom José ascended to the throne in 1750, the Portuguese bank of the Guadiana was deserted south of Castro Marim: Vila Real de Santo António was the brainchild of the Marquês de Pombal, who ordered the town to be built in five months in 1774, on the site of a settlement flushed away by a tidal wave *c.* 1600. This was to be the headquarters of the pilchard- and tuna-fishing industry: to ensure the success of his venture, Pombal ordered Monte Gordo to be burnt flat. The layout follows that adopted by Pombal in the reconstruction of Lisbon—wide streets cut into squares—but bears none of Lisbon's elegance.

Vila Real de Santo António is grim, grimy, grid-patterned and geared to Spanish daytrippers. The one mitigating feature is that some streets run east–west and hence look distinguished at sunrise and sunset, while goats graze on the edge of town. Guestrooms get booked up quickly.

The gently winding Guadiana, smooth and banked with rich greenery, is navigable as far as Mértola: you should ask the tourist office if there are any boats making this stunningly beautiful journey.

★★Hotel Apolo, Av. dos Bombeiros Portugueses, ✆ 44448 (*moderate*), on the edge of town towards Faro, is basic with tacky trimmings and an electric shoeshine machine. In high season, it's expensive for what you get. **★★★Hotel Guadiana**, Avenida de República, ✆ 511482 (*inexpensive*), is a hotel in the grand style with several national flags flapping outside and a sweeping staircase within. The large air-conditioned rooms are tastefully furnished and thoroughly modern with a television in every room. The manager is a friendly soul, who gently regrets the building of the bridge to Spain. Good value. Angolan varnished-wood female heads line the staircase of **Residencial Matos Pereira**, 57 Rua Dr. Sousa Martins, ✆ 43325 (*cheap*), one street inland from the Praça Marquês de Pombal, leading to decent rooms with carved wooden beds and firmly religious pictures. Pokey **Residencial Baixa Mar**, 3 Rua Teofilo Braga, ✆ 43511 (*cheap*), just around the corner from the riverfront, smells like a hospital, with metal beds, although some rooms have balconies.

There are several restaurants on the bank of the Guadiana, but none of them is remarkable, aside from the large and often excellent **Caves do Guadiano**, 90 Avenida de República (*expensive–moderate*) which serves superlative seafood.

Up the River Guadiana

Castro Marim

Sheep wade through the marshes 4km north of Vila Real de Santo António, and emerge with dirty underbellies. Their shepherds hail from Castro Marim, a little town set in the lee of a hill topped by a semi-circular **fortress**, built by Dom João IV on foundations laid by Dom Afonso III in the 13th century. Dom João IV was also responsible for the construction of the **Fortress of São Sebastião** on a hill opposite.

Dom Dinis granted Castro Marim to the recently founded Order of Christ, and it served as their headquarters until their removal to Tomar in 1334.

The town is more impressive from a distance than close to; the only feature of interest is the **Reserva do Sapal** nature reserve, whose headquarters are in the former fortress, and who map a marshy 7km walk.

Alcoutim

Some 44km north of Vila Real de Santo António, the village of Alcoutim rests on the bank of the River Guadiana, mirrored across the water by the Spanish village of Sanlúcar de Guadiana, close enough to hear the braying of a Spanish donkey. The dogs of Alcoutim do not tire of barking at foreigners, its chickens do not cease from pecking between the cobblestones set unevenly and steeply between houses edged with geraniums.

By 1688, Alcoutim had long been a centre for smuggling tobacco and snuff into Portugal from Spain. When the superintendent of the Junta do Tabaco discovered a hoard of the stuff, 'the whole population rose in arms'; the superintendent and his cronies were chased from the village by a crowd which included its governing officials.

One corner of the otherwise plain 14th-century ruined **castle**, at the highest point in the village, is planted with daisies and set with trestle tables: it makes a lovely place to picnic, overlooking a poultry yard and the river. A 17th-century low relief of John the Baptist is locked in the corner of the **Igreja Matriz** by the river. Next door, a restaurant doubles as Alcoutim's only *pension*, in summer. If you want to stay in the village earlier in the year, to see the spring flowers, ask around for a room.

A newly built road follows the river for 14km south from Alcoutim, before turning inland to emerge just south of the village of Odeleite. It makes a fabulous walk.

House of Burgundy

1128/39–85	Afonso (Henriques) I
1185–1211	Sancho I
1211–23	Afonso II—Uracca (1220)
1223–48	Sancho II
1248–79	Afonso III
1279–1325	Dinis—Isabel of Aragon (1282)
1325–57	Afonso IV
1357–67	Pedro I—Blanca of Castile (1328)
	—Constanza of Castile (1336)
	—?Inês de Castro
1367–83	Fernando—Leonor Teles (1372)

House of Avis

1383–85	João I (Regent)—Philippa of Lancaster (1387)
1385–1433	João I (King)
1433–38	Duarte
1438–81	Afonso V
1481–95	João II—Leonor (1471)
1495–1521	Manuel I—Isabel of Castile (1497)
	—Maria of Castile (1500)
	—Leonor of Spain (1518)
1521–57	João III
1557–78	Sebastião (Sebastian)
1578–80	Cardinal Henrique
1580	António, Prior of Crato

House of Hapsburg

1580–98	Philip II of Spain (I of Portugal)
1598–1621	Philip III of Spain (II of Portugal)
1621–40	Philip IV of Spain (III of Portugal)

House of Bragança

1640–56	João IV
1656–67	Afonso VI—Isabel of Savoy (1668)
1667–83	Pedro II (Regent)—Isabel of Savoy (1668)
	—Maria of Neuberg (1687)
1683–1706	Pedro II (King)
1706–50	João V—Maria-Ana of Austria (1708)
1750–77	José
1777–92	Maria I—Pedro III (1760)
1792–1816	João VI (Regent)—Carlota Joaquina of Spain (1784)
1816–26	João VI (King)
1826–28	Pedro IV

Rulers of Portugal to 1910

1828–34	Miguel
1834–53	Maria (da Glória) II—August of Leuchtenberg (1834)
	—Ferdinand of Saxe-Coburg-Gotha (1836)
1853–55	Ferdinand (Regent)
1855–61	Pedro V
1861–89	Luís—Maria-Pia of Savoy
1889–1908	Carlos
1908–10	Manuel II

Language

If you have a basic knowledge of Latin and French or Spanish, you should be able to make sense of written Portuguese, which is a Romance language. Pronunciation is another matter: Portuguese is diabolically difficult to speak. Plunge on in. The Portuguese are far too polite to make fun of your attempts, and most people will be delighted that you've made the effort. (Also, they are fond of reminding visitors that Portuguese is the seventh most widely spoken language in the world.) English is not uncommon in the cities and tourist areas, but it's just as alien to the Portuguese as their language is to us; French is a more useful *lingua franca*, since the Portuguese learn it as their second language.

Some anthropologists reckon that the Portuguese made their pronunciation as different as possible from Spanish, to emphasize their own identity. It may take several flagons of local wine before you can get your tongue around the vowels. A single stressed syllable (denoted by an acute accent or a circumflex) tends to swallow up the rest of a word. The tilde ('[en]+[en]') is most commonly used as 'ão', which produces a nasal 'ow' as in 'cow'. Consonants tend to be slurred. 'C' is soft before 'e' and 'i', but hard before 'a', 'o', and 'u'. 'ç' is pronounced 's'. 'J' is pronounced like the 's' in 'leisure'. 'G' sounds the same when it comes before 'e' or 'i'—otherwise it is hard, as in 'get'. 'Lh' takes on the sound of 'ly', 'qu' of 'k'. 'S' is pronounced 'sh' when it comes before a consonant or at the end of a word. 'X' also sounds like 'sh'.

Greetings

good morning	*bom dia*
good afternoon or evening	*boa tarde*
goodnight	*boa noite*
goodbye	*adeus*
see you later	*até logo*
yes	*sim*
no	*não*
please	*por favor*
thank you	*obrigado (when spoken by a man)*
	obrigada (when spoken by a woman)
excuse me	*com licença*
I am sorry	*desculpe*

Common Phrases

please help me	*ajude-me por favor*
Do you speak English?	*Fala inglês?*
How much is it?	*Quanto custa?*
Where is the toilet?	*Onde ficam os lavabos?*
I am in a hurry	*Tenho pressa*
Why?	*Porquê?*
Where?	*Onde?*
How are you?	*Como vai?*
I'm lost	*estou perdido*
I don't understand	*não compreendo*
What do you call this?	*Como se chama isto?*

Asking Directions

Is this right for...?	*Vou bem para?*
Can you direct me to...?	*Pode indicar-me o caminho para...?*
the railway station	*a estação*
round trip	*ida e volta*
the centre of the city	*o centro da cidade*
bus-stop	*paragem de autocarro*
railway station	*estação ferroviária*
taxi rank	*ponto de táxi*
police	*pol'cia*
hospital	*hospital*
chemist	*farmacêutico*
museum	*museu*
church	*igreja*
beach	*praia*

Accommodation

a single room	*um quarto simples*
a double room	*um quarto de casal*
with private bathroom	*com banho*
bring me	*traga-me*
a towel	*uma toalha*
soap	*sabonete*
toilet paper	*papel higiénico*

Restaurant

the menu	*ementa*
breakfast	*pequeno almoço*
lunch	*almoço*

dinner	*jantar*
the bill	*a conta*
Is service included?	*O serviço está incluindo?*
the wine list	*a lista dos vinhos*

Time

What time is it?	*Que horas são?*
when	*quando*
do you open?/do you shut?	*abrem? /fecham?*
When will it be ready?	*Quando fica pronto?*
immediately	*imediatamente*
yesterday	*ontem*
tomorrow	*amanhã*
today	*hoje*
this afternoon	*logo à tarde*
this evening	*logo à noite*
one night	*uma noite*
one day	*um dia*
midday	*meio dia*
midnight	*meia noite*
now	*agora*
later	*mais tarde*

Money

Can I have	*Pode dar-me*
the bill	*a conta*
the receipt	*o recibo*
the change	*o troco*
Can you change?	*Pode trocar?*
Do you take traveller's cheques?	*Aceitam traveller's cheques?*
a bank	*um banco*
What is the rate of exchange?	*Qual é o câmbio*
signature	*assinatura*
notes	*notas*
coins	*moedas*
money	*dinheiro*

Post Office

What is the postage?	*Quanto é a franquia?*
on this letter	*nesta carta*
postcard	*bilhete postal*
parcel	*volume*

| by air mail | *por via aérea* |
| stamps | *selos* |

Measurements

big	*grande*
bigger	*maior*
small	*pequeno*
smaller	*mais pequeno*
long	*comprido*
short	*curto*
cheap	*barato*
expensive	*caro*
beautiful	*belo*
ugly	*feio*

Everyday Purchases

Do you sell...?	*Vendem...?*
films for this camera	*filmes para esta máquina*
newspapers	*jornais*
books	*livros*
magazines	*revistas*
in English	*em inglês*
ballpoint pens	*esferográficas*
postcards	*postais*

Days of the Week

Sunday	*domingo*
Monday	*segunda-feira*
Tuesday	*terça-feira*
Wednesday	*quarta-feira*
Thursday	*quinta-feira*
Friday	*sexta-feira*
Saturday	*sábado*
Holidays	*feriados*

Chemist

Have you anything for...?	*O que têm para...?*
bad sunburn	*queimaduras de sol*
colds	*constipações*
constipation	*prisão de ventre*
diarrhoea	*diarreia*
sore feet	*pés doridos*

Numbers

one	*um*
two	*dois*
three	*três*
four	*quatro*
five	*cinco*
six	*seis*
seven	*sete*
eight	*oito*
nine	*nove*
ten	*dez*
eleven	*onze*
twelve	*doze*
thirteen	*treze*
fourteen	*catorze*
fifteen	*quinze*
sixteen	*dizasseis*
seventeen	*dezassete*
eighteen	*dexoito*
nineteen	*dezanove*
twenty	*vinte*
twenty-one	*vinte e um*
thirty	*trinta*
forty	*quarenta*
fifty	*cinquenta*
sixty	*sessenta*
seventy	*setenta*
eighty	*oitenta*
ninety	*noventa*
one hundred	*cem*
one hundred and one	*cento e um*
one thousand	*mil*

Colours

white	*branco*
black	*preto*
red	*vermelho*
blue	*azul*
green	*verde*
brown	*castanho*
yellow	*amarelo*

Architectural Terms

Municipal town hall	*Câmara*
Mother Church/parish church	*Igreja Matriz*
viewpoint	*miradouro*
pillory	*pelourinho*
villa/country seat	*quinta*
public square	*rossio*
cathedral/diocese	*sé*
manor house	*solar*
keep	*torre de menagem*

Restaurant and Menu Vocabulary

Coffee and Tea

a small, black coffee	*bica*
a tall glass of white coffee	*galão*
decaffeinated coffee	*Nescafé*
tea	*chá*

Poultry and Game — *Aves e Caça*

chicken	*frango*
hen	*galinha*
turkey	*peru*
partridge	*perdiz*
rabbit	*coelho*

Meat — *Carne*

lamb	*anho*
steak	*bife*
kid	*cabrito*
mutton	*carneiro*
rumpsteak	*entrecosto*
ham	*fiambre*
liver	*figado*
suckling pig	*leitão*
wild boar	*javali*
deer	*veado*
tongue	*lingua*
fillet	*lombo*
pork	*porco*
kidneys	*rins*

bacon	*toucinho*
beef	*vaca*
veal	*vitela*

Fish	***Peixe***
tuna	*atum*
salt cod	*bacalhau*
carp	*carpa*
grouper	*cherne*
sole	*linguado*
bream	*pargo*
scabbard fish	*peixe-espada*
hake	*pescada*
small bass	*robalo*
red mullet	*salmonete*
mackerel	*cavala*
sardines	*sardinhas*
salmon	*salmão*
trout	*truta*

Shellfish	***Mariscos***
cockles	*amêijoas*
shrimps	*camarões*
prawns	*gambas*
rock lobster	*lagosta*
cuttle fish	*lulas*
octopus	*polvo*

Vegetables	***Legumes***
garlic	*alho*
rice	*arroz*
potatoes	*batatas*
onions	*cebolas*
carrots	*cenouras*
mushrooms	*cogumelos*
cabbage	*couve*
cauliflower	*couve-flor*
peas	*ervilhas*
spinach	*espinafres*
broad beans	*favas*

beans	*feijão*
peppers	*pimentos*

Fruit	***Frutas***
plums	*ameixas*
pineapple	*ananás*
figs	*figos*
orange	*laranja*
apple	*maçã*
pear	*pêra*
grapes	*uvas*

Cooking	***Preparo***
roasted	*assado*
boiled	*cozido*
stewed	*estufado*
fried	*frito*
smoked	*fumado*
grilled	*grelhado*
stew	*guisado*
braised	*nas brasas*
on the spit	*no espeto*
baked	*no forno*
mixed (i.e. salad)	*mista*

Other	
butter	*manteiga*
cheese	*queijo*
bread	*pão*
ice	*gelo*
pepper	*pimenta*
salt	*sal*
olive oil	*azeite*
vinegar	*vinagre*
beer	*cerveja*
red wine	*vinho tinto*
white wine	*vinho branco*
table wine	*vinho de mesa*
water	*água*

Selected Bibliography

I feel like a dwarf on the shoulders of giants: I owe an enormous debt to numerous literary sources, which I have not been able to acknowledge in the text. The editions listed are those I have used. The following have been invaluable:

Azevedo, Carlos de, *Churches of Portugal* (Scala Books, 1985).

Bradford, Sarah, *The Story of Port* (Christie's Wine Publications,1983).

Ellingham, Mark, etc., *The Real Guide: Portugal* (Prentice Hall, 1989).

Gallop, Rodney, *Portugal A Book of Folk Ways* (C.U.P., 1961). Popular anthropology.

Gil, Júlio, *The Finest Castles in Portugal* (Verbo, 1986).

Livermore, H.V., *A New History of Portugal* (C.U.P., 1969).

Read, Jan, *The Wines of Portugal* (Faber and Faber, 1987).

Robertson, Ian, *Blue Guide: Portugal* (Ernest Benn, 1984).

Smith, R.C., *The Art of Portugal 1500–1800* (Weidenfeld and Nicholson, 1968). Professorial overview of the arts.

Vieira, Edite, *A Taste of Portugal* (Robert Hale, 1988). Anecdotal cookbook.

Whol, Helmut and Alice, *Portugal* (Scala Books, 1983). Incisive and independent-minded text to accompany glossy photographs.

À Descoberta de Portugal (Seleções do Reader's Digest, 1982). Clipped descriptions of villages, with longer pieces on local quirks.

The Fine Wines of Portugal (Decanter Magazine, 1987).

Guia de Portugal Vol I, II, and III (Biblioteca Nacional de Lisboa, 1924, 1927). Detailed exegesis of everything, everywhere.

Guia de Portugal Vol III (1985), IV i (1985), IV ii (1986), V i (1987), V ii (1988) (Fundação Calouste Gulbenkian). Modern editions of the above series.

Tesuros Artísticos de Portugal (Seleções do Reader's Digest, 1976). Facts about monuments and art.

This book owes much to the following:

History

General

Marques, A.H. de Oliveira, *History of Portugal* (2 vol) (Columbia, 1972).

Nowell, Charles, *A History of Portugal* (Van Nostrand, 1952).

Payne, S.G., *History of Spain and Portugal* (University of Wisconsin Press,1973).

Trend, J.B., *Portugal* (Ernest Benn, 1957).

Specific

Alarcão, J. de, *Roman Portugal* (Aris and Phillips, 1988).

Cheke, Marcus, *Dictator of Portugal: Marquis of Pombal* (Sidgwick and Jackson, 1938).

Cheke, Marcus, *Carlota Joaquina, Queen of Portugal* (Sidgwick and Jackson, 1947).

Francis, David, *Portugal 1715–1808* etc. (Tamesis, 1985).

Hanson, C., *Economy and Society in Baroque Portugal 1668–1703* (Macmillan, 1981).

Read, Jan, *The Moors in Spain and Portugal* (Faber and Faber, 1974).

Robinson, Richard, *Contemporary Portugal* (George Allen and Unwin, 1979).

The Discoveries

Boxer, C.R., *The Portuguese Seaborne Empire 1415–1825* (Hutchinson, 1977)

Crone, G.R., *The Discovery of the East* (Hamish Hamilton, 1972).

Sanceau, Elaine, *The Perfect Prince* (Livraria Civilização, 1959).

Ure, John, *Henry the Navigator* (Constable and Co, 1977).

Monographs

Delaforce, Angela, *The Solar de Mateus* (unpublished ms.).

Goffen, Rona, *Museums Discovered: The Calouste Gulbenkian Museum* (Woodbine Books, 1984).

Guides

Baedeker's Portugal (The Automobile Association, 2nd Edition).

Ellingham, Mark, etc. *The Rough Guide to Portugal* (R.K.P., 1987).

Lowndes, Susan, and Bridge, Ann, *The Selective Traveller in Portugal* (Evans, 1949).

Raposo, Francisco Hipólito, *Beira Alta, Estremadura e Ribatejo* and *O Minho* (Mobil, 1987). Detailed local guides.

Raposo, Francisco Hipólito, *Alto Alentejo* (Mobil, 1986). As above.

Articles in Journals, Periodicals, and Newspapers

Amorim, Roby, *The Welcoming Chimney* (*Atlantis*, November/December 1986).

Bairrada, Eduardo Martins, *Pavement Artists of Lisbon* (*Atlantis* January/February 1987).

Barrett, Frank (*The Independent*, 22 July 1989).

Blum, Patrick, and Smith, Diana *Financial Times Survey: Portugal* (*Financial Times*, 11 Oct 1989).

D'Orey, Leonor, and Teague, Michael, *In the King's Service* (*House and Garden*, November 1986).

Jardim, Bela, *Pillories* (*Atlantis*)

Newby, Eric, *Insider's Guide to Lisbon* (*The Observer Magazine*).

Smith, Diana (*Financial Times*, 19 September 1987, 7 January 1988).

Miscellaneous

Cabral, Martim (ed.), *Portugal: Business Partners in Europe* (De Montfort, 1986).

Campbell, Roy, *Portugal* (Max Reinhardt, 1957).

Macaulay, Rose, *They Went to Portugal* (Penguin, 1985).

Pina-Cabral, João de, *Sons of Adam, Daughters of Eve* (Clarendon Press, 1986).

Watson, Walter Crum, *Portuguese Architecture* (Archibald Constable, 1908).

Literature

Bell, Aubrey (trs.), *Four Plays of Gil Vicente* (C.U.P., 1920).

Camões, Luis Vaz de, *The Lusiads* (Penguin, 1985).

Garrett, Almeida, *Travels in My Homeland* (Peter Owen/UNESCO, 1987).

Macedo, H. (ed.), *Modern Poetry in Translation 13/14 Portugal* (Modern Poetry in Translation, 1972).

Pessoa, Fernando, *Selected Poems* (Penguin, 1988)

Pires, José Cardoso, *Ballad of Dogs' Beach* (Dent, 1986).

Queiroz, Eça de, *The Maias* (Dent, 1986).

Saramago, José, *Baltasar and Blimunda* (Cape, 1988)

Primary Sources

Alcobaça and Batalha (Centaur Press, 1972).

Azurara, *Chronicle of the Discovery of Guinea*

Beckford, William, *Recollections of an Excursion to the Monasteries of Lopes, Fernão,* The English in Portugal (Aris and Phillips, 1988)

Index